455

Popular Mechanics
SATURDAY MECHANIC

Also from *Popular Mechanics*

Popular Mechanics Home How-To

Popular Mechanics Home How-To:
Plumbing and Heating

Popular Mechanics Home How-To:
Weatherproofing and Insulation

Popular Mechanics Home How-To:
Home Repairs and Improvements

Popular Mechanics Home How-To:
Outdoors and Gardens

Popular Mechanics
101 Quick Home Improvement Tips

Popular Mechanics
Home Answer Book

Popular Mechanics
Encyclopedia of Tools & Techniques

Popular Mechanics SATURDAY MECHANIC

The Editors of
Popular Mechanics

Cliff Gromer
Project Editor
Contributing Illustrators: Adolf Brotman,
Ron Carboni, Don Mannes,
Russel Von Sauers, Fred Wolff

HEARST BOOKS
NEW YORK

POPULAR MECHANICS
Editor-in-Chief: Joe Oldham
Managing Editor Production: Deborah Frank
Graphics Director: Bryan Canniff
Home Improvement Editor: Steven Willson
HEARST BOOKS
Editor: Michael Mouland
Assistant Editor: Timothy Hazen

It is the policy of William Morrow and Company, Inc., and its imprints and
affiliates, recognizing the importance of preserving what has been written, to
print the books we publish on acid-free paper, and we exert our best efforts to
that end.

Library of Congress Cataloging-in-Publication Data

Popular mechanics Saturday mechanic / the editors of Popular
    mechanics.
        p.   cm.
    Includes index.
    ISBN 0–688–12963–3
    1. Automobiles—Maintenance and repair.   I. Popular mechanics
(Chicago, Ill. : 1959)
TL152.P654   1994
629.28'722—dc20   93–29734
                                                       CIP

Printed in the United States of America

First Edition

1 2 3 4 5 6 7 8 9 10

BOOK DESIGN BY MICHAEL MENDELSOHN OF MM DESIGN 2000, INC.

CONTENTS

FOREWORD

For over ninety years, car owners have turned to *Popular Mechanics* for advice on making their cars run better and on how to solve problems—both major and minor—that arise in the course of car ownership. In fact, *Popular Mechanics'* car care articles have consistently been among the best read of all the diverse features that have appeared in the magazine. So it seemed to be a natural to assemble a "best of" collection of *Popular Mechanics'* recent auto maintenance and repair articles under one cover.

As anyone who has ever owned an automobile knows, a car thrives on proper and regular maintenance, and timely repair. Without these, the comfort, performance, and enjoyable driving experiences built into the car quickly erode into a nightmare of squeaks and rattles, mushlike handling, and balky operation. And, while some people prefer to hire professionals, many others opt to save time and money by doing the work themselves, which is why this book was created. In its pages, you'll find everything from the proper way to jump-start a dead battery, to resealing a leaky engine, to replacing a clutch. This volume covers your car from bumper to bumper with a broad range of topics that will enhance the engine and drivetrain performance, handling, braking, safety, and appearance of your vehicle—whether it be a compact, sports, or full-size model, two-wheel-drive or 4 × 4. Whether you're breaking out the brand-new wrenches from your first tool set or sliding under a car on your creeper for the umpteenth time, you'll find this book to be an indispensable reference source, packed with easy-to-follow, step-by-step instructions that take the mystery out of auto maintenance and repair and save you money. Should you choose to turn the work over to a professional, the following pages will also decipher the language of auto technicians and body-repair pros so that you can intelligently discuss the work to be done.

So whether you are a do-it-yourselfer or a do-it-for-me person, our goal is to help you maintain the value of your car, truck, van, or sport-utility, and realize all the performance, efficiency, and driving pleasure that was engineered into it.

—JOE OLDHAM
Editor-in-Chief
Popular Mechanics

MAINTENANCE BASICS 1

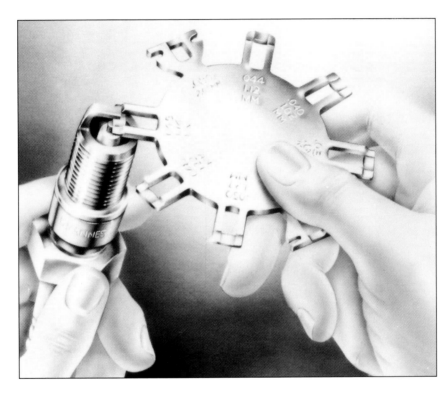

Tools of
THE TRADE

To a mechanic, "tools" fall into two important categories: "hardware" tools, the implements that actually do the job, and "software" tools, the books and other publications that provide the information necessary to do the job. To work on your own car with any measure of success, you'll have to stock your garage with some of both.

STRATEGIES AND INSTRUCTIONS

There's no good excuse for a driveway mechanic to be without the factory service manual for his automobile. General auto repair manuals that cover a variety of makes are less expensive than several factory manuals if you have more than one car to work on. You can usually buy the factory manual through your car dealer's parts counter. For some cars, more than one instruction book is necessary to fully cover drivetrain as well as body and electronics.

THE SERVICE MANUAL

Most factory service manuals begin with a general information section, usually with charts that tell you how to interpret your car's VIN number. You'll be able to pinpoint the specs of the engine installed, the plant at which the car was built, and similar data. Other charts interpret body ID plates with paint and interior color codes as well as trim levels. Other general information will include overall specs, fluid capacities of the various systems, and even data on bolt ID and torque. This chapter should also show the correct jack and lift points for raising and supporting your car.

The general information section is often followed by a maintenance and lube chapter. Use this material in conjunction with our car care plans to tailor the maintenance routines to your specific vehicle.

The rest of your service manual is divided into chapters, each of which covers one specific system,

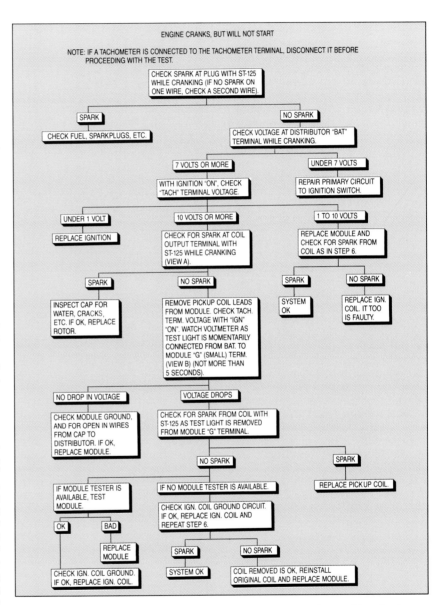

1 "Trouble tree," found in service manuals, takes you to the problem in the fewest steps.

such as heating and ventilation, or a group of systems, such as emissions controls.

Most manual chapters include three types of information. First, where applicable, many chapters begin with a short explanation on how a particular system operates. This information can help when it comes to making logical decisions

about the possible causes of a given problem.

Next comes diagnostic information. This troubleshooting material can be very general and somewhat brief or it can be incredibly specific and detailed. Typical of the first kind of diagnostic directions are those for engine mechanical diagnosis. Here you'll find lists of possible causes that relate to a symptom. For example, in the 1985 Celebrity manual there are eight potential problem areas listed under the heading "Excessive Oil Loss."

Much more complicated are the diagnostic procedures for driveability problems. Some makers, such as GM, instruct you to begin the diagnosis of a driveability problem by triggering the diagnostic mode of the computer system. You progress from there to troubleshooting individual systems with test lights, ohmmeters, and the like, and sometimes finish up checking symptom-organized lists of possible causes.

Other manufacturers, notably Chrysler, begin diagnosis of computer-controlled engine driveability problems with visual checks. In either case, you have to read the manual material carefully and do things in the right order. The procedures work on a process-of-elimination basis. If you don't begin at the beginning, you throw the whole diagnostic plan out of whack.

At some point, the troubleshooting of complex systems is sure to include a diagnostic "tree diagram" (see Fig. 1). To follow our example of this type of diagram, you obviously begin by performing the test in the box at top. Then, depending on whether you find "spark" or "no spark," you proceed on to one of several "branches." Notice that every path eventually concludes with a repair or with a "system OK."

The third type of information, usually at the end of a service manual chapter, is on repairs. It often doesn't include tasks considered simple by professional mechanics.

THE TOOLBOX

How many tools do you need to service your car? Frankly, as many as you can afford. Realistically, however, you can get by with a fairly basic set if you intend to do only maintenance jobs. But if you're going to perform complicated repairs you'll need a lot of special tools, many of them designed to do just one specific job.

Plier Tools

From among the vast number of plier tools, you'll need at least three basic types: a conventional slip-joint plier, a pair of side-cutters for

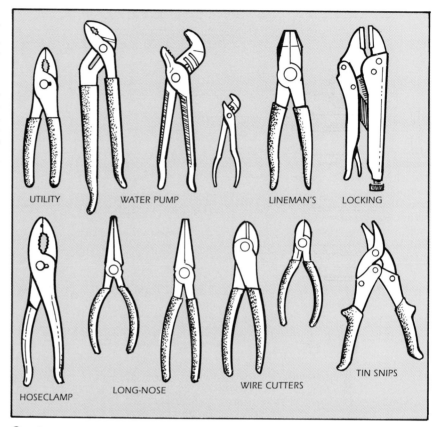

2 Pliers are handy for many specialized jobs. Just don't use them when what you really need is a wrench or socket.

cutting and stripping wire and—among many other uses—prying out cotter pins, and a pair of long-nose or needle-nose pliers.

Once you have the basic three you'll eventually want to expand your plier drawer (Fig. 2). You might first add a locking plier; the most common type is sold under the Vise-Grip trademark. Among many other possible uses, this tool can be clamped tightly around a stripped bolt for removal or it can be used to hold parts in place for welding. Lineman's pliers with insulated handles are useful for various electrical-system chores. Water-pump pliers offer nearly parallel jaws and lots of leverage. A second pair of long-nose pliers can be sharpened for service on snap rings, or special snap-ring pliers are available as well. Small side-cutters can be of use when working with delicate components. Hose-clamp pliers are grooved to grab the spring-type hose clamps that are standard equipment on many cars. Wire strippers/terminal crimpers (not pictured) are very useful pliers with a

row of split circles on the jaws for stripping wires of various gauges and a special crimping area behind the jaws for attaching solderless wire terminals. Tin snips, available for cutting left-hand curves, right-hand curves, and straight cuts, are a necessity if you're going to do serious bodywork.

Screwdrivers

For servicing today's cars, you'll need an assortment of flat-blade and Phillips screwdrivers in various sizes. You'll ruin a lot of screwheads if you use the wrong-size driver. In addition to various-sized tips, you'll need some variety in handle lengths. Cheap screwdrivers are not well suited to driving screws, so buy high-quality tools that will not distort the screwheads.

For most cars you'll also need a couple of Torx-style screwdrivers, distinguished by their six-point drives. On some cars, you'll need this type of screwdriver to replace a headlight bulb or seatbelt housing.

Our favorite screwdriver is a

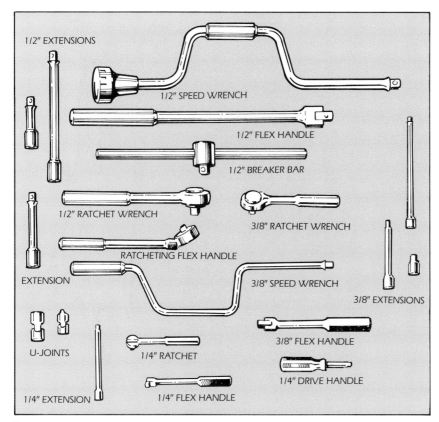

1/2" EXTENSIONS

1/2" SPEED WRENCH

1/2" FLEX HANDLE

1/2" BREAKER BAR

1/2" RATCHET WRENCH

3/8" RATCHET WRENCH

RATCHETING FLEX HANDLE

3/8" SPEED WRENCH

EXTENSION

3/8" EXTENSIONS

U-JOINTS

1/4" RATCHET

3/8" FLEX HANDLE

1/4" DRIVE HANDLE

1/4" EXTENSION

1/4" FLEX HANDLE

3 Whether you need to turn sockets fast, really tight, from an odd angle, or from far away, there's a special ratchet, extension, or handle to do it.

8-POINT

12-POINT

4-POINT

6-POINT

4 Twelve-point sockets will fit hex and square nuts. However, they have a tendency to round off tight hexes.

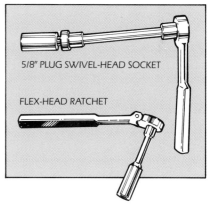

5/8" PLUG SWIVEL-HEAD SOCKET

FLEX-HEAD RATCHET

5 Swiveling wrenches with spark plug sockets fit cramped engines.

high-quality, flexible-shaft ratchet job with interchangeable bits of tool steel. The extra bits fit in the handle, and are available in every size and style you might need. Angle screwdrivers, with a tip mounted perpendicular to the shaft, are useful for screws that can't be reached with anything else.

Socket Tools

Square-drive tools are probably the most important for someone who intends to service automobiles. To begin, you'll need both ⅜-in.-drive and ½-in.-drive ratchets and breaker bars (Fig. 3), at least one short and one long extension for each drive, and a complete set of standard sockets for each. If your car is fully metric, you may want to purchase just metric sockets at first. If your car includes both metric and inch sizes, you'll need a set of each.

You'll need a spark-plug socket of either ¹³⁄₁₆-in. or ⅝-in. size. Don't just use a deep socket for this purpose. Spark plug sockets have a special rubber insert to hold the insulator,

helping prevent breakage while giving you a means to lift the plug away from the engine without dropping it.

A torque wrench is also a necessity, as it should be used for everything from installing wheels to tightening cylinder head or manifold bolts. The most common and least expensive type has a pointer attached to the drive head that rests against a scale near the handle. More expensive types replace the scale and pointer with a dial. A style used by many mechanics has a rotating handle with a scale of torque figures on the tool. You dial in the torque figure you want by turning the handle. Then, when you tighten the bolt, the wrench will click to signal you when you reach the specified figure.

Eventually, you'll want to add universal joints, which can be fitted at the end of an extension; speed handles; T-handles; additional extensions; and a ¼-in. ratchet, extension, and screwdriver handle for smaller capscrews. Adapters that allow the use of ⅜-in.-drive sockets on ½-in.-drive ratchets (or

various other combinations) can also be handy at times. You'll want to expand your socket set to include hex or Allen drive sockets, sockets for large slotted screws, deep-well sockets, universal-joint "swivel" sockets, and ¼-in.-drive sockets, all in both inch and metric sizes.

You'll also want to supplement your standard twelve-point sockets with some eight-, six-, and four-point sockets (Fig. 4). Six-point sockets are needed when you have to loosen a bolt with rounded corners where the twelve-point might slip. Our ⅜-in.-drive deep-well sockets are of the six-point type. Thick-wall six-point sockets (usually black for identification) are available for use with impact wrenches. Eight- and four-point sockets are for removal of square plugs. If you have the eight-pointers, you really don't need the fours.

If you can't reach the spark plugs on your engine with a conventional plug socket, extension, and ratchet, you may need either a swivel-head plug socket or a ⅜-in.-drive ratchet with a jointed hand that can be rotated to a different angle in respect to its handle (Fig. 5).

Wrenches

A basic set of combination wrenches—box at one end and open end on the other (Fig. 6)—will get you started in this department. Use a box wrench when you don't have clearance for a socket. Open-end wrenches are really only suited to running down a bolt or backing it out, as they slip quite easily, ruining both the bolthead and your knuckles.

Fig. 7 shows how an open-end wrench should be used, handle angled away from the direction of rotation. Once the bolt is rotated, the wrench is slipped off, slid around in a counterclockwise direction and reinserted. Once you've practiced this technique, an open-end can be used to turn a bolt very quickly. When loosening a fastener with a combination wrench, break it loose with the box end, then flip the wrench around and run out the bolt with the open end.

Once you have a basic wrench set, you'll want to expand with some other types. Those that have a

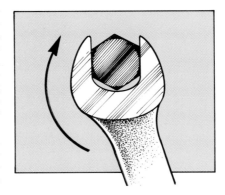

7 Turn one flat, pull back, turn again, and you can really move!

box on both ends generally have a greater offset than the combos, making them useful for certain problem areas. Both box and open-end wrenches are available in a variety of lengths. You'll also find box wrenches shaped like a crescent for inaccessible bolts, box wrenches that ratchet, and sockets attached to a handle with an open-end opposite. We frequently use a very thin open-end "tappet" wrench for any double-nutted bolt or stud or in tight spots.

You'll also want tubing wrenches (not pictured), which are like a six-point open-end with one side missing. Once slipped over a tube, the five remaining points of the wrench can loosen the soft nut on the end of the tube without rounding it off. Special L-shaped box wrenches that can be driven with a ratchet are available for loosening hard-to-reach distributor clamp bolts.

You might be better off without adjustable crescent wrenches, as these tools are most likely to round off a hexhead. But it's good to have a couple of them around in different sizes for those times when you have to turn a simple-to-reach, not-very-tight bolt, the size of which you are not sure.

Hammers

Hammers must be used with great restraint when working on a complicated machine like an automobile. But you will need one from time to time (Fig. 8). Begin with a ball-peen for tapping your drift or making a center-punch mark, and supplement it with a rubber mallet for hanging things into position. Eventually, you'll want to add a brass hammer for driving lugs into hubs and similar tasks. A plastic-head hammer is useful for dislodging somewhat delicate parts. Finally, you'll want a good hand sledge to drive a large chisel into a large rusty nut.

You'll want to have some chisels, punches, and drifts that you can hit with your hammers. If you work on cars regularly, you'll undoubtedly have to chisel off a rusted nut or bolt before long, probably on a shock absorber. Drifts are used for removing pins from shafts, studs, or hubs. A center punch is necessary to provide a spot to start a drill bit in steel or aluminum.

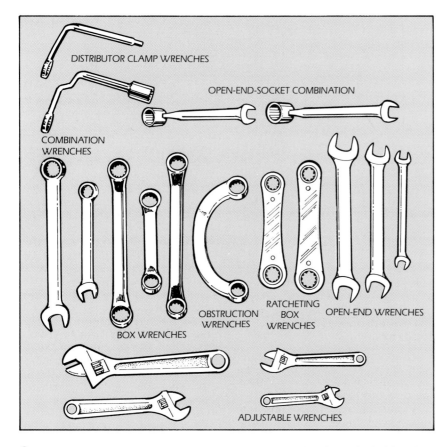

DISTRIBUTOR CLAMP WRENCHES

OPEN-END-SOCKET COMBINATION

COMBINATION WRENCHES

BOX WRENCHES

OBSTRUCTION WRENCHES

RATCHETING BOX WRENCHES

OPEN-END WRENCHES

ADJUSTABLE WRENCHES

6 Use adjustable wrenches as a last resort—they're hard on both the bolthead and your knuckles. Use the box wrenches whenever you can for the same reason.

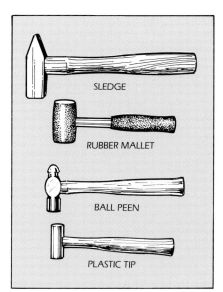

8 If you're looking for a claw hammer, it belongs in the woodshop, not the garage.

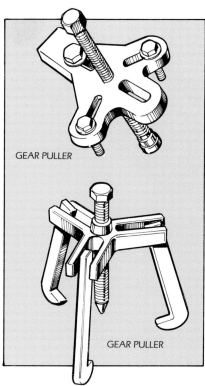

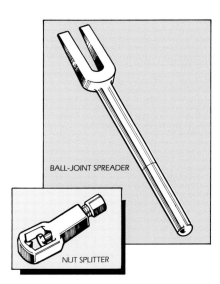

9 Don't even think of prying off a pulley or harmonic balancer with a screwdriver—use a puller. Nut splitter is great for exhaust nuts. Ball-joint tool is affectionately known as a "pickle fork."

You'll need only a couple of files at first. A small ignition-point file is good for cleaning up spark plugs or even repairing the threads on a small screw. One medium-size flat file will also come in handy for smoothing rough edges or flattening slightly distorted surfaces. Later, you'll want to add a rattail for smoothing out holes and a three-sided file for getting into corners. A hacksaw and a couple of high-quality, fine-tooth blades will come in handy if you have to shorten a bolt or fabricate a bracket.

An assortment of tool-steel high-quality drill bits and a ½-in. or ⅜-in. chuck electric drill is also necessary.

Pullers and Pluckers

Hub pullers, nut splitters, gear pullers, pickle forks, and other devices of this ilk probably won't be purchased until you need them. Sooner or later you will undoubtedly want them, however.

A good three-pronged gear puller (Fig. 9) can be used for removing a variety of hubs and gears. This tool is available in several sizes to suit various applications. A puller with slots through which bolts can be inserted is useful for removing any type of hub with threaded holes, such as a steering wheel hub or engine damper pulley. Various other pullers, including slide-hammer de-vices for removal of rear-drive axles, are also available. Some of them can be rented for one-time use.

A nut splitter is a good substitute for a chisel when you have to remove a rusted nut. A ball-joint spreader and rod-end separator, commonly known as pickle forks,

are necessary for suspension-system work. The ball-joint spreader has the wider slot between its prongs.

Oil Change and Lube Tools

An oil filter wrench is, of course, an absolute necessity for any driveway mechanic. Before you buy, make sure you get one that will work on your car, as there are numerous types available (Fig. 10).

Most of the long-handled metal-band jobs work great where there's room for them, but on most cars there isn't. The best of these are ad-justable for different type filters.

A handy oil filter wrench is the type that has a sturdy nylon strap attached to a piece of square tubing with a ½-in. hole down the center. The strap is placed over the filter and the tubing is rotated counter-clockwise until the strap snugs up. Then a ½-in. square drive extension and ratchet are used to continue ro-tating the tubing until the filter is loosened.

In addition to a filter wrench, you'll want an oil-can spout, if you can't get oil in plastic bottles with built-in spouts.

Precision Tools

Every home mechanic should have at least a good pair of vernier cali-pers for determining the size of pins, bolts, and other similar items as well as a set of feeler gauges and a wire gauge for checking spark plugs. If you're going to rebuild en-gines, you'll need much more, in-cluding micrometers, snap gauges, a dial indicator and magnetic base, a depth micrometer, and—ideal-ly—a dial-bore gauge. A good ring compressor will also be needed for engine work. The best type is a ta-pered sleeve for each bore size. If you plan on assembling cylinder heads, you'll need a valve-spring compressor.

The dial indicator and magnetic base are probably worth having even if you never touch the inside of an engine as it is useful for gaug-ing a lot of different things, such as ball-joint wear and even wheel-bearing adjustment.

Other Good Stuff

Sooner or later you'll want to invest in a battery charger. A small, 10-amp

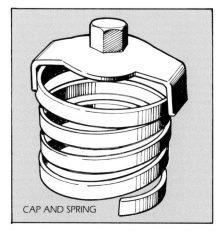

CAP AND SPRING

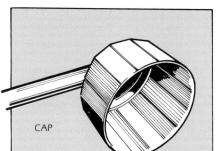

CAP

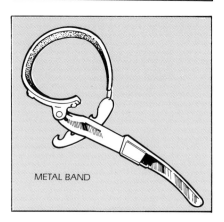

METAL BAND

NYLON STRAP

POUR SPOUT

10 Get the filter wrench that fits your car. Pour spout is optional nowadays.

job can bring a partially discharged battery to full charge in a few hours. You'll need at least a 6-amp model for decent performance. In addition, you'll need a battery post and terminal cleaning tool. You can use a knife for this job, but the special cleaning tool is inexpensive and does a better job. You'll need a timing light to perform tuneups. If you're willing to suffer, you can use the cheap kind that attaches only to the plug wire. A power timing light, which provides much more illumination and is immeasurably easier to use, costs about three times as much.

And you can't get by without a miniature analyzer, which includes a tachometer, ohmmeter, voltmeter, ammeter, and dwell meter. Use it for tuneups, charging-system troubleshooting, general electrical-system troubleshooting, and a wide variety of other jobs.

A good set of taps and dies is expensive but necessary when you have to straighten out the threads on a mangled bolt or clean the threads in a rusty cylinder block. Finally, don't forget to be nice to your tools. You don't have to get into public displays of affection, but you should wipe off the grease each time you use one. And you should have an organizational plan for keeping everything in its place, whether you have a twelve-drawer top-and-bottom tool chest or a two-drawer mini toolbox. Knowing where something is when you need it can cut your creeper time in half. It also makes it easier to tell when something is missing.

How to Perform a
SAFETY INSPECTION

In an effort to keep unsafe automobiles off the road, most states conduct annual safety tests. However, it's a good idea to perform your own safety inspection in your driveway and not wait for that annual test.

- Check the inflation pressure of each tire. It should be at least what the carmaker recommends but no higher than the tire's maximum pressure, which is embossed on the sidewall.

There should be at least ³⁄₁₆ in. of tread, and there should be no signs of uneven wear. When the wear bars begin to show or if there are signs of mechanical trouble—scalloped, feathered, or other odd tread wear—replace the tire.

- Pop the trunk and check the spare, the jack, its handle, and the lug wrench.
- Turn on the lights and walk around the car. Check the headlights, on both high and low beam, and all marker lights and taillights.

Replace any burnt-out, dim, or flaring bulbs.

If replacing the bulb does not cure the problem, check the socket and the wiring connector.

- With the back of the car against the garage door or wall, step on the brake pedal and look in the rearview mirror. You should see the glow of the brake lights.

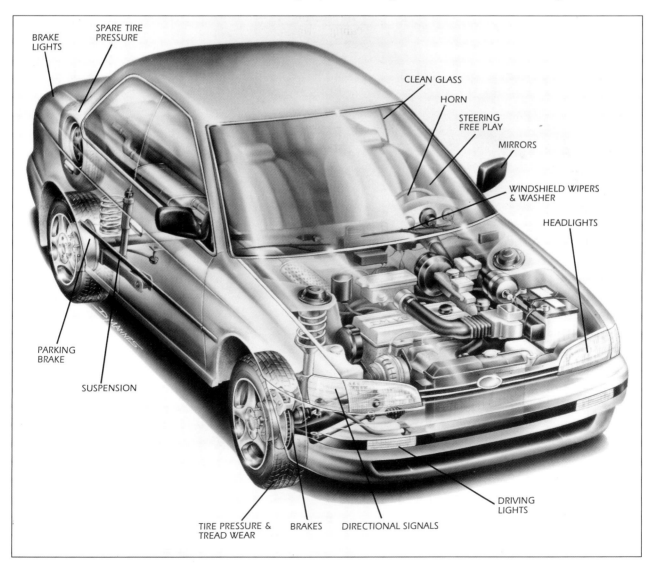

BRAKE LIGHTS
SPARE TIRE PRESSURE
CLEAN GLASS
HORN
STEERING FREE PLAY
MIRRORS
WINDSHIELD WIPERS & WASHER
HEADLIGHTS
PARKING BRAKE
SUSPENSION
TIRE PRESSURE & TREAD WEAR
BRAKES
DIRECTIONAL SIGNALS
DRIVING LIGHTS

- Turn on the ignition and check the directional signals. Also check the four-way hazard flashers. If they do not work, replace their relay.
- Press the horn button. If the horn is weak or nonsounding, check the wiring under the hood.
- While you're still in the driver's seat, check the steering without the benefit of the power assist. Gently turn the steering wheel left and right, feeling for free play.

In rack-and-pinion systems, there should be virtually no movement of the steering wheel that does not move the front wheels.

With other systems, there should be no more than about 1 to 2 in. of free play in the steering wheel.

If the steering wheel feels sloppy, check the components under the car.

- With the engine running, but the car not moving, tromp the brake pedal.

The pedal should be firm under foot and should not continue to sink as you press on it.

- Put the car in gear and accelerate quickly. Again, stomp the brake.

The car should stop short, without veering left or right, with most of its weight transferring to the nose. If the car pulls, or one brake locks, check for a sticking caliper, warped rotor or improperly adjusted drum brake.

- Park the car on an incline and engage the parking brake. Put the transmission in NEUTRAL. The brake should hold the car. If not, adjust the brake's cable.
- Use the windshield washer to clean the windshield. The spray should be full and powerful, covering the glass. The wipers should clean the glass without streaks. Replace the rubber inserts if they do not do the job. Top up the reservoir.
- Clean and check all windows and mirrors for nicks, chips, or cracks.

How to Pass Your STATE INSPECTION

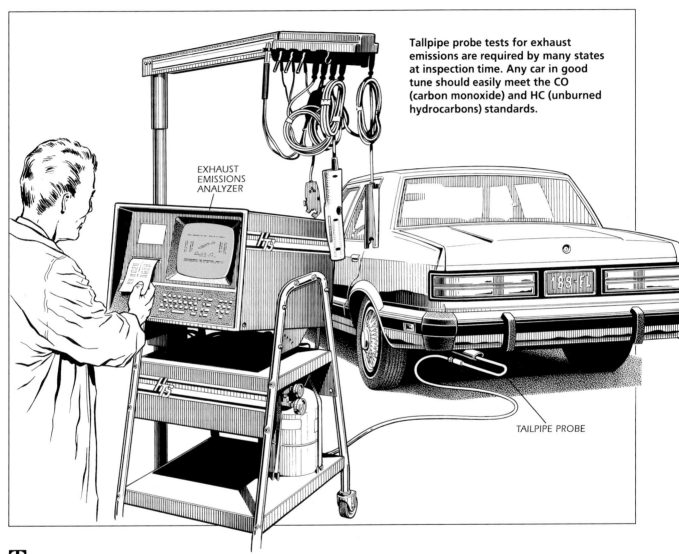

Tailpipe probe tests for exhaust emissions are required by many states at inspection time. Any car in good tune should easily meet the CO (carbon monoxide) and HC (unburned hydrocarbons) standards.

EXHAUST EMISSIONS ANALYZER

TAILPIPE PROBE

The annual ritual of state motor vehicle inspection can fill any car owner with anxiety. For the enthusiast who has modified his car, there's the question of compliance. Even the suburban commuter with a factory-spec family sedan may have some concern. Will the exhaust emissions meet regulation? Will I have to wait through long lines again because of a misaimed headlight that I could have adjusted at home in a few minutes?

Those worries are not without some justification. Fact is, in some states with periodic motor vehicle inspection programs nearly one-third of all cars fail to meet safety or emissions standards their first time through. Presently, nearly half of all states require regular inspections, and another ten stipulate that the car's condition must be checked whenever ownership changes. And strict exhaust emissions standards mean that virtually all car owners are subject to at least a tailpipe sniffer test on a regular basis.

The good news is that with regular engine maintenance and a straightforward check of safety items you can catch nearly all of the potential failures that might turn up in a state inspection. The exact procedures and standards of inspections vary greatly from state to state, of course. In the past, state-run facilities were commonplace, but private repair shops are increasingly assigned this task. These shops are generally licensed by the state's Department of Motor Vehicles and continually audited by that agency. Certified mechanics follow guidelines in the regulations handbook when making their inspection.

Preparing your car to pass state inspection can save you more than just time, too. In general, the inspection fees charged by private garages are regulated by the state, and they're often far less than the shop's normal hourly labor rate. Taking New York as an example, the maximum fee runs to $17 and the procedure takes a half hour to do properly. To avoid losing money on the time spent performing inspection service, the mechanic has an understandable incentive to fail items that may be on the borderline of compliance. The car owner isn't obligated to have his car repaired at the inspecting shop, but the mechanic hopes he will, to avoid the inconvenience of moving the car to a second repair shop. You'll have to decide how much you trust the inspecting mechanic's ethics.

TAILPIPE SNIFFERS

As more American cities become concerned with air-quality standards, requirements for checking the performance of each car's emissions control system are adopted. In some cases, a visual check to ensure that all the emissions control devices are present may be performed. Other states use an exhaust-gas analyzer to determine carbon monoxide (CO) and hydrocarbon (HC) levels. This requires that a probe be placed in the tailpipe with engine running at normal idle speed.

The tester prints out a tape of the CO and HC readings, usually making one copy for the car owner and one for inspection station records. Each time the tailpipe test is performed, the equipment should check the validity of its own calibration against reference gases.

Any car with a good-running, properly equipped engine should be able to pass the emissions segment of a state inspection. If it hasn't been tuned up recently, this is the time to do it. Make sure that the idle speed and ignition timing are at the manufacturer's spec. Experienced Saturday mechanics will immediately recognize the important areas requiring attention. A dirty air filter could cause an overly rich condition, raising the CO level beyond allowable tolerances. A sticking choke on carbureted engines would have the same effect. Bad spark plugs or ignition wires will create a

misfire, raising HC levels and probably causing a failure.

An illuminated CHECK ENGINE light is a sure tipoff that the engine's fuel management system has detected a problem.

Use the procedures outlined in your factory shop manual to check for trouble codes in the memory of the engine control computer. An O_2 sensor failure, for example, could certainly make for high emissions levels. In general, the relatively low cost of these sensors makes it smarter to replace them rather than to attempt a cleanup of the fouled sensor.

Even portions of the emissions control equipment designed to lower oxides of nitrogen levels, which are not measured by the test equipment, can affect the other pollutants that *are* checked. For example, a leaking EGR valve or a vacuum leak might well cause a lean misfire condition, raising HC readings high enough to provoke a test failure.

Ideally, an engine should be thoroughly warmed up to operating temperature before the emissions test is performed so that the catalytic converter will be operating and the choke will have opened.

Inspections for the presence and operation of emissions control devices are generally limited to the most common systems in use. Obviously, the catalytic converter must be present and its air supply line (if originally equipped) should be properly connected. On converter-equipped cars, the fuel inlet restrictor (Fig. 1) must be in place to prevent the use of leaded gas, which would poison the catalyst.

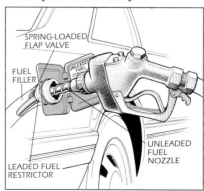

SPRING-LOADED FLAP VALVE

FUEL FILLER

UNLEADED FUEL

UNLEADED FUEL NOZZLE

LEADED FUEL RESTRICTOR

1 A missing or modified leaded fuel restrictor in the fuel filter will cause a catalytic-converter-equipped car to fail state inspection.

In the engine compartment, visual checks are performed to determine that all control devices are still in working order, provided the car was equipped with these devices when it was built. The PCV system has to be in working order. The EGR valve must be installed to factory specs and all vacuum hoses connected. A thermostatic air cleaner must have its manifold heat pipe in place, and any holes drilled or punched in the housing will result in a failure. The air injection pump, along with its drive belt, diverter valves, and plumbing, must be present. The evaporative canister must be properly located and connected.

If your car has all of the proper equipment in place and still fails the state sniffer test, it may be eligible for repairs under the factory warranty. Many components are covered by federal law requiring up to five-year/50,000-mile coverage of emissions control devices.

There are also a number of chemical compounds sold at auto parts stores that are designed to help cars pass the inspection tests. The trouble is, these gas tank additives will only mask the symptoms, not cure the condition causing the high pollutant levels. It's better to fix the problem properly to assure optimum gas mileage and prevent any further damage to the engine.

EXCEPTIONS TO THE RULE

Realizing that the high costs of bringing some older or high-mileage cars into emissions compliance might not be economically feasible, most states have provisions for exemptions. After failing the initial test, the owner must follow set repair procedures and submit to a second test. He can then get a waiver of emissions inspection provided the inspector certifies that control devices are in place and the second test shows an improvement in pollutant levels. Some states place a cost limit on the amount of money an owner must spend trying to bring the vehicle into compliance, but there is no limit for the cost of repairs to correct previous tampering with the control devices.

SAFETY CHECKS

The traditional periodic safety inspection covers many easily

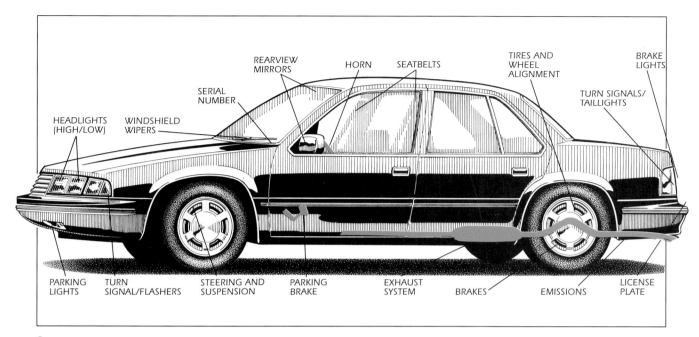

2 Safety check points you should look over before inspection time include all lights, glass, and mirrors, as well as mechanical components.

checked items such as operation of the horn and turn signals, as well as some tougher points like the brake performance and headlight aim (Fig. 2). Start your checks with the lighting system, making certain that all headlamps, taillamps, stop lamps, turn signals, side marker lights, license plate lights, and reverse lights will illuminate and that all lenses are in good condition. Four-way flashers must work as well. If you have added auxiliary spot or fog lamps, they must be wired to a switch separate from the headlamps.

Several methods are in use for verifying proper headlight aim, but you can pass the test in most states by adjusting them yourself (Fig. 3). Park the car on a flat, level surface with the headlights twenty-five feet from a vertical wall. Draw a line on the wall parallel to the ground at the height of the headlight centers. Make a mark where the car's centerline intersects this parallel line. Using the diagram, turn the headlight's adjusting screws to aim their brightest spots below the line marking the headlight centers and slightly toward the right side of the road. If you have single headlights, this will bring your high beams in as well. If you've got quads, adjust the high beams so the center of the bright spot is straight ahead.

All windows must be made of approved safety glass and free of exposed sharp edges (Fig. 4). In general, any star-shaped stone chip larger than 3 in. diameter, or any crack longer than 11 in. in the area covered by the windshield wipers, will be a cause for rejection. All mirrors must have unbroken glass.

UNDERNEATH THE CAR

The safe control of a vehicle is directly related to the condition of its tires and suspension. Tires must not have any visible cuts, bulges, or exposed cord. The minimum acceptable tread depth is $\frac{1}{16}$ in., measured at four points. Note that in many

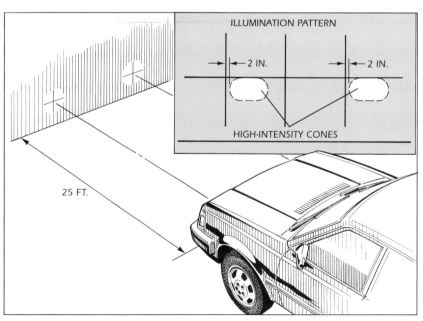

3 Headlight aim requires parking the car 25 ft. from a wall and adjusting the beams to fall below the line between the lights' centers and slightly toward the right side of the road.

13

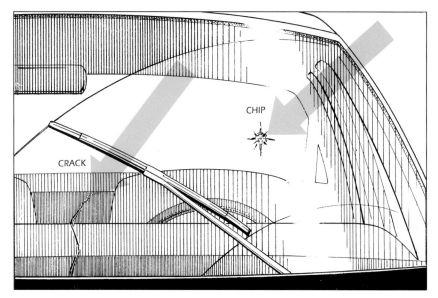

4 Any large star-shaped stone chip or long crack in the wiped area of the windshield glass will cause a rejection. Minor chips or cracks out of the driver's line of sight are usually okay.

For the most part, it isn't the outright stopping performance of the brakes that's tested but the equal braking power at all four wheels and the physical condition of the components.

Testing the brakes for equalization in state-run facilities can be done on sensitive, calibrated equipment, but all you need to do in preparation is assure that the car will stop straight, without pulling left or right. The private repair shop will also perform a visual inspection to look for leaks at the wheel cylinders, calipers, or brake fluid hoses. Disc brakes will be failed if a pad's friction material is cracked or if the wear sensor is in contact with the rotor (Fig. 7). Drum brake linings must be at least ¹⁄₁₆ in. thick, or at least ¹⁄₃₂ in. above any rivethead. Cracks in the rotors or drums will also cause rejection.

Several tests of overall brake system condition are also used. These can be performed by the car owner before taking the car in for inspection. The pedal must have a reserve of at least one-third of its possible travel when depressed under normal foot pressure with the engine running (on cars fitted with power brakes). The pedal must also hold its position without sinking for at least sixty seconds. Then, the vacuum is depleted from a power-brake-equipped car by pumping the pedal several times with the engine off and holding foot pressure against the pedal. When the engine

states the readings are taken in two adjacent tread grooves showing the most wear and at a similar point at least 15 in. away on the circumference. You can use a coin to gauge the tread depth and transfer your measurement to a ruler, or you can look for the tread wear indicators which are molded into the tread pattern (Fig. 5).

The condition of the tire tread area will also give you some indication as to the wheel alignment. Look for feathering and scalloping patterns which indicate that the toe-

in is out of adjustment (Fig. 6). In most cases, state inspection procedures don't use the standard toe-in measurements in fractions of an inch. Instead, a scuff gauge is used, driving the car over a pad to determine the amount of sideways slippage of the front tires. A reading of more than thirty feet per mile will result in rejection.

BRAKE CHECKING

Braking systems are the largest category of state inspection failures.

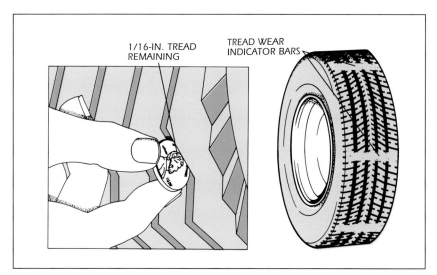

5 It's exactly ¹⁄₁₆ in. from Lincoln's head to the rim. Tread wear indicators will also show when the tire is worn beyond safe use.

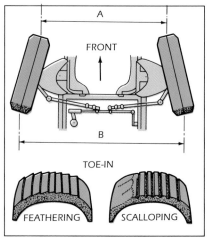

6 Difference between measurement A and B is toe-in. Wear patterns of the tire will show the need for an alignment.

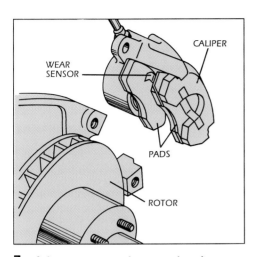

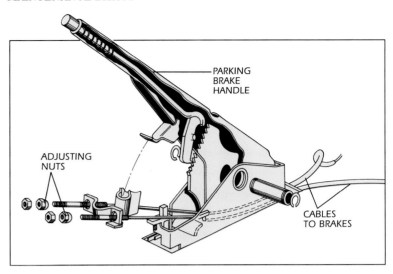

7 If the wear sensor is contacting the brake rotor, the brakes will be rejected in state inspection. Replacing the pads is called for.

8 Adjustment of the parking brake can be done by tightening the cables attached to the brake lever. Turn both adjusting nuts the same amount.

is started, the pedal should fall slightly.

Operation of the parking brake is checked by setting the brake and running the engine slightly above idle speed with the automatic transmission in DRIVE or a manual transmission in LOW gear and the clutch lightly engaged. To avoid failing inspection, the car can't move forward. If it does, adjust the cables controlling the parking brakes by tightening (Fig. 8).

Suspension system checks vary greatly from state to state. Some actually require an inspection of ball joints and tie rods for looseness, while others accept a measurement of steering wheel free play as a guide to front-end condition. In those cases, a maximum of 2 in. of free play with power steering (or 3 in. with manual steering) is allowed before rocking the steering wheel can be detected at the front wheels.

There should also be no binding or excessive tightness anywhere in the steering system. Additionally, all springs and torsion bars should be mechanically sound and the shock absorbers or struts and their mounts must not be broken or missing.

How to Choose the
RIGHT ENGINE OIL

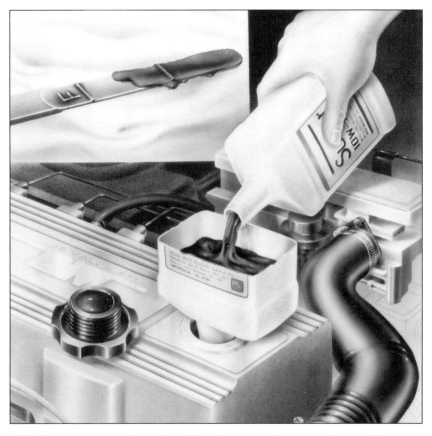

Add oil as necessary to keep the oil level between the FULL and ADD marks on your dipstick.

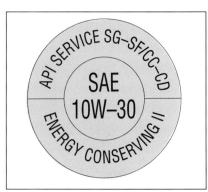

This oil is API-rated as SG (gasoline), as well as CD (diesel), and it's energy conserving.

Of all the maintenance you perform on your car or truck, none is more important than changing its engine oil. Regardless of what you own and what type of driving you do, change the oil—and filter—every 3,000 miles.

Just as critical as draining the old, contaminated oil is replacing it with the right amount of the right oil—oil that's correct for your car.

Sticking with a name brand helps ensure the oil itself is of high quality and that it has the necessary additives to perform up to snuff.

The first critical oil specification is its SAE *viscosity* rating. Viscosity describes how the oil flows at a given temperature.

Oil's viscosity changes with temperature. When hot, the oil thins and flows more easily. When cold, it thickens. Additives minimize the viscosity changes. A "W" after a viscosity rating indicates winter and describes how the oil behaves at 0°F.

Multiviscosity oils behave like a thin, low-viscosity oil when cold and a thick, high-viscosity oil when hot. A single-viscosity—straight weight—may not adequately lubricate at one temperature extreme or the other.

A quality multiviscosity oil that covers all temperature extremes of where you live and drive will do the trick. Check your owner's manual to see what viscosity oils are recommended for the temperature ranges you're going to be driving in.

Since thinner oils flow more easily than thicker ones at the same temperature, the thinner oils have less friction. Reducing internal engine friction improves performance and reduces fuel consumption. Many newer, lower-viscosity blends are labeled "Energy Conserving."

Synthetic oils flow more easily than many natural oils, which further reduces friction—especially at extremely low temperatures. (They are also more resistant to high-temperature breakdown.) If you live where winter temperatures stay at subfreezing levels, a quality synthetic may better lubricate your engine, especially at startup.

Synthetic oils tend to be more expensive than natural ones. Don't think this is an excuse or a reason to extend oil-change intervals.

Synthetic oils tend to flow so easily that even an otherwise minor oil leak can become a hemorrhage.

The other oil specification of concern is its *service* classification. This letter-grading system is set by the American Petroleum Institute (API).

Service indexes beginning with "S" are for gasoline (spark-ignition) engines. Those beginning with "C" are for diesel (compression-ignition) engines. Many oils are rated with both an "S" and "C" classification.

Higher-letter oil is better than lower. If your owner's manual recommends SE oil, you can use SF but not SD. API's current highest-rated oils are SG and CD.

How to Change a FLAT TIRE

Loosen all lugnuts before jacking up the car. Remove the loosened nuts, saving the one farthest from the ground for last.

No matter how careful and conscientious you may be, sooner or later you are bound to face the inconvenience of a flat tire.

To help ensure that a flat tire is no more than an inconvenience, be prepared to deal with this eventuality. Each time you check your tires and their inflation—at least twice a month—check the spare. Mini-spares typically require about 60 psi. Use a tire-pressure gauge calibrated at least that high. Buy a good gauge and keep it in your glovebox.

Be sure that your car or truck is always equipped with a working, suitable jack, its handle or handles, and a lug-nut wrench. Carrying a cross-type lug-nut wrench is a good idea, since the wrench's design offers secure and ample two-handed leverage.

Equip your car or truck with either safety flares or a reflective-plastic warning triangle.

It's also a good idea to carry a

small wheel chock—even a block of wood, 4 × 4 × 4 in. If you drive off-road or along roads without paved shoulders, carry a piece of ½-in. plywood, two feet square, to place under the jack.

Other small items that can be handy when changing a flat are a brightly colored folding rain poncho, work gloves, a flashlight, and some waterless hand cleaner.

Besides having all the equipment necessary for changing a flat tire, be familiar with the procedure. Different vehicles need different types of jacks. Know how to use your car's jack and where it should be placed under the car—a reinforced section of underbody, suspension component, or frame rail.

Should you get a flat tire, pull safely off the road and set the parking brake. Do not stop on a narrow shoulder, bridge, or in a tunnel. If there is no safe place to stop, keep driving—slowly, in the right lane, four-way flashers on—until you can pull off the road.

A car sitting on a jack is unstable at best. Do as much work as possible with the car sitting on the ground. When the car is being jacked up, it should be empty—no passengers.

Remove everything needed to change the tire. Set the flares or reflective triangle between you and oncoming traffic.

Remove any wheel cover or hubcap to gain access to the lug nuts. Some wheel covers have locks or hard-to-spot pry slots. Check your owner's manual. The jack handle or lug-nut wrench generally has a flat tip for removing the cover.

Loosen all of the lug nuts. If you cannot loosen a tight nut, first be sure that you are turning it in the correct direction. Check your owner's manual to be certain that none of the lug nuts have lefthand threads.

Position the wrench on the nut so you can safely step on the wrench, using the weight of your body to help loosen the nut.

After all the nuts have been slightly loosened, position the wheel chock at the tire diagonally opposite the flat.

Position the jack according to the carmaker's directions. Jack up the car so the flat tire clears the ground by 2 to 3 inches.

Remove the loosened lug nuts, saving the one that's farthest from the ground for last.

Remove the flat tire and place it next to the car, then position the spare on the wheel studs.

Put the lug nuts back on, the one farthest from the ground first. Anti-seize compound, or even oil on the threads and chamfer of the nut, will make removal easier next time. Tighten the nuts just enough so the wheel is snug. Snug them in a crisscross pattern.

Lower the car back to the ground and remove the jack.

Use the wrench to finish tightening the nuts, in a crisscross pattern.

Remove the chock. Replace the cover, then stow the flat, the jack, its handle, the wrench, the wheel cover, and the reflective triangle.

How To Replace
WIPER BLADES

If you wait until the next time it rains to discover that your car needs new windshield wiper blades, you may end up needing more than just wiper blades.

You can replace your wiper blades either with exact duplicates from the new-car dealer or with lower-cost universal (or nearly so) replacements from an auto parts store. Depending on the blade, you may be able to replace just the rubber squeegee.

The rubber that actually wipes the water is normally the only piece that wears out. This is called the squeegee or blade refill. The blade is the frame that holds the squeegee in place, and the wiper arm swings the blade back and forth across the windshield.

Before buying replacement blades:

- Measure the length of the blade. Replacements are marked by length, in inches.
- Determine how the blade is connected to the wiper arm.

Depending on the make, model, and year of your car or truck, the blade can be attached to the wiper arm in one of several different ways. Universal-type replacement blades are usually packaged with several different types of connectors—match yours when you install the blade. Here are the most common connectors:

- Bayonet-type mounts have the wiper arm going straight into a hinged receptacle on the blade. Release a locking tab and pull the blade straight off the arm.
- Hook-type mounts have wiper arms with a U-shape at the end. The hook goes over a pin or hinged sleeve in the middle of the wiper blade. Flip the blade over the hook, and slide the blade off the hook. Some have a locking tab which has to be released.

- Pin mounts have the blade and arm parallel to each other, attached by a steel pin. Depress the small locking tab next to the pin, and slide the blade away from the arm.

If you choose a duplicate wiper blade from the dealership, reverse the procedure and you're done. If you opt for a universal replacement, select the proper connector adapter and install it on the wiper blade as needed.

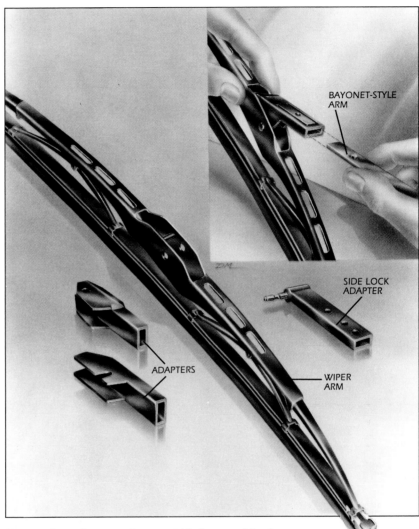

Many universal-type replacement blade assemblies have adapters to mate with many different styles of wiper arms—use the one that's appropriate for your vehicle.

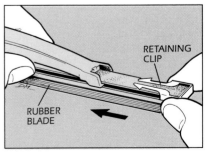

Replace just the rubber portion by sliding it into the blade until the clip seats.

If your wiper blade accepts refills, replace just the old squeegee once you've taken the blade off the arm.

Most squeegees have locking tabs at one end or the other. Squeeze them closed (pliers are helpful), and slide the refill out of the blade's frame.

Some blades have a locking tab on one of the blade links. Press in the locking button, and slide the locking link along with the squeegee off the rest of the blade. Remove the locking link from the squeegee.

Thread the new squeegee through the fingers of the blade frame. Be sure both edges are threaded until it locks in place.

Anytime you're working on the wiper blades, take care not to bend or twist the wiper arms. And always take care not to scratch the windshield—don't operate the wipers on a dry windshield; the grit will etch the glass.

How to Check
DRIVEBELTS

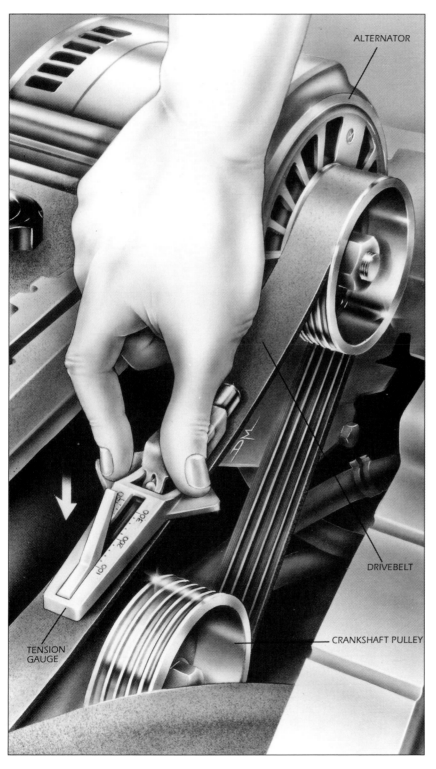

ALTERNATOR

DRIVEBELT

CRANKSHAFT PULLEY

TENSION GAUGE

Though the fan belt is gone from just about every car these days, your car still has other belts under the hood. These drive the alternator, air-conditioning compressor, power-steering pump, and water pump.

Some drivebelts are single V-belts riding in a deeply grooved pulley. Some are poly-V belts with several grooves and ribs riding in matching grooves in the drive pulleys.

On some engines, belts may be used to drive more than one accessory. Many new cars use a single belt for all of the accessories.

Regardless of the type or number of belts under your hood, they should be inspected at least four times a year.

Inspect the sides of V-belts for glazing, cracks, and tears.

Check the ribs of poly-V belts for breaks in the ribs, cracks, and missing chunks of rubber.

Any damaged belt must be replaced, but it's good practice to replace any drivebelt after four years. Even if the drivebelt appears to be in good condition, it may be weak internally.

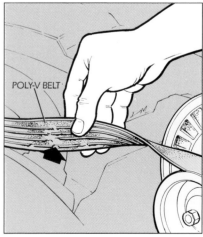

POLY-V BELT

Check the undersides of all belts by twisting the belt along its entire length.

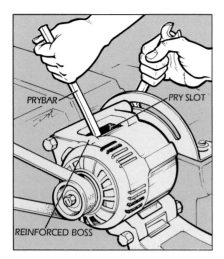

PRYBAR   PRY SLOT

REINFORCED BOSS

All accessories have a tensioning provision including reinforced sections and pry slots.

Replacement belts should match the original belt in size and thickness.

New poly-V belts must have the same number of ribs as the original.

Check the tension of all drivebelts using a belt-tension gauge.

Inexpensive, simple-to-use gauges are available at auto parts stores. The distance between pulleys on today's engines is too small to accurately judge a belt's tension by merely pressing it between two pulleys.

All drivebelts have a provision for tensioning the belt. However, it may not be obvious at first glance. When several accessories are driven by a single belt, there may be only one adjustment. Either only one of the accessories can be moved in its bracket, or there is a separate idler pulley which does not drive anything, but serves only to tension the belt. On cars with a single belt, the tensioner may be spring-loaded and automatic. If the belt is too loose or too tight, replace the tensioner.

Many accessories or their brackets have special tabs or slots for a wrench or a ratchet drive specifically for moving the accessory. If you must pry on an accessory, take care to pry only on the appropriate, reinforced section or you may damage it.

Do not overtighten a belt. Too much belt tension accelerates wear of the accessory's bearings and shaft. Too little tension allows the belt to slip in its pulleys.

How to Tune Up ANTENNAS

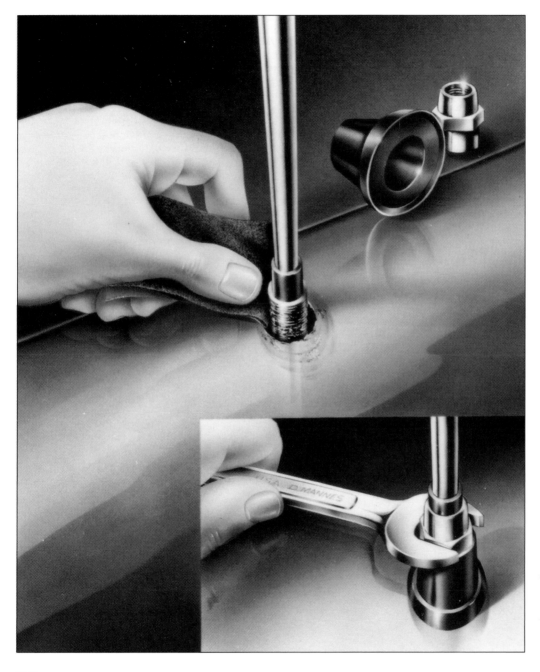

The source of fuzzy sound from your car radio can often be traced to the antenna. The fix is an easy one.

Your car radio's sound quality depends on the antenna. Some cars have the antenna embedded in the windshield or even in the roof, but most have a mast-type antenna. And, while some masts are fixed, most are telescopic. Regardless of type, here's what you should do to ensure a clean signal.

Thoroughly clean the extended mast of bugs and road grime. Then wipe it dry.

Lightly lubricate all moving sections with a petroleum-based penetrating solvent. Wipe away excess lubricant. Do not use silicone-based lubricants, since silicone is not conductive.

The antenna must be grounded to the car. Therefore, even light rust at the antenna's base can deterio-

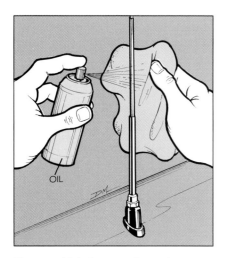

Clean and lubricate a telescoping antenna using a petroleum-based lubricant.

rate radio performance. Undo the antenna's base mount to check.

Remove any rust from the fender or roof mounting hole and the antenna's base clamp, using emery, sandpaper, or a small wire brush. Check and then clean the swiveling bottom clamp on antennas that are so equipped.

Make certain the base gaskets—including sealing washers on mounting screws—are intact. Do not overtighten the mounting nut or screws, or you may distort the car's sheet metal around the hole.

Check that a fixed-mast antenna makes good contact with the base. Use a small open-end wrench on the hex-shaped bottom of the mast to unthread the mast from the base.

Clean any rust or grime from the base connection's threads. Reattach the mast to the base, snugging but not overtightening it to the base threads.

Check the wire connectors at the connections of an integral windshield antenna. Clean corrosion from them. Recrimp loose connectors.

The antenna cable runs from the antenna to the radio. Cars with a rear-mounted antenna may have an extension cable between the radio and the antenna—check any intermediate connections. Make sure the cable end is clean and tight in the radio jack. If necessary, spray the jack connector with contact cleaner and gently recrimp the connector end.

How to Check
EXHAUST SYSTEMS

Probe rusty spots of exhaust plumbing to make sure corrosion is only on the surface.

A routine inspection of your car's exhaust system—two or three times a year—can do more than keep your car performing properly and quietly. It can save your life. Odorless carbon-monoxide gas leaking into your car can make you drowsy or ill. With time, it can kill you.

Though you need no sophisticated tools to inspect the exhaust, you do need goggles or safety glasses to protect your eyes from falling pieces of rusted metal. Also, you'll obviously want a sturdy floor jack and safety stands to raise your vehicle and allow you to work underneath it.

Always perform exhaust system work when the engine and exhaust are cool. Begin the inspection in the engine compartment, then work your way back under the car.

Under the hood, check the exhaust manifold—there are two if your engine is a V6 or V8, one for each cylinder head—which is the part of the exhaust that bolts up to the engine.

- Look for loose or missing mounting bolts or nuts on the manifold.
- Check manifold mounting flanges for cracks.
- Check that the gaskets between the manifold and engine are not broken or missing. Carbon stains on the manifold or the engine adjacent to the manifold indicate a leak.
- Examine connections to components of the emissions-control system, including the tubes or pipes from the manifold(s) to the EGR (exhaust gas recirculation) valve. Look for rusted-through holes, cracks, and deep dents or kinks.
- See that the oxygen sensor—threaded into the manifold—is properly snugged in and not showing any signs of leakage. Check that its wiring is properly connected.

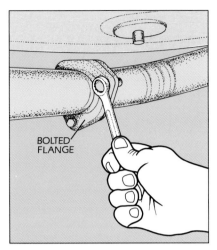

Don't force exhaust system bolts. If the nut or bolt is too tight, use penetrating oil first.

Next, slide underneath your rig. Be sure that it is properly and securely sitting on safety stands. Then:

- Check the connection at the end of the exhaust manifold. Remember, V-type engines have two manifolds. These connections are often spring-loaded. Be sure that the nuts are secure, and that the springs and the gasket—often a sealing ring—are intact.
- Follow the exhaust pipe from the manifold to the catalytic converter, or primary muffler, on to the connecting pipes, the secondary muffler, and finally the tailpipe. Run your gloved hand over each pipe and muffler, feeling for holes, cracks, or deep dents.
- Use an old screwdriver to jab at each pipe, connection, and muffler. If you can poke the screwdriver through the surface rust, the component should be replaced.
- Check all clamps and hanger brackets. Tighten any loose nuts or bolts. This requires the correct-size box wrench or socket. You may have to treat the nuts and bolts with penetrating oil before attempting to turn them. Otherwise, they may break off.
- Twist and inspect all rubber hangers. Cracked, chunked, or broken hangers should be replaced.

How to Check
SUSPENSION SYSTEMS

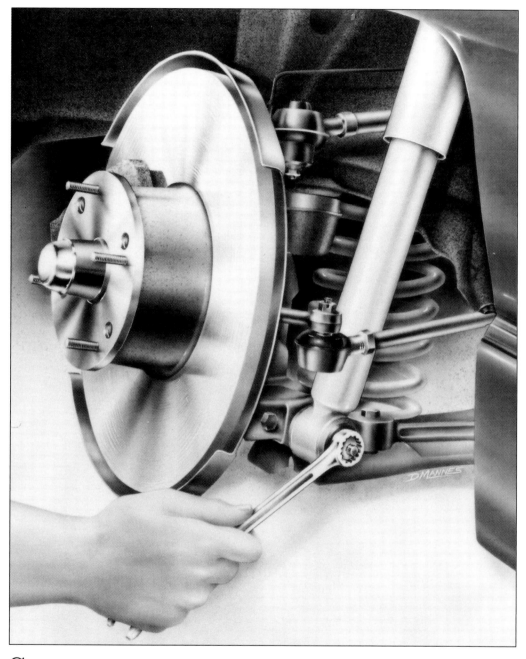

With the wheels off and the car on stands, you can check the tightness of the suspension bolts.

Severely worn shock absorbers and springs do more than make you seasick as your car wends its way down the road. They can dangerously deteriorate your car's handling, and cause tires and other components to wear prematurely. To prevent such an extreme condition, inspect your vehicle's suspension at least twice a year.

You must work underneath your car to check the springs, shock absorbers, and the various links and rubber mounts that compose the suspension. To do that safely and easily, you must raise the car and place it on safety stands. Make sure the safety stands are on a stable base—either a concrete garage floor or 2 × 2-ft. pieces of ½-in. plywood.

To inspect the front suspension, chock the rear tires before raising one front wheel with the jack.

27

Place a safety stand under a solid frame member or mounting point. Lower the car onto the safety stand.

Jack up the front wheel on the other side, and place a stand in a matching spot on that side. Lower that side of the car onto the stand. For added safety, leave the partially raised jack in contact with the car.

Slide under the car and look at each wheel's spring and shock absorber.

Check that the spring is properly seated, top and bottom.

Check for cracks or obvious deformation of the coils.

Check the shock-absorber tubes for dents, dings, and cracks.

Carefully inspect the shock absorber for signs of leaking oil on the tubes.

Inspect the upper and lower mounts of the shock absorber for loose or missing mount bolts, and missing or broken rubber bushings.

If mount bolts are loose, tighten them. But if any mounts are broken or if any of the shock absorbers or springs are physically damaged, they must be replaced. In fact, if one front (or rear) shock absorber or spring is bad, both front and rear units should be changed as a pair.

Check all the rubber bushings that mount the metal suspension components to the chassis as well as to each other.

Bushings that are more than slightly cracked and dried or are missing chunks of rubber must be replaced.

Check that the bushing mount bolts are snug.

Dry, squeaking bushings can be lubricated with some aerosol silicone. Apply the silicone sparingly.

Inspect all the metal rods, links, and arms, including the antiroll bar, for dents, bends, and cracks.

Check that all mount nuts and bolts are secure.

After inspecting the front suspension, lower the car and repeat the process at the rear.

With the car back on the ground, push down on each corner of the car in turn, and let the spring and shock absorber bounce it back up. If any corner of the car bounces more than twice, that shock absorber is due to be replaced.

To check the shocks, push down on one end of each bumper and observe the reaction.

How to Maintain
LOCKS AND HINGES

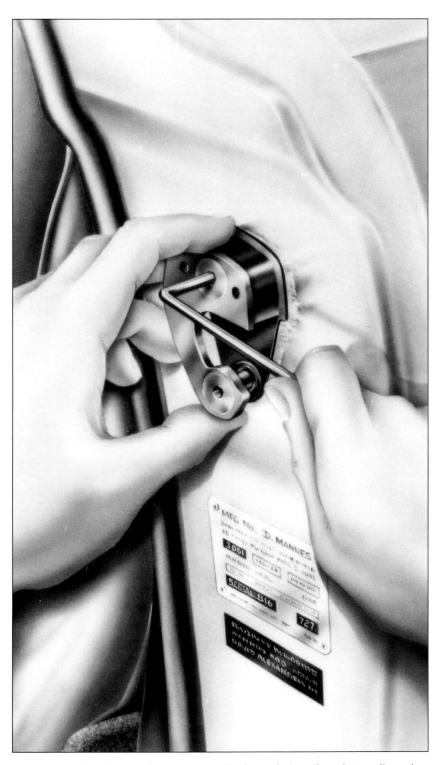

A groaning car door irritates you each time you open it. And a hinge or lock that freezes can leave you stranded. Fortunately, it's easy to keep all doors and locks working smoothly and quietly. A twice-a-year maintenance regimen is all that's needed.

Different areas require different lubricants. The ones to use are:

- Waterproof white grease. Do not use multipurpose lithium grease, which is too thick. Nonstaining grease protects upholstery and clothing.
- Clean engine oil.
- Graphite-based lock lubricant. This can be a powder, a squeeze tube, or an aerosol.

Before you apply any new lubricant, clean off the old, caked-on, dirt-laden lube. Use a grease-removing solvent such as mineral spirits on a clean rag or an aerosol degreaser with a finely adjustable spray nozzle. Read any cautions on the label. Dry all the parts before lubricating.

Generally, more closely assembled parts, such as hinge pivot pins, should be oiled. Parts with larger clearances, such as latches and sliding metal pieces, should be greased.

Use a small amount of graphite-based lube on all of the lock cylinders.

Poorly aligned, Ill-closing doors may need to have their striker plates adjusted.

Squirt a small amount of oil onto the pin that goes through the door hinge.

Oil each hinge on each door, as well as the hinge pins of the trunk lid (or rear hatch) and hood.

Don't forget the pivot pins of the fuel-filler door.

Open and close the doors, trunk, and hood several times to work in the oil. Wipe off any excess oil.

If a door, trunk lid, or hatch does not close smoothly, or if it does not properly line up with the rest of the car, its latching mechanism, or striker, may need to be adjusted.

With the door, trunk lid, or hatch closed, see if it has to be moved in or out to align with the adjacent

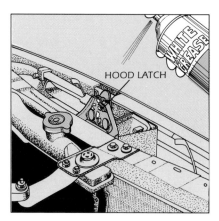

White grease is best for hood and trunk latches. Be sure to wipe off any excess.

body panels. Partially loosen the striker's mounting screws on the car body. Move the striker *slightly* in the direction needed—either in or out—and snug down the mounting screws. Recheck the alignment.

Grease the hood latch and the hood hinge springs.

Open and close the hood and trunk lid several times. Wipe away excess.

Since even the thinnest oil holds dirt and grit that can jam a lock, use graphite to lubricate all locks. Hold the lock open with the tip of a key to spray into the lock. Insert, twist, and remove the key a few times. Then wipe it clean.

How to Replace Your SPARK PLUGS

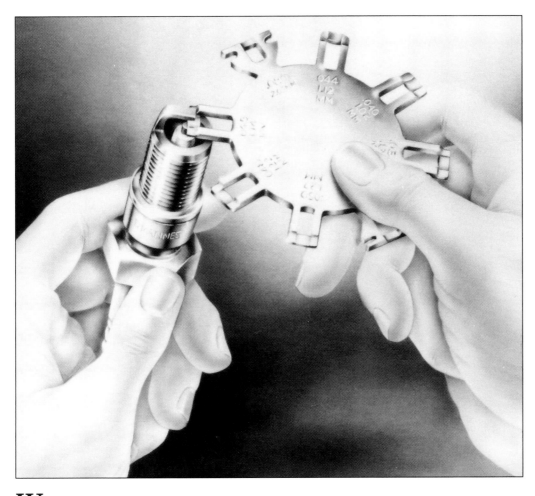

Use a spark-gap tool to measure and adjust the gap between the spark plug's electrode.

While your owner's manual gives the carmaker's recommendation for spark-plug replacement intervals, play it safe by changing plugs at least once a year. The task is relatively inexpensive, since new spark plugs cost a few dollars, and installation is relatively simple.

To do the job right, you'll need a ratchet, a spark-plug socket sized for your plugs, and a few extensions to allow you to reach all the plugs. You'll need a special spark-gap tool to measure and adjust the gap between the plug's electrodes. You also might need a spark-plug boot puller, silicone spray, and some antiseize thread compound. Naturally, you'll need the right number of new plugs. Check your owner's manual for the specified spark plug.

Some plugs have long threaded portions, others short. Plugs also are made in several different diameters. Some plugs require a metal ring gasket to seal the plug against the engine, others do not.

The wrong plug can damage your engine. Don't experiment with plugs that look close.

Work on a cool engine, and change one spark plug at a time, starting at one end and working in order. To begin, disconnect the spark plug's wire from the plug. Do not pull the wire—you can break it internally. Twist and tug on the heavy boot that covers the plug.

Use a special spark-plug wire pulling tool or a looped piece of wire for boots you can't grasp. Next, remove the plug. You may have to

rap the ratchet handle with the heel of your hand if the plug is in tight.

Before removing the plug totally, blow air through a hose to remove dirt and debris from around the base of the plug.

After extracting the old plug, inspect it. Its electrodes should be golden brown. Heavy black or blistered white deposits indicate a problem. If there are no problems, prepare to install the new plug.

Check the electrode gap. The tuneup decal under the hood lists the correct gap. Adjust the gap as necessary by gently bending the hooked side electrode as needed.

Put a dab of antiseize compound on the plug's threads to help the plug come out easily next time.

If the replacement plugs have

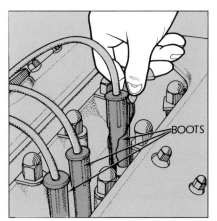

You may need to use a special tool to remove stubborn spark-plug connector boots.

gaskets, be sure there's one on the new plug. Also be sure the old gasket came off along with the old plug.

Thread the new plug in by hand to avoid crossing the threads. Use a piece of hose slipped over the top of the plug, or use the spark-plug socket without the ratchet handle.

Snug the spark plug down with the ratchet, but don't overtighten it, or you may damage the plug.

Before reattaching the spark plug's wire, spray some silicone into the boot. This makes it easier to remove the wire the next time.

Place the boot over the tip of the plug and push it home, making sure that the metal connector inside the boot connects to the plug.

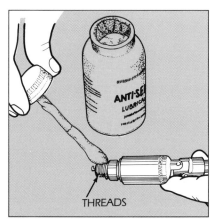

Use antiseize compound on the threads of new plugs to facilitate their removal.

How to Check
WHEEL BEARINGS

Periodically spin the raised nondrive wheels of a car. Release the parking brake if these are rear wheels.

The bearings in your car's non-drive wheels need to be periodically inspected, cleaned, and lubricated. To perform this service, jack up the end of the car that you will be working on, and support it on safety stands.

Spin the raised wheels—the parking brake must be released if you are inspecting the rear wheels. The wheel should spin smoothly with no squeaking, shrieking, grinding, or rattling. Do not confuse the scraping noise of brake pads dragging on the brake rotor with bearing noise.

Be certain that the wheel's lug nuts are snug, then grasp the tire at top and bottom and try to rock the wheel in and out. You should not be able to feel any discernible movement. If you can feel any looseness or roughness, or if you have not cleaned the bearings and repacked them with grease in 30,000 miles or so, disassemble and clean them.

With the tire and wheel off, pry the dust cap from the middle of the hub. If the nut is held by a cotter pin, remove and discard it. Install a new cotter pin later. If your car uses a special lock-nut, use a long punch to unlock it from the slot in the axle. Use a new nut when you reassem-ble. Use a socket on a ratchet to undo the nut. Rock the hub to remove the retaining washer and outer bearing.

Slide the hub off the axle and place it on two blocks of wood. Use a long drift or punch to knock the grease seal out of the back of the hub. The inner bearing will fall out with the seal.

Thoroughly clean all the pieces with mineral spirits. Allow the bearings to dry by themselves on a clean cloth.

Carefully inspect each roller and the thin metal cage that holds them. Also inspect the bearings' outer

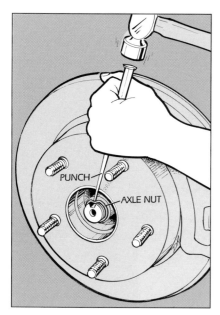

Wheel bearings on many new cars have a nut that is peened into a locking groove and must be discarded after it is removed.

A bearing that shows chips, spalling, or deep scratches must be replaced.

races—the hard metal ring that is pressed into the hub—that the rollers run against. Any deep scratches, spalling, chips, or heat discoloration means the bearing must be replaced.

Pack the cleaned bearings with fresh wheel-bearing grease. Do not use multipurpose grease. Force the grease into and around all of the rollers. Also fill the cavity in the wheel hub at least one-third full with grease.

Place the inner bearing back in the wheel hub and install a new seal. Use a ball-peen hammer against a block of hardwood or a hockey puck to seat the new seal.

Carefully slide the hub onto the axle shaft, and replace the outer bearing and the retaining washer. Spin the hub as you tighten the retaining nut. Check your carmaker's specifications for tightening the retaining nut.

Insert a new cotter pin—loosening rather than tightening the nut to align the nut's slots if necessary—and bend over its ends or peen down the tab of a new nut for cars that use special locking retaining nuts.

How to
DEGREASE YOUR ENGINE

A clean engine makes for easier maintenance, and runs cooler to boot.

Accumulated underhood dirt and grease can cut into your engine's performance. But even a moderate coating of grit and grime will cut into your enthusiasm for basic engine maintenance. The bonus is it's easier—problems are quick to spot and correct in a clean engine.

Degreasing even the most neglected engine is easy—and inexpensive. Follow these steps:

Begin by carefully shopping for a quality engine degreaser. Buy one that's environmentally safe and biodegradable. Cleaners that are slightly caustic will lightly etch aluminum components, making them look new.

Next, protect body panels and electrical components from engine cleaner and water.

Cover fenders, grille, and windshield with plastic trash bags.

Seal the air intake, carb opening, or throttle housing with plastic.

Wrap the distributor cap, exposed connections on the ignition coil, and starter motor.

Assess how grime-covered the engine is. Even the most potent cleaners have trouble cutting through a quarter-inch of caked-on grease. Use a gasket scraper or putty knife to scrape accumulations of crud. Dig caked-on dirt and mud from crevices, using an old screwdriver.

Now apply the degreaser to the engine, firewall, fender liners, and the rest of the engine compartment. Follow the directions on the cleaner: Some recommend being used on a cold engine, some a warm engine.

Engine cleaners are still potent chemicals. Wear safety goggles and a pair of rubber or vinyl work gloves.

Use a strong stream of water to wash off the cleaner. Attack specific, stubborn spots individually.

Use a wire brush and water to clean corrosion from battery terminals and tray. If there's a lot of white chalky buildup, wipe the battery and connections with a baking-soda-and-water paste, then hose it clean.

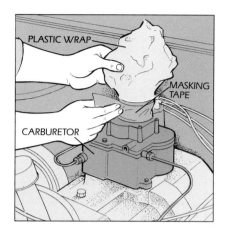

Cover carb inlet and distributor with plastic or foil to keep dirt and water out.

Stubborn dirt will need scrubbing with a brush. Be careful near carb and distributor.

Rinse off the engine degreaser with plenty of water from the garden hose.

How to Replace a
BATTERY

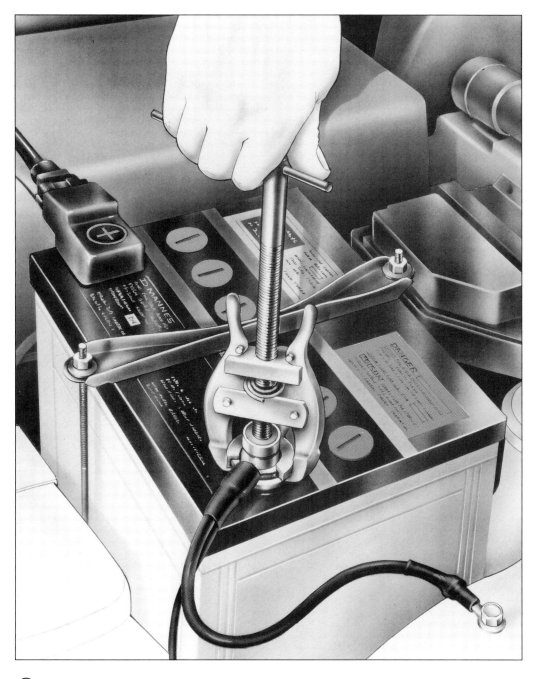

Begin by undoing the ground cable connection. On all modern vehicles this is the negative post.

Over time, a battery loses its ability to hold the charge given to it by the alternator. As the chemicals in the battery age, the battery may not have even the energy to start the engine. Sensible maintenance suggests you replace the battery before you're stranded some cold, lonely night.

Test the battery's strength using a voltmeter. With ambient temperature of about 70°F, the meter should read at least 12 volts.

Or, if the starter motor groans or quickly loses verve as it struggles to crank the engine, the battery may be ready to be replaced. But before condemning your battery, inspect the rest of the charging system (see next chapter, "How to Check Your Charging System").

You can buy an exact duplicate of your car's battery from the dealership or a quality replacement from an auto parts store or large discount chain.

Before you decide to take on the relatively simple task of replacing your vehicle's battery, remember that an automotive battery is filled with sulfuric acid. Spilled acid can burn your skin and eat through clothing. Wear work gloves, eye protection, and old clothing when replacing a battery.

Buy a replacement battery that is rated as powerful enough to start your engine. The strength of auto batteries is rated in Cold Cranking Amps (CCA) and Hours Reserve.

Check that the positive and negative battery posts are at the same corners of the new battery as the old and that the new battery will sit securely in the battery tray.

Also check that your existing battery holddown bracket will work on the replacement battery. If you're not sure, or if the bracket is corroded, replace that as well as the battery.

Begin by first undoing the ground-cable connection from the battery post. On all modern vehicles, this is the negative post.

Loosen the nut and bolt holding the clamp connection to the post or remove the bolt if the battery has side terminals.

Twist the cable clamp to loosen it on the post. If it is tight, use an inexpensive puller tool made for the job. Lay the cable aside. With the ground disconnected, it is safe to undo the positive cable clamp.

Remove the battery bracket. This may be held in place by wing nuts and require no tools, or it may be held by one or more hex nuts, requiring the correct-size socket or wrench. Lift out the old battery and carefully place it aside.

Clean any corrosion from the battery tray and its compartment. A mixture of baking soda and water neutralizes acid corrosion. Flush with clean water.

Place the battery in the tray, with the terminal posts at the proper corners. Reattach the holddown clamp or bracket and snug it in place.

Clean the cable connections before attaching them to the new battery. An inexpensive wire brush, available at auto parts stores, does a fine job.

Connect the positive cable to the battery's positive terminal. Be sure the cable clamp is squarely on the post, and snug the nut and bolt.

Connect the ground cable to the battery's negative terminal post, and snug the nut and bolt.

For side-terminal batteries, clean both surfaces of the cable end and the threads of the cable bolts before attaching them. Again, connect the positive cable first.

Coat the connections with petroleum jelly to retard corrosion.

How to Check Your CHARGING SYSTEM

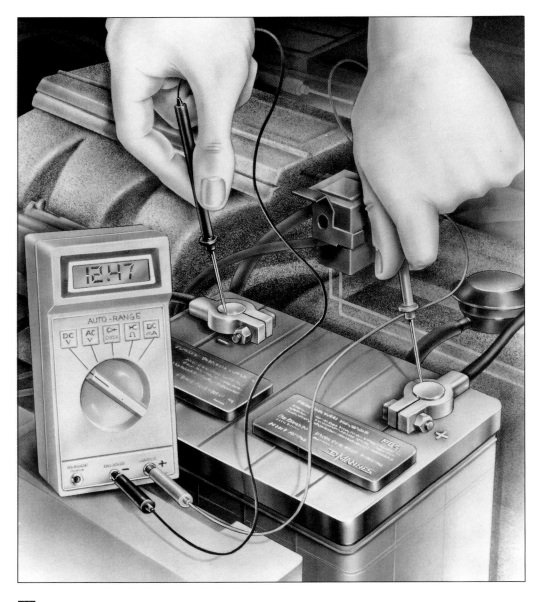

A voltmeter is used to test components powered by the alternator.

The electrical power for the ignition, electronic fuel injection, engine computer, lights, heater fan, and sound system is all generated by the alternator. The alternator also charges the battery, which is needed to supply the electricity necessary to get the car started. You should check the charging system periodically.

While thorough testing requires a voltmeter, you may also make some simple but effective charging system checks using a 12-volt test light.

Start at the battery, but be careful. The battery is filled with corrosive sulfuric acid and, when it is charging, it produces explosive hydrogen gas—do not smoke or bring an open flame near a battery.

Make sure the cable connections at the battery are snug and corrosion free. An inexpensive battery-terminal cleaning brush does an excellent job of cleaning these connections.

If the battery has removable cell caps, be sure that there is the correct amount of electrolyte in the cells. Add distilled water as necessary. Also be sure the cables themselves and the connections to the starter and the engine or chassis are intact.

Disconnect the battery's ground terminal and attach a voltmeter to the battery's two terminals.

When the outside temperature is about 70°F, the voltmeter should read at least 12 volts. If not, the battery needs to be charged or replaced.

But first check the alternator.

Inspect the alternator drivebelt for cracks, missing chunks, and glazed surfaces. Also check the belt's tension. When tensioning an alternator belt, do not pry on the alternator housing. You can easily crack the alternator's soft aluminum housing.

Next check the alternator's output. If you have a voltmeter, connect it to the battery and start the engine. With the engine running at about 2,500 rpm and all accessories off, the meter should read about 14 to 15 volts. If the reading is higher, the voltage regulator may be defective.

With the lights and accessories on and the engine running at 2,500 rpm, the meter should read 12 to 13 volts. If not, the alternator may be defective.

Double-check by connecting the voltmeter's positive lead to the BAT terminal on the alternator and the negative to a ground on the engine.

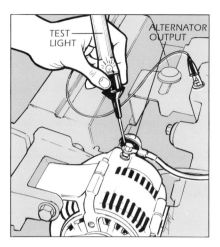

Check the connection between the alternator and battery using a grounded test light.

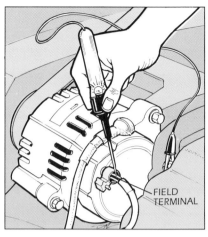

On GM cars, a test light should glow brightly at all terminals with the engine running.

The voltmeter should read no less than 12.5 volts, engine running and accessories on. If it reads less, the alternator is defective. If it reads more than about 13 volts, there may be a problem with the voltage regulator.

If you have a GM car or truck, a

test light should glow dimly when touched to the alternator's Terminal 1 and brightly when touched to the BAT terminal with the engine off. With the engine running, the test light should glow brightly at all the terminals.

How to Use a
VACUUM GAUGE

As your engine's pistons go down during the intake stroke, they cause a drop in air pressure inside the intake manifold. That drop in pressure, or partial vacuum, draws in the air your engine needs to mix with fuel for combustion. In fact, the speed of a gasoline engine is controlled by regulating the flow of air into the engine. The accelerator pedal is attached to a throttle plate in the intake airstream. The more air, the more fuel to mix with it for more power and speed.

Thanks to the throttle plate, you can measure the partial vacuum created by a running gasoline engine, and that measurement is an accurate and handy indicator of the engine's condition. All you need is a vacuum gauge. Most automotive vacuum gauges are packaged with a length of vacuum hose and various adapters. The adapters allow you to connect the gauge to engine vacuum hoses of varying inside diameters.

Vacuum is measured as inches of mercury and the gauge is marked "in.-Hg." with the scale typically running from zero to 30. Many vacuum gauges also double as low-pressure testers, for checking mechanical fuel pumps, and have a second scale marked in psi. However, the pressure scale has no bearing on vacuum.

Here's a step-by-step guide for using a vacuum gauge:

For an accurate reading, attach the gauge to a hose that is subject to the engine's full vacuum—one connected to the intake manifold between the throttle plate and the engine. Good choices are the hose to the distributor and power-brake booster. Bad choices are components that don't get vacuum all the time—such as various emissions controls.

To ensure that the engine is running properly with the gauge attached, splice the gauge connection into the vacuum source hose with a T-connection. If you must disconnect the vacuum source hose from a component to attach the gauge,

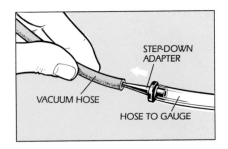

STEP-DOWN ADAPTER

VACUUM HOSE

HOSE TO GAUGE

An adapter allows the gauge's larger hose to connect securely to a smaller vacuum hose.

disconnect it from a component that is not related to engine performance, such as the power-brake booster. Remember to reconnect the hose when you're done.

With the gauge attached and engine fully warmed and idling, whip open the throttle briefly and let it snap shut while watching the gauge. The needle should drop to about 5 to 7 in.-Hg. and then quickly rise to its reading.

A healthy engine reads about 16 to 22 in.-Hg. (check your car's service manual) at sea level. Deduct 1 to 2 in.-Hg. for every one thousand feet of altitude. If the gauge reads steady but appreciably lower—about 5 to 7 in.-Hg.—look for a vacuum leak. Recheck the gauge connections. Then look at the intake manifold and other vacuum hoses.

A steady but low reading in the 10- to 14-in.-Hg. range indicates low compression—as from worn piston rings—or incorrect ignition timing.

A reading that is steady but higher than about 22 in.-Hg. could indicate a blocked air intake. Remove the air cleaner element and retest.

If the gauge needle swings back and forth wildly, between about 10 and 20 in.-Hg., there is probably a problem with the engine's valves.

A smooth fluctuation of the needle—in cadence with the engine's idling—points to a leaking head gasket and lost compression.

If the vacuum drops to nearly zero and then climbs back to near normal after you whip the throttle, check for exhaust system restrictions.

How to Use a
TEST LIGHT

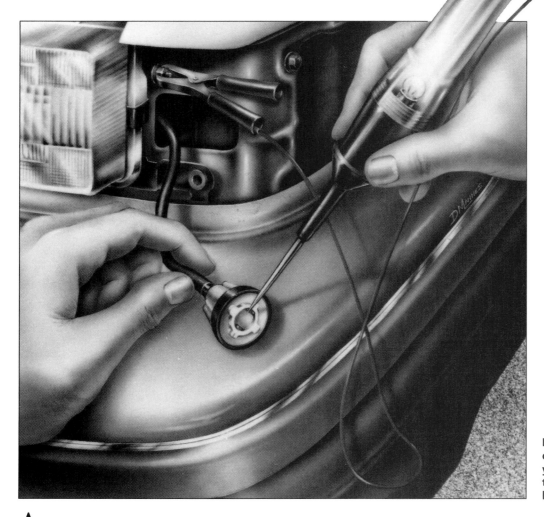

If the electrical circuit is hot, then your connection tester's lamp will light up.

Although you can make a test light with wire and a bulb, you'll be better off buying one. When shopping, there are certain things to look for.

Make sure you buy an automotive test light, not a household one. Automotive electrical systems are 12-volt, direct current (DC), while household electricity is 110/120-volt, alternating current (AC).

One of the leads should be a long wire of at least 14-gauge thickness, with a heavy alligator clip at the end so you can easily reach the area where you need to work. The other lead should be a pointed metal probe that can cleanly pierce the insulation of wires you need to test and probe into wire connectors.

Test lights work on a simple idea: By connecting the light to both ground and to a power source, you complete an electrical circuit, and the bulb in the test light glows. If the bulb doesn't light up, there's a problem.

Before attempting to trace any problems, always check that the light is working. Connect the light to your car's charged battery. If the light doesn't go on, change its bulb and/or check its leads.

Whenever an electrical component stops working, first check its fuse. See your owner's manual for the location of the fuse panel, usually under the dash in a kick panel.

Make sure the ignition and the switch for the suspect part are on.

Connect the light to a good ground, such as a metal bolt or bracket.

Probe both sides of the fuse with the test light. Modern, color-coded plastic spade fuses have small test holes.

If only one side of the fuse illuminates the test light, the fuse is blown. If both sides light, the fuse is good.

If the fuse is good, you can use the test light to see if the component itself is bad or if there's a bad connection or broken wire between the fuse and the component. Since at least one wire that goes to the component has to carry electricity to it, that wire will be "hot" when the switches are on.

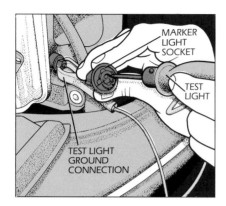

Be sure the circuit you're testing is actually turned on at the switch.

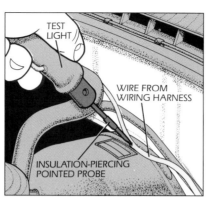

Use the sharp probe to pierce the plastic insulation of the wires.

Ground the test light near the nonworking light or accessory. With the test light's metal tip, probe the wire connector where it attaches to the component. The light should go on in at least one connection. If not, there's a break in the circuit.

Electric circuits need a ground connection to be complete. Use the test light to check these as well.

Connect the light to the component's ground wire or connection. Touch the light's probe to the battery's positive terminal, or another known "hot" source. If the light doesn't glow, the ground is bad.

How to Service
BRAKES

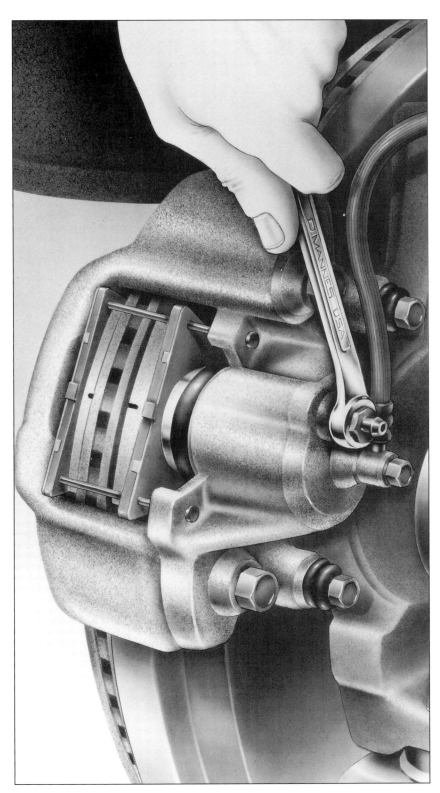

Each time you step on the brake pedal, you count on the brake system to slow or stop your car or truck. If the brake system fails, it can be disastrous. However, some regular inspections and periodic maintenance should keep the brakes working for the life of your vehicle.

Every late-model car or light truck uses disc brakes at the front wheels. These do most of the braking and wear more quickly than the rears. They are also easy to maintain.

Check the master cylinder for a sudden drop in fluid level and signs of leaks. Next, place the vehicle on safety stands. Remove the front wheels.

Inspect the brake hoses for leaks, cracks, chafing, or other damage.

Check the hose fittings and connections for corrosion or leaks.

Inspect the discs (also called rotors) for deep grooves, cracks, surface unevenness, or other damage.

Check how much friction material is left on the brake shoes themselves. Most disc brake shoes have built-in wear indicators in the form of a deep groove down the middle of the friction material. As the ma-

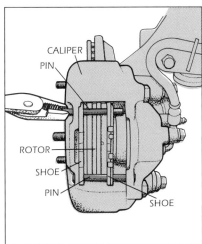

Shoe replacement requires undoing a couple of pins and sliding out the shoes.

terial wears away, the groove disappears. Many brake systems also offer an audible brake-lining wear indicator which shrieks if the brake shoes are dangerously worn.

If everything checks out all right, put the wheels back on. However, if it has been more than two years since the brake fluid has been flushed from the brake system, it's a good idea to replace it with fresh fluid. The fluid in the brake system collects water and impurities which can damage the system. And if the brake shoes are worn, they must be replaced.

To flush the old brake fluid, attach a small hose to the bleeder fitting on the brake farthest from the master cylinder—the right rear. Place the other end of the hose in a container.

Loosen the fitting nut and have a helper step on the brake pedal.

Close the fitting while he still has the pedal down. After he releases the pedal, top up the master cylinder.

Repeat the operation three times, or until the brake fluid becomes water-clear. Next, do it at the left-rear brake. Then go to the front brakes.

To replace worn disc brake shoes, undo any retaining clips holding the pins that run through the caliper. Remove the pins from the caliper.

With the pins out, the only thing holding the brake shoes is the pressure from the caliper piston. Carefully push the piston back into the caliper, using either a large C-clamp or a large screwdriver or pry bar. Don't pinch the piston's boot.

Pull the old brake shoes out of the caliper, noting which is the inner shoe as well as the presence and position of any clips or backing plates.

Put the backing plates over the new brake shoes and apply a thin coat of antirattle paste to the backs of the new brake shoes or backing plates.

Slide the new shoes in place.

Clean and reinstall the pins.

Reattach any retainers.

How to Use a
MULTIMETER

You may never have considered the idea, but you might want to purchase an electric multimeter. These handy little devices measure electric voltage, amperage, and resistance and allow you to find short circuits, broken wires, defective switches, and even failing—or failed—electric motors. If you so desire, and gain some proficiency, you can even use a multimeter to diagnose problems with your car or truck's fuel injection and ignition systems.

Before you step up and lay down your good money for an electric multimeter, you must understand that there are two basic varieties—and the differences between the two can be critical.

The first type, and probably the least expensive, is an analog meter, with a needle that sweeps back and forth across a scale. The second, more preferable, and slightly more costly, type has a digital readout instead of a needle. However, the critical difference is not the difference between the needle or digital readout; the important difference is the multimeter's own internal resistance.

As with every piece of electrical equipment, multimeters offer resistance to the electricity that flows through them as they make their measurements. The old-fashioned meters have a low resistance, and are called low-impedance meters. The newer, digital types have a higher resistance, and thus are called high-impedance meters.

Since newer cars use transistorized circuits that are also low-resistance, a low-resistance meter may give an inaccurate reading, or worse, possibly damage some of your car's electronic circuits by allowing high current to flow through the meter's circuits.

When shopping for a meter, besides looking for one with high impedance, look for a meter with long test leads and, if possible, a ground test lead with a clip at one end. High-impedance, digital multimeters are available at electrical supply stores and auto parts stores for under about $20.

To use the meter, first turn it on and then set the selector to the appropriate scale—for working on your car, that would most likely be the DC voltage, and if your meter has a high- and low-voltage setting, select the low (0–20 volt) range.

Connect the ground—that's the negative and usually black—to a solid ground near where you're working. That means a clean, not painted, not rusty bolt or bracket on the engine or chassis. Then touch the positive, or red, lead to the electric source, such as the battery's positive terminal.

If the battery is good, the meter should read about 12.6 volts. Start the car, and the voltage should rise to 13–14 volts if the charging system is working correctly.

You can use the voltage function to troubleshoot any 12-volt circuit—lights, power windows or antennas, starter. With the black lead connected to ground, switch on the troublesome accessory and check for voltage at the accessory's connection. Assuming there is no reading, keep moving the meter's positive probe along the accessory's wire toward the switch or fuse until you get a 12-volt reading. As soon as the reading goes from zero to 12, you have found the problem. If the reading does not go to 12 volts until you get to switch, the switch is probably defective.

In addition to measuring voltage, you can use a multimeter to measure a component's electrical resistance—whether an item is in the car or on the workbench. By checking the resistance of an electrical motor, you can determine if the motor is beginning to fail. You can also check the resistance of spark plug wires to determine if the wire is damaged internally or if the insulation is beginning to come apart and allowing high-voltage electricity to leak out.

For instance, almost any electrical motor used in an automobile will have a resistance to ground of almost zero—often less than a single ohm. And a spark plug wire should read several thousand ohms per foot of length. In the case of the motor, a high resistance—say 3,000 ohms—would indicate a burned-out motor. A spark plug wire might read an infinite resistance, indicating an internal break.

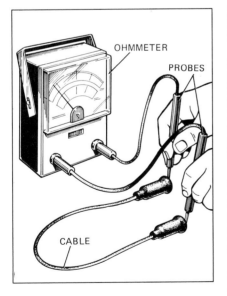

Check your spark plug leads with the ohmmeter function on a multimeter. A typical reading is about 10,000 ohms for resistor-type wires.

How to Aim HEADLIGHTS

If you never disturb the aim of your car's headlights, you should never have to reaim them. However, it may take less than you think to disturb their aiming accuracy.

Obviously, if the front of the car or truck is involved in even a seemingly insignificant fender-bender, the headlights may be out of whack. Less obviously, each time you replace a sealed beam or halogen bulb in a composite headlight, the accuracy of the light's aim might be affected.

Therefore, periodically, and after replacing a light, you should check the headlight aim.

Before beginning, be sure that the tires are all properly inflated, there is no huge load in the trunk or cargo bed, and the springs aren't sagging. Also, the vehicle must be parked on a level surface.

All headlights have adjusting screws, in addition to their mounting or retaining screws. However, you may have to remove a trim ring or bezel to gain access to them. You will find one along the top or bottom edge of the light that adjusts the beam up and down, and another similar screw on either side of the light that adjusts it left and right. The adjusting screws are spring-loaded.

Some newer models have bubble-type level sight glasses built into each headlight housing. To aim these, turn the adjusting screws until the bubble is centered in the marks in the sight glass.

If your car or truck is not equipped with these sight-glass levels, try the following procedure:

- Pull the car or truck right up against a flat, light-colored wall.
- Make chalk marks on the wall opposite the center of each headlight. If you have a four-headlight system, make the marks in front of all four lights.
- Move the car away from the wall and make large, easily seen crosses through the chalk marks.

Many newer cars have built-in levels for aiming the headlights. Be sure the vehicle is parked on a dead-flat, level surface. Consult your owner's manual for correct settings.

- Park the car or truck so the lights are twenty-five feet away from the wall.
- Turn on the headlight low beams—the outer two or upper two in a four-light system. The bulk of the light pattern should fall just below and to the right of the crosses that correspond to the centers of these lights.
- Turn the appropriate adjusting screw in or out, in quarter-turn increments, to move the beam as needed.

On two-light systems, adjusting the low beam should also adjust the high beam. On four-light systems, however, you have to repeat the process with the separate high-beam units. Since the low beams will also be on when you switch to high beams, you must block their light so you can clearly see the high-beam pattern on the wall. Mask the low-beam units with a small piece of wood or heavy cardboard. The center of the high beams' light should fall about 2 in. below the center of the crosses on the wall.

Double-check your headlight aim by driving down a dark road. The low beams should illuminate the road only in front of the car. The high beams should light up the road up to about three hundred feet ahead of you, as well as illuminating trees and lampposts along the right shoulder.

48

How to Check
UNDERHOOD FLUIDS

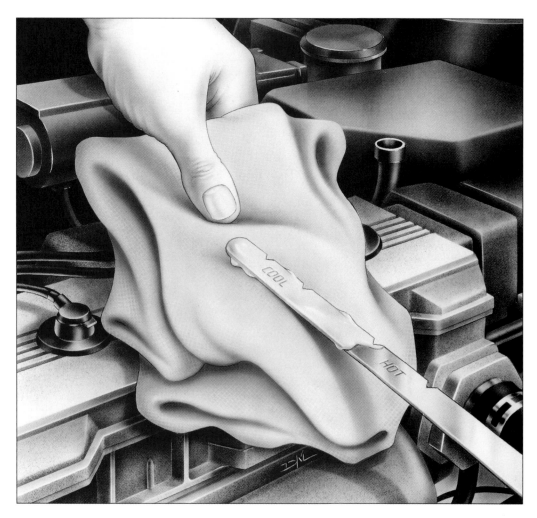

Transmission dipstick should typically be checked with the transmission completely warmed up, engine idling in Park. Check your owner's manual for details, use the specified type of ATF, and *don't* overfill.

One of the most basic maintenance procedures is also the most important—checking all of your car or truck's vital fluids at least once every week.

The best time to do this is after you've just driven several miles, so the fluids and components are at their normal operating temperature. For accuracy, your car or truck should be parked on a level surface. All the items you'll need to check are located under the hood, and the full routine should take less than five minutes.

Begin with the engine oil.

- Locate the engine-oil dipstick. Cars equipped with manual transmissions usually have just one dipstick. Automatic transmission–equipped cars have a second dipstick for checking the transmission fluid level.
- Pull the dipstick entirely out of its tube in the engine and wipe it clean using a cloth or paper towel.
- Inspect the stick's bottom end if you are not familiar with it. The metal stick will have markings—possibly notches, holes, hatch marks, or lines—indicating a full level and a low level. The dipstick may also indicate an acceptable area between them.

- Reinsert the dipstick into its tube. Be sure that it is fully seated, and remove it again.
- Check the oil level on the stick.
- If the level is low, add only enough oil to bring the level up to—but not above—the FULL mark. If the level indicates the crankcase is a half-quart low, do not add a full quart of oil. Add a half-quart, or wait until the level drops to a full quart low. Oil added above the FULL mark will leak out.
- When adding oil, use a name brand of quality oil that meets

the specifications listed in your owner's manual.

- Locate the oil filler cap on top of the engine. After removing the cap and adding oil, wipe up any spills and retighten the cap securely.
- Recheck the oil level and fully reinsert the dipstick.

Next, check the transmission oil or fluid level. Most cars and trucks with an automatic transmission have a dipstick similar to the engine oil dipstick. On some cars, automatic transmission fluid is checked with the engine idling, on others the engine must be off. See your owner's manual.

- Remove the dipstick, wipe it clean, reinsert it fully, and then pull it out to check the fluid level.
- Add fluid only if the level is low. Too much fluid in automatic transmissions can lead to shifting problems.

- With most cars, the transmission fluid gets poured down the dipstick tube. Use a long-necked funnel or a funnel attached to a length of hose for access to the tube.

Checking the engine coolant level on most cars now merely involves looking at the coolant recovery reservoir mounted to one side of the radiator. The reservoir usually shows level indicators when the coolant is cold and when it is hot.

- If your car or truck does not have a reservoir, remove the radiator cap and check the level in the radiator. Do not open the radiator cap until the radiator is cool to the touch or you may be severely scalded by hot, pressurized coolant.
- Add a 50/50 mix of antifreeze and water to raise the coolant level to an inch below the radiator neck to allow room for coolant expansion.

- If your car has a reservoir, pour the coolant directly into the reservoir; there is no need to open the radiator cap.

Brake fluid can be checked by looking at its level in the master cylinder's reservoir. On all modern vehicles, this reservoir is translucent—you need not open it to see the fluid.

On vehicles with disc brakes, it is normal for the brake-fluid level to go down as the brakes wear. There is no need to keep topping up the brake fluid as long as the level remains above the MINIMUM mark. A sudden drop in level indicates a problem—have it checked.

On cars with power steering, you can check the level of the power steering fluid by removing the cap from the fluid reservoir. The dipstick is attached to the cap. The level is checked with the engine off. Most dipsticks have marks indicating the correct fluid level when the fluid is cold or hot.

How to Inspect Your TRANSMISSION

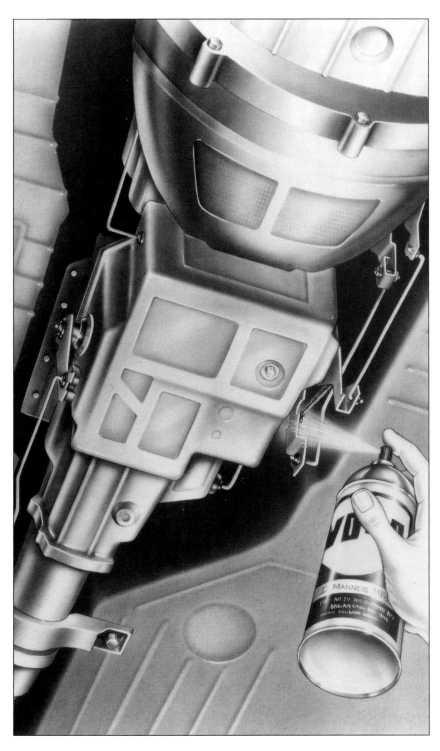

While your engine might be at the top of its game, your transmission may not be taking full advantage of the engine's output. If you neglect the transmission, you are not fully maintaining your vehicle's drive-train.

Begin by checking level and quality of the lubricant in the transmission.

Most automatic transmissions have a dipstick so you can check fluid level. This check may be done with the engine running and idling, or the engine off—check your owner's manual.

Some manual gearboxes for front-wheel-drive cars have dipsticks. On some, the dipstick may be the speedometer cable. Check your owner's manual.

Manual gearboxes on rear-wheel-drive vehicles do not have a dipstick. Check the oil level from underneath. Remove an inspection plug on the side of the gearbox housing—the oil level should be up to the bottom of the plug's hole.

Top up the transmission, if necessary, using the lubricant specified by the carmaker. Some manual gearboxes may require a specific grade of oil or possibly automatic transmission fluid. There are different types of automatic transmission fluids—only use the type specified in your owner's manual.

Do not overfill any gearbox, automatic or manual. If you overfill a manual gearbox, you can increase internal drag, and create leaks.

In addition to checking the level of the transmission's lubricant, check its quality. Most carmakers recommend draining and refilling the gearbox lubricant periodically.

Automatic transmissions also have an internal filter to keep crud from getting into the sophisticated transmission valve body. This filter must be periodically cleaned or replaced. This requires draining the fluid first, and possibly removing the transmission oil pan.

Next check the exterior of the gearbox.

Raise the car and put it on safety stands or ramps.

Check the operation of the various shift linkages of your automatic or manual transmission. Lubricate the pivots with a water-resistant, light lubricant.

Look for leaks at seals and gaskets. A leaking seal must be replaced. You may be able to cure a leaking gasket by tightening the bolts.

Be sure that any vacuum tubes are connected, and not cracked or torn.

Also inspect all the linkages that control the transmission's operation.

Check shift linkages to see that they are clean and not sticking. Have a helper move the shift lever through all quadrants as you check the linkage movements.

On automatic transmissions with a mechanical, throttle-operated kickdown, have your helper tromp the accelerator pedal (engine off) while you check the operation of the kickdown linkage.

On manual transmissions, have your helper step on the clutch pedal. Check the clutch linkage operation to see that it moves smoothly.

Use an aerosol cleaner to remove corrosion and built-up grease and grime from the joints of the linkage. Use a brush if needed.

Lubricate the linkage joints with a light oil or water-resistant white grease.

How to
JUMP-START YOUR CAR

Sooner or later, it happens to all of us—either we leave the headlights on inadvertently and drain the battery, or our faithful car or truck simply refuses to start. For whatever reason, you're reduced to using jumper cables to provide power to start your engine. In spite of how simple it seems when the man from the auto club does it, there is a wrong way and a right way. The wrong way can potentially damage your car, or the car belonging to your well-meaning helper, or, worse yet, injure one or both of you. Here's the right way:

If your car has simply refused to start for some undetermined reason, and you've discharged the battery while trying to start it, there's no reason to think that simply hooking up a second battery and trying again will do any good. So the first thing to do is to try to figure out what the problem is, and correct it to give you a fighting chance of lighting a fire the next time.

This means checking for fuel and spark. Modern cars are complex—refer to the chapter "What to Do When Your Car Won't Start," and do the troubleshooting first.

On the other hand, leaving the lights on all night gives you a basically sound vehicle that needs only a jump to get going.

Start by selecting your jumper cables. This might not be possible if you're stuck by the side of the road—you'll use the cables you can borrow. But when you go to purchase a set, look for two things. Buy a set of cables that is long enough to go from your battery, whether it's on the right or left side of your engine compartment, to the battery on the opposite side of a booster car's engine compartment—plus about three feet. Better yet would be a set long enough to go to a booster car parked directly behind you—but that might take up a lot of trunk space. Next, look for thick, copper cables. Thinner, aluminum cables are lighter, but will overheat rapidly if your engine needs to be cranked over for more than a few seconds.

Quality cables will outlast your car, so don't be cheap. Store them in a plastic bag to keep corrosion from damaging the clamps.

Once you're ready to actually begin, start by positioning the booster car close enough to your car to stretch the cables. Look under the hood to see where in the engine compartment the battery actually is. Some vehicles have the battery in the trunk. Some vehicles have the battery in an inaccessible position in the engine compartment—but these generally have a terminal block, clearly marked in red, that has a big cable that leads to the battery positive terminal. Simply treat this terminal as if it were the battery's positive post.

Do be careful not to tangle the cables, some important part of your anatomy, or your necktie into the running vehicle's fan or belts. Be sure both vehicles are parked in a safe position, out of traffic. Leave enough room between them to walk if you need to. Open both hoods. If you can find it easily, adjust the idle of the booster vehicle to about 1,500 rpm. A dime slipped between the throttle stop and the idle set screw is good, or you can simply have an adult sit in the driver's seat and hold the accelerator down a fraction.

Turn off all electrical switches in both cars, except for the engine of the booster car, and the parking lights for illumination if it's dark. Start by hooking the red battery cable between the two batteries' positive terminals. These terminals will be clearly marked on the plastic of the battery's case with plus signs (+). Don't assume that a red terminal is the positive side—someone may have inadvertently replaced the ground cable with a red-banded cable intended for the positive post.

Be sure the jumper cable's black terminal doesn't contact the red terminal—clamp the black terminal onto the cable a foot or so back from itself to keep it clear of the red terminal if necessary. Many cars have plastic covers slipped over the battery posts to prevent shorts and

delay corrosion, so you'll need to pull those back and out of the way to achieve good metal-to-metal contact.

Now clamp one of the cable's black terminals to the battery ground (−) post. Which end first? It doesn't really matter—but the second black terminal should attach to some ground point away from the battery. What constitutes a good ground? A radiator or radiator shroud is thin and often poorly grounded. Same with bright trim. An alternator bracket or the corner of a cylinder head is perfect.

Go ahead and make the final connection at your chosen ground point. If you wear glasses, fine. If not, look away or borrow some shades. If you get a loud, two-inch-long spark, you've got the polarity reversed, so quickly yank the cable back and reverse your final connections. It is normal to get a couple of

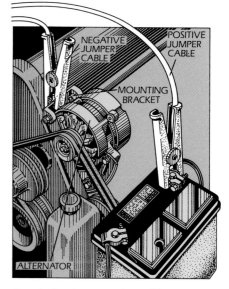

Attach the clamp on the red jumper cable lead to the positive (+) post on the working car's battery; then attach the other end to the positive post on the dead battery. Next, attach the negative (black) cable to the working battery's negative (−) post, and attach the other end to a good ground—a bolt on the engine or the chassis—on the disabled car.

small sparks when making the correct connection.

WARNING! Once in a great while, the hydrogen gas that's collected inside a battery will explode when ignited by a spark—that's why we suggest making the final connection away from the battery. An exploding battery is actually a fairly mild explosion—but it will throw sulfuric acid for twenty feet. Be careful and make any unnecessary personnel stand back. If you've been trying to start a car and have worked the battery hard, it will emit hydrogen gas. Wait a few minutes for it to dissipate. Removing the battery caps will help.

If you've made the connection, the booster car will show a slight drop in idle speed. Don't try to start the stalled car immediately—you'll have better success if the booster car's alternator charges up the flat battery for several minutes. If the battery is completely dead, ten minutes wouldn't be too long.

Now start the disabled vehicle. After it's run for a couple of minutes, you can remove the cables.

Don't shut off the formerly disabled vehicle until it's had a chance to charge up the battery. Try to use as few electrical accessories, such as the air conditioner or rear window defogger, as possible during the charge-up period. If your charging system and battery are in good condition, a minimum charging period of about twenty minutes will be sufficient to charge up the battery for a normal restart. But to fully charge the battery, the engine should be run for at least an hour.

How to Replace
SHOCK ABSORBERS

How do you know the shock absorbers on your vehicle are done for and need to be replaced? If your car bottoms out over bumps that never made it do so before, or sways excessively in turns, then the shock absorbers are probably worn. The time-honored test is to pump the suspension up and down by pushing down on the bumper with one foot. If the fender bobs up and down a couple of times after you let go, then the shocks are probably gone.

Only in America do we call them *shock absorbers*. We do so in error—shock absorbers don't absorb shocks. The rest of the world calls them *dampers*, and that's a more appropriate name. Their function is to control the action of your car's springs or torsion bars by damping out overtravel as the suspension moves up and down.

Another diagnostic test is to visually inspect the shock absorber. Signs of oil leaking from the shock is grounds for immediate replacement. Oil? Shocks work on a simple hydraulic principle: Oil is forced to flow through small holes—called *orifices*—in the shock as the suspension moves up and down. The oil resists being crammed through the holes, which creates the shock's damping forces. There is only a small amount of oil inside the shock's tube, and any significant loss will reduce its efficiency. And once the oil starts to weep from the seal, it's a rapid degeneration into failure. Shocks with corroded or bent damper rods, or rods that show a deterioration to their shiny, plated finish, are candidates for the scrap heap as well.

At any rate, you've decided to replace your shocks. If you have MacPherson struts (as most cars do nowadays), replacing the shocks inside the struts is more complicated —consult your service manual, and beg, borrow, or rent a set of spring compressors to deal with that high-energy coil spring surrounding the strut.

Park the car or truck on a paved surface. Block the wheels on the other end of the vehicle, and raise the end you're working on clear of the ground. You'll be working under the car, so make sure it's secure on sturdy jack stands. As an added safety measure, throw the removed wheels under the car (in the center) to hold it off you in case you do manage to knock it off the stands. Did you remember to loosen the lug nuts before you raised the vehicle clear of the ground?

Most shock absorbers are very straightforward in their mounting. Most of the time you can simply remove the mounting hardware and install the new parts. If the fasteners are rusted, douse them liberally with penetrating oil and let them set for twenty-four hours. Extreme cases might require a nut splitter or a hacksaw. Heating the fasteners with a torch may also work, but you'll probably cook the rubber bushings. We strongly recommend using new locknuts regardless, and replacing rubber bushings if they look at all weather-checked or deteriorated.

Some shocks have the suspension's bump stop incorporated into their design, often in the form of a rubber collar surrounding the

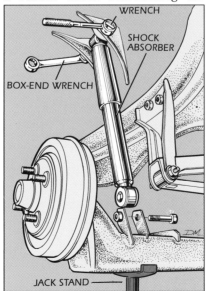

Replacing a shock on the rear of most vehicles is simple and easy. Support the vehicle on jack stands, unbolt the old shock, and bolt in the new one.

shock's main actuating rod. There may or may not be a boot or shield of some sort, intended to keep road grime and water away from the delicate chrome plating on this rod. Some rear suspensions have the fasteners for the shock's upper mount buried inside the rear interior panels or inside the trunk. If there are no access panels, it might be necessary to remove a considerable amount of interior to get a wrench on the upper mounting nut.

If there is a spring mounted concentrically with the shock, you'll need the aforementioned spring compressor to get the spring parted from the shock. *Don't* try to disassemble the unit without one— there's enough energy potentially stored in that spring to send a wrench sailing into your neighbor's backyard, not to mention where it could send your teeth. (See the chapter "How to Replace MacPherson Struts.")

Gas shocks are common nowadays. These devices have high-pressure nitrogen gas trapped in the same chamber with the damping oil. The purpose of the nitrogen is to prevent or reduce the number and size of the bubbles in the oil as the shock moves up and down rapidly. The bubbles move much more readily through the shock's metering orifices, interfering with its carefully tailored dampening characteristics. The downside of this is that the pressure inside the shock makes the shock rod constantly extend itself to its full length. This type of shock is invariably shipped with a nylon strap or wire holding it into a shorter, collapsed configuration. Leave this strap untouched until the new shock has been set in place and the hardware is at least finger tight. If not, you'll have a tough time compressing the shock in order to line up the mounting holes.

Always replace shocks in pairs, even if one seems to be okay. It's very important that both have identical damping rates, or your car will develop handling problems as the suspension bounces differently left to right.

How to Use the New A/C REFRIGERANT

New automotive a/c systems use Refrigerant-134a, which is not compatible with old R-12 systems. Not only does the refrigerant canister itself have a different connector (inset), but the system requires different gauge manifolds with large, quick-disconnect fittings and even different hoses—none of which fits the old-fashioned a/c systems.

It happened just recently, so you probably didn't even notice. But if you now try to buy a small can of air-conditioning R-12, you'll be told that it was taken off the market for environmental reasons, that not much is being produced, and that only professionals can buy it. You've surely also heard that the automobile industry worldwide is rushing to install redesigned air-conditioning systems with a new product—environmentally more acceptable R-134a. These moves affect service of both existing and new cars.

R-12, commonly called Freon, which is DuPont's trade name for it, is a chlorinated fluorocarbon, or CFC. The chlorine atoms in CFCs that get into the air (such as leakage from auto a/c systems) make their way up to the stratosphere, about twenty miles above the earth, where they interact with and work to erode the ozone layer, which protects us from the sun's harmful ultraviolet rays.

By international agreement, Refrigerant-12 production was cut sharply. It stops in 1995. The R-12 that is currently being made is primarily committed to uses other than servicing cars. Some is for new cars, because all the cars and assembly lines just can't change so fast.

Small cans (once 14 ounces, now 12 ounces) of R-12 legally are supposed to be sold only to professionals who are both trained and certified in recycling R-12 and have the equipment to do so because it is now illegal to vent R-12 to the atmosphere. The recycling equipment pulls the R-12 from a car's a/c system, purifies it, and puts it back in the car, along with any additional R-12 that's needed after a leak has been repaired.

You'll see cans of R-134a on the shelves for sale next to the cans of R-12, but R-12 and R-134a cannot be mixed or interchanged. Air-conditioning systems that use R-134a have been designed not to accept R-12. The diameter and threads of the connector fittings are different in an R-134a system from those in an R-12 system. Even the connectors and hoses are different so you cannot mistakenly try to add R-12 to an R-134a system and vice versa. In fact, using the wrong refrigerant can seriously damage an a/c system.

A loophole in the law permits you to buy large cans (20 pounds or more) of R-12. The large cans actually available are 30 pounds, and with the current R-12 tax of $3.35 a pound and the price of R-12 soaring, you could spend hundreds of dollars. In addition, R-12 must be stored carefully to minimize leakage, and even then, you might find there's been a substantial loss years later when you try to use it. Your best bet is to get a leak fixed and enjoy the cool air on a consistent basis.

In any case, it now makes good dollars-sense, as well as good ecological sense, to fix a leaking system. Most leaks are at O-ring fittings—a low-cost repair—and many others also are in the under-$100 category, not including replacement R-12. If you're planning to hold on to your car or truck, you can justify spending more.

Even if the refrigeration part of the system needs repair, it may not require a lot of R-12. The loss of even less than a half-pound of refrigerant is enough to cause a major reduction in a/c performance.

All this means that you can expect to run into difficulties when you service your vehicle's a/c system. As production of R-12 ends, re-cycling has been stepped up—even to the point of scavenging R-12 from cars in wrecking yards. But the simple reality is that there is not enough R-12 around to service all the cars that need it. You already may be facing the possibility of not being able to find any R-12 at any price.

What are you to do if you can't get R-12? You could convert the system to another refrigerant, but there is no other refrigerant you can just "drop in" to an R-12 system and have it work satisfactorily and safely. Any alternative refrigerant requires some system modifications and/or special procedures to work.

Conversion to R-134a is the choice of the auto industry, and GM is including brochures in its new cars saying it will convert cars whose systems fail under warranty if R-12 is "no longer available or affordable."

Retrofit procedures and parts required have been developed by carmakers and the SAE. However, the specifics of the conversions will vary widely between cars—even among different years and models of the same make.

But beware: There's a lot of "home-brew" refrigerant out there that is being sold as a "drop-in" substitute for R-12. No carmaker approves any one of them. These universal refrigerants have performance, safety (some are flammable), and toxicity problems. Even a "safe" blend, such as one DuPont is testing, has a high leak rate and it "disassociates" (comes apart at the seams, so what's left is chemically different from what was put in) when it leaks. Remember, you cannot simply top off your a/c system with a blend.

No professional repair shop—other than the installer—will touch a system with a blend. And any shop that would install a home-brew blend is one you should avoid in the first place. Don't let anyone talk you into a blend, period.

Several blends contain R-22, a household/commercial refrigerant, which is being sold by itself in auto parts stores. Your old R-12-can tap will fit the R-22 can, so you could put pure R-22 into an R-12 system—a terrible mistake. A/C performance will suffer, the system will leak, and the compressor will fail pretty quickly.

Also consider that a competent and properly equipped professional can't—and won't knowingly—touch a system filled with some strange brew, because he can't pull the blend into an R-12 or R-134a recycling machine without contaminating his equipment.

If your system was not properly identified, or you didn't tell the shop what alternate refrigerant you had used, and it later learns that your system damaged its equipment, you could be legally liable. Planned conversions to R-134a, for example, include R-134a adapters that cover existing service fittings, so a shop shouldn't make a mistake.

How to
STORE YOUR CAR

You've just received orders and you're going to be spending the next three years on foreign soil. And you just know that your brand-new ZR-1 isn't going with you. You also know that you're definitely *not* going to leave the keys with your kid brother while you're gone.

Whether you're going to put your new or like-new car, pickup truck, or motorcycle in storage for a few months or a few years, you can help guarantee that it will be in the same primo condition when you take it out of storage as it was when you put it in.

You'll also have a minimum of grief getting it back on the road.

DRIVE IT BEFORE YOU PARK IT

While you can easily coat various external surfaces to seal them from the ravages of moisture and exposure, short of totally disassembling your car, you can't quite as simply protect internal surfaces. But there are critical unseen areas that must be protected from corrosion, rust, and the formation of varnishes and gums. Drive far enough and long enough to thoroughly warm up all of the vehicle's vital fluids—engine oil, transmission fluid, gear oil, and engine coolant. Then, drive home

Squirt clean engine oil into each cylinder's spark plug hole to coat the cylinder walls. Spin the engine to oil the combustion chambers and piston rings.

and drain everything. Draining all the fluids while they're hot removes any corrosive moisture and sludge with them.

Naturally, replace the engine oil filter. Replace the fuel filter as well. Then refill with fresh lubricant.

Next, flush and refill the cooling system. Either drain the old coolant from the radiator and engine block or use a reverse-flush kit, with a special flushing Tee installed in a heater hose.

Once the cooling system is completely free of old coolant and rusty water, refill the system with a fresh 50/50 mix of antifreeze coolant and water. Check the protection-level chart on the coolant container.

Remember, a mix that's purely antifreeze is not as potent as one that has some water in it, due to the chemical reactions of the ingredients. Also, the anticorrosion additives in the coolant rely on the presence of a certain amount of water to do the job, so don't go any stronger than 70 percent coolant and 30 percent water.

With fresh coolant in the engine and new lube in the engine, transmission, and drive axle, go for another drive. Again, the purpose is to fully lubricate all internal moving parts and seals. This time, drive to a filling station that you've known and trusted for years to have pure fuel in clean tanks. But before filling your car, pour a fuel-stabilizing additive into the fuel tank.

Fuel stabilizers are designed to prevent stored gasoline from breaking down, forming varnishes and gums inside the fuel system. If your auto parts store doesn't stock a fuel stabilizer, try an outdoor power equipment dealer, where it's sold for lawn and yard equipment. Add as much stabilizer as needed for your vehicle's fuel tank. Then fill the tank with fuel, and drive just enough to mix the stabilizer and pump it into the carburetor or fuel injectors.

While totally draining gas from the tank and running the engine until the carburetor, fuel pump, filter, and lines are empty also prevents the buildup of varnish, it leaves room inside the fuel system for condensation to build. The condensation causes corrosion. A full tank leaves no room for condensation or corrosion in the fuel system.

Add fuel-stabilizer additive to prevent varnishes inside the fuel system.

Now you can drive home to finish the storage procedures.

BATTEN DOWN THE ENGINE

Further protect the inside of your car's engine by putting a coat of oil on surfaces that normally aren't heavily lubricated.

Once the engine is cold, remove the spark plug from each cylinder. Then squirt several shots of clean engine oil into all the cylinders through the spark plug holes. Apply antiseize compound to the spark plugs' threads, and reinstall the old plugs in the cylinder head. Disconnect the ignition, leaving off all the plug leads and the leads to the distributor or control module. (If you have an electronic ignition, you should check the service manual for the appropriate way to disable the ignition. Simply pulling the high-tension leads may cause spark box failure.)

Turn the ignition key to spin the engine several times. This not only ensures that the oil in the cylinders covers the cylinder walls for the entire piston stroke, it forces the oil up into the combustion chamber and onto the valves, to help protect those surfaces.

Coat each ignition system connection component with dielectric grease as you reinstall all the wires. Also, disconnect the battery leads and coat all the terminals, including the exposed terminals on the starter, with petroleum jelly. Remove the battery from its tray and attach it to a trickle charger, away from the car.

Besides protecting all electrical connections with petroleum jelly or silicone to seal out moisture, apply silicone spray to all accessible hoses—fuel lines, coolant hoses, vacuum hoses—to help prevent them from drying out.

To help prevent rust and corrosion of unpainted metal parts—such as the throttle linkage, exhaust manifold, clamps, and brackets—coat them with petroleum jelly, silicone, or penetrating oil.

Last, to discourage mice and other small creatures from taking up winter quarters in your engine compartment, roll fist-size packets of camphor balls in cheesecloth. Place the camphor packets around the engine compartment, tucking some in corners near the firewall and against the felt or foam sound-deadening material on the hood's underside.

Tape a plastic bag over the air-cleaner intake and exhaust pipe exit to prevent mice and squirrels from nesting or storing seeds inside.

UNDERSIDE UP

To prevent the tires from developing a flat side while resting in the same spot for so long and to ease the load on the springs, shock absorbers, and the rest of the suspension, your car or truck should be stored sitting on safety stands.

Make sure your stands are large enough to securely hold your rig off the ground. Each stand should have a broad base and large enough cradle, as well as being rated to hold at least one fourth of the vehicle

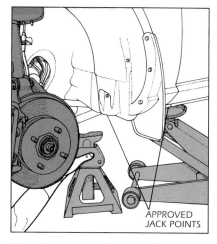

APPROVED JACK POINTS

Place the car on safety stands for the duration of the storage.

weight. Jack up your car or truck so that when it's resting on the safety stands, the bottom edges of the tires all clear the ground by an inch or so. You don't need the vehicle towering above the ground. It should be just high enough for the tires to rotate freely. If you're storing the car on an unpaved surface, use lengths of wood long enough to prevent the stands from sinking into the surface as the seasons progress.

Place each safety stand carefully. Support your vehicle under frame rails or other structural members, not under axles or suspension components. If you place the stands under an axle, the weight of the vehicle will still compress the springs and shock absorbers. With the safety stands under the vehicle's frame, the wheels, springs, shocks, and suspension components all hang free, holding only their own weight.

With your rig up in the air, remove all four wheels and tires, and lay them aside for now. Slide underneath and inspect the entire underbody. Remove any clumps of wet or dry leaves, grass, caked-on mud or anything that could trap moisture, helping in the formation of rust.

Look for any bare metal areas and seal them. If appropriate, prime and paint them, otherwise coat the surfaces with silicone, penetrating oil, or another water barrier to prevent rust and corrosion. Key areas to protect include steel suspension components, brake drums, wheel spindles, and bearing covers, as well as disc brake calipers and rotors. Also protect exposed shift linkages and non-stainless-steel exhaust pieces.

While you're underneath, coat all rubber surfaces with silicone spray to keep them from drying out. This includes suspension bushings, fuel lines, the lower radiator hose, brake lines, and constant-velocity joint and steering rack boots.

Last, check for grease fittings on suspension and steering components as well as at the driveshaft universal and slip joints. If there are any fittings, grease them with the recommended lubricant. And then hang some more camphor and cheesecloth packets around the undercarriage to help discourage nesting.

Now, before putting the wheels and tires back on, clean the inner and outer sidewalls of the tire, and

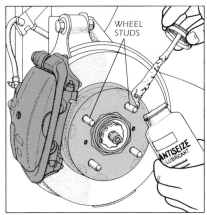

Coat the wheel studs' metal threads with antiseize compound.

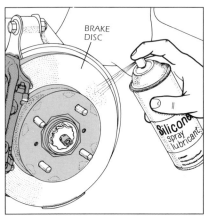

Coat rotors and calipers and other exposed metal parts with silicone.

apply silicone to both. Also, clean both sides of all the wheels. Put a coat of wax on the cleaned wheels, but don't buff it off. Apply antiseize compound to the threads of the wheel-mounting studs, and reinstall the wheels and snug up the lug nuts, torquing them to specifications. Then coat the nuts' outer surfaces with wax. Make sure the tires are all inflated to the correct cold-inflation pressure to help them keep their shape, and cap the valve stems. Then reinstall any wheel covers.

Double-check that the car is high enough off the ground so that the wheels are all hanging freely to prevent flat-spotting the tires.

A CLEAN BODY

Next, thoroughly clean the car, inside and out. In fact, detail the car as though you were about to be taking it to a car show. With one im-

portant difference—don't make it shine.

Thoroughly and carefully wash the car. Remove the license plate brackets and luggage racks that can trap dirt and moisture, and clean the areas they normally cover.

Store these pieces in the trunk, along with the radio antenna mast, if it is not the type that fully retracts, and the windshield wiper arm assemblies. By removing the wiper arms, you relieve the pressure on their holddown springs. But be sure to coat the exposed wiper shafts with petroleum jelly to protect them from corrosion after you've finished washing the car.

Take extra time to be sure to totally remove any stains. Bird droppings, tree sap, dead bugs, and globs of road tar and other substances can etch the car's finish if given months—or years—to work at it. Use a chemical solvent, like bug and tar remover, to completely clean all stubborn spots. Then, wash and rinse the car again to remove any residue of the solvent. Dry the car, using chamois or old terry-cloth towels. Then inspect the finish carefully.

Check for any chips, nicks, or scratches in the paint. Any damage down to bare metal will surely rust —possibly through—given enough time in storage. Treat any bare spots with a rust stabilizer, then prime the area and, after the primer dries, touch up the damage with the correct color body paint.

Next, apply a moderate coat of wax. However, unlike what you normally do, cover the entire car at once and then simply let the wax

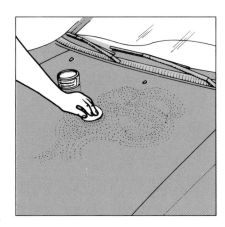

Place a moderate coat of wax on the car's finish, but don't buff it off.

dry to a haze. You won't buff off the wax until you take the car out of storage.

Similarly treat all chrome surfaces of your car—wire wheels, grilles, headlight bezels—with a quality chrome polish. Also treat plastic and vinyl surfaces with an appropriate polish. Protect weatherstripping around the windshield and backlight, as well as all the doors and the trunk, with silicone.

GO INSIDE

Next, do a thorough cleanup of the car's interior. Wash and vacuum all upholstery, carpets, and floor mats. Clean and polish the dashboard, door panels, armrests, pedals, shift lever, window crank, and door levers. After cleaning, coat all noncloth surfaces with the appropriate polish. Spray the clean upholstery and carpeting with a cloth protector.

Be totally sure there's no water trapped anywhere inside the car. Otherwise, it will not only be a source of rust and corrosion, the moisture will encourage mildew to develop. Make certain all vent holes, such as the bottom of the doors and under the cowl, are clear to allow moisture to escape. As an added antimildew measure, spray some household disinfectant into all the heater/defroster/air conditioning vents, as well as into the fins of the heater core and air conditioning evaporator.

Before sealing up the interior, place a couple of open boxes of baking powder around the passenger compartment. Place one box under the front seats, one in the rear, and one under the dash to absorb odors. Then close all the windows, and close the doors.

If your car is a convertible, close the top and install any zippered-in windows or side curtains. Besides helping to seal the interior, this installation will help prevent the convertible top and the car's side curtains from cracking at the folds.

Next, clean the trunk or cargo area of station wagons and hatchbacks. Again, be very careful that there are no pockets of water or moisture anywhere. Clean and dry the rain channel around the trunk or hatchback opening. Remove the spare tire and jack from their storage well, and be sure that area is dry.

Clean all interior plastic, vinyl, or leather surfaces with the appropriate product. Shampoo the carpets and cloth seats.

Before reinstalling the spare, inflate it to its proper pressure. But to keep the spare from getting misshaped in storage, lay it flat on the floor of the trunk or cargo area, out of its mounting bracket.

Place an open box of baking powder in the trunk to absorb moisture and odors. Be sure that the weatherstripping is coated with silicone, and close the trunk lid.

COVER IT UP

Whether you store your car inside, as is preferable in a heated, humidity-controlled garage, or in an unheated barn, chicken coop, carport, or out in the yard, put a quality cover over the car. A cover not only keeps dirt and dust off the car, it shields the car from the sun's ultra-violet rays, the ozone, and other airborne pollutants. Logically, the more of the car you can cover, the better.

It's critical then that your cover is the correct size for your car or truck. While you can have a cover custom tailored to fit your rig, you can also buy a more-or-less universal one off the shelf. Custom-made covers not only protect all of your car, they fit snugly, leaving less room for moisture or critters to get underneath. A well-fitted cover also stands a better chance of staying in place if the car is outdoors and subject to wind and weather. If you buy a ready-made cover, make sure that it's the correct size for your car. The cover has to slip over and under your car's front and rear bumpers and under the rocker panels on both sides of the rig.

Regardless of which type of cover you select, make sure it's made of a soft material that won't scratch the car. In addition, the cover should be lint-free and tightly woven to prevent dirt and dust from passing through. Yet, it should allow air to pass through so moisture won't settle under the cover.

Before putting the wraps on your car, be sure that you've properly sealed it, and that the radio antenna is either lubricated with penetrating oil and fully retracted or removed and in the trunk with the wiper arms.

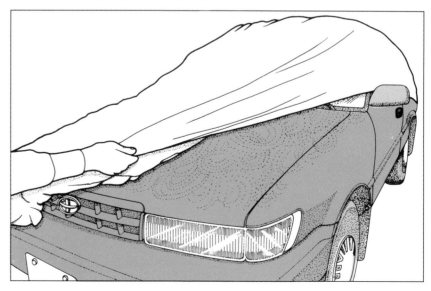

Seal the entire car with a cover to keep out dirt, dust, and moisture.

ENGINE 2

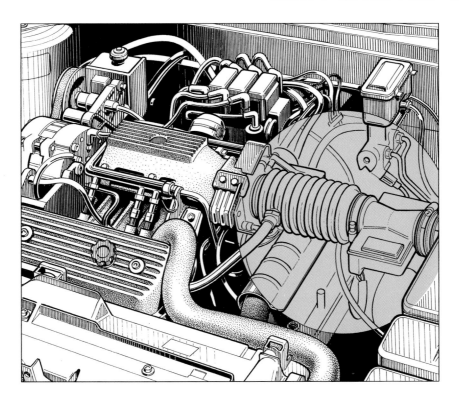

What to Do When Your Car WON'T START

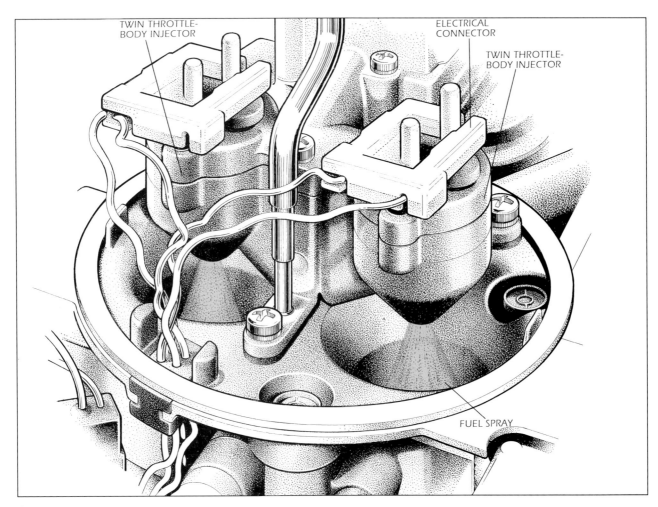

TWIN THROTTLE-BODY INJECTOR

ELECTRICAL CONNECTOR

TWIN THROTTLE-BODY INJECTOR

FUEL SPRAY

1 First check for throttle-body injection operation: injectors should spray fuel when engine is cranked.

It seems like it only happens when you're ten minutes late for an important appointment. You hop in your car and turn the key. Nothing. The engine turns over fine, but it won't start. What to do?

COVERING THE BASICS

Before you even pop the hood, make sure you've covered the essentials—like putting fuel in the tank and using the proper starting technique.

A fuel gauge that reads FULL doesn't always indicate a full tank. If you can't remember the last time you filled up, and the gauge is still pinned to the F mark, try pouring a few gallons of gas into the tank before you look for a more complicated problem. On many cars, the fuel gauge will read FULL continuously if the sending unit isn't properly grounded.

If your engine is carbureted and the tank is empty, prime the engine by pouring a few tablespoons of gas down the carb. But reinstall the air cleaner to prevent a backfire that could start a fire. Fuel-injected engines will usually prime themselves if the key is left in the ON position for a few seconds.

Improper starting techniques can also leave you with a no-start, par-

ticularly in cold weather. Most carbureted cars are started by pressing the throttle to the floor, releasing it, and turning the key with your foot off the throttle. On some cars two pumps are necessary in colder weather. Most fuel-injected cars are started with your foot off the throttle—pumping does nothing. Check your owner's manual for detailed starting information.

FUEL OR SPARK?

Two things are necessary to make any gasoline-burning engine run: fuel and spark. Once you're satisfied that the problem is not simply an empty fuel tank or incorrect starting technique, you can tell whether it's due to a lack of fuel or spark with a visual check.

Although simple in most cases, the procedure is not the same for throttle-body fuel-injected, port-injected, and carbureted engines.

THROTTLE-BODY FUEL-INJECTED

Begin your routine by turning the key to the ON position and noting the CHECK ENGINE light. (The name varies, but all recently produced engines have some type of light to indicate computer system problems). The light should be illuminated with the key in the ON position. If not, there is probably a basic power-supply problem and you should consult your factory service manual for further directions.

If the CHECK ENGINE light came on and your car has throttle-body fuel injection, remove the air cleaner and have a helper crank the engine while you observe the fuel injectors. You should see fuel spraying from the injectors while the engine cranks (Fig. 1).

If you do see fuel spray, disconnect the injector (or injectors— some have two) and have your helper crank the engine again while you observe. If one or more of the injectors sprays while it is *disconnected*, the injector or injector seal is faulty and must be replaced. In this case, the no-start is caused by flooding, and you should remove the plugs, clean them with dry-cleaning fluid or spark plug cleaner, and crank the engine with the plugs out and the new injectors disconnected for a few seconds before attempting to start it.

If, while cranking the engine with the harness disconnected, there was not visible fuel spray—but you did see fuel spray when you cranked with it connected—the problem is not due to a lack of fuel. Proceed to *Checking for Spark*.

If you didn't see any fuel spray the first time you cranked the engine—with the injector harness connected—disconnect the injector harness and connect a test light across the harness connector. Special inexpensive test lights that plug into the harness are available for this purpose at auto parts stores.

Crank the engine with the test

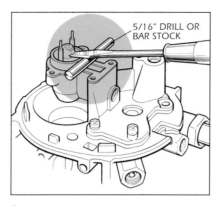

2 Use fulcrum for screwdriver to pry injector from GM throttle-body injector.

light connected. It should blink on and off, indicating that voltage is being supplied to the injector and the lack of fuel is due to either a faulty injector or a fuel-delivery problem. To determine which, turn the ignition off for at least ten seconds and install a fuel-pressure gauge on the Schrader valve found on your engine's fuel-supply line or on the fuel-filter case.

On some cars, you'll have to use a high-pressure gauge, like the ones sold specifically for fuel-injection diagnosis. But check your manual to be sure. Some TBI systems operate at low pressure, so all that's needed is a gauge with a Schrader valve attachment.

Within a few seconds after turning the ignition on, the fuel system should pressurize. If it does, the no-start problem is due to a faulty injector(s) that should be replaced (Fig. 2).

If it doesn't pressurize, the problem is due to a bad pump, a plugged in-line or in-tank filter, a restricted

fuel line, or (on cars with in-tank pumps) a leaking fuel pump coupling (Fig. 3).

PORT FUEL-INJECTED

The procedure differs for port-injected engines because you can't see the injectors without removing them from the intake manifold.

Because of this, most manufacturers recommend that you begin trouble-shooting by checking the computer's memory for trouble codes. To do this, consult the appropriate chapter in your factory service manual.

If no trouble codes are stored, skip to the section below to check for spark.

If you find that spark is okay, disconnect an injector harness connector from one of the injectors and connect a test light. As noted above, special fuel-injection test lights are sold for this purpose. Crank the engine while you watch the light.

If the light blinks on and off, install a fuel-injection pressure gauge on the Schrader valve, which is probably located somewhere on the fuel rail. Turn on the ignition and note fuel pressure after the pump stops running (a few seconds in most cases). Pressure should be 30 to 40 psi on most port-injected engines. If it's not, check your service manual to make sure this spec is correct for your system. If you conclude that low fuel pressure is a problem, the cause would be comparable to TBI fuel problems mentioned earlier.

If pressure is okay, and all previous checks yielded passing grades, go to the section *Other Possible Problems*.

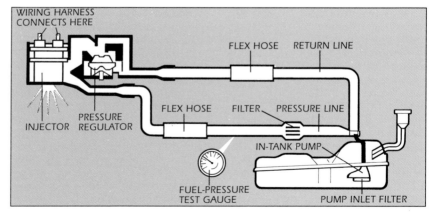

3 Fuel-pressure test gauge is attached at Schrader fitting (see text for location).

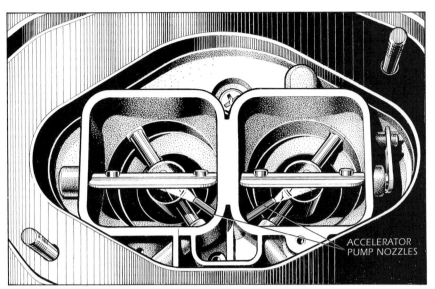

4 Snap the throttle open and watch the carb accelerator pump nozzles for fuel spray.

CARBURETED ENGINES

If your carbureted engine fails to start, check to see that the warning lights or CHECK ENGINE light comes on when the key is in the ON position. If it doesn't, there's a wiring problem.

If the lights come on but the engine won't start, remove the air cleaner. If the engine hasn't been running for six hours or more, the choke should be almost fully closed. If it isn't, open the throttle. The choke should snap closed. If it doesn't, it's either dirty, broken, or misadjusted.

If the choke seems to be working, look down into the carburetor. While holding the choke open, move the throttle rapidly to the full open position. You should see fuel squirt from the accelerator pump nozzles within the carb (Fig. 4). If you see fuel, proceed to the section *Checking for Spark*.

If you don't see fuel squirt from the accelerator pump nozzles when you open the throttle, check once again to make sure there is fuel in the tank, then remove the fuel filter and check for restriction. On many cars the filter can be found behind the carburetor fuel inlet nut. Use two wrenches while removing the fuel line—one on the inlet nut, one on the fuel-line nut. It's best to use a special tubing wrench on the fuel-line nut if you have one, as this type of wrench is less likely to slip on the

nut. Place a rag on the manifold under the fuel-line connection before you unscrew it. There should be visible evidence of filter contamination if it's bad enough to cause a no-start.

On cars with in-line filters, place a rag under the filter and release the hose clamps that secure it in the fuel line. With this type filter it's difficult to tell if it's contaminated (unless it's see-through plastic), so you may just have to replace it to tell if it's the culprit.

If the fuel filter checks out okay, check fuel-pump capacity by connecting a hose from the fuel-inlet line to a suitable, unbreakable container. Crank the engine. The fuel pump should supply a half-pint or more of fuel in fifteen seconds. If the pump can't deliver enough or delivers none at all, it should be replaced.

It's also possible that the line leading to the pump or the inlet sock in the tank is restricted. You can determine if either of these is the cause by filling the carb float bowl manually, starting the engine, and then checking fuel-pump pressure and vacuum.

Before you remove a fuel pump, always disconnect the battery's negative cable to prevent the possibility of an electrical spark igniting any spilled fuel. When installing a new pump, make sure the pump push rod or drive cam properly contacts the pump lever.

If you found that the fuel-pump

capacity was okay but there is no fuel squirting from the accelerator pump nozzles, the problem is inside the carb. On most cars, you can remove the carb air horn for basic inspection without removing the carb from the engine.

To remove the carb air horn (the upper part of the carburetor), disconnect the fuel line, throttle, and choke linkage along with any other linkage rods that connect the carb base to the carb air horn.

Then, being extremely careful not to drop anything into the carburetor, remove the screws that join the air horn to the float bowl; some screws may be hidden within the air horn.

Once all of the screws are removed, you should be able to carefully lift the air horn off the carb base. The float assembly, and in some cases the accelerator pump, will come off with the air horn. Turn the air horn upside down so that the float is facing you.

The float, needle, and seat control the amount of fuel flowing into the carb. When the carb fuel bowl is full, the float rises and pushes the needle into its seat, preventing any more fuel from entering the float bowl until some of it is burned in the engine. If the float is jammed in the up position (down with the air horn turned over), the needle will stay in the seat and no fuel will enter the carb.

Another possibility is a needle that sticks in its seat when the float drops. You can check for this by turning the air horn so that the float is facing down. The float should drop and the needle should move out of its seat. If it doesn't, it's stuck and it should be replaced. Wear has probably led to a ridge that causes the needle to stick in its seat. Replace it. Adjust float height before reinstalling the air horn (Fig. 5).

If the float bowl was full of fuel when you removed the air horn, examine the accelerator pump. On many carbs you'll find the pump hanging from the air horn. It consists of a rawhide or neoprene piston that pushes fuel through a chamber and into the accelerator pump nozzles. If the piston has deteriorated, fuel won't squirt out and starting will be difficult, if not impossible.

Some carbs have a diaphragm-type accelerator pump rather than a

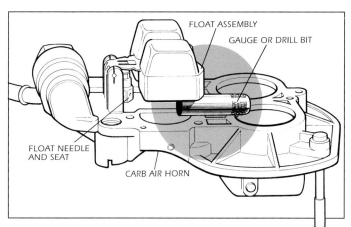

5 Invert air horn to check float height with drill bit or appropriate gauge.

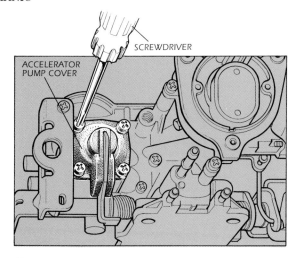

6 Remove the accelerator pump cover to check for a torn or leaky diaphragm.

piston. This type pump is usually attached to the carb base with screws. Check for a torn diaphragm by removing the pump assembly (Fig. 6).

CHECKING FOR SPARK

Once you've determined that enough fuel for starting is available—or with port-injected engines before you check for fuel—you can perform a very simple test to see if the second element necessary for starting an engine is available: ignition spark.

In the good old days of simple cars with points and condensers, all you had to do to check for spark was pull the coil wire from the distributor tower and hold it near the ground while cranking the engine. If it sparked, you did the same thing with one of the plug cables to make sure voltage was getting past the rotor and distributor cap.

With today's high-power ignitions, you could end up with a serious electrical shock or damaged ignition components if you check for spark in this manner. Nowadays you need a special spark-test tool, but the job is still an easy one. This tool is available at most auto parts stores, or any GM dealer. Ask for the ST-125 spark tester. Because spark checks are an important part of many diagnostic routines, no serious driveway mechanic should be without this tool.

To check for spark, remove one plug cable from a spark plug with the ignition turned off. Twist the boot a little if you have to. Install the spark tester on the end of the cable and attach the clamp to a good ground. Then, while your helper

cranks the engine, watch the end of the spark tester. A well-defined spark should arc from the tester's center electrode to its housing (Fig. 7).

If you see a spark, check several other cables in the same way. If they all check out okay, you can be sure that a lack of spark is not preventing the engine from starting.

If there is no spark, remove the distributor cap and make sure the rotor turns when the engine cranks. If it doesn't, the pin that secures the distributor gear to the shaft is probably broken and the distributor will have to be removed for repair. It's also possible that the camshaft timing belt or chain is broken. If the rotor turns and there is no spark, check for broken or disconnected pickup wires. If everything looks okay, further diagnosis of the electronic ignition system is necessary.

OTHER POSSIBLE PROBLEMS

If your troubleshooting finds that the engine is supplied with both fuel and spark, you'll have to look elsewhere for the starting problem.

On many fuel-injected engines, a throttle-position sensor (TPS) that sticks in the wide-open throttle position will cause the computer to go into the CLEAR FLOOD mode. This results in a lean fuel mixture that makes starting difficult, if not impossible.

If the coolant sensor on a computer-controlled engine fails in such a way that its circuit opens with the ignition off, the computer will think that the outside temperature is extremely cold. In warm weather, this condition can cause flooding, which will result in a no-start (Fig. 8).

Water in fuel-system components can cause a no-start in cold weather, particularly if you get a load of gas that was blended for warm weather. The best cure is a warm-up indoors. If you have recurring trouble, add a can of gasoline winterizer.

An EGR valve that sticks open can cause an overly lean air/fuel mix during cranking, resulting in a no-start. Remove a suspect EGR valve and make sure its pintle is firmly against its valve seat (Fig. 9).

If an engine's camshaft timing chain or belt jumps one or more

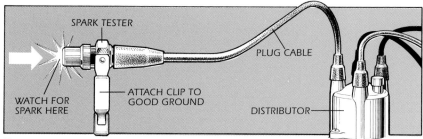

7 Use the spark tester to avoid electrical shock and damaged ignition components.

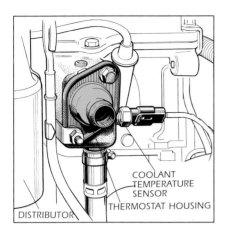

8 On Chrysler 2.2L engines, coolant temp sensor is in the thermostat housing.

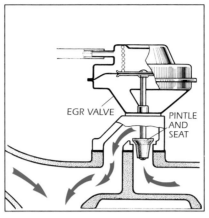

9 Remove the EGR valve to check the pintle for proper seal against the seat.

teeth on the gear or pulley because of wear, the engine will usually only snort and backfire when you attempt to start it.

To see if an engine has jumped time, turn the crank until the ignition timing mark on the crank pulley is aligned with the pointer on the engine, then remove the distributor cap.

The rotor should be pointing to the terminal in the distributor cap for the first cylinder in the firing order or the cylinder 180° across the cap. If not, the engine has jumped time, or—as explained earlier—the distributor's drive gear pin has sheared.

How to Solve
HOT-START PROBLEMS

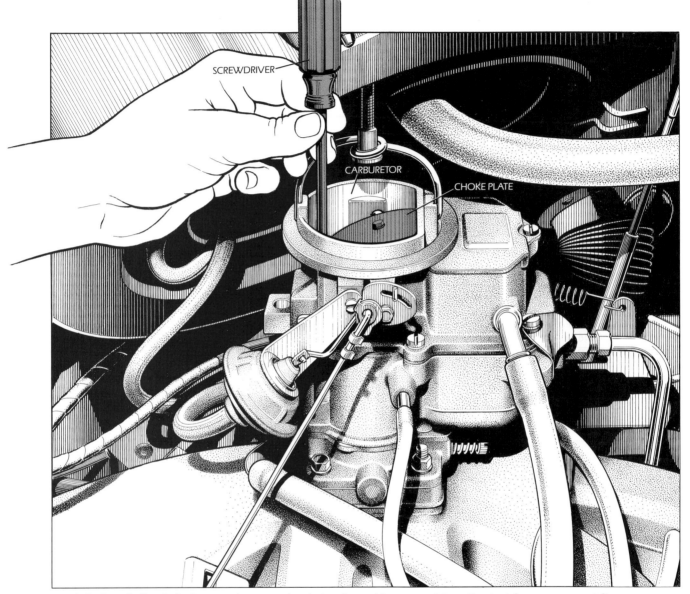

SCREWDRIVER

CARBURETOR

CHOKE PLATE

Quick fix for a balky choke is to wedge open the choke plate with a screwdriver. See text for a permanent fix.

It's a hot day in the middle of August. You park your car for thirty minutes or so while you do a bit of shopping. When you return you discover that the car, which started easily on the coldest mornings last winter, won't start now.

Hot-starting problems are a common source of driver distress. Because they sometimes go away when the engine has cooled completely, they can be very difficult to diagnose.

Hot-start problems can be divided into two categories: those that cause the engine to crank so slowly that it won't fire and those that make the engine hard to start but don't affect cranking speed.

HOT START, SLOW CRANK

Here, when you turn the key to the START position, the engine sounds like it's turning one revolution at a

time with a pause between each. The engine may suddenly begin to crank faster, or it may just continue cranking laboriously until the battery is dead.

If it occurs only once, it may be due to nothing more than a discharged battery or inoperative charging system. If it occurs often when the battery is fully charged, it may be the result of high cranking circuit resistance, internal engine problems, cooling system problems,

HIGH CRANKING RESISTANCE

When corrosion or loose connections in the starting circuit raise circuit resistance, your battery might have a tough time cranking the engine. And, because resistance increases further when underhood temperature is high, the problem may be noticeable only on hot summer days.

Before even attempting to diagnose the problem, clean the battery posts and terminals as well as the connection points on the starter motor, starter relay, and/or solenoid. Reinstall the terminals and make sure all connections are tight. Start the engine and warm it to maximum operating temperature by driving it slowly for at least half an hour. Then check starter positive and negative circuit resistance by measuring voltage drop.

To check positive circuit voltage drop, connect the positive cable of a voltmeter that reads in tenths of a volt to the positive battery post and the negative cable to the terminal on the starter (see Fig. 1). On starters with external solenoids (including most GM cars), connect the negative lead to the large copper connector that joins the solenoid to the starter. Crank the engine with the meter attached. It should read less than .5 volt if circuit resistance is within limits.

If you get a reading in excess of .5 volt on a car with an external solenoid, attach the negative probe of the voltmeter to the BAT terminal on the solenoid where the battery cable is attached. If there is less than .5 volt to this point with the engine cranking, but more than .5 volt at the bridge between the starter and solenoid, the resistance problem is within the solenoid.

High solenoid resistance is very common on some older GM cars. The problem is due to a buildup of corrosion on the brass disc that transmits voltage to the starter when the solenoid engages. Newer Delco solenoids have an improved design contact plate.

If positive circuit resistance was excessive at both points, the problem is in the positive battery cable or its connections. Replace the cable and recheck all terminals for corrosion.

Check negative circuit resistance by connecting the voltmeter's negative lead to the negative battery post and the meter's positive lead to the starter housing. Make sure you make contact with the bare metal of the housing. When the engine cranks the ground circuit, voltage should drop less than 0.2 volt. If not, check all connections again and replace the ground cable if necessary. If the ground circuit cable is attached to the frame, make sure that the cable joining the frame and engine is in good condition. By connecting your voltmeter's positive lead to various points in the ground circuit you can usually pinpoint the problem area.

EXCESSIVE SPARK ADVANCE

Slow crank/hot problems are frequently caused by a combination of high resistance and excessive advance, so it's a good idea to check spark timing even if you think you've solved your problem with a solenoid or cable replacement.

First, attach a tachometer and make sure idle speed is at specification. Then, check the timing following the directions on your vehicle information label or in your shop manual. If the manufacturer provides a range of acceptable timing, adjust to a figure at the lower end of the range.

On cars with mechanical advance, check the centrifugal weights inside the distributor to make sure that corrosion isn't causing them to stick when the engine is hot.

COOLING SYSTEM PROBLEMS

Believe it or not, serious cooling system problems can cause hot start/slow crank problems. If coolant passages surrounding engine cylinders are blocked with sludge and corrosion, heat from the pistons won't be transferred to the coolant (see Fig. 2). This causes the pistons to expand to the point where friction between them and the cylinder walls makes the engine difficult to turn.

This can sometimes be remedied by a power backflush combined with a cooling system cleaner. In severe cases, cylinder block replacement may be the only solution.

Ordinary overheating problems can also cause an engine to crank slowly when hot, so check the cooling system thoroughly.

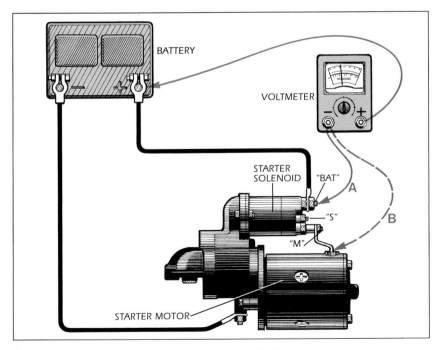

1 To check resistance on starters with external solenoids, connect meter as shown.

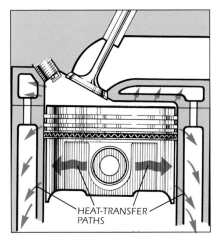

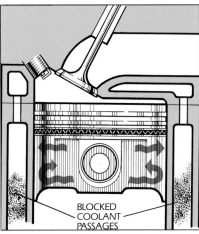

2 Heat flows easily from piston to coolant in normal cooling system (top). In clogged system, piston can expand enough to drag.

INTERNAL ENGINE PROBLEMS

Any internal engine problem that produces friction can cause the engine to crank slowly. And since most clearances tighten up when the engine is hot, it's most likely to happen then.

You can tell if your engine is hard to turn by removing the plugs and attempting to turn the front crankshaft bolt with a torque wrench. It should break away at 90 lb.-ft. or less and should turn with the application of 70 lb.-ft. or less.

Internal engine damage might occur in combination with, or as a result of, blocked cooling system passages. The torque-wrench test can't tell you for sure that the problem is due to one or the other. So before disassembling your engine or asking the mechanic to do so, make sure you've exhausted more conventional remedies.

FAST CRANK, NO HOT START

What about cars that crank fast when the engine is hot but still won't start? This problem is usually the result of a choke system failure, a fuel flooding problem, a serious vacuum leak, fuel starvation, or an intermittent electrical failure. If your car is in need of a tuneup, do that before looking for more unusual causes.

CHOKE PROBLEMS

The scene is repeated over and over again in supermarket parking lots during the heat of summer. After a futile attempt at starting his car, the driver jumps out, throws up the hood, unscrews the air cleaner and jams a screwdriver between the choke plate and carb body (see page 70). After starting the car, he reverses the procedure, slips behind the wheel and drives away.

The culprit could be an incorrect choke adjustment, but you must also consider the carburetor flooding problems discussed below. Although the screwdriver holds the choke flap open, that may only be necessary because of engine flooding.

Choke adjustment and cleanup, though, are the first two things you should consider. Make sure the engine is cold. Use a small solvent brush and a can of carb cleaner, or an aerosol can of carb cleaner, to remove all the varnish and accumulated dirt from the linkage arms and choke assembly.

Because there are a number of different choke mechanisms on carburetors, we can't provide exact directions or specs for checking each. So to do this job properly, you'll need a service manual. Most choke systems require at least three adjustments: vacuum break, choke flap closing, and fast idle. Some call for as many as five or six different adjustments.

On most systems, a temperature-sensitive bimetal coil, mounted either on the carb body or within a stove on the intake manifold, opens and closes the flap. On some, the coil is heated electrically; on others, exhaust heat is used. Adjustment is frequently accomplished by turning the housing that surrounds the bimetal coil until a pointer aligns with a specified point on a scale that is attached to the carb body. On others, the housing is mounted in a fixed position and adjustment is made by bending a linkage rod or lever. Sometimes the correct choke flap position must be gauged with a rule, or with a drill bit or rod gauge.

On most carbureted cars, the choke housing is mounted with rivets or slotless screws to discourage tampering. To remove rivets drill them out. To remove slotless screws, make a slot in each with a hacksaw blade (see Fig. 3).

Choke flap sticking can become a problem on very old carburetors or poor rebuilds if the choke flap bushings have worn to the point where the flap won't stay in one position and can't be adjusted properly.

BOWL VENT BOILOVER

When you park your car, heat from the engine is transferred to the fuel remaining in the carb float bowl. The temperature increase is accompanied by rising pressure. This pressure has to be relieved or fuel will be forced into the intake manifold. Once the manifold becomes soaked with fuel, the engine floods and can only be started by holding the throttle and choke flap wide open. If you're greeted with a powerful gasoline odor when you open the hood, the engine is most likely flooded.

On most cars, the float bowl is vented to the evaporative emissions canister. The vent must be open when the engine is shut off or high

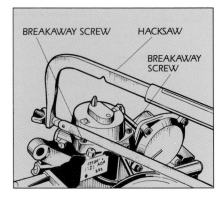

3 Remove carb from engine if necessary to cut slots in choke housing screws.

pressure within the bowl will force fuel through the carb metering circuit.

Check the bowl vent and any connecting hoses for possible blockage. If they're okay, take a look at the canister. If the bottom of the canister is open, you can usually replace its filter. If a closed canister drips fuel from the bottom, replace it and troubleshoot the evaporative emissions system (see your service manual).

INTERNAL CARB LEAKS

If you find that your bowl vent system is okay but your engine continues to flood when it's shut off hot, the carburetor probably has an internal leak.

Before you invest in a new carb, make sure your engine is running at normal temperature. Even a good carburetor may spit fuel into the engine if it's running 30° or 40° above normal.

VACUUM LEAKS

If your engine is hard to start hot but does not seem to be flooded with excess gasoline, a vacuum leak could be the problem. Check all hoses for splits, kinks, and other signs of damage. If they're old and brittle, replace them. Make sure all hoses are connected in the manner illustrated on the emissions information label (see Fig. 4).

In addition to making hot restarts difficult, a vacuum leak will cause a rough idle. To find a vacuum leak that is not the result of an obviously defective hose, use a needle-nose pliers to squeeze off each vacuum hose near its source while the engine is idling. When the roughness clears up, you've found the leak. If the hose itself is okay, the component it's attached to may be bad.

An EGR valve that sticks open qualifies as a vacuum leak, as it allows the engine to draw air through the exhaust passages when you're trying to start it. On most engines you can check the EGR valve by applying vacuum to it with a hand-held vacuum pump while the engine is idling. When the vacuum signal causes the valve to open, the engine will idle roughly. When you release the vacuum, the valve should close and proper idle should be restored. If the application of vacuum to your

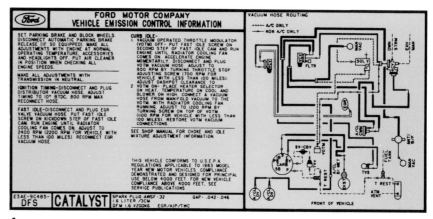

4 Decal in engine compartment shows vacuum hose routing and spark advance specs.

EGR valve does not cause it to open, check your service manual for EGR test procedures.

FUEL STARVATION

While excess fuel is a common cause of hot-start problems, they also can be the result of fuel starvation. In these cases, the engine cranks until the pump has filled the float bowl sufficiently. Then it finally starts.

You can tell if your engine is getting a supply of fuel by removing the air cleaner and looking down the carburetor barrels. (Do this while the engine is off and the starting problem is present. Take care not to burn yourself on hot engine parts.) While holding the choke flap open, crack the throttle. You should see

fuel shoot out the accelerator pump nozzles (see Fig. 5). If you don't, check the fuel filter, fuel pump, and carburetor float adjustment.

ELECTRICAL PROBLEMS

Some electronic parts can fail temporarily when underhood temperatures are high. Unlike our previous examples, the engine will start only after having cooled off for an hour or two.

The most likely offender in these cases is the electronic ignition module. Off-brand discount-priced modules seem to be more likely to fail than name brand or original equipment types. Applying dielectric silicone grease to the underside of GM modules reduces the chance of heat damage and hot restart problems

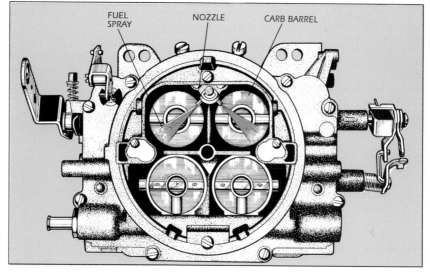

5 Fuel should spray from accelerator pump nozzles when throttle is opened manually.

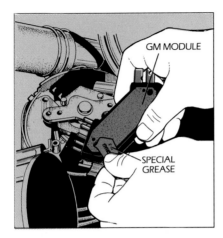

6 Dielectric grease on the back of GM ignition modules can prevent heat damage.

(see Fig. 6). Have a mechanic test the old module before you buy a new one; these expensive electronic parts cannot be returned.

FUEL-INJECTED ENGINES

Because most injection systems remain pressurized after the engine is shut off, a fuel injector that sticks open can flood the engine and foul one or more plugs. Given enough time, the fuel evaporates and the engine starts easily. But for the first hour or so after shutoff, starting can be extra tough.

On port-injected engines (one injector per cylinder), a sticking injector can sometimes be located by checking the plugs half an hour after shutoff. If a plug is fouled or wet, it's likely that the injector for that cylinder is leaking.

A lack of wet plugs doesn't necessarily rule out dripping injectors. A visual check of the injectors is the best test. On throttle-body injection systems (central injectors within a carblike body), the injectors are easy to observe and you can simply warm the engine, shut it off, remove the air cleaner, and watch the injector(s) to see if there's a drip. On some port-injected systems you can lift the injectors and fuel rails out of the ports to watch for drips.

A check of system pressure is also useful in tracking down leaking injectors. If pressure drops continuously after the engine is shut off, a leaking injector could be the cause. But other problems—like a faulty fuel pump check valve, a leaking pump connection, or a bad pressure regulator—can cause pressure loss as well.

On most systems you can measure pressure by attaching a fuel-injection pressure gauge to the Schrader valve, which looks like a tire valve. When attaching the gauge, wrap a rag around the gauge connector to catch any pressurized fuel that squirts out.

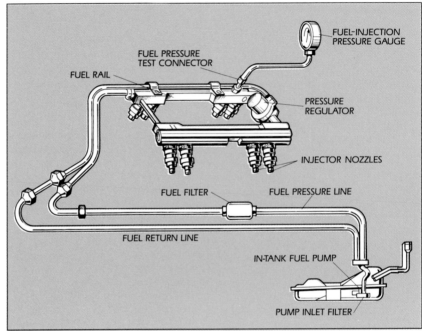

7 To check for leaking fuel-injector nozzles, attach pressure gauge to Schrader valve.

How to Solve
HESITATION PROBLEMS

Does your car procrastinate? When you jab the throttle floorward does your engine draw an empty breath, sag, think about it for a moment, and then finally respond? If so, you have a hesitation problem, or—in mechanic's jargon—tip-in stumble.

Besides the annoyance factor, engine hesitation can be extremely dangerous in severe cases. When you mash the pedal to cross a busy intersection, you want your car to move *right now*. Fortunately, the condition is fairly easy to diagnose and repair.

If the hesitation is present only when the engine is cold, it's caused by a defect in the choke, EFE, or heated intake air systems. We'll limit the discussion to warm-engine hesitation.

PLAN OF ATTACK

On late-model cars with computer control systems—that includes most cars built since 1981—check for trouble codes in the computer system before you move on to other kinds of diagnostic work. You'll find instructions in the fuel injection, carburetor, or driveability and emissions chapters of your service man-

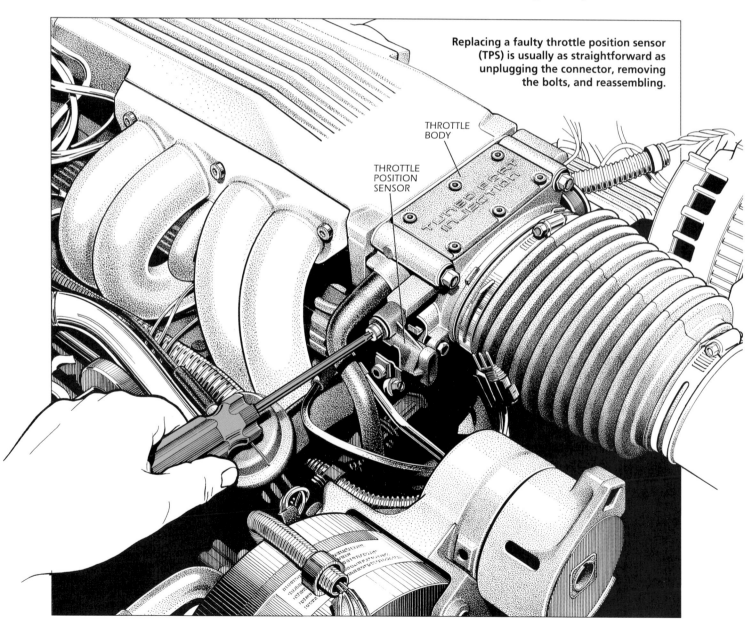

Replacing a faulty throttle position sensor (TPS) is usually as straightforward as unplugging the connector, removing the bolts, and reassembling.

THROTTLE BODY

THROTTLE POSITION SENSOR

ual. If you do find that a trouble code has set, perform the indicated troubleshooting routine that corresponds to that code.

If the problem has not been diagnosed by the engine computer, move on to the checks that follow. Of course on cars without a computer system, you'll begin with the visual checks described below. Notice that the routine differs in some places, depending on whether your engine is fuel injected or carbureted.

BASIC VISUAL CHECKS

Because a vacuum leak can cause the fuel mixture to be excessively lean, it is a prime cause of hesitation. In some cases—but not all—a vacuum leak may also cause a rough idle.

Begin your visual check by examining all vacuum hoses for splits, kinks, and improper connections. (You can determine where each hose should be connected by studying the vacuum diagram on the Vehicle Emissions Control Information Label.)

A cracked or split hose is sometimes difficult to detect by sight alone. But if a hose is split or cracked, it will also cause rough running at idle. So vacuum leaks can sometimes be located by squeezing off each vacuum hose with hose-crimping pliers (available at auto parts stores) or a similar device. Simply close off the hose as near as possible to the vacuum port that it connects to. If a rough idle clears up, you've located a leak.

Once you're sure that all the vacuum hoses are okay, check for air leaks at the base of the carburetor or throttle body. First, make sure the bolts or nuts are reasonably tight. Don't make them as tight as you can get them—as you could break one. If access room allows it, use a torque wrench and tighten them to spec. If you can't reach the fasteners with a torque wrench, use a box wrench or open-end wrench that is about 8 or 9 in. long, and tighten with moderate pressure.

If the bolts seem to be tight enough, spray some carb cleaner around the base of the carb or throttle body with the engine idling. If the idle smooths out somewhat or its speed changes even momentarily, there's a leak, and you'll have

to replace the gasket. Remember that engines with electronic idle-speed control will automatically correct the idle, so the change resulting from the carb cleaner blocking the vacuum leak will be less pronounced than on an older engine with mechanical idle-speed adjustment. Carb cleaner is highly flammable, which is why it works. Don't spray it near the distributor or alternator, or you could lose your eyebrows.

On all cars, check for air leaks at the intake manifold gasket. You can use the carb-cleaner spray. On fuel-injected cars with airflow sensors, check carefully for air leaks at all intake locations between the sensor and the engine.

Make sure you carefully examine any ducting between the airflow meter and throttle. If the ducting is attached with screw clamps, make sure they're secure, but not so tight that they dig into the ducting (Fig. 1). Check intake manifold bolts and those that join the ram tubes to the intake manifold for tightness (Fig. 2).

Check the oil filler cap for proper sealing. On some cars with closed PCV systems, or with limited-intake PCV systems, a loose or leaky oil filler cap can cause hesitation.

Make sure your EGR valve isn't passing exhaust gas at idle. This can cause leaning of the mixture and hesitation. If you're in doubt, check by temporarily replacing the EGR gasket with a solid piece of cardboard. If this cures the hesitation problem, your EGR valve is dirty or defective. Don't leave the cardboard in place—spark knock problems will result.

IGNITION TIMING

There are other factors that can cause a lean mixture, but many are common either to carbureted or fuel-injected engines only, so we'll deal with those later. For now, let's consider another likely cause of tip-in stumble—incorrect ignition timing. If ignition spark is not advanced enough to burn the initial charge, you'll get a hesitation that is virtually identical to one caused by a lean mixture.

You'll need a good timing light, of course. And you'll also need a tachometer to adjust idle speed. You can find the correct timing and idle specification for your car on the Vehicle Emissions Control Information Label found in the engine compartment. The label will also provide some instructions in regard

1 Check ducting between airflow meter and throttle unit of a port-injected engine.

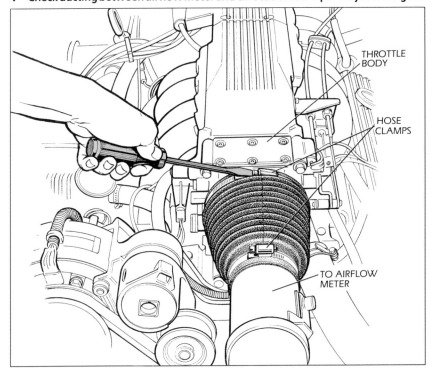

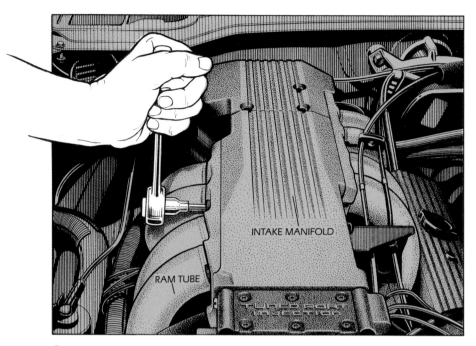

2 A vacuum leak between the airflow meter and intake valve can cause hesitation.

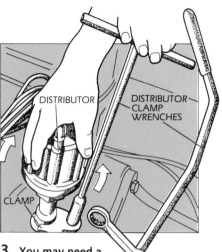

3 You may need a special wrench to loosen the distributor clamp bolt and adjust timing.

to any vacuum hoses that have to be disconnected when you check the timing. On fuel-injected cars with idle-speed control motors or idle air valves, consult your manual for instructions on idle-speed adjustment.

Timing is adjusted by loosening the distributor clamp and rotating the distributor one way or the other (Fig. 3). For example, if the distributor rotation is clockwise, rotate counterclockwise to *increase* advance.

Next, check the ignition wires for cracking, hardness, and proper connections at both distributor and spark plugs. Ignition problems are usually more common to rough running than hesitation symptoms, and it's a long shot here, but a hesitation that is accompanied by rough running can be caused by an ignition problem.

Check the spark plugs to make sure they're not fouled. (If they are, the fouling may only indicate that your hesitation is not really hesitation, but rather rich-mixture "blubbering.")

Check all low-voltage wiring for proper connections, paying particular attention to wires going to fuel injectors. Look for corroded terminals or cut wires. Again, a low-voltage electrical problem will usually cause rough running in addition to hesitation.

CARBURETED ENGINES

Hesitation problems are probably more common to carbureted engines than to fuel-injected engines. This is true because carburetors depend on a rather failure-prone device—the accelerator pump—to enrich the mixture when you first mash the throttle. In many cases, a bad accelerator pump will also cause difficult starting when the engine is cold.

The accelerator pump is located within the carb, and it's difficult to determine whether or not it works by just looking at it. Your best bet is to see if the pump produces any *results*.

Here comes the fun part. To see if the pump delivers any fuel when you open the throttle, you'll have to climb up on top of your engine—or at least on top of the fender—so you can peer down into the carburetor with a flashlight while you open the throttle. The engine should be cool and turned off, of course. When climbing around the engine compartment, take care that you don't crush any wire connectors or other delicate components.

Aim the flashlight down the carb primary barrels. On four-barrel carbs, or staged two-barrel carbs, the primaries are the smaller barrels. Inside you should see one or two little nozzles that point down toward

the center of the barrel. These are the accelerator pump nozzles. Now, while holding the flashlight so that you can see the nozzles, open the throttle briskly to the full-open position. The accelerator pump nozzle(s) should deliver a substantial stream of fuel to the carb barrel. If nothing happens, or just a few drops dribble out, either the accelerator pump is bad, or something is limiting the accelerator pump's fuel supply.

Before you dig into the carb, check the fuel filter and fuel pump. If the pump can't fill the carb's fuel bowl completely, the accelerator pump may not be able to draw a full charge.

The fuel filter is either in the fuel line or behind the carburetor inlet nut (Fig. 4). If you haven't replaced it in the last few thousand miles, do so now. Don't change the filter on a hot engine. Let it cool down first. And use rags to catch any spilled gasoline.

To check the pump, you'll need a fuel-pump pressure gauge. Install the gauge by disconnecting the fuel line at the carb. The gauge kit should come with adapters for connecting the gauge to a neoprene line or to a threaded steel line. Run the engine at idle. The gauge should show between 4- and 7-psi fuel pressure. If it does, check pump volume by holding the disconnected fuel line in a graduated container while a helper runs the engine. Record how long it takes the pump to deliver a pint of fuel.

A typical fuel pump on a carbu-

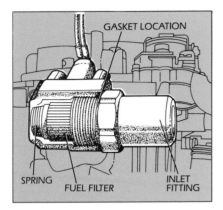

4 Typical GM carb fuel filter shows spring and location of potentially leaky gasket.

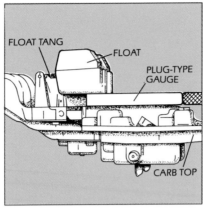

5 Most carb kits use cardboard plug gauges to check the float adjustment.

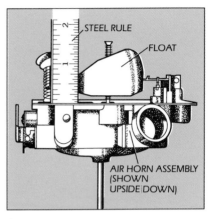

6 You can also use a steel rule to check float height on most carbs.

reted engine should produce a pint of fuel in thirty seconds. Some V8 engines require a pint every twenty seconds. You can find a spec for your engine in the manufacturer's service manual. The fuel should be relatively free of air bubbles. If it's not, there may be a pinhole in the fuel line between the tank and pump. If either fuel pressure or volume is below spec, the fuel pump should be replaced.

If both the fuel pump and filter have been eliminated as potential problems, you'll have to dig into the carb or replace it with a rebuilt. Rebuilts are expensive, however, and there's no reason why you can't rebuild your own carb. And since rebuilding kits are relatively inexpensive, there's little point in disassembling your carb without installing a rebuild kit. What's more, the kit comes with a new accelerator pump, which is probably what you need. Aside from a bad pump, other likely sources of the problem are incorrect float adjustment or a clogged passage.

The kit will come with at least cursory instructions. You'll also find instructions in your service manual. Take extra care in adjusting float height. You can use the plug gauge that comes with the kit (Fig. 5), or a steel rule (Fig. 6).

There are two relatively common types of accelerator pumps, and your carb is likely to have one or the other. One is a diaphragm, the other a plunger. The diaphragm is attached to the outside of the carb (Fig. 7), the plunger type is within the carb and hangs from linkage on the bottom of the carb air horn or top cover (Fig. 8).

Some recent carbureted engines with computer control are also fitted with a throttle-position sensor (TPS) like that described in the fuel-injection section below. Because this device helps the carburetor deliver the extra fuel needed for acceleration, it can be a cause of hesitation. If your engine is equipped with a TPS, your service manual will include adjustment and replacement instructions in the carburetor chapter.

FUEL-INJECTED ENGINES

On a fuel-injected engine the throttle position sensor or TPS bears primary responsibility for telling the computer that you've just opened the throttle, and that it ought to hurry up and increase the fuel supply.

The TPS is a potentiometer that is connected to the throttle shaft of a fuel-injected engine's throttle body or throttle. Wires connect the TPS to the engine's fuel-injection computer.

As the throttle valve is opened, the amount of current passing through the TPS to the computer increases. Thus the computer can tell when you hammer the throttle home, and it will provide more fuel. If the TPS fails, or its wiring is defective, it won't tell the computer what's going on and the engine will hesitate. In many cases, this condition will set a trouble code and turn on the CHECK ENGINE light. On most GM cars, a defective TPS will set code 21 or 22.

But a TPS that just binds or sticks may cause hesitation without setting a code, so make sure you check

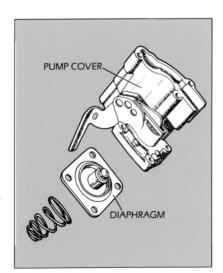

7 Accelerator pump from a Chevette carb is typical of the diaphragm type.

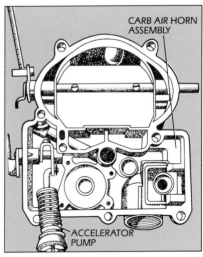

8 Plunger-type pumps can be serviced after the air horn is removed.

that this device is operating correctly.

Some early fuel-injected import cars with Bosch electronic fuel injection have a TPS, but don't set trouble codes. On these cars you can usually tell whether or not the TPS is working by checking output voltage with the throttle opened and closed. You'll find instructions in your service manual, but in general, the voltage should increase as the throttle is opened.

Installing a new TPS is usually quite easy, but varies from car to car. On a GM car with port fuel injection, disconnect the battery's negative cable. (Never work on any electronic control system without disconnecting the battery's negative cable.) Disconnect the TPS electrical connector and remove the TPS Torx screws, along with the lockwashers and retainer (see page 75).

To install the new unit, hold the throttle valve in the normal closed idle position, and install the TPS. Reinstall the retainers, screws, and lockwashers using a thread-locking compound. Then reattach the electrical connector and adjust, following the instructions in your shop manual.

If you're satisfied that the TPS is not the source of the problem, check fuel pressure. Checking fuel-injection system pressure has become an integral part of troubleshooting almost any kind of engine-performance problem.

To check fuel pressure, you'll need a fuel-injection pressure gauge. GM, Ford, and Chrysler engines with port injection have a fuel-pressure gauge attachment point, so you simply connect the gauge to this port. (For Chryslers with TBI, see below.)

In most cases, the gauge point is a Schrader valve, like the kind you'll find on a tire. On TBI cars, the fuel-pressure gauge point may be right on the throttle body. On many port-injected cars, it's on the fuel rail. On 2.5-liter, GM four-cylinder engines, you'll find the gauge point between the fuel filter and throttle body. On 1.8- and 2-liter fours with TBI, the gauge point is under the car near the fuel filter.

On Chrysler products, you have to relieve pressure before checking. Do this by loosening the gas cap and removing the wiring harness connector from one fuel injector. Then ground one injector terminal with a jumper and connect another jumper between the second terminal and the positive post of your battery.

Leave the wires in place for ten seconds. To attach the pressure gauge to a Chrysler TBI system, remove the fuel-intake hose from the throttle body and attach the pressure gauge between the filter hose and throttle body.

On those Chryslers, start the engine and take a pressure reading. TBI systems should produce 34 to 38 pounds; port-injection systems are 52 to 55 pounds.

With Ford and GM products, you'll have to supply electricity to run the pump. You should not attempt to check fuel pressure with the engine running. On a GM car, just connect a jumper between the positive battery cable and terminal G of the ALCL connector under the dash. On Fords, disconnect the electrical connector to the fuel pump, which is located just forward of the fuel tank. Then connect a 12-volt jumper to the connector to run the pump.

Compare your pressure reading to the specification in your service manual. Most Ford and GM fuel-injection systems of the high-pressure variety should produce between 35 and 45 psi. GM TBI units are low pressure and will pump up about 9-psi fuel pressure.

How to Cure
ENGINE RUN-ON

Your secondhand car has been a faithful servant for years, ferrying you to and from work without problems. But one day everything changes as you pull into your parking space and switch off the engine. Your motor emits an annoying *ka-thunk-kathunk* and continues to blow chunks for a full minute after you twist the key.

This phenomenon is often labeled dieseling because diesels run

Excess carbon buildup in the combustion chamber can be blown out by running distilled water into the engine while it runs at very fast idle.

without the benefit of ignition spark—and so will a gasoline engine, sort of.

WHAT'S HAPPENING UNDER THE HOOD?

It takes two things to make an engine run: fuel and spark. With a carburetor and a mechanical fuel pump, fuel will continue to be pumped into the carb's float bowls, and then sucked into the engine as long as the engine continues to tick over—regardless of whether there's any spark to actually start the fire in the cylinders. We know of a fellow who forgot to take a car out of gear

as he was towing it cross country. The tank was full when he left, and very empty when he arrived.

Under the wrong circumstances, spark isn't necessary to ignite any gasoline pumped into the engine. The most common cause is a hot spot in one of the cylinders. The hot spot might be a sliver of head gasket poking out into the combustion chamber, an incandescent accretion of carbon, or even an overheated portion of the cylinder head itself. As the fuel/air mixture is sucked into the cylinder, its temperature is below the point where the hot spot is hot enough to ignite it. But as the piston rises and the mixture is com-

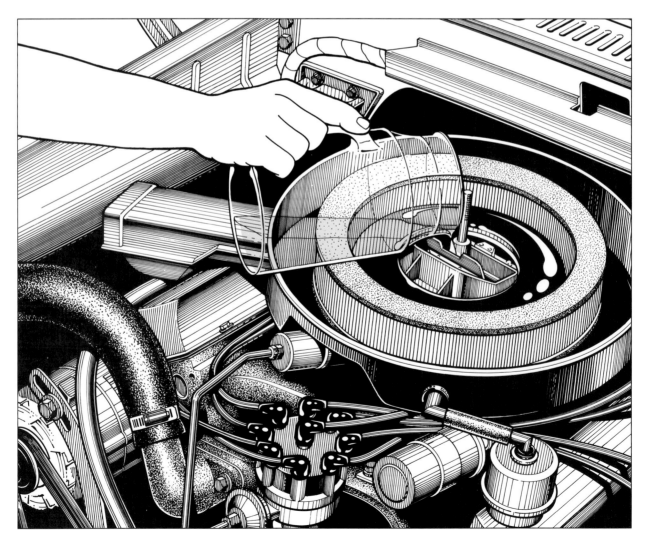

80

pressed, the temperature of the mixture will rise and you've got combustion.

Mind you, the piston is probably still headed uphill when the bang happens, making for a very inefficient event, thermodynamically speaking. But it can be efficient enough to make even a V8 engine gain enough momentum to spin over with only one cylinder chugging along.

Dieseling won't melt your engine or crack your block—it really sounds worse than it is. One exception to this might be if your engine is prone to backfiring when it's dieseling. This is caused by unburned fuel pooling in the exhaust and igniting well downstream of the valves. A really good backfire can blow a hole in a marginal exhaust system.

If you have an occasional, minor problem with dieseling, try this: Just leave the car in DRIVE instead of putting it in PARK when you shut it off. The extra drag of the transmission will probably reduce dieseling to a few shakes. Another ploy is to fan the throttle a few times, drowning the engine in excess fuel. This can cause problems if you want to restart the engine in a few minutes, however. The extra fuel can wet the plugs.

WHY DOES DIESELING HAPPEN?

Dieseling can have several causes. Perhaps you are using cheap off-brand gasoline. Saving a few pennies per gallon can be a disaster in the long run. Higher-octane gasoline is *harder* to ignite, which is a measure of its resistance to detonation in a running engine. Low-octane juice is therefore more likely to be ignited by a hot spot. Exacerbating this is the tendency for a detonating engine to run hotter.

Perhaps your mechanic increased your idle speed to help you squeak through your emissions test. Bad move. A higher-than-recommended idle speed may emit fewer hydrocarbons, but it may also make just enough power when your engine is dieseling to let the engine tick over to the next compression stroke—then the whole thing starts over.

The idle-speed sniffer test is a simple one. If your car can't pass it without bumping up the idle, then there's good reason to suspect other problems. Odds are that a proper tuneup will vastly improve the dieseling situation—as well as your gas mileage.

CHECK FUEL MIXTURE AND TIMING

In a coughing car, the causes are less important than a cure. One cause may be an overly rich fuel mixture. Check your mixture settings to see if this is the problem.

While you're at it, reset your engine timing. A poorly timed motor may misfire and deposit a film of carbon inside your cylinders. Also, an engine that's timed incorrectly will tend to run hotter.

Armed with a timing gun, attach the red lead to your battery's positive terminal, the black to the negative, and place your spark lead onto the lead to the No. 1 cylinder. Check the manual and see if any vacuum hoses should be disconnected, crimped shut, or plugged. Also check for the correct idle speed setting. Start your engine and idle it long enough for it to warm up fully—it might be a good idea to start this project when the engine is already warm.

Now illuminate the timing mark with your timing light. If the timing is off, shut down the engine and loosen the clamp nut on the distributor or holddown. Then rotate the distributor to line up the timing marks. A tiny dab of white paint on the timing marks and indicator arrow will make them much easier to see. If the timing is off, you should check the ignition points and dwell angle before finalizing the timing, as resetting the dwell angle will also change the ignition timing.

COOL IT DOWN

A less-than-perfectly efficient cooling system can raise the temperature of the cylinder head and combustion chamber enough to cause dieseling. If your car has no temperature gauge, but only an overheat warning light, you may not have any indication of overheating.

Start with the obvious. Look for leaves, bugs, birds, or mud plugging the radiator fins. Be sure the fan shrouding, airdam, or any internal baffling near the radiator is in place.

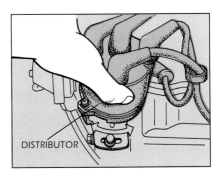

An engine with incorrect ignition timing will run hotter. Change the timing by slewing the distributor.

Check the level of coolant in the radiator—not the level in the overflow tank. When the radiator is cool to the touch, remove the pressure cap. If your system has an overflow tank, water should fill the radiator completely. If your vehicle has no tank, then the level should be within an inch or so of the top—if the radiator cap is in the middle of the top of the radiator. If the cap is on one side near the top, the coolant should be within about 2 in. of the fill neck. Top the system with a 50/50 coolant/water mix. If the level slowly sinks during the next week or so, start looking for leaks.

One overlooked spot for leaks is the hose between the radiator neck and the overflow tank. Check for cracks in the tank as well.

If your dieseling problem is bad when driving in the city, but okay on longer trips, you may have a fan-related problem. Air moving through the radiator may be adequate at freeway speeds, but insufficient to cool the engine in traffic. Check the viscous coupling if your vehicle uses one. Grab the fan blades (while the engine is shut off, obviously). There should be some resistance to motion, rather than the fan freewheeling. If the fan moves very easily, look for evidence of leaking silicone fluid around the fan hub.

If your vehicle uses an electric fan, be sure the fan is working and that the thermostatic switch is turning the fan on and off at the correct temperature.

If all else fails, replace, or at least check, the thermostat. Don't try to make your engine run cooler by using a lower-temperature thermostat, though. Just replace it with a new one of the correct type and temperature rating.

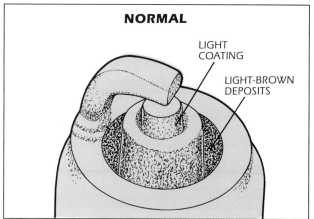

NORMAL

A normal spark plug will show fine, light-brown deposits and a sharp, clean electrode gap.

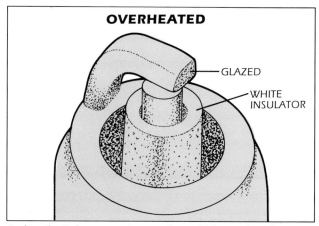

OVERHEATED

A plug that's been running too hot will have glazed-looking electrodes and may have shiny spots on the insulator.

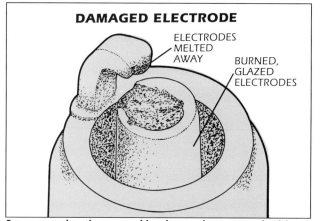

DAMAGED ELECTRODE

Severe overheating caused by detonation or poor ignition timing can actually melt and erode the metal electrodes.

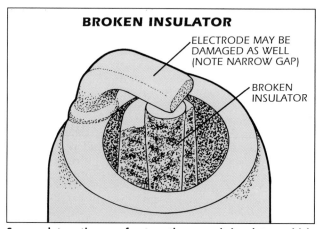

BROKEN INSULATOR

Severe detonation can fracture the ceramic insulator, which in turn can damage the electrode, closing the electrode gap.

PLUGS

Spark plugs live in the heart of your engine, directly inside the combustion chamber. Consequently, the traces of combustion by-products that gather can tell you many things about the efficiency of your engine. Too many cars, especially of older vintage like your dieseling carbureted classic, have severely neglected plugs. If your plugs haven't been changed for a couple of years or a lot of miles, you may not be able to glean much from reading them.

Here's how to do a proper spark plug change:

Start by using compressed air, high-pressure water, or even a sharp stick and a can of carb cleaner to clean the area on the head that surrounds the plug socket. You don't want any dirt falling into the plug hole—it could cause problems if it made it into the cylinder—and it might strip the threads if dirt catches on them and doesn't fall all the way in.

Get an old shoebox or a piece of cardboard, and punch holes in it to correspond with the plugs on your engine. Remove the plugs with a socket wrench, and insert them into the corresponding holes in the box, electrode-end up.

If you're in a dark, dingy garage, get a good light or move out into the sunshine. Using a magnifying glass, examine each plug carefully.

Start by comparing the plugs to one another. If all the plugs look pretty much the same, fine. If one or more plugs has a substantially different appearance, then there's some anomaly in your engine causing it. One plug that's oil-fouled would make you suspicious of the rings or valve guides in the corresponding cylinder. One cylinder that's obviously much hotter is probably running lean, most likely from a manifold vacuum leak near the runner for that cylinder. Check for obvious leaks like a deteriorated grommet on the PCV valve. Any leanness caused by a vacuum leak will make the engine run hotter, as well as the single cylinder closest to the leak.

If all the plugs look about the same, check the gaps. They should be within specifications, and the electrode corners should be flat and square. Electrons are more likely to jump from a sharp corner than a round one, reducing the voltage necessary to initiate a spark. Look for evidence that the plug is firing electrically—a shiny, bare-metal appearance at the corners of the electrodes.

Any cylinder that's not firing at all will have a wet, gasoline-smelling surface. Or perhaps it's oil-fouled—see if the gas evaporates from a

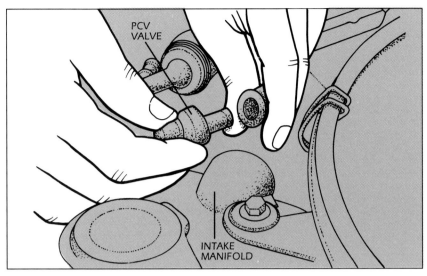

A deteriorated PCV valve grommet or hose can cause a vacuum leak, lean fuel mixture, and subsequent overheating.

warm plug within a few minutes. If you've wisely elected to change the plugs on a cool engine to save yourself from horribly burned fingers, try flicking your Bic lighter and evaporating the gas. Oil fouling will remain, gasoline fouling will dry up.

A dieseling engine might well show evidence of an overheated plug—one (or more) with white, glazed-looking deposits baked onto the surface of the insulator. Or you may find small metallic-looking spheres just barely large enough to see.

Reinstall or replace the plugs. Be sure the new plugs are the correct type and heat range. Put a small dab of antiseize compound on the threads, being careful to keep it away from the electrodes or insulator.

ANTIDIESELING SOLENOID

Some older cars regulate engine run-on with an electrical antidieseling solenoid, located at the base of the carburetor. This shuts off the supply to the carb's idle circuits when the ignition is turned off.

If the valve is corroded or fouled by debris, or the return spring is rusted through or worn out, the valve may stay open and permit the engine to diesel. Unscrew the valve and check the appearance and operation of the plunger, as well as the bore where it seats. If you replace the valve, be sure it's operating properly or the engine won't idle. A

previous idling problem may have prompted someone to disable the solenoid as a quick-fix solution.

HIGH-REV ENGINE CLEANING

If resetting your motor's fuel mixture and timing doesn't help, there are a few alternatives.

If you own a high-revving sports car with a manual transmission, you can literally blow out carbon deposits with a procedure called an "Italian tuneup." For many years there wasn't a maximum speed limit on the Autostradas or freeways in Italy. An owner of a high-performance car that used the cruder ignition systems of the day might have considerable difficulty with fouled plugs after a few days of low-speed driving in the city. A trip to a neighboring city on the Autostrada would raise the combustion chamber's temperatures high enough to literally burn away the carbon accumulation on the plugs and restore performance. The term has stuck around—although modern, fuel-injected cars with high-energy electronic ignition systems really don't need this kind of exercise.

Remember to obey your state highway traffic laws, but the essence is to warm up the car thoroughly, find a relatively traffic-free chunk of freeway, and slow down to 30 mph or so below the speed limit. Then downshift and bring the revs up to as fast as you dare. Repeat this a half-dozen times or so. This will

not only clean off the plugs, but also burn or loosen some of the thick, crunchy carbon accumulation on the head and piston crown.

WATER-INJECTION CARBON REMOVAL

Face it, most of us don't drive sports cars. For lower-revving six- or eight-cylinder engines, or if you live in an urban area where there's no appropriate place for a high-speed run, there is a variation that works just as well. You'll need a small-mouthed soft-drink bottle or some container that will allow you to dispense a thin stream of water; a couple of pints of distilled water; and an assistant.

With the car thoroughly warmed up and idling, remove your air filter and expose the carburetor.

Let the engine warm up until the radiator water is around 200° F. Fill the bottle with lukewarm distilled water. Now have your assistant sit behind the wheel and idle it at about 2,500 rpm above normal idle. If your car lacks a tachometer, do it by ear: That's about the speed your engine turns over at 70 mph.

Keeping your fingers and hair clear of the open carb throat and the whirling fan blades, carefully pour water into the open ports of the carburetor. With your free hand, signal your assistant to gun it. Every time he or she guns the engine, trickle about three tablespoonfuls of water into the carb.

Pour an even amount of water into each carburetor barrel. You must also wear eye protection to prevent any stray water from being fanned back into your face.

You may be surprised by what flies out of the tailpipe. Greasy black smoke will signal that your engine is cleansing itself of its internal carbon.

Be *very* careful not to add too much water to the carburetor at once—it's a long shot, but enough water cascading into the cylinder all at once might take up the volume between the head and piston. While steam and combustion gases are compressible, water is not.

And if there's no room left when the piston hits Top Dead Center, the consequences include a broken piston, bent crankshaft, or twisted rod.

The actual carbon removal is

caused by the thermal shock of water exploding into steam inside the cylinder. This will literally pulverize much of the carbon, which then blows out of the exhaust.

Of course, do this outdoors. Curious onlookers should be shooed away from the tailpipe, lest they receive a face full of toxic goo. We also suggest that you avoid doing this near sensitive surfaces, like the laundry hanging on the line or a white-painted garage door.

Continue the technique of rev-pour-gun-goo until the black smoke stops. If the vehicle continues to emit smoke after several pints of water, check with your mechanic, who may tell you it's time to get out while you're still ahead.

WHAT ABOUT FUEL INJECTION?

Fuel-injected engines generally don't run on after the key is turned off. Think about it—the electric fuel pump is not generating any fuel pressure, and the electrically activated fuel injectors aren't being triggered. Once in a great while it can happen—but only on an engine that's running so sick that the dieseling is one of the minor symptoms.

There's a certain amount of fuel under pressure in the fuel lines and fuel rail—enough to turn over the engine for a few seconds. And if one or more of the injectors—including the cold-start injector, if your vehicle uses one—is leaking, then it's possible that it will provide enough fuel to let the engine run on.

How to Smooth a
ROUGH IDLE

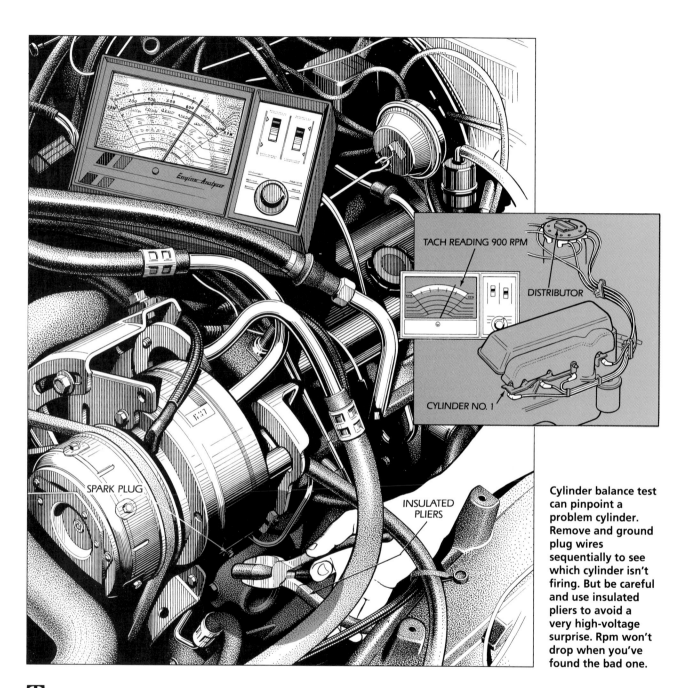

TACH READING 900 RPM

DISTRIBUTOR

CYLINDER NO. 1

SPARK PLUG

INSULATED
PLIERS

Cylinder balance test can pinpoint a problem cylinder. Remove and ground plug wires sequentially to see which cylinder isn't firing. But be careful and use insulated pliers to avoid a very high-voltage surprise. Rpm won't drop when you've found the bad one.

There are a lot of little car problems or malfunctions that you can learn to live with. There are others, however, that make driving unpleasant and sometimes lead to more expensive failures if ignored. One of these is a rough idle. In its most benign form, a rough idle may be nothing more than a slight vibration and spitting from the exhaust. More severe cases may shake the vehicle so hard that other parts threaten to rattle off. Eventually the hydrocarbon-laden exhaust will ruin the catalytic converter and O_2 sensor.

WHAT'S GOING ON?

When an engine idles roughly it's because one or more cylinders are running out of sequence, inefficiently, or are completely dead. If the misfire clears up above idle, you can usually rule out internal engine problems right away. An engine may seem to run okay at high rpm even with a misfire because the increased speed masks the roughness. Before attempting any diagnosis, make sure timing and idle speed are adjusted to spec. Then check to see that the choke (if any) closes when the engine is cold and opens when the engine is warm.

ENGINE CONTROL SYSTEM

Most cars produced since 1981 have a computerized engine control system. The computer will record trouble codes when engine operating faults occur. Some manufacturers, including Ford and Chrysler, suggest that the computer system troubleshooting routines should be performed after conventional diagnosis. GM instructs its mechanics to check for computer-system trouble codes and carry out the indicated diagnostic operations prior to conventional troubleshooting. You'll find detailed instructions for diagnosing GM, Ford, and Chrysler computer systems in your factory service manual.

The most important thing to remember in respect to computerized engines is that conventional troubleshooting and computer-system diagnosis are interrelated. In other words, a fault such as a vacuum leak can be uncovered through normal diagnostic routines, yet it might set a trouble code in the computer's memory.

VACUUM LEAKS

Sometimes a rough idle can be cured with a visual inspection. This is particularly true if the engine has just been worked on, as it's easy to leave a hose disconnected or mix up the engine's firing order.

To check vacuum hose connections, find the vacuum hose diagram for your car, probably in the engine compartment somewhere, frequently on the Vehicle Emissions Control Information Label. Make sure all hoses are connected as indicated on the diagram. Make sure they fit tightly on their respective pipes. If not, replace them or, if they're larger hoses like those used for power brakes and are in good condition, secure them with screw-type hose clamps (Fig. 1). Visually check every hose for kinks or splitting.

1 Secure larger hoses with screw clamps to cure misfire from vacuum leaks. Tighten until rubber extrudes through clamp.

Once you're sure all the vacuum hoses are in good shape and properly connected, have the engine running at idle and squeeze each hose closed near the point where it connects to its vacuum source (Fig. 2).

If the idle smooths out when you squeeze off the hose, either the hose itself is leaking or the component it's connected to is defective.

When you're certain that the vacuum hoses and the components they're attached to are not causing the rough idle, check the intake manifold gaskets by spraying nonflammable solvent on them while the engine is running. If the idle smooths out, the manifold gaskets are leaking and you'll have to remove the manifold to replace them. While the intake manifold is off, check it for cracks or warpage.

Check the bolts that hold the carb or throttle body onto the intake manifold (Fig. 3). These bolts frequently come loose and can cause a rough or erratic idle. Check the carb base or throttle-body gasket by spraying nonflammable solvent on it like you did for the intake manifold.

Most cars produced since 1975 have exhaust gas recirculation valves (EGR). If the valve sticks open at idle or if an improper hose connection causes vacuum to be applied to it at idle, it will make the engine run rough. To check, warm the engine fully, disconnect the vacuum hose to the valve, and plug the hose. If this clears up the idle, the hose is improperly connected or

there is a fault in the valve's vacuum control system.

If disconnecting and plugging the EGR vacuum supply doesn't clear up the idle, remove the EGR valve and cut out a piece of cardboard to the same shape as the base of the valve. Cut holes for the bolts but not for the valve's ports. Grease both sides of the cardboard and reattach the valve to the engine with the cardboard under it, blocking the exhaust and intake passages. With the valve's vacuum hose disconnected and plugged, start the engine. If the idle is now smooth, the valve is defective and must be replaced. If the idle is still rough, the valve is not at fault. Unbolt the EGR valve, remove the cardboard, and reinstall the valve with a new gasket.

IGNITION WIRE ROUTING AND CONDITION

A check of ignition wire routing is next. Determine the firing order for

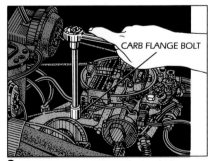

2 Squeezing off vacuum lines with pliers can isolate a suspect component. Use smooth-jawed pliers or cover with rag.

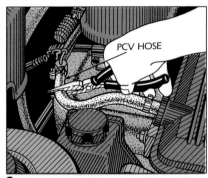

3 Loose carb or throttle-body base bolts can be a source of vacuum leaks. Chase leaks with nonflammable spray solvent.

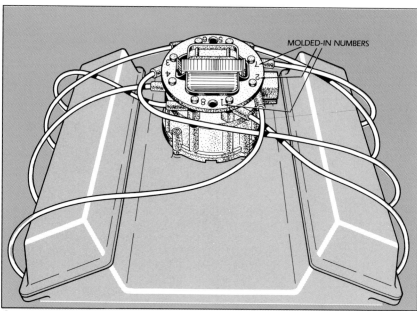

4 Connect plug wires according to sequence on distributor cap and intake manifold.

your engine and make sure all the plug wires are connected properly.

The firing order for most engines is stamped on the intake manifold, or you should check the shop manual. On late-model GM engines, it's marked on the plug wire retaining ring (Fig. 4).

On GM and Chrysler V8s, cylinder No. 1 is farthest forward on the left bank of the engine. Left bank means the left side as you would see it from the driver's position. The other cylinders on the left bank are 3, 5, and 7. On the right bank are 2, 4, 6, and 8.

On Ford V8 engines, cylinders 1, 2, 3, and 4 are on the right bank; 5, 6, 7, and 8 are on the left bank. The same two numbering systems apply to the various makers' V6 engines. Inline six- and four-cylinder engines are simply numbered front to rear.

To check firing order, simply take the first number in the order, usually 1, and trace that wire back from the corresponding spark plug to the distributor cap. Then, moving around the distributor cap in the direction of distributor rotation, check to see that each wire is connected to the proper spark plug. If you don't know the direction of distributor rotation, remove the cap and bump the engine with the starter to see which way the distributor shaft rotates.

For example, if you were check-ing plug wire connections on a Chevy V8, you'd find that the firing order is 1, 8, 4, 3, 6, 5, 7, 2. The rotation is clockwise, and No. 1 cylinder is front, left bank. So you'd trace the wire from the front, left-bank cylinder back to the distributor cap. Then you'd locate the next wire on the cap in a clockwise direction and make sure it was attached to the spark plug for the No. 8 cylinder, the last one on the right bank.

As you check, examine each wire for cracks, hardness, or splits. Make sure that the wires are securely connected and that the terminals are free of corrosion. Sometimes you can detect bad wires by watching the engine idle at night, as you'll see blue sparks where the current arcs to ground. If you're not sure about the condition of the wires and if they're several years old, replace them. For high-voltage ignition, like GM HEI or Ford EEC IV, use the same 8-mm silicone-jacketed wires that the car was originally equipped with.

While silicone-jacketed wires are much more expensive than conventional types, they also offer much better insulation and will last much longer. The silicone-jacket wires are available in 7-mm size for conventional ignition systems. On cars with computer systems or radios, make sure you get carbon-core, TVRS-type wire.

CYLINDER BALANCE TEST

If the visual or computer system tests don't uncover the cause of the rough idle, a cylinder balance test can determine which cylinders are misfiring. You'll need a tachometer and a pair of pliers with insulated handles. Remove the air cleaner and plug the vacuum line or lines that are joined to it. Connect the tachometer and unplug the idle speed control motor, if there is one (most computerized systems have this).

Then, while watching the tach, pull the plug wire off the No. 1 cylinder's spark plug and hold the wire terminal next to the cylinder head so it can arc to ground. Note how much the engine speed drops when you remove the wire (see page 85). Continue in the same way, checking each cylinder for rpm drop.

If the engine speed doesn't drop on one or more of the tested cylinders, or if it drops much less than it did on the others, the cylinder is probably not running or it's running very poorly (see chart, Fig. 5).

If you don't see the spark arc to ground when the wire of a dead cylinder is removed, attach the wire terminal firmly to the end of a screwdriver and hold it by the insulated handle with the shaft close to a clean metal ground while an assistant starts the engine.

For cars with high-energy ignition, use a spark tester instead of the screwdriver to prevent shock. Spark testers are available from GM dealers (ask for the ST 125 tester) or from most auto parts stores.

The wire attaches to one end of the tester and the other end has a clamp that you attach to ground before starting the engine. In either case, you should see spark when the engine is running. If you don't, the wire or the distributor cap is defective.

Replacing both the cap and wires is an almost certain cure if you're not getting spark at one or two wire ends, but you can check individual wires with an ohmmeter if you wish. Connect the meter leads to each end of the wire. Resistance should be less than 30,000 ohms for most applications (Fig. 6). If you're not sure about the condition of a wire, compare its resistance reading to a known good wire. Examine the cap for cracks or corrosion. Replace it if you're not certain of its condition.

	ENGINE RPM PLUG WIRE	ENGINE RPM PLUG WIRE	
CYLINDER	ON	OFF	CONCLUSION
1	900	825	OK
2	900	835	OK
3	900	900	NOT RUNNING
4	900	840	OK
5	900	890	VERY WEAK
6	900	830	OK
7	900	820	OK
8	900	835	OK

5 Cylinders should show similar rpm drop when wires are off.

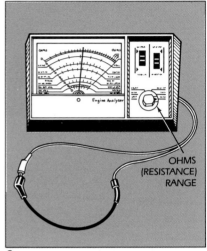

OHMS (RESISTANCE) RANGE

6 Check the resistance of the spark plug wires with an ohmmeter. Resistance should be no more than 30 Kohms.

If you do see spark but the cylinder failed the balance test, either the plug is bad, there's an intake manifold vacuum leak that you missed, an internal engine problem is affecting that cylinder, or the cylinder is not getting fuel.

Remove the plug for the cylinder in question. If it really wasn't running and the cylinder was getting fuel, the plug should be black and wet. Replace it with a good plug, start the engine, and repeat the balance test.

LEAN MISFIRE

If the plug is okay and your car is equipped with port fuel injection, listen to the injector for the weak cylinder as the engine idles. Use a stethoscope or a piece of hose. You should hear the injector open and close rapidly. Compare its sound to that of the other injectors. If it doesn't open and close, turn off the engine, unplug the injector, and connect a test light to the harness connector. Crank the engine; the light should flash on and off. If it does, the injector is bad. If it doesn't, there's a problem in the wiring or in the engine computer system. Repair as necessary or repeat the computer system diagnostics. If the light does flash, the injector is probably just dirty. In many cases if one injector is

dirty, the others are as well. This may be evidenced by numerous cylinders showing marginal rpm drops on the power balance test.

Sometimes dirty injectors can be cleaned by adding a can of injector cleaner to the fuel tank. One such product, which seems to be more powerful than most others, is available through Chevron filling stations. At about $8 a can, it is also considerably more expensive than other injector cleaners.

Some manufacturers of port-injected vehicles recommend the Chevron product and supply it through their parts department. Remember, however, that there is always some danger in using any high-powered solvent in that it could cause deterioration of fuel-system parts on some vehicles. All owners of injected cars, both throttle-body and port, should use fuel that includes a detergent.

On carbureted or throttle-body-injected cars, it's not likely that one cylinder could be totally fuel-starved unless there's an internal engine problem. However, the engine can idle roughly because of intermittent lean misfire on all or some cylinders. On V6 or V8 engines with dual-plane intake manifolds, you may sometimes find the misfire and poor power balance readings on one bank only. This means that the idle circuit on the side of the

carburetor that feeds that bank or the injector on that side of the throttle body is clogged or misadjusted.

CHECKING THE VALVE TRAIN

If a valve for a particular cylinder doesn't open or close, the cylinder won't run. To check valve-train parts, remove the valve cover on the side of the engine with the dead cylinder. Check the two pushrods, rocker arms, and valve springs for that cylinder. Look for bent pushrods, broken rockers, broken valve springs, misadjusted rockers, or—on engines with ball-and-socket rockers like the Chevy V8—a rocker stud that may have pulled out of the head. A stuck valve is fairly common on engines that have been in storage for a considerable amount of time.

If you find a broken spring, you can pressurize the cylinder with a spark-plug hole air-hose adapter and an air compressor. This will prevent the valve from falling into the engine when the spring is removed.

Then use one of the widely available "on engine" valve-spring compressors to remove the spring and replace it with a new one. You may need to hold the engine in position with a wrench on the front pulley when you pressurize the cylinder.

A stuck valve can usually be

freed up by squirting penetrating oil on the guide and then pushing on the valve. Sometimes a few taps with a plastic or brass mallet, square on the end of the valve stem, may be necessary to loosen the stuck valve.

Bent pushrods are easy to replace on most engines. If the pushrod is damaged, check the rocker arm carefully for galling or burrs, and shine a flashlight down into the camshaft valley to make sure the lifter is secure and hasn't hopped out of its bore.

If you don't see any signs of valve-train damage, rotate the engine with a wrench on the front pulley and watch both valves for the offending cylinder to make sure they open and close. If one or both don't open, either the camshaft has been worn flat, the rocker arm adjustment is backed off, or—with ball-and-socket rockers like those on a Chevy V8—the stud may have pulled out. If the stud has pulled partway out, remove it by removing the rocker arm and stacking washers on the stud until you have just enough room to screw on the nut. Then run the nut down, raising the stud. If you get to the end of the stud's threads before it's out of the head, add more washers. Install a new stud using an anaerobic stud and bearing retainer compound.

Put a nut on the end of the stud and tap it in carefully. Don't start the engine for at least twenty-four hours.

If the camshaft is flat, you're in for a major repair job. Consult your shop manual for instructions on removing and replacing the cam. You can be sure that you'll have to remove the radiator and grille. And remember, all those metal filings from the old cam are in the engine. You might end up spinning a bearing or wiping out the new cam. A complete engine rebuild is best. If you don't want to go that far, at least pull the oil pan and clean it. Then flush the engine's valley with solvent before installing the new cam. While you've got the pan off, you ought to have a look at the bearings and oil pump.

OTHER INTERNAL PROBLEMS

If the valve train checks out okay, the cause of the misfire is probably a compression leak, either a bad head gasket, a burned valve, or extremely bad rings. Check compression with a compression gauge and compare it to other cylinders. If down more than 30 percent, it could cause a rough idle.

Pressurize the cylinder with a spark-plug hole air-hose adapter and a compressor. Then listen for the air leak. If the culprit is an exhaust valve, you'll hear it in the exhaust pipe. If it's an intake valve, you'll hear air rushing out the throttle. If it's the rings or a broken piston, you should hear air through the oil filler hole. You'll hear at least some sound of air rushing in all these places; you have to compare them to see which is the real source. A bad head gasket will usually produce air bubbles in the cooling system. Remove the thermostat housing to check for them.

How to Cure SPARK KNOCK

Just ahead is a steep hill. You're driving in high gear and your car begins to lose speed. You squeeze the accelerator toward the floorboards and you're rewarded with little or no engine response and a noise like marbles in your hubcaps.

You wish it were that simple. Unfortunately, what you're hearing is the death rattle of spark knock. What it means is that uncontrolled combustion in your engine is trying to beat your pistons, rings, and rod bearings to death.

But not to worry. Unless you're riding around in a pumped-up muscle car with 10 or 11:1 compression ratio, you can probably solve the problem with some systematic diagnostic work and, in most cases, minimal repairs.

THE ROOT OF THE PROBLEM

We call this pinging noise spark knock because everyone else calls it spark knock, and we want you to know what we're talking about. But, in truth, spark knock is not a very accurate name for this condition because it's not always related to spark or spark timing.

Spark knock is usually the result of *detonation*. Detonation occurs when a second combustion-chamber flame front is ignited some time after normal ignition. Now the air/fuel mixture is burning on both sides of the chamber and there's some unburned mix between the two flame fronts. Heat and pressure rise far more rapidly than in normal combustion, due to the two flame fronts. Eventually, the heat and pressure cause the unburned gases to explode violently, pounding the top of the piston, the ring lands, and the bearings.

This second flame front is caused by preignition. Preignition occurs when a hot spot on the chamber or spark plug causes the mix to ignite before the ignition spark occurs. Preignition can also occur spontaneously if overall combustion chamber temperature is already so high that the heat buildup that results from compression of the mixture brings it to combustion temperature.

Now here's the part that confuses even some knowledgeable technicians. The high cylinder pressure that preignition causes can produce spark knock noise even if detonation doesn't occur. In this case, the noise you hear is caused by the piston slamming into a wall of high pressure as it rises on the compression stroke. Preignition that occurs without detonation is usually less damaging than detonation, but it can still cause premature engine failure, and it robs horsepower.

In either case, the fix is the same, so a total understanding of this complex subject isn't absolutely necessary. In the following sections, we'll

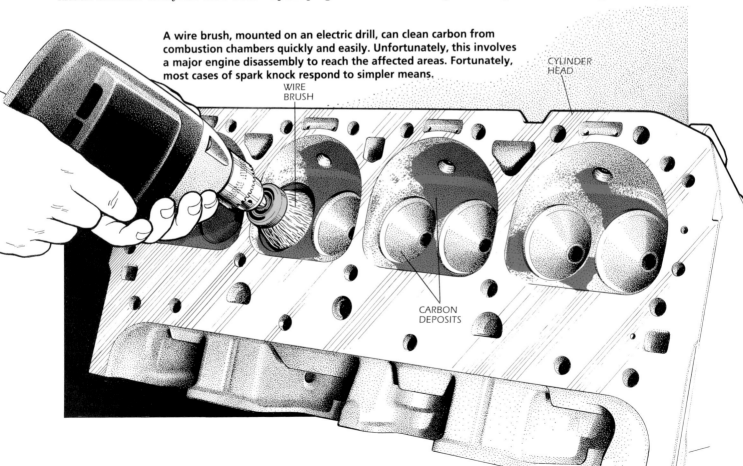

A wire brush, mounted on an electric drill, can clean carbon from combustion chambers quickly and easily. Unfortunately, this involves a major engine disassembly to reach the affected areas. Fortunately, most cases of spark knock respond to simpler means.

WIRE BRUSH

CYLINDER HEAD

CARBON DEPOSITS

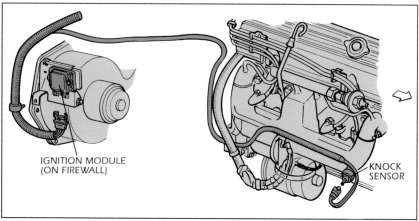

Some high-performance engines are fitted with a knock sensor. Knock control systems retard ignition timing.

provide a general guide for eliminating the dreaded death rattles of spark knock. If your car does not have a knock sensor, you can skip the first section.

If you have a Hearst Motor or factory service manual, you can supplement this guide with the information you'll find there. Look for the troubleshooting guide in the engine driveability section and see what it has to say about spark knock, detonation, or preignition.

KNOCK SENSORS

Some of today's high-performance engines are fitted with a knock sensor. This usually consists of a sensor device that can detect the vibration caused by spark knock and a control microprocessor. In most cases, the microprocessor for the knock sensor system is the same one that controls ignition timing. And when the sensor detects knock, the computer retards timing until it goes away. There is, of course, a penalty in fuel economy and power, because retarding the timing makes the engine less efficient.

Some of the best knock sensor systems are selective, meaning they localize the knock problem to one or more cylinders and retard ignition only for the offenders. In these cases, the penalty in fuel economy and performance isn't as severe.

A few knock sensor systems used on turbocharged engines reduce boost rather than retard timing. This will also curb spark knock, as it can be a function of both cylinder pressure and ignition timing.

If the knock sensor circuit fails,

you might experience severe spark knock in some driving situations. Troubleshooting procedures frequently call for tapping on the engine block with a small hammer while watching for ignition retard with your timing light. On turboboost systems with a boost gauge, drive the car in a manner that usually generates spark knock (uphill in high gear at moderately low rpm with a wide throttle opening, for example). As you drive, watch for boost reduction when spark knock occurs.

On the most advanced systems, a circuit failure will frequently set a trouble code in the microprocessor's memory. If this has occurred, your CHECK ENGINE light should be illuminated. See your service manual for details on reading and interpreting trouble codes.

What if your knock sensor circuit is working overtime? In other words, if conditions exist that are causing spark knock even in normal driving, your engine computer could be retarding the timing most of the time, resulting in loss of power and efficiency. Suspect this if your car is a lot more sluggish than it used to be for no immediately apparent reason.

If this is the case, you should check for some of the other conditions, outlined below, that can cause spark knock and correct them as needed.

SPARK STUFF

Many of the spark knock problems are caused by incorrect spark plug heat range or incorrect ignition tim-

ing. Check your plugs to make sure that they're the correct heat range. A spark plug that is too hot can cause preignition problems.

If you don't know what plug your engine is supposed to use, check with your parts store counterman. Sometimes a manufacturer will change the recommended plug number after the car is in service, so make sure you're consulting an up-to-date listing.

Changing to a spark plug that is colder than the recommended one can sometimes help cure preignition problems, but the cold plug can cause other driveability problems. If the correct plug runs so hot that it causes preignition, you have a problem somewhere else. In this case, the plug heat is a symptom, not a cause.

Take a look at all the plugs while you're at it. Heavy deposits or hot spots on the electrodes or insulators can cause preignition. If the plugs don't look good, clean or replace them.

When you've determined that your plugs are okay, check initial and total ignition timing. If timing is too far advanced, heat and pressure will build up too soon and spark

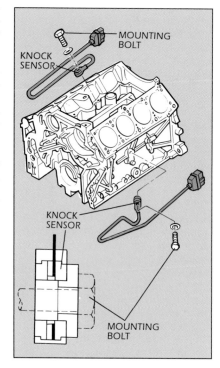

Many vehicles have only one sensor. This system has one for each cylinder bank.

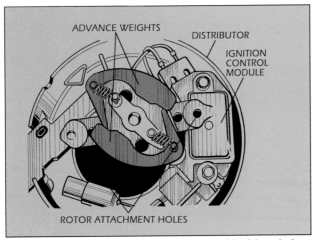

If the advance weights bind in an advanced ignition timing position, spark knock can result.

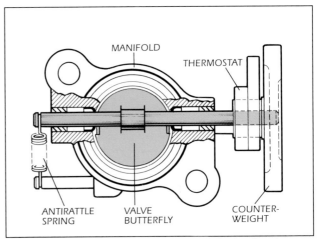

Check the fully warmed engine temp. If the intake air preheating remains on after the engine warms, spark knock can result.

knock will result. Your timing should be set to the amount recommended by the manufacturer. Retarding it beyond this point may help eliminate spark knock, but if everything else is okay, you shouldn't have to.

An exception would be extremely high-compression engines (10:1 or higher) from the 1960s. With some of these, which were engineered for high-octane leaded fuel, you might have to retard timing or resort to other measures to make them run knock-free on premium unleaded or a 60/40 mix of premium unleaded and regular leaded, or you might have to use an octave-boosting fuel additive.

If ignition timing is at spec, check for binding of centrifugal advance weights on cars equipped with a distributor. This is common on GM cars where the centrifugal weights are directly below the rotor. If the weights stick in the fully advanced position, spark knock can result.

If one of the springs on the distributor's advance counterweights breaks, the initial advance and total advance may be correct, but the large total advance can come in at much too low of an rpm. So a physical check of the advance mechanism may be in order. If the distributor shaft bushings are worn enough, the shaft may cock sideways enough to upset timing at higher rpm. Be sure the vacuum advance or retard hoses are intact, not leaking or crimped, and that they are connected to the correct vacuum port on the manifold or carb. A vacuum tap on the side of the carb that sees a port just below

the lip of the throttle butterfly will see vacuum only after the throttle is open far enough. Manifold vacuum taps will signal the advance mechanism anytime there is vacuum, which may be too soon.

ENGINE OVERHEATING

If your timing and plugs are okay, it's time to turn your attention to the cooling system. If you haven't been flushing and refilling it once a year, you may have some deposits of guck in the cylinder heads that cause localized overheating and spark knock. We've seen some extremely severe cases of spark knock that were caused by a dirty cooling system.

Do a flush and refill with a 50 percent solution of antifreeze. If the system is extremely dirty, you may have to find a technician who has a power backflushing machine, or use some cooling system cleaning chemicals, or both.

Once everything is clean, check the fully warmed engine temperature and compare it to the manufacturer's spec. If you don't have an engine temperature gauge that reads in real numbers, you can install one. Just replace the cooling system warning light pickup with the gauge pickup and mount the gauge under your dash. If you don't want to install it permanently, you can just hang it somewhere while you take a test drive.

If the running temperature is 10° or more in excess of specs, you should take steps to lower it.

High operating temperature can be caused by an incorrect or defective thermostat, slipping fan belt, bad water pump, collapsing radiator hose, or defective fan clutch.

HEATING THE CHARGE

If the air/fuel mix is overheated going in, the chances of spark knock problems are multiplied. There are two systems that can easily cause excessive preheating of the mix: intake hot-air and early fuel evaporation (EFE). Some cars have both, some have one, others have neither.

Intake hot-air systems draw air from a stove atop the exhaust manifold. On many cars, this system is controlled by a vacuum motor. The vacuum supply that actuates the motor is turned on and off by a thermal switch in the air cleaner. When the intake air is cold the motor closes a door in the air cleaner, and the engine draws its air supply from the stove. When things warm up, the door is supposed to open, allowing the engine to draw cool air. If the door doesn't open, spark knock can result.

If your hot-air door is closed and your engine is warm, check for vacuum at the vacuum motor. If you find vacuum, the thermal switch is defective. (There should be no vacuum supply when the engine is warm.) If you don't have vacuum to the motor, the door is probably stuck closed.

EFE supplies heat to the base of the intake manifold to aid in fuel vaporization. Some systems use an

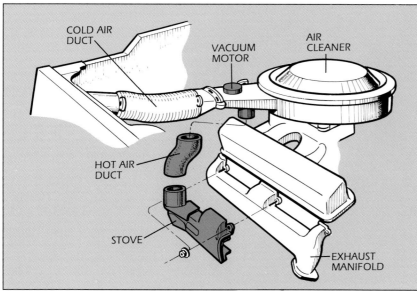

This EFE system directs exhaust gases through the intake manifold with a valve in the exhaust manifold.

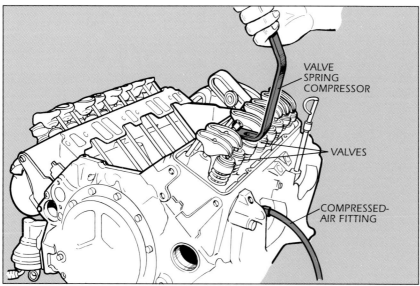

This tool allows removal of Chevy V8 valve springs with the cylinder heads on the engine.

burning a quart of oil every couple hundred miles.

It turned out that oil was getting into the combustion chambers, combining with the charge and causing preignition of the mix, probably due to a lowering of the gasoline's octane number. An on-car seal replacement job solved the problem completely.

You can purchase a special tool that will allow you to compress and remove valve springs without removing the heads. Your auto parts store or dealer parts department should have it. You'll also need a compressed-air supply and a spark-plug hole/air hose adapter. Auto parts stores should have this, too.

Filling the cylinder with compressed air while the piston is at the top of its travel on the compression stroke (both valves closed) will allow you to remove the springs. If you remove a spring and its retainer without filling the cylinder with air, the valve will drop into the cylinder, perhaps necessitating removal of the head.

EGR

A defective exhaust gas recirculation system will almost always cause spark knock. EGR routes a certain amount of exhaust gas back into the intake system to help lower combustion chamber temperature. If the EGR system is broken or disabled, the engine is likely to develop spark knock problems.

Some people disable EGR in the hopes of improving engine performance. On today's cars and with today's gasoline, it has the opposite effect.

The most basic EGR valves use a vacuum signal to open the valve. Because they draw the signal from just above the carburetor or throttle body throttle plates, the signal is not present at idle. A temperature control switch in the vacuum line prevents exhaust gas recirculation when the engine is cold.

You can check this type of EGR in a few minutes. Warm the engine and run it at 2,000 rpm. Check for control vacuum to the valve. If there is none, the thermostatic switch is defective.

Then, with the engine idling, apply vacuum to the EGR valve with a hand vacuum pump. The engine should stumble or die. If there is no

electric grid below the carb to supply this heat. If the heat remains on when the engine is warm, an overheated mix will result.

Other EFE systems route exhaust heat to a passage in the intake manifold. This type uses a valve in the exhaust pipe that closes when the engine is cold by means of a bimetal spring like those used on choke systems. When the valve is closed, exhaust is routed into the intake manifold passage, warming the manifold and the mix. These valves

can sometimes stick in the closed position, particularly on cars that are not driven on a regular basis.

VALVE SEALS

One of the worst spark knock problems we ever encountered was due to a case of bad valve seals. The car, a 1970 Javelin with a V8 engine, would rattle like it had marbles in the hubcaps with just a little squeeze on the throttle. It was also

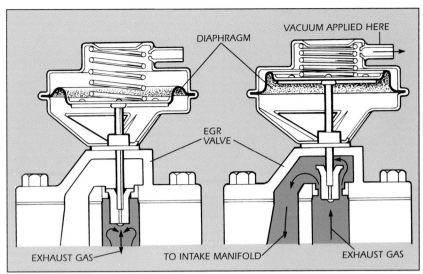

DIAPHRAGM

VACUUM APPLIED HERE

EGR VALVE

EXHAUST GAS

TO INTAKE MANIFOLD

EXHAUST GAS

When the EGR valve is open, exhaust gases are mixed with the air/fuel charge.

CARBON BUILDUP

Carbon accumulation in the combustion chambers and on the piston tops can cause detonation or preignition due to a resulting increase in compression ratio and/or hot spots in the carbon. Various top-engine cleaners are available that will remove a lot of this. Sometimes disassembly and a wire brush cleanup are required to completely solve the problem of heavy deposits.

VACUUM LEAKS

Vacuum leaks can cause spark knock in some cases because they lean out the mixture and lead to localized burning of the mix. This kind of spark knock problem would usually be accompanied by rough idle.

Small vacuum leaks are tough to pinpoint. Check all vacuum hoses for deterioration and hose connections for a snug fit. Apply carb cleaner to gaskets and hose connections while the engine is idling.

Just remember that this stuff is flammable—don't set your eyebrows on fire by spraying carb cleaner near the distributor or any other electrical sparks.

change in performance, the EGR valve is defective or the valve's exhaust supply is blocked.

To determine which, feel the underside of the valve diaphragm while vacuum is applied. (Wear gloves—it's hot.) If it doesn't move, the valve is defective. If it moves, but there is no change in idle when the valve is opened with the engine running, the EGR passages are plugged.

Other EGR systems are more complex. Some are regulated at least partly by exhaust backpressure. Some are computer controlled by means of a switching solenoid. Some are even more complicated, like the three-stage system used on some Mitsubishi (Chrysler) 2.6-liter four-bangers. If your system isn't a simple valve and vacuum switch arrangement, check the diagnostic procedures in your service manual.

How to Knock Out
ENGINE KNOCKS

STETHOSCOPE

VALVE COVER

An automotive stethoscope can help you pinpoint a knock or rattle before you start tearing things apart.

At first, you pretend not to hear that dull metallic banging noise pounding out from under the hood. "I'm just imagining it," you tell yourself. But it persists, and as thoughts of dreaded big-dollar repair bills continue to muddy your disposition, you realize you're going to have to *do* something about the death knell. But it's too soon for despair. More often than not, an apparent engine knock proves to be something else. What's more, even a real knock can sometimes be repaired without great expense or difficulty.

ENGINE KNOCKS WHEN COLD

This type of noise is a banging or dull metallic thud, not a ticking or rattling noise. The sound in-creases when engine torque is applied, but disappears after two or three minutes of running time.

One common cause of this noise is a faulty Early Fuel Evaporation (EFE) valve (Fig. 1). On cars so equipped, the valve is located in the exhaust manifold and closes when the engine is cold to divert hot exhaust gases to the intake manifold. If the valve bushings are worn, it may bang against the manifold. When torque is applied, load increases and exhaust volume is greater. Thus, the banging is louder. When the engine warms up, the valve opens, and the noise disappears.

You can usually determine if the EFE valve or another component is making noise by listening to it through a stethoscope or length of heater hose (see illustration above). Automotive stethoscopes are available at better auto parts stores. To use the stethoscope you simply touch the probe to the area of the engine or part in question. A hose is used in much the same way: one end to your ear, the other on the part. When using a hose, take care that you don't touch any spark plug wires as you might be treated to a high-voltage slap in the head.

When checking for a noisy EFE valve, compare the sound heard at the valve with what you hear at a location on the engine block. If the noise is more pronounced near the valve, it's probably the source.

While a faulty EFE valve is a wel-come find when diagnosing a cold-

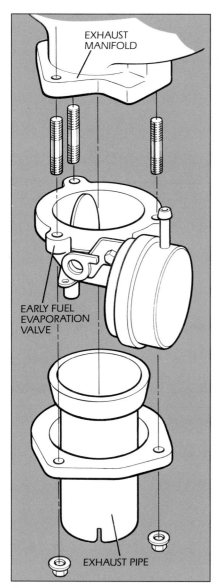

1 The Early Fuel Evaporation valve can produce a noise that sounds like rod knock.

The solution is not an attractive one, as it calls for disassembly and rebuilding of the engine. That's why some dealers will try to tell you that the noise doesn't matter. And, from their point of view, it doesn't, as the car will probably be out of warranty by the time the condition deteriorates to the failure point.

ELIMINATING PISTON SLAP

If you're determined to repair a piston-slap problem yourself, the best fix is to bore the cylinders and install new, oversize pistons. Ask the machine shop to bore to the minimum oversize that will clean the cylinders. Once the block has been bored, carefully check piston size and cylinder bore size to make sure clearance falls within production tolerance. Cylinder bores can be measured with a snap gauge and micrometer or—as a superior alternative—with a dial bore gauge and a micrometer (Fig. 2). Mike pistons on the skirts about 1 in. below the oil ring or wherever the manufacturer specifies (Fig. 3).

Sometimes, quite similar to the sound of excessive piston clearance is the noise caused by a bent connecting rod. In this case, the engine can sometimes be repaired by merely replacing the rod and its piston with new components, but check carefully for damage to the cylinder wall.

Hone the cylinder before installing the new piston and rod, and com-

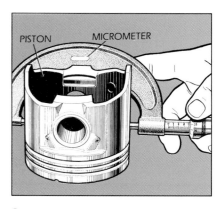

3 Mike pistons on the skirts, opposite wrist pin, and about 1 inch from the top.

pare ring end gap to the specs found in your service manual. On most cars you can do this job without actually removing the engine block. But make sure you thoroughly wash the honed cylinders with soapy water, rinse and wipe dry, and oil the fresh surfaces immediately. Of course, you must check all clearances, including piston to cylinder, connecting rod bearing, and, on V8 and V6 engines, the side clearance between the big ends of the two connecting rods on the journal in question.

ENGINE KNOCKS WHEN WARM

A heavy engine knock that occurs only when the engine is warm or whenever the engine is running un-

engine knock, the classic cause of this type of noise is a serious one: One or more of the cylinders is too big for its piston. As the piston warms up, it expands and the noise disappears. Increased load causes the piston to slap the walls harder, increasing the noise.

On very old engines, this clearance is the result of cylinder wall and piston wear. On newer engines, it is more often a manufacturing defect. Manufacturing tolerances are narrow (example: .0007 to .0017 in. for a 1985 Camaro V8) and engines that are out of spec can occasionally slip by.

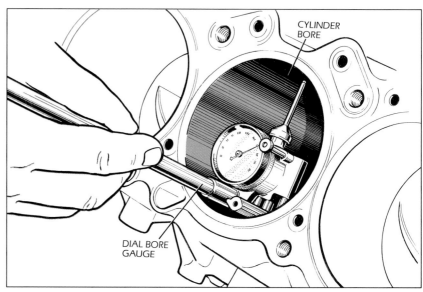

2 A dial bore gauge will measure cylinder size, taper, and out-of-round.

der load can be caused by some relatively innocent problems.

One example comes immediately to mind. It was a 1970 Tempest with high mileage. A distinct knocking noise developed gradually. It sounded like a seriously worn bearing, and it looked like the engine's days were numbered. But a quick check with a stethoscope suggested that the noise was coming from the bell housing area. A trip under the greasy side confirmed this. The cause? Loose torque converter bolts that were easily replaced.

Other causes of a heavy knock include the very common exhaust system throb, caused by an exhaust system component coming into contact with the body or chassis. In many cases, the noise is only heard under load. The cure is simple: relocation of the offending member by means of hanger adjustment.

Another possibility is a broken crankshaft balancer or pulley hub. You can usually detect this condition by watching the crank pulley while the engine is running. The runout caused by a loose fit will probably be visible. However, you may have to remove the pulley to confirm the problem. This job is a tough one on most rear-drive cars as it requires removal of the radiator. On some cars you may have to lift the engine. Check your shop manual before attempting to remove the crankshaft pulley on a front-drive car.

On cars with a mechanical fuel pump, a worn pump pivot can produce a muted banging noise that sounds like a much more serious internal problem. The condition is fairly common on GM V8 and V6 engines. You can use your stethoscope or length of hose to verify a noisy pump.

Excessive rod bearing or main bearing clearance is the classic worst-case cause. Again, if the engine is new, excessive clearance is a manufacturing defect. If it's an oldie, wear is the culprit.

DIAGNOSING AND REPLACING WORN ENGINE BEARINGS

You can confirm excessive clearance by removing the oil pan and checking clearance with the deformable clearance-checking plastic available at auto parts stores. The

most widely available product of this type is called Plastigage. Purchase a size that bridges the maximum clearance spec for your engine. For example, the maximum main bearing clearance for most modern Chevy V8 rod bearings is 0.003 in. Therefore, you would want to use Plastigage that is sized for a 0.002-in. to 0.005-in. range, or thereabouts. To check rod bearing clearance, you simply unbolt the bearing caps, one at a time. (If you intend to remove more than one rod or main cap at a time, you must mark the main caps and both lower and upper parts of the rods with number stamps. (They are *not* symmetrical or interchangeable, and *must* be installed in their original orientation and location.) With the bearing cap off, pull down on the upper part of the rod to make sure it's seated on the crank. Then wipe the bearing clean and lay the gauging material across the full width of the cap bearing. Reinstall the cap, torquing it to spec. This will compress the plastic gauging material. Do not rotate the crank while the material is in place. Remove the cap and compare the width of the compressed gauging material to the scale on its package.

Checking main bearing clearance is the same except that you'll have to push the crankshaft up against its upper bearing halves. To do so, support it at both ends with screw jacks or small hydraulic jacks.

To measure clearance, insert Plastigage in the lower main bearing caps as described above or, if the engine is out of the car, on the crank journal. Torque the cap in place, and compare your reading to the specs in the service manual (Fig. 4). On most engines, specs for front and rear main bearing clearances differ from those for center bearings.

Once you've confirmed that clearance is excessive, you can replace upper and lower bearing inserts with new ones. Undersize bearings are available to compensate for minimal crankshaft wear. However, if the crank is excessively tapered or worn, engine removal and crank grinding will be necessary.

You can sometimes detect excessive crank wear, particularly on the main journals, by looking for ridges at the edges of the part of the journal that contacts the

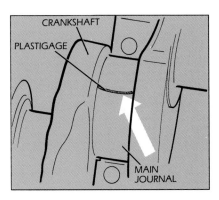
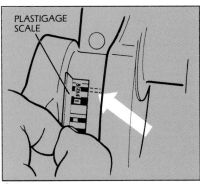

4 Clean journal and bearing, lay strip of plastic gauging material across journal (top). Torque rod or main cap, remove and measure bearing clearance directly with scale supplied with Plastigage (above).

bearing. If the bearings have oil grooves in the center, a ridge will form there when the crank wears excessively. Any ridge that can't be easily polished away, as described below, is cause for concern. To mike the crank, you would have to remove it from the car.

Rod journals can be checked for wear with a micrometer. Simply remove the two caps from a journal (make sure they're numbered) and push the pistons up into the block. If the valves are closed, you may have to remove the spark plug. Measure the journal and compare its size to the service spec in your service manual. Mike each journal in several spots to determine if it is out-of-round or tapered. For example, the service tolerance for out-of-round on most Chevy V8s is 0.001 in. maximum.

To remove upper main bearings make a tool out of a small cotter pin as illustrated in Fig. 5. Make sure the bent pin lies flush against the crank. Then rotate the engine so that the bent pin contacts the side of the bearing shell opposite the

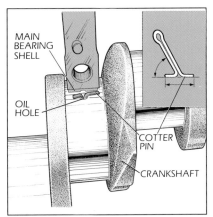

5 Insert bent cotter pin in crank oil hole, rotate crank to remove the bearing shell.

bearing tang. Continue turning the engine until the bearing shell is pushed out.

If crank bearing surfaces are less than perfect, lightly polish them with No. 400 emery cloth and solvent. Push each rod journal's connecting rod or rods and the attached pistons up into the engine, away from the crank. Loop a strip of wet emery cloth over the journal and pull it back and forth in even strokes, using lots of solvent. Make sure you polish evenly, all the way around each journal. To polish main bearings, pass the emery cloth behind the journal and have a helper rotate the crank as you polish.

Once the crank has been lightly polished, wash it thoroughly with solvent. Use an oil squirt can filled with solvent to flush the crank's oil gallery bores. Lube the upper bearing half with clean engine oil and rotate it into place with your bent cotter pin. Make sure the bearing tang seats in the block. Check clearance with the Plastigage as described above. If clearance is okay, lube the lower bearing with clean engine oil, reinstall the cap, and torque to the manufacturer's specification.

ENGINE KNOCKS LIGHTLY WHEN HOT

A faint engine knock that is heard only when the engine is hot can be the beginning of serious trouble in that it is sometimes caused by excessive rod bearing clearance. More often, however, it is the result of a relatively simple problem such as

the previously mentioned loose torque converter bolts. Slight exhaust leaks at the manifold can also produce noise that may resemble a knock under certain conditions.

If the noise is extremely load sensitive—if it is loudest when climbing a hill in high gear—it is probably spark knock. The causes of spark knock include excessive ignition advance, engine overheating, an overly lean condition, combustion chamber carbon accumulation, fuel of insufficient octane rating, an engine hot air or EFE system problem, and—most common of all—an inoperative EGR system. (See previous chapter.)

ENGINE KNOCKS AT IDLE WHEN WARM

Noises that are most noticeable at idle may vary from a dull knock to a loud ticking or clattering. An idle knock that is noticeable only for a few seconds and then goes away is often the result of hydraulic lifter bleed-down. This condition is due to wear within the lifter that allows oil to bleed out when the car is parked for a few hours or more. The only fix is lifter replacement. However, the mating of new lifters with an old cam can also cause excessive wear. The best choice is to learn to live with the noise or to replace the lifters and camshaft.

Excessive main bearing end clearance (or thrust clearance) that exceeds specification may also cause noise right after startup. End clearance can be checked by inserting feeler gauges between the crank and crank thrust bearing (the one that wraps around its cap as shown in Fig. 6). Make sure the crank is pushed up tight against the opposite side of the thrust bearing while checking. You can move it forward or backward by rapping with a rubber or wooden mallet. Replacing the thrust bearing is the fix for this problem, but it's best to replace all main bearings along with the thrust bearing.

Excessive piston wrist pin clearance will produce a rhythmic clatter when the engine is warm. Sometimes it is most pronounced upon deceleration when the engine is revved in NEUTRAL. Again, if the noise is present in a new engine, it's due to a manufacturing defect. If it

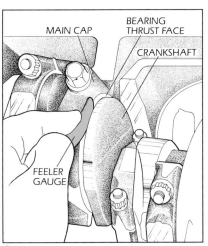

6 Check thrust clearance between the thrust surface and the crank cheek.

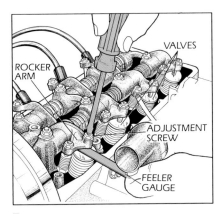

7 Even engines with hydraulic lifters may require occasional valve lash adjustment.

becomes a problem in an older engine, the pistons and rods will have to be removed and oversize wrist pins installed.

The most common causes of engine ticking noises at idle include noisy accessory bearings and engine valve-train problems. If the noise is coming from the valve train, you can usually pinpoint it to one side or the other of a V8 or V6 with your stethoscope or hose as shown in the illustration on page 95.

On engines with adjustable rockers, eliminating a valve-train noise may be only a matter of adjusting the clearance or "lash" in the valve train to approximately zero. To adjust clearance, you simply unlock the adjustment screw by turning its jam nut open with a box wrench,

98

setting the clearance with feeler gauges and a screwdriver, and tightening the jam nut without disturbing the clearance (Fig. 7).

Other engines use an adjustable ball-and-socket pivot, but the principle is the same. Overhead cam engines often use shims instead of adjustable rockers, and unless you're willing to invest in a handful of shims and a special tool to sneak them in under the cam, the best you'll be able to do is find the loose ones, and turn the actual adjustment over to a mechanic.

Check your service manual to determine which valves can be set at each crankshaft position. If you don't have a service manual, rotate the engine and watch each valve's pushrod. Turn the crank another 30° or so after the pushrod for the valve being adjusted has dropped to its lowest point, then adjust that valve.

If you can't solve a noisy valve-train problem by adjusting the valve, you'll have to remove and check parts until you find the offenders. Look for galling or rough spots on rocker arms, worn rocker shafts, bent pushrods (on cam-in-block engines), broken valve springs, and valve stem tip wear.

If all valve-train parts look okay, but valve-train clearance is obviously excessive on one or more valves, the cause is most likely camshaft and lifter wear. If you replace a cam, you should replace all the lifters as well. Or, on overhead-cam engines, replace the rockers or bucket lifters as required. Then remove and flush the oil pan to get most of the metal shavings out of the engine. Replace the oil filter before starting the engine and change the oil and filter again after running the engine for fifteen minutes. Don't allow the engine to idle at less than 1,500 rpm when it is first restarted following camshaft replacement.

How To
STOP STALLING

Engine stalling is more than annoying. Depending on when and where it happens, it can be downright dangerous.

LOOKING FOR CLUES

The circumstances that cause an engine to stall are very important, because they can point you in the right diagnostic direction. So before you start digging under the hood, think about the events that led up to the stalling. We'll cover a variety of different types of problems, explain the symptoms that usually precede the shutdown, and provide some troubleshooting strategies.

On cars with computer engine control systems, including most domestics produced since 1981, the problem that caused the stalling may have turned on the dashboard CHECK ENGINE light. GM wants you to check the computer system for diagnostic codes before you perform other troubleshooting work. Ford and Chrysler recommend that you first try to find common causes of the engine performance problem,

then troubleshoot the computer system only if the problem is not resolved. In any case, you'll find complete instructions for performing the diagnostic routines in GM and Chrysler service manuals. For Fords, you need the Emissions Diagnosis manual for the appropriate model year.

ENGINE DIES AS LOAD INCREASES, WARM ENGINE

Suppose your engine stalls just as the throttle is opened to crest a

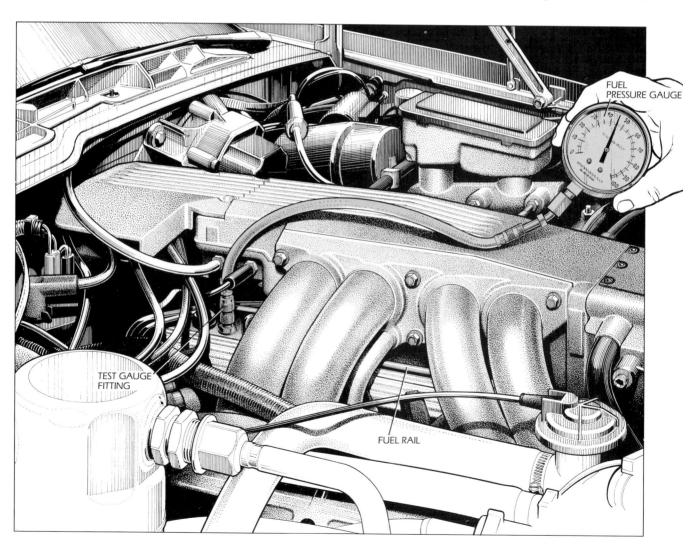

Multiport-injected cars have a fitting on the fuel rail to check fuel pressure. Use the correct high-pressure gauge and be careful not to spray fuel onto a hot engine.

hill—when the going gets tough, it quits. In less extreme cases, the symptom may only be a surging.

The most probable cause of this type of failure is fuel starvation. The fuel system is capable of providing adequate fuel under low-load situations but can't keep up when the demand is high. Fuel starvation may be more prevalent when temperatures are high, but will almost always be affected by load. On fuel-injected engines, fuel starvation stalling may be more sporadic and might not seem to be load sensitive. Diagnosis of a fuel starvation problem differs depending on whether your engine is carbureted or fuel-injected.

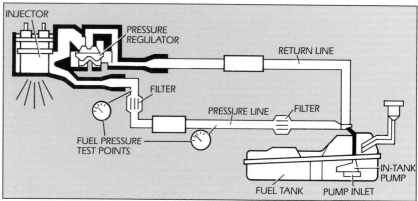

1 Schematic of throttle-body injection system shows several points to meter fuel pressure.

CARBURETED ENGINES

On carbureted engines, the first thing to consider when you have a fuel delivery problem is the fuel filter. On most carbureted cars it's either in the fuel line or behind the carburetor inlet nut. If it isn't new, replace it before you look for more complicated solutions. Change the filter only when the engine is cold, and place a rag under the filter before disconnecting it.

To start, look for a fuel filter spliced into the fuel line. This type filter is usually attached to the line with short lengths of neoprene hose, and replacement is simply a matter of loosening the clamps and installing the new filter. Be sure to install it with the arrow pointing toward the carburetor.

If the filter isn't in the fuel line, it's probably behind the carburetor inlet nut. Use two wrenches to remove the fuel line from the inlet nut—one to hold the nut and one to turn the fuel line. With fuel line off, remove the inlet nut. Be prepared to grab the filter when the nut is unscrewed, as there is probably a spring behind the filter. Note any difference between the front and rear of the filter. Many have a check valve on one side. The new filter must be installed with the check valve pointing in the same direction.

If the new filter doesn't solve the problem, pump pressure should be tested. After disconnecting the fuel line at the carburetor, attach a fuel-pressure gauge. Run the engine at idle on the fuel in the carb float bowl and read pressure. For most cars, it should be between 4 and 7 psi. If pressure is too low, replace the pump.

If pressure was up to spec, check the pump output volume. After disconnecting the fuel line from the carb, hold it in a graduated container. Have an assistant run the engine and record how long it takes the pump to deliver a pint. Don't spill fuel on a running engine as it could easily ignite.

At idle speed, most pumps should produce a pint in about thirty seconds. Most V8 engines require a pint every twenty seconds. Check the spec in your service manual. If the fuel is full of air bubbles and output is below spec, there may be a small hole in the line between the tank and the pump.

If the pump pressure was okay, but output is not what it should be, suspect a restricted fuel line, clogged tank, clogged purge canister or tank vent. To see if the fuel supply has been contaminated, transfer the fuel from your pumping test to a clear glass container and examine it for water, particles, or other signs of contamination.

If the fuel supply is contaminated, the tank should be removed and flushed. For safety reasons, this job is best left to a professional who has a fuel-tank evacuation system. If you feel you must do it yourself, run the car completely out of gas first and take care that no flames or sparks are present in the area where the tank is removed. If done in a garage, make sure any pilot lights are shut off. After the tank has been cleaned, replace the fuel filter and blow out the fuel line and fuel return line.

FUEL-INJECTED ENGINES

As noted above, a fuel starvation stalling problem on a fuel-injected engine may not always seem as obviously load-related as it does on a carbureted engine. In fact it may resemble an intermittent electronic stalling problem as described below. In less extreme cases it may only result in high-speed surging.

On fuel-injected engines, begin your diagnosis by checking pressure. You'll need a fuel-injection pressure gauge. On GM and Ford engines, the gauge must be connected to the pressure-checking port or gauge point provided for this purpose. In most cases the gauge point is a Schrader valve, similar to that used on tires. On some throttle-body fuel injection (TBI) cars (those with one or two injectors mounted in a central carburetor-looking throttle-body unit) you'll find the gauge point right on the throttle body. On most port-injected cars (those with one injector per cylinder), it's on a fuel rail—the unit that delivers fuel to the port injectors (see illustration on page 100). On 2.5-liter GM engines with TBI, the gauge point is between the fuel filter and throttle body. On 1.8- and 2-liter GM fours with TBI, it's under the car near the fuel filter (Fig. 1). Attach the pressure gauge to the gauge point.

Because the electric fuel pump won't run without a distributor reference signal, you have to supply electricity to the pump. To do this on GM cars you apply positive battery voltage to the ALCL terminal G. The ALCL connector is under the dash near the steering column on

101

most GM cars (Fig. 2). Ford recommends that you disconnect the electrical connector to the fuel pump. This connector is located just forward of the fuel tank. Attach a 12-volt jumper to the connector to run the pump for the pressure test. An adapter harness is available for this purpose from Ford. Make sure that there are *no* fuel leaks before attaching any electrical connectors under the vehicle.

Compare your pressure reading to the manufacturer's specification. Many fuel-injection systems are of the high-pressure variety and should produce 35 to 45 psi. GM specifies more than 40 psi for most of its port-injection systems. Low-pressure systems, such as the GM TBI units, should produce at least 9 psi.

Ford recommends that the fuel pressure measurement be augmented by a check of pump capacity. This is accomplished by disconnecting the fuel return line at the fuel rail and replacing it with a hose. The hose is then inserted in a calibrated container of at least one-quart capacity and fuel is allowed to flow for ten seconds. Don't attempt this test without checking specific instructions in your factory service manual. You'll find them in the fuel pump section, group 24 to 35 in most Ford manuals.

To check fuel system pressure on Chrysler products, you must first relieve pressure. To do so, loosen the gas cap and remove the wiring harness connector from any injector. Then ground one injector terminal with a jumper wire and connect another jumper between the second terminal and the battery positive post. After ten seconds, remove both jumper wires. Measure pressure on multipoint systems at the gauge point on the fuel rail. On TBI systems remove the fuel intake hose from the throttle body and attach the pressure gauge between the fuel filter hose and throttle body.

On both Chrysler systems, you can start the engine to take a pressure reading. TBI systems should provide 34 to 38 pounds pressure; multipoint systems should provide 52 to 55 psi. If pressure of any fuel-injection system is not up to spec, replace the in-line filter and recheck. But before doing this or any other parts replacement work on a fuel-injection system, be certain to

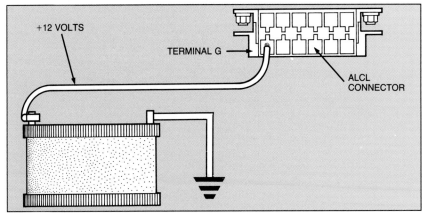

2 Voltage applied to terminal G of ALCL connector will operate fuel pump for testing.

relieve system pressure following the specific directions for your car as outlined in your service manual. On Chryslers you can relieve fuel pressure as described above.

If fuel pressure is not up to spec after replacing the filter, block the fuel return line by squeezing off the flexible hose section. Disconnect the injector on GM TBI units. Then check fuel pressure as before and note reading. If it is not up to spec, either the electric pump, the coupling hose (where applicable), or the pump inlet filter is defective. If pressure is now okay, the problem is the fuel-pressure regulator (the fuel meter cover on GM TBI units) or there is a restriction in the line between the pump and gauge.

ENGINE CHUGGLES, SPUTTERS, AND DIES

This condition is typified by a rough blubbering. It is usually at its worst when the engine is idling or at low speeds and begins to clear up as the throttle is opened fully. The engine may belch black smoke out of the tailpipe, and you will probably smell gasoline. Eventually the engine will die at idle or low throttle. All these symptoms are the result of too much fuel being delivered to the cylinders.

On carbureted engines an overly rich condition is most often the result of a faulty carb float system. Either the float has a leak and sinks to the bottom of the float bowl or the float needle doesn't seal against the needle seat (Fig. 3). To check for a leaking float, remove the carb air

horn—the top part—and shake the float to see if it's full of gas. If so, it must be replaced. If it's not a brass float, it may be saturated with fuel. This is also grounds for replacement.

If the float is okay, examine the float needle and seat. Any visible wear is reason for replacement.

On computer-controlled carbureted and fuel-injected engines, the condition will probably set a trouble code. In addition, the control system will compensate for the condition so the symptoms will not be as severe as on a nonelectronic system and will probably not cause stalling, but will cause poor economy and ragged operation.

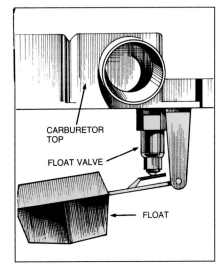

3 Check float for leaks, or better yet, weigh it to be sure it hasn't soaked up fuel.

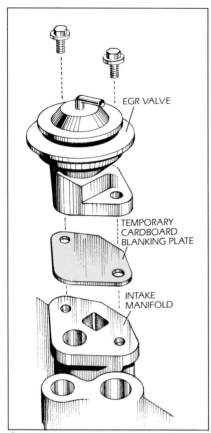

4 Replace EGR valve gasket with cardboard shim temporarily to check valve.

ENGINE RUNS ROUGH, STALLS AT IDLE

This type of exaggerated misfire condition may seem similar to the overly rich engine described above, but it differs in that there will be no black smoke emissions and no smell of gasoline. In addition, the symptoms are more typified by roughness at idle rather than blubbering. Stalling occurs at idle or just as the throttle is opened slightly from the idle position. These symptoms can be caused by anything that makes the engine extremely lean, such as a substantial vacuum leak. But the most common cause of these symptoms is an EGR valve that won't shut off at idle.

To confirm that your EGR valve is allowing exhaust gases to enter the intake manifold at idle, disconnect and plug its vacuum hose while the engine is idling. If this eliminates the misfire and solves the problem, there is a defect in the EGR control system, possibly a mis-

routing of a vacuum hose or a bad vacuum switch.

If disconnecting the vacuum hose doesn't smooth the idle, shut the engine off, remove the EGR valve, cut a piece of cardboard that will fit between the valve and the engine to block off its exhaust port and outlet port, and reinstall the valve with the cardboard in place (Fig. 4). If this cures the problem, remove the valve and the cardboard and replace the valve. (If you merely leave the cardboard in place, you'll have other problems, including spark knock that could ruin your engine.)

ENGINE STALLS WHEN COLD

An engine that dies repeatedly when cold is suffering from an overly lean cold-start fuel mix, a slow idle, or a lack of warmup assistance.

Begin by checking for vacuum hose leaks, then make sure the hot-air tube is connected to the air cleaner of cars that are equipped with a hot-air system. Make sure that the air cleaner is tight and that the air cleaner/carb gasket is in place.

Check hot-air system operation by watching the damper door in the air cleaner as the cold engine is started. It should swing closed and block off outside air. If it doesn't,

apply at least a 7-in. vacuum to the door's vacuum motor and see if the door closes (Fig. 5). If it still won't close, the vacuum motor is bad or the door is stuck. If it closes, trap vacuum by kinking the hose and see if it will remain closed. If it doesn't, the vacuum motor diaphragm is bad and the motor assembly should be replaced. If the motor checks out okay, the temperature sensor that supplies vacuum during warmup is bad.

On most carbureted engines and some fuel-injected ones, warmup driveability is enhanced by an Early Fuel Evaporation (EFE) system. This system is either a mechanical one that delivers heated exhaust to the intake manifold or an electric one that provides heat under the carb by means of an electric grid.

Mechanical systems depend on a valve in the exhaust stream to close and divert exhaust flow to the intake manifold passage. The valve may stick because of corrosion and must be lubricated as part of your maintenance procedure.

In most cases the valve is vacuum actuated. The control vacuum is switched on by a temperature sensor. If you find that the valve won't close, check for vacuum at the supply hose. If it's present and the valve is not frozen in place, replace the vacuum actuator and valve assem-

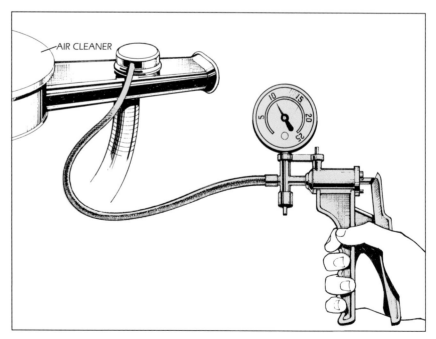

5 Use a handheld vacuum pump to cycle the motor that's built into the air cleaner to operate the thermostatic valve.

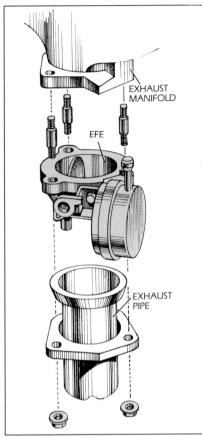

6 Early Fuel Evaporation (EFE) valve routes hot exhaust gases through intake manifold.

bly (Fig. 6). If vacuum is not present, replace the temperature sensor and/or check the vacuum hose for serious leakage or obstruction.

On electric systems, check for voltage between each side of the heater switch and a good engine ground when the engine is cold and the ignition is on. You'll find the

heater switch somewhere in a coolant passage and connected to the electric grid with a wire.

If there is voltage at both sides of the heater switch, check for voltage where the heater grid connects to the harness to make sure the wiring is okay. On systems with a ground wire, check for voltage across the two terminal connectors.

If there is voltage between the connector and a good engine ground but not between both sides of the connector, the ground wire is bad. If voltage is present across the connector, the grid is probably bad (Fig. 7).

RANDOM AND INTERMITTENT STALLING

Usually there are no symptoms other than the very annoying tendency of the engine to suddenly die. This condition is almost always due to an electronic failure, but because it usually cures itself soon after it happens, it is difficult to diagnose. If you're lucky, it will set a failure code in the engine computer system of late-model cars, giving you a head start on tracking it down. For example, if it sets a no distributor reference signal code, the problem might be in the distributor pickup coil or Hall-effect sensor, depending on which your engine has.

In general, the troubleshooting charts for the various codes won't help you locate the specific source of an intermittent because it may not be present while you're performing the diagnostic routines. Sometimes you might have to make an educated guess, replace a part, and hope for the best. The parts counterman at your dealership

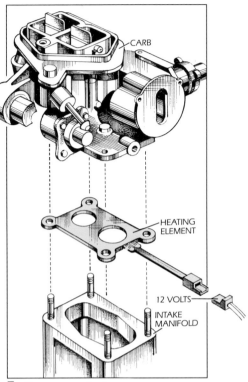

7 Some manufacturers use electrically heated grid to warm fuel in cold engines.

might be able to tell you what the most likely cause of a specific intermittent trouble code is.

Sometimes you may find that intermittent failures occur more often when temperatures are high. In some cases, these are caused by faulty electronic ignition modules. If, for example, the module of a GM HEI distributor was installed without proper application of insulating silicone lubricant, it may fail intermittently.

How to Find VACUUM LEAKS

The vacuum created in an intake manifold when the engine is running isn't really a vacuum—it's pressure that is less than whatever the atmospheric pressure happens to be outside the engine's induction system.

So, if outside atmospheric pressure is 14.7 pounds per square inch but 11.5 inside the manifold when the engine is running, the 11.5 is called vacuum. Consequently, when we talk about a vacuum leak, what we really mean is atmospheric air leaking into a lower pressure area. Auto manufacturers put "check for vacuum loss" at the top of troubleshooting charts.

"I estimate that vacuum leaks and damaged vacuum components account for at least 60 percent of the engine driveability problems we're seeing," Dick Emrich says. He's a resident instructor at the General Motors Training Center in Moorestown, New Jersey. "That's why we emphasize the importance of vacuum to our students and teach them several methods they can use to track down disruptions. Leaks are sometimes very elusive."

The check is threefold: (1) to be sure that air isn't leaking into the intake tract, (2) to see that components that need vacuum to function are really tapping into manifold vacuum, and (3) to be sure no component that is getting the vacuum supply it needs is damaged or malfunctioning.

Depending upon which components are affected, the problems a disruption in vacuum causes are stalling, hard starting, hesitation (also known as sag and stumble when accelerating), too fast an idle, rough idling, surging, lack of power, missing, backfire, poor fuel economy, dieseling (engine run-on when the ignition is turned off), pinging (detonation, preignition, and spark knock), failure to pass a state emissions test, and a hydrogen sulfide (rotten egg) odor from the exhaust.

Components that need vacuum to operate are found all over the

Although technically not a vacuum leak, even a minor air leak between the mass airflow sensor and the throttle plates can make your engine run really rough.

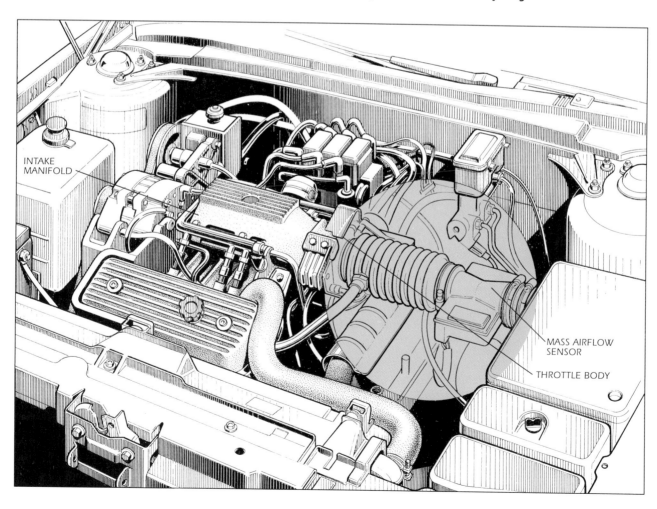

INTAKE MANIFOLD

MASS AIRFLOW SENSOR

THROTTLE BODY

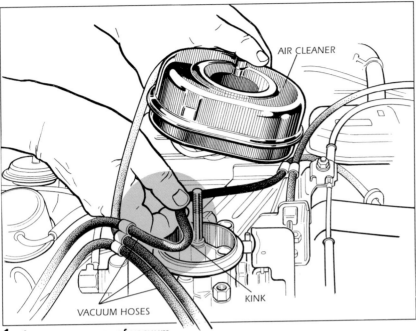

1 A common source of vacuum-related driveability problems is pinched vacuum lines.

modern vehicle, meaning cars and light trucks built since 1970. The greatest number of these components, however, are found in 1975 to 1984 models.

Since about 1985, electronics has assumed the role of supplying power to some components that once used vacuum, but vacuum is still necessary for plenty of parts on 1985–88 cars and light trucks.

Depending on the engine, these are the exhaust gas recirculation valve, positive crankcase ventilation valve, fuel pressure regulator, distributor vacuum advance, air cleaner vacuum motor, deceleration valve, choke vacuum break, throttle modulator, manifold absolute pressure sensor, charcoal canister purge valve, air by-pass valve, antibackfire valve, dashpot throttle stop, distributor modulator valve assembly, exhaust heat control valve, and a variety of vacuum switches, valves, and regulators.

Nonengine parts also use vacuum created by the engine. These include the brake booster, automatic transmission, cruise control, and climate control system.

Vacuum created inside the engine by the action of the pistons gets to parts through hoses connected to fittings (vacuum taps) on the carburetor (or EFI throttle body) and/or intake manifold. These hoses are the weakest links in the system, so it's with them that you begin to troubleshoot.

SOUNDS AND SIGHTS

Don't get scared off by what seems to be a jumble of spaghetti in there. Although vacuum hoses seem to be everywhere, one that's leaking is not always that hard to pick out.

A leaking hose sometimes announces its existence with a hiss or whistle. To make it easier to pinpoint which hose among the many you see is creating a vacuum loss, use a 4-ft. length of $5/16$-in. vacuum hose as a stethoscope. With the engine idling, hold one end of it to your ear and move the other end slowly over each vacuum hose, in turn. Be sure to scan around each component and vacuum tap to which the hose connects. The leak might be there.

If a vacuum hose is leaking where it connects to a tap on the engine or to a fitting of the component, see if it's just loose, and push it on the rest of the way. If not, the defective hose or component should be replaced.

Keep in mind that a hose doesn't have to be leaking for it to be the cause of vacuum loss that affects the operation of a vehicle. It could be blocked. This possibility is more likely when an engine performance problem develops immediately after you've done some work on the engine. You may have kinked or closed off a hose by accidentally shoving a part, such as the air cleaner, down on it (Fig. 1).

The chance of a hose getting clogged with debris is remote, but to make sure it hasn't happened, remove the hose and blow through it.

SQUEEZING IT OFF

If a vacuum leak is severe enough to cause a misfire or rough idle, *and* it's not caused by a bad connection to the source of the vacuum (like the manifold or carb), you can sometimes localize it with a pair of pliers. Actually, anything that will squeeze the hose shut without permanently damaging it will do.

This method works best with non-computer-controlled vehicles, as the computer will try to compensate for the lost vacuum, and the idle may very well not be affected. But if the leak is severe enough, even the computer won't be able to compensate.

Use the pliers to squeeze the hoses close to the manifold or vacuum supply. If the idle quality picks up, the leak or malfunctioning component is outboard of the clamp. You can then move the clamp along the hose, away from the manifold, following any branches in the line. Or it's possible that the component, say a cruise control or choke pull-off, is defective and leaking. If so, then you'll be able to pinch the hose right next to the suspect component and still see a change in idle.

CHART CHAT

Use the vacuum hose routing chart mounted in the engine compartment (Fig. 2) to identify vacuum hoses and vacuum components. If it's missing or obliterated, you'll have to trace each hose back from its fitting on the engine to find branch hoses and vacuum components that intersect with it. This means first removing the air cleaner to locate the vacuum taps on the carburetor or throttle body and intake manifold (Fig. 3).

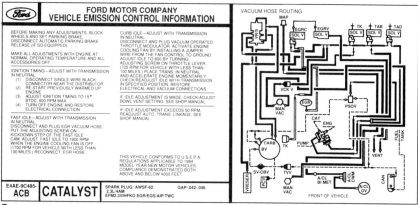

2 This engine compartment sticker
will show you how that underhood spaghetti connects.

OTHER LEAK POINTS

Not all vacuum leaks originate at the hoses. One common point is the carb or throttle body attach bolts. Intake manifolds can become loose where they meet the head. This type of leak can sometimes be found by spraying carb cleaner (*not* brake cleaner) on the suspect area. If the idle smooths out or picks up, the carb cleaner is being sucked in and burned. The vacuum leak has made the mixture too lean, so the extra fuel you spray in makes it richer momentarily, and you've found the leak. Be careful, since carb cleaner is highly flammable (which, of course, is why it works).

Unfortunately, this method is less effective on computer-controlled systems, as the computer sees the lean mix and compensates automatically.

Fortunately, tightening the offending bolts near the leak often seals it up. If not, you may have to replace the gasket involved.

USING A VACUUM GAUGE

There's no substitute for a vacuum gauge if you're troubleshooting a rough-running engine. If you're in the market for one, consider a handheld vacuum pump that incorporates a gauge. As a gauge, it can help you determine if engine vacuum is to specification and also if there is a non-vacuum-related defect. As a detection instrument, it can help you to find a leaking vacuum hose and damaged vacuum components (Fig. 4). Let's see how each is done.

Vacuum gauges are calibrated in terms of inches of mercury (in./Hg) instead of atmospheric pressure, to make them easier to read. They are

set to give a reading of zero when the engine is off, instead of whatever the atmospheric pressure happens to be where the test is being made.

You need to know the exact vacuum specification for your engine. The range of 17–21 in./Hg, which is recommended by many general automotive repair manuals, is no longer applicable to most modern engines. Using it can lead to false test conclusions.

For example, the Buick 3.8-liter V6 engine with plenty of valve overlap has a normal vacuum of 15 in./Hg. Overlap means that during a combustion cycle the exhaust and intake valves in a cylinder are open simultaneously for a brief period. At high engine speeds this actually increases power, but at idle speeds it reduces vacuum somewhat. If you refer to that 17–21 in./Hg range on this engine, you may go in search of a vacuum leak that doesn't exist.

In checking vacuum with a vacuum gauge, keep in mind that specifications in service manuals are sea-level readings. That reading will drop by 1 in./Hg for every 1,000 ft. you are above sea level. For example, a reading of 20 in./Hg in New York City (sea level) would be a reading of 15 in./Hg in Denver (5,000 ft. above sea level) for the same engine. So, if you're in Denver and take the service manual reading as gospel, you could go wrong.

To see if the vacuum developed by the engine is up to spec, you have a few choices. You can disconnect a vacuum hose from a vacuum tap

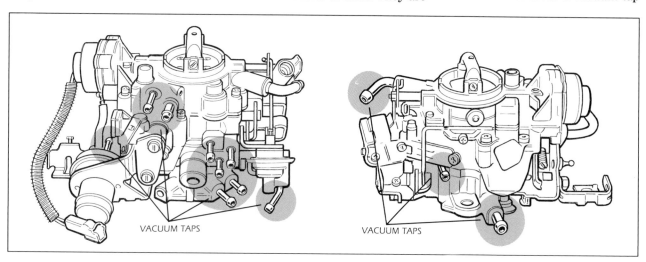

3 As if twelve vacuum taps weren't enough to have to deal with, some of these have several tees branching from them.

on the carburetor, TBI, or intake manifold and connect the gauge to the fitting. Or you can disconnect the vacuum hose from the brake booster, remove the check valve, and connect the gauge to the end of the hose—you will probably have to use an adapter to do this. Or you can disconnect a vacuum hose from an engine vacuum component and connect the gauge to the end of the hose—again, you'll probably have to use an adapter.

If there's any leak between the gauge and the source of vacuum, a true reading won't be obtained.

There's another important point here: Make sure the source of the vacuum into which you tap the gauge is manifold vacuum—not ported vacuum. Manifold vacuum is true engine vacuum. Ported vacuum is less than manifold (true) vacuum and will, therefore, lead to an erroneous test reading. A manifold vacuum tap is positioned below the carburetor or TBI throttle plate. A ported vacuum source lies above the throttle plate.

And there's still another precaution. If you decide to attach your gauge to a vacuum hose, see that the hose doesn't use a vacuum restrictor or vacuum delay upstream of where the gauge is connected (Fig. 5). This will affect the reading.

Start the engine and allow it to warm up. With the engine running at idle speed, the vacuum gauge should show a normal reading that holds steady. The gauge needle should neither waver nor drift.

Then, open and close the throttle rapidly. The gauge needle should drop below 5 in./Hg, bounce up to 2 or 3 in./Hg above normal, and then settle at normal.

Suppose the needle holds steady at idling speed, but stays in the 4- to 7-in./Hg range. There's a loss of vacuum from the engine itself. Most often this loss is caused by loose carburetor or TBI mounting bolts, or a bad gasket between the carburetor or throttle body and intake manifold. Hopefully, that is. Otherwise, piston rings may be worn or there may be a loss of vacuum around the valves. Do a cylinder leakdown test to check out non-vacuum-related defects.

Suppose the vacuum gauge needle doesn't show a normal reading, but neither does it show a loss of

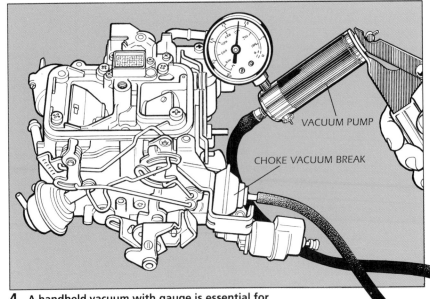

4 A handheld vacuum with gauge is essential for diagnosing problems.

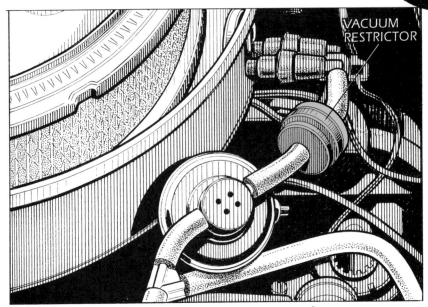

5 Be sure your gauge taps into a vacuum line upstream of any vacuum restrictors. Otherwise, the gauge readings will be misleading.

vacuum. This is what you may be up against:

- *A steady reading at idling speed of 8 to 14 in./Hg:* Ignition timing isn't set properly or there's a compression leak past the piston rings. A vacuum gauge needle that wavers slowly by 2 to 6 in./Hg from normal also suggests a compression leak.

- *A sharp back-and-forth fluctuation at idling speed of about 5 in./Hg from normal:* Suspect a leaking head gasket or worn valve guides.
- *A slow drifting at idling speed of about 5 in./Hg from normal:* The carburetor is not adjusted correctly.
- *A steady reading at idling speed above normal:* There's a restriction in the air-intake

system. Look for a clogged air filter or sticky choke.

- *A reading that drops to near zero when the throttle is opened and closed rapidly and rises but doesn't hit normal:* Look for a restriction in the exhaust system.

Along with cracked hoses and a bad carburetor (or TBI) gasket another cause of engine problems because of vacuum disruption is a split vacuum-component diaphragm. In other words, the component won't work although it's getting vacuum. To compound the problem, air is leaking into the intake, making the mixture lean.

It takes patience to find out if there is a bad part. You may have to test all of them until you finally hit the one you're looking for. Discon-

nect the hose from the vacuum fitting of each component, attach the hand-vacuum pump to the fitting, and apply vacuum. If the gauge needle doesn't rise or rises and falls, the part is defective.

ABOUT MPFI

Just because your engine has a multipoint fuel injection (MPFI) system, don't think you're off the hook. It too has engine vacuum taps that feed vacuum components. But as critical—and even more devious—is any leak at a point downstream of the mass airflow sensor. It will present you with an engine performance problem that will make you want to pull your hair out. If more air is sucked into an MPFI engine than the mass airflow sensor is sup-

posed to let in, it will cause performance trouble in spades.

Okay, technically it can't be called a *vacuum* loss—the pressure in this area is usually not much less than atmospheric, and certainly isn't as low as inside the manifold. But it is downstream of the airflow sensor, so it's unaccounted for by computer.

Finding leaks here can be tougher, because there's usually no noise associated with them. You'll simply have to look for loose hose clamps, cracks hiding in the accordion pleats of the connecting piping, or cracks in plastic tubes. The carb cleaner trick sometimes works, but in order to keep from singeing off your eyebrows, be sure not to spray too near the distributor or the wiring.

How To Diagnose
ENGINE COMPRESSION LEAKS

H ave you ever been forced to live with a powerplant that just wouldn't idle smoothly, even after a tuneup and carburetor adjustment? Or how about that older, high-mileage engine that still runs reasonably well, but lacks the punch it once had and drinks fuel as though it had a hole in the gas tank?

In both cases the culprit very well may be poor sealing of cylinder pressure within the powerplant. A pressure leak is most likely to occur at the rings, the valves, or the head gasket. But pressure can leak through cracks in cylinders or cylinder heads as well. And, of course, severely damaged pistons or worn piston ring grooves (lands) will serve as escape routes for precious cylinder pressure.

Correct cylinder pressure is essential to satisfactory vehicle operation. If an engine is unable to compress the air-fuel mixture as much as it should, the affected cylinder will not operate at maximum efficiency and the engine will lose power. And since a wider throttle opening will be required to propel the car at a given rate, more fuel will be consumed.

If only one or two cylinders have a defective compression seal, the engine will lope or miss while idling. If cylinder pressure is leaking through an intake valve, backfire may result at some speeds.

CHECK THE
IGNITION SYSTEM

A check of ignition system components should always precede any attempts to diagnose an internal engine problem. This should include at least spark-plug cleaning,

Your engine's compression can leak past the valves, around spark plug threads, past the piston rings, through cylinder-wall or combustion-chamber cracks, or around the head gasket.

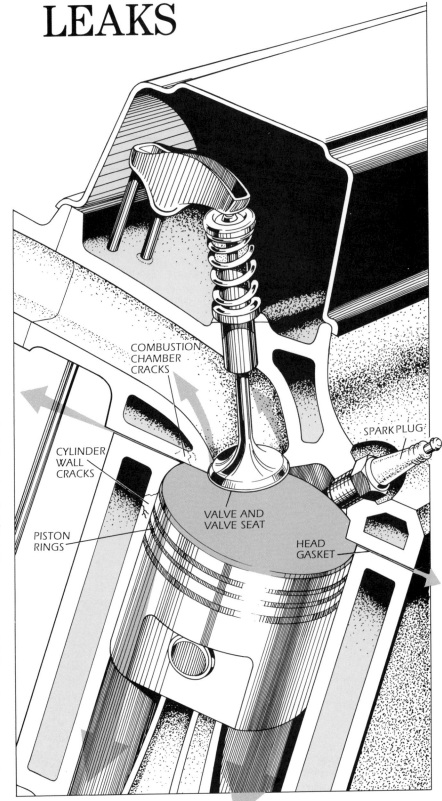

COMBUSTION CHAMBER CRACKS

SPARK PLUG

CYLINDER WALL CRACKS

VALVE AND VALVE SEAT

PISTON RINGS

HEAD GASKET

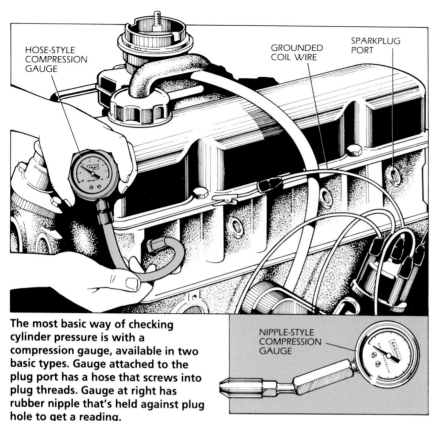

HOSE-STYLE COMPRESSION GAUGE

GROUNDED COIL WIRE

SPARKPLUG PORT

NIPPLE-STYLE COMPRESSION GAUGE

The most basic way of checking cylinder pressure is with a compression gauge, available in two basic types. Gauge attached to the plug port has a hose that screws into plug threads. Gauge at right has rubber nipple that's held against plug hole to get a reading.

inspection, and regapping, and a check of all secondary components, including cap, wires, and rotor.

Spark plug condition can sometimes provide clues regarding internal engine condition.

Oily wet plugs with large deposits of carbon sometimes indicate defective piston rings, but the same condition can result from a number of other problems that are not related to ring sealing. Plugs that are slightly darker than others may indicate a poor compression seal, but again the same condition can be the result of various other problems.

If the internal problem is simply one of oil control, replacing or cleaning the plugs will probably make the engine perform better for a while, but if the same plug fouls again within a couple of thousand miles, you can assume that a serious oiling problem exists.

Oil consumption problems are by no means always related to compression sealing problems, but a check of the compression seal should be performed when an oil consumption problem is noted.

Some mechanics check fuel system components before checking compression seal when a misfire or power loss problem arises. However, carburetor diagnosis is usually more difficult than internal engine diagnosis—unless you're equipped with an emissions analyzer—so the typical Saturday mechanic will usually try to rule out compression seal problems as a cause of misfire or poor power before turning to the carburetor.

CHECKING CYLINDER PRESSURE

The most basic method of checking for a compression leak is by measuring cranking cylinder pressure with a compression gauge.

Compression gauges are generally available in two basic types: One is fitted with a rubber nipple that is held against the plug hole to obtain a reading, while the other has a hose attachment that is screwed into the plug hole. The second type is easier to use, but with some care either can be used satisfactorily on most engines. On engines where access to the plug holes is limited, the hose type must be used.

Before beginning a compression test, remove all of the spark plugs. If you don't have a remote starter switch that you can wire between the battery and starter relay or solenoid, you'll have to have a helper crank the engine from inside the car.

You have to make sure that your battery remains fully charged for the complete test, because compression readings will drop if the engine cranks noticeably slower. The best solution in this case is to perform the test while the battery is connected to a charger.

Open the throttle valves and choke valve completely. You should provide some means of holding them open. The throttle can sometimes be held open by placing an appropriately sized object between the idle screw and fast idle cam. With the throttle all the way open, the choke unloader should push the choke partway open. You may need a piece of wire to hold it all the way open.

Disconnect the negative wire from the coil and cover the terminal end of it with insulating electrical tape. On GM HEI ignitions disconnect the BAT terminal from the distributor. Turn the key to the ON position, even if you're using a remote starter switch.

One caveat: Many late-model electronic ignition systems won't take kindly to disconnecting the high-tension side of the coil. You'll need to disable the ignition system some other way to prevent damage to the electronic ignition amplifier. Generally, you can unplug the connector to the ignition amplifier or the distributor—but you'll need to check the service manual for your specific model and year of vehicle to be sure. Don't say we didn't warn you.

With the compression gauge in place on the first cylinder to be tested, crank the engine five times or until you get a maximum reading. Write down the gauge reading. Move on to the next cylinder and take a reading, cranking the engine the same number of times you did for the previous reading. Continue until all cylinders have been tested.

INTERPRETING GAUGE READINGS

All of your readings should be within 75 percent of your strongest cylinder. Furthermore, the pressure reading of each cylinder should equal the minimum suggested by the vehicle manufacturer. Minimum pressures are found in the spec tables of most general auto repair manuals.

With a small four-cylinder engine, however, you may want all of your cylinders to fall within 85 or 90 percent of each other. On a large V8, strong cylinders can compensate easily for their weaker brothers, but a small engine may suffer a considerable loss of performance and smoothness with a compression loss of 25 percent in one cylinder. It's all a matter of how fussy *you* are about the way your car runs, weighed against the cost of repairing the compression leak.

LOCATING LEAKS

The compression test won't tell you where the engine is leaking compression, just that a leak exists.

Mechanics used to squirt oil in the cylinders in an attempt to distinguish valve leaks from piston ring leaks, but this method will only reveal grossly leaking valves, because the oil volume raises the cylinder pressure and may therefore mask a slight valve leak. On the other hand, the oil may fail to seal seriously worn or damaged rings, causing you to conclude erroneously that the valves are the source of the problem. It can also mask a leaking head gasket.

The best method of pinpointing compression leaks is an air test, which can be performed with either a cylinder leakage tester or homemade air test device. The idea here is to pressurize each cylinder with compressed air and then look for the spot where it leaks out.

PERFORMING AN AIR TEST

A homemade air tester can be fashioned from an air hose, a regulator, and a spark-plug hole/air hose adapter. This last item is threaded to fit the plug hole on one end and has an air hose connector on the other end. You should be able to purchase one at your local auto parts store. If your air compressor develops less than 90 psi, you won't need the regulator.

A commercial cylinder leakage tester will provide more than just an indication of where the leak is located. It will also tell you what percent of the compressed air charge is leaking out of the cylinder. This can help you determine how serious the leak is.

The cylinder leakage tester offers another advantage. If your engine has a bad compression ring seal and an internal oiling problem (the two don't necessarily go together), a cranking compression test may fail to reveal a poor compression seal because of the presence of oil in the cylinder.

In this case, the cylinder leakage tester can help you diagnose a compression leak, because it is not as easily fooled by the presence of oil in the cylinder as the compression gauge. However, the homemade air tester cannot measure the seriousness of a compression leak. All it can do is locate it.

DETERMINING TDC

The air leak or cylinder leakage test must be performed while the cylinder being tested is at Top Dead Center on its compression stroke. There are several ways to determine TDC.

The crankshaft pulley or flywheel of your engine is marked for No. 1-cylinder TDC. If the No. 1 cylinder is on compression stroke, the distributor's rotor should be pointing to the No. 1 plug wire. (Check a manual if you don't know how the cylinders of your V8 engine are numbered. Nearly all four- and six-cylinders are numbered front to rear.)

If you have good access to the crank pulley, you can mark it for Top Dead Center of the other cylinders. TDC of an eight-cylinder occurs every 90°. TDC of a four-cylinder occurs every 180°.

If you have a six-cylinder engine, TDC occurs every 120°. A flexible tape measure can be used to measure the circumference of the pulley. The circumference is then divided by half the number of cylinders, and the pulley is marked in increments of a length equal to the quotient.

For example, on a six-cylinder's pulley, measuring 18 in. in circumference, the TDC marks would occur every six inches. One mark is already there. You would make two additional marks.

Assuming that the firing order is 153624, the mark that you make 120° counterclockwise will be TDC,

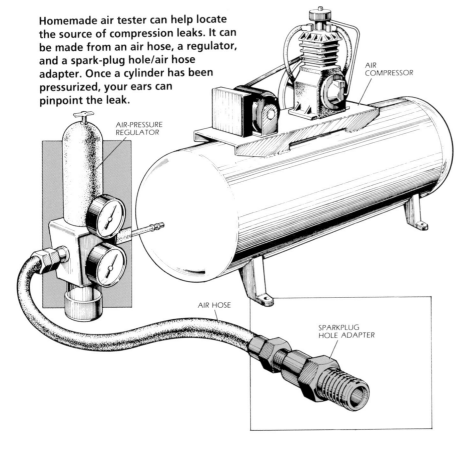

Homemade air tester can help locate the source of compression leaks. It can be made from an air hose, a regulator, and a spark-plug hole/air hose adapter. Once a cylinder has been pressurized, your ears can pinpoint the leak.

AIR-PRESSURE REGULATOR

AIR COMPRESSOR

AIR HOSE

SPARKPLUG HOLE ADAPTER

cylinder 5. The second mark that occurs as you continue to rotate the engine clockwise will be TDC, cylinder 3. On the engine's next clockwise rotation, the original TDC mark will be for cylinder 6. The second mark will be TDC/2, the last mark TDC/4.

Another method is to use some type of device to signal you as each cylinder rises to the top.

Some mechanics use a whistle that has been inserted into the end of a hose that is attached to one of those previously mentioned plug-hole/air hose adapters. When the contraption is screwed into the plug hole and the engine is turned, the whistle will shriek loudly on the compression stroke, but will stop abruptly as TDC is reached.

On some engines, you can easily see the top of the piston come up in the bore on compression and exhaust. You can tell which stroke (compression or exhaust) the engine is on by removing the distributor cap. If it's on compression stroke, the rotor should be pointing to the spark plug wire for the cylinder in question.

Once you're sure that the engine is on TDC for the cylinder to be tested, screw the adapter into the plug hole, adjust the air pressure regulator to 70 or 80 pounds, and attach your air hose to the adapter. If you're using a cylinder leakage tester, set the leakage meter at zero before connecting the test hose to the spark-plug adapter. If the engine is not exactly at TDC, the air pressure may force the piston down in the bore. If that happens, you may have to use a wrench to hold the engine in place while you perform the test.

LISTENING FOR LEAKAGE

With the air supply connected to the cylinder, listen for compression leakage through the exhaust pipe, crankcase oil filler hole, carburetor opening (with the PVC hose disconnected), adjacent spark plug holes, and the edges of the cylinder head sealing areas.

A leak through either of those last two locations suggests a bad head gasket. If air seems to be rushing out the carburetor, you have a bad intake valve.

Leaking exhaust valves will produce a hissing noise in the exhaust

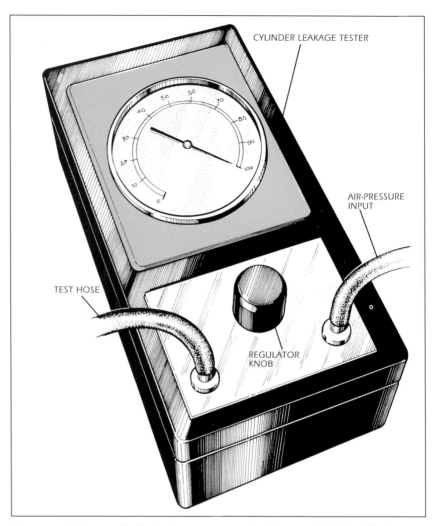

A commercial-type cylinder leakage tester can help locate a leak. It will also show what percentage of the compressed air is leaking past the rings.

pipe. If you detect air hissing out through the oil filler hole, the rings are worn.

After listening for air leakage at all locations mentioned above, remove the radiator cap and look for bubbles in the coolant. Their presence would indicate a leaking head gasket or cracked cylinder head.

Remember that you're looking for the point of *excessive* leakage. There will always be some leakage past the rings. If jiggling the engine with a wrench on the front pulley increases the size of the leak significantly, the ring lands may be worn.

Exhaust valve leakage can be caused by dirt on the seat.

Some mechanics like to tap firmly on the top of the exhaust valve stem with a brass hammer while checking cylinder leakage. This will release a burst of air past the valve which can

help dislodge any particles that may be creating a leak. It can also temporarily seat a valve that may not seat well under operating conditions, because of a worn valve guide. So this practice can be somewhat deceiving. If you do stop an exhaust valve leak in this manner, crank the engine two complete revolutions and see if the leak recurs. If it does, the problem is probably the result of a worn guide.

USING A COMMERCIAL TESTER

If you're using the commercial cylinder leakage tester for the air leak test, you'll get a percentage reading of cylinder leakage.

The leading manufacturer of this type of equipment specifies 20 percent or more as a failure level. Race car engine builders usually look for less than 5 percent cylinder leakage. Again, it's all a matter of how fussy you are. Most high-quality production engines that we have tested leak less than 10 percent.

When testing a cylinder that showed evidence of oil fouling on the spark plug, allow the air hose to remain connected to the cylinder for at least five minutes. This will blow excess oil past the rings, if the ring seal is poor, allowing a more accurate reading.

After the No. 1 cylinder has been leak-tested, continue checking other cylinders that failed the cranking compression test.

You may want to test all cylinders if you have a commercial leakage tester. You should obviously leak-test any cylinders that showed evidence of oil fouling. If you marked your crankshaft pulley for TDC locations, the second cylinder in the engine's firing order should be tested after No. 1. Simply rotate the engine to the next mark.

As explained previously, it will take two full revolutions to bring all cylinders to TDC. If you're using the whistle or eyeball method to determine TDC, you can simply move on to the next cylinder on the bank.

PLUGGING THE HOLE

Once you have determined the source and the seriousness of a compression leak, you have a repair decision to make. Some leaks may not be worth repairing.

For example, a leaking compression ring that falls right at the 25 percent failure figure on the cranking test and produces perhaps 30 percent leakage with the commercial cylinder leakage tester may not be worth repairing, particularly on an older vehicle. On the other hand, a leaking exhaust valve that produces the same loss of pressure may be worth repairing due to the fact that the job is much less costly and time-consuming, particularly if you can replace your own cylinder head.

If you find that your engine needs new piston rings, a complete engine rebuild is called for. The powerplants of fifteen or twenty years ago were frequently reringed right in the car. The mechanic simply pulled the heads, dropped the pan, and knocked the pistons out. He would then hone the cylinder walls while standing on a fender, install new rings on the pistons and new bearing inserts on the rods and drop them in.

If your mechanic tries to tell you that he can repair your late-model, small-displacement engine in such a manner, find a new mechanic. Today's engines are built to much closer tolerances, and, consequently, repairs involve considerably more precise measurements and expert machine work.

Don't take a chance on haphazard repairs. If your engine failed in original equipment form, you certainly don't want it rebuilt to specs that are even looser than the original equipment specs.

How to Service Your COOLING SYSTEM

Servicing your cooling system is a straightforward, low-tech job. Proper timely flushing and filling of your radiator with the correct antifreeze coolant will keep your engine running cool and prevent corrosion in your cooling system.

July. You've driven almost halfway to your first vacation in years. But as you reach the mountains, you notice that when the car begins to climb, so does the temperature gauge. Before long, the gauge is pegged and steam billows from under the hood as you pull over to the side of the road. And as the sun sinks slowly into the west, so does your vacation.

Chalk up this failed cooling system to wear. But the problem is not a worn-out hose or water pump. It's worn-out antifreeze.

Ethylene glycol, which makes up over 95 percent of the antifreeze, doesn't wear out, but the additive package does. Or more accurately, the additives become exhausted.

One of the additives to get used up is silicone silicate. It protects soft aluminum engine parts—cylinder heads, for example—from the ravages of hot and rapidly circulating coolant. As the engine heats up, silicone silicate bonds to aluminum parts to form an extremely hard protective barrier. Without it, the soft aluminum dissolves into the heated

coolant, travels to the insides of the radiator, and then sticks to the radiator tubes. Eventually, the tubes plug up and the engine overheats.

The bonding of silicone silicate to aluminum components is not a one-time event. Every time the engine heats up and cools down, some of the silicone silicate loses its bond and falls off the aluminum. Antifreeze makers add extra silicone silicate, and it rebonds to the area immediately. But eventually, the extra silicone silicate gets used up—and the antifreeze is worn out. It's

115

not how many miles you drive, it's how many times you start your engine, warm it up, and then cool it down that determines how long antifreeze lasts.

Antifreeze manufacturers recommend flushing and refilling the cooling system with a fresh mixture of antifreeze and water every two years—more often for cars that make frequent short trips.

Other additives that protect against rust and neutralize acids also lose their effectiveness over time.

LEFTHAND THREADS

RADIATOR

DRAIN PETCOCK

Don't be fooled—the drain cock on your radiator has lefthand threads, and may require more leverage than your fingers to open.

FLUSHING

Some people mistakenly believe that removing the lower radiator hose and letting as much used coolant as possible drain from the engine and radiator is sufficient before installing new coolant. But that can leave as much as half of the old coolant in the engine, hoses, and heater. Some engine blocks have plugs that allow coolant to be drained, but they are often difficult to get to. Even if you find them, they're usually frozen in place.

Removing and replacing half the coolant is better than ignoring the system completely. Unfortunately, installing half of the new antifreeze means you're installing only half of the new additives—which means your cooling system could wind up short of the additives it needs.

The only way to remove *all* of the old coolant, as well as rust, acids, and other contaminants, is through backflushing. In this procedure, fresh water is forced through the system in the direction opposite to normal coolant flow. This flushes the old coolant and much of the contaminants backward through the system and out the radiator cap. When the water coming from the radiator cap opening runs clear, the cooling system is then clean.

The easiest way to backflush a cooling system is to permanently install a flushing tee in the heater inlet hose. The tee allows you to attach a garden hose to the heater hose to flush clean water through the engine and radiator. A threaded cap fits over the tee to seal it between flushes. Flushing tee kits are available at most auto parts stores.

Before you start flushing, there are a few words of caution: Never open a warm, pressurized cooling

system, or you risk the chance of burning yourself severely. Also, most front-wheel-drive and many rear-wheel-drive vehicles have electric radiator fans that can turn on unexpectedly—even if the radiator is not warm. To be safe, avoid the fan or disconnect it before you start.

To flush the system using a tee, open the radiator petcock and drain the radiator completely. If the radiator doesn't have a petcock, remove the lower hose at the radiator. Draining the radiator lowers the level in the cooling system sufficiently so you can install the tee without spilling coolant all over the engine.

To install the tee, find the heater inlet hose. It travels from the firewall to the engine block. The outlet hose connects to the water pump.

Use a sharp knife to sever the inlet hose in an accessible area, then fit the tee into each end of the hose and secure it with the hose clamps provided with the tee kit.

Next, close the radiator petcock (or reinstall the lower hose), and refill the radiator with fresh water. Then connect the garden hose to the tee.

Before you turn on the hose, install the coolant deflector (supplied with the kit) into the radiator cap opening, start the engine, turn the heater on high, and then turn on the garden hose. The old coolant will immediately begin to gush from the radiator. After the coolant is out and the water runs clear for about two minutes, shut off the engine, then turn off and disconnect the garden hose.

Most cars today have a coolant recovery tank mounted to the fender well. When backflushing, you should also remove the tank and drain the old coolant.

When you flush your cooling system, keep in mind that antifreeze is highly toxic. It also tastes quite sweet, and pets or small children may try to drink it. For that reason, never leave coolant in drain pans or puddles.

Antifreeze makers recommend discarding coolant in contained sewage systems, such as septic systems or sanitary sewers. Check with your local municipality sewage plant or the local EPA office for their recommendations.

The ethylene glycol, as we mentioned earlier, is not worn out and could easily be recycled by redistilling it to remove contaminants. Unfortunately, we don't know of anyone who does so on a commercial level. But the time will come when antifreeze is recycled as a matter of course, along with engine oil and batteries.

CLEANING DIRTY SYSTEMS

If the cooling system in your car hasn't been properly maintained over the years, simple backflushing will not be enough to clean the system. If the old coolant is severely discolored and the radiator tubes and cap opening show evidence of rust and other deposits, consider cleaning.

There are three types of cooling system cleaners on the market. The

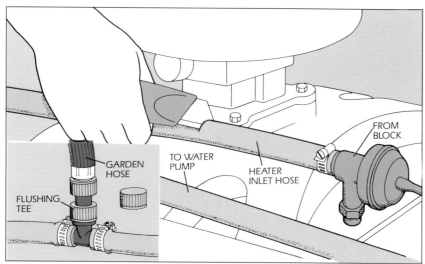

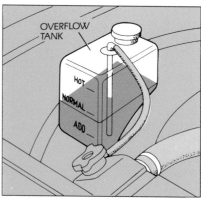

Check the coolant overflow reservoir at least weekly for the proper fluid level.

Splice the flushing tee into the heater inlet hose at a point just before it enters the engine block.

so-called heavy-duty two-part cleaners, which consist of a powdered acid-based cleaner, followed by a neutralizer, should *not* be used in an engine containing aluminum components because the harsh alkalies in the neutralizer are too hard on the aluminum. It's especially critical that acid-based cleaners be avoided if your car has an aluminum radiator, since these cleaners can eat through the thin aluminum tubing in a very short time. Ten-minute fast flushes won't hurt aluminum components, and they do a good job of cleaning mild rust and greasy contaminants as well as some of the coarser deposits, but they won't be able to thoroughly clean a severely contaminated system.

Both the acid-based cleaner and the ten-minute fast flush should be installed before you backflush the system.

Chelator-based cooling system cleaners, such as Prestone Super Radiator Cleaner and Peak Performance Radiator Cleaner, do the best job of cleaning modern cooling systems, especially those with aluminum components. Though they cost slightly more than other cleaners, their effectiveness is worth the added expense. Their only other drawback is that ethylene glycol neutralizes the cleaner's effectiveness, so it must be added to a system that has already been flushed completely with water to assure that all the ethylene glycol has been removed from the system.

In addition to cleaning rust and scale, chelator-based cleaners also do a good job of cleaning solder corrosion, commonly known as solder bloom. These hard, white deposits that look a little like flower buds can plug up the radiator tubes if allowed to grow unchecked.

After you've flushed the system, and nothing but clean water is inside, add a quart of chelator cleaner. (Add two quarts for systems with twelve or more quarts capacity.)

Because chelator cleaners take time to work, you'll have to drive the car for three to six hours before the system is clean. However, you don't have to do all that driving at once. When the cleaner has finished doing its job, flush the system a second time to remove the cleaner.

With all cleaners, it's important to remember that coolant flow through the radiator only occurs when the engine needs to rid itself of excess heat. During cold weather, even if the temperature gauge says the engine is at normal operating temperature, most or all of the coolant may be recirculating in the engine block—effectively bypassing the radiator. Even the best cleaners won't clean the radiator unless hot coolant is flowing through it. For this reason, it's best to use cleaners during warm weather. Check the radiator for coolant flow by squeezing the upper radiator hose. When it's hot and pressurized, the coolant is flowing through the radiator.

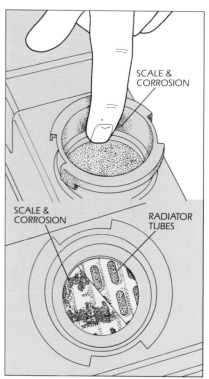

Check the radiator filler neck and the radiator tubes regularly for signs of corrosion.

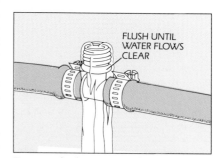

Turn on the heater, and flush the system until clear water flows from the tee.

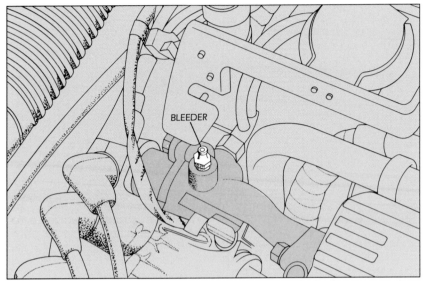

Many vehicles require air bleeding from a fitting on the head. Check your manual.

REFILLING THE SYSTEM

Coolant is a mixture of antifreeze and water. The more antifreeze you add, the more freezeup and boilover protection you get. So, why not forget the water and fill with pure antifreeze? There are several reasons. First, freezeup and boilover protection begins to reverse itself if you add much more than 70 percent antifreeze. Pure antifreeze will actually turn to frozen slush at a higher temperature than a 50/50 mix of antifreeze and water. And many of the additives in antifreeze won't be-

come active until water has been added. That means you won't get proper corrosion protection unless the system contains water.

Also, pure antifreeze doesn't conduct heat as well as water, which means that pure antifreeze can't transfer engine heat to the radiator as readily, and overheating results.

For most cars, adding a 50/50 mix of antifreeze and water offers sufficient protection from freezeups and boilover. A 70/30 mix is the maximum recommended concentration of antifreeze in any cooling system.

Typically, a 50/50 mix of good

quality antifreeze and water protects against freezing down to −34°F. And the boiling point is raised to 265°F if the car has a radiator cap that holds 15 pounds of pressure. With a 70/30 mixture, freezeup won't occur until the thermometer drops to a bone-chilling −84°F, and boil over is forestalled to 276°F (see Cooling Capacity Chart below).

To determine how much antifreeze you should add for the freezeup and boilover protection you wish to achieve, consult your vehicle owner's manual for the cooling system's total capacity. For a ten-quart system, you would add five quarts of antifreeze to achieve a 50/50 mix. Or add seven quarts for a 70/30 mix.

Quality pays. You should also make sure to buy a good quality antifreeze. Often, heavily discounted brands are already diluted with as much as 50 percent water. Read the label.

The rule here is that if the antifreeze costs half the price of others, it probably has less than half the protection. You can verify this by looking at the freeze point chart on the back of a discount brand. At the 50/50 mix point, it may only show protection down to −16°F compared to −34°F for a name brand.

To add antifreeze to a freshly flushed system, first drain the radiator of water and close the petcock. Then, with the flushing tee cap re-

Maintaining a 50/50 mix of coolant and water gives optimum freeze protection and cooling performance.

COOLING CAPACITY CHART								
Cooling system		Quarts of antifreeze required						
Capacity (QTS.) 3	4	5	6	7	8	9	10
6	−34°							
7	−17							
8	−7	−34°						
9	0	−21						
(9.5 liters) 10	4	−12	−34°					
11	8	−6	−23					
12	10	0	−15	−34°				
13		3	−9	−25				
14		6	−5	−17	−34°			
15		8	0	−12	−26			
16		10	2	−7	−19	−34°		
17			5	−4	−14	−27		
18			7	0	−10	−21	−34°	
19			9	2	−7	−16	−28	
(19 liters) 20			10	4	−3	−12	−22	−34°

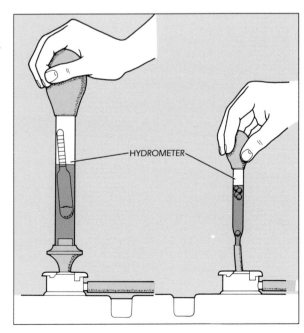

HYDROMETER

moved, pour the antifreeze into the radiator. As the radiator fills, clear water will escape from the flushing tee. As soon as you see antifreeze escaping from the tee, stop pouring and reinstall the tee cap and radiator cap.

To mix the coolant, start the engine and let it warm up while the heater is set on high. Many modern front-wheel-drive cars, such as Hondas, and mid-engine cars, like the Toyota MR2, have coolant bleed screws mounted on the engine. These screws allow air to escape from the areas that are higher than the radiator cap.

To bleed excess air, open the screw to let out the air after you first start the engine. When coolant flows from the screw, tighten it.

If you have doubts about whether your car has one or more bleed screws, consult a repair manual. Failure to bleed the system can cause air locks, which can lead to overheating and boilover. Don't trust that the air will all eventually find its way to the radiator and out the vent. If the manual calls for bleeding and you don't do it, you run the risk of meltdown.

Got the appropriate amount of undiluted coolant into the system? If the system was drained completely, there should be no problem. Or was there enough water lingering to make the system full too soon? If that's the case, let the engine warm up and then cool down completely.

With the coolant thoroughly mixed, drain the radiator partially and then add additional pure antifreeze. Allow it to mix in the engine again. Then, after the engine has cooled down, test the protection level with an antifreeze hydrometer.

There are two types of hydrometers. One has a scale that reads the level of protection. The other has little balls. The number of floating balls indicates the level of protection which is listed on the hydrometer's package.

To use either type of hydrometer, dip the end in the coolant and draw enough liquid into the clear glass tube until the gauge or balls float. Add more straight antifreeze as needed, and repeat the mixing procedure until you've reached the proper level of protection.

What to Do When Your Car OVERHEATS

It's hot. You're in bumper-to-bumper traffic, creeping along at a couple of miles per hour. Hot fumes from the car in front of you are being sucked through the cooling fins of your radiator. The temperature gauge climbs. Steam starts curling out from under your hood.

This is the kind of trouble you don't need. A little bit of diagnosis and repair time can put your cooling system into tip-top shape.

DIAGNOSIS

Coolant spurting out from under your hood or puddling on the ground every time you shut your car off is a sure sign of cooling system problems. However, other cooling system problems may only make themselves known in terms of high coolant temperature and boilovers.

Does coolant escape before your car overheats, or only after the temperature gauge has redlined or the warning light has switched on? Your answer will help determine where you should begin looking for a problem.

PRELIMINARY CHECKS

If your cooling system loses coolant before your engine overheats, begin by looking for obvious visually detectable leaks. With the engine running, check all hoses in the cooling system (Fig. 1). While you're at it, look for cracking, drying out, or soft spots that may cause future problems. Carefully examine the exposed radiator. If drips are detected near a hose connection, make sure it's not just a loose clamp. Check the thermostat housing, the radiator drain plug, the coolant recovery tank, heater control valves, and the heater core. Sometimes a leaking heater core will spill coolant into the car's interior.

Raise the car on jack stands or ramps, following the manufacturer's recommended jacking proce-

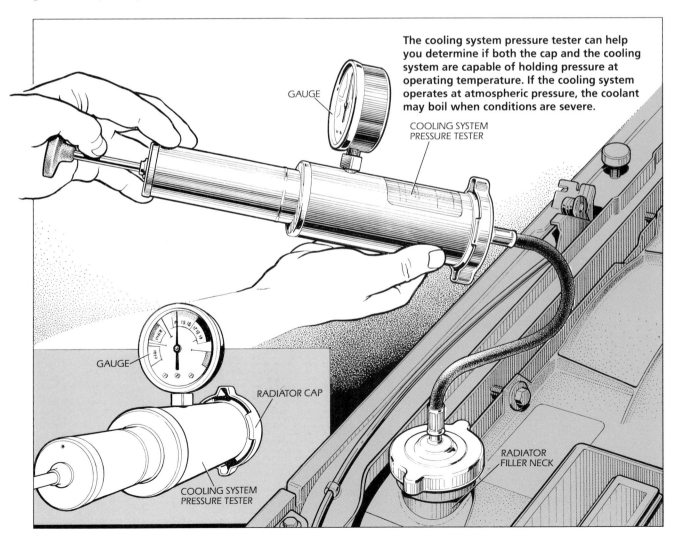

The cooling system pressure tester can help you determine if both the cap and the cooling system are capable of holding pressure at operating temperature. If the cooling system operates at atmospheric pressure, the coolant may boil when conditions are severe.

GAUGE

COOLING SYSTEM PRESSURE TESTER

GAUGE

RADIATOR CAP

COOLING SYSTEM PRESSURE TESTER

RADIATOR FILLER NECK

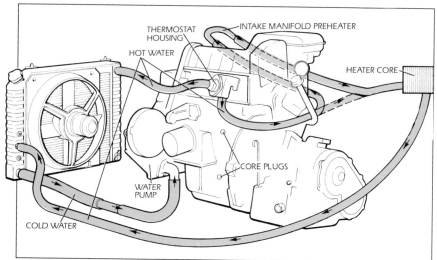

1 Water is circulated through block and head by pump, while part is routed to heater core and intake manifold. As engine warms, thermostat opens, sending heated water to radiator. Cool side of radiator returns water to inlet side of pump.

dure. Then, crawl underneath and look for signs of leaking core plugs. You won't have to run the engine to check the core plugs, as the drip should continue for a while after the engine is shut off. What's more, you should find some residue or other visual indication at the point of the leak. If you can't see all the core plugs in the side of the block, use a small dental mirror or a pocket mirror. Some cars have core plugs on the back of the engine block that are hidden by the bellhousing. If one of these plugs leaks, coolant will run out through the vent hole in the bottom of the bellhousing.

COOLING SYSTEM PRESSURE TEST

If your coolant loss isn't due to an immediately obvious leak, you'll have to pressure test the cooling system to determine if there really is a leak (remember, your coolant loss could be just a result of overheating). The pressure-test tool is available at all auto parts stores. It's indispensable for any home mechanic who wants to be able to diagnose cooling system problems.

The tool allows checks of both radiator caps and the cooling system. An adapter is provided for testing the cap. The cap is actually more than a cap (Fig. 2). It's really a system pressure regulator with an internal valve and seal and an external safety valve. The internal

valve vents to the recovery tank when pressure in the cooling system exceeds the cap's rating. A second seal keeps air out, but opens to rapidly vent steam in the event of a boilover. A cap that won't keep the system pressurized will lead to loss of coolant as it heats and expands into the recovery tank. What's more, an unpressurized system lowers the boiling point of the coolant, which can result in boilover and coolant loss.

To check the cap, simply attach it to your tester using the adapter and pump up pressure until the tester gauge indicates the amount of pressure specified for your vehicle's cooling system. That figure

is in the manufacturer's service manual (or in a general repair manual, like the *Motor Manual*). If the cap won't hold pressure to the specified figure, it must be replaced. Once you're sure the cap is okay, attach the tester to the radiator neck and pump the system up to the pressure specified. If pressure remains steady, the system is leak free.

INTERNAL COOLANT LEAKS

If you can't find an external leak, you should look for a coolant leak inside your engine. You can detect many internal coolant leaks using a cylinder pressurizing tool. This is the same tool that is used to pinpoint compression leaks. It allows you to pressurize cylinders with air. (If air can leak out of the cylinders, coolant can leak into the cylinders after shutdown.)

The part of the tool that you need for this test is the spark-plug air-hold adapter—nothing more than an air fitting that screws into your plug hole. You'll also need an air compressor or a large air tank pressurized to about 100 psi. You can purchase the air hold from an auto parts store, or you can make one by welding an air fitting to the base of an old spark plug.

To test, remove the upper radiator hose, thermostat housing, and thermostat. Reinstall the housing without the thermostat and top off the system with coolant.

Remove the plugs and install your air-hold adapter into the number one plug hole. Turn the engine to TDC compression stroke for the

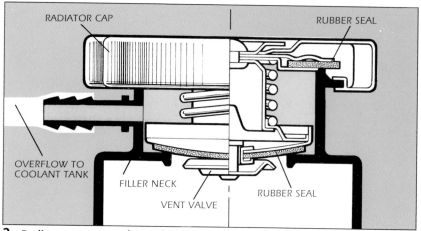

2 Radiator cap vent valve maintains a seal, so system becomes pressurized as the temperature rises.

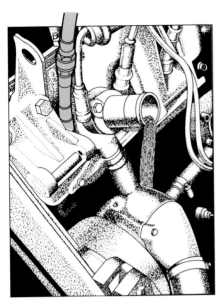

3 Use compressed-air fitting to pressurize cylinders and find failed head gaskets or cracked blocks leaking into water jacket.

number one cylinder. Attach your air-compressor hose or the outlet hose of a pressurized air tank to the air-hold chuck/plug adapter. If your engine's well worn and loose, or you have all the plugs out, you may have to hold the engine with a wrench on the harmonic balancer bolt to keep it from turning. Prop the end of the wrench on something solid—there's plenty of force generated when the air hits the cylinder.

Watch for bubbles of air in the outlet neck (Fig. 3). A cylinder that produces bubbles has a leaking head gasket, cracked cylinder wall, or cracked combustion chamber. This kind of internal leak allows combustion gases to escape into the coolant while the engine is running and probably allows coolant to escape into the engine after shutdown.

If you don't want to attempt this test yourself, have a professional mechanic check for combustion gases in your coolant with an emissions analyzer. With the engine running, he can hold the probe of the analyzer over the open radiator. If combustion gases are escaping into the cooling system, he'll get a reading.

Of course, some internal coolant leaks could be in parts of the water jacket that are not exposed to combustion pressure. These leaks will allow coolant to mix with the oil.

This is usually detectable by oil condition. Look for discoloration of the oil: It can turn milky or light brown. In less severe cases, you might only notice foam or scum on the dipstick.

UNEXPLAINED BOILOVER

What about the cooling system that passes a pressure test and holds coolant just fine until engine temperature reaches blast furnace level? In this scenario, the problem is due to something that prevents the normal exchange of heat between engine and coolant, and/or coolant and air. It could be due to something that prevents the effective circulation of coolant or air through the radiator.

Begin by taking a long, hard look at that radiator.

Is the shrouding missing or damaged? Does your car have a front airdam that is designed to push air up through the radiator? If so, is it torn or twisted out of shape? Is something blocking the car's grille?

Carefully examine the radiator surface. Has it been repaired following extensive collision damage? If so, a number of tubes or cells may have been closed. Some radiators consist of coiled cells. Others are

made up of tubes joined by heat-dissipating fins (Fig. 4). If insects and other debris clog the cooling fins or coils, air won't be able to pass through, and heat won't be exchanged.

Working your way back, take a look at the fan. If it's an electric fan (Fig. 5), it must switch on when the engine reaches a certain temperature. Your service manual can provide a spec, but, obviously, the fan should switch on before the engine overheats. To check it, simply run the car until coolant temperature comes up to the upper end of the normal range and see what happens.

If the fan doesn't work, either the coolant switch that operates it is bad, or the fan motor is shot. You can tell which it is by hot-wiring the fan to the battery. If it won't run, it's bad. If it runs on direct battery current, the switch is probably defective.

If you have an engine-driven fan, check for missing or misshapen blades. Any fan damage is grounds for replacement even if it doesn't cause a cooling problem, because loose or damaged blades can be deadly if they come off when the engine is running and you're bent over the hood.

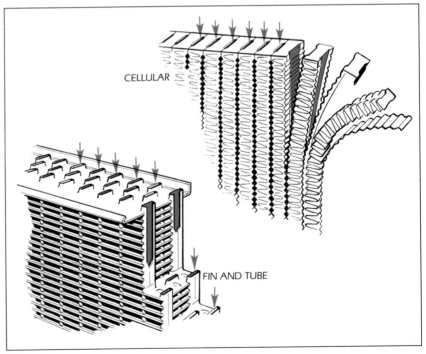

4 Radiators and most heater cores are of cellular construction. Fin-and-tube radiators route the coolant through the tubes.

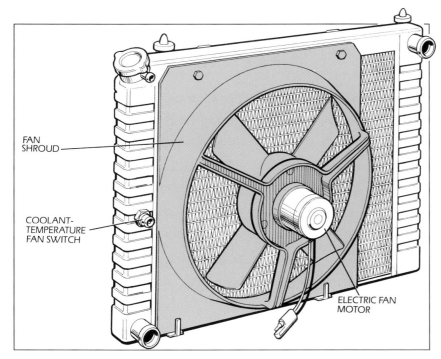

FAN SHROUD

COOLANT-TEMPERATURE FAN SWITCH

ELECTRIC FAN MOTOR

5 If the coolant-temp switch fails, the electric fan won't run when the engine warms.

Most engine-driven fans are clutched (Fig. 6), so they partially disengage at low temperatures when they're not needed. If the clutch slips after warmup, the engine will overheat.

To check your fan clutch, start the engine cold and listen to the fan as the engine warms. When the clutch begins to engage, the sound of the engine should change noticeably as load increases. You can speed engine warm-up by limiting the flow of air through the radiator. To verify your diagnosis, have a helper shut off the warm engine while you watch the fan. If the clutch is engaged, the fan should stop spinning immediately.

CIRCULATION CHECKS

Water pump failure is certainly among the leading causes of overheating, and if your overheating problem is severe and sudden, the pump may well be the culprit. On the other hand, the thermostat (Fig. 7) is just as likely to be the source of your problem.

To determine whether or not your pump is pumping and your thermostat is opening, simply warm the engine to operating temperature with the radiator cap removed. When and if the thermostat opens, coolant should start flowing through the radiator. You'll be able to detect the flow quite readily just by looking through the cap opening. If the engine reaches the point of overheating and nothing is moving in the radiator, either your thermostat isn't opening, or your water pump isn't pumping.

To determine which, you can remove the thermostat after everything has cooled down. As noted above, you'll probably find it under the connector neck housing that joins the upper radiator hose to the engine. If it's not there, check your service manual for specific information.

To test a thermostat, check for the proper spec in your service manual. Then suspend the thermostat and a thermometer in a pan of water. Heat the water and note the temperature at which the thermo-

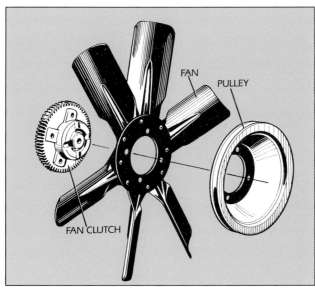

FAN

PULLEY

FAN CLUTCH

6 If the viscous-coupled fan clutch fails, overheating can result.

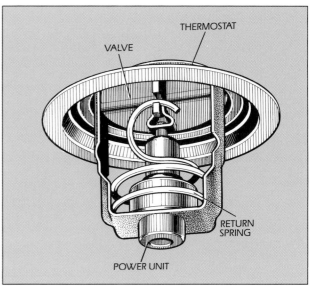

THERMOSTAT

VALVE

RETURN SPRING

POWER UNIT

7 Power unit will push valve open when coolant temp rises to correct temperature.

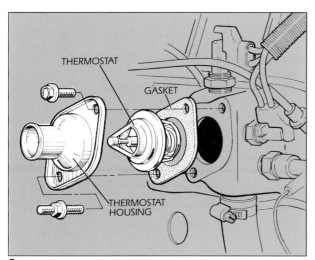

8 Install thermostat with power unit aimed toward engine block.

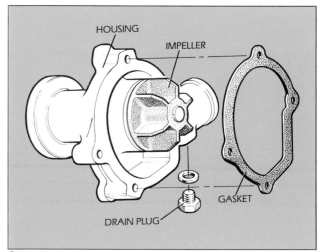

9 Some water pumps are installed with a conventional gasket and gasket sealer.

stat opens. If it doesn't open at all or opens only partially at the specified temperature, it is the cause of your overheating. (If it opens too soon, it could cause inefficient heater operation and engine condensation.)

Replace a bad thermostat with the recommended unit. Don't think you're doing your engine a favor by installing a thermostat that opens at a lower temperature. A cool-running engine allows condensation of water vapor and subsequent sludging of oil. For the same reason, never operate an engine without a thermostat.

When installing a new thermostat, note which end of the unit goes toward the engine and make sure it fits in the housing recess (Fig. 8). Remove all old gasket material, and use a new gasket or high-temp silicone gasket material as recommended by the manufacturer. If you use a gasket, *lightly* coat both sides with a nonhardening gasket compound. Reinstall the water neck and torque the bolts to the recommended fig-

ure. Don't overtighten: It's easy to crack the neck.

If the thermostat is okay, but there is no coolant flow in the radiator after the engine has warmed, the water pump is defective and should be replaced (Fig. 9).

If flow in the radiator is okay, check the water pump drive belt for signs of slippage. Even a slightly slipping belt can contribute to overheating at high engine speeds.

An incorrect water/antifreeze solution can allow premature boiling of the coolant. If your coolant contains less than 50 percent antifreeze, you're not maximizing your boilover protection. As you increase the percentage of antifreeze above the 50 percent mark, the boiling point rises. However, as antifreeze percentage rises above a 68 percent concentration, freeze protection is lost. Furthermore, a coolant mix that leans too high to the antifreeze side will not dissipate heat as effectively.

Thus, our recommendation is a 50/50 antifreeze/water mix for most parts of the country, including

places where the temperature might never drop below freezing. For extremely cold areas, where temperatures might drop to 30° below zero or lower, use approximately 65 percent antifreeze, 35 percent water.

COOLING SYSTEM BLOCKAGE

Okay, everything seems to be working fine, but your engine still overheats. It could simply be the result of dirt and deposits restricting the flow of coolant through your engine and radiator.

If you've been following proper maintenance procedures, which include annual backflushing and refilling of the cooling system, dirt shouldn't be a problem. But if you've neglected your cooling system, some of the passages in your engine could be blocked by corrosion. A professional power backflush and chemical treatment might solve the problem. But teardown could be necessary if other solutions fail.

How to Diagnose
HEATER PROBLEMS

It's a midwinter night as cold and as dark as an attorney's heart. You've scraped the windows clear while the car warmed up in the driveway—but you've gone several miles, the temp gauge has crept well above the peg, and you realize that even though the heater is on full blast, frost is creeping back across

If you need to replace a stuck-open thermostat, scrape off the old gasket while plugging the hole with a rag. Don't use gasket sealer, as it may clog the stat.

the windscreen. It's also creeping up your leg from your totally numb toes. Your heater fan is blowing noisily—but the air issuing from it is as cold as a meat locker.

Your heater has always worked fine before—time to get into a heated garage, make some hot coffee, and find the problem.

Even on a day with ambient temperatures close to zero, the temperature of the air in the floor register with a warmed-up engine should reach at least 120° to 130° F. Start with the easiest items to check. The

blast of cold air says the blower circuit is working, but if there is no airflow, start with a check of the fuse. Or the system may have a low-coolant-temperature lockout switch to keep the blower off, and this switch is misbehaving. If it has a lockout, quick-check the blower circuit by hitting DEFROST, which (usually) overrides it.

If the blower is working, check the floor heater outlet to see if hot air (or any air) is really coming out. The outlet may be blocked by carpeting or a silencing pad that has

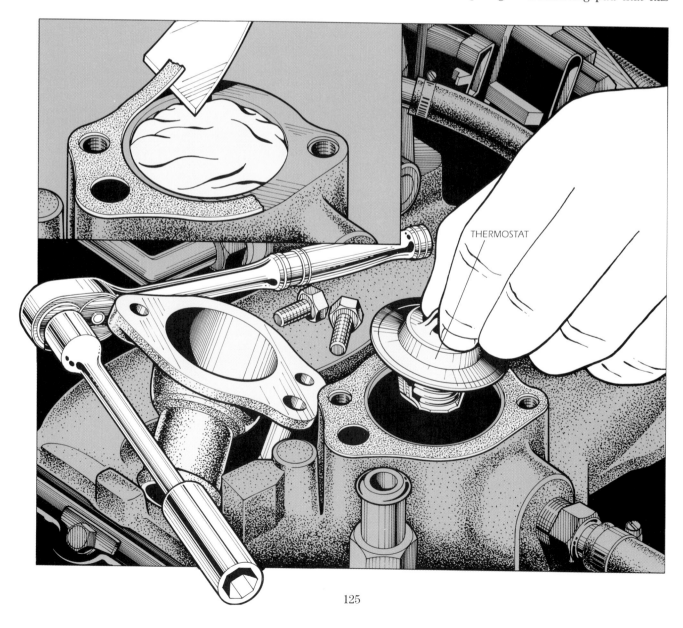

THERMOSTAT

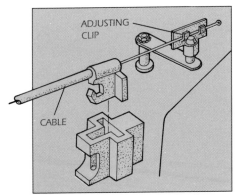

Adjust the heater control cable by moving the cable's end in its retaining clip.

slipped out of position, or an under-dash piece of duct work may have come out of its mating part.

Is the temperature door on the heater case swinging fully into the HOT position? Almost all cars have a flap door in the heater case that regulates heat by controlling airflow (a few, such as most VWs, control heat by modulating coolant flow through a heater valve on the inlet hose). With the cable setup, move the temperature lever from COLD to HOT and then feel for resistance and listen for flap-door movement in the heater/air-conditioning case. If there's no flap-door movement, the cable may have come off the retainer pin on the flap-door link. On many vehi-

cles, the door and its operating linkage and/or motor are accessible by removing either an under-dash acoustic panel or the glovebox.

If you hear the flap door move, but you don't hear it lightly slap against both ends at the COLD and HOT positions, it needs adjustment. There are almost infinite variations of temperature-cable adjustments, but usually the adjustment is something obvious, even if it's such a rare item as a turnbuckle. However, the most common setup—also used with cable-controlled heater coolant valves—is the cable housing in a retaining clip or bracket, either a spring type, a knurl on the cable housing (to hold it in the clip), or a U-bracket with a screw retainer. Readjust it by disengaging the cable housing and setting the flap door (or heater coolant valve shaft) in one extreme position (hot or cold, depending on the design), then reinstall the housing in the clip or bracket so there is no bowing or kinking.

Many domestic cars and some imports have a so-called self-adjusting cable clip for the temperature door. Move the temperature lever or rotary knob to the COLD or HOT position, depending on the design, then push the temperature door to the full COLD or full HOT position, and a pin on the flap-door link will carry the clip with it to the proper position.

If you're not absolutely sure which way to adjust a cable, refer to a service manual to get an exact sequence of operations. In some cases, the bell crank has a second cable to the heater coolant valve, so if you adjust one, you may have to adjust the other. This is common on Honda vehicles.

If the temperature door is operated by an electric motor, usually either it works or it doesn't, and is obviously silent and immobile when it doesn't. Occasionally there's a bad connection, but more often the motor has failed. However, problems with plastic gears in the motor assembly are possible, and even though the motor is alive, the defective gears will probably produce clicking or grinding noises. Replacing a defective motor is not just a matter of unbolting the old and installing the new. There may be an adjustment necessary and there often is an electronic calibration sequence, so refer to a service manual.

On GM cars, you may find that something as simple as an operating rod from the flap-door arm to the motor's arm has popped out of its plastic retainer. After making sure the door itself moves freely (by moving the rod in and out), just snap the rod back in so the threaded end protrudes about ¼ in. from the end of the retainer.

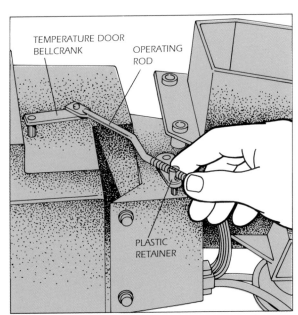

Some vehicles adjust the heater's temperature doors by means of a plastic clip and an operating rod.

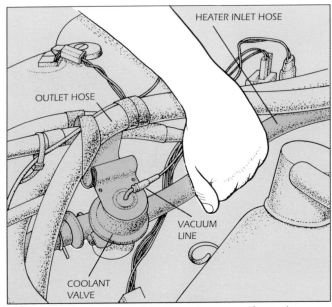

Check to see if the heater inlet hose is warm—if not, the coolant valve may be plugged or stuck.

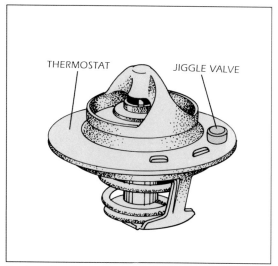

Replace the thermostat only with the correct type and temperature rating.

It may be necessary to remove a large access panel to get to the heater core, temperature doors, and a/c evaporator.

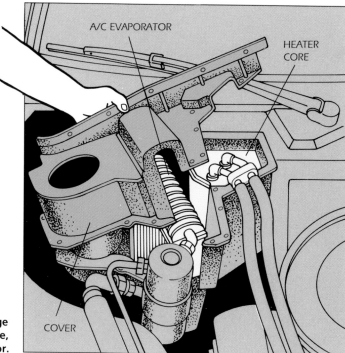

On cars with automatic temperature control, a defective sensor could put the system out of control. Run the temperature setting up to the highest number possible, typically 85° to 90° F, where it should bypass the sensors and go into a maximum heat mode. If it now starts producing hot air, an ambient and/or in-car sensor is the problem. With the in-car sensor, the fault usually is a disconnected air supply hose (or a defective motor circuit for a tiny fan) that draws interior air over the sensor. A simple test: Locate the sensor grille in the dashboard and with the system turned on place a small sheet of paper against it. The paper should be held in place by the air being sucked into the grille.

If the system passes these preliminary checks, next find out if the engine has warmed up, which it should do within a few miles even on a cold day. If you have a temperature gauge, fine. If you have only an overheat warning light, look instead at the electric radiator fan—if your car has one. If it goes on long before the engine is obviously warm, it will keep the coolant temperatures down. The usual reasons: a stuck relay or a defective coolant temperature switch or sensor.

On a car with a fan clutch, check to see if it's locked up. Start and run the cold engine for a few seconds, by which time it should free up. Stop the engine and try turning the fan by hand. If it's very difficult to turn, replace it.

If the fan operates normally, put your hand on the heater hoses close to the engine compartment firewall—the inlet hose anywhere after the heater coolant valve, if used. With the engine running long enough to be fully warmed up and the temperature lever at HOT, they both should feel hot, with the outlet hose (to the water pump or radiator) just slightly cooler. If neither is hot, feel the radiator's upper hose. If it isn't really hot, the engine isn't warming up and the thermostat is likely to be the problem.

Remove the thermostat and suspend it by a piece of wire in a pot of water with a radiator thermometer in it. Heat the water and watch the valve in the stat. If it starts to open at more than 20°F (about 12°C) below the number stamped on it, replace it. If the stat is at the water pump inlet, it is supposed to be rated at 10° to 15°F below a stat that's located at the cylinder-head outlet (typically around 180°F, 82°C) versus 195°F (88° to 89°C).

A replacement stat on a car today must duplicate the original, or the latest factory design, not just fit in. The correct thermostat may have a bypass valve to control a passage that regulates warmup. To ensure full warm-up, the stat might use a rubber seal or a tight-fitting valve to prevent coolant "leakage" from the engine to the radiator. There may be a "jiggle valve" to help balance system pressures and purge air bubbles.

To replace the thermostat without introducing problems or leaks, first carefully scrape the old gasket from the sealing surface. Use a rag to prevent bits of gasket from falling into the neck. If the manifold or head is aluminum, don't leave any scratches behind. If the old gasket is really stuck, try one of the spray-can gasket-loosening solvents. Use a new gasket when you torque down the bolts—but if you must use gasket cement, use it very sparingly or you could cement the thermostat shut with what squeezes out.

If you find that the coolant *does* get hot, find out why it apparently isn't going through the heater. Check both heater hoses for kinks and reposition them if necessary.

No kinks? Trace one heater hose to the engine and if there's a heater-coolant valve, move the temperature lever to HOT; with the engine warmed up and running, the hose should be hot on both sides. If it's hot on the engine side only, the valve isn't opening. If it's vacuum-

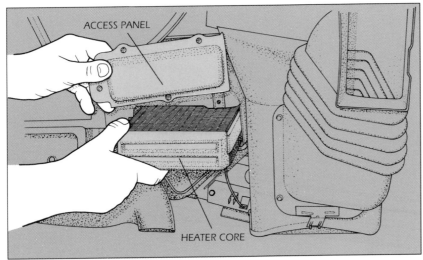

Some vehicles make the heater core accessible from inside the passenger compartment, underneath the dashboard.

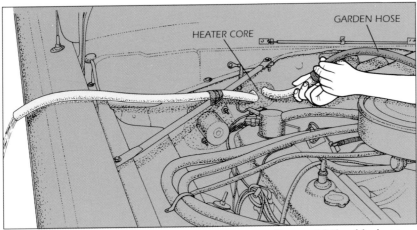

Backflush the heater core with water to remove any flow-restricting blockage.

operated, disconnect the hose and feel the hose end for vacuum with the temperature lever in the HOT and then the COLD positions (there should be vacuum in one position, usually at COLD). If the vacuum supply is constant (on or off), there is a defect in the control-valve circuit. On many cars the feed is from a vacuum valve in the dashboard control head. On others, moving the temperature lever operates a cable to the temperature door in the under-dash heater/air-conditioning case, and at that door is a vacuum valve controlled by a link.

If you determine that the heater valve is not opening properly even though the vacuum feed is correct, replace the valve, which typically is just spliced into the heater inlet hose and held in place by clamps.

If there's a cable control, look at the heater-coolant valve for an adjuster, often just a curved bracket holding the cable housing. Slide the cable housing in or out, whichever you have to do to eliminate any bows or kinks, so the lever movement turns the valve shaft enough to open the valve. Then reinsert the cable housing in the bracket.

Is the heater inlet hose hot and the outlet hose much cooler? The heater is either plugged or loaded with trapped air. Here's a test you should run only briefly so only a small amount of coolant comes out of the system. Disconnect the heater outlet hose from the water pump (or ra-

diator bottom tank), aim the end into a large pail, and plug the hose fitting with a rubber stopper (or a piece of hose, pinched off with a clamp). Run the engine with the heater on and the temperature lever set to WARM or HOT. You should see a heavy, solid flow of coolant from the hose end. If the flow starts out as a trickle, then increases to a steady flow, air has been trapped in the cooling system. Reconnect the hoses and fill the system carefully, opening any coolant air bleeds.

Many cars are notorious for trapping air, and you may have to follow a specific procedure to get the system full—and then repeat it several times. Filling with the front of the car jacked up (so it's clearly the high point of the cooling system) often helps, but is not always a complete answer.

If you can get the system filled, but the problem recurs, it could be combustion gases leaking past the head gasket into the cooling system, forcing coolant out and filling its space. There are inexpensive testers that go into the radiator neck and make any bubbling (indicating exhaust gas) easier to spot, but a professional mechanic's chemical-type combustion leak detector is a much surer indicator.

If the light/intermittent flow from the heater outlet doesn't get better quickly, the heater core is plugged. The heater has smaller tubes than a radiator, so if the cooling system has been neglected, it could clog first.

Many GM and some Ford cars have heater cores that are not difficult to replace. The core may be in the engine compartment, where removing a large plastic cover provides access. Or, although it's under the dash, there's an easy-to-remove access panel. It's worth checking a repair manual to find out. Of course, if the a/c must be discharged and the evaporator removed first, see a professional, who can pull the CFC-based (Freon) R-12 into a recycling machine instead of venting it to the atmosphere.

Before you commit yourself to replacing a clogged heater core, however, try to backflush it. Clamp spare pieces of heater hose to the necks, aiming the inlet neck hose away from the engine. Force a garden hose gun tip into the outlet neck, and let water flow through, varying the pressure at the household bibcock. Hopefully, this will dislodge enough dirt to clear the tubes, and you'll see a reasonable flow from the heater inlet neck.

Don't use compressed air, because heater core tubes can't take a lot of pressure. Even pros will try it only as a last straw, warning that the heater could end up leaking.

Occasionally, there will be good flow with a garden hose, but after you reconnect everything, the heater still barely performs. There could be a hot coolant supply problem, even if the heater hoses are routed smoothly. How can you tell? Warm up the engine and repeat the check with only the heater outlet hose disconnected and aimed into a pail. Still a weak flow? Either the cooling system itself is plugged or the water pump is weak. If sharply revving the engine improves the flow, the water pump is suspect. If it doesn't, try flushing the cooling system. But if the flow is not improved, either a slipping, loose, or eroded impeller on the water pump is a likely problem on a high-mileage car, particularly if the cooling system has been neglected (unless you're in a cool area, the engine probably overheats in warm weather). Some radiator shops can test coolant flow rate on the car, but where the pump is suspect and it's accessible, many will pull it for inspection.

Good flow of hot coolant from the heater? And the temperature door checked out? Now you're into tough diagnosis. One not-so-rare answer is a dislodged heater-core seal or baffle inside the heater case, allowing cold air to bypass, instead of going through, the heater. If the heater core ever was replaced, someone may not have secured the seals properly.

Still searching? You may find your car has an unusual heating system design feature that isn't working. Many 1986–88 GM cars with manual a/c, for example, have what is called a "slave door," an additional flap door that opens to allow extra airflow through the heater. If the flap door doesn't move, perhaps because the vacuum hose from the dashboard control head to the diaphragm unit is kinked or disconnected, that could cause a major-league drop in hot-air output.

Also, many late-model cars include separate ducts to provide heat for the rear-seat passengers. This draws a lot of heat from the front registers, which makes it important for the entire system to work at peak efficiency.

How to Troubleshoot Your
EGR SYSTEM

What automotive part has gotten the most bad press in the past fifteen years? Taking blame for multitudes of engine problems—including hard starting, stalling, hesitation, surging, spark knock, missing, rough idle, lack of power, and backfiring—is the EGR valve. Its purpose is to limit the quantity of oxides of nitrogen (NOx) engines spew into the atmosphere. To keep down NOx levels, it's necessary to keep combustion chamber temperatures below 2,500°F by in-

jecting exhaust gas into the intake system. This dilutes the fuel/air mixture, lowering temperatures dramatically. The tricky part is knowing when to inject, because EGR is unnecessary at idle or full throttle. Modern carburetors and fuel injection systems are calibrated with EGR in mind, so a malfunctioning EGR system (or a missing one) can lead to serious spark knock.

EGR control components include

time-delay valves, coolant or ambient temperature vacuum switches, back-pressure transducers, vacuum-amplifiers, timers, electric-pulse solenoids.

EGR systems rank high on the list of automotive systems misdiagnosed by both Saturday and professional automotive mechanics.

Many believe a system has failed if they feel no movement from the EGR valve diaphragm as engine speed is increased. Under

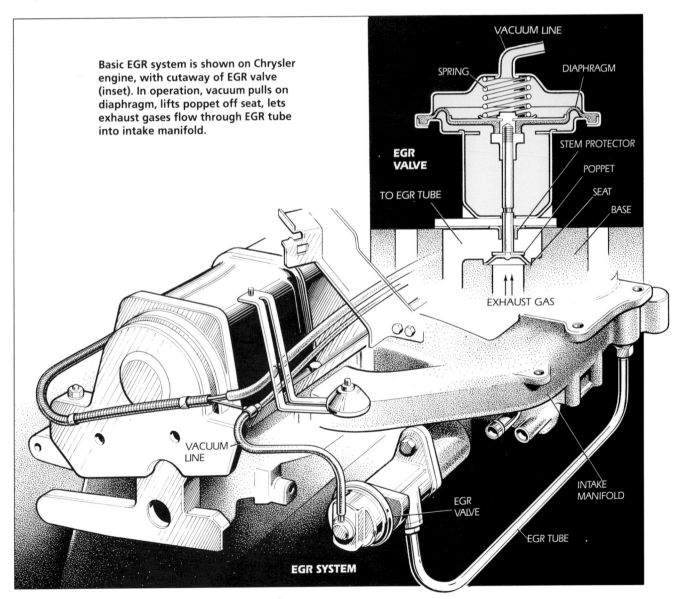

Basic EGR system is shown on Chrysler engine, with cutaway of EGR valve (inset). In operation, vacuum pulls on diaphragm, lifts poppet off seat, lets exhaust gases flow through EGR tube into intake manifold.

some conditions, feeling no change is normal.

Accurately troubleshooting the EGR system in your vehicle hinges on your knowing how it is supposed to work and which components control the valve. The following is a description of some of the main EGR systems used by Chrysler, Ford, and General Motors over the past ten years.

CHRYSLER SYSTEMS

Most Chrysler Corp. cars and light trucks built in the U.S. use one of two types of EGR systems: venturi-vacuum or ported-vacuum. With the venturi-vacuum system, vacuum is drawn from a port tapped into the venturi of the carburetor or throttle body. Because the pull of venturi vacuum by itself is not strong enough to raise the EGR valve diaphragm off its seat, Chrysler uses a vacuum amplifier.

In addition, there's a coolant-controlled temperature valve or timer to prevent the EGR valve from opening when the engine is cold or started, which would cause hesitation or stalling. A charge temperature sensor (CTS) may keep the delay timer from beginning its countdown until the fuel mixture in the intake manifold is above 60°F. The delay timer, controlled by a solenoid, delays the vacuum signal from thirty-five to ninety seconds.

TROUBLESHOOTING CHRYSLER EGR

Start a *cold* engine and let it run between 2,000 and 3,000 rpm. Watch the stem of the EGR valve (Fig. 1). It should not move.

Let the engine warm up for two or three minutes. Increase engine speed to between 2,000 and 3,000 rpm as you watch the valve stem. It should now move.

If the stem acts this way, the EGR system is working properly. But if the stem doesn't move when it's supposed to, either the EGR valve is bad or vacuum is not reaching the valve.

To test the valve, disconnect the hose from the valve hose connector and attach a hand vacuum pump securely to the connector. Pump up vacuum; then, hold it at a steady reading. If the EGR valve stem still doesn't move, replace the valve.

Even if the stem moves, there still may be a slow loss of vacuum because of a pinhole in the diaphragm, so apply vacuum and squeeze the hand vacuum pump hose closed. The valve stem should stay open as long as the hose is clamped. If the stem falls, replace the valve.

If hand-vacuum-pump testing confirms that the EGR valve is in good shape, check the rest of the system. First, examine the entire length of vacuum hose from the EGR valve to wherever the hose ends. Replace or straighten cracked or kinked hoses.

If the vacuum hose ends at a part that screws into the radiator, cylinder head, intake manifold, or water pump housing, you're dealing with a coolant-controlled EGR temperature valve (CCEGR). When the engine is cold the CCEGR vacuum switch should shut off the flow of vacuum to the EGR valve. To test, make sure the engine is fully cold (shut off for at least twelve hours), and the ambient temp in the shop is below 80°F or so. Then connect a hand vacuum pump to the connector nearest the threads and pump up vacuum. There shouldn't be more than a 1-in. drop in vacuum in one minute. If it's too warm in the shop, you'll have to remove the switch and immerse it in ice water or put it into the refrigerator.

Replace a bad CCEGR with one the same color (and temperature value) as the one your car was originally equipped with.

The EGR valve hose may go to a vacuum amplifier. Coming off this circular component are one or two other hoses. If there is one hose, it goes to a solenoid that controls a delay timer. Two hoses go to the timer solenoid and a charge temperature sensor, respectively. The CTS senses the temperature in the intake manifold. Here's how to test these components:

- *Vacuum Amplifier*—Trace and disconnect the hose going to the CCEGR from the amplifier, or if there's no CCEGR, from the carb or throttle body. Attach a vacuum pump to the hose, and start and warm up the engine. Apply 2 in. of vacuum with the pump. The valve stem should move and the engine should idle roughly. If not, replace the vacuum amplifier.

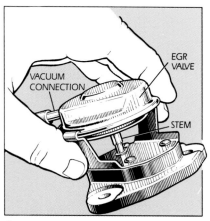

1 Watch stem of EGR valve for movement when diagnosing EGR system problems.

- *CTS*—With the engine cold, disconnect the two wires and connect the ohmmeter across the terminals. If the resistance is 10 ohms or more, replace the CTS.
- *Delay timer solenoid*—Disconnect the wire going to the timer at the solenoid to uncover a two-prong connector. Attach a jumper wire from one prong to ground. Attach a jumper wire from the battery and touch it to the other prong. If the solenoid doesn't click, replace it.
- *Delay timer*—For stalling or rough idle in the first minute of operation, suspect a faulty timer. With the engine cold and turned off, disconnect the vacuum hose at the EGR valve and reattach it at once. Start the engine and rev it up between 2,000 and 3,000 rpm. Watch the EGR valve stem as you keep time using a watch with a sweep hand. If the timer is black, the stem shouldn't move for thirty-five seconds; orange, sixty seconds; red, ninety seconds.

CHRYSLER PORT-VACUUM EGR

A small coolant-temperature-operated switch, called a coolant vacuum switch (CVS), won't admit ported vacuum from a fitting just above the throttle plates to the EGR valve until the engine has warmed up. Troubleshoot these components with a hand vacuum pump the way

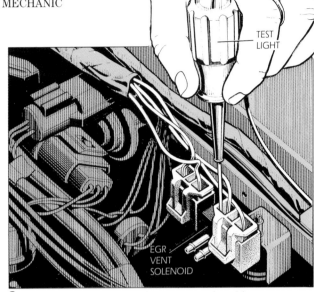

2 Damaged vacuum lines can disable an EGR system; be on the lookout constantly for kinked or cracked hoses.

3 Use test light to ground EGR vent solenoid; it should click if solenoid has power, is electrically okay.

we've just described for a venturi vacuum system.

FORD SYSTEMS

Most FoMoCo engines in 1974 and later, U.S.A.-built vehicles without microprocessors have one of three types of EGR systems: ported vacuum, remote back-pressure transducer, or integral back-pressure transducer. Trace the vacuum hose from the EGR valve. If it connects to a part having several hoses attached to it, that part is a vacuum switch and you have a remote back-pressure transducer system. Otherwise, you're dealing with a ported

4 Clamp close-fitting socket with extension into tailpipe to build back-pressure.

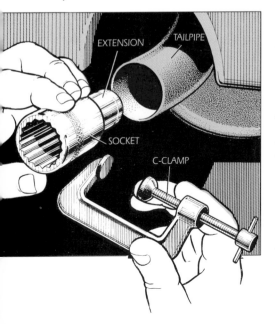

vacuum system (3-in. vacuum motor), or an integral back-pressure transducer system (4-in. vacuum motor).

Begin testing a back-pressure transducer system by disconnecting the vacuum hose at the EGR valve. Start the engine and press your thumb over the hose. If the engine is a 2.3-liter, run it at 3,000 rpm. If it's a 1.6-liter, run it at 4,000. With all other engines, press the accelerator pedal down once and release it. You should feel vacuum at the hose end. If not, and the hoses are okay, replace the back-pressure transducer, which lies between the EGR valve and the intake manifold.

You still have to test the EGR valve. Reattach vacuum hose and build up exhaust system back-pressure by inserting socket into tailpipe (Fig. 4).

Remove the vacuum hose at the EGR valve and attach a vacuum pump to the valve. With the engine idling, apply 6 in. of vacuum. The EGR valve diaphragm should move, and the engine should start to run roughly. If so, clamp the vacuum line to the pump and hold it for thirty seconds. Not more than 1 in. of vacuum should be lost. If any of these tests fail, replace the EGR valve.

MICROPROCESSOR SYSTEM

Ford-built vehicles with microprocessor control systems have electronically controlled EGR systems.

A sensor called the EGR valve position sensor, which is mounted on top of the EGR valve, receives signals from the microprocessor through two solenoids to control the opening and closing of the valve. Let's call one the control solenoid and one the vent solenoid.

To check this system, first test the EGR valve by disconnecting the vacuum hose connected to the valve and attaching a hand vacuum pump. Apply vacuum and hold it for thirty seconds. If vacuum drops more than 1 in. in that time, replace the valve.

If the valve tests okay, but spark knock persists on the road, test the electrical part of the system. Begin at the EGR vent solenoid (Fig. 3), which is the solenoid having the small vent. Connect the pigtail end of a test 12-volt light to a convenient ground and turn on the vehicle ignition switch, but don't start the engine.

Probe the electrical connectors at the solenoid with the tip of the test light. If probing both wires with the test light doesn't make the light glow and the solenoid click, replace the solenoid. Test the control solenoid the same way. Now, make sure solenoids hold vacuum.

To test the vacuum-holding ability of the control solenoid, disconnect the vacuum hose from the solenoid and attach a hand vacuum pump. Seal the vent of the vent solenoid with tape or a finger to keep vacuum from escaping.

Pump up vacuum and energize the control solenoid with the test

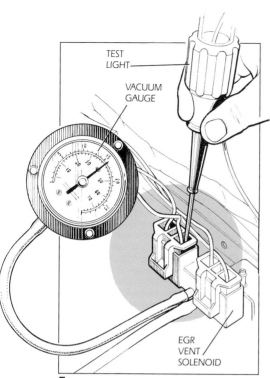

5 Vacuum gauge readings should not drop more than an inch during testing.

GM SYSTEMS

Most GM engines with and without Computer Command Control (CCC) have one of three types of EGR valves: single diaphragm (or port), positive back-pressure, or negative back-pressure (see Fig. 6).

Warm up the engine. With a six- or eight-cylinder engine running at 2,000 rpm or a four-cylinder engine running at 3,000 rpm, pull the vacuum hose off the EGR valve and place your finger tightly over the end of the hose.

If you don't feel vacuum, there's a bad hose or a defective vacuum component. If vacuum is present, reconnect the hose, reach beneath the valve, and put your finger on the diaphragm. It will be either rubber or metal.

If rubber, you're dealing with a single-diaphragm EGR valve which opens and closes in response to ported vacuum. Test this valve by alternately opening and closing the throttle. If the diaphragm moves up and down (if it doesn't, replace it), attach a hand vacuum pump and apply vacuum (Fig. 7). If vacuum doesn't hold, replace the valve.

Positive back-pressure EGR valves are controlled by both vacuum and exhaust back-pressure. Test it with the engine warmed up and running at a fast idle. Disconnect the vacuum hose from the valve, insert a golf tee in the end of the hose and place a finger on the valve diaphragm. The diaphragm should stay down and engine speed

should increase. Reconnect the vacuum hose and feel if the diaphragm rises. Engine speed should decrease.

Note: You may feel a slight vibration from the diaphragm plates of both positive and negative back-pressure EGR valves. This is normal. Take the valve off the engine. Apply 10 in. or more of vacuum to the valve with a hand vacuum pump. The diaphragm should not rise off its seat.

Maintaining vacuum, aim a stream of low-pressure air into the valve's exhaust outlet (Fig. 8). If the diaphragm doesn't open completely, clean the exhaust passage if it's heavily coked, or replace the valve.

A negative back-pressure EGR valve is controlled by a combination of manifold vacuum, ported vacuum, and negative exhaust back-pressure. Test it with the engine off.

Disconnect the vacuum hose from the EGR valve and push up on the diaphragm plate as you place a finger tightly against the EGR valve hose connection. If the diaphragm drops in less than twenty seconds, replace the valve. Repeat the procedure as someone cranks the engine. If the diaphragm doesn't drop, replace the valve.

GM EGR CONTROL UNITS

Most GM engines use a thermal device that controls vacuum to the EGR valve. Engines without CCC employ a coolant-temperature-sensing switch, an engine-heat-

light. If vacuum drops, the control solenoid is bad. Replace it.

Test the vent solenoid by continuing to hold the vent closed and maintaining vacuum on the control solenoid. Energize the vent solenoid with the test light. As you do, unblock the vent. Vacuum should not drop, meaning that the vent solenoid has closed and vacuum is being retained (Fig. 5).

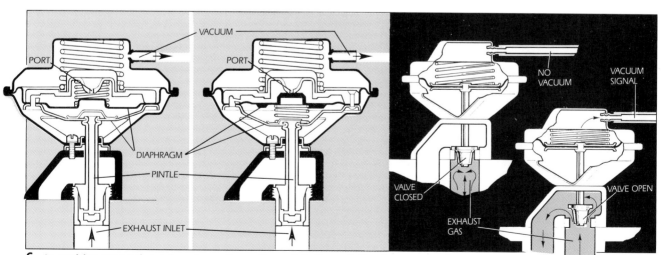

6 In positive-type valve exhaust, gas flows through hollow pintle, closes port, allows vacuum to open pintle. In negative, vacuum pulls diaphragm port open, keeps pintle closed unless exhaust pressure keeps it shut. In single-diaphragm type, vacuum opens valve.

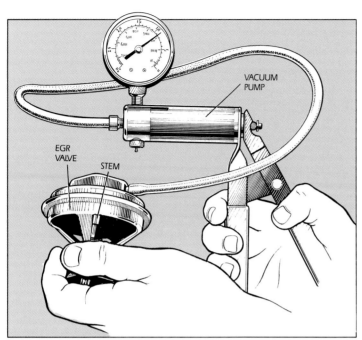

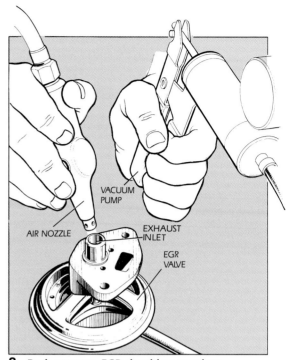

7 Apply vacuum to EGR valve, watch stem move up. Diaphragm should then hold vacuum steady, not leak down.

8 Back-pressure EGR should open when compressed air is blown in exhaust inlet.

sensing switch, or a combination coolant and engine switch.

If the EGR valve responds positively to tests, make sure the rest of the system is not causing your engine problem by checking hoses; then, by replacing the control switch.

The EGR control system of GM engines with CCC on pre-1983 and many post-1983 vehicles consists of a solenoid and a thermal sensor. To test them, connect a vacuum gauge to the end of the hose at the EGR valve and start the engine. Open and close the throttle a few times. There should not be a vacuum reading until the engine gets warm.

If there is a reading, remove the wire at the solenoid. If this makes vacuum disappear, replace the thermal sensor. If the vacuum reading persists, suspect a bad solenoid. Beginning in 1983, GM started using a Pulse-Width-Modulated EGR System that pulsates up to 32 times per second on 2.8-, 3.0-, 3.8-, 5.0-, and 5.7-liter engines. If you find that an engine-driveability problem is not due to a bad EGR valve, get help to determine if it's one of the control units.

How to Replace
FILTERS

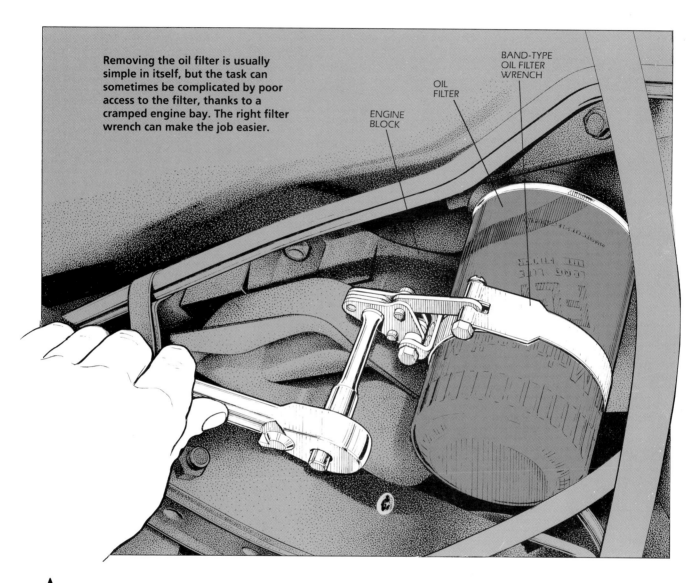

Removing the oil filter is usually simple in itself, but the task can sometimes be complicated by poor access to the filter, thanks to a cramped engine bay. The right filter wrench can make the job easier.

BAND-TYPE
OIL FILTER
WRENCH

OIL
FILTER

ENGINE
BLOCK

Although today's cars are protected by more self-diagnostics and fail-safe systems than ever before, the first line of defense dates back to the origin of the species.

They're hardly high-tech, but filters stand guard in most of your car's systems, trapping oil contaminants, turning back dirt in the fuel system, and shutting the door on airborne abrasives trying to make their way into the induction system.

Considering their importance, and how easily they can be maintained or replaced, it's worthwhile to make a regular filter patrol part

of your car care routine. In terms of making your car run better longer, the time it takes pays higher dividends than any other routine maintenance chore you can tackle.

OIL FILTERS

Locating the oil filter remains easy on almost all cars. It's threaded onto the exterior of the engine, and you'll just have to look (sometimes hard). The only noteworthy exception: On some late-model General Motors cars with 2.5-liter four-cylinder engines, it's in the oil pan (loosen a

giant plug to drain the oil, then remove the plug and pull out the filter with pliers).

To be able to remove the filter, you'll need to raise the car, either with drive-on ramps or a hydraulic jack to lift the car by a crossmember, followed by safety stands under the suspension arms.

Carmakers' recommended filter replacement intervals vary, but you can't go wrong changing the filter whenever you change the oil—at least twice a year, every three to four months or 3,000 miles if you do a lot of short-trip, heavy-load, or

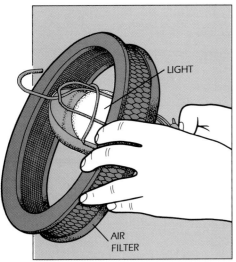

Inspect your air cleaner regularly for signs of plugging or a torn paper element.

stop-and-go driving. Removing the old oil filter should be a straightforward operation if you have a filter wrench that fits in and on. The old strap wrenches are "universal," in that they grasp the filter body and will work on any filter within a broad size range.

If a strap wrench won't fit in, you may need an end-cap wrench, which usually fits into even the tighter quarters on some cars. The

end-cap wrench locks against flutes on the end of the filter. Even if you have a wrench that's the right diameter for your car's filter, you must also make sure the flute pattern of wrench and filter also match. If you installed the old filter with that wrench, there's apparently a match. However, if you buy a different brand replacement filter this time, bring along your wrench to make sure it will work.

If you don't have a wrench, and need an end-cap, check the wrench you buy against a filter of the same brand that's on your car. Then get a replacement filter with the same flute pattern (it need not be the same brand). Or buy a universal end-cap wrench with spring-loaded "fingers" that lock against several flutes, enough to loosen the typical filter within its specified range.

Some filter designs will last a bit longer or remove slightly finer dirt particles, but if you use any name-brand or major store brand and change the filter at reasonable intervals, you should never encounter an oil filtration problem. Always buy a filter recommended in the maker's current catalog for your car's engine, model, and year. Just because a different number looks the same doesn't mean it is, and it may give you problems with installation, or

eventually work loose and leak, even if it doesn't leak immediately.

If the wrench is a strap-type, position it on the filter as close to the base as possible. Place a drain pan under the filter, and if the filter is recessed, make a trough of aluminum foil so when you loosen the filter any oil flows along the trough into the drain pan rather than on the ground, or, even worse, onto a wiring harness, before dripping onto the ground. Or you can wrap the harness with foil to protect it.

Having a problem trying to loosen a badly stuck filter? If the filter simply distorts without loosening when you use an end-cap wrench, you've got to put a wrench around the filter right at the base, even if there isn't much room to turn a handle. You may be able to do it with chain-type locking pliers, a plumber's strap wrench, or an oil filter strap wrench, but for a real problem the best choice is a pair of oil filter removal pliers, such as the Vim V-240 and V-241 (Durston Manufacturing Co., LaVerne, CA 91750). Our favorite universal tool is actually the 24-in. Channelock pliers, which costs about forty bucks but has plenty of other uses around the shop.

Once you have the old filter off, check to make sure the rubber gas-

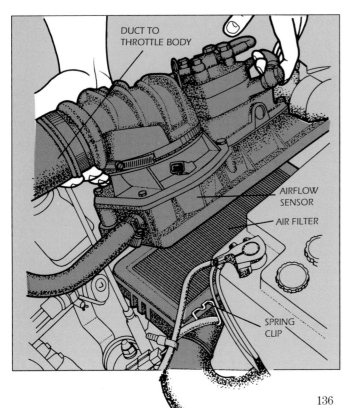

Remote air cleaners can be hard to access, and the spring clips hard to release or fasten properly.

When inspecting the air filter, also check the PCV systems filter, if there is one.

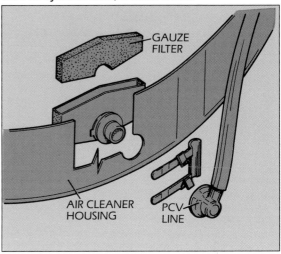

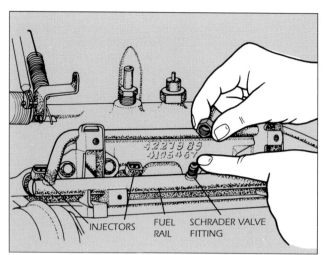

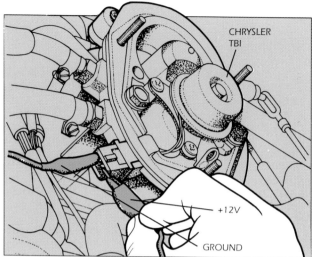

Relieve fuel system pressure before opening up any high-pressure fuel filter fittings. Keep a fire extinguisher handy.

On some Chrysler products, relieve fuel pressure by jumping the injector to 12V for ten seconds or so.

ket came off with it. If it didn't, reach up and dig it out. If you don't, you'll have an oil leak, as the two gaskets will distort when squeezed together. Clean the filter mounting surface with a cloth.

Apply a thin film of clean oil to the new filter's gasket, then thread on the filter. It should thread on smoothly. If you encounter resistance, stop, as you may be cross-threading. Be careful not to scrape the filter over anything as you're worming your way through the engine compartment up to the filter mounting pad—you don't want to collect any dirt and inject it directly into your engine. If the filter is more or less vertical, prefill it with clean oil, to reduce the interval between engine start and establishing oil pressure.

Once you have the filter threaded on, run it down until you feel it just make contact with the mounting surface. Install the wrench (flip over a strap wrench so the band closes when the wrench is turned in the clockwise direction). Then make note of some emblem on the filter body for reference and tighten the filter about a three-quarter-turn more. You might be able to do this by hand, so avoid distorting the filter with tools if you can.

Replace the drain plug, replacing the gasket washer if necessary. After adding oil, start the engine and check for leaks near the base of the filter.

A word about oil filter interchangeability: Don't. Just because a filter seems to screw on to the oil

filter flange and has sufficient mechanical clearance doesn't mean it's safe to use it.

There are a number of similar filters with slightly different thread pitch and gasket diameters—different enough to pass cursory examination, but fail under pressure by blowing off the threads some cold morning or popping a gasket on a hot day.

Some filters have an internal pressure relief valve, intended to by-pass oil flow if the filter medium becomes totally plugged by sludge. The theory is that some dirty oil is better than no oil at all, or having the paper filter burst under the strain and dumping a quart of sludge straight into the engine. Some filters have no such valve, as they're intended for engines that have an internal relief valve.

There may indeed be some substitution possible—and the filter manufacturer's interchange table should be your guide. For instance, there's a larger Ford filter, intended for trucks, that is a direct replacement for the standard PH-8 Ford spin-on.

Another option is a remote filter adapter, with lines running up to a filter mounted on the fenderwell or firewall. The easy access makes a filter change a standup job, and if you mount the filter so it's upright, it's a clean job as well.

AIR FILTERS

The air filter always used to be atop the carburetor or throttle body, un-

der an easily accessible cover held by a wing nut. Every couple of years, you simply took off the wing nut, lifted the cover, removed the old element, cleaned out the housing, and installed the new one.

If you live where there isn't any dust or airborne dirt to speak of, check the filter annually. Dusty conditions shorten the interval considerably, and if you drive on unpaved roads, every three months is more like it.

Lower hoodlines mean filter housings located away from the carburetor or throttle body. If you aren't sure where, trace the large, flexible air duct from the top of the engine until you come to a large metal or plastic housing with a cover, and it's probably there.

In many cases, the filter cover is held by spring clips, and you may have to work in with a screwdriver to release and reengage the clips. Some filter covers also hold a section of the fuel-injection system, so you may have to unplug a wiring connector for working clearance. If you do, inspect its retainer carefully so you don't break a plastic tang taking it off. When you refit a connector, be careful not to bend any terminals.

Inspect the filter, and if there's only one dirty spot, opposite the intake air snorkel, just tap the filter against a workbench to remove loose dirt, then turn the element and reinstall. Of course, if you live in an area where there's a lot of airborne sand, it may not darken the element. In that case, hold a shop light up to the inboard side of the element. If the filter is clear, you should see uniform lines of light shine through at the pleats.

Here again, get the *exact* filter element specified for your car. If a filter is just slightly smaller, it won't fit the housing properly and unfiltered air can leak into the engine between the element and the housing.

When you're changing the filter, also look in the housing for a small gauze filter used on older carbureted engines to clean the intake air for the Positive Crankcase Ventilation (PCV) system. If this gauze filter is dirty, pull it out and install a new one.

At the same time, check the ductwork connected to the air filter housing. Of course, it should be connected at both ends, but it also should be free of any tears. A torn or loose hot-air duct for a thermostatic air cleaner can allow cold air to leak in and affect driveability until the engine is warm. A torn or loose duct from the air cleaner to the carburetor or throttle body allows unfiltered air to get in. On cars with airflow sensors, leaks permit unmeasured airflow, which can result in a lean fuel mixture, leaving you with a driveability problem you'll have a hard time tracing.

GASOLINE FILTERS

The gas filter is usually under the hood, and if you trace the fuel line from the carburetor or fuel injectors, you'll come to it. Not under the hood? Well, maybe it's underneath, such as just forward of the gas tank on some models. In these cases, you'll have to lift up the rear of the car for access.

Many carmakers don't recommend specific fuel filter replacement intervals. However, even without apparent driveability symptoms, it's a good idea to change the fuel filter every two years.

There are some close brushes with high technology on cars with fuel injection, because you must relieve system pressure of anywhere from 15 to 60 psi (depending on the type of system) before you can change the filter. This is unlike carburetor systems, which operate on modest pressures in the 3- to 6-psi range, with little or no residual pressure. However, dealing with the higher pressures of fuel-injection systems needn't frighten you.

If your fuel system has a tire-type service valve, called a Schrader valve, installed to simplify connection of a pressure gauge, just remove the cap, wrap a towel around the valve to collect fuel spray, and

depress the pin. Safety glasses, please. When the fuel stops spraying out, the pressure is relieved.

A similar setup is used on fuel-injected Hondas—a threaded plug that can be removed to install a pressure gauge. The plug is on the fuel rail (tubing) next to the pressure regulator, and all you have to do is hold a fitting with one wrench while you loosen the plug with a second wrench. Wrap the fitting with a towel to collect seeping fuel, of course.

You may be able to remove a fuel pump fuse, followed by cranking the engine for ten seconds. With the pump disabled, the pressure will be dissipated. This may set a trouble code in your engine computer, but don't worry, because it shouldn't cause the CHECK ENGINE light to repeatedly come on. You could disconnect the car battery for about a half-minute to erase the code—not a bad idea for general safety if you're disconnecting fuel lines or operating a Schrader valve under the hood. However, most engine computers have sophisticated programs that include adaptive learning. It means the computer has adjusted the engine controls for your driving style. Disconnecting the battery erases this data, and it will take perhaps one hundred miles

Now you can remove the fuel filter itself by carefully unscrewing the appropriate fittings and clamps that hold it in place.

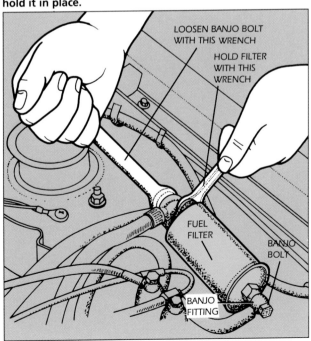

Some carburetors are equipped with a small filter where the fuel line enters the carburetor body.

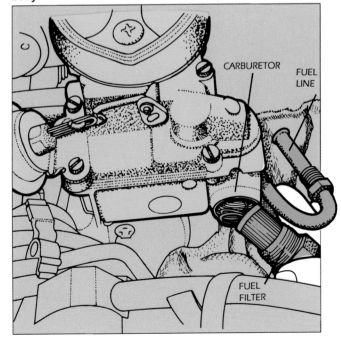

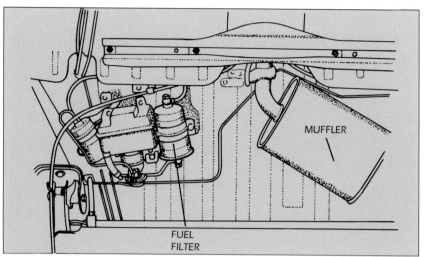

Can't find the filter in the engine compartment?
It may be under the car, just ahead of the fuel tank.

of driving for the computer to re-learn.

There are other methods to re-lieve system pressure. On Chrysler throttle-body injection systems, there is no Schrader valve, so un-plug the injector's wiring connector and hot-wire the injector with jumper wires—one to battery posi-tive, one to ground—for just a few seconds, and you'll open the injec-tor long enough.

Or, check a wiring manual for the fuel pump ground location. You can also get underneath the back of the car and trace the fuel pump wiring to the ground connection (typically a black wire), and disconnect it. Dis-connecting the ground may be one of the least convenient ways to stop the pump to relieve system pressure by cranking, but you can use the technique on just about any car.

Finally, here's another universal method. Very gradually loosen a fuel line or fuel hose clamp at a joint, well wrapped in a towel, and let the fuel seep out. This is what we do, but we're careful, and we keep a fire extinguisher nearby.

The exact procedure for taking out the old filter varies, but it should be obvious. Standard fittings that thread together are the most widely used on both carbureted and fuel-injected cars. Just hold one fitting while you loosen the other (which one to hold should be obvious). Many fuel-injected engines have banjo fuel filter fittings that get their name from their shape. A bolt goes through the banjo with gaskets on top and bottom. These gaskets should be replaced when you change the filter.

If the filter is clamped to hoses, you may be able to loosen the clamp and reuse it, but do this only if it's a worm-drive type. With all others, in-cluding the spring-wire type, dis-card the clamps and install new ones. In fact, the only way you can get some clamps off is to chop them apart with side-cutter pliers.

On most carbureted GM cars, the filter is in a carburetor boss. Discon-nect the line, then remove the fuel line fitting for access.

A cheap, ineffective fuel filter may allow dirt to damage some pretty expensive components, so don't gamble. A quality aftermarket brand should be considerably cheaper than original equipment, because you can buy it from a parts store (with a generous discount structure) instead of a car dealer. However, if there is no reputable aftermarket re-placement, spend the extra money for an original equipment replace-ment.

How to Give Your Engine a VALVE JOB

There are a lot of good looking seven- to ten-year-old domestically built cars out there that might deliver another decade of use. Unfortunately, a large percentage of these six- and eight-cylinder machines don't run as well as they look. When the light goes green, these oldies are left in the lurch. In most cases, burned valves and poor valve seating due to worn guides are the culprits.

A good valve job and guide replacement can put one of these engines right back in the pink. However, the machine work and the new parts are expensive enough on their own. Add the cost of having the heads removed and replaced (R + R)

and you're talking more money than you'd want to spend on a ten-year-old buggy. The solution is to do the R + R yourself, then find a top-notch machine shop to prepare the heads.

You'll need a complete set of mechanic's tools, as well as a torque wrench, a compression gauge, masking tape, a ballpoint pen, a grease pencil, a gasket scraper, some nonflammable solvent, and a pan to wash parts.

DO YOU NEED A VALVE JOB?

While the symptoms described above are a good sign that your car may need a valve job, a compres-

sion test and/or cylinder leakage test can provide better evidence.

To test engine compression, remove the spark plugs and prop the throttle valves and choke valve completely open. Disconnect the wires from the coil and make sure they don't short out. On GM HEI, disconnect the BAT terminal from the distributor.

Hold the compression gauge snugly against the plug hole of the first cylinder to be tested and crank the engine five times or until you get a maximum reading. Write down the number and repeat for all cylinders. If one or more do not fall within 75 percent of the strongest, you have bad compression.

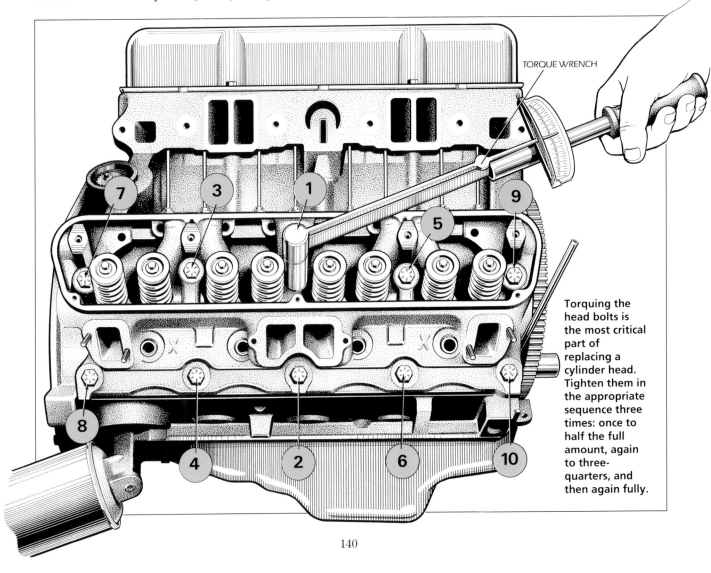

TORQUE WRENCH

Torquing the head bolts is the most critical part of replacing a cylinder head. Tighten them in the appropriate sequence three times: once to half the full amount, again to three-quarters, and then again fully.

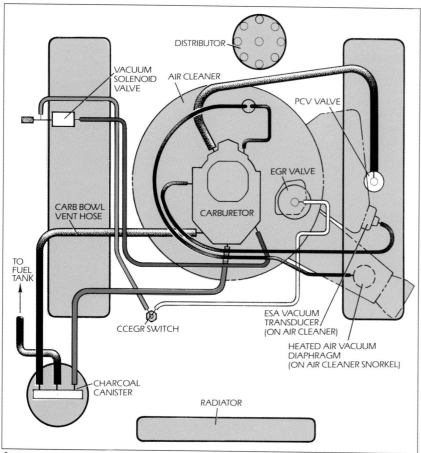

DISTRIBUTOR

VACUUM
SOLENOID
VALVE

AIR CLEANER

PCV VALVE

EGR VALVE

CARB BOWL
VENT HOSE

CARBURETOR

TO
FUEL
TANK

CCEGR SWITCH

ESA VACUUM
TRANSDUCER
(ON AIR CLEANER)

HEATED AIR VACUUM
DIAPHRAGM
(ON AIR CLEANER SNORKEL)

CHARCOAL
CANISTER

RADIATOR

1 Typical vacuum hose routing diagram: Don't panic! Just keep track.

You can usually get a somewhat better idea of the cause by squirting a couple of spoonfuls of oil into the offending cylinder through the plug hole. If valves are the leaking point, the compression reading should only rise slightly or not at all when the compression test is repeated. If compression rises to normal with the oil in the cylinder, worn rings are probably at fault.

REMOVING ACCESSORIES

Before you start unbolting things, study the underhood layout. Note which accessories are bolted to the cylinder heads or restrict access. Study the wiring and vacuum hoses. Since you'll be removing the carb and intake manifold as one unit on most cars, some hoses can remain in position.

Refer to the vacuum hose diagram located somewhere in the engine compartment (Fig. 1). If you can't find this label or if the diagram doesn't make sense to you, photo-

graph the engine to get a good perspective on all areas where there are hoses and wires.

Before doing anything else, disconnect the battery's negative cable. If you haven't already done so, remove the spark plugs. Label each plug wire by writing the cylinder number on a piece of tape and folding it around the end.

On most cars you'll have to move the air-conditioning compressor. Determine where the compressor's brackets attach to the engine and move the compressor to the side of the engine compartment without disconnecting its wiring or hoses.

On some cars you'll have to remove the alternator, air pump, and steering pump as well. The steering pump should just be unbolted and relocated in the engine compartment as the a/c was. If necessary, you can remove the alternator from the car, but make sure you label all wires with tape.

On some engines, including Chevy V8s, the distributor passes

through the intake manifold and must be removed. Before doing so, turn the engine to the firing position for the No. 1 cylinder (the mark you use to set ignition timing) as indicated on your front pulley. Use a wrench on the crankshaft pulley bolt to turn the engine.

Find the spark-plug wire for the No. 1 cylinder, and, with a grease pencil, mark its location on the cap and on the distributor, right below the cap. Remove the distributor cap with all the plug wires in place, disconnecting only the coil wire from the center tower. If the distributor's rotor isn't pointing to the spot you marked for the No. 1 cylinder's wire, rotate the engine one complete revolution. Note the positioning of the distributor and, if you can, mark it and the intake manifold so you can relocate it precisely.

Once the distributor has been marked for repositioning, disconnect the wire that joins it to the coil or ignition wire harness and label it. Remove the distributor clamp and distributor. Reinstall the distributor cap with all its wires connected and store the unit in a dry place on your workbench.

Disconnect every vacuum hose and wire that will prevent removal of the intake manifold and/or cylinder heads and label each (Fig. 2). Using a rag to catch spilled gasoline, disconnect the fuel line. Use two wrenches; one on the fuel line nut, a second on the fitting it screws into. On some cars you'll have to remove other components or accessories as well. These may include the AIR pump or AIR system diverter valve, cruise-control components and ignition

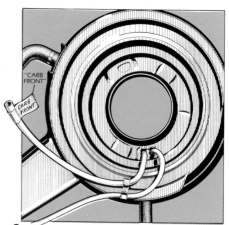

2 Label each and every one of the hoses and wires before you remove it.

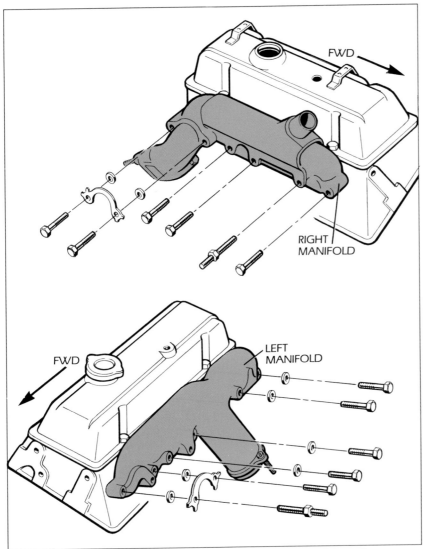

3 Don't be surprised if years of rust have reduced the size of the exhaust manifold bolts considerably, say from 9/16 in. to 3/8 in. or smaller. And they'll be hard to turn, too.

coil. But if any of these parts are attached to the intake manifold in such a way that they don't prevent its removal, leave them in place.

UNBOLTING THE MANIFOLDS

Before you can remove the intake manifold, the engine coolant must be drained. To drain the engine and radiator, remove the radiator cap and open the petcock at the bottom of the radiator. When the flow stops, open the petcock at the bottom of the engine block or remove the lower radiator hose to drain the coolant.

When the coolant has drained,

unbolt the intake manifold. The engine must be completely cold before any components are unbolted or parts warpage may occur. Make sure you've removed all the bolts and check for any debris on the manifold that could fall into the engine. Then, grab the manifold front and rear and pull up hard. If you can't find a place to grasp the manifold, you can pull on the carb, but be careful not to bend any linkages. On some engines with separate valley covers you can insert a pry bar under the manifold runners if it is stuck. On others, including Chevys, you can't because the manifold doubles as a valley cover.

Once the manifold has been re-

moved, unbolt the valley cover (if applicable) and cover the engine valley with a rag.

The exhaust manifolds are next. On most cars, the best strategy is to unbolt the manifolds from the heads (Fig. 3). Check for locking tabs next to the bolt heads. These must be bent back with a small screwdriver before the bolts can be loosened. On some engines, the manifold bolts are almost impossible to reach. If this is the case, unbolt the exhaust pipes from the manifolds and remove the manifolds along with the heads.

OFF WITH ITS HEADS

Before unbolting the heads, you'll have to remove the valve covers and valve train parts. It's essential that you arrange some sort of system for keeping valve train parts in order because rocker arms and pushrods mate to each other as they wear. If your engine has rocker stands, like some Fords and most Chryslers, simply mark the stands for each side before unbolting them. If you have stamped rockers on studs like those used on Chevrolets, unbolt each rocker and tie a wire through the rocker, nut and ball joint, then attach a label to each with a number on it. Shipping tags work well.

Once the rockers have been removed, find an old shoe box, punch sixteen small holes in the bottom (for eight-cylinder engines), and number each hole for a corresponding spot on the engine, inserting each pushrod into its appropriate hole. With valve train parts removed, loosen the head bolts. Make a note of the location of any bolts whose threads are coated with sealant. With all the bolts removed, the heads should come off fairly easily, since gasket sealers are usually not used. If you can't get the heads off, check to make sure you've removed all the bolts.

Once the heads are off, examine them and the gaskets for signs of combustion gases leaking past the gasket's sealing ring. Save the gaskets so you can match them up to the new ones.

CHOOSING A MACHINE SHOP

Don't take your heads to any auto parts store that happens to have a machine shop in the back. Instead, find an advanced, well-equipped shop that specializes in engine machine work. The most sophisticated are frequently those that do high-performance work. Explain to the counterman that, in addition to a valve job, you want the head gasket surfaces checked for straightness, the guides checked, and the spring pressure checked and adjusted. If the man in the machine shop doesn't know what you're talking about, find a new machine shop. If the head surfaces aren't straight, have them resurfaced. If they're cut more than .010 in., the intake manifold gasket surfaces will have to be machined as well.

PRIOR TO REASSEMBLY

While you're waiting to get your heads back, wash all other parts in nonflammable solvent. If you have stand-mounted rockers, disassemble them. String the rockers, washers, and springs on wires so they can be kept in order. Check all valve train parts for ridges or flaking that indicate excessive wear and replace as necessary. Check pushrods for straightness by rolling them on a flat surface.

Clean the block decks of all carbon and dried gasket compound with a gasket scraper. (If your engine is aluminum, use a soft brush and gasket solvent.) Make sure all deposits are removed, but don't scratch the deck surface. If you have one, use a bottoming tap to clean the head bolt hole threads. If your head gaskets were blown, check the block decks for straightness with a straightedge and feeler gauge. Check with the straightedge positioned lengthwise and then across the deck. If you can slip a .004-in. feeler gauge under the straightedge anywhere on the block, you're in trouble (Fig. 4). For inline sixes, the limit is .006-in.

However, if the engine deck variation is only slightly more than 0.003 in. and the car's age and condition don't justify a full engine rebuild, you might want to try buttoning things up and hoping for the best.

Today's sophisticated head gaskets can frequently hold things together even with parts that are warped beyond normal tolerances.

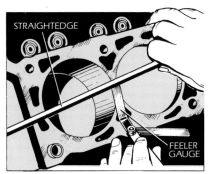

4 Check the head for warping with a good metal straightedge and feeler gauges.

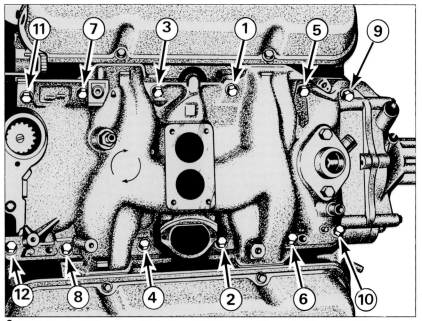

5 This Chevy V6's torque sequence is common to all five-bolt-per-cylinder engines.

REASSEMBLY

Use premium, brand-name head gaskets for reassembly. The latest designs include silicone sealing beads around water and oil holes and a stainless-steel ring around the bore. Compare the new gaskets to the original ones to make sure that oil and water holes correspond. The new head gaskets and all the other gaskets needed can be purchased in a "head set." Embossed shim-type gaskets or metal-faced sandwich gaskets should be sprayed lightly with a nonhardening gasket compound. Those with special coatings and/or sealing beads should be installed as is.

Intake manifold gaskets should be attached to the heads with fast-drying adhesive so they'll remain in place while the manifold is installed. Use a light coating of gasket adhesive on the manifold side. Valve cover gaskets should be attached to the valve covers with the fast-drying adhesive. Exhaust manifold gaskets are installed dry.

To install your heads, place the new gaskets over the dowel pins on the engine block. Make sure that the correct side is facing up; most gaskets are marked. Carefully locate each head on the dowel pins. Lubricate the head bolts and screw them in by hand. Pay attention to the length of each bolt. Some engines may have bolts of three or four different lengths. If some of your head bolts screw into the water jacket, apply a light coating of thread seal-

6 Tighten to half torque first, then full. Remove the carb, if needed, to use socket wrench.

ant to the threads of these. Run the bolts down with a speed handle until they're just touching the head. Then, starting with the center bolt and working your way out in a clockwise circle, tighten all the bolts to half the head bolt torque spec.

When every bolt has been torqued, repeat the process, tightening each to an amount 50 percent higher than the first figure. Finally, torque all bolts, in sequence, to the final figure. For example, if the head torque spec is 80 lb./ft., torque the heads to 40 lb./ft., then 60 lb./ft., and finally 80 lb./ft.

Install the intake manifold next. If your manifold doubles as a valley cover, attach the end seals to the block with heavy-duty, fast-drying adhesive, like 3M 8001 weather-stripping cement. Allow the adhesive time to dry before installing the manifold.

Apply silicone gasket sealer on top of the seals before carefully lowering the manifold in place. Lube the manifold bolts, then torque

them in sequence (Fig. 6) to half the specified figure, then full tightness.

Lube the valve train parts with engine oil and install them, tightening fasteners to the torque specs indicated.

Most engines with hydraulic lifters require no valve lash adjustment. However, some with ball-and-socket rockers do require adjustment. On engines with rocker stands you may have to shim the stands if the heads were resurfaced, by an amount equal to what was removed from the heads.

Install the valve covers, taking care not to overtighten the bolts. Attach all vacuum lines and wires, then reinstall all accessories. If you removed the distributor, position it according to your reference marks with the rotor pointing to the mark for the No. 1 cylinder. Fill the engine with new antifreeze mixed 50/50 with water. Then, after starting the engine, check the timing with a timing light.

If the engine runs rough after the timing has been corrected, make

7 Adjustment procedures for ball-and-socket rockers differ; read the shop manual.

sure that the rocker arms are allowing the valves to close when the lifters are on the base circle of the cam. If they're not, adjust or shim accordingly.

After the engine has warmed fully, allow it to cool completely, then remove the valve covers and retorque the heads to the final spec. Do this again after driving the car for 500 miles.

How to Solve
OIL PRESSURE PROBLEMS

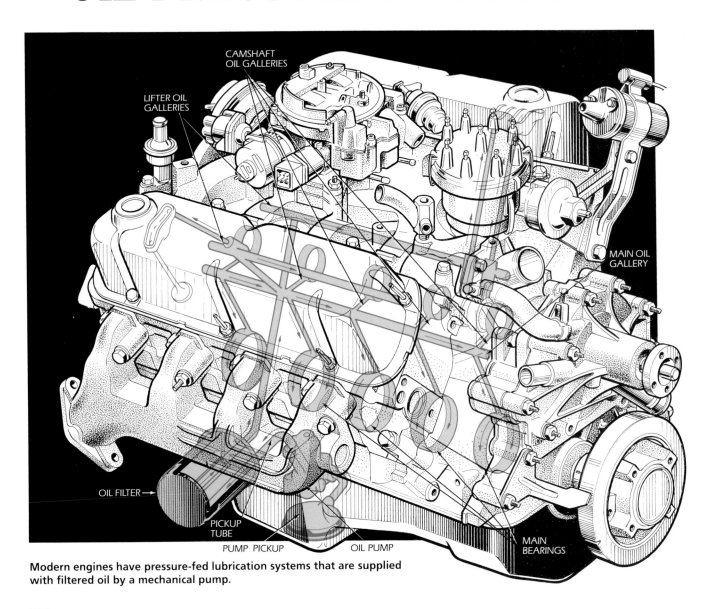

CAMSHAFT
OIL GALLERIES

LIFTER OIL
GALLERIES

MAIN OIL
GALLERY

OIL FILTER →

PICKUP
TUBE

PUMP PICKUP

OIL PUMP

MAIN
BEARINGS

Modern engines have pressure-fed lubrication systems that are supplied with filtered oil by a mechanical pump.

The first thing you notice might be the soft glow of an idiot light when your engine is idling. Or perhaps the needle of your oil pressure gauge has begun to drop out of the safe range. Or maybe you've just noticed that your engine ticks and clatters much more than it used to. They're all clues that could point to an oil pressure problem. If you don't act right away, extensive engine damage can result.

A magnified view of an engine's crankshaft journal and bearing sur-faces makes it very easy to under-stand why a loss of lubricant can be so critical. Although these surfaces appear completely smooth to the naked eye, they're actually covered with little peaks and valleys. If the journal and bearing come into di-rect contact at high speed, the re-sulting friction quickly generates heat that can cause the metal parts to seize.

On the other hand, if these mov-ing parts are separated by a film of lubricant, the sliding friction is re-placed by fluid friction. Because the molecules of the lubricant move freely when they encounter high or low spots on the machined parts, they offer little resistance to move-ment. Consequently, heat genera-tion is minimized, protecting the surfaces.

DELIVERING THE LUBE

Modern automobile engines are equipped with a full-force lubrica-tion system that pumps oil to most

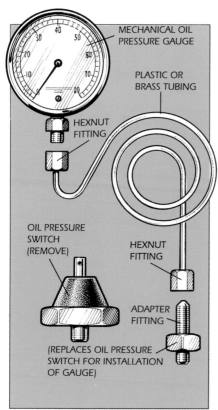

1 To read the actual engine oil pressure, install a mechanical gauge in place of the stock idiot light or indicator.

moving parts (see illustration on page 145). Oil is drawn into a pump through a mesh screen submerged in the oil pan.

In most systems, the pressurized oil is first pumped through the filter. The filter or filter mount is equipped with a bypass valve so flow will not be interrupted if the filter clogs.

The filtered oil is then pumped into the main oil gallery. Oil is usually supplied to hydraulic lifters and main bearings by means of passages connected to this gallery. Oil routed to the lifters is then directed up to the rest of the valve train, via a separate passage or through the pushrods. Main bearing lube travels through drilled passages in the crankshaft journals to the connecting rod bearings. Oil spray from between the connecting rod pairs, or in some cases, from a small passage in one side of each rod cap, lubricates the cylinder walls and piston pins.

Low oil pressure is the result of problems in the pump or delivery circuit. If the pump can't supply enough oil to fill the galleries, pressure will be low. If there is an overly large opening in the circuit that allows oil to escape too easily, low oil pressure will result. Improper oil viscosity or oil dilution can also make pressure readings drop below spec, as pump efficiency is dramatically affected by the thickness of the lube.

CHECKING OIL PRESSURE

If you feel that your engine's oil pressure is lower than it should be, you can confirm your suspicions with a remote gauge.

Purchase a mechanical-type oil pressure gauge and installation kit from an auto parts store (Fig. 1). The installation kit will include a number of pipe fitting adapters, one of which can be installed in your engine in place of the idiot light switch. If your car already has an oil pressure gauge, install the adapter in place of the stock gauge sending unit. The pressure test will confirm the low reading of your stock gauge.

Manufacturers' specifications for oil pressure vary. To be absolutely sure that your engine's lube system is operating reasonably close to full capacity, you should check oil pressure test specs for your car in a general service manual or in the vehicle manufacturer's manual.

Generally, two figures are given, one for idle oil pressure and one for 2,000-rpm pressure. In most cases, your pump should be able to provide about 10 psi at idle with a fully warmed engine and 25 psi or more at 2,000 rpm. Some makers, however, call for considerably more pressure.

If your test finds that oil pressure is okay but the idiot light continues to glow, replace the oil warning light switch. If a new switch doesn't turn the light off, check the oil light switch circuit for problems.

SOLVING LOW-PRESSURE PROBLEMS

If you found that oil pressure was below the recommended figure at idle but within the acceptable range at higher speeds, check the engine idle speed. It may be below specs.

Oil pressure that is somewhat low at one or both test points can be caused by motor oil that is of incorrect viscosity or has been diluted with gasoline. Try an oil change, using the manufacturer's recommended oil viscosity for the weather conditions.

If the oil change solves your pressure problems and you find that the drained oil is heavily diluted with

2 Oil pan removal may be blocked by steering linkage, requiring the engine to be jacked up. Attach gaskets and seals securely before reinstalling.

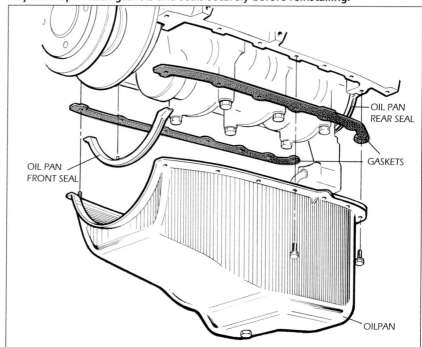

gasoline, find the cause of the dilution before putting the car back in service. It may have been caused by an engine misfire that allowed unburned fuel to run down past the rings, or, on carbureted cars, it may be the result of a ruptured fuel pump diaphragm.

A clogged oil filter can also cause a loss of pressure. If your filter has been on the car for more than a few thousand miles, change it and re-test.

PULLING THE OIL PAN

Having eliminated simple causes, further diagnosis requires removal of the oil pan on most powerplants (Fig. 2). On some engines, however, the oil pump is externally mounted and can be checked without removing the pan. If this is the case on your engine, proceed to the section headlined "Checking the oil pump."

On some cars, oil pan removal is a simple task, but on most it is quite difficult and may involve loosening the engine mounts and jacking or lifting the engine. The starter motor or other components may have to be removed to get to the pan bolts.

Specific instructions for oil pan removal are found in both general service manuals and vehicle manufacturer manuals. On some "short skirt" type engines, the pan will have to be dropped more than a few inches before it will clear the main caps, crank counterweights, and oil pump.

CHECKING THE OIL PUMP

If your engine suffered a total loss of oil pressure, the cause is most likely a broken oil pump drive.

Most oil pumps are driven by a shaft that joins the pump to the distributor drive gear or by an intermediate shaft that is fitted with a gear and driven by the cam. If the drive mechanism breaks, a total loss of oil pressure will be the result. Another possible cause of total oil pressure loss is a missing oil gallery plug.

In addition to the simple causes mentioned previously, partial loss of pressure can be the result of a worn pump, a clogged pump pickup, a hole in the pickup tube, a broken tube, or excessive bearing clearance. Less likely causes for partial loss of pressure include leaking gal-

lery plugs and porous block castings.

Since you have to remove the oil pan on most engines to check any of the more likely causes, you ought to check all of them before buttoning up. On high-mileage engines, low pressure is frequently caused by a combination of pump and bearing wear.

Once the pan is off, remove the pump from the engine. It's held in place on the block or on a main bearing cap by one or more bolts (Fig. 3). In most cases, the pickup tube is attached only to the pump, although on some engines it may be retained by a bolt. On engines with external pumps, the pickup is usually bolted to a machined surface inside the crankcase.

If the pickup tube is pressed into the pump, leave it in place. If it's pinned or bolted to the pump, remove it for inspection. Examine the pickup and pickup tube for possible air leaks. Check also if there is clogging of the pickup screen.

Disassemble the oil pump by re-

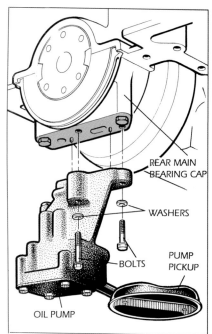

3 Most oil pumps are located inside the pan, bolted to a main bearing cap. Torque to correct spec when reinstalling.

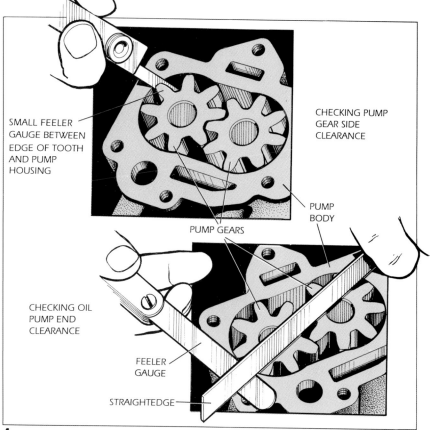

4 On spur-gear-type pumps, critical clearances to be checked are those between the gear edge and housing, and between gear ends and the bottom plate of the pump.

147

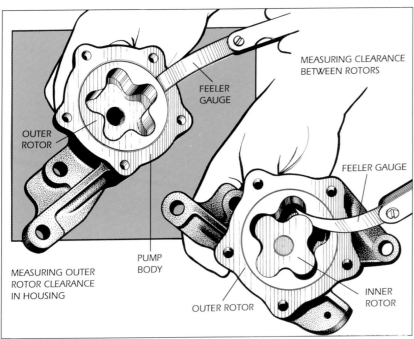

MEASURING CLEARANCE BETWEEN ROTORS

FEELER GAUGE

OUTER ROTOR

MEASURING OUTER ROTOR CLEARANCE IN HOUSING

PUMP BODY

FEELER GAUGE

OUTER ROTOR

INNER ROTOR

5 Lobed rotor-and-ring-type oil pumps must have clearances checked between the outer rotor and pump body, and between the inner and outer rotor lobes.

moving its bottom cover. Hold the pump in a vise between two pieces of wood or brass jaws. On some engines that have externally mounted pumps, the cover (as well as the gears and relief valve) can be removed without unbolting the pump from the engine.

On the pump cover or body, you'll probably find a hexhead or expansion cup plug. The pump relief valve and spring are installed behind this plug. Remove the plug, valve, and spring, and check to see how the valve moves in its bore. If you find that it is stuck in its bore or fits so loosely that you can move it sideways any discernible amount, it could be the problem. Replace the valve and the pump or cover as necessary.

If your oil-pressure test found that pressure was okay at idle but lower than specified at a higher speed, a weak relief valve spring might be the source of your trouble. Some manufacturers provide a specification for relief valve spring length. (A weak spring will be shorter than a good one.) Measure your spring and compare it to spec.

Under the pump cover, you'll find the pumping mechanism. Two types are commonly used. One utilizes a driven, lobed inner rotor that turns

a surrounding lobed ring or outer rotor. The other variety uses two spur-type gears, one of which is attached to the driveshaft.

Inspect the gears, pump cover, and pump body for signs of wear and scoring. Obvious damage is grounds for replacement. If you're in doubt about pump condition, check clearances with a feeler gauge.

To check a spur-gear-type pump, measure clearance between the top of the gears and the pump body's gasket surface using a straightedge (small steel ruler) and a feeler gauge (Fig. 4). Lay the edge of the rule across the gasket surface and insert the feeler gauge between it and the gears. You'll find specifications in a service manual. Using a narrow feeler gauge, check clearance between the edge of the pump gear and the pump body.

If your car is equipped with a lobed rotor-and-ring-type pump, you should at least check clearance between the center rotor and the pump body gasket surface, between the outer rotor and case, and between the inner rotor lobes and outer rotor lobes (Fig. 5). Chrysler also provides specs for checks of cover flatness, rotor thickness, and outer rotor diameter.

Measure clearance between the center rotor and gasket surface with a straightedge and rule. Check clearance between the high points of the two rotors and between the outer rotor and the pump body with a feeler gauge. For the 2.2-liter Chrysler, the specs are .01 in. (maximum) and .014 in. (maximum), respectively.

Check cover flatness with a rule and feeler gauge, laying the side of the rule across the center of the cover and inserting the feeler gauge into any low spots below it. If the pump is not up to spec, it must be replaced.

Before reinstalling a spur-gear-type pump, pack the gear cavity tightly with petroleum jelly. Fill lobe-and-ring-type pumps with motor oil.

CHECKING BEARING CLEARANCE

As bearing clearance gradually increases because of normal wear, the lube oil escapes more easily from the force-fed circuit and pressure drops. Because some of the lube escapes prematurely, certain parts don't get enough. If main bearing clearance, for example, is excessive, the rod bearing oil supply will be inadequate.

The bearing clearances of an assembled engine can be checked using a plastic gauging material (Fig. 6). This product, which is best known by Perfect Circle's trade name Plastigage, will provide accurate measurement of bearing oil

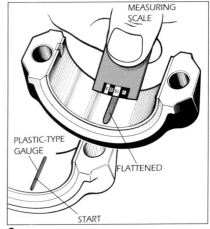

MEASURING SCALE

PLASTIC-TYPE GAUGE

FLATTENED

START

6 Plastic clearance gauge starts out round, is crushed flat when bearing cap is torqued.

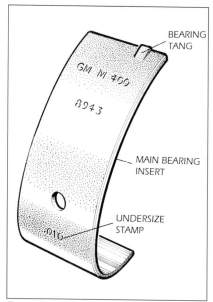

7 Back side of the bearing insert is stamped to indicate undersize dimension.

clearance when it's crushed between the bearing and the crankshaft (Perfect Circle, Dana Corp., P.O. Box 455, Toledo, Ohio, 43692). Purchase two different sizes of the material at an auto parts store so you can measure clearances from .002 in. to .006 in.

To check main-bearing clearance, remove main caps two and four (on five-main-bearing engines) or two, four, and six (on seven-main-bearing engines). Insert paper shims that are at least .010 in. thick between these bearings and the crank and reinstall the caps. This will lift the crank off the other bearings to check clearance.

Remove each of the other bearing caps one at a time and wipe all oil from journal and bearing. Then, place a piece of the gauging material on the center of the bearing in such a way that it spans the width of the bearing. Install the cap, torque it to spec, and remove it without turning the crank. Now, compare the crushed strip of gauging material to the scale on the package. This will give you the clearance figure.

If the strip is so wide that it's off the scale, or if it hasn't been flattened at all, use a different-size gauging strip to get an accurate reading.

Check clearance of the other main bearings in the same way. Then, move your paper shims to journals one and five or one and seven and check the clearance of the bearings that previously supported the shims. Record all the numbers on a piece of paper, along with the part numbers and any size indication on the bearings (Fig. 7).

Check rod bearing clearance in a similar manner. Remove rod caps one at a time. Place the gauging strip on the rod cap bearing and reinstall, torquing to spec.

If you have a micrometer, check the rod throws for taper and out-of-round by measuring each throw at both ends and at points on the circumference that are 90° apart.

Compare your figures to manufacturer's specs. If rod journal taper or out-of-round are in excess of what the manufacturer allows, the engine will have to be rebuilt.

However, if the crankshaft is otherwise okay, but clearance is in excess of manufacturer's allowance, you can probably tighten it up by replacing the bearings with "undersize" bearings. (Undersize bearings are actually larger than standard; they're called undersize because they're for use with undersize cranks.)

For most applications, bearings are sold in standard as well as .010- and .020-in. undersize. In each of these sizes, bearings can be purchased with an additional .001-in. or .002-in. undersize. The extra bearing material makes up for too much clearance.

Determine which bearings you need by calculating how much the present clearance exceeds ideal specified tolerances. Go to the parts store armed with bearing part numbers and any undersize indication that may have been found on the back of the bearings. A knowledgeable counterman will have no trouble helping you choose the proper replacements for your crankshaft's bearings.

After installing the new bearings, check all clearances again. Check all rod and main bolt torque readings twice, and reinstall the oil pan.

How to Cure
EXCESSIVE OIL
CONSUMPTION

Y ou push on the throttle when the light turns green. A cloud of noxious blue smoke quickly forms behind you. The six or seven cans of oil that are in your trunk roll toward the rear and bang against the bulkhead. Your fellow motorists hurl insults at you as they pass by. The nation's petroleum reserve is in jeopardy.

Some oil consumption problems are the result of serious engine damage—like holes in pistons, for example. But similarly severe oil loss can be caused by relatively simple problems and can be fixed just as simply.

OUTY OR INNY?

The first step is to get down on the ground and have a good look at your parking space. If there's a puddle of oil, you can assume that at least some of your difficulty is caused by an external leak.

If you don't find any oil on the ground, inspect the underside of your car. If everything rear of the engine is coated with wet oil, suspect a gusher that only activates when the engine is running. But make sure you don't confuse leaking trans oil or differential oil with engine oil.

If, on the other hand, your engine's leak is internal, oil will be drawn into the combustion chamber when you drive and your car will smoke. When will it smoke?

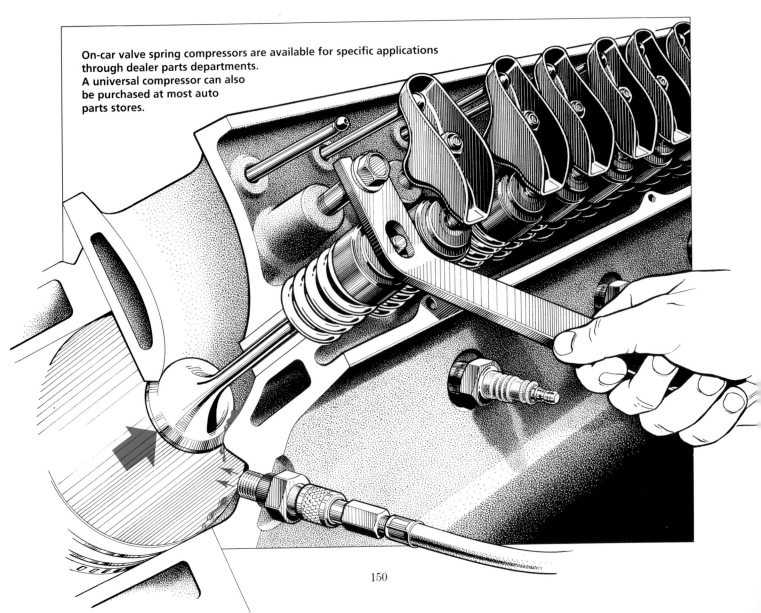

On-car valve spring compressors are available for specific applications through dealer parts departments. A universal compressor can also be purchased at most auto parts stores.

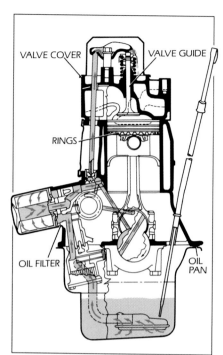

There are plenty of potential internal and external leakage points on an engine.

Perhaps at idle, when accelerating, when decelerating, after long periods of idle, or right at startup. Pinpointing the driving condition that generates smoke can help you track down the cause.

INTERNAL LEAKS

Smoke is the most obvious symptom of internal oil consumption, but not the only one. Oil mixing with the air/fuel charge can cause spark knock. And, when the engine operates low on oil much of the time, clicking and clacking noises—along with accelerated wear—will result.

There are several ways that oil can get into the combustion chamber: through the valve guides, the piston rings, the PCV system, or past a blown head gasket. On some engines, particularly V8s where the intake manifold does double duty as a valley cover, oil can leak past the intake manifold gaskets.

Here's where that smoke can help you shorten the list. If your tailpipe smokes only when the car is first started after several hours at rest, valve guides are probably the culprit. Ditto if the smoke belches out only when the engine is first accelerated after extended idling.

If the engine smokes throughout the rpm range, worn or stuck oil rings are the likely cause.

Although these rules can help you narrow down an oil-consumption problem, they aren't hard and fast. For example, as guide wear increases, smoke may be obvious at all speeds and loads.

Removing all the spark plugs may help you localize the problem. What you're looking for are the heavy, black, oily deposits that indicate oil consumption. If they're limited to one or two cylinders, you can focus your troubleshooting on those cylinders.

PCV SYSTEM

The PCV system allows crankcase gases to escape to the intake manifold where they are drawn into the engine and oxidized. One PCV system hose joins the PCV valve and engine crankcase (via the rocker cover on most applications). The PCV valve is connected to the intake manifold. On some systems, the valve may be located at the rocker cover end of the hose, but its function is the same.

Under high engine-vacuum conditions, such as idle or light load, crankcase gases flow through the PCV valve into the intake manifold. On most PCV systems, a second hose connects the crankcase (again via the rocker cover) to the engine air cleaner. In many cases, a small separate filter is provided for the PCV hose. This hose allows fresh air to be drawn into the crankcase as the gases are purged.

If the PCV valve clogs, crankcase gases won't be purged, pressure will build up, and oil may be pushed back up the fresh-air hose into the air cleaner. In some cases, the high crankcase pressure may allow oil to be pushed past oil rings that might otherwise be adequate.

You can check the PCV valve by disconnecting it from the crankcase end, starting the engine, and checking for vacuum at the valve with the engine idling. Next, remove the valve from its hose and shake it. You should hear a rattling sound. If you don't feel vacuum at the valve and/or the valve won't rattle, replace it and check the hose for obstruction. Since the valve is quite inexpensive, it might be a good idea to replace it in any case. (Always replace the PCV valve at your 15,000-mile maintenance intervals.)

If the PCV system continues to deliver an excessive amount of engine oil to the air cleaner even when the PCV valve is functioning correctly, it may be that the engine's compression rings have worn to the extent that the crankcase is over-pressurized. A cranking compression or leakdown test can help you verify this.

Valve Guide and Seal Failure

Even if smoke emissions suggest that your problem is a likely case of oil-ring leakage, you'll probably want to check the valve guides and valve seals first as this can be accomplished without removing the cylinder heads.

The valve guides are the bush-

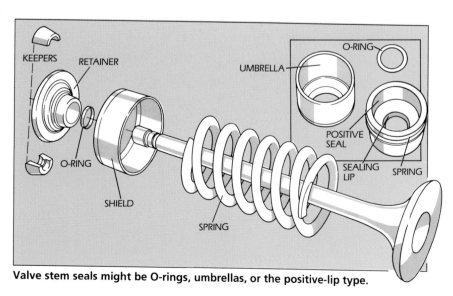

Valve stem seals might be O-rings, umbrellas, or the positive-lip type.

151

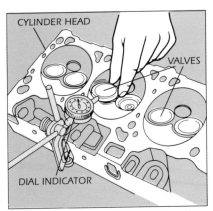

Measure valve guide clearance on the chamber side of the head with a dial indicator.

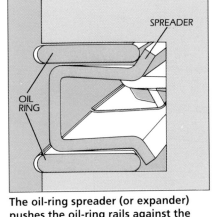

The oil-ring spreader (or expander) pushes the oil-ring rails against the cylinder wall.

ings that support the intake and exhaust valve stems. When the valves open and close, they slide up and down in the valve guides. The valve seals limit the amount of oil that reaches the top of the guide. Both guide wear and seal failure will allow oil to enter the combustion chamber via the guides.

There are two ways to check valve guides and seals. One way requires removal and disassembly of the cylinder head(s). The other easier way is an on-the-car method. To do the job the easy way, you'll need an air compressor and a spark-plug hole/air chuck adapter. This last item plugs into an air hose disconnected on one side and screws into the spark-plug hole on the other side. This allows you to pressurize each cylinder while you remove the valve keepers and retainer to check the seal and guide.

In addition to the compressor and adapter, you'll need a new rocker cover (or cam cover) gasket, a set of engine valve seals, some quick-drying gasket adhesive, and some nonhardening gasket adhesive.

You'll also need an on-the-engine valve spring compressor. There are several types available. Some are specific to a certain type of engine. Others are universal. Most auto parts stores carry this tool.

To check the guide, carefully re-route or disconnect any wiring or tubing that might interfere with rocker cover removal. Tag any lines that you disconnect, so you'll be able to reconnect them properly.

Remove the rocker cover(s) and screw the air hose adapter into the first spark-plug hole. (If you've isolated the problem to certain cylinders, you can move right to those locations.) With the adapter in place, turn the engine until that cylinder is at Top Dead Center (the highest point of piston travel) on its compression stroke. You can tell when the cylinder is approaching Top Dead Center/compression stroke because air will come shooting out of the adapter. When the airflow stops, you've reached approximate Top Dead Center, which is close enough for our purposes here.

On cam-in-block engines or overhead-cam engines with rocker-arm actuated valves, remove the rocker arms from the first cylinder's valves. On some engines, including most domestic V8s, this is merely a matter of unscrewing the jam nut from the shaft that supports the rocker. On other engines, you'll have to unbolt a rocker shaft that supports the rocker arms for the entire bank of cylinders.

On overhead-cam engines where the cam is positioned directly above the valves, you'll have to disengage the timing belt or chain and remove the cam. Procedures vary widely here. Consult your service manual for specific cam removal instructions.

Once rocker arms or camshafts are out of the way and you can see the top of the valves, connect your air compressor hose to the adapter. If the engine turns because of air pressure pushing down on the piston, you'll have to hold the crankshaft in place with a wrench on the front pulley bolt or with a screwdriver wedged against the flywheel ring gear. A helping hand may be necessary here.

With the cylinder pressurized, tap the retainer of the intake valve with a worn socket and hammer, locating the socket over the end of the valve stem in such a way that it contacts the retainer but not the keepers. Compress the valve spring and retainer with the compression tool and remove the keepers. Use needle-nose pliers if your fingers are too big to grasp them. Make sure you don't drop a keeper into the engine.

Once the keepers have been extracted, remove the valve spring and retainer. Air pressure will prevent

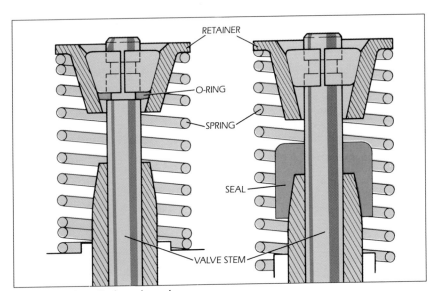

O-rings are installed on the valve stem, and umbrellas or lip seals fit over the guide.

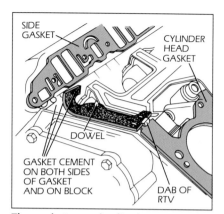

The gasket must be firmly cemented to the block before installing the manifold.

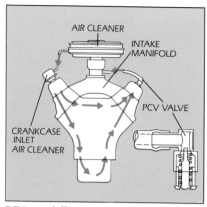

PCV can deliver engine oil to air cleaner if the valve fails to purge the crankcase.

the valve from dropping into the cylinder.

Examine the valve stem seal. If it's an umbrella stem seal, you'll find it on top of the valve guide. If it's an O-ring seal, it should be in the second groove on the valve stem, just below the keepers. In either case, the seal should be soft and pliable. If it's hard or cracked, it may be the cause of your oil-consumption problem. Upon reassembly, replace all valve stem seals.

To check the intake guide, release the air pressure from the cylinder while holding the top of the valve stem. Be careful. If you drop the valve, you might have to disassemble the engine to retrieve it. Try wiggling the valve stem back and forth. If it moves a visible amount, the guides are excessively worn, and the heads will have to be removed for guide replacement and grinding of the valve seats.

If you're not sure whether clearance is excessive, mount a dial indicator perpendicular to the valve stem and wiggle the stem. A typical intake valve specification calls for 0.001- to 0.003-in. valve stem clearance from the factory. The high-end tolerance for used parts is about 0.004 in. on most engines.

Check the exhaust guides in a similar manner, but note that exhaust guides are usually engineered with a bit more clearance than the intakes. Here, a slight amount of lateral movement is okay. More than 0.005-in. clearance is excessive on most applications.

If the guides are okay, reinstall all valve train parts with a new valve seal. If your engine is equipped with

O-ring-type seals, you can push them into the proper groove with a keeper half before the split keepers are installed. If you found cracked or broken seals, they could be the sole cause of even serious oil consumption.

Attach the rocker cover or cam cover gasket to the cover with fast-drying adhesive. Apply nonhardening gasket compound to the engine side of the gasket before installing.

If you found excessive guide wear, the head(s) will have to be removed for guide replacement and valve-seat grinding. (Because the guides locate the valves in respect to the seat, you can't replace the guides without grinding the seats.)

OIL RINGS

Once you're certain that an internal oil-loss problem isn't due to some simpler cause, you may have to bite the bullet and consider the oil rings. But before you do, perform a quick compression test with a handheld gauge. Crank each cylinder four or five times with all plugs removed and compare readings. If one cylinder is way off (and one spark plug was oil soaked), you might be looking at a blown head gasket, a hole in a piston, broken rings, or other major damage.

If all cylinders are quite low, both the compression rings and oil rings may be worn. As noted earlier, worn compression rings can cause oil loss through the PCV system and/or past seals and marginal gaskets.

If all cylinders are okay, you may still have worn oil rings. Oil rings sometimes fail (or stick) before the compression rings are worn out, and bad oil rings can help mask bad compression rings by providing plenty of lube to seal the gaps.

Of course the only cure for worn oil and/or compression rings is an engine rebuild, but sticky oil rings can sometimes be loosened. If you want to give it a try, fill the crankcase with SAE 10W oil and a thin oil additive meant to free sticking lifters and oil rings. (Don't use a viscosity booster.)

Drive the car for at least thirty minutes. If engine temperature doesn't reach the maximum end of the allowable range, cover part of the radiator with a piece of paper. Before the engine cools down, drain the oil and refill with your normal engine oil, such as a 10W-30. This treatment is somewhat hard on the engine, but when a total rebuild is your only alternative, it may be worth a try.

EXTERNAL LEAKS

If you're simply losing oil rather than burning it, the fix may be less expensive. But it can be equally difficult.

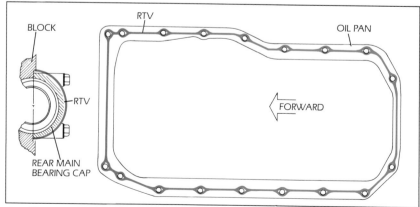

A uniform, unbroken bead of RTV must be applied inside of the bolt holes.

Because there are so many locations from which oil can leak, it's sometimes hard to find the gusher.

If the oil drip is evident while the car is parked, wash the underside of your car with soap and a high-pressure hose to remove the oil that has probably been blown all over the underside of your car while driving. Then, clean your engine with one of the commercially available engine cleaners. You may have to apply the cleaner several times to clean a really filthy engine. Make sure you protect all electronic parts with plastic bags.

With engine and undercar clean, cover your garage floor or driveway with white paper. Engine oil leaks will leave dirty spots. Automatic trans fluid leaks will leave pink or light brown spots. You can usually locate the leak by concentrating on the area right above the spot on the paper. Likely sources include rocker or cam covers, timing cover, oil pan, fuel pump gaskets, and, where applicable, intake manifold end seals. This last location is found only on some V-type engines where the intake manifold seals the valley, an arrangement that is seemingly quite prone to leakage. This is particularly true in cases where the manifold has been removed for service, as the end seals can be quite difficult to install.

If normal methods fail to uncover a leak, try a black-light kit. This oil-detection device comes with a fluorescent oil additive. You simply add the fluorescent stuff and let her leak. Once the oil with additive has leaked, you aim the black light at various locations until the glowing oil can be seen.

Quite a few engines use RTV sealants in place of regular gaskets in some oil-sealing locations. Bathtub caulk is for bathtubs—get an RTV sealer intended for automotive use at the auto parts store. Apply a continuous bead inside of the component's bolt holes.

Some gasket makers supply a conventional gasket for certain applications that were originally RTV from the factory. In many cases, the gasket provides a superior seal. If an RTV joint has failed, you might ask your auto parts counterman whether or not a conventional gasket is available.

How to Reseal a
LEAKY ENGINE

Drip, drip, drip, drip. Day and night, week after week, your car works tirelessly, trying to create a small-scale replica of the La Brea tar pits on your garage floor. Where is the oil coming from?

You've tried tightening engine and transmission oil pan bolts. You've replaced the valve cover gaskets and manifold end seals. You've checked the oil filter's O-ring seal. You've searched for easy-fix solutions, but no luck. The oil, blown by the wind when you drive, drips from just about everywhere in the general vicinity of your engine, as well as coating the back end of your car—and the front

ends of those behind you—with small droplets of oil.

After investing a pocketful of quarters at the local car wash to clean the engine, you're able to localize the leak. The source of all that yuck is a leaking front or rear crankshaft seal.

It's time to bite the bullet and dedicate an afternoon or two of messy, but reasonably simple, repair effort to the cause of keeping the oil in the pan. (Replacement of front and rear crankshaft seals does vary somewhat from car to car, so you may have to consult the manufacturer's factory service manual for specifics.)

CRANKCASE FRONT COVER SEAL REMOVAL

The seal on the front of the crankshaft is usually the more reliable of the two crank end seals. But it does fail, and replacement is relatively easy on rear-drive cars. On many front drivers, it requires lifting—or even removal of—the engine and may be a job best left to a pro. The 2.2-liter and 2.5-liter Chrysler engines require special tools for seal removal.

On some rear-drive cars, the radiator is so close to the front pulley and drive belts that you'll want to remove it before attempting to serv-

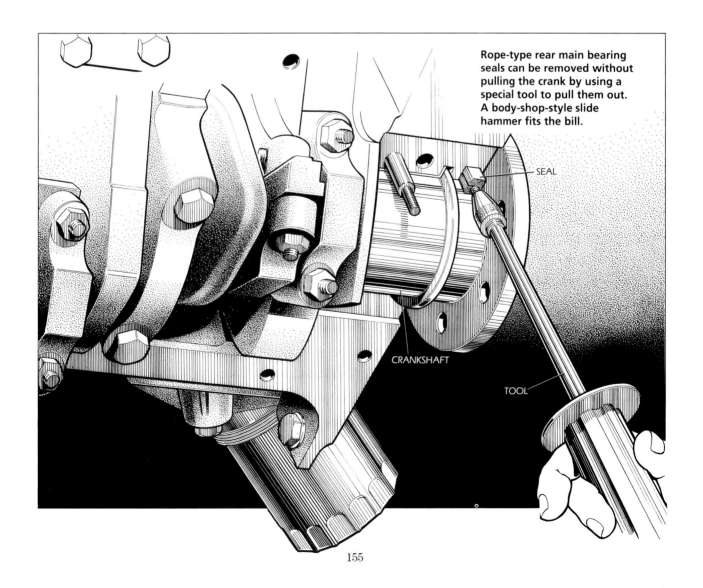

Rope-type rear main bearing seals can be removed without pulling the crank by using a special tool to pull them out. A body-shop-style slide hammer fits the bill.

SEAL

CRANKSHAFT

TOOL

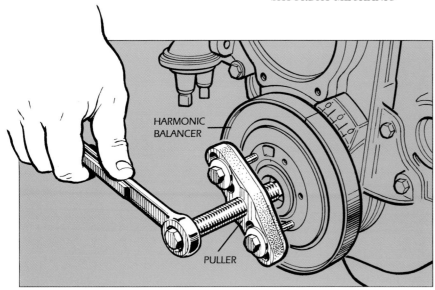

1 A hub puller for removing the crankshaft hub can be rented from auto parts stores.

ice the crankshaft seal. On others, you can do the job with radiator in place. On most cars, you'll have to remove the fan shroud. On many applications, you'll be able to remove and replace the seal without removing the front crankcase cover, or timing cover, as it's frequently called.

Begin by removing the fan, drivebelts, and crankshaft pulley. The pulley is usually secured to the heavy crankshaft harmonic balancer—that big round wheel on the front of the crank—by several small bolts. This balancer is sometimes called a harmonic damper, and on other vehicles it's not used at all. There's simply a pulley or hub that bolts onto the crankshaft directly.

On some cars, you'll have to remove the water pump to provide good access to the balancer and seal. Whatever you have, we'll be referring to it as a hub, and it's got to come off. Once the pulley is off, remove the retaining bolt. That's the big bolt in the middle. On stick-shift cars, you can put the transmission in gear and apply the parking brake to keep the crank from turning while you wrench the bolt off.

On automatics, try wedging a big pry bar in the transmission torque plate (flywheel) after removing the trans bellhousing dust cover. If there is no dust cover, look for an access hole on the engine side of the trans bellhousing. If you have a big air compressor and a ½-in.-drive im-

pact wrench, you can usually spin the bolt off without holding the engine.

You'll probably need a hub puller (Fig. 1). A puller designed specifically for this purpose can be purchased at most auto parts stores. Some stores will rent the tool.

Install the puller on the hub with the two or three bolts provided. Once the bolts have been threaded well into the hub, turn the shaft screw in to remove the hub.

Inspect the area of the hub that rides against the seal. If it's worn or grooved, you'll need a new hub.

Pry the seal out of the cover with a large screwdriver (Fig. 2). *Don't* scratch the crankshaft surface. Find an object that you can use to drive the seal into the cover. It should contact the outer metal portion of the seal all the way around. A used disc-brake piston works on some applications, but a pipe fitting, large socket, or even a piece of wood will do.

CRANKCASE FRONT COVER SEAL INSTALLATION

Be sure the seal's bore is clean and free of burrs. Oil the outer diameter of the seal lightly to ease the way. Don't use gasket sealer, RTV, or anything else but clean oil. Lightly tap the seal in, with the spring/lip side inside.

Generally, seals are installed with the part numbers legible from the outside, as is the case here. If you've got it started straight, no problem. But if there's a burr, or you start it crooked, you stand the chance of tearing the rubber coating off the metal insert. It'll still seal to the rotating crankshaft, but oil will seep between the timing cover and the seal body almost as fast as the old seal leaked it. However you do it, push the seal home until it sets flush with the appropriate lip in the bore. That's probably also flush with the surface of the timing cover. But you may want to measure the seal and the bore beforehand to get an idea of how deep it's supposed to go.

Align the hub keyway with the crankshaft key and reinstall the hub on the crankshaft. Don't pound on the outer area of the hub. You could knock it off-center and cause an out-of-balance condition. If you have to beat the hub back on, use

2 Use a large screwdriver to carefully pry the seal out of the front cover.

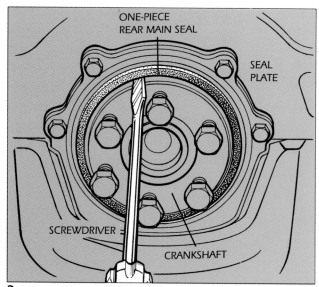

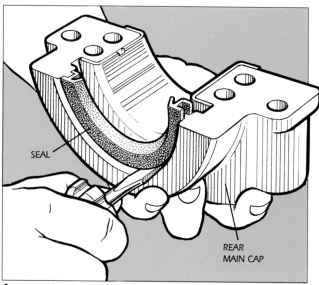

3 A one-piece rear main seal can usually be pried out with a screwdriver without removing the seal plate.

4 Pry lower half of rear main seal from the cap with a small screwdriver.

discretion and tap lightly near the center using a wooden block and alternating from side to side. Check for burrs and misaligned keyways if it seems like there's too much effort involved. A light film of grease might help.

Better yet, use a hub puller that can also be used as a hub installer. This will make sure the thing is started on straight, which is most of the battle.

ONE-PIECE REAR MAIN SEAL REMOVAL AND REPLACEMENT

Some engines, including the GM 2.0-liter and 2.5-liter four-cylinder engines, 2.8-liter and 3.1-liter six-cylinder engines, and the Chrysler 2.2-liter, 2.5-liter, and 2.6-liter four-cylinder engines, as well as most late-model Ford and GM engines, have a one-piece rear main seal that can only be accessed from the back of the engine. Thus, to service these seals, the transmission must be removed, a good-sized job.

If you do decide to brave removing the tranny, replacement of the seal itself is quite easy. Don't even attempt removal of an automatic transmission without a trans jack. This device can be rented from most tool rental stores.

Ramps or proper jack stands are a must here. Be sure to block the wheels, as well as setting the parking brake. You'll need to remove the

driveshaft, which obviates the use of PARK to keep the car from rolling off and squishing you.

Metal-jacketed one-piece rear main seals can be removed by punching a hole in the seal cover with a sharp awl. Then, screw a threaded slide hammer into the seal. Yank the assembly out of the block. If there's not enough metal to allow for the use of a slide hammer, pry the seal out with a screwdriver, but take care not to scratch the crankshaft's seal surface (Fig. 3). Some of these engines have a removable seal carrier that can be unbolted from the block to allow you to replace the seal while standing up comfortably at a proper workbench, rather than lying on your back in the driveway. Be sure to replace the gaskets or seals associated with the seal carrier, if you go this route.

Installing the new seal is similar to installing a front seal—you have to find a large round metal cup or similar object that will mate with the circumference of the seal. The seal is then tapped into its recess in the engine block.

Install the seal with lip or spring (if applicable) pointing toward the engine. Lubricate the seal with clean engine oil.

Most vehicle manufacturers provide a special tool for installation of the one-piece rear main seal. This tool locates on the back of the crank by means of dowel pins or bolts and pushes the new seal into its bore via

a screw-jack mechanism. Again, getting the seal started in straight is half the battle. Don't use sealer of any sort between the seal and the bore where it rests.

TWO-PIECE REAR MAIN SEAL REMOVAL

There are two types of two-piece rear main seals in use today. One type is called a rope seal, because the packing-type seal resembles a rope. The other type is a molded-rubber lip seal. Removal and replacement of molded-rubber seals is time-consuming, but not very difficult. Removal and replacement of the rope-type seal is a lot tougher, and sometimes not completely successful, unless the engine is completely disassembled.

Some manufacturers, however, specify a molded-rubber seal as replacement for the original rope seal. One such application is the Chrysler V8. At least one gasket manufacturer, on the other hand, recommends against this procedure, claiming that the manufacturing tolerances for rope-seal engines aren't accurate enough to ensure a good oil-tight job when the rope seal is replaced with a molded-rubber seal. We'd say that rather than trying to install a new rope seal—a job that's touch-and-go at best—we'd opt for using the recommended replacement molded-rubber seal.

You're going to start with the

157

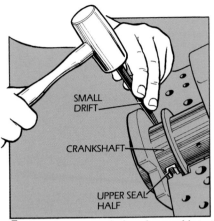 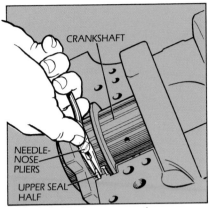

5 Tap the rear main bearing seal into the block (left), then tug on the protruding edge with needle-nose pliers while turning the crank to spin it out (right).

most difficult part of this job: oil pan removal. The parts you have to remove to get the pan off vary somewhat from car to car, but you can tell by crawling under there and eyeballing the situation. You should also consult your factory manual, which will provide a detailed list of everything that has to come off first. On all cars, you should start by disconnecting the negative battery cable.

On most Chevy V8 applications, for example, you'll continue by removing the air cleaner and the upper fan shroud.

Next, block the rear wheels, check to make sure the transmission is in PARK or in gear if it's a manual. Then raise the vehicle and support it securely on ramps or jack stands in factory-recommended jacking locations. Once it's up in the air, drain the oil pan.

On that Chevy, you'll have to disconnect the Air Injection Reactor (AIR) hose at the converter pipe. Then, disconnect the AIR pipe at the exhaust manifold. Remove the exhaust crossover pipe at the manifold and at the point where it joins the catalytic converter.

Remove the starter and the flywheel cover. Then, disconnect the transmission oil cooler lines at the transmission oil pan. Next, remove the engine mount bolts that run through the mounts from front to rear. This allows separation of the mount for lifting of the engine.

Unbolt the oil pan and lower it as far as possible. Turn the crank until the forward crankshaft throw and counterweight are tucked up into the block and not extending downward. Jack the engine up at the front of the trans bellhousing. Then, reinstall the engine mount through bolts under the mounts so that they hold the engine in a slightly elevated position. You now should be able to wiggle the oil pan out of there. On some vehicles, you may need to remove the crossmember or more of the exhaust system.

If the oil pump is mounted on the rear main bearing cap or in a position that interferes with access to the rear main bearing cap, you'll have to remove it. In most cases, this is just a matter of removing one or two bolts and lowering the pump and pump driveshaft.

Next, determine if the seal is in the rear main bearing cap or in a seal carrier behind the bearing cap. Then remove the main bearing cap or seal carrier. Pull the oil seal out of the bearing cap by prying it from below with a small screwdriver (Fig. 4). If the seal is in a seal carrier, there will be some other gaskets on the sides of the carrier. Remove these as well.

To remove the upper half of a molded-rubber rear main bearing seal, tap one edge with a small drift or screwdriver, pushing the edge of the seal up into the block. This will push the other edge of the seal out of the block. Tug on the protruding edge as you turn the crank and rotate the seal out of the engine block (Fig. 5).

To remove the upper half of a rope seal (which will be replaced with a molded-rubber replacement seal), screw the threaded end of a small slide hammer into one end of the seal and tug on the seal while you turn the crankshaft toward the slide hammer (see illustration on page 155). You can also try tapping on the opposite side of the seal with a drift that is almost as wide as the seal. On rebuilt engines, some rope seals are glued in place. If this is the case, you might be in for quite a struggle.

TWO-PIECE REAR MAIN SEAL INSTALLATION

Once the seal halves have been removed, clean all sealant and other junk from the bearing cap or seal carrier and the crankshaft. Inspect all surfaces for nicks or burrs that could interfere with the seal.

There are several types of tools intended to ease rope seal installation. You can make a sort of shoehorn out of shim stock to prevent nicking the seal. But it requires feeding the seal in carefully, turning the crank over while doing so, and has the danger of nicking the crank seal surface. Try to find the Chinese-handcuff type of tool that pulls the seal over the top of the crank. Coat the seal lips and bead with engine oil. Whichever tool you use, pull or push the seal around the crankshaft into the engine block. When the seal has been rolled all the way in and is flush with the block on both ends, remove the tool.

Install the other half of the seal in the bearing cap or seal carrier.

Install any additional gaskets as required. Glue them to the carrier with a gasket compound that dries fully (Fig. 6). After the gasket cement has dried, use an RTV engine gasket compound on the other side of the gaskets. Apply RTV sealant to the mating ends of the seal. Make

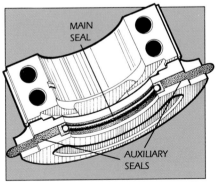

6 Some rear main bearing caps and seal carriers are grooved for auxiliary seals.

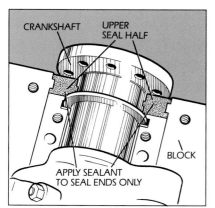

CRANKSHAFT UPPER SEAL HALF

BLOCK

APPLY SEALANT TO SEAL ENDS ONLY

7 Coat the mating ends of a two-piece rear main seal with RTV sealant.

sure you use high-temperature, oil-resistant RTV (Fig. 7). Install the rear main bearing cap or carrier and torque to the manufacturer's specification.

If the rear main bearing cap is the thrust bearing, tighten the cap to approximately 10 lb.-ft. initially and tap the crankshaft rearward and forward to align the thrust surfaces before torquing the bearing cap to full tightness. Check for proper end play after the cap is fully torqued.

Clean the oil pan and oil pump with solvent and a brush. Reinstall the pump with a new gasket.

Make sure the oil pan mating sur-faces are flat. If the area around each bolt hole protrudes, flatten it using a piece of wood and a brass hammer. When the pan is dry, glue the pan gaskets and seals in place with a quick-drying gasket compound. Apply a thin coat of RTV engine sealant to the top side of the pan gasket and seal, making sure that you fill any cracks between joints. Install the pan and torque the bolts to specification. Install all the pan bolts a few threads with your fingers before you tighten any of them, and then work side to side, tightening them gradually.

How to Check Out a TURBOCHARGER

Disassembling a turbocharger is pretty straightforward business—just be careful, as the slender turbine blades are fragile. If you're lucky, you'll be able to use an open-end wrench on the turbine end of the shaft.

It's your turn to ferry Mother-in-law to her weekly Mah-jongg night, and she's running late. Not a problem. You've got a turbo under the hood—just the ticket to make up a few extra minutes.

Suddenly, there's a buzzing noise. Power goes down, and a cloud of blue smoke goes up in your mirrors. What gives?

You've blown your turbo. Not only is Mom going to be late, you just *know* this is going to set your bank account back a few dragons. Say as much as $2,000, depending on the manufacturer and the dealer's parts department.

Take heart. All is not lost. In spite of their high-tech basis in thermodynamics, turbos are actually simple creatures. With some respect for the extremely close tolerances involved, it's possible to rescue many blown turbochargers, possibly for less than $100 and some simple hand labor.

THEORETICALLY

As you nail the throttle, hot exhaust gases rush through the exhaust (turbine) housing, spinning the turbine wheel with energy from the otherwise wasted heat in the exhaust. The turbine wheel is mounted on a shaft that drives a compressor wheel. The compressor takes air in through the air cleaner and pushes it into the intake manifold. This extra air causes intake manifold pres-

160

sure to be higher than without the extra push.

When the intake valves open, pressurized air rushes into the engine's cylinders while the carb or injection adds fuel to match. And your relatively small powerplant pumps out horsepower more typical of much larger engines.

Turbochargers operate under very taxing conditions. And failures are not uncommon. However, many total failures can be prevented if you recognize the symptoms early and do something about it. There are a number of symptoms that indicate possible turbocharger problems. We'll outline some of them here and then show you how to rebuild a turbocharger.

LOW BOOST

One common turbocharger problem is a lack of boost—first noticed as a loss of engine power at full throttle.

If your car is equipped with a boost gauge, as most turbocharged cars are, you'll immediately notice any drop in boost pressure. If your car is not equipped with a boost gauge, you can check boost by installing a pressure gauge tap in the intake manifold and routing a hose to the passenger cabin. Then, while driving the car at full throttle under heavy load, check the boost reading on the gauge. If it's significantly less than manufacturer's specs, you have a problem.

Before condemning the turbo, check for a clogged air filter, an obstruction or leak in the duct that joins the turbo's compressor outlet to the intake manifold, an intake manifold gasket leak, a leak or obstruction in the exhaust system, or a wastegate problem.

Wastegate leakage is a common cause of low boost pressure. The wastegate is a device that opens to divert exhaust at a predetermined level of boost to prevent overboosting. Wastegate leaks are usually caused by carbon accumulation around the wastegate itself. A weak or broken return spring or a defective wastegate control canister (wastegate actuator) can cause the wastegate to open too early, preventing full boost.

However, a control canister failure will usually result in overboost. And because overboost can cause serious detonation problems, it could damage your engine. Other

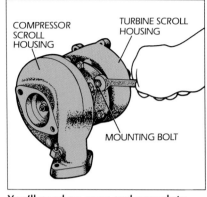

You'll need an open-end wrench to disassemble the scroll housings.

causes of wastegate-related overboost include an obstructed hose between the compressor and the control canister, a leaking canister, and a canister diaphragm failure.

On a lot of newer applications, the wastegate canister operation is computer regulated by means of a solenoid. If the solenoid fails to open, overboost can result. If the solenoid fails to close and never limits the application of boost pressure to the canister, low boost pressure may be the result.

If you've ruled out other potential causes and the turbocharger seems to be at fault, you can disassemble it to determine the extent of damage and whether or not a fix is practical. Sometimes a loss of boost is merely the result of dirt accumulation on the compressor blades. More often, it's the result of damaged compressor or turbine blades.

The working parts of the turbo —shaft, compressor, turbine, and bearing housing—can sometimes be purchased without the two scroll housings. This assembly is known as a cartridge. If you decide to replace the cartridge, see the rebuild instructions that follow in regard to disassembly of the housings.

If either the turbine housing or the compressor housing is damaged, the turbo can't be rebuilt in the field and should be replaced. In many cases, turbine or compressor failure damages the housings as well.

TURBO NOISE AND VIBRATION

Strange noises or vibration at the turbocharger usually indicate failure of the turbocharger bearings

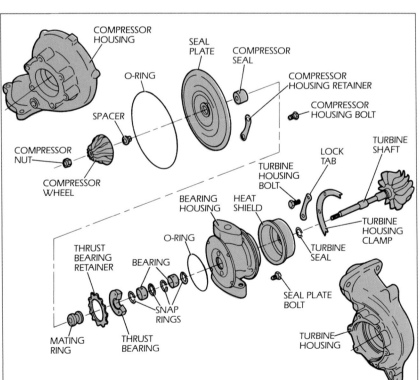

An exploded view of a typical Garrett T3 turbo. Expect to see some minor variations.

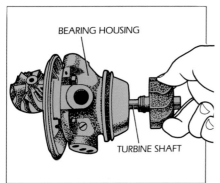

The turbine shaft can be withdrawn once the compressor nut and wheel are removed.

and/or damage to rotating parts that have caused an out-of-balance condition. In most cases, the damage to the turbo is fairly serious by the time things start shaking and shrieking. A cartridge replacement will usually be necessary to cure a vibration or noise problem. Sometimes, an accumulation of dirt on the compressor can cause imbalance.

EXHAUST SMOKE

Perhaps the most common signal of impending turbo failure is a puff of smoke when you first start the car in the morning. This condition can worsen quickly to overall smoking and eventual loss of turbo boost. Smoke is the usual first hint that something is going wrong. And it signals the best time for you to try to do something about your turbo problem. In many cases, total turbo failure will occur within 5,000 miles of the time when smoke first appears in the exhaust.

But before you dig into the turbo, consider some other possible causes of smoke. Of course, an internal engine problem can cause smoke. Valve guide wear causes a smoking condition similar to that caused by turbo seal failure, though it rarely comes on all at once.

Even turbo-related smoking may be caused by something other than failed turbo seals. On a diesel, a clogged air filter can lead to pressure considerably below atmospheric on the compressor side of the turbo. This can cause oil to be drawn past the compressor seal. On the other hand, a clogged turbo oil-return pipe can cause excessive

oil pressure and eventual loss of oil past the turbo's seals into the intake and exhaust systems.

But the most likely cause of turbo-related exhaust smoke is coking of the turbine shaft due to overheating of the lubricating oil. The abrasive fried oil (coke) grinds away at the turbo's shaft bearings. Once the bearings have worn, the shaft wobbles. This causes failure of the seals that separate the turbine and compressor from the oil-pressurized center bearing housing. Once oil enters the turbine and compressor housings, it's drawn into the intake manifold and exhaust systems.

The relatively easy fix for this condition is seal and bearing replacement. A number of aftermarket manufacturers provide replacement parts for passenger-car turbochargers. One that we are aware of (Turbo City, Inc., 1137 W. Katella Ave., Orange, CA 92667; (714) 639-4933), sells a rebuilding kit intended for someone who has never rebuilt a turbo. The kit includes all the seals, bearings, O-rings, thrust plates, and gaskets needed to rebuild a turbo, as well as instructions outlining the job.

That same company sells complete turbos and turbo cartridges (the working parts exclusive of the scroll housings). They will also rebuild your turbo for you if you want to ship it to them.

TURBO REBUILD

The rebuild procedure is easy for the experienced driveway technician, as the instructions provided with the rebuild kit are fairly good.

The unit we rebuilt was the Garrett T3, the most common passenger-car turbo in the world. The only other type you're likely to encounter is the Mitsubishi turbo, which is used on Mitsubishi and late-model Chryslers. The Mitsubishi and Garrett turbos are very similar, as are the rebuild procedures.

Before beginning the disassembly of the damaged turbo, we found that a brief examination of the new parts provided in the kit was helpful. This way, you'll recognize the parts you'll be replacing as you remove them.

Before you start to disassemble the turbo, mark the four main sec-

tions—turbine scroll, bearing housing, seal plate, and compressor scroll—with a scribe so you can reassemble them in the same relative positions. Disassembly of the turbo begins with removal of the wastegate control canister or actuator, then the turbine and compressor housings.

Next is removal of the compressor nut from the turbine shaft. This can be tough because the shaft rotates freely in the bearing housing. If you try to jam it by sticking something in the turbine or compressor blades, you'll ruin them. All turbo shafts are manufactured with a hex at the opposite (turbine) end of the shaft, but this is frequently ground away when the turbine shaft and wheels are balanced.

The turbo we rebuilt still had enough of the hex intact to permit restraint of the shaft with an open-end wrench. If you're not that lucky, hold the turbine wheel with a thick towel. If that doesn't work, try wrapping an old V-belt around the turbine wheel a couple of times. Then, hold the belt while you loosen the compressor nut. Turbo City does not recommend that you use an impact wrench, as it can bend the shaft.

The rest of the disassembly process is easy. First, you'll extract the turbine wheel and shaft from the turbine side of the bearing housing. If the shaft is coked, you may have to carefully tap on the compressor end with a plastic mallet. (Our moderately coked shaft came out with a

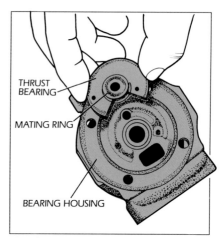

The thrust bearing (thrust plate) and mating ring can be lifted from the bearing housing.

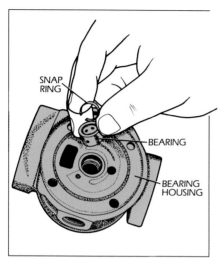

After the snap rings are removed, the bearings will slide out of the bearing housing.

light tap or two.) The compressor spacer will then slip right out of the compressor end of the seal plate. The turbine heat shield can be lifted from the bearing housing on the turbine side.

Next is removal of the seal plate from the bearing housing, followed by removal of the compressor seal from the seal plate. The compressor seal in our turbo was a multipart drop-in unit. The top piece is simply lifted off the three locators in the housing. The internal part, along with the spring that preloads it, must be rotated until its notches align with the locating teeth in the housing.

Earlier turbos may have a press-in positive seal. Use a vise and socket to remove this type of seal.

Some turbos located upstream from the throttle body, like Saabs and Volvos, may have a dynamic seal that is very similar to the piston-ring-type seal found on the turbine side of the bearing housing.

Turning your attention to the bearing housing, lift off the thrust bearing, the mating ring, and the O-ring that you'll find on the compressor side of the bearing housing.

You should use a good pair of snap-ring pliers to remove two outer snap rings (C-clips), one from each side of the bearing housing. Once these have been extracted, the bearings will slide out.

Finally, remove the turbine seal from the seal groove in the turbine

shaft. Make sure you don't nick the edges of the seal groove.

Check all turbo parts for unusual wear. The instructions will point you to several areas of concern: the bearing housing bore, the turbine shaft seal groove, the compressor and turbine blades.

Clean all parts in a glass-beading machine or in cold carburetor dip. If you have neither, your local auto parts store or mechanic will probably be willing to do a cold dip for you. Any good machine shop should have a glass-beading machine. This gadget looks like a sandblaster, but uses smooth microscopic glass beads to remove carbon and rust without damaging the metal surface.

If not, you can purchase a moderately sized container of cold-dip cleaner along with a small parts basket at your auto parts store. Just make sure the can is big enough to dunk the housing scrolls. Give all the parts at least a four- or five-hour soak. You may have to brush some of the hardened coke deposits, but take care not to get the cold-dip solvent on your hands—it dissolves organic matter.

Before reassembly, check the diameter of the turbine-shaft bearing journals. For a T3, they should measure 0.3997 in. to 0.4000 in. The shaft in our T3 measured 0.3990 in. A call to Turbo City revealed that some previously rebuilt turbos may have 0.0010-in. or 0.0015-in. undersized shafts. Turbo City immediately sent

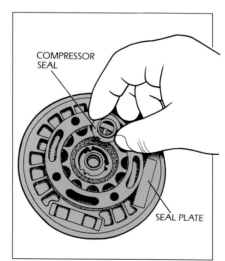

Rotate the positive multipart seal to release it from the seal plate.

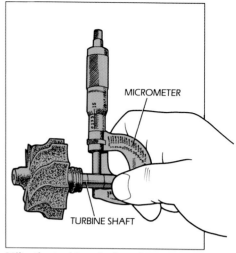

Mike the turbine shaft and compare this measurement to specs in your instructions.

us a set of 0.0010-in. oversized bearings for the rebuild—as they'll do for any customer who discovers an undersized shaft.

Of course, if your turbo has never been rebuilt, it is highly unlikely that it would be fitted with undersized components. The Turbo City bearings, by the way, are bronze severe-service units. The pieces they replace, in most cases, are normal-service aluminum bearings.

With a 1.0-in. snap gauge and micrometer or vernier caliper, check the diameter of the bearing housing bore at the point where the turbine seal contacts it. It should measure 0.6220 in. to 0.6223 in. When assembled on the turbine shaft, the diameter of the turbine seal ring (piston ring) should measure 0.709 in. to 0.711 in.

Assembly is basically the opposite of disassembly. Make sure you coat the shaft and thrust bearings with engine oil. Take care when installing the turbine seal on the turbine shaft. It must fit in the groove and rotate freely. Don't force the turbine seal into the bearing housing. When it is properly centered, it will slide in easily.

Tighten the compressor wheel nut to 18 to 20 in.-lb. plus 90°. When you reassemble the housings, make sure the compressor and turbine wheels do not contact any part of either housing. Install the wastegate actuator bracket before you bolt the turbine housing in place.

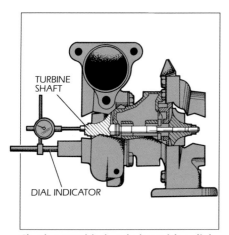

TURBINE SHAFT

DIAL INDICATOR

Check assembled end play with a dial indicator along the length of the turbine shaft.

When reassembly is complete, you should check some other clearances, including axial end play (0.001 in. to 0.004 in.). Radial bearing clearance (the shaft's up-and-down movement) should measure 0.0030 in. to 0.0065 in. Check radial clearance with a dial indicator. On some turbos you can touch the shaft with the dial indicator's probe through the oil hole in the bearing housing. With the correct new bearings and a shaft that specs out on journal diameter, this measurement should be okay.

After installing your rebuilt turbo on the car, clean the oil inlet line thoroughly. Don't use RTV sealer on the oil inlet line connections—it can clog oil passages.

Change the engine oil. Then, preoil the turbo by cranking the engine with the coil wire disconnected. (On GM HEI systems with an integral coil, disconnect the distributor BAT wire while cranking.)

Once the oil pressure has come up, reconnect the ignition and start the engine. Let it idle for three or four minutes before test-driving the car.

To prevent bearing wear in the future, run the engine at idle speed for about thirty seconds before you switch off the ignition. This will prevent loss of oil pressure to the bearings while the turbo is spinning at high speed.

How to Replace a CATALYTIC CONVERTER

Yo've fought your way through boulevard traffic for what seems like long enough for the next payment on your sled to become overdue. At last, you swing onto the freeway entrance, with the wind blowing in your hair. Hmmm . . . not very twisty here. So, you do what any red-blooded vehicle owner would—leadfoot the accelerator pedal and brace yourself for the welcome surge of speed that seemed so easy last week. Instead, your car picks up a mere one mile an hour. And the driver behind you is frantically gesturing toward your tailpipe.

Red-faced, you hop out and see sparks dancing out of your tailpipe. No, you're not a victim of a demonically possessed exhaust system. Your car has fallen prey to a mal-function of a most-misunderstood component of your emissions control system: a clogged catalytic converter.

CATALYTIC CONVERTER OPERATION

A bubble of metal located after your engine's exhaust manifold, the catalytic converter is designed to re-

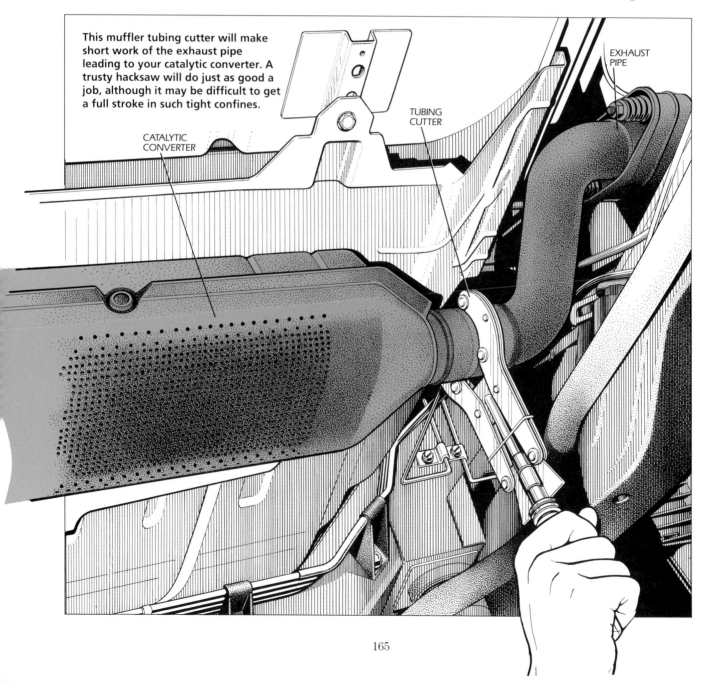

This muffler tubing cutter will make short work of the exhaust pipe leading to your catalytic converter. A trusty hacksaw will do just as good a job, although it may be difficult to get a full stroke in such tight confines.

CATALYTIC CONVERTER

TUBING CUTTER

EXHAUST PIPE

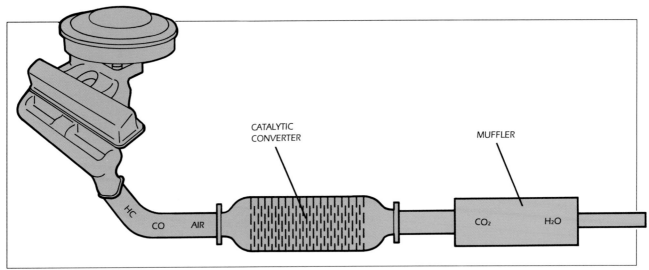

Some catalytic converters use excess air in the exhaust stream to oxidize excess pollutants.

duce hydrocarbon (HC) and carbon monoxide (CO) emissions into carbon dioxide and water vapor. The converter also purges oxides of nitrogen (NOx) vapors from the exhaust. It is called catalytic because precious-metal catalysts inside the converter react with these toxic gases on the large surface area of an ingenious honeycomb coated with less than a gram of the catalytic material.

Most vehicles made after 1980 use this so-called monolithic converter. If your car is pre-1980 vintage, it's more likely you'll have a pellet-type converter. Pellet converters contain thousands of tiny grains of ceramic reactants that produce a similar result.

A catalytic converter is a tiny combustion chamber. Your vehicle's air management valve adds fresh air to the exhaust gases inside the chamber, heating the converter's insides to speed up the catalytic reaction. Additionally, the engine management computer only lets air into the converter when the engine is heated. A fuel-rich mixture from a cold engine can cause the converter to overheat, and after a period of time, melt down. So can the excess hydrocarbons from a poorly running, misfiring engine.

This leaves goopy chunks of partially melted matrix inside the converter. They rattle around the inside of the converter and eventually clog the exhaust flow. A worst-case sce-

nario can blow out your head pipe after the converter is completely blocked.

Catalytic converters are also sensitive to what some mechanics call lead poisoning. Exhaust from leaded gasoline gunks up the honeycombed monolith by coating the precious-metal catalysts with metallic lead, rendering it dysfunctional. This will leave your converter with serious intestinal blockage as well.

A final cause behind cranky converters is nature itself—rust can eat away the converter casing. While the device can still operate, the unprotected elements are so superheated that one vehicle owner lost his entire lawn in a fire that was caused by his converter.

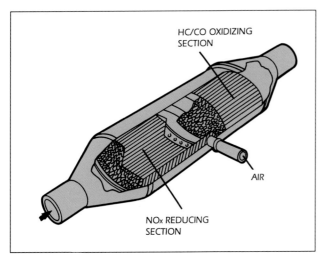

Other designs inject a volume of fresh air into the converter to permit oxides of nitrogen (NO_x) to be reduced in a separate chamber.

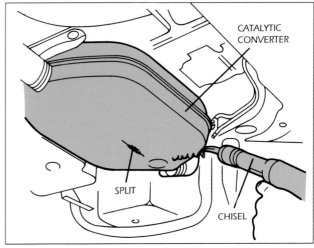

In some cases, it's possible to repair a damaged outer shell by chiseling off the casing and crimping on a new one.

You might conclude that the main beneficiary of emissions controls isn't the environment—it's your mechanic's pocketbook.

GETTING TO THE BOTTOM OF IT

Yet, it's not necessary to fork out the $300 to $500 most service departments charge for converter replacement. Replacing your own converter is almost as easy as installing a new muffler. But, no surprise, there are a few caveats before you begin.

As always, use proper ramps or jack stands to lift the vehicle high enough for access to its underpinnings. Don't improvise, unless you feel capable of bench-pressing a ton or so. You'll be working directly underneath the parts you're wrenching on, so use some sort of eye protection to prevent flakes of rust from finding their inevitable and painful way into your eyes.

Be sure your vehicle has sat, engine off, for at least two hours before you begin. Since the converter is a miniature combustion chamber, it runs hotter than your engine. Even if your engine is cold, the heat-hungry demons inside your converter may still be cavorting.

There are no published generic diagnostics for a blown converter. Most service mechanics simply test-drive the vehicle and feel the engine lug. You can also tap the converter with a rubber mallet. Loose monolithic elements will rattle inside the housing. This tells you that the precious metals have flaked off the honeycomb and are threatening to invade your tailpipe.

A brief examination of the converter housing will also reveal corrosion and scoring caused by road damage. Rarely, an off-road odyssey may have even scraped open the metal shell and exposed the monolith.

A simple rustout or scrape of the converter's outer skin may not seem immediately perilous, but there are sound reasons to avoid leaving the converter's inner shell exposed to the elements. First off, it leaves the inner shell exposed to road salt, air, and other potentially damaging foreign substances or objects. Second, the loss of insulation will make the converter take longer to warm up to its effective operating temperature,

spewing excess pollutants all the while it's slowly digesting the parts of itself that have warmed up. Third, converters run *hot*—hotter than the rest of the exhaust system because the reactions inside the converter are producing even more heat than the manifold is pumping in.

Fortunately, many converters can be reskinned by simply chiseling off the old outer skin and insulation, and crimping on a new outer shell from the dealership.

For the same reason, it's really important to replace or repair any metal heat shields in the area of the converter, whether they are intended to protect the interior and floor of your own vehicle or to keep heat from melting the pavement beneath the converter when you park.

IS THIS TRIP REALLY NECESSARY?

A loyal, obsessive Saturday Mechanic disciple, you of course want to check your plugged converter against the numbers. You simply need a vacuum gauge, which measures your engine's health in inches of mercury.

Attach the vacuum gauge anywhere you can find unmetered vacuum on the intake manifold or throttle plate. On GM/BOC (Buick, Oldsmobile, and Cadillac) vehicles, the air-conditioning and cruise-control ports are ideal. Look for a vacuum fitting that springs from the manifold itself, or from the carb or throttle body well below the throttle plates. Tee in before any gadgets in the line, as they may restrict the vacuum flow—you want pure unadulterated manifold vacuum.

For most cars, a normal reading with the engine idling is about 17 to 19 in. of mercury. A converter problem, or for that matter any exhaust restriction, will reduce this when the engine revs up.

Once you have attached the gauge, increase the engine speed beyond 2,500 rpm. Mechanics vary on this figure; some like to rev it beyond 3,000. A normal, unblocked exhaust system will read within three pounds of idle. A clogged system will show a reading that's well below this and often sputter and miss.

For example, if your engine shows 18 in. of mercury at 1,500 rpm, revving it up should create 15 in. at 2,200 to 2,500 rpm. If the vacuum meter reads below 15 in., you may have a blocked exhaust system caused by a malfunctioning converter.

For an even more positive diagnosis, there are exhaust pres-

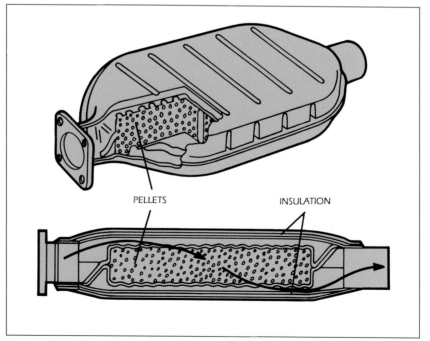

This pellet-type converter, a design that's giving way to honeycomb types, uses ceramic pellets coated with catalyst metals.

PELLETS

INSULATION

sure gauges that screw into the exhaust manifold at the fitting for the O₂ sensor.

At any rate, you've decided the problem has to be the converter. The next step is to replace the converter. A basic enough procedure; there are, nevertheless, a few key details to master.

REMOVING AND REPLACING YOUR CONVERTER

Most catalytic converters are attached to the exhaust system by a set of clamps and flanges. There is both a converter inlet and an outlet attachment. The first step is to remove these clamps. This is where the fun begins, particularly in cold-weather regions.

Four-figure temps and salt-fed rust can eat away boltheads and wreak havoc on vulnerable flanges. To detach corroded bolts, you might try a torch to heat and loosen them. Don't be afraid to heat the fittings cherry red. Those of you without a torch will have to resort to more conventional measures, like nut splitters, penetrating oil, and a few well-chosen phrases. Plan on replacing all of the hardware from the beginning—it's rare that you can get much of it apart in any shape to be reused. You'll make better headway when the replacement is already waiting on the bench, and you're not trying to rescue some old chewed-up bolt.

Many domestic vehicle converters are actually welded to the exhaust system. In this case, you can use a pipe cutter or hacksaw to remove the inlet and outlet points. Cut just inside the welds so your installation is not hampered by excess traces of the old converter.

You must also detach the air hose that runs from your manifold to the converter. Typically, a clamp or flange subassembly is all you need to remove. Think hard about replacing at least a few feet of this hose, while you're in the neighborhood.

CONFIRMING THE WORST

There is a final check before you finally bolt up the expensive new pieces. Clamp a length of pipe to the system inlet and outlets, bridging the converter's place in the exhaust system. Reattach the vac-

uum gauge, and rev it up. You should see the vacuum settle at an appropriate value, well above the one with the slagged converter corking things up.

But do not—and we mean it—do not drive the vehicle yet. The Environmental Protection Agency requires that all post-1979 vehicles on the road possess a functioning catalytic converter. Squirrels, pine trees, and asthmatic emissions checkers will haunt you for eternity if you do not comply with this simple regulation.

Now, it's time to replace the converter. Simply repeat the removal steps in reverse. Mechanics are mixed on their preference for the exact steps. Suffice to say that the new converter must be securely attached at both inlet and outlet ports, and the manifold air hose must be clamped in place.

Start by assembling all the flanges and slip-joints loosely, with all the hardware started and gaskets in place, but without tightening anything even finger tight. Make sure everything is hanging straight and level, with plenty of clearance—exhaust systems move around a lot.

Be sure any slip fittings telescope at least 2 in. into each other, and clamp the center of the overlap. Try buttering up the hardware with some antiseize compound as well. You *might* need to disassemble this stuff at some point a year or three down the pike—when the remaining exhaust system corrodes away, for example, which it will do sooner or later. The antiseize compound

will make your life much simpler when that day arrives.

AFTERMARKET CONVERTERS

A visit to your dealership parts department will reveal that a new catalytic converter can cost you as much as $300—each, if you're unfortunate enough to have two. Yet there are a number of very good aftermarket converter kits available. Priced at $125 to $150, these kits include a so-called universal catalytic converter and a conversion kit. You *must* purchase the right kit for your vehicle. You'll find these converters, along with plenty of good advice as to what other parts you will need, at the local auto parts store.

To this end, aftermarket manufacturers publish catalogs that recommend connector pipes for attaching their products to your vehicle. A lifetime warranty applies to many aftermarket converters.

GO FOR THE CAUSE—NOT JUST THE SYMPTOM

Auto companies design catalytic converters to last the lifetime of the vehicle. Emissions testing labs, such as GM's Milford Proving Grounds, batter converter prototypes with months of all-weather tests that evoke secure nods of approval from engineering management.

When your catalytic converter goes bad, the reason is usually that your engine is not functioning properly. Don't be a Saturday mechanic

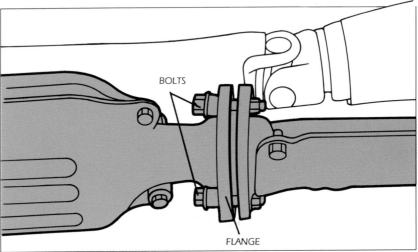

Separating corroded fasteners is the toughest part of converter replacement. Have fresh replacements on hand.

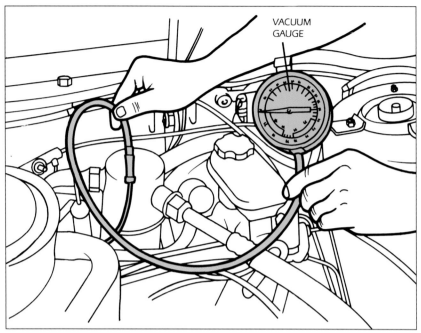

A plugged converter will show up on a vacuum gauge as abnormal vacuum readings, indicating that there's back-pressure in the system.

who installs a new converter, only to discover his car or truck lugging after a few months of city driving. To prevent future converter damage, it is essential that you discover why your engine is malfunctioning.

WASTE NOT, WANT NOT

At some point in time, catalytic converters will consume virtually all of the worldwide production of rhodium, one of the catalysts. Fortunately, rhodium, platinum, and other scarce elements are pretty easy to reclaim from the slag in your converter. Many salvage lots will even *give* you a few bucks for your old converter, because they sell them in bulk to someplace that melts them down and re-refines them for the few grams of precious metals in them. At worst, take the hulk down to a muffler shop and see if they mind you throwing it onto the pile of converters that they send off to be recycled.

How to Replace a TIMING BELT

You're humming down the turnpike at 55 mph. The engine has never run better, purring like the proverbial sewing machine. But then it suddenly quits—almost as if someone had turned off the ignition. As you dodge traffic while trying to coast to the shoulder, you repeatedly crank over the engine, but it doesn't even try to catch.

Now what?

Your car has just broken a camshaft timing belt.

Timing belts were first introduced in the mid-sixties. Since then, they have gained broad acceptance. Today, more than five hundred models of cars and light trucks are equipped with belts.

Before the introduction of timing belts, overhead-cam engines used timing chains. But belts have many advantages over chains—not the least of which is lower design, engineering, and production costs.

Timing belts also take up less room, and they run much quieter than chains. They also weigh less and require no lubrication. Overall, belts are also much less complicated

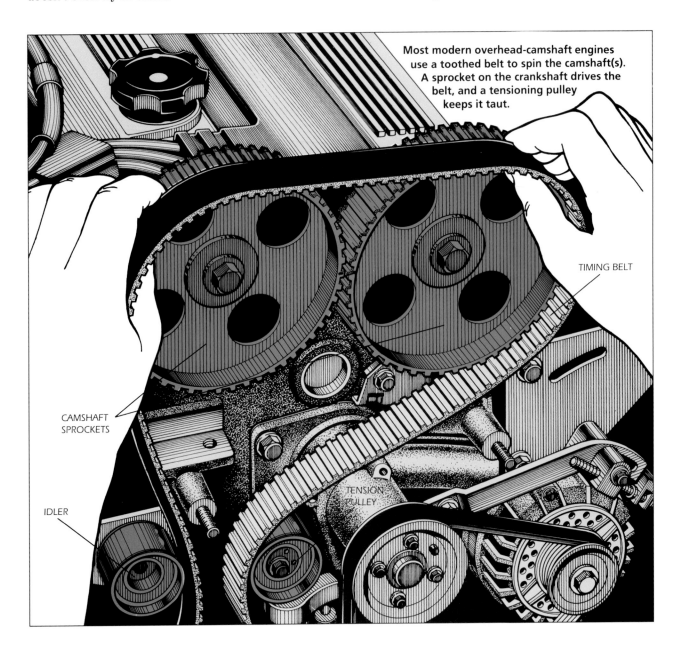

Most modern overhead-camshaft engines use a toothed belt to spin the camshaft(s). A sprocket on the crankshaft drives the belt, and a tensioning pulley keeps it taut.

TIMING BELT

CAMSHAFT SPROCKETS

TENSION PULLEY

IDLER

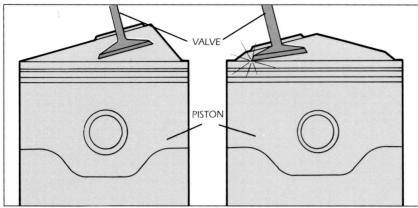

In noninterference engines (left), the fully open valve cannot foul against the top of the piston. In the interference type (right), the valve can hit the piston.

than chain designs, and they also often serve to drive other components, such as the water pump, distributor, oil pump, and fuel pump.

The timing belt keeps the upper and lower halves of an engine connected and running in perfect sync: The crankshaft spins the timing belt, which, in turn, spins the camshaft to open and close the valves. The result is the elegantly timed sequence of the four-stroke-cycle engine—intake, compression, power, exhaust. When the timing belt breaks, the four-stroke cycle becomes a no-stroke cycle and the engine quits.

INTERFERENCE VERSUS NONINTERFERENCE

In the world of broken timing belts, there are only two important kinds of engine designs: Interference and noninterference. Noninterference, or free-running, engines are designed with a little extra clearance between the tops of the pistons and the fully open valves inside combustion chambers. This little-noticed design feature only becomes significant when the timing belt breaks. The extra room prevents an open valve from contacting a piston.

In an interference engine, there isn't any extra clearance: When the timing belt breaks, the pistons strike the open valves—usually with catastrophic results.

How much damage occurs depends on how fast the engine is running when the belt lets go. Damage can range from a couple of bent valves at low rpm, to broken valves,

damaged pistons, scarred cylinder walls, and a cracked cylinder head at a higher rpm.

When the timing belt breaks in a noninterference engine, installing a new belt is all that's needed to restore a healthy four-stroke cycle.

Why would any car company design an interference engine? There's good reason: Adding the necessary clearance in the combustion chambers to make an engine a noninterference design sacrifices compression. Lower compression means less efficiency and lower horsepower.

In all, about 40 percent of the engines with timing belts are higher compression, interference designs. As the demand for engine efficiency

increases in the coming years, expect the percentage of interference engine designs to increase.

BELT FITNESS

Of course, the key to avoiding a belt problem lies in keeping it in good shape and replacing it at the manufacturer's recommended interval. How long a belt ultimately will last depends on many factors. Chief among these is how well the engine is designed. The less torque loading, or vibration, placed on the belt, the longer it will last. Oil, dirt, and heat also significantly reduce belt life.

In the early days of timing belts, many carmakers didn't bother specifying when a timing belt should be changed. But over the years, they've learned that the timing belt should be changed at specified intervals. For example, on early Ford Escorts with the 1.6-liter engine, Ford issued a recall that specified a belt change at 24,000 miles.

Fortunately, carmakers have been able to significantly reduce torque loading. And better shielding from heat, dirt, and oil has made for longer-lasting belts. The belts themselves also have been improved. Most timing belts are constructed of neoprene. But many newer cars are now equipped with belts constructed of a new material known generically as HNBR (Hydrogenated Nitrile Butadiene Rubber). (Gates Rubber Co. calls it HSN for Highly Saturated

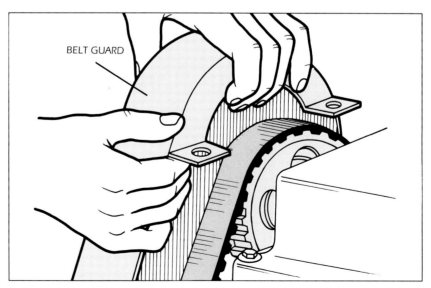

First, remove a plastic or stamped metal belt cover for access. You might also have to remove some accessories or drivebelts.

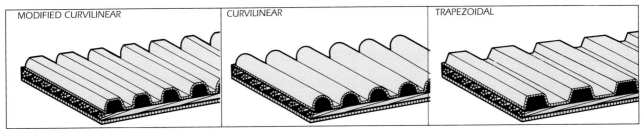

Carmakers use three distinct belt-tooth profiles. Replacement belts must have the same tooth profile as the original.

Nitrile.) No matter what it's called, this material stands up to heat and oil contamination much better than neoprene.

With all of the improvements to engines and their timing belts, many manufacturers now typically call for timing-belt replacement at 60,000 miles. A few carmakers are even talking about increasing the interval to 90,000 miles on new models in the coming years.

Don't bother trying to inspect a timing belt. Beltmakers used to have all kinds of visual inspections to determine if a belt was going bad or whether a used belt was worth reinstalling or not. But given the relatively low price of a belt—roughly $30 to $60—and the potential for engine destruction should the belt fail, it simply makes sense to change the belt at the recommended interval, or even near the recommended interval if you are doing other engine work that would make changing the belt easier. If your car

doesn't have a recommended interval, Gates Rubber Co. recommends changing the belt at 60,000 miles, or sooner.

It's also penny wise and pound foolish to reinstall a used timing belt for any reason. And if you ever find a timing belt that is oil soaked, you should replace it as soon as possible.

REMOVING BELTS

By and large, changing a timing belt is fairly straightforward. But the procedures vary widely depending on engine design, make, and model. What follows is a general procedure. To change the belt on your car or light truck, consult a service manual for specific instructions.

Begin by disconnecting the cable from the ground terminal of the battery. Next, remove the distributor cap, then rotate the engine by hand until the timing mark on the crankshaft pulley is aligned with the 0°

mark on the timing scale. At the same time, the distributor rotor should be aligned with the index mark on the distributor housing, which indicates that the rotor is in the firing position for No. 1 cylinder.

After you've rotated the engine to the No. 1 firing position, remove any items that interfere with removing the timing-belt cover. These may include accessory drivebelts, radiator hoses, the radiator, the crankshaft pulley, or even an engine mount on some poorly designed front-wheel-drive models with a transverse-mounted engine.

The timing cover usually is made of sheet metal or plastic. Remove the bolts that hold it to the engine and lift it off.

Once the cover is off you can see the timing belt. Double-check that the engine is in the proper firing position by looking for marks on the camshaft sprocket and the crankshaft pulley. Many engines have a small dot or indexing line on the

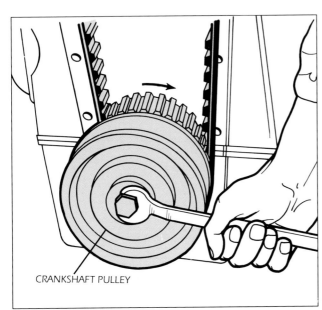

Turn the engine by hand to align the timing marks before removing the old belt.

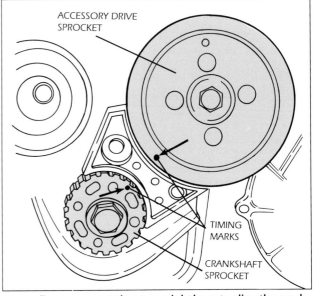

Depending on your engine, you might have to align the crankshaft sprocket with a mark on an accessory drive sprocket.

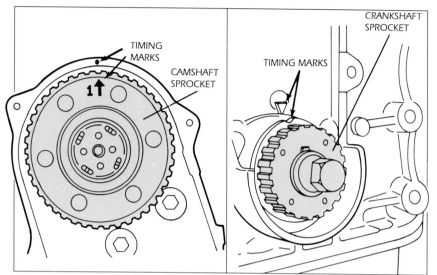

Align marks on the sprockets with marks on the block and cylinder head.

pulleys that align with corresponding marks on the block or head. The same is true of the accessory shaft. On some engines, the indexing mark on the camshaft sprocket aligns with the parting line of the first camshaft bearing tower.

Check the belt and immediate areas for signs of oil or other fluid leakage. Possible areas of leakage include the crankshaft main seal, the accessory-shaft seal, and the cam seal. All three seals are located behind their respective timing-belt pulleys. Oil leaks also can come

from the front of the cam cover and the oil pan. It is imperative that oil leaks be repaired before the belt is replaced.

To remove the timing belt, loosen its tensioner. On some cars, this may require a special tool. For instance, on early Ford Escorts, a special offset wrench is needed to reach a tensioner bolt that is directly behind an engine mount.

Many engines have a spring-loaded tensioner. If that's the case, loosen the bolts holding the tensioner, then pry the tensioner away from

the belt and retighten the bolts so the tensioner remains off the belt.

With the belt tension relieved, the timing belt should slide off the camshaft and crankshaft pulleys fairly easily. However, heat and miles may have the belt sticking in its grooves—pry it off with an old screwdriver or small pry bar if necessary.

Once the timing belt has been removed, do not rotate the crankshaft or camshaft. This is especially critical with interference engines because turning either shaft independently of the other can cause the pistons to contact the valves, resulting in engine damage.

GETTING BELTED

Since their introduction, timing belts have been designed with three different profiles: trapezoidal, curvilinear, and modified curvilinear. All three look strikingly similar. The teeth must also be spaced properly and the belt must be the proper width. If any one of these factors isn't perfect, the timing belt is likely to self-destruct in a very short amount of time. That's why the part number must match exactly.

Timing belts are extremely tough when they're installed on the car. But they're rather fragile if they are twisted or bent into any configuration other than the one they were

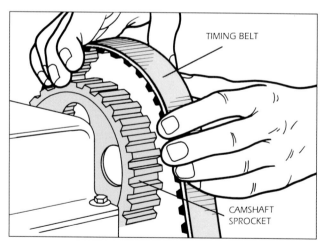

With the belt tensioner fully loosened, the replacement belt should slip into place by hand. Be careful not to rotate the sprockets as you install the belt.

With the new belt in place, check the timing marks and readjust the tension pulley. Proper belt tension is critical.

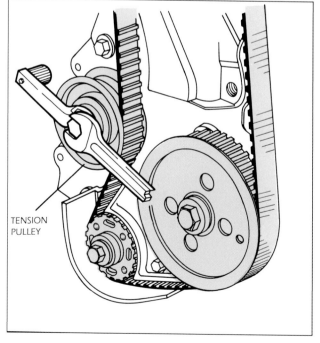

designed for. That's why timing belts, unlike regular belts, are sold in a box.

INSTALLING BELTS

Never try to force or pry a belt over the sprockets when installing it. If the belt doesn't go on easily, either you have the wrong belt or the idler pulley is not loose enough.

After you slide the timing belt into position, make sure that the belt is properly installed around each of the sprockets and that the teeth on the belt mesh properly with the teeth on the sprockets.

On engines with spring-loaded tensioners, loosen the tensioner fasteners so the idler pulley contacts the belt. Be careful not to let the pulley snap against the belt—this might cause damage.

Whatever you do, don't try to guess the proper belt tension. Proper belt tensioning is a critical measurement and belt life will suffer if it isn't done correctly.

Once proper belt tension is restored, verify that all the indexing marks on the accessory shaft, crankshaft, and camshaft pulleys are still aligned. Then, using a wrench on the crankshaft pulley, rotate the en-gine—in its normal direction of operation—at least two complete revolutions. If you run into any hard resistance, it's possible that the timing is off—so recheck the position of all the timing marks and try again. If they aren't off, loosen the belt tensioner and reinstall the belt so the marks align and repeat the retensioning procedure before turning the engine over by hand again.

After the belt is properly tensioned and the marks align, reinstall the timing cover, pulleys, and the other items you removed, start the engine, and you're done.

DRIVETRAIN 3

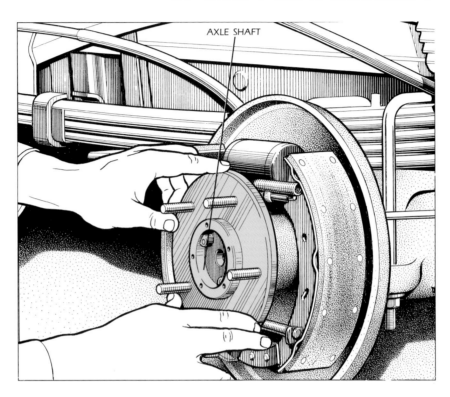

AXLE SHAFT

What to Do When Your AUTOMATIC TRANS WON'T SHIFT

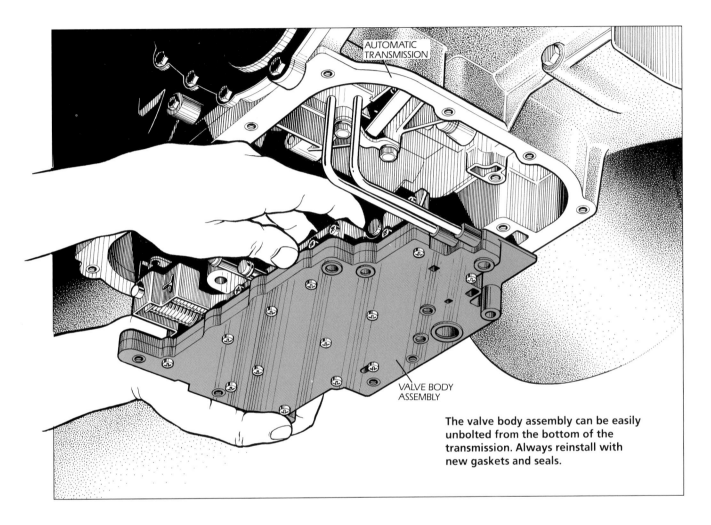

The valve body assembly can be easily unbolted from the bottom of the transmission. Always reinstall with new gaskets and seals.

Maybe the first thing you notice is that pause when you pull the shifter back into DRIVE on a cold morning. Maybe there's a long, slow shift between first and second, or perhaps even no shifting at all. Automatic transmission trouble. It's enough to send shivers up your spine.

Sometimes, if you're an experienced driveway technician and you haven't let the problem progress too far, you can resolve some slippage and shifting problems without removing the transmission from the car.

But be forewarned: If a slippage problem continues over an extended period of time, clutch and/or band wear and damage will result, necessitating a costly professional teardown. And remember, a lot of automatic transmission problems cannot be resolved *without* teardown. But experience suggests that the percentage of those that can be solved on the creeper is significant enough for you to have a go at it.

One more preliminary note: If your engine isn't running correctly, fix it *before* you attempt to repair a trans slippage or shift problem.

Some engine problems, like a vacuum leak, can dramatically affect transmission operation.

CHECK THE FLUID

Before you start looking for a problem, you should check the condition of the trans fluid. If it smells like rotten eggs and appears grossly discolored, it's probably already too late for a quick fix. But some of the fluid used today turns rather dark and smells pretty bad even in normal use, so don't condemn your trans on

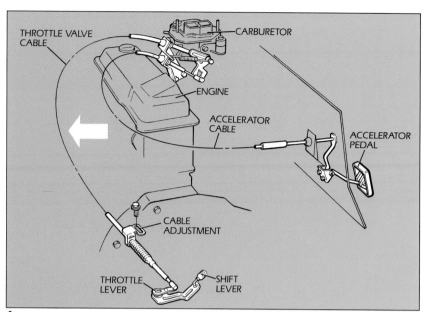

1 Many cars are equipped with an adjustable throttle valve cable or linkage that helps determine shifting. If the adjustment is incorrect, shifting problems can result.

the basis of fluid condition alone unless it's extreme.

Other things you should look for while checking the fluid are air bubbles or a milky pink color. Air bubbles suggest that a suction line is leaking. This can cause erratic shifting, but usually won't cause a constantly repeatable slippage or shifting problem. A milky color indicates that water has gotten into the fluid somehow. If this is the case, you can attempt a fluid and filter swap, but chances are that the water has already caused seal failure or other internal damage.

Of course, a low fluid level can cause shifting and slippage problems. Make sure you check the fluid level following specific recommendations in your owner's manual. In most cases, this means checking the fluid level with the transmission hot, the car parked on level ground, the engine at slow idle speed, and the transmission selector lever in PARK. It requires at least fifteen miles of highway driving to bring the fluid to what is considered hot temperature. Some manufacturers also provide a cold dipstick position for checking, but this isn't as accurate as a hot fluid check.

If you do find a low fluid level, check carefully for leaks. They may be hard to pinpoint because the airstream under the car spreads the

fluid all over. Many leakage problems, including rear seal, bad pan gasket, leaking cooler lines, and even transmission case porosity, can usually be resolved without removing the trans.

Among the most common causes of trans fluid leaks are bad cooler lines. These connect the trans to the oil cooler that is usually located in the radiator. The lines are under pressure and a pinprick leak can make quite a mess. Because they sometimes rub against chassis parts and are subjected to a lot of road debris thrown up by the wheels, they can easily fail.

CHECKING THE TV CABLE

No, we're not talking about the cable that brings television into your cave. We're talking about the throttle valve cable (or linkage) that helps determine when and if your transmission will shift on most cars. If it's out of adjustment, it can cause slippage, erratic shifting, or no shifts.

If your car has a TV cable or linkage, you'll find it between the throttle linkage and the transmission linkage (Fig. 1). It modulates the operation of valves within the transmission depending on how hard you're pushing on the throttle pedal.

Once you've located the TV cable

or linkage, make sure it doesn't bind or stick. If it does, see if you can determine why and correct the problem. With mechanical TV linkage, a little lubrication may be all that's needed.

Often, a sticking TV cable is due to a sharp bend in the cable, damaged housing, or misaligned bracket parts.

When you've determined that the cable or linkage mechanism works smoothly, you can adjust it. You can find specific instructions for your adjustment in your Motor or factory service manual. There are too many variations to cover here.

VACUUM PROBLEMS

If there are any vacuum lines connected to your transmission, check them for splitting, cracking, or loose ends that could cause leaks. If the lines are connected to a device that looks something like the vacuum advance mechanism on a distributor, your trans has a vacuum modulator that could be causing your problems (Fig. 2). A bad modulator will cause harsh and delayed upshifts or no upshifts. On some cars it can also cause an early upshift.

Some modulator failures will also cause exhaust smoke, as trans fluid may be drawn into the engine. Because all modulator failures will cause at least some fluid to be drawn into the modulator vacuum line, you can check your modulator by removing the vacuum line and looking for fluid at the modulator/vacuum line connection. If the modulator is leaking, replace it.

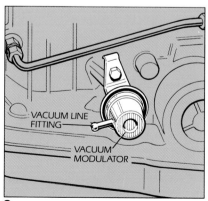

2 To check for a bad modulator, remove the vacuum line from the modulator and look for trans fluid at the connection point.

SHIFT LINKAGE

The next thing to check is shift linkage adjustment. If the linkage detents prevent the transmission valves from moving into place, all kinds of shifting problems can result. To adjust the gearshift linkage of most cars, shift selector lever to PARK. Then, disconnect linkage from trans. Locate the trans shift lever in PARK.

With trans and linkage in PARK, locate the linkage on the trans shift rod, shortening or lengthening the linkage until it fits. If your car has a cable linkage, the cable adjuster changes the linkage length. If your car has mechanical linkage, you'll probably find a rod that screws in or out of its rod end or a stud and nut that slide in a slot.

If you can't determine how to adjust the linkage by eyeballing it, check your shop manual. This may also be necessary with some Fords, which are adjusted with the selector lever in the DRIVE position.

PRESSURE TEST

How do the pros diagnose automatic transmission problems? The best technicians test-drive the car, then pressure-test it. By comparing symptoms and pressure reasons, they can usually narrow down the possible causes of a shift problem. The pressure test is performed by attaching a gauge to pressure ports on the outside of the transmission case (Fig. 3).

You can determine probable causes of slippage and shifting problems by pressure-testing your transmission, but you'll need some special tools to do the job. First, you'll need a tachometer. Second, you'll need one or more pressure gauges. For some models, a 150-psi gauge will suffice. For others, you'll need a 300-psi gauge. Third, you'll need a Motor or factory service manual, which provides a chart showing you how to interpret the results.

Once armed with all the necessary tools and charts, drive the car fifteen miles to raise fluid to operating temp.

Then, raise the vehicle securely on heavy-duty jack stands, or better yet, on a car hoist that allows the drive wheels to turn. Consult your service manual for specific jacking instructions, and don't attempt this

job unless you can raise and support the car in the approved manner.

Install an engine tachometer and position it so that you can read it while you test. Disconnect the TV cable and shift cable or linkage from the transmission levers so they can be controlled from outside the car. Finally, attach the gauges to the ports required for the test being conducted, and perform the tests as described in your manual.

In interpreting the results, you can limit possible sources of the problem according to what pressure readings you obtain in the various prescribed tests. For example, on most cars, if you have correct pressure minimum and maximum on any one test, you can assume that the pump and pressure regulator are okay.

On many cars, if you have low line pressure in all positions and on all tests, you may well have a clogged filter, which is easy to repair. Of course, this condition can also be caused by a bad pump or stuck regulator valve. Other results may suggest leakage in one particular circuit. Sometimes, a circuit leakage problem can be corrected by replacing or cleaning the valve body and/or spacer plate—another job that can be performed with the

transmission in the car (see the illustration on page 177).

Some repairs not listed here can be made in the car on certain transmissions. If your pressure test points to a specific part as a possible cause, check your service manual to see if it's a job you can do yourself. Many shop manuals have a section devoted to in-car service that lists all parts that can be replaced without pulling the trans.

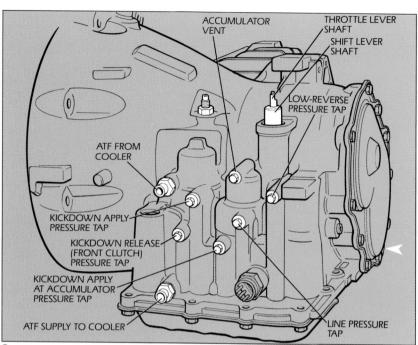

3 This Chrysler transaxle is fitted with a number of pressure ports on the outside of the transmission case for checking fluid pressure in various hydraulic circuits.

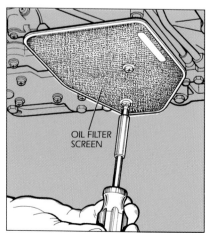

4 Most transmission filter screens are secured to the valve body with a couple of screws. This is the only filter in the system.

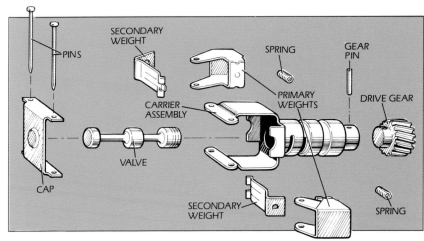

6 General Motors' THM 125 governors are calibrated at assembly, so individual parts other than the drive gear shouldn't be replaced.

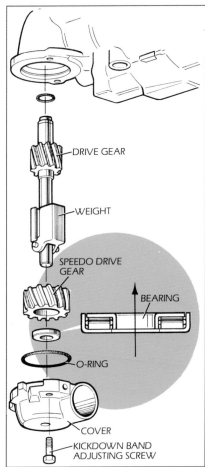

5 The governor can be removed by unbolting the governor cover and dropping the governor assembly out of the transaxle case.

FILTER AND FLUID SWAP

If the pressure test reveals low line pressure in all positions, you might try a filter and fluid swap before resorting to a costly out-of-the-car teardown. Even if you're not equipped to do the pressure test, but you have shifting or slippage problems, and your trans fluid and filter haven't been changed in the past 20,000 miles or so, the procedure can sometimes provide a fast and inexpensive fix.

If your trans has a drain plug in the plan, you're all set. Just make sure you have a huge drain pan to hold the ten or more quarts of trans fluid.

If your trans doesn't have a drain plug, you can remove all the pan bolts except two in two opposite corners of the pan. Then, with a

drain pan under the opposite corner, slowly unscrew the two remaining bolts. Allow the opposite corner of the pan to drop gradually as the fluid pours out. You may have to tap the pan a bit to break the gasket seal, but make sure the two remaining bolts are still well into the trans before you begin to drop the corner of the pan.

When the fluid has drained, carefully remove the two remaining bolts while supporting the pan.

Once the pan is off, you can remove and replace the filter pickup screen (Fig. 4). If it's clogged with friction material, you may have found the source of your problems.

Some clutch material in the pan is normal. Even a little bit of metal from thrust surfaces is normal in

some transmissions. A large quantity of clutch material and metal is, of course, a sign of other more serious problems.

GOVERNOR

A bad governor can cause shifting at incorrect speed or no first-to-second shift. Some transmissions have a port for checking governor pressure.

Some governors, including many of those on GM transmissions, can be cleaned or repaired without removing the transmission from the car (Fig. 5). On some models, you'll have to drop the driveshaft and the trans tailshaft (while supporting it with a jack) to remove the governor.

Possible governor faults that

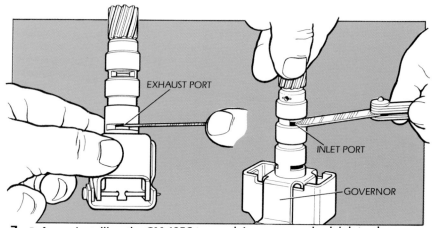

7 Before reinstalling the GM 125C transaxle's governor, check inlet valve opening with weights extended completely outward. It should be 0.020 in. Check exhaust opening with weights held tightly inward. It should also be 0.020 in.

could cause no shifting are numerous. On most cars you can look for binding weights, missing springs, missing or damaged O-rings, and bad drive gears (Fig. 6).

Some governors, including the illustrated GM 125C governor (Fig. 7), require adjustment of fluid circuit inlet and exhaust ports.

VALVE BODY

If the governor itself seems okay, but symptoms and pressure tests suggest a governor problem, it could be that one of the governor oil circuit orifices in the valve body spacer plate is plugged. Other pressure-test results that seem to indicate a leaking or clogged circuit might also be caused by a valve body or spacer problem.

The valve body and spacer plate can be removed with the trans in the car (see illustration on page 177), but unless you find obvious blockage, it's going to be tough to tell if you've accomplished a cure without road testing.

To get the valve body off the trans, you'll have to remove the oil pan, filter, and shift mechanism.

BAND ADJUSTMENT

Most GM transmissions don't have band adjustment capability. A lot of Ford and Chrysler transmissions do, however, and some models have a band adjustment procedure as scheduled maintenance.

In many cases, band adjustment can help solve a minor slippage or sloppy shifting problem—but only if you get to it before the situation has gotten out of hand. The longer a band slips, the more it wears. And when the friction material is gone or deteriorated, no amount of adjustment is going to help.

Some bands, like the intermediate band on the pictured Ford C5 transmission (Fig. 8), can easily be adjusted with a torque wrench while the trans is in the car. For most band adjustments, which require torque in the neighborhood of

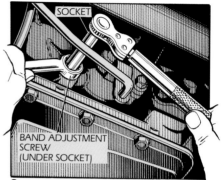

8 Band adjustments are done by loosening the locknut, adjusting the screw with a socket, and tightening the jam nut.

10 ft.-lb., an in.-lb. torque wrench is recommended.

The procedure usually calls for loosening a locknut, then tightening the band adjustment screw to a specific torque figure. Once the torque figure has been reached, the screw is backed off a specific number of turns, then held in position while the locknut is tightened.

How to Cure
DRIVELINE VIBRATIONS

You climb in your car to go to work, just like you do every morning. After starting the engine, you immediately shift into reverse and there's that noise again—a loud bell-like clank—as the transmission engages.

Actually, the noise is not transmission-related at all. What's more, it's not expensive or difficult to fix. Backing out of the driveway every day for a few years with a rapidly idling, stone-cold engine has simply pounded out one of the driveshaft universal joints. The noise sounds so expansive and expensive because rear-wheel drivelines can rival good ventriloquists in amplifying and then tossing sounds all over as

they travel up and down the drive-shaft.

A rear-wheel driveline's ability to throw sounds can give even seasoned mechanics nightmares—where loose torque converter-to-thrust-plate bolts mimic an engine rod knock, or a seemingly clunking rear suspension actually turns out to be worn splines on the transmission output shaft and driveshaft yoke.

DRIVELINE DIAGNOSTICS

Consider any components—from the engine mounts all the way back to the road wheels—to be fair game

when you're looking for mysterious driveline sounds or vibrations.

Many driveline noises tend to change in frequency, pitch, or speed. If the noise change is dependent on engine speed, it means the noise is most likely engine-related. If the noise occurs in some gears and not others, look for transmission problems. If the noise changes according to vehicle speed, you'll probably find its cause somewhere between the transmission output shaft and the rear wheels.

Clunks, clanks, bangs, and bongs usually occur during acceleration or deceleration and most often relate to excessive wear or play in a driveline part. To check out these noises,

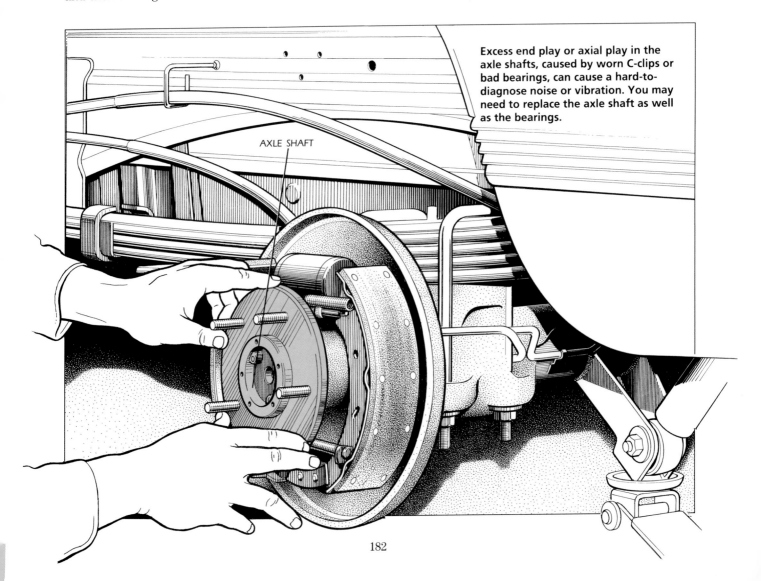

Excess end play or axial play in the axle shafts, caused by worn C-clips or bad bearings, can cause a hard-to-diagnose noise or vibration. You may need to replace the axle shaft as well as the bearings.

AXLE SHAFT

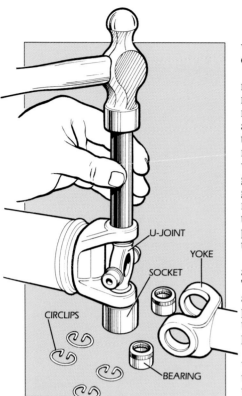

Use an old wrist pin and socket to lightly drive out old U-joint bearings.

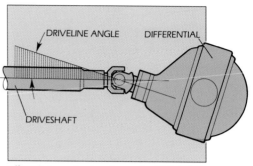

Vibration under load may be U-joints binding at excessive driveline angles.

drive the car on smooth pavement at varying speeds, being sure to make several left and right turns.

With automatic-transmission cars, engage and disengage the transmission while the car is stopped and note whether you hear bangs or clunks shifting into drive or reverse.

If you hear driveline noise in manual transmission cars only when the clutch pedal is depressed, suspect a bad throwout bearing.

As you drive, shift to neutral and let the engine idle. If the noise disappears, it's most likely engine-related.

GETTING YOUR BEARINGS STRAIGHT

If you hear a whirring or a grinding noise from the rear of the car, and the noise changes in frequency or volume when making turns, the cause is most likely a rear-axle bearing.

To change a rear-axle bearing, you have to remove the axle from the housing. The most common methods of holding an axle in the housing are with a C-shaped retainer inside the differential, or

with a bolt-on flange at the outer end of the axle housing.

To remove axles with a C-shaped retainer first, drain the gear oil and remove the differential cover. Next, remove the differential pinion shaft and pinion gears to gain access to the retainer. You'll see the C-shaped retainer on the end of the axle shaft where it fits into the differential side gear. With the differential pinion gears removed, there is just enough room to push in the axle sufficiently to allow the C-shaped retainer to be pulled out. Once the retainer is out, the axle slides from the housing.

Unfortunately, the axle also acts as the inner race for the bearing. That means if the bearing is bad, the axle's bearing surface is probably pitted, galled, or grooved, and both the bearing and the axle must be replaced.

To remove axles that are held with a bolt-on flange, simply remove the fasteners holding the flange to the housing and attach a slide-hammer puller to the lug-nut studs on the end of the axle. After a few tugs on the slide hammer, the axle and bearing should pop out of the housing. A pressed-on retainer holds the bearing onto the axle, but most automotive machine shops will remove the old bearing and retainer and press on new parts. And always replace bearing seals when changing a bearing.

PEEK UNDERNEATH

Once you've noted any noises during your road test, it's time to crawl underneath for a closer inspection.

Begin by checking the tires. Abnormal tire wear, such as cupping or signs of obvious imbalance, can cause driveline noise. This is also a good time to look for roadway paraphernalia, such as wire, string, or rope, that may have wrapped itself around the driveshaft.

U-JOINT POINTS

The most common cause of rear-wheel driveline noises is worn or damaged U-joints. To check, set the parking brake, then firmly grasp the driveshaft near the rear U-joint. *Any* side-to-side or up-and-down movement in the joint indicates excessive wear or failure in the U-joint bearings.

Other than the stone-cold backup

syndrome mentioned earlier, U-joints usually fail after the seals holding the lubrication in the needle bearing cups fail. Once the seals let go, the grease quickly flies out and the needle bearings fail. It's easy to tell when a seal has failed because there is a telltale line of grease on the floor pan in line with the failed joint.

U-joints can also bind, which can cause noise or imbalance of the driveshaft. Sometimes, tapping the U-joint with a soft-faced hammer will loosen a binding U-joint and the problem will disappear. If so, the U-joint should be removed and inspected, then replaced or re-lubricated.

Removing and installing universal joints is not difficult. After removing the driveshaft, remove the clips that retain the U-joint bearing cup into the driveshaft yoke, propeller shaft, or mounting flange. Using a press or large-diameter punch and hammer to push on one cup will push the other cup out on the opposite side.

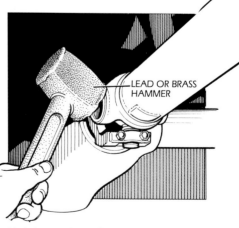

Lightly tapping a frozen U-joint may free it temporarily.

To install a U-joint, press the new cups in place after the U-joint spider is installed in the driveshaft. If you don't have a press, auto machine shops will also replace U-joints.

BAD VIBRATIONS

Vibration or imbalance problems that change with engine speed are usually confined to the torque converter on automatic transmissions, or the clutch and flywheel on manual transmissions. Balance problems that occur after the transmission output shaft are vehicle-speed sensitive and, aside from tire imbalance, can usually be traced to the driveshaft.

It's not difficult to distinguish between driveshaft and tire imbalance. Because the driveshaft spins ahead of the differential, it rotates 2.5 to 3.5 times faster than the tires do—with a corresponding difference in the frequency of the imbalance. You'll also feel driveshaft imbalance more in the seat and floor pan, because the vibrations don't have to travel up through the suspension springs before reaching the body and interior.

A driveshaft that is dented, bent, or missing its balance weight (usually located near the rear U-joint) causes driveshaft imbalance. You should also inspect the companion flange on the differential. If a U-joint lug has sheared off, the U-joint can ride off-center, causing imbalance.

Removing and replacing the driveshaft without returning it to its

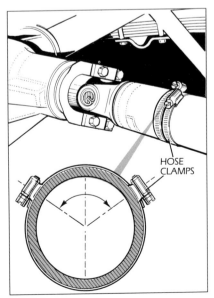

HOSE CLAMPS

Rebalance a driveshaft on the car by systematically adding weight with hose clamps.

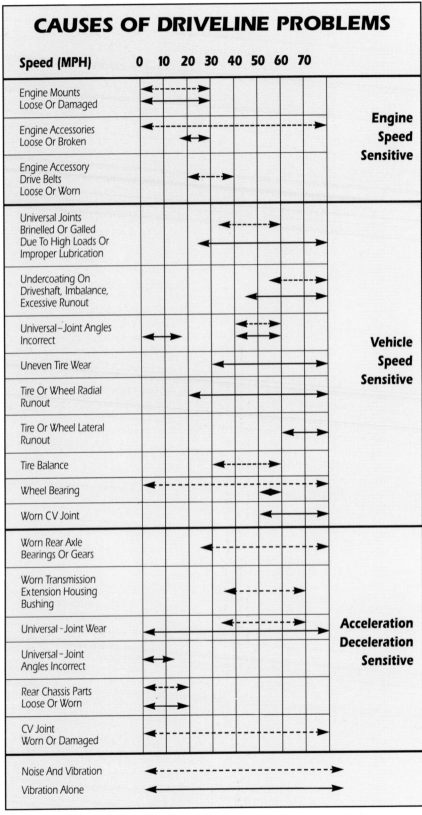

CAUSES OF DRIVELINE PROBLEMS

Speed (MPH)	0	10	20	30	40	50	60	70	
Engine Mounts Loose Or Damaged	←	-	- →	→					Engine Speed Sensitive
Engine Accessories Loose Or Broken		←	↔	-	-	-	-	→	
Engine Accessory Drive Belts Loose Or Worn				←	- →				
Universal Joints Brinelled Or Galled Due To High Loads Or Improper Lubrication					← - →	→			Vehicle Speed Sensitive
Undercoating On Driveshaft, Imbalance, Excessive Runout						← - →	→		
Universal-Joint Angles Incorrect	↔					← - ↔			
Uneven Tire Wear					←			→	
Tire Or Wheel Radial Runout					←			→	
Tire Or Wheel Lateral Runout							↔		
Tire Balance					← -	→			
Wheel Bearing	←	-	-	-	-	◆	→		
Worn CV Joint						↔			
Worn Rear Axle Bearings Or Gears					← -	-	-	→	Acceleration Deceleration Sensitive
Worn Transmission Extension Housing Bushing						← - →	→		
Universal-Joint Wear	←					← - →	→		
Universal-Joint Angles Incorrect	↔								
Rear Chassis Parts Loose Or Worn	← - →								
CV Joint Worn Or Damaged	← -	-	-	-	-	-	→		
Noise And Vibration	← -	-	-	-	-	-	→		
Vibration Alone	←							→	

184

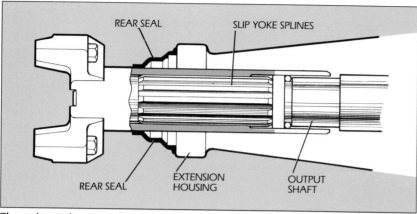

REAR SEAL

SLIP YOKE SPLINES

REAR SEAL

EXTENSION
HOUSING

OUTPUT
SHAFT

Thumping noises may emanate from a dry or worn set of output shaft splines.

original location can also cause driveshaft imbalance. For this reason, you should always mark the driveshaft with chalk and make a corresponding mark on the differential companion flange, so you can return the driveshaft to the same position. You should also mark a clutch, pressure plate, and torque converter before removing them for the same reason.

Sometimes you can cure driveshaft imbalance problems by simply rotating the driveshaft's location in the differential companion flange. Try rotating it one-quarter turn at a time to see if the imbalance goes away. If that doesn't work, mount two large hose clamps around the driveshaft near the differential end. The screws on the clamps will act as balance weights. Start with the screws opposite each other and gradually rotate the clamps so the screws get closer together and the imbalance disappears. If rotating the screws to one side of the shaft doesn't work, try rotating them to the other side. Failing that, many automotive machine shops and frame shops have the ability to balance driveshafts off the car.

THUMP-BUMP IN THE NIGHT

As the rear suspension moves up and down, the driveshaft swings in an arc. This means the driveshaft must get shorter and longer as it travels through the arc. For this reason, the front of the shaft is usually splined, and it slides into corresponding splines on the transmission tailshaft. A thump-bump sound can occur when going over bumps that can be traced to these splines. If the splines

get dry, they bind as the driveshaft gets longer and shorter. Eventually, a step wears into the splines, and the result is a thump-bump as the driveshaft moves in and out.

To inspect the splines, remove the driveshaft, then look at the splines inside the driveshaft yoke and on the transmission output shaft. The step is usually found on the yoke. The only cure is to replace it. Far more serious are stepped splines on the output shaft, because the transmission will have to be disassembled and the output shaft replaced.

DIFFERENTIAL EQUATIONS

If you hear clunks—especially around corners—and the U-joints

are okay, the problem may be excessive axle end play. To check for excessive end play, simply jack up the car and pull in and out on the rear wheel. If the axles are held into the axle housing with C-shaped retainers, the retainers or the groove in the axle may be worn and end play is the result. On Fords, you can reduce end play by putting shims behind the C-shaped retainers. On GM cars, you'll have to replace the axle, the retainer, or both.

Chuckles, chatters, ticks, clicks, whines, and whistles can all get their start in the differential. Chuckles and chatters can occur if the differential gear lube is low, or on limited-slip differentials, if the wrong gear lube is installed. Chatters can also occur if the differential (spider) gears are assembled too tightly. You'll also get chattering if the differential's limited-slip shim packs are too tight.

Differential whine can be traced to a few causes. Many ring and pinion gearsets are "timed" so each gear tooth on the ring meshes with a corresponding tooth on the pinion. If they don't, the result is whine. To check timing, remove the differential cover and look for witness marks on the pinion and ring gear. When you rotate the gears, the marks should align.

Other causes of whine are incorrect pinion bearing preload, an im-

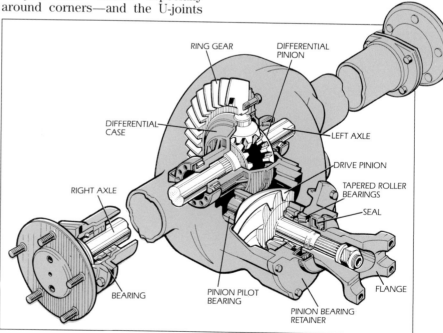

RING GEAR

DIFFERENTIAL
PINION

DIFFERENTIAL
CASE

LEFT AXLE

DRIVE PINION

TAPERED ROLLER
BEARINGS

SEAL

RIGHT AXLE

FLANGE

BEARING

PINION PILOT
BEARING

PINION BEARING
RETAINER

Noisy differentials may require partial disassembly to diagnose some problems.

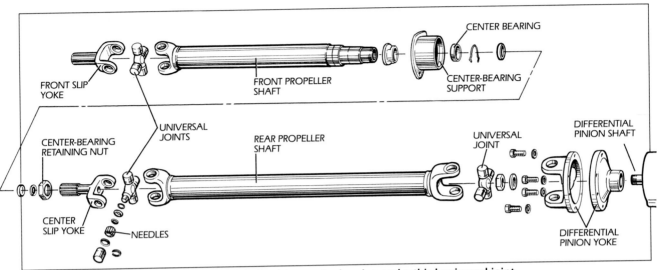

Some larger vehicles use a two-piece driveshaft with a center bearing and a third universal joint.

proper wear pattern on the ring and pinion gearset, or improper differential bearing spread. All of these problems should be checked and repaired by a qualified differential specialist.

One source of whine—usually loudest in the passenger compart-ment—can come from the middle of the driveshaft on some cars, such as early GM models and many Volvos. Because these cars have a two-piece driveshaft, the front half is supported by a bearing that's mounted around the driveshaft.

To check the center support bearing, remove the driveshaft (you'll usually have to remove the bearing mounting bolts to do this). Rotate the bearing to see that it operates smoothly and freely, with no noise. The rubber isolator between the bearing and its mount should also be free of play and cracks.

How to Maintain and Repair
FOUR-WHEEL DRIVE

Over hill, over dale—until you bend a wheel, bust a ball joint, or fry a wheel bearing.

Four-wheel-drive trucks are a lot of fun because they can take you places a car can't. But there's a price to pay in increased maintenance and repair, especially if you spend a lot of time sloshing through mud or pounding over rocks. Dirt and moisture are natural enemies of all bearings and joints, and you have to keep them clean and well lubricated if you want to keep rolling.

In addition to the wear and tear of off-road use, many 4×4 owners who have installed different wheels, tires, or suspension parts are plagued with steering shimmy problems.

In the following sections, we'll explain how to repair or install a steering damper for shimmy control, how to check for bent rims, and how to service 4 × 4 ball joints and wheel bearings.

SHIMMY CONTROL

Every time you drive over a small bump in the road, the tire involved gives the steering linkage a good smack. When a 4 × 4 is equipped with large wheels and tires, road shock forces may be multiplied. These forces cause motion in the steering linkage—shimmy, which is a frightening shaking of the tires and steering wheel.

A steering damper, attached to the tie rod on one end and the frame or front axle housing on the other, can greatly reduce the abuse (Fig. 1). Nothing more than a shock absorber, the steering damper arrests the motion that feels like you're losing control.

CHECKING AND REPLACING A STEERING DAMPER

Many 4 × 4s come factory-equipped with a steering damper. Because of its importance and because of the constant abuse to which it is subjected, check damper condition on a regular basis.

Each time you lube your front end, inspect the damper mountings. At each end of the damper, you'll

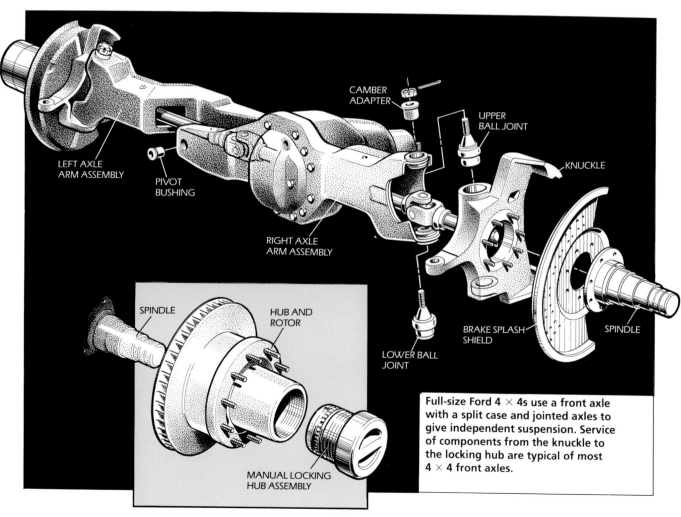

LEFT AXLE ARM ASSEMBLY
PIVOT BUSHING
RIGHT AXLE ARM ASSEMBLY
CAMBER ADAPTER
UPPER BALL JOINT
KNUCKLE
LOWER BALL JOINT
BRAKE SPLASH SHIELD
SPINDLE

SPINDLE
HUB AND ROTOR
MANUAL LOCKING HUB ASSEMBLY

Full-size Ford 4 × 4s use a front axle with a split case and jointed axles to give independent suspension. Service of components from the knuckle to the locking hub are typical of most 4 × 4 front axles.

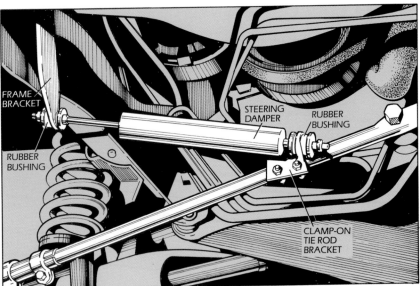

1 Steering shimmy problems, often exaggerated by oversize tire installation can be brought under control by installing a hydraulic steering damper on the linkage.

find rubber bushings. If the bushings are worn or deteriorating, they must be replaced.

Check the damper for signs of fluid leakage or a bent shaft. A light film of fluid near the shaft seal is sometimes normal, but the damper should not drip fluid. A leaking damper or one with a bent shaft must be replaced. If the damper is old and you're not sure about its condition, or if shimmy is a problem, install a new one.

If you've outfitted your rig with big mud tires, you probably need some help hanging on to the steering wheel.

Retrofit steering dampers are available from a number of companies. One principal supplier is Moog Automotive (P.O. Box 7224, St. Louis, MO 63177).

To install the steering damper, loosely attach the mounting brackets in the spots indicated in the instructions. Extend the damper and assemble the mounting bushings, washers, and nuts. The damper should be almost horizontal, with the shaft end slightly higher than the cylinder end. Make sure the damper has adequate clearance in respect to chassis parts, hoses, and so on. Tighten the mounting bolts, then turn the wheels to make sure the shock doesn't prevent full wheel movement.

CHECKING FOR BENT WHEELS

For those who really beat on their 4 × 4s, bent wheels are a common problem. If you experience a roughness or vibration immediately after an off-road trip, chances are you've smacked up a wheel. If you manage to cut a tire while bouncing around off-road, you should always check the wheel for damage.

Measure wheel runout with a dial indicator. If possible, radial and lateral runout should be measured on both inboard and outboard sides of the wheel (Fig. 2). If the wheel design makes the outboard measurement impossible, check inboard runout only. Check lateral runout with the indicator positioned perpendicular to the face of the wheel, against the smooth surface on the far edge of the rim. Check radial runout with the indicator mounted parallel to the wheel, against the flat part of the inner rim. Replace steel wheels if radial runout exceeds 0.040 inch or if lateral runout exceeds 0.045 inch. Replace aluminum wheels if either radial or lateral runout exceeds 0.030 inch.

BALL JOINT INSPECTION

Most manufacturers recommend that you check ball joints on a reg-

ular basis. For serious off-road use, check them every time you lube the steering and suspension parts. Some trucks, including Toyotas, do not have ball joints. Instead, the steering knuckle is mounted on cone-type bearings. If lubed on a regular basis, these should not require adjustment.

To check conventional ball joint suspensions, raise the truck with a jack positioned under the front differential housing. Chock the wheels and place jack stands under the axle, just inside the springs or in the positions recommended in your service or owner's manual. Rock the tires in and out and watch for side-to-side movement of the ball joint studs. Check for vertical looseness by attempting to raise each tire with a pry bar while watching the studs. Any easily noticeable movement is excessive.

On Ford minitrucks, check for side-to-side movement only. Watch the gap between the spindle and axle jaw while checking. More than 1/32-inch movement is excessive.

You'll need a fish scale to check the joints of full-size Chevy or GMC light trucks for binding (Fig. 3). Remove the wheels, then disengage the connecting rod and tie rod so that each knuckle assembly can be rotated independent of the other. Attach the scale's hook to the tie rod mounting hole of one of the steering knuckles. Then, with the

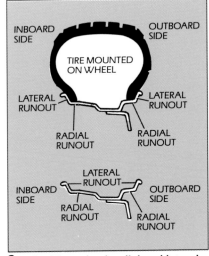

2 Checking wheel radial and lateral runout is done best with a dial indicator and the tire dismounted from the wheel.

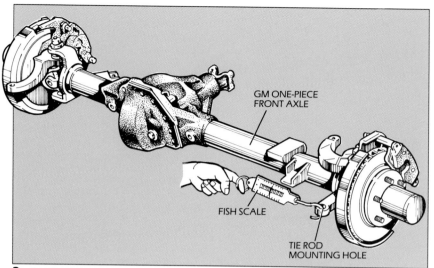

3 To check for binding in ball joints, measure the turning effort with a fish scale hooked to a tie rod mounting hole. The fish scale reading should not exceed 25 pounds.

knuckle assembly in the straight-ahead position, pull the scale toward the differential center section. Watch the scale to see how much force is needed to keep the knuckle turning after breakaway. For most trucks, it should not exceed 25 pounds.

BALL JOINT REPLACEMENT

To replace a ball joint on trucks with a one-piece or Ford-type front axle, you have to remove the locking hubs, the hub/rotor, and the spindles before you can disengage

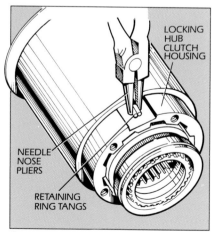

4 Removal of most locking hubs requires disengagement of hub retaining ring. Use needle-nose pliers to compress ring tangs.

the knuckle and ball joint from the front axle. For many trucks, including full-size Chevy, Ford, and Dodge and the Ford minitrucks, you'll need a ball-joint press to remove the joints from the knuckle. Before you can get close to the ball joints, you'll need a special spanner wrench to remove the wheel bearing outer locknut and a large socket for the adjusting nut. A torque wrench is needed to adjust the wheel bearing.

The replacement of the joint is the same as on a passenger car.

HUB REMOVAL, INSPECTION

The removal of either automatic or manual-locking hubs is fairly easy and is necessary for ball joint service or wheel bearing lube. A few examples follow. The procedures for other trucks are very similar, but there are quite a few different types of hubs that have been used over the last fifteen years. Even within one model year, different type hubs were used on some vehicles.

Disassembly of automatic locking hubs is somewhat complex, and there are too many steps and too many different procedures for us to cover them here. But it's a job you should be able to do if you have the factory service manual for your truck. Automatic locking hubs should be disassembled and lubed with automatic trans fluid, or as recommended, every 24,000 miles.

When disassembling an automatic hub, never remove the brake band from the drag sleeve and detent.

Disassembly of manual hubs is easy, and it's a good idea to pull them apart, clean the parts, check for galling, chips, or excessive wear, and reassemble them whenever you have them off for wheel bearing or ball joint service. Lube the parts with a coating of automatic transmission fluid or multipurpose grease, depending on manufacturer recommendation. Use a multipurpose grease or white lithium grease on the O-ring seals.

To remove the automatic locking hub used on most late-model Dodge trucks, unscrew the five cover screws, using a Torx T-25 driver. Remove the cover, along with the bearing race spring assembly, the sealing ring, the seal bridge retainer, and the bearing components. Locate the wire retaining ring on the outer edge of the hub clutch housing, squeeze it together with needle-nose pliers and pull the remaining parts from the spindle (Fig. 4).

To remove the automatic locking hubs used on Ford Bronco II and Ranger, unscrew the retainer washers from the lug nut studs, then pull the hub assembly off the spindle. Remove the snap ring from the end of the spindle shaft, then remove the axle shaft spacer, needle thrust bearing, and the bearing spacer. Being careful not to damage it, pull the cam assembly off the wheel bearing adjusting nut along with the thrust spacer and needle thrust bearing (Fig. 5).

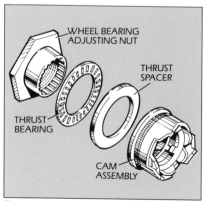

5 Take extra care not to damage the cam assembly when removing automatic locking hubs from Ford Bronco II/Ranger axles.

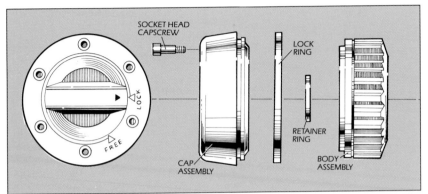

6 To remove Ford manual locking hubs, the lock ring located in the groove of the wheel hub must first be taken out with needle-nose pliers. Then you can slide the hub off.

To service the Ford manual hub used on Bronco, F-150, and F-250, disengage the cap from the hub by unscrewing the six socket head capscrews (Fig. 6). Next, remove the snap ring from the axle shaft. Then locate the lock ring that is seated in the groove of the wheel hub, and use a pair of needle-nose pliers to remove this ring. The body assembly should then slide out of the wheel hub. You may have to use a puller to remove the body assembly. To service the manual hubs used on Jeep CJ and Scrambler, remove the hub bolts and tabbed lockwashers along with the hub body and gasket. Remove the retaining ring from the axle shaft, then the hub clutch and bearing assembly. When reinstalling the hub, use a new gasket. Do not turn the hub dial until it has been reinstalled.

WHEEL BEARING SERVICE

If you keep your truck out of the mud and water, a wheel bearing and spindle bearing lube job every 12,000 miles is adequate, but if you're continuously blasting through the muck, you should do it at least twice as often. As noted previously, you'll need a special tool—a spanner wrench for the wheel bearing outer locknut—to service the wheel bearings on most trucks (Fig. 7). You'll also need a gigantic hex socket (2⅜ in. for many types) to remove the wheel bearing adjusting nut, and a torque wrench.

T-Trucks have permanently lubed, sealed wheel bearings. These bearings are part of a one-piece hub and bearing assembly that bolts

right up to the steering knuckle. If they fail, the entire unit is replaced.

To service the wheel bearings on most other 4 × 4s, remove the locking hubs as described above, then remove the brake caliper and hang it out of the way. Next, remove the wheel bearing lock-nut, lock ring, and adjusting nut. Pull the hub and disc assembly from the spindle. The outer wheel bearing cone and roller assembly will slide out as the hub is removed.

Unscrew the spindle retaining nuts. Then remove the spindle from the knuckle studs and axle shaft. You may have to tap the end of the spindle lightly with a soft hammer to disengage it (Fig. 8). If there's a thrust washer behind the spindle, note its position and mark one stud and washer hole, so the washer can be reinstalled in the same position.

Clean any old grease from the needle bearings inside the spindle and from the spindle bore seal. If the bearing is in good condition, thoroughly lubricate the needle bearing and pack the spindle face that mates with the spindle bore seal using a high quality multipurpose bearing grease. Reinstall the spindle over the axle and torque the retaining nuts to spec (20 to 30 ft.-lb. for most Ford and Dodge light trucks, 65 ft.-lb. for Chevy and GMC trucks).

Pry the grease seal out of the back of the hub and discard it. Remove the inner bearing cone. If the bearings have to be replaced rather than just repacked, you should drive the bearing cups out of the hub and replace them as well. In most cases you should be able to knock them out with a long brass dowel rod and

a hammer, but for some hubs you may need a slide hammer and puller device to yank them out.

Lube the bearings with multipurpose bearing grease after cleaning all old grease from the bearings and hub. Pack the cones and rollers with the grease. If you don't have a bearing packer, work as much lubricant as possible between the rollers and the cages. Then, position the inner bearing cone and roller in the inner cup and install a new grease seal, carefully tapping it into place with a large socket or cup that fits just within its perimeter. Position the hub and disc assembly on the spindle, install the outer bearing assembly and the adjusting nut.

WHEEL BEARING ADJUSTMENT

Before reinstalling the locking hubs, you have to adjust the wheel bearings. Using the spanner wrench

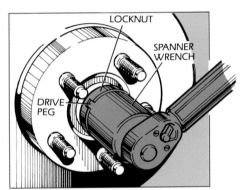

7 A four-prong spanner wrench helps to remove the outer wheel bearing locknut.

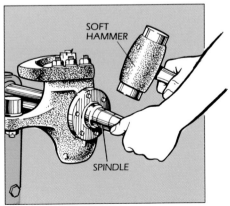

8 A soft hammer may be needed to disengage front spindle from knuckle studs.

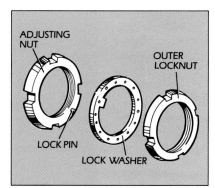

9 Wheel bearing locknut peg fits into spindle groove. Hole in lockwasher engages pin.

socket and a torque wrench, tighten the bearing inner adjusting nut to 50 ft.-lb. while rotating the wheel back and forth. Loosen the nut and re-tighten to the same spec. With GM automatic hubs, retighten to 35 ft.-lb. Back off the adjusting nut 45°, then install the lockwasher by turn-ing the inner adjusting nut until the lock pin slips into the nearest hole in the lockwasher (Fig. 9). Install the outer locknut and tighten it to 150 ft.-lb. (160 ft.-lb. on GM). If you want to make sure you've got it right, check wheel end play with a dial indicator. It should be less than 0.006 inch.

LOCKING HUB INSTALLATION

To reinstall Ford and Jeep manual locking hubs, assemble parts in the reverse order of the procedure found above in the section "Hub re-moval and inspection." After install-ing Jeep hubs, raise the front of the truck, turn the hub dials to "4 × 2," and rotate the wheels. If the wheels don't rotate freely, check the hub in-stallation and make sure the dials are fully in "4 × 2" position.

To reinstall Dodge automatic locking hubs, check to see that the drag sleeve retainer washer is in po-sition between the wheel bearing adjusting nut and the locknut. Make sure that the spacer and retaining ring are in position on the axle shaft, then install the automatic locking hub into the wheel hub, aligning the drag sleeve slots with the tabs on the drag sleeve retainer washer. Align the outer clutch housing splines with the splines of the wheel hub. Then, loosen the cover screws three or four turns and push in on the cover to allow the retaining ring to expand into the rotor hub groove. Using your Torx T-25 driver, tighten the cover screws to 40 to 50 in.-lb.

To reassemble Ford minitruck automatic hubs, install the locknut needle bearing and thrust washer in the order of removal and push the cam assembly onto the locknut by lining up the key in the fixed cam with the spindle keyway. Install bearing thrust washer, needle thrust bearing, and axle shaft spacer. At-tach the snap ring to the end of the spindle, then install the locking hub assembly over the spindle by lining up the three legs in the hub assem-bly with the pockets in the cam as-sembly.

How to Service CV JOINTS

Constant-velocity joints are taking the place of universal joints that Saturday mechanics know so well. In a rear-drive car, U-joints connect the driveshaft to the transmission and rear axle, allowing the axle to move up and down on its suspension. In a front-drive car, CV joints connect the drive axles to the transaxle and front wheels.

Four CV joints are used—one at each end of each axle—to allow the front wheels to move up and down with the suspension, and to steer through angles of about 20°.

The old type of universal joint from rear-wheel-drive cars would not take the abuse of the front-drive

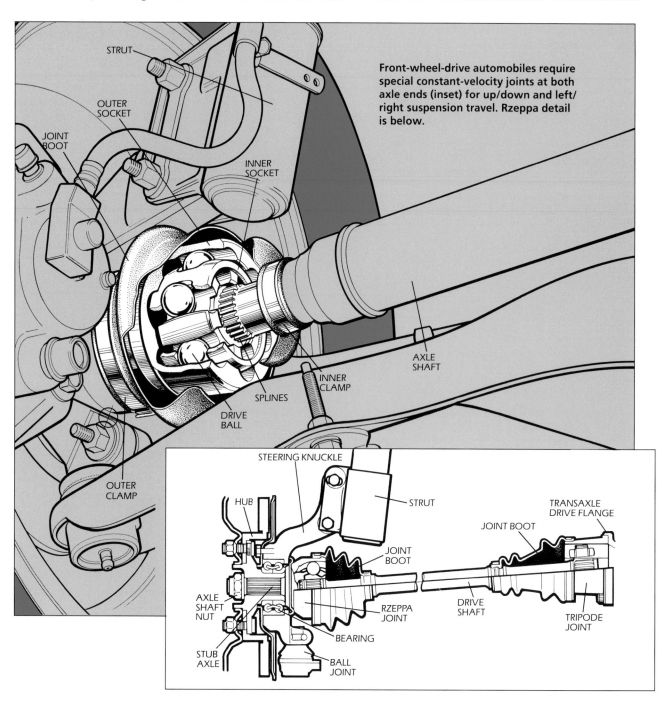

Front-wheel-drive automobiles require special constant-velocity joints at both axle ends (inset) for up/down and left/right suspension travel. Rzeppa detail is below.

STRUT

OUTER SOCKET

JOINT BOOT

INNER SOCKET

AXLE SHAFT

INNER CLAMP

SPLINES

DRIVE BALL

OUTER CLAMP

STEERING KNUCKLE

STRUT

HUB

JOINT BOOT

TRANSAXLE DRIVE FLANGE

JOINT BOOT

AXLE SHAFT NUT

RZEPPA JOINT

DRIVE SHAFT

TRIPODE JOINT

STUB AXLE

BEARING

BALL JOINT

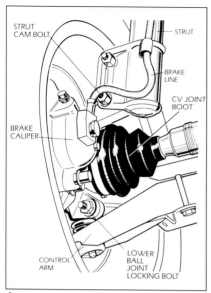

1 Protective boots enclosing CV joints must be flexible and have an unbroken seal to keep out destructive road grit.

system. Furthermore, a shaft driven by a conventional U-joint will not maintain a constant velocity unless it is perfectly aligned with the driving shaft. If the conventional U-joint is flexed, the driven shaft speeds up and slows down as it rotates.

So, for FWD cars, a joint is needed that not only will deliver power at sharp angles, but also will not cause serious vibration and make driving unpleasant.

There are two types of joint that fit the bill. One, the Rzeppa joint, achieves these goals by joining the two shafts with a ball and groove arrangement. The second, called a tripode or tri-pot joint, joins the shafts with grooves and roller bearings. Tripode joints are usually found at the inboard ends of most FWD driveshafts, while Rzeppa joints are generally used at the outboard ends.

Both types are quite durable, but there are certain precautions that must be taken with these units to ensure long life.

Because the CV joint flexes farther than the older U-joints, it requires a softer seal to protect the innards from the grime, dirt, and salt that splash up from the road. The easiest method of protecting the unit is to cover it with a boot similar to the old U-joint covers used on Chrysler cars from the 1930s through the '60s.

As with the old Chryslers, if this boot should rupture, all of the abrasive junk on the road collects on the lubricant in the joint and begins to act more like a grinding compound than a lubricant.

Taking care of a front-wheel-drive car, then, begins with getting the car on a lift or being able to get under it safely a few times a year to check the CV joint boots for damage. You should do this before winter sets in, then once during the winter and again in the spring. If you do an oil change and lube at 3,000-mile intervals, check the boots as part of this service.

Cold temperatures and accumulated ice and snow can tear a perfectly good boot to shreds in a matter of minutes.

CV JOINT INSPECTION

During the inspection, the wheels must be free to rotate so that you can see all the way around the boot. The clamps on each end of the boot should be checked to be sure that they are tight and not rusted through or broken (see Fig. 1). The boot material, a rubbery substance, should be flexible to the touch. A boot that's hard and brittle is likely to rupture soon and should be replaced. Grease spray around the joint is a sure sign of a damaged boot.

There should be no signs of tears or holes in the boot, since any hole will allow water and dirt to enter the joint. A damaged boot must be replaced immediately.

If the boot is torn, check the lube inside for grit or particles by rubbing a bit of it between clean fingers. If grit is present or if the car has developed symptoms of joint failure, the shafts will have to be removed for joint service. A boot that has become soft and mushy should also be replaced.

Serious joint damage can usually be detected when driving. A clicking noise when turning indicates a worn or damaged outboard joint. A clunk during acceleration indicates a worn or damaged inboard joint. And shudder or vibration during acceleration usually indicates a damaged or sticking inboard joint.

On the other hand, if a boot is only slightly damaged or worn and there's no indication of further problems, the boot alone can be replaced. There's more than one way

to do the job. You can install a factory original boot or one of the new aftermarket quick-fit boots.

QUICK-FIT BOOTS

With the quick-fit boots the job can be done without removing the axle because the boots come with a lengthwise split in them. You simply cut the clamps that hold on the old boot and use a knife to cut the old boot off the car. In the package of the new boot you will find a container of lubricant to be used on the joint once you've cleaned it. The new boot is slipped in place and the end clamps are loosely attached to position the boot.

A special bonding solvent supplied in the kit is applied to the edges of the split (Fig. 2). The edges are tied together and in forty to sixty minutes the solvent will cure, permanently sealing the seam. Simply finish tightening the end clamps and you're on your way. The quick-fit boot is available from most parts stores.

If your inspection revealed that the joints are damaged or contaminated with grit, or if you decide to replace the boots with conventional factory units, you'll have to remove the driveshaft and joint assembly.

You may decide that you don't want to attempt this job yourself. On some cars, you will need a two- or three-leg hub puller to push the shaft out of the steering knuckle. On

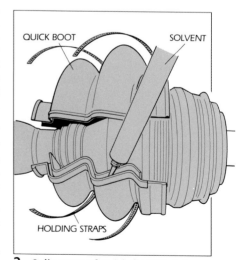

2 Split seam of quick-fit CV joint boot is permanently joined with a special bonding solvent that's supplied in the kit.

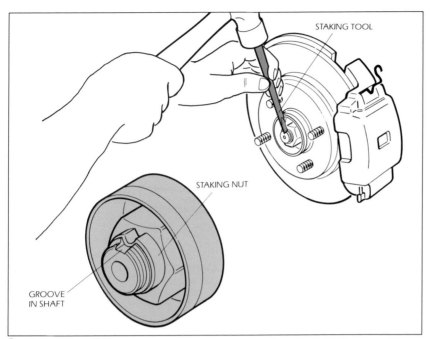

3 Staked axle shaft nuts are removed by unthreading. Restake them as shown with a rounded chisel edge.

the nut is tightened, the neck of the nut is staked in place.

When removing this type of nut, make no attempt to relieve the staked portion, just unscrew it as found. You can make a tool from a small cold chisel to stake the nut on reassembly. Grind the sharp edge from the chisel, leaving a rounded edge. The recommended radius is $\frac{1}{16}$ in. Place the tool directly over the groove in the shaft and, wearing safety glasses, use a couple of solid hammer blows to complete the staking (Fig. 3).

The third type of self-locking nut uses a nylon insert to keep it from backing off the shaft once it's tight.

You should replace a staked nut as well as a self-locking nut each time they are removed.

Once the axle nuts have been loosened, jack the car up by the frame and place stands under the frame in the locations shown in a shop manual, letting the wheels hang free. Remove the wheels and finish removing the hub nut and washer.

other cars, particularly GM models, it may be difficult to pry the inner CV joint away from the transaxle without a special tool. If you do decide to have a professional do the job, find one you know, or one who's NIASE (National Institute of Automotive Service Excellence) certified in front end and suspension work.

If you decide to do it yourself, you must obtain a factory service manual or general auto repair manual that includes specific, detailed instructions for performing this service on your particular vehicle.

REMOVING THE AXLE

The procedure begins with the removal of the large axle shaft retaining nuts that are found where the front-wheel bearing nuts would be on a rear-wheel-drive car. This is best done by loosening the nuts while the car is still on the ground. These nuts are usually torqued to between 180 and 225 lb.-ft. and require a good heavy socket and a long breaker bar.

Chock the wheels, apply the emergency brake, and put the car in gear or an automatic transmission in PARK.

There are three methods of locking the axle nut to the shaft—with a cotter pin (just like the front-wheel retaining nut on a rear-

drive car), a staked nut, or a self-locking nut.

The staked nut looks much like a castle nut—one that could be used with a cotter pin—except that it doesn't have the cotter-pin grooves. The threaded portion of the shaft has a groove cut into it and, once

CHRYSLERS AND FORDS

On Chrysler and Ford vehicles, remove the nut that connects the tie rod to the steering knuckle, then separate the rod end from the knuckle. Take care not to tear the

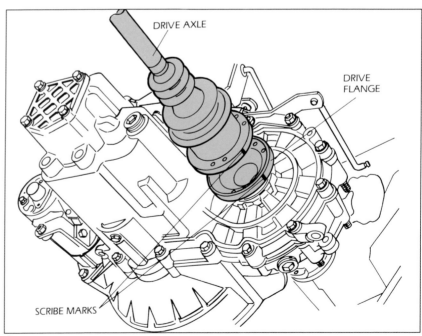

4 Drive axles bolted to transaxle should be scribed for proper alignment on reassembly.

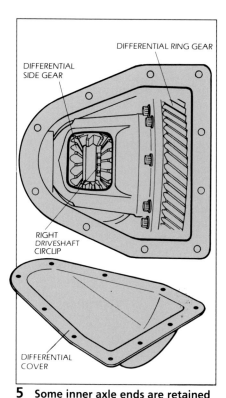

DIFFERENTIAL RING GEAR

DIFFERENTIAL SIDE GEAR

RIGHT DRIVESHAFT CIRCLIP

DIFFERENTIAL COVER

5 Some inner axle ends are retained by circlips. Release the clips after the differential cover has been removed.

rubber seal on the tie-rod end.

Remove the pinch bolt that holds the ball joint to the steering knuckle and use a pry bar to separate the lower control arm and ball joint from the steering knuckle. If the car is equipped with a front sway bar, unbolt it before you try to separate the ball joint from the knuckle. Don't use a pickle fork on the ball joints or tie-rod ends unless you plan to replace them, as the fork will tear the seals.

Attempt to move the knuckle assembly and strut away from the driveshaft, allowing the shaft to drop out of the hub. If the shaft won't release from the hub, get a puller that can be attached to the wheel studs on the hub. Use the puller's screw jack to push the shaft out of the hub.

Determine the method used to hold the inner ends of the shafts to the differential. There are three common methods: a flange to which the half-shaft is bolted, a stub shaft that enters the differential and is held in place with a circlip, or just stub shafts that enter the differential. The latter are held in place with thrust bearings in the hub assembly.

Stub shafts are common on General Motors and Ford vehicles.

On all Chryslers, except those equipped with the A-412 transaxle, the speedometer drive gear must be detached from the transaxle before the right-side driveshaft can be removed.

If the inner axle end is held in place by a bolted flange (Fig. 4), as on some Chrysler and Volkswagen cars, mark the flanges with a scribe to ensure their proper relationship when you reassemble them. The attaching bolts on this type are socket-head (Allen) capscrews. Use a good ⅜-in.-drive socket-head wrench with a ratchet to remove the screws and a torque wrench to reinstall them. The socket-head screws may be hidden behind protective plastic caps on some Chrysler models. Apply 33 lb.-ft. of torque to the screws during reassembly.

When there are no flanges on the inner ends of the drive axles, the differential cover may have to be removed to relieve the pressure on the circlip that retains each shaft. This arrangement is used on early Omni/Horizon models.

OMNI/HORIZON AXLES

To begin with, the procedure is the same: Loosen the hub nut; jack up the car and support it on stands with the wheels and suspension hanging free; then remove the hub nut, washer, and wheel. Next, place a drain pan under the differential cover. Loosen the bolts and remove the cover. Rotate the driveshaft until the circlips' ends are visible (Fig. 5). Squeeze the tangs of each circlip with a pair of needle-nose pliers and push the stub shaft into the side gear by prying with a screwdriver inserted between the stub shaft and the differential pinion shaft.

Release the ball joint and tie-rod end as described below. Separate the splined end of the shaft from the knuckle by pushing the knuckle away from the CV joint. Remove the driveshaft assembly from the vehicle by pulling outward on the inboard CV joint. Don't pull on the shaft.

When reinstalling the differential cover, Chrysler recommends that you use the silicone RTV gasket material in a tube. After all traces of the old gasket material have been removed from both mating surfaces,

draw a bead of the RTV material on the cover, going completely around the cover and making a circle around each bolt hole.

Allow the material to skin over—about five minutes—and install the cover loosely. Just snug the bolts up a bit more than finger tight and allow the material to set for about five more minutes. Then finish the job by torquing the bolts to 12–15 lb.-ft. for Chrysler-built cars.

Removing the third type of axle shaft requires the use of a couple of

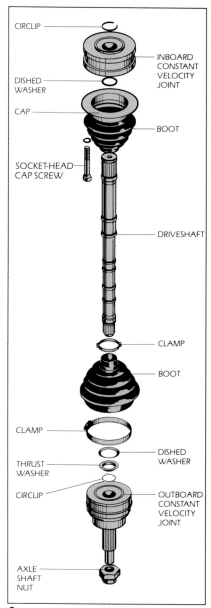

CIRCLIP

DISHED WASHER

CAP

SOCKET-HEAD CAP SCREW

INBOARD CONSTANT VELOCITY JOINT

BOOT

DRIVESHAFT

CLAMP

BOOT

CLAMP

THRUST WASHER

CIRCLIP

DISHED WASHER

OUTBOARD CONSTANT VELOCITY JOINT

AXLE SHAFT NUT

6 CV joints may be serviced individually after the axle has been removed. Disassemble the CV joints by removing circlips.

O-ring pullers. Some auto parts jobbers who carry rebuilt axle shafts or a stock of CV joints will either lend or rent the tools to you. You still must remove the axle hub nut and washer as before, as well as the wheel.

GM JOINTS

When removing CV joints on GM cars, you should disengage the steering knuckle from the strut rather than from the control arm (see illustration on page 192). Before the strut can be disengaged, the brake line must be disconnected from the strut and the caliper must be detached and supported.

You must also mark the cam bolt on the strut mount so it can be reinstalled in the same position to retain wheel alignment (Fig. 1).

A special adapter is used with a slide hammer to remove the stub shaft end (inner end) from the differential of a GM FWD car. You should have a drain pan handy, as fluid will leak from the differential.

The next step requires a puller that resembles a steering wheel or harmonic balancer puller. It is used to force the axle shaft out of the front wheel hub. Don't use a hammer here since the blows would probably ruin the front wheel bearings, which cost over $100 each.

Once the shafts are on the bench, you must determine whether to replace them with rebuilt units or to disassemble them and replace only the CV joints and boots. (The CV joints would be making noises if they are defective or worn out—noises like snapping on turns or grinding and backlash when applying the throttle or letting the car coast.)

CV joints that need replacement can also cause a shimmy in the steering system. If you've managed to get the shafts out of the car and know that the joints will need to be replaced, you should consider replacing the entire axle shaft assemblies with rebuilt units. (A rebuilt shaft assembly for the right side of an Omni, for example, carries a list price of about $240, while the parts needed to rebuild the shaft in the shop carry a list price of about $195). Then the procedure boils down to bolting in the rebuilt shaft, which is already assembled and lubricated.

REPLACING CV JOINTS

However, if you are adventurous, you can remove the CV joints and install new ones on the axle. To perform the job, you must have a service manual with specific instructions for your car.

Most CV joints are held together by a series of circlips which, when removed, allow the joint to be disassembled (Fig. 6). Before disassembling the joint, make sure your work area is really clean. Cover the entire work surface with a piece of towel. The thickness of the towel will stop any pieces that drop from bouncing and becoming lost.

Some axles have balance weights (Fig. 7) which should not be removed.

Without a doubt, servicing front-wheel-drive components is a more involved job than many home mechanics are willing to take on. In some cases it may require special tools to torque the axle shaft nuts (which must be tightened to 225 lb.-ft.), pullers to remove the driveshafts, or equipment to realign the front end after unbolting and reinstalling front strut components. But regular inspection and maintenance of the CV joint boots, coupled with the knowledge of how these parts function, will go a long way toward making life with front-wheel-drive cars easier and less costly.

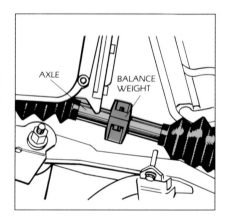

7 To prevent unwanted vibrations, axle balance weights should not be removed.

How to Replace a CLUTCH

This is the afternoon you've been dreaming about. The sky is crystal blue and the mountains beckon on the horizon. But traffic on the freeway is thick and moving at a frustrating five below the limit. Suddenly, you see your opportunity develop as a gap appears in the morass of Sunday drivers. You deftly knock the shift lever down a notch to third gear, release the clutch, and tromp the gas pedal.

But all you get is a 350-horsepower scream of wasted power as you watch the tach needle jump

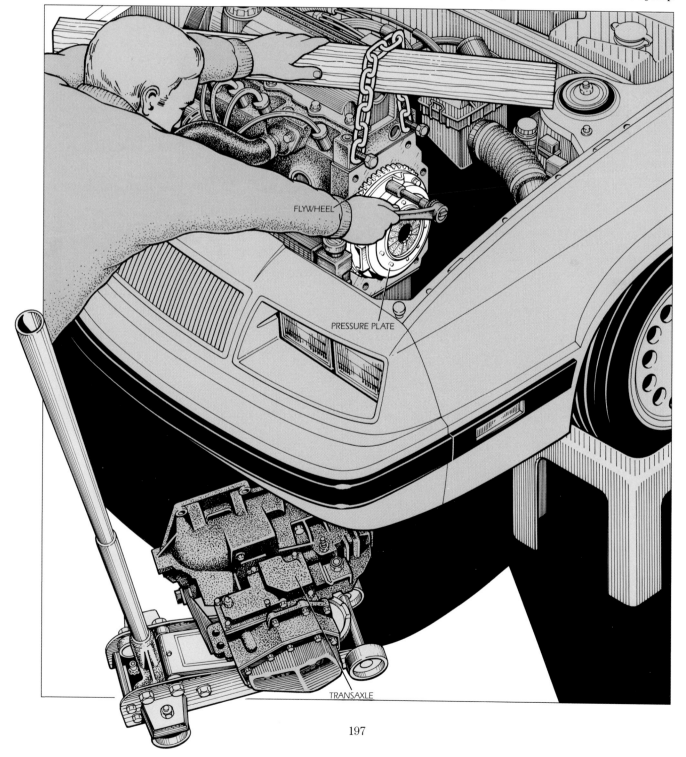

FLYWHEEL

PRESSURE PLATE

TRANSAXLE

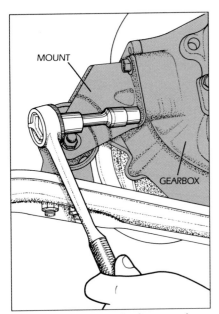

Support the engine of a front-engine car before undoing the transaxle mounts.

to six grand while the speedometer needle slowly creeps up from 50 mph, accompanied by the acrid smell of fried clutch.

THE WEAK LINK

No matter how sophisticated your car or truck—whether it is equipped with front-wheel drive, rear-wheel drive, or all-wheel drive, be it a fuel-frugal econobox or a tire-smoking rocket sled—if it is equipped with a manual transmission, it also has a clutch.

And sooner or later the clutch will wear out and need to be replaced.

Actually, the term *clutch* used here refers to the entire assembly that channels engine power to the transmission. The clutch assembly consists of the engine's flywheel, a covered spring-loaded steel disc called the pressure plate, a friction disc referred to as the clutch disc, and a release-bearing assembly commonly called the throwout bearing.

The pressure-plate assembly is bolted to the flywheel and sandwiches the friction disc between matching surfaces on the flywheel and pressure-plate disc. The center hub of the friction disc is splined to the transmission's input shaft. The friction disc can slide fore and aft

on the shaft, but when it rotates, so does the shaft.

When the clutch is engaged, the heavy springs behind the steel pressure plate squeeze the friction disc solidly against the flywheel.

When the clutch is disengaged—when you step on the clutch pedal—the release bearing is forced against fingerlike levers which release the spring force of the pressure plate. This allows the friction disc to slide away from the flywheel, disconnecting the transmission from the engine.

Each time you engage the clutch, the friction disc briefly slips—as it begins to contact the spinning flywheel, the friction disc must catch up to the flywheel in speed. This slipping action, as well as the normal function of maintaining friction between the pressure plate and flywheel, wears away the friction material. In addition, with time and use, the springs in the pressure-plate assembly weaken, loosening their grip on the friction disc.

Eventually, the clutch disc will begin to constantly slip between the flywheel and the steel pressure plate. That slippage is exaggerated by sudden and severe loads on the clutch—hard acceleration, pulling a heavy load, or climbing a steep hill.

Normal use also weakens the springs in the hub of the friction disc. These springs absorb the rotational shocks when the friction disc engages the flywheel. Time also takes its toll on the release bearing, which spins along with the clutch each time you step on the clutch pedal. And as the miles accumulate,

the surfaces of the flywheel, pressure plate, and clutch disc can form ridges, cracks, and scores. In addition, a leaking seal can saturate the clutch with oil.

Weak hub springs or an oil-saturated, glazed, or otherwise damaged friction surface cause uneven clutch engagement, which results in chatter.

PUT IN SOME SLACK

As the clutch wears, the linkage that operates it should be adjusted to ensure that the disc fully engages and disengages. Press down the pedal with your hand and use a ruler to measure how far the pedal travels before it starts moving the clutch. Either judge the difference in pedal resistance between the relatively light force of the return spring and the heavier resistance of the clutch itself or remove the return spring altogether to make the check. Typically, pedal free play can vary from 1/2 in. to 1 in.

Adjusting the free play in the linkage is usually done at the release-bearing fork on the clutch/flywheel housing. On vehicles with hydraulically activated clutch linkage, the adjustment may be made near the clutch pedal and the master cylinder or the release fork and the slave cylinder.

To restore the linkage's free play, you typically need to loosen a locknut or remove a retaining clip and then thread in or thread out the adjusting nut or rod. Tighten the locknut and remeasure the pedal's free play.

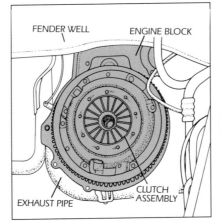

On a transverse-engine car, the flywheel and clutch are accessible from a wheel well.

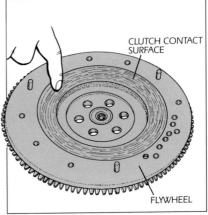

Check the flywheel's friction contact surface for scores, cracks, and severe heat bluing.

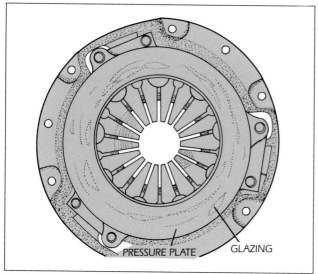

Glazing on the pressure plate can be from weak or broken pressure-plate springs.

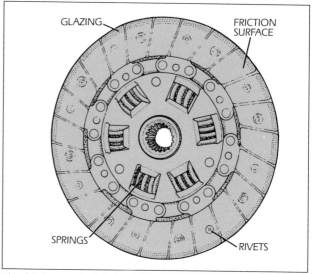

The friction material should be above the rivetheads. Weak hub springs cause chatter.

GETTING TO THE HEART OF IT

If adjusting the clutch linkage does not cure the problem, you're going to have to delve deeper. On almost all vehicles, this means removing the clutch assembly to inspect it. Once you've gone to the trouble of removing the clutch, you'll probably replace all of the parts.

Removing the clutch almost always means removing the transmission. And in front-wheel-drive cars, the task requires the removal of the transmission/differential unit—the transaxle—and this often involves removing both axle shafts.

And with most 4WD sport/utility vehicles and pickup trucks, removing the transmission involves the added complexity and weight of the four-wheel drive's transfer case.

Depending on how many mounts your vehicle's engine sits on and where they are placed, you may have to support the engine before you begin removing the transmission. Most front-drive cars rely on mounts on the transaxle to help carry the engine.

You can support the engine with an engine hoist. Or you can tie the engine to a beam (a solid 4 × 4 does fine) lying across the engine compartment. Take care not to rest the beam on sheet-metal or any non-structural steel. Also be sure not to let the beam foul against any accessories.

Once the weight of the engine is supported, you can begin.

Unless you have a pit in your garage floor or have a vehicle that sits tall off the ground, you will have to raise the vehicle to gain access beneath for you to work and to slide the transmission or transaxle out from under it. Jack up the vehicle and place it on safety stands. If the transmission can be removed without taking off any wheels, you can drive the vehicle onto work ramps.

MAKING THE DISCONNECTION

Before removing the transmission from the engine, you must uncouple the transmission from the rest of the drivetrain. In the case of a rear-wheel-drive vehicle, this means removing the driveshaft from the rear of the transmission. With 4WD sport/utility vehicles and trucks, you must disconnect the front driveshaft as well. With a front-wheel-drive vehicle, you must remove the axle shafts that attach the transaxle to the front wheels.

On many vehicles, once the driveshaft or drive axles are removed from the transmission, there is nothing to prevent all of the transmission oil from pouring out of the housing. Some manufacturers recommend draining the oil from the transmission before removing it. Others recommend merely plugging the shaft or axle opening after removing the

drive axles or driveshaft. However, if you have not replaced the gearbox oil within the recommended interval, drain the old oil and refill the transmission with fresh lubricant.

Before disconnecting the driveshaft at the rear universal joint, mark the position of the driveshaft in the U-joint's yoke to maintain the drivetrain's balance when you reassemble. Once the driveshaft is disconnected at the rear, you can slide it forward into the transmission housing to gain enough space to clear the rear axle unit. Then slide the driveshaft out from the transmission. Take care not to damage the splines on the front end of the shaft, the transmission's rear oil seal, or the front universal joint.

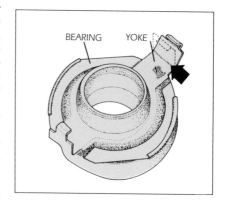

Cracked or broken yoke or a worn release-bearing hub causes chatter or slipping.

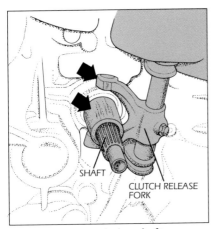

Damage to transmission shaft or bearing fork can snag the release bearing.

The procedures for removing the drive axles for front-wheel-drive vehicles vary from make to make. Depending on your car, you may have to remove the front wheels, the brake rotors, the lower strut mounts, or other suspension links. You will also have to remove the nut or retaining clips at the ends of the shafts.

The axle retaining nut on some front-drive cars is self-locking and, once removed, must be discarded. Likewise, the retaining clips used on the ends of some drive axles must be replaced once removed as well.

However, once any retaining clips or nuts are removed, the drive axle should pull straight out of the transaxle. As with a rear-wheel-drive vehicle, take care not to damage the oil seals in the transaxle or the splines on the ends of the axle. In addition, with a front-wheel-drive vehicle, be sure not to damage the constant-velocity joints at each end of the drive axle. Take care not to pinch or tear the CV-joint boots.

You must also disconnect the clutch and shift linkages as well as the speedometer cable from the transmission before you can remove the gearbox from the engine. If your vehicle has a hydraulically activated clutch linkage with the slave cylinder mounted on the transmission which requires you to disconnect the slave from the master, you will have to bleed the system the same way you bleed the brake system after you've reinstalled the transmission. Also, depending on your vehicle, you might have to remove the starter motor.

Once the transmission is free, you can unbolt it from its mounts and from the engine.

Before you slide the transmission off its locating dowels and away from the engine—which often requires some initial persuasion with a small pry bar—have the transmission properly supported by a floor jack with a large cradle or by a transmission jack. A front-wheel-drive transaxle or a transmission with a transfer case can weigh a few hundred pounds.

Once the transmission is removed from the engine, you can remove the clutch itself.

Partially loosen the bolts through the pressure plate that hold the clutch assembly to the flywheel. The springs in the pressure plate will push the plate out against the bolts. As you finish loosening and removing the bolts, the friction disc will slip down.

Be prepared to catch both the pressure plate and the friction disc when you remove the final bolt.

FALLOUT FOR INSPECTION

With normal wear, the friction surfaces of the clutch disc should be worn, and if the clutch had been slipping badly, expect it to be glazed as well. The metal surface of the pressure plate may also show some heat bluing from slippage. Replacing them with new parts will solve the problem.

Inspect all the parts to determine if there is a problem other than from normal wear.

If even one of the disc-hub springs is broken or weak—possibly even loose—the clutch will chatter when engaged.

Oil soaked into the friction disc would cause chattering. It also indicates a leak at either the engine's rear main oil seal or the transmission's front oil seal.

Remove the flywheel from the engine to inspect the engine's oil seal for signs of leakage. If the seal is suspect, replace it. Also inspect the flywheel. If the flywheel is glazed, burned, cracked, or scored, it must either be resurfaced or replaced. If your engine uses a pilot bearing in the center of the flywheel's hub, check that bearing. Replace it if it is at all suspect.

Remove the clutch-release bearing from its fork. Clean the trans-

mission's input shaft and inspect it. If the surface around the shaft that the bearing rides on is deeply scored or worn, the bearing will stick, causing partial or uneven clutch engagement. If the splines of the input shaft are damaged, the friction disc will stick. If there is any damage to the transmission shaft, it must be replaced. Also inspect the shaft's oil seal for leakage. Replace a leaking seal.

Operate the release-bearing fork —it should move freely and easily throughout its entire range. If it binds, it can prevent the clutch from fully engaging or disengaging.

Inspect the release bearing and its hub carefully. Spin the bearing—it should move freely, quietly, and smoothly. Even if the release bearing seems good, replace it as a preventive measure. If the surface of the bearing's hub is scored or worn, the bearing will not slide smoothly on the transmission shaft—replace it.

PUTTING IT ALL TOGETHER

When installing the flywheel on the crankshaft, be certain that you follow the manufacturer's recommendations—some makers use flywheel mounting bolts that must be replaced if removed. Others use a special bolt locking plate.

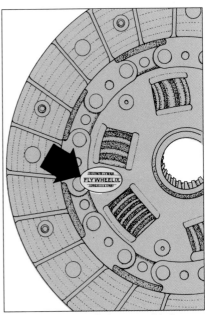

Take care to install the new friction disc with the proper side against the flywheel.

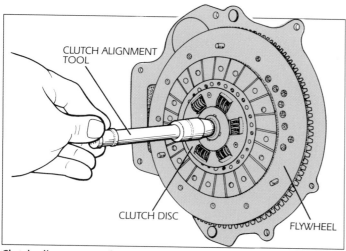

Clutch alignment tool centers the clutch friction disc on the flywheel so the transmission input shaft will install properly.

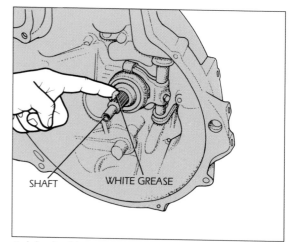

A dab of white grease on input shaft keeps bearing and clutch disc sliding freely.

With the flywheel in place and properly torqued down, you can install the new clutch disc and pressure plate. It is critical that the clutch friction disc be perfectly centered on the flywheel. To align the disc on the flywheel, use an old transmission input-shaft stub or an aligning tool.

This tool consists of various pilots which thread on a large dowel and a sliding cone-shaped sleeve which slips over the dowel.

Attach the pilot that fits snugly in the hole in the center of your engine's flywheel onto the dowel. Place the pilot firmly into the flywheel. Slip the friction disc over the dowel.

Note that the splined center hub of the friction disc is not the same on both sides. Take care to mount the friction disc with the side marked FLYWHEEL toward the engine.

Place the pressure plate over the friction disc and just start its bolts. Slide the cone-shaped sleeve over the dowel handle so the cone goes into the splined hub of the friction disc. Firmly hold the sleeve against the friction disc to center it. Tighten the pressure plate's mounting bolts in a crisscross pattern, according to the manufacturer's specs.

Before installing the new release bearing, lightly coat the splines of the transmission's shaft with multipurpose grease. Also fill any grease cavity in the release bearing or its hub according to your vehicle maker's specifications. Install the new release bearing—again taking care to install it so the rotating part of the bearing will bear against the pressure release fingers of the pressure plate.

Slide the transmission back under the vehicle and raise it so the input shaft is level with the center of the clutch assembly. Carefully align the transmission shaft with the clutch and slide the transmission against the engine. Slowly rotate the transmission's output shaft as you go. When the splines of the transmission's input shaft align with the splines of the clutch friction disc, the transmission should slide home.

Align the transmission housing, rotating it as necessary on its shaft, and replace the housing bolts.

Then reassemble everything you have removed, adjust the linkage for the new clutch, and you're ready to get the power back to the wheels.

ELECTRICAL AND ELECTRONIC SYSTEMS 4

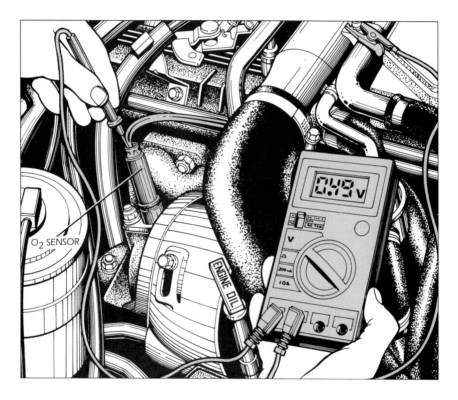

O₂ SENSOR

ENGINE OIL

How to Track Down
INTERMITTENT ELECTRICAL PROBLEMS

You turn the ignition key to crank the engine, and it barely turns over. Visions of explaining to your spouse why you're late getting home again send a cold chill down your spine. Finally your engine catches. Bad battery? Well, maybe not.

Hit the horn button to warn a suicidal bicyclist and all you get is a click—which the biker ignores. Dead horn? That's the least-likely possibility.

Pull the headlight switch at night and faint beams barely light the road ahead. Step on the gas and the headlights brighten. Bad charging system? Not likely.

Turn on the radio and there's nothing but static. Something wrong with the radio? Good chance there's not.

Every one of these problems could be nothing more than a corroded or poorly connected electrical ground. Virtually every electrical circuit in your car depends just as much on the ground side to com-

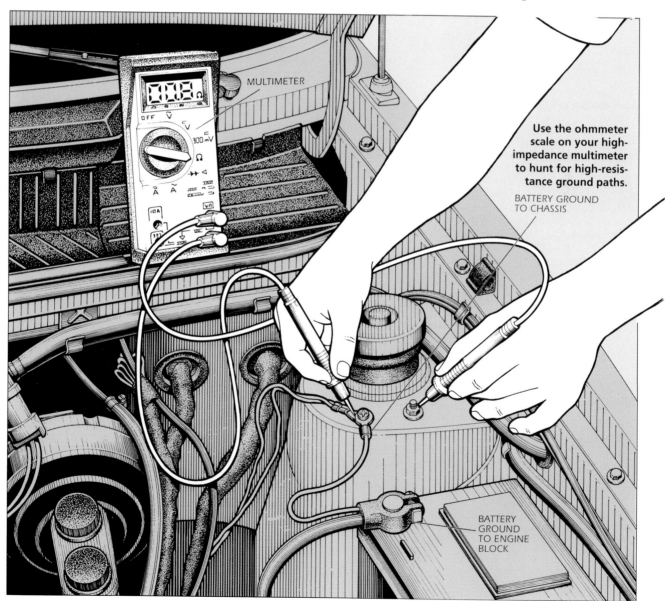

MULTIMETER

Use the ohmmeter scale on your high-impedance multimeter to hunt for high-resistance ground paths.

BATTERY GROUND TO CHASSIS

BATTERY GROUND TO ENGINE BLOCK

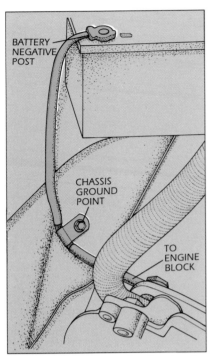

BATTERY NEGATIVE POST

CHASSIS GROUND POINT

TO ENGINE BLOCK

Corrosion can compromise the chassis ground in the center of this cable.

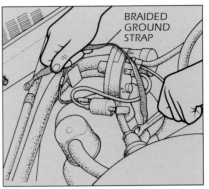

BRAIDED GROUND STRAP

Check for corroded or missing ground straps between the engine and firewall.

lutely correctly in order to cure the problem.

Sometimes the bad ground will be something you can see, but more often it's something you can't. Today's electrical and electronic systems are so sensitive that an acceptable ground of yesterday is a problem of today. And when it comes to electronics, you can't rely on the old rule that a bad ground only results in poor performance. A ground may be a reference for an electronic circuit, and if the ground is bad, it can result in more current flow and the subsequent frying of transistors. This means that even if you find and replace the bad part, the problem will recur unless you trace and correct the bad ground.

Use a digital multimeter to check grounds, but be careful to select a meter with a "high-impedance" 10-megohm rating (low current flow so it's computer-safe). Suitable multimeters start at less than $50, with professional brands costing about $120 to $400. The more expensive professional models are higher quality and have a lot of special features, some including rpm and plug-in thermocouples for temperature measurement. So base your decision on the overall range of work you plan to do.

If the problem is slow cranking, test the battery ground cable. Set the meter to VOLTS, connect the positive lead to the battery ground terminal or post, and the negative lead to the engine or, if possible, to the starter housing. Have someone crank the engine and the meter will

read whatever voltage isn't being used in the starter circuit. If it's more than 0.4 volt, either the connection or the cable is bad. If it's a split cable (one branch to a ground on the body, the other to a ground on the engine), a 0.5-volt drop is tolerable. If you find an excessive drop, it could be in either branch.

Look for a corroded terminal or frayed wiring at the battery end, damaged insulation (perhaps from battery acid droppings), and/or frayed wiring on each branch. Also inspect each ground connection with the meter—positive lead to the bolt holding the cable end, negative to the adjacent metal on the body or engine. Crank the engine and the reading should be less than 0.2 volt.

On some cars, there's a single ground cable from the battery's negative post, but it goes into a connector with two or three branches.

plete the circuit as it does on the positive wiring.

A bad ground is not only common, it's the cheapest repair you can make. Yet the failure to find and fix bad grounds leads to many unneeded parts replacements, including expensive computers and sensors. So if there's even a possibility that the ground could be responsible, it's worth looking into. However, finding a bad ground can be difficult. And the repair must be done abso-

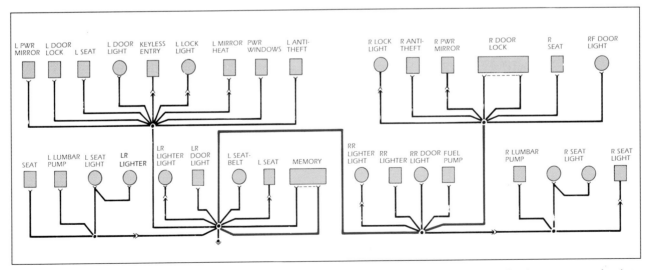

L PWR MIRROR · L DOOR LOCK · L SEAT · L DOOR LIGHT · KEYLESS ENTRY · L LOCK LIGHT · L MIRROR HEAT · PWR WINDOWS · L ANTI-THEFT · R LOCK LIGHT · R ANTI-THEFT · R PWR MIRROR · R DOOR LOCK · R SEAT · RF DOOR LIGHT

SEAT · L LUMBAR PUMP · L SEAT LIGHT · LR LIGHTER · LR LIGHTER LIGHT · LR DOOR LIGHT · L SEAT-BELT · L SEAT · MEMORY · RR LIGHTER LIGHT · RR LIGHTER · RR DOOR LIGHT · FUEL PUMP · R LUMBAR PUMP · R SEAT LIGHT · R SEAT LIGHT

If the fuel-pump ground is marginal, opening a rear door kills the motor because the courtesy light shares a ground point.

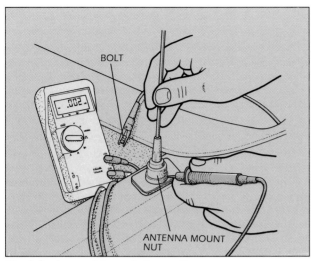

Check for low resistance between the antenna mount and a good chassis ground, like this mounting bolt.

Some antennas rely on spring-loaded lugs to ensure contact with the sheet-metal fender.

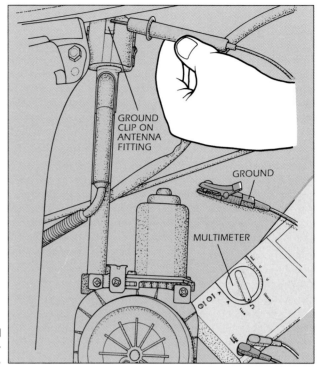

The branch to the starter may be fine and the engine will crank normally, but one of the other branches may be bad. This can cause a variety of general electrical-circuit problems. Disengage the connector and inspect each branch terminal for a bent or damaged tab or poor connection between the wire and the terminal.

There are two grounding variations that suffer from special problems. One (used on many Fords) is a single cable from battery to engine, but with about an inch of insulation stripped away at the midpoint. A clamp is wrapped around the cable and bolted to the car body to provide the second ground. The clamp and the wiring under it may corrode and affect both body electrical circuits and engine cranking.

There may be a second grounding cable—often a braided metal strap—far from the battery that goes from the engine or transmission to the body, a setup used by both Chrysler and General Motors. This type of cable may be at the firewall, perhaps partly under the air-cleaner housing or elsewhere nearly out of sight, even underneath the car. Frayed, corroded, even damaged by rocks, it can hang by strands for a while, until there aren't enough strands to complete the cir-

cuit with a minimum voltage drop. The result is similar to the bad branch problem. Or, it may be that a mechanic removed a secondary strap or cable to gain access to a part for a repair job, then forgot to put it back in place. Everything may seem okay, but you soon discover otherwise.

SENSITIVE GROUNDS

Electronic circuits are sensitive to poor grounds, but so may be garden-variety electrical circuits. Example: The power windows, power seats, power mirrors, and interior lights don't work, and the engine stalls when you open any door. This actually happened on a 1990 Lincoln Continental, and the single, simple cause of all this misery was a bad ground. All these systems—and the in-tank electric fuel pump—share the same ground.

Occasionally we see cases where turning on one accessory affects the operation of another, because they share the same weak ground. Result: The electrical current finds another way to complete the circuit—through the other accessory.

When the car is suffering from a problem that involves just one or a few circuits, you really need a manual with charts that show all the

components that share the same ground (or if a circuit has a single "dedicated" ground) and where the ground is located. Sometimes the regular shop manual has the diagnostic diagrams. In other cases (such as Ford), it's in a separate manual. The charts also show the ground wiring that is part of a common splice and where that splice is located. That's important because several splices may use just one ground, and that's exactly what occurred in this case.

If only the systems or components with ground wiring up to a splice are affected, you know you have to check only the splice. If failed systems share a common ground but different splices, you know the splices are good and you only have to check the ground.

However, the locator lists or illustrations are important because you can't guess. In the case of the '90 Continental, the ground is partly under the front seat, not exactly the place you would think to look for the end of a fuel-pump circuit.

It's true, however, that some electronic circuits are considered so sensitive that they have two grounds—a setup called redundant grounding. It would seem unlikely that a problem could result if one fails, but there are problems all the time where all that's wrong is a single ground weakness (not even a complete break).

You can test an electronic circuit ground with an accurate multimeter set for VOLTS. If there's a choice (as opposed to an auto-ranging meter that picks the appropriate range for the reading), set it on the 0–2 volt scale, activate the circuit, and you should get a zero reading. Even 0.1 volt is too much.

Using an ohmmeter to take a resistance reading at the ground connection is a good alternate method, and it can be done with the circuit off, which takes the variability of voltage out of the picture. With many circuits, a voltage-drop reading is difficult or impractical, so resistance is the way. But it also can be difficult to get an accurate resistance reading unless you're careful. Repeat a check several times to verify a reading. Make sure you test at the same spots and use a needle probe you can dig in, instead of a clip that may make inconsistent contact. You can buy meters with leads that convert from an alligator clip to a needle probe.

Unless the meter is auto-ranging, begin by selecting a medium ohms scale (0–100 or 0–200) and touching the lead clips or probes together. If you have to set the range, be careful not to pick 0–100K or 0–200K, which is simply too high to give you an accurate reading. You should get a resistance reading of no more than 0.2 ohm, and preferably less (hopefully zero). If you can't get this reading, and the meter uses a dry-cell battery, the battery probably is weak. Any resistance meter will have an internal battery.

Touch the ground terminal and the adjacent metal and you also should get a similarly low reading. If you're checking an electronic system ground wire from its origin to the adjacent sheet metal, the reading should be no more than 5 ohms.

RADIO GROUNDS

Although a blown fuse is the most common cause, many no-reception problems can be traced to a bad ground, either for the radio itself or for the antenna. Many people change spark plugs and wires to get rid of ignition noise or static when a weak antenna ground is the problem.

Access to the radio ground often requires removing the radio itself, but with today's front-service dashboards, that's rarely a problem. Typically, you pry out a plastic trim piece held by spring clips, then remove a few screws and pull the radio forward. On some, there's a clearly separate ground wire to a nearby bolt. On others, the radio's plug-in harness includes one ground wire (usually black). Probe the ground wire terminal with one ohmmeter lead, and touch the other to a nearby body ground to make the test.

Testing an antenna ground often is very straightforward and the fixed antenna mast is the easiest. Check resistance from the shield around the bottom of the mast to the engine compartment sheet metal while gently trying to rock the mast side to side. There should be no more than a half-ohm reading. Be careful not to measure resistance from the trim that rests against the fender. It usually has a rubber gasket under it and is insulated, not grounded.

If the car has a retracting antenna mast (power or manual) in the rear quarter panel or front fender, locate the motor/gear mechanism or housing and look for either a ground cable (typically used with plastic body panels) or grounding/retaining clip or tab. Make a resistance check looking for no more than 0.5 ohm. With a rear quarter panel antenna, the access is in the trunk. With a front fender antenna, you have to remove a few screws from the wheelwell liner to reach the ground.

On cars with an antenna that retracts into a roof pillar, and no external grounding shield, remove the trim piece for access to the antenna holder that provides the ground.

When the static is intermittent and the resistance reading is good, recheck while you try to wiggle or push on each section of the antenna assembly. If the resistance reading suddenly shoots up, the ground is not secure.

If the external parts of the antenna assembly have a protective coating, it

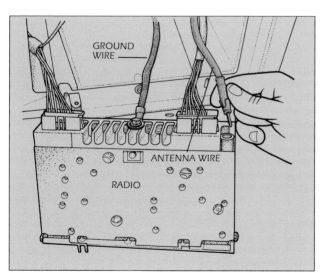

It's amazing how many poorly performing radios are grounded only by the antenna cable, rather than a proper ground strap.

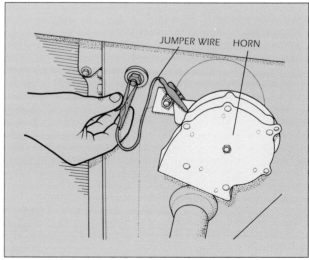

You can use a jumper wire to diagnose a poor ground connection on a high-current device like the horn.

may insulate the metal from the ohm-meter leads. You'll have to dig in with a pin probe.

Problem with the antenna ground? There may be rust on the body hole. Clean it with a wire brush, then delay a recurrence by applying a coat of nonhardening sealer to the underside of the trim.

If there is no AM reception and the FM is very weak and noisy, the problem is likely to be a break in the center wire of the antenna cable. If you check resistance between this and the cable housing, it should be infinite. Gentle wiggling of the center wire tip and flexing the cable may suddenly produce a low reading, indicating that the center wire is intermittently making contact.

FIXING 'EM

Repairing other weak grounds often requires no more than just tightening a loose screw or wire-brushing away some corrosion from the threads. However, even clean threads that feel tight actually may be making loose contact, particularly if a bolt isn't threaded all the way up. A missing washer may be the problem.

Or if a ground connection originally came with a star washer that has been lost, get another one. It will dig in and restore the low-resistance contact that's necessary.

And just to prove that high tech can throw you another curve, don't use a star washer on a bolt or nut that didn't originally come with one. It may have a special protective/conductive coating that the washer—or even wire-brushing—will destroy, and the bolt or nut soon will corrode and the grounding problem will return.

Grounds—or for that matter any electrical connections—that are exposed to the elements probably could benefit from a shot of protective grease, but plain old white lithium grease or even Vaseline work just as well.

We used to be satisfied with good grounds. Now they have to be great, and if you give them the attention that matches their importance, you can make them that way.

How to Check Your
TROUBLE CODES

A technician uses an expensive scan tool to access the computer's trouble codes.

They all laughed when you opened the hood of your late-model computer-controlled fuel-injected car. They know that only the cognoscenti at the dealership have been inculcated with the secret codes that hide the darkest secrets of your engine's operation. They know that only with thousands of dollars worth of inscrutable test gear, covered with flashing lights and arcane symbols, could the furthest depths of engine management be probed. How dare you attempt to repair your car armed with little more than a Radio Shack voltmeter?

They're wrong. It's true that well-trained pros use computerized "scan" testers (starting at $750) and oscilloscopes with gas analyzers (around $35,000) to locate the tough problems, but most repair shops just look for the trouble codes generated by the engine computer's self-diagnosis system. You can do that yourself—without the pros' expensive equipment.

Besides managing your engine, modern automotive computers also monitor themselves, their sensors, and the systems they control. When the computer detects a problem within its purview, the problem is logged into the computer's memory and assigned a code number. And while at one time only General Motors' systems provided easy access to those trouble codes, today every make of car does.

However, there is no industry-wide standard for trouble codes; you can't use one maker's trouble

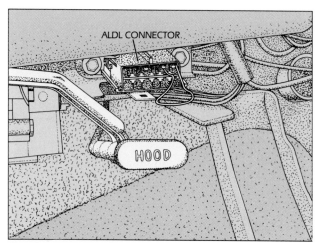

Shorting two pins of the ALDL connector will send a General Motors' computer into its self-test mode.

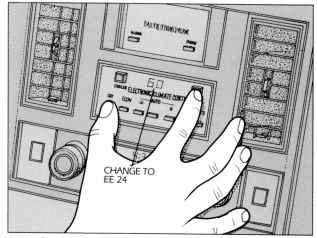

Enter the diagnostic mode by simultaneously pressing the off and heat buttons on the air-conditioning panel.

codes for another car. For example, while Code 44 on GM cars means an oxygen-sensor problem, it means no trouble in the computer system on many Nissan products.

With a quality repair manual—either from the factory or from an aftermarket publisher—you can get the trouble codes and know what each one means. Better manuals also provide a precise procedure for you to check out the code—using equipment you probably already have, such as fused jumper wires, computer-safe test lights (about $10 each), and digital volt-ohmmeters (as little as $30 for the basic-but-good model).

The manual is also your source for the location of various computer-system parts—including the computer itself. You'll find most computers under the dash or behind a kick pad, but some are under a passenger's seat and still others (most Chrysler and some General Motors) are under the hood. So the parts-location illustrations in the manual are important.

General Motors led the industry with its underdash diagnostic plug and the CHECK ENGINE dashboard light. Other makers soon followed, and the POWER LOSS light on Chrysler products in the mid-to-late 1980s and the SERVICE ENGINE NOW on some GM cars serve the same purpose. Import companies and Ford were late to adopt the CHECK ENGINE light, but still have provided trouble codes.

If your car is equipped with a CHECK ENGINE light or the equiva-

lent, wait for the light to go on and stay on for a few seconds, to be sure the computer has logged a trouble code. Some computers also log codes for intermittent problems and may even briefly flash the CHECK ENGINE light at the time they're logged.

WHAT YOU'LL NEED

Before you attempt to access your car's computer, understand that if you follow the test procedures improperly, you may damage some very expensive components. Don't say we didn't warn you!

Before you begin, be certain that you have the *correct* service manual or information for your specific vehicle. Simply connecting a jumper wire incorrectly can be enough to do electronic damage. Now, properly armed and warned, here is what's needed to access the memory of your late-model car's computer and see if there are any trouble codes:

- **General Motors**—With the ignition on, bridge the diagnostic plug's end terminals—possibly using a paper clip—that have a white/black and a black wire. The CHECK ENGINE light should flash, or pulse, out a code starting with 12 (light pulse, brief pause, then two light pulses). This means "no ignition signal to the computer," which is correct since the engine isn't running. This is a simple check of the self-diagnosis capability.

Then the light will pulse all codes detected, with a moderate pause between each one. It may repeat the codes twice. All the GM trouble codes are two digits each.

In addition, Cadillac and Cadillac-built front drives—Buick, Riviera/Reatta and Olds Toronado—provide a digital readout of trouble code information on the Fuel Data Center. With the ignition on, simultaneously press and hold the OFF and WARM(er) buttons on the a/c panel. After all the panel indicators light up, release the buttons. On most models, any intermittent engine codes (with the letter E as a prefix) are displayed first, followed by current trouble codes (prefix EE). The service manual also can lead you into a more comprehensive diagnosis, all without the use of special testers.

- **Chrysler**—(*Note:* Since most pre-1991 Jeeps and the Eagle Premier do not have Chrysler-designed computer systems, the following procedures are not applicable to those vehicles.) Without starting the engine, cycle the ignition key on and off, on and off, then on again. The POWER LOSS or CHECK ENGINE light will pulse out the codes. A No. 55 (five pulses, pause, five pulses) indicates that the test is over.

- **Ford**—Only models equipped with the EEC III or EEC IV engine computers (check your car's underhood tuneup decal) have self-diagnostic capabilities. In addition, Ford did not install a CHECK ENGINE dashboard warning light until later EEC IV cars.

If your car has an EEC III system (mid-1980 to 1983), you will need a vacuum gauge. A manual vacuum pump makes the job simpler, but is not necessary. Connect the vacuum gauge between the emissions' diverter valve and its solenoid. Then with the engine fully warmed and idling, apply 20 in. or more of vacuum to the Manifold Absolute Pressure (MAP) sensor's vent neck for one minute. If you don't have a vacuum pump, attach a hose to a vacuum source on the intake manifold. Release the vacuum and the self-test will run automatically.

All the codes will be pulsed out by the jumping needle on the vacuum gauge. First the needle will pulse an engine number equal to half the number of engine cylinders (twice for a four-cylinder, four times for a V8, and so on). Early in the test, engine vacuum and idle speed will rise, and after about two minutes, both will fall. Then the needle will pulse out any trouble codes. A Code 11 (pulse, pause, pulse) is a pass. If your car has an EEC IV computer, you must locate two underhood diagnostic connectors. One has five terminals, the other only one. Hook up a jumper wire and an analog voltmeter to the connectors and the car battery as directed by your manual. The engine should be cold and not running, but the ignition should be on. The voltmeter needle should flick the engine

cylinders code during the test, and any trouble codes or Code 11, which means no trouble code found, at the end of the test.

You can also test for cylinder balance on EEC IV–equipped cars with sequential port fuel injection. See the service manual procedure following the engine-running test. Many 1991–1992 Ford models have three-digit trouble codes, in addition to the two-digit ones.

- **Toyota**—If the CHECK ENGINE light goes on with the engine running, connect a fused (under 10-amp) jumper from a test terminal, often labeled "T," or "TE-1," to the "E-1" terminal (electrical ground) of an underhood plug. The engine must be off; ignition on. The dashboard warning light will pulse out any codes and keep repeating them. If the

Trouble Codes

Code	Description	Code	Description
11	Pass	**44**	Thermactor air upstream during self-test
12	Rpm not within self-test upper rpm limit band	**46**	Thermactor air not bypassed during self-test
13	Rpm not within self-test lower limit band	**51**	-40° indicated ECT-sensor circuit open
13	D.C. motor did not move (2.3/2.5/1.9L CFI)	**52**	PSPS circuit open
13	D.C. motor does not follow dashpot (2.3/2.5/1.0L CFI)	**52**	PSPS did not change states
14	PIP circuit fault	**53**	TPS circuit above maximum voltage
15	ROM test failed	**54**	-40° F indicated ACT—sensor circuit open
16	Rpm too low to perform fuel test	**55**	Key power circuit low
18	Loss of tach input to processor-SPOUT circuit grounded	**57**	NPS circuit failed open
19	Failure in EEC reference voltage	**61**	254° F indicated ECT—circuit grounded
21	Indicates ECT out of self-test range	**63**	TPS circuit below minimum voltage
22	Indicates MAP/BP out of self-test range	**64**	254° F indicated ACT—circuit grounded
23	Indicates T.P. out of self-test range	**67**	NPS circuit failed closed—A/C on during self-test
24	Indicates ACT out of self-test range	**67**	NDS circuit open—A/C on during self-test
25	Knock not sensed during dynamic response test	**72**	Insufficient MAP change during dynamic response test
29	Insufficient input from V.S.S.	**73**	Insufficient TP change during dynamic response test
31	EPT/EVP below minimum voltage	**74**	BOO switch circuit open
32	EVP voltage out of static limit	**75**	BOO switch circuit closed—ECA input open
32	EGR valve not seated (PFE)	**77**	Operator error (dynamic response/cylinder balance test)
33	EGR valve not opening	**78**	Power interrupt detected
34	Insufficient EGR flow (1.9L, 2.3L T/C EFI/2.3L, 3.8L CFI)	**81**	AM2 circuit failure (OCC test)
34	EVP voltage above static limit (SONIC)	**82**	AM1 circuit failure (OCC test)
34	Defective EPT sensor (PFE)	**84**	EVR circuit failure (OCC test)
34	Exhaust pressure high/defective EPT sensor	**85**	CANP circuit failure (OCC test)
35	EPT/EVP circuit above maximum voltage	**87**	Fuel pump test failed (OCC test)
41	EGO sensor circuit indicates system lean-no EGO switch detected	**89**	CCO circuit failure (OCC test)
42	EGO sensor circuit indicates system rich-no EGO switch detected	**91**	EGO sensor input indicates system lean (cylinders 5-8)
43	EGO lean at W.O.I.	**92**	EGO sensor input indicates system rich (cylinders 5-8)
44	Thermactor air system inoperative (cylinder 1-4 dual EGO)	**94**	Thermactor air system inoperative (cylinders 5-8, dual EGO)
		98	Hard fault present, ***FMEM MODE***
		99	Idle not learned, ignore codes 12 and 13

Warning! Your trouble codes will probably vary from these Ford codes—but this list is typical of what you might see on your vehicle.

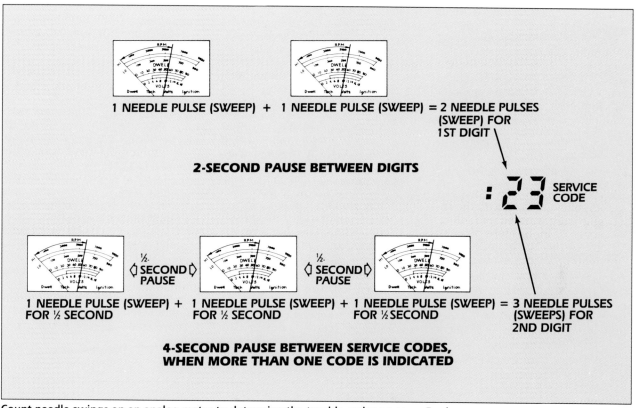

1 NEEDLE PULSE (SWEEP) + 1 NEEDLE PULSE (SWEEP) = 2 NEEDLE PULSES (SWEEP) FOR 1ST DIGIT

2-SECOND PAUSE BETWEEN DIGITS

:23 SERVICE CODE

1 NEEDLE PULSE (SWEEP) FOR ½ SECOND + ½-SECOND PAUSE + 1 NEEDLE PULSE (SWEEP) FOR ½ SECOND + ½-SECOND PAUSE + 1 NEEDLE PULSE (SWEEP) FOR ½ SECOND = 3 NEEDLE PULSES (SWEEPS) FOR 2ND DIGIT

4-SECOND PAUSE BETWEEN SERVICE CODES, WHEN MORE THAN ONE CODE IS INDICATED

Count needle swings on an analog meter to determine the trouble codes on some Fords.

light just blinks once every quarter-second, there are no codes stored. To check the control unit of the automatic transmission, use the same underhood plug—the OVER-DRIVE light will do the pulsing.

- **Honda**—If the CHECK ENGINE light goes on, find a two-terminal connector under the

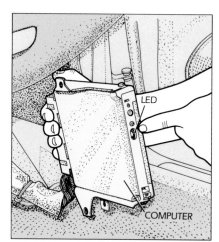

This Nissan's computer must be removed from under the dash to see the LED flash.

right side of the dash. Bridge the connector's terminals and the CHECK ENGINE light pulses out the codes. Single-digit trouble codes are displayed by a series of short blinks. For double-digits, it's longer pulses for the first digit, short ones for the second (three long pulses followed by one short is 31). Late-model Accords do not have a CHECK ENGINE light. On these cars, you must pull back the carpet under the dash on the passenger's side, turn on the ignition, and watch an LED on the computer body it-self blink out the trouble codes.

- **Nissan**—Depending on the model, your car may use one of several self-diagnosis sys-tems. However, they are all ac-cessed—with the ignition on and the engine off—by one or two LEDs on the side of the en-gine computer, found either under the dash or the passen-ger's seat depending on the model. Older models have one red and one green LED. Newer models just have a red one.

A mode-selector screw next to the LED(s) on most models allows you to choose from several diagnostic fea-tures. Turn the selector screw fully clockwise and wait for the LED to flash. The number of times indicates test mode. Then turn the screw fully counterclockwise and wait again. When you're in the trouble-code mode, any codes will pulse out. Where two LEDs are used, the red pulses the first digit, the green the second (two red pulses and one green equal Code 21). On units with just one red LED, long pulses are for the first dig-it, short ones for the second.

DECODING

Knowing the trouble codes does not necessarily mean you know what the trouble is. For instance, a code indi-cating a problem at the oxygen sen-sor may mean the sensor or its wiring is bad. But it may also mean that there is too much, or too little, oxygen in the exhaust for the computer to cor-rect the situation—possibly indicating a disconnected vacuum hose or leaking fuel injectors.

Mechanical problems seemingly unrelated to the computer may also precipitate a trouble code. For example, if the thermostat sticks open, coolant temperature is abnormally low, and the computer may be tricked into concluding that coolant temperature is normal but the coolant-temperature sensor is defective.

It is critical, therefore, that you have the proper manual for your car. The right manual will lead you through the diagnosis very specifically, step by step, until you pinpoint the problem.

TURNING OFF THE LIGHT

After you've fixed the problem, you must turn off the CHECK ENGINE light and clear the computer's memory of the trouble. The procedures for clearing the codes from memory vary—check your manual.

However, it may be necessary to disconnect the computer by either pulling its fuse or disconnecting the battery for about thirty seconds. Be aware that you also lose any fuel and ignition running adjustments the computer has made (along with the radio station preselects). It can take up to one hundred or so miles of driving for the computer to remake those adjustments. Until it does, your car may not perform well, even though all problems were repaired.

There are some nonengine computers that require a specific procedure to clear a code. These systems have backup circuits to hold the code even if the car battery is disconnected.

One alternative to an expensive scan tool is to use your laptop computer and a software package called Diacom. Diacom connects the parallel port of your computer to the diagnostic connector of your GM, Ford, or Chrysler product. Depending on the capabilities of your car's on-board computer, you can read trouble codes or monitor many vehicle functions in real time, or trap them in memory for later perusal or printout. Call Rinda Technology at (312) 736-6633.

Low-cost computer testers for do-it-yourself use are perhaps one to three years away, but when they come, they'll enable you to do an even better job. Right now there are a few simple devices on the market in the $30 to $40 range, but basically they consist of nothing more than a connector, a fused jumper wire, and an LED, boxed with a short manual that has the breakdown of the codes and some short instructions on how to perform the tests. They work—but they're no substitute for an inch-thick factory shop manual and a certain amount of common sense. In the meantime, learn to use the engine computer self-diagnosis and you'll do more than you ever thought possible.

How to Maintain Your CHARGING SYSTEM

You're still miles from home on a classic dark and stormy night when you realize that the road in front of you is rapidly getting dimmer.

You pull over, and as the engine goes to idle the BAT warning light on the dashboard flickers—just before the engine coughs and dies.

The problem? Something is awry in your car's charging system.

The electricity that powers the ignition system, fuel injection, computer, lights, and accessories all comes from your car's alternator. In addition to all these operating tasks, it also recharges the battery. Whenever the engine is running, the alternator is spinning, making electricity.

The pulley on the front of the alternator drives a shaft-mounted electromagnet, called a rotor. The rotor gets the current it needs to energize its magnet from the battery, through brushes that contact slip rings on the rotor shaft. As this electromagnet spins, its magnetic field induces current flow through tightly wound wire coils surrounding the rotor inside the alternator. These coils are wound around an iron core, and together the windings and core compose the stator. As engine speeds increase, the current in the rotor increases with it, producing a simultaneous increase in voltage from the stator.

Left unchecked, the alternator would keep producing more and more voltage as engine speed increased. Too much voltage will boil the battery and blow fuses. Too little will not charge the battery or run the accessories. That's where the voltage regulator comes in. The voltage regulator limits the alternator output and prevents overcharging the battery in the process. The regulator operates by limiting the amount of current going to the rotor windings. Though voltage regulators used to be electromechanical devices that used vibrating—and often adjustable—contact points to limit current flow, modern regulators are small, sealed electronic devices that use diodes to control

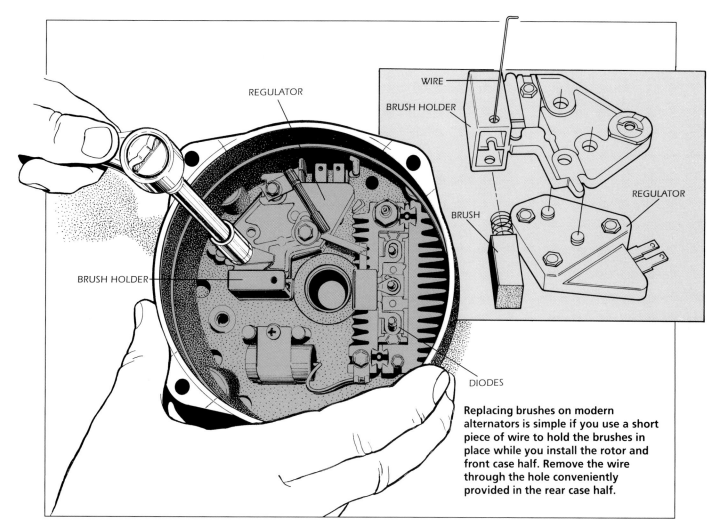

REGULATOR

WIRE

BRUSH HOLDER

REGULATOR

BRUSH

BRUSH HOLDER

DIODES

Replacing brushes on modern alternators is simple if you use a short piece of wire to hold the brushes in place while you install the rotor and front case half. Remove the wire through the hole conveniently provided in the rear case half.

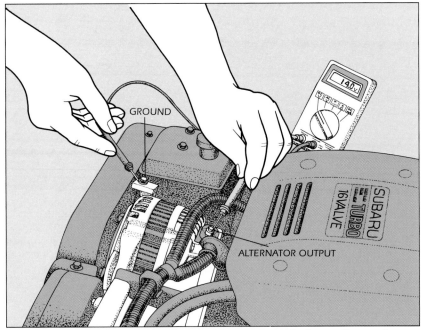

Be sure to check voltage at the alternator's output terminal as well as at the battery.

alternator output. In fact, in many late-model cars the regulator is integrated into the alternator.

The electromagnet in the rotor is made of wire windings surrounded by interlocking metal fingers, which are the alternating magnetic poles. As the rotor spins inside the stator, the magnetic poles are constantly reversing the direction of the current flow in the stator. It's this changing of direction that creates alternating current (AC), rather than direct current (DC).

But since your car's electrical system requires direct current, the AC must be converted to DC before it leaves the alternator. This is done by diodes, which act as electrical one-way valves.

The third component of the charging system is the battery. The battery stores the electricity needed to start the engine and to provide a small amount to energize the alternator's rotor while the engine is running.

Remember, electricity only flows in a complete loop. If there is a problem anywhere in the charging system, the entire system goes down. When you're diagnosing a charging system problem, you must consider the battery, the alternator, the voltage regulator, and all of the wire and connections between them.

BATTERY BASICS

The battery relies on the alternator to replenish its power, so a weak—or dead—battery may point to a problem elsewhere in the system or could be the cause of the trouble. In any case, it's an excellent place to begin your diagnosis.

Automotive batteries store electricity chemically. The box we generally call a battery is really six smaller cells, connected in series. Each of these smaller cells consists of electrodes immersed in a water/sulfuric-acid solution, called electrolyte. The electrodes are alternating plates of lead and lead peroxide. Nonconducting porous separators between the plates prevent short circuits within the cells. The chemical reaction between the sulfuric acid and the lead plates causes the flow of electrons between the electrodes.

The chemical reaction that creates electricity also produces a certain amount of lead sulfate, which gets deposited on the electrodes. When the battery is being recharged, the chemical reaction is reversed—the lead sulfate breaks down and rejuvenates the electrolyte.

As time goes on, however, the lead-sulfate coating on the electrodes is too heavy to be broken down completely. Over time, the electrolyte grows weaker and the electrodes become less conductive.

Like other chemical reactions, the lead-acid reaction in your battery slows as temperatures go down. A fully charged battery is at maximum strength when the temperature is about 70° F. A battery that's got enough zap to start your car on a warm spring day may not get the job done when the mercury drops to the freezing mark or lower.

Before checking your battery, ensure that it is fully charged. If the battery isn't a sealed, maintenance-free type, you can check the strength of the electrolyte in each cell. Remove the vent caps and check to see if the electrolyte level is up to the bottom of the fill neck in each vent. If not, add distilled water. Drive the car for a while to thoroughly mix the water with the electrolyte. Then use a hydrometer to test the specific gravity of the solution. The electrolyte of a fully charged battery should be between 1.27 and 1.29 at about 70° F.

Check the state of the electrolyte in a sealed battery by checking the built-in indicator eye.

Disconnect the battery ground cable and attach the battery to a charger. When the battery charger shows that the current draw is less than 1 amp, the battery is charged. Double-check by using the hydrometer. Remember, battery strength is inverse to ambient temperature—do this diagnosis on a warm battery. And any time you're handling a battery, keep in mind that it's filled with acid. Wear eye protection, and flush spilled electrolyte from your skin immediately.

Also remember that a charging battery produces hydrogen gas, which can explode if exposed to a spark. Some manufacturers recommend removing the battery caps to allow hydrogen to dissipate, while others recommend leaving them in place. If you do remove them, cover the holes with a clean shop towel to prevent dirt and foreign objects from contaminating the electrolyte.

With the battery charged and warm, connect a voltmeter to its terminals. The voltmeter should read at least 12 volts. If not, replace the battery. Be sure to turn in the old battery when you buy the new one. The battery supplier will properly dispose of the battery. Do *not* sim-

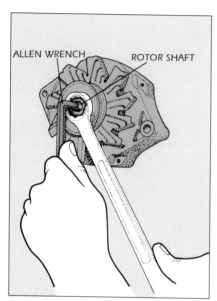

Remove the pulley by holding the rotor with an Allen wrench and turning the nut.

ply toss out the old battery with the trash. It contains lead and acid, both toxic substances that are very harmful to the environment.

If the battery is putting out more than 12 volts, reconnect its ground strap and disconnect the ignition system, leaving the voltmeter attached to the terminals. Have a helper crank the engine for fifteen seconds, while you check the voltmeter. A healthy battery should put out at least 9.6 volts at about 70°F. If not, it is weak and must be replaced.

If the battery passes the voltage tests, clean its terminals and connectors. Use an inexpensive wire brush designed to clean both the terminal posts and the cable clamps. If your car has a side-terminal battery, make sure that the cable mounting surfaces and the attaching bolts are clean and corrosion-free.

Even though the advent of the so-called maintenance-free sealed batteries has greatly cut down on battery corrosion, it's still a good idea to coat the battery connections with white grease or petroleum jelly—after they have been connected—to prevent a buildup of corrosion on the terminals. Clean the surface of the battery with detergent and warm water to remove surface dirt, which, in damp weather, can drain your battery by becoming an electrical path.

Check the other ends of the battery cables. Make sure that the ground strap is intact and that it is snugly attached to the car's chassis or engine and that the mounting bolt is not rusted. Check that the positive cable is secure, intact, and connected properly at the starter switch or junction box. Again, be sure that the cable terminal end is solid and that the mounting nut is rust-free and snug.

ALTERNATELY SPEAKING

If the battery is good—or if a replacement quickly runs down—suspect the alternator or the voltage regulator.

To check those components, leave the voltmeter hooked up to the battery—which should still be holding more than 12 volts.

Start the engine and run it at 2,000 to 3,000 rpm. With the lights, heater, defroster, and other accessories off, the voltmeter should read about 2 volts higher (typically 14 to 15 volts, check your car's specs) than it did with the engine off. If the voltmeter reads *more* than 2 volts higher, suspect the voltage regulator.

With the engine still running at 2,000 to 3,000 rpm, switch on all the lights and accessories. Now the voltmeter should read about 0.5 volt more than when the engine was not running. If the voltage now is not at least 0.5 volt more than at rest, there's one more test to try before condemning the alternator.

Shut the engine down and disconnect the voltmeter leads from the battery. Connect the voltmeter's positive lead to the BAT terminal on the alternator and the negative to a good ground. Restart the engine, turn on all the lights and accessories, and bring engine speed up to 2,000 to 3,000 rpm. If the voltage reading still fails to increase by at least 0.5 volt, there is a problem with the alternator. But if the voltmeter now indicates an increase of more than 0.5 volt, suspect the regulator.

DRIVEBELT BASICS

Another common culprit in low alternator output is the engine's accessory drivebelt. A slipping belt is all that's needed to reduce alternator speed and output to unaccepta-

ble levels. Many new-model cars use a single multi-V serpentine belt to drive all the engine accessories. These belts use a single spring-loaded tensioner to ensure proper tension. If the belt seems slack, the tensioner might be sticking or otherwise defective. Also, check to make sure there are no cracks or missing pieces between the belt's grooves.

If your alternator is driven by a V-belt, check the belt's tension. Thanks to today's tighter engine compartments and shorter distances between belt pulleys, the only way to accurately check drivebelt tension is with a special gauge, available at auto parts stores. Compare the reading against your car's specs. Also check the belt for glazed sides, cracks, and missing chunks. If you haven't replaced the belt in two years, it's a good idea to replace it now, regardless of how good it may look.

If the belt is loose, tighten it. If the belt drives more than only the alternator, ascertain which accessory—or idler—pulley is the one that pivots and adjusts tension. Take care when tightening the belt not to overtighten it. A belt that is too tight accelerates bearing wear in the accessory. Don't pry against the sides of the alternator to tension

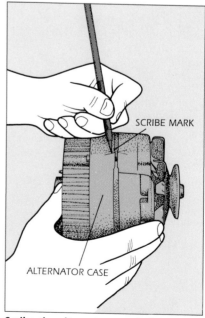

Scribe the alternator case halves to ensure bolting them back together correctly.

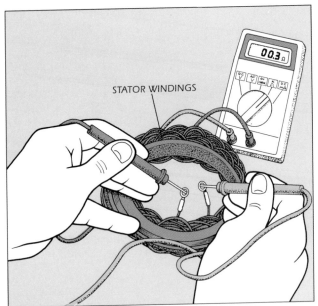

An ohmmeter is the proper instrument to check for electrical continuity through the stator windings. You should expect to get a low-resistance reading.

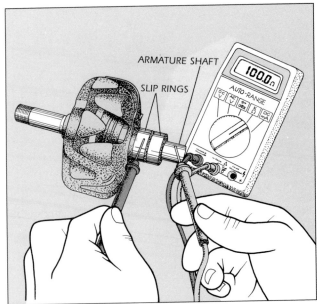

Check carefully for possible short circuits between the alternator's slip rings and the rotor itself. Correct readings in this instance should show a very high resistance.

the belt. Either pry on a special boss on the housing, or look for a tab or hexhole designed to accept a wrench for you to tension the belt.

Next, inspect all the wiring connections. A loose or corroded connection causes voltage drop, reducing the alternator's effective output.

However, if the belt and wiring are good but alternator output is not, the alternator must be repaired or replaced. Or, if the alternator output is higher than it should be (as outlined above), the regulator must be replaced. There are no repairs to be made to a modern, sealed electronic voltage regulator.

If your car does not have the voltage regulator built into the alternator, chances are you'll find the unit either on the firewall or near a strut tower on the fender well, where it may be hidden by another component. Disconnect the wiring, labeling it if necessary, and remove the regulator's mounting bolts. Clean the mounting surface and bolts before installing the replacement.

However, if the problem is the internal voltage regulator or the alternator, you must disassemble the alternator. Start by disconnecting the battery ground connection. Then, remove and label the wires from the back of the alternator. Next, loosen the drivebelt and slip it

off the pulley. Then remove the bolts holding the alternator in its bracket.

Next, mark the mating halves of the alternator's housing, using either a scribe or permanent marker (on a clean, dry surface). Then remove the long through-bolts that hold the housing halves together.

The front and rear of the housing should separate easily. If they need a little persuasion, tap lightly on a reinforced section of the housing with a soft-headed mallet—taking care not to damage the soft aluminum housing. Within the alternator housing, you will find the diodes and the brush holder—possibly along with a resistor and radio-noise-suppressing capacitor—as well as the voltage regulator (on units with internal regulators).

Next, remove the pulley from the end of the rotor shaft. Hold the shaft with an Allen wrench while loosening the pulley retaining nut. With the nut off, the pulley, fan, and any spacers slip off the end of the rotor's shaft. Slide the rotor out of the front half of the alternator housing.

Before removing the stator assembly, scribe mating marks on it and on the alternator housing. Then, disconnect the stator winding's terminals from the diodes and slip the stator out of the alternator housing.

Besides checking the rotor for

obvious damage—such as a bent shaft—you can test the electromagnet's windings for internal breaks. Connect an ohmmeter to the brushes' slip rings on the rotor shaft. There should be some continuity between the rings. Depending on the alternator, the ohmmeter should read anywhere from 2 to a few hundred ohms. Next, test that there is no continuity between either of the slip rings and the rotor itself.

Inspect the stator windings in the same manner. Connect an ohmmeter between any two of the stator's coil leads—there should be continuity between the leads. Repeat the test with all combinations of the terminals. Next, test between each of the terminals and the stator's iron core. There should be zero continuity.

If the rotor or the stator fails any of the tests, replace the alternator.

If they both pass, test the diodes. Alternators typically have either three or six diodes. Each of the diodes must be tested. If the diodes are individually accessible, simply connect the ohmmeter to both sides of the diode and note the reading. Then, reverse the polarity and note the meter reading. If the diode is good, the meter will show continuity in one direction and not in the other. It may be necessary to un-solder one end of the diodes if they are preassembled.

If the diodes are embedded in a mounting plate, hold the meter probes to the diode terminals and to their joint mounting tab, or first to the terminal marked BAT, and then repeat the tests with the probe held to the terminal marked GND. If any of the diodes are bad, replace the assembly.

While alternator brushes nor-mally last well past the life of the unit, inspect them for cracks, chips, and wear. Be sure that their backing springs are good and have the ten-sion needed to hold the brushes against the rotor shaft's slip rings. The slip rings should be regular—not overly grooved—and shiny. Out-of-round, burned, or heavily worn slip rings are grounds for a new or re-built alternator.

If all the alternator tests prove good, but the voltage regulator is defective, replace just the regulator.

To reassemble some alterna-tors—like GM's Delcotron—you must first depress the brushes fully into the brush holder and keep them there while you slip the rotor shaft back into the housing. To hold the brushes, insert a stiff piece of wire—a straightened paper clip will do—through a hole in the back of the al-ternator housing and through the holes in the brush holder. After the al-ternator is reassembled, and you're sure the rotor shaft is spinning prop-erly, slip out the wire. The brushes will pop up against the slip rings.

Reinstall the alternator. Replace the drivebelt and properly tension it. Then, reattach the wiring to the back of the alternator and recon-nect the battery's ground cable.

How to Fix
LEAKY FUEL INJECTORS

Burble, spurt, rumble. Burble, spurt, rumble. At idle, your engine shakes and stumbles, at speed it lacks power and smoothness, and your gas mileage is sinking slowly. You've completed all the standard diagnostic routines as outlined previously. You've got good spark and compression on the cylinders that are misfiring. Could it be the fuel injectors?

Or maybe you've been chasing down a hard-starting problem. The engine cranks fine and has plenty of spark, but won't start after a hot soak. Could it be the fuel injectors?

A fuel injector is a simple device. Basically, it's a valve that is opened and closed by a solenoid. Fuel injectors usually fail in one of four ways:

- They become partially clogged with fuel/air deposits and deliver a lean, uneven mixture.
- They fail to fire due to an electrical failure.
- The solenoid quits, and the injector fails to fire even though it's getting voltage.
- The injectors drip after the engine is turned off and cause a flooded no-start condition.

In the following sections, we'll look at each of these situations and explain what you can do to get your buggy back in shape. We'll talk about two basic kinds of injection systems—multipoint systems with one injector for each cylinder, and

throttle-body injection (TBI) systems with one or two injectors mounted in a central throttle body.

STUMBLE OR MISFIRE

An uneven and sometimes intermittent stumble or miss is frequently the result of dirty, partially clogged fuel injectors. However, it can also be caused by a variety of other conditions, including lack of compression in one or more cylinders, lack of ignition spark in one or more cylinders, or fuel starvation. Before you begin chasing down a fuel injector problem, remove and examine all the spark plugs and check the engine compression.

Because a lean misfire may cause

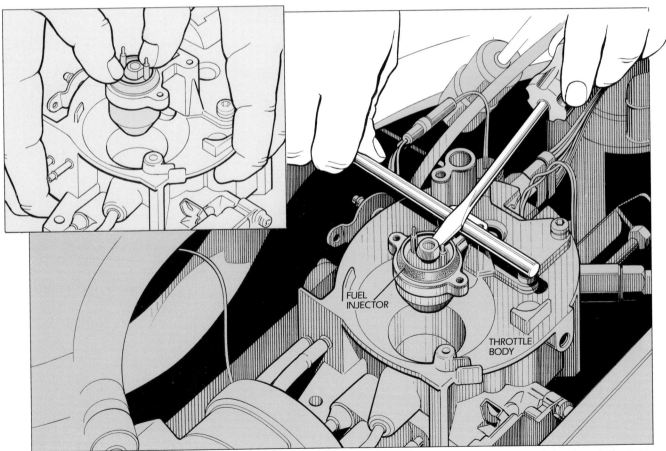

With the old meter cover gasket in place, locate a ¼-in. drill bit as shown and pry the injector out of the throttle body by using a screwdriver. After installing the seal and filter, push the new injector down into the throttle body.

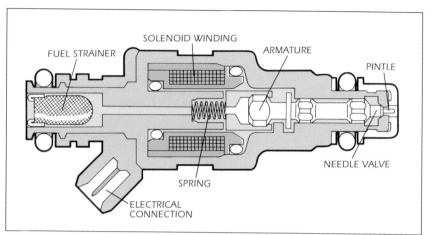

Solenoid pulls up plunger to spray fuel from pintle, which closes under spring pressure.

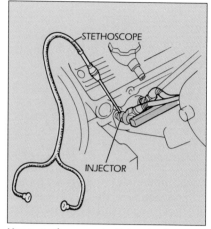

Use a stethoscope to listen to the injector as it opens and closes.

one of the plugs to appear wet or discolored, you can't assume you have a spark problem on the basis of spark plug condition alone—so test each spark plug cable for voltage with a spark tester. Spark testers are available (ask for the ST 125 tester) from most auto parts stores.

Attach plug wires one at a time to one end of the tester. Attach the other end of the tester, by means of its clamp, to ground. Start the engine and watch the tester to see if you get spark. If you don't, the wire or the distributor cap is defective.

If spark is good and the compression gauge reading of each cylinder is within 25 percent of the others, you can start looking for a fuel mixture problem.

But before you turn your attention to the injectors, make sure that a vacuum leak isn't the cause of the lean condition. To check vacuum hose connections, find the vacuum hose diagram for your car. It's probably in the engine compartment, frequently on the Vehicle Emissions Control Information Label. Make sure all hoses are connected as shown on the diagram. Make sure they fit tightly on their respective pipes. If not, replace them, or, if they're larger hoses like those used for power brakes and are in good condition, secure them with hose clamps. Visually check *every* hose for kinks or splitting.

Once you're sure all the vacuum hoses are in good shape and properly connected, grab your needle-nose pliers and, with the engine running at idle, squeeze each hose closed near the point where it connects to

its vacuum source. If the idle smooths out when you squeeze off the hose, either the hose is leaking or the component it's connected to is defective.

Check the intake manifold gaskets by spraying nonflammable solvent on them while the engine is running. If the idle smooths out, the gaskets are leaking, and you'll have to remove the manifold to replace them. While the intake manifold is off, check it for cracks or warpage.

On cars with multipoint fuel injection and a mass airflow sensor, check the air-inlet ducting for leaks in bellows connectors and other mating surfaces that are downstream of the airflow meter.

On carbureted cars, or cars with throttle-body injection, check the bolts that hold the carb or throttle body onto the intake manifold. These frequently come loose and can cause a rough or erratic idle. Check the carb base or throttle-body gasket by spraying nonflammable solvent as you did for the intake manifold.

Everything okay? Now let's have a look at those injectors.

MULTIPOINT INJECTORS

Using a stethoscope or a piece of hose, listen to each injector while the engine is running. If you use a piece of hose, make *sure* it doesn't touch a plug wire. Black hose is a good conductor and can deliver a shock to your ear—no fun.

You should be able to hear the injector open and close rapidly. The sound of a good injector is crisp and

metallic. One that is partially clogged with deposits on the seat or pintle will produce a dull, muffled sound. Compare the sound of each injector to that of the other injectors.

If your stethoscope diagnosis found one injector that opened and closed with a muffled sound, the injector is probably dirty and could be the cause of a misfire or stumble.

You may find that one injector makes no noise at all. If so, turn off the engine, unplug the injector electrical harness connector, and attach a 6-volt test light to the harness connector. You might want to purchase a test light (noid light) sold specifically for checking fuel injectors. This tool will plug right into the harness connector.

Crank the engine. The light should flash on and off. If it does, the injector is bad or the plug is severely corroded. Clean the connector and reattach it. If the injector still won't fire, it's defective and must be replaced.

If the light doesn't flash—indicating no power to the injector—there's a problem in the wiring or in the engine computer system. On many applications, the injector wiring harness is grounded. Make sure the ground connection is good.

If the wiring checks out okay, perform a computer system diagnostic routine. You should find instructions for this in your service manual.

On most cars, the computer system can be diagnosed without special equipment. While the routines are usually elaborate, they're not

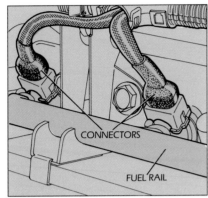

Check the fuel injector electrical connectors for a good fit and clean contacts.

necessarily difficult if you can follow a tree diagram. If you don't have specific instructions or the right equipment for your car, don't diagnose the computer system. Get professional help.

TBI DIAGNOSIS

On carbureted or throttle-body-injected cars, it's not likely that one cylinder is totally fuel-starved—unless there's an internal engine problem. However, the engine can idle roughly because of intermittent lean misfire on all or some cylinders. And, if a TBI injector doesn't deliver any fuel, you'll have a no-start problem to deal with.

When the engine is cranking, the TBI injector should spray fuel. If it doesn't, attach that 6-volt test light to the connector to see if it's being supplied with electricity. If not, a check of the wiring and possibly the computer system is called for.

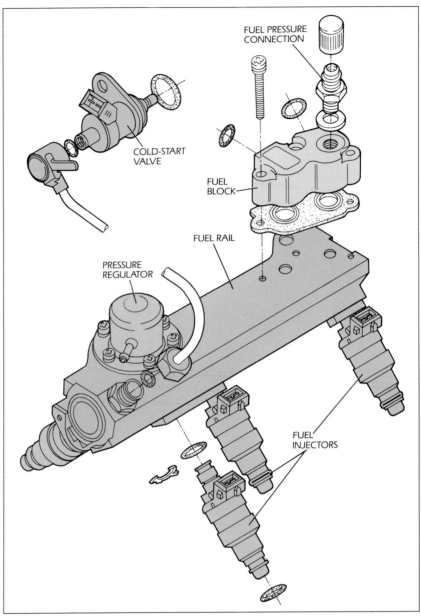

This GM fuel rail is removed along with the injectors. Note the location of the fuel pressure connection for gauge attachment.

Some injector system harnesses, like this Chrysler unit, are connected to ground.

If the power supply checks out okay but the TBI unit doesn't spray, check fuel pressure. To check pressure, attach a high-pressure gauge to the fuel supply Schrader valve, or other connection point as indicated in your service manual. Then turn off the ignition for about thirty seconds and turn it on again. Note the reading on the gauge immediately after the ignition is turned back on.

If fuel pressure is good, the injector is bad. If fuel pressure is below specs for your car, or if there is no pressure, you have a problem in the fuel supply system—possibly the pump or the fuel pressure regulator.

At medium throttle, the TBI spray should be cone-shaped and consistent. If it is even slightly irregular, driveability problems can occur. Sometimes a cleanup can restore good performance. Sometimes replacement of the injector is necessary.

FUEL INJECTION CLEANUP

Sometimes dirty injectors can be cleaned adequately by adding injector cleaner to the fuel tank. Follow the directions on the can.

The best way to clean a fuel injection system is by removing the injectors from the engine and having a professional clean them on a specialized flow-tester/cleaner. Some repair shops are equipped with on-car injection cleaning systems that can do a good job, but don't allow for visual spray-pattern checks. There are also some simple injection cleaning systems inexpensive enough that the driveway mechanic might consider purchasing.

Injector designs have improved to the point where they're now much more resistant to clogging. On older cars where injector clogging is a recurring problem, replacement of the injectors with new aftermarket or original equipment (OE) units might be the best alternative.

DRIPPING FUEL INJECTORS

A fuel injector that sticks open can flood the engine and foul one or more plugs. Given enough time, the fuel evaporates and the engine starts easily, but for the first hour or so after shutoff, starting can be tough.

On port-injected engines (one injector per cylinder), a sticking injector can sometimes be located by checking for fouled or wet plugs half an hour after shutoff.

The absence of wet plugs doesn't necessarily rule out dripping injectors. A visual check of the injectors is the best way to test. On TBI systems, the injectors are easy to observe, and you can simply warm the engine, shut it off, remove the air cleaner, and watch the injectors to see if there's a drip. On some port-injected systems, you can lift the injectors and fuel rails out of the ports to watch for drips.

A check of system pressure is also useful in tracking down leaking injectors. If pressure drops continuously after shutoff, a leaking injector could be the cause. But other problems—like a faulty fuel pump check valve, a leaking pump connection, or a bad pressure regulator—can cause pressure loss as well.

PORT INJECTOR R AND R

If you find that electrical current to an injector is okay, but the injector

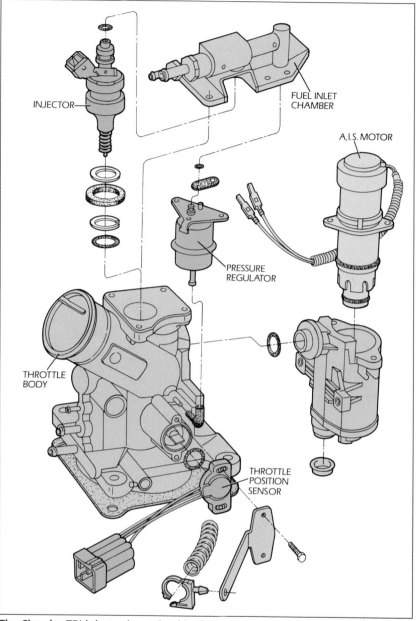

The Chrysler TBI injector is retained in the throttle body by the inlet chamber.

still doesn't fire, it should be replaced with a new unit. Or you may decide to remove your injectors for professional cleaning or replacement with the later-model aftermarket types that are less prone to clogging.

In either case, the removal and replacement job can vary from being relatively easy to quite complex. We'll provide some examples here. For instructions specific to your model, use this guide in combination with your service manual.

Prior to working on a fuel injec-

tion system, disconnect the battery's negative cable. (In fact, we recommend disconnecting the negative cable whenever you work on your car. It's good insurance against accidental shorts or spark-induced ignition of gasoline fumes.) On Chrysler systems, you'll have to disconnect the cable after you've relieved fuel pressure.

Before you can remove an injector from most fuel injection systems, you have to relieve the fuel system pressure. In most cases, this can be done with a fuel pressure gauge and bleed-off hose. The gauge is attached to a valve on the fuel rail, frequently a Schrader valve, and system pressure is released. Wrap a rag around the connector while attaching the gauge to prevent fuel spillage.

Chrysler has specific instructions for relief of fuel pressure in its multipoint systems. Loosen the gas cap and remove the wiring harness connector from one fuel injector. Then ground one injector terminal with a jumper, and connect another jumper between the second terminal and the battery's positive post. Leave the wires in place for ten seconds.

On many cars, the removal of the fuel injectors is quite simple. The rail and injector assembly can be removed from the engine as a unit once the fuel lines and electrical connectors have been disengaged.

On some cars, you'll have to remove quite a few other components before you can get to the fuel rail. On some Toyotas, for example, you'll have to remove the distributor and air-intake chamber before the fuel rail.

In most cases, the injectors are retained in the fuel rail by lock rings. On GM cars, this lock ring is disengaged by turning it clockwise and locked by turning it counterclockwise. On some applications, no snap rings are used and the injectors are retained only by their seals. On these, it's important not to drop any injectors when you lift the fuel rail off the intake manifold.

All injection system O-rings and seals should be replaced when the unit is serviced. You must use O-rings intended for this purpose. Some O-rings are made of materials that are not tolerant of gasoline.

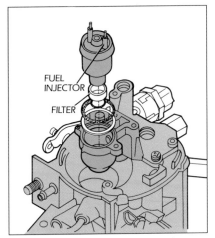

The GM TBI unit commonly used includes a single injector. Some V8 TBIs have two.

Loosen five screws to remove the fuel meter cover from the GM throttle body.

TBI R AND R

The TBI R and R is relatively easy because there's not much stuff in the way. The procedure varies somewhat from car to car. We'll cover the most common application here—the GM TBI. Before beginning any injector R and R, make sure you relieve fuel system pressure as described earlier.

After removing the air cleaner and the electrical connector, unbolt the fuel meter cover. Do not remove the four screws that secure the pressure regulator to the bottom of the fuel meter cover. There's a giant spring lurking in there.

Leave the fuel meter gasket on the throttle body so you won't damage the casting, and lift the injector from the throttle body using a screwdriver and ¼-in. drill bit as shown. Remove the O-ring and washer from the fuel meter body in-

jector cavity and the small O-ring from the nozzle end of the injector. Rotate the injector fuel filter until you can remove it from the base of the injector.

Lube a new small O-ring, and push it on the nozzle end of the injector until it is flush against the fuel filter. Install the steel washer in the fuel meter body. Lube a new large O-ring, and install it on top of the washer. The O-ring should be flush with the top of the fuel meter body casting.

Install the injector in the cavity, aligning the raised lug on the injector base with the notch in the fuel meter body cavity.

Install the fuel meter cover using a new gasket. Apply anaerobic thread-locking compound to the fuel meter screws. Reinstall the injector's electrical connector and air cleaner.

How to Troubleshoot
THROTTLE-BODY FUEL
INJECTION

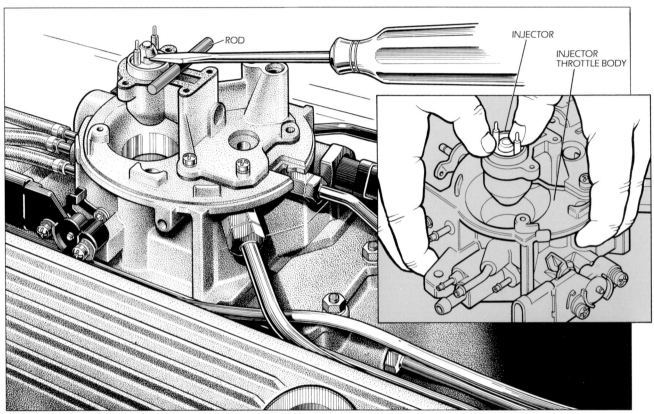

Stubborn injectors can be gently pried from the throttle body with a screwdriver and a small bar, drill bit, or screwdriver handle as a fulcrum. Replace with finger pressure (inset).

If you think troubleshooting throttle-body injection (TBI) is too complex for the Saturday mechanic, you're wrong. It's a relatively simple system to handle. And test instruments cost only about $60.

However, before you turn your attention to a TBI system in hopes of solving a performance problem, be sure to check other possibilities, such as vacuum loss, bad electrical connectors, and ignition-related malfunctions. These cause trouble much more often than the TBI.

SIMILARITIES AND DIFFERENCES

On the surface, TBI looks like a carburetor system (Fig. 1). It's mounted on the intake manifold as a carburetor would be, and it may have that large familiar-looking air cleaner over it, as a carburetor does. Once you remove the air cleaner, the differences become apparent.

When the throttle body is uncovered, you notice one (single-point) or two (dual-point) fuel injectors. Or you might see two throttle bodies, each with one fuel injector (Fig. 2).

In addition to the fuel injector(s), there are other parts of a TBI system that can be troublesome: in-line fuel filter between the fuel tank and throttle body, fuel-pressure regulator, electric fuel pump, fuel sock in the fuel tank, and the idle-speed control.

In addition to these, you can't approach TBI without considering the electronic system that controls it.

The electronic system calculates the fuel requirements of the engine and gets the fuel injector or injectors to deliver the amount of gasoline necessary for the engine to run efficiently. When considering the TBI as a possible cause for an engine performance quirk, the important point to remember about electronics is that a malfunction with the control unit (computer) or with a sensor can cause the same problems that a fault in the TBI system can cause. Therefore, if the tests described below result in a clean bill of health for the TBI, check out the electronics. If the CHECK ENGINE light on the dash is lit,

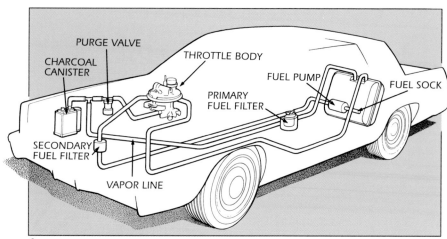

1 Throttle-body injection layout is similar to that of carburetor systems.

refer to the manual for the procedures for interrogating the computer for its diagnostic codes before you try any troubleshooting on your own.

LIGHTING THE WAY

When your TBI-equipped engine won't start, first determine whether the fuel injector is being energized so it opens and sprays gas into the engine. An accurate, easy-to-use test instrument is the TBI Injector Harness Tester (Fig. 3). This test light costs less than $10, and you can order one from Borroughs Tool & Equipment Corp., 2429 North Burdick St., Kalamazoo, MI 49007, or from Kent-Moore Tool Group, 29784 Little Mack, Roseville, MI 48066.

To use the test light, disconnect the wire harness that connects to the fuel-injector electrical terminal and plug the test light into the wire harness connector. Crank the engine. If there are two fuel injectors, test both.

Does the test light give pulsating flashes? If not, there's an electrical failure or a problem with the electronic control system.

But if the light flashes, the reason the engine doesn't start lies with the injector itself, fuel pump, in-line fuel filter, or fuel sock. To get a line on which it is, check the tip of the fuel injector as someone in the car cranks the engine.

You should see gas spraying from the fuel injector, but look closely because it's sometimes difficult to pick up the spray. If you don't see gas spraying, the problem is with the fuel-delivery system.

Furthermore, if you're having a performance problem—something other than the engine is not starting and the spray of gas from the fuel injector is not in the shape of a well-defined cone—there is a TBI-related problem. TBI-related performance problems can include hard starting, stalling, hesitation, rough idle, fast idle, dieseling (engine run-on), lack of power, and poor mileage.

In testing to determine which part of the fuel-delivery system is causing the trouble, establish whether the malfunction is with the injector or another component. You

can do this by analyzing fuel-system pressure, but to do this test you may first have to relieve pressure in the system. If you don't relieve the pressure, you'll get sprayed with gas as you loosen fittings to connect the pressure gauge.

Most manufacturers have a fuel-pressure diagnostic valve in the fuel line. If your car has one, you can tap the pressure gauge into the valve, avoiding the need for relieving fuel-system pressure.

RELIEVING FUEL-SYSTEM PRESSURE

Although manufacturers suggest different ways of doing this, you won't go wrong following this procedure:

1. Place an automatic transmission in PARK—a manual gearbox in NEUTRAL—and engage the parking brake.
2. Remove the fuel pump fuse from the fuse panel if there is a fuel pump fuse. If not, look for a wire harness connector near the fuel tank. Pull apart the connector to disconnect the electric fuel pump.
3. Start the engine. When the engine stalls, crank it for five seconds.

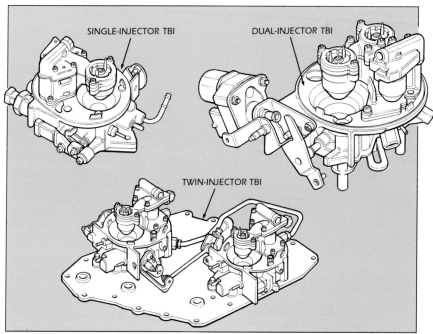

2 Dual-injector TBI has single throttle body, two injectors and venturis. Twin style uses two single injectors.

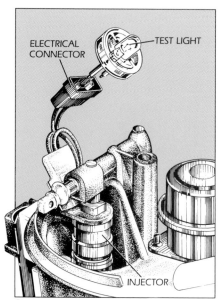

3 This inexpensive test light will flash if TBI electricals are okay.

Do the test in the following way. (If your system is equipped with a fuel-pressure diagnostic valve, you can just attach the gauge to it, rather than depressurizing the system and disconnecting lines to insert a gauge.)

1. If you disconnected a vacuum hose from the throttle body when you removed the air cleaner or air inlet duct, block the vacuum port to prevent vacuum loss as you crank the engine. Vacuum loss can result in a false reading.

2. Disconnect the fuel-inlet line from the throttle body. That's the one coming from the in-line fuel filter. The other line you see at the throttle body is the fuel-return line. More about this one later.

3. Connect the fuel-pressure gauge between the end of the fuel-inlet line and the throttle body (Fig. 4).

4. With the fuel pump reactivated, turn on the ignition switch but do not crank the engine. Wait two seconds, note the pressure-gauge reading, and turn off the ignition switch. Or, you can jumper 12V to the fuel pump with clip leads. On most GM cars, you can jumper to the ALCL connector under the dash. At any rate, the reading will be one of the following:

(a) A reading in line with the normal specification, indicating that there's nothing wrong with this TBI system except maybe the fuel injector (see below).

(b) A zero reading, in which case the engine won't start.

(c) A reading lower than that specified, in which case the engine has one or more of the aforementioned driveability problems.

(d) A reading higher than that specified, in which case the engine will flood.

ZERO FUEL PRESSURE

The malfunctions that result in a zero fuel-pressure reading are a

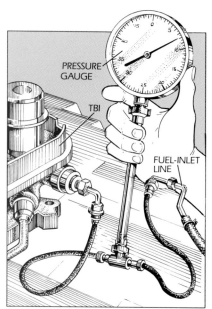

4 Disconnect fuel lines (shown), or use test fitting to attach pressure gauge.

damaged fuel line; breakdown in the fuel pump electric circuit, including the fuel pump relay; bad fuel pump; and clogged fuel filters.

Examine the fuel line for damage first. Doing this is relatively easy—look for a kinked or crushed line.

Then check the fuel pump fuse. If it's blown, and you replace the fuse only to have it blow again, there's a short in the fuel pump circuit.

Listen to the fuel pump. After the ignition switch has been off for several minutes, put your ear close to the fuel tank as someone turns the switch back on. Or, you can jumper the pump as described earlier. Do *not* crank the engine. If you hear humming or whirring, even momentarily, the fuel pump and fuel pump relay are okay. Turn your attention to the fuel filters.

Relieve fuel-system pressure and take another pressure test, but this time place the pressure gauge between the outlet side of the in-line fuel filter and fuel line. If pressure is now normal, a part of the fuel line from the filter to the throttle body which you can't see is crushed or kinked.

If pressure is still zero and the in-line fuel filter hasn't been replaced in a while, do that now.

The in-line filter can be found under the rear of the car on the frame rail, against the outside of the fuel tank, or in the engine compartment.

That's it, except for these few tips:

- Although fuel pressure has been released, a little gasoline may spray when you disconnect a fuel fitting, so wrap a cloth around your hand and the wrench to collect it.
- Whenever you reconnect a fuel fitting, don't reuse the O-ring seal. A used seal might cause a leak. Buy several new ones, because you may have to disconnect the fitting a few times during the course of TBI servicing.
- Keep in mind that once you allow fuel-system pressure to build up, you have to release it before disconnecting any part of the system again.

FUEL-SYSTEM PRESSURE TEST

A fuel-system pressure gauge should cost you less than $50 from an auto parts dealer or from one of the two companies mentioned on page 226.

You'll need specific data concerning the pressure developed by your TBI system. This spec is in the service manual. Don't guess at it. Depending on the system, pressure can be between 9 and 39 psi. Make sure the gauge is appropriate for the fuel-pressure spec for your system.

If you can't spot it easily, trace the fuel-inlet line back from the throttle body.

To replace the filter, relieve fuel pressure and disconnect the fuel line from each side of the filter. Make sure the new filter comes with seals for the fuel-line fittings. Screw the fittings to the filter by hand and give them a quarter-turn with a wrench. Turn on the ignition switch and check for leaks. If replacing the in-line filter doesn't help, then there's the fuel sock to consider. It's on the end of the fuel pickup in the gas tank and will have to be removed to be serviced (Fig. 5). The fuel sock is *supposed* to be self-cleaning, but they have been known to foul and cut off the supply of gas.

Suppose you get no response from the fuel pump when you listen to it. Then, check the fuel pump relay before diving into the gas tank to replace the pump. A wiring diagram from the car's service manual will make it easier to pinpoint the relay.

Once you find it, disconnect the wire connector to see if terminals are clean and tight. Use a test light to make sure current reaches the relay.

Push the probe of the test light into the connector so it makes con-

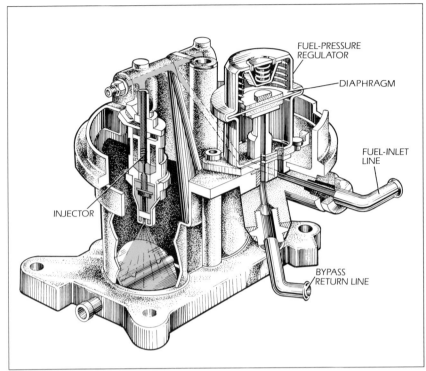

6 Rubber diaphragm in regulator may be replaceable— if not, replace the entire regulator.

tact with the terminal. Turn on the ignition. If the test light doesn't glow, there's an electrical failure. But if the test light shows that current is reaching the relay, check the relay output to the pump. If voltage is present at the pump contacts, then you'll have to replace the pump.

LOW FUEL PRESSURE

Conditions that will cause a low fuel-pressure reading are a clogged in-line fuel filter, restricted fuel-delivery line, a dirty fuel sock, and a faulty fuel-pressure regulator. If the in-line fuel filter hasn't been replaced in some time, that's a good place to begin.

It's easy for a fuel line to be damaged, so examine it along its length from the fuel tank to the throttle body.

If you've still not found the reason for low fuel pressure, the next step is to service the fuel sock. Some vehicles have an access port through the trunk floor, but you may have to drop the tank. Empty the tank safely first, and remember that gasoline fumes are dangerously explosive.

HIGH FUEL PRESSURE

Suppose you get a fuel-pressure reading in excess of what the manual stipulates. It doesn't happen too often, but when it does there are two good reasons. The fuel-return line is kinked somewhere between the throttle body and fuel tank and is restricting the flow of gas back to the tank. This results in high pressure and flooding. Or, the fuel-pressure regulator is defective, and not bleeding off excess pressure back to the tank.

FUEL INJECTOR

Performance problems often associated with a malfunctioning fuel injector are hard starting, rough running, and black exhaust smoke when the engine finally starts—also dieseling (engine run-on). Dieseling indicates that an injector may be stuck partially open.

When the fuel-pressure test shows a normal reading but there is a problem that could be fuel system related or when the spray pattern you observe while watching the injector is suspect, add a fuel-injector cleaner to the fuel tank. Use one rec-

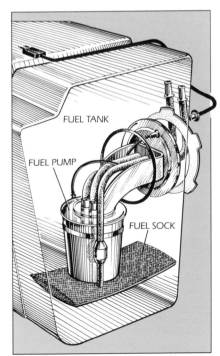

5 In-tank filter sock and pump may require tank removal for service.

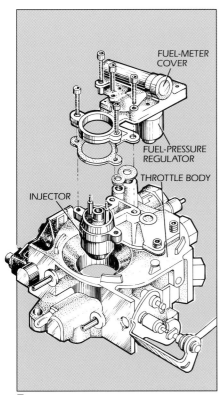

7 Remove fuel meter cover for access to regulator or fuel injector.

1. After relieving pressure in the system and removing the air cleaner, disconnect the electric connector from the fuel injector.
2. If the injector is held by a bracket, remove the screw to free it.
3. Try to pluck the injector from the throttle body with your fingers. If the injector doesn't come out, get something to use as a fulcrum, such as a small screwdriver or a round piece of metal stock. You also need a screwdriver with a fairly long shank. Place the fulcrum across the front of the injector, put the screwdriver over the fulcrum so the tip of the screwdriver engages the ridge around the injector, and press down. The injector will pop out (see illustration on page 225).

To install a new injector, lubricate the O-rings with automatic transmission fluid. Then, look for a guide pin on the injector, line it up with the crevice in the throttle body, and push.

OTHER COMPONENTS

Three other parts you may have to deal with are the fuel-pressure regulator, idle-speed control, and throttle-position sensor.

- The fuel-pressure regulator is set at the factory. When it goes bad, the reason is usually a tear in its diaphragm (Fig. 6). A damaged fuel-pressure regulator will often leak gas and cause the engine to flood.

Indications of a bad regulator (in addition to a performance problem) are gas odor and spark plug tips wet with gas.

The fuel-pressure regulator is part of the fuel-meter cover on top of the throttle body (Fig. 7). Up to now, the entire cover assembly of many TBI units had to be replaced when the regulator failed. Now, manufacturers are issuing replacement diaphragms.

- A faulty idle-speed control causes rough, unstable idle and stalling at idle. This is one component of most throttle-body injection systems that will put a trouble code into the computer when it fails. To replace a bad idle-speed control, disconnect the wire terminal and unbolt the device.

- Although the throttle-position sensor (TPS) is a part of the electronic control system and not the throttle-body injection system, it's attached to the throttle body and is usually associated with it.

If the TPS goes bad, the air/gas ratio is disrupted and an overly rich fuel mixture will occur. This can mean rough idling, stalling or hesitation on acceleration from a standstill, black smoke, and poor fuel economy.

The TPS is screwed to the side of the throttle body. Unscrew it and install a new one, but just be sure you get the correct TPS for the kind of throttle body on the car. It may need to be adjusted to spec, but some vehicles are self-adjusting.

ommended by the manufacturer of your car.

Using a cleaner is often an easy, inexpensive way to get rid of dirt in the injector that is gumming up the works. However, if this doesn't resolve the problem and testing ignition, vacuum, and so on turns up nothing, you may want to remove the injector(s) for testing by a shop that has an injector tester. Here is what's involved in removing the injector(s):

How to Troubleshoot Your
ELECTRONIC IGNITION

Traffic is backed up six deep behind you at the stop sign, but your car has stalled and simply refuses to start. Twisting the key again only serves one purpose—heating up the already-smoking starter motor even more, which mirrors the steam coming from your ears. Your ignition system has failed.

On many cars, the old no-start diagnosis—check for spark and then for fuel—may not work. If some computers detect a severe fuel-system problem, they refuse to permit a spark, even if the system is capable of doing so. However, in such cases a trouble code will be set.

So today the opening routine for no-start, hard-start, or even misfire and hesitation is always to look for a trouble code (see the chapter "How to Check Your Trouble Codes"). And

Check the gap between the magnetic sensor and trigger wheel using a feeler gauge.

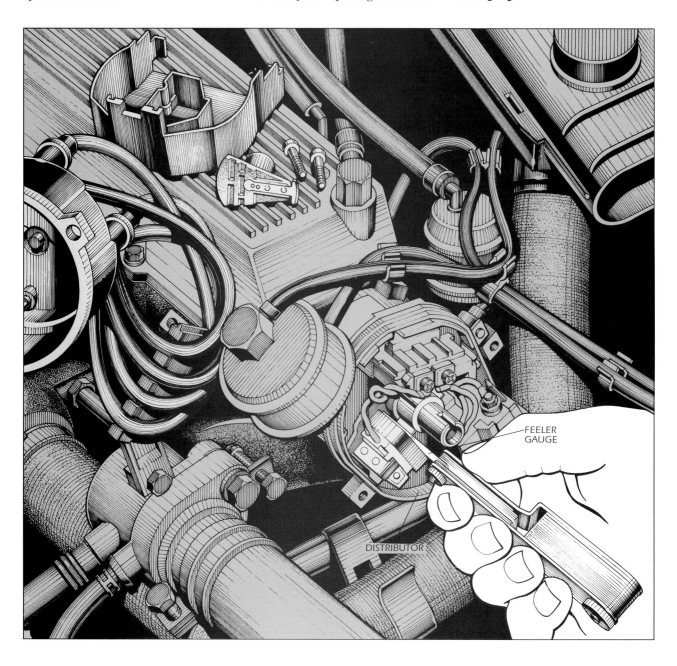

FEELER GAUGE

DISTRIBUTOR

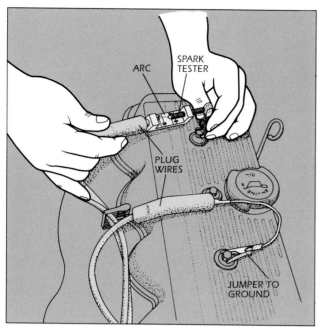

Most distributorless ignitions require that you ground the other plug lead from the same coil to check for spark.

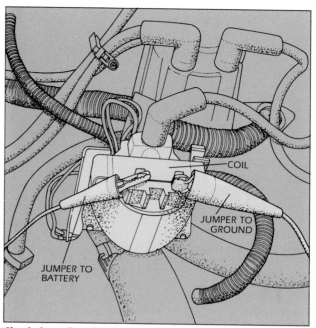

Check the coil on distributor-type ignitions by bypassing the electronics completely. See text and the next illustration.

because many computers distinguish between a "hard" (current) failure and one that merely is stored in memory from who knows when, you can see if the code is related to the problem.

When the computer detects a major failure of a sensor, it adopts one of two strategies. If possible, it simply substitutes an average value for the missing sensor signal and uses other sensors to guide its decisions. The results may be so good, you just think that performance is off a bit.

However, if it can't, or if the failure may significantly increase engine emissions, the computer will go into a "limp-home" mode. The engine keeps running but obviously poorly. The CHECK ENGINE light goes on, and if you shine a timing light on the timing marks, you'll see very little or no change in the number of degrees of ignition advance, even if you rev the engine way up.

The computer does not monitor the ignition secondary circuit—spark plugs, wires, distributor cap, rotor, etc.—and in fact, can detect only some failures in the ignition primary circuit (the low-voltage part of the system), such as a very badly shorted or opened circuit. The computer also knows if it doesn't receive a signal from an electronic ignition module on engines with a

distributor. For problems such as these, the computer can set a trouble code.

If you don't find a code, check for spark. And the best way to do it on today's systems is one spark plug wire at a time with a low-cost spark tester. The best plug testers have adjustable gaps so you can set them for the peak voltage of a particular system.

No spark? Or is there a weak or intermittent spark? The problem has to be in the ignition system itself, beyond the diagnostic capability of the computer.

WITH A DISTRIBUTOR

If the engine has a distributor, it also has a single ignition coil, a sensor called a pickup coil in the distributor, a distributor cap and rotor, and an electronic module—either on the distributor or elsewhere in the engine compartment.

The first place to check, even for no spark at the plugs, is inside the distributor cap. Electronic ignition produces high voltage, and high voltage arcing around is something like a lightning storm in that tiny area. Look for corroded electrical contacts and any physical deterioration, particularly cracks around

any mounting screws and contacts. If you find anything suspicious, replace the part. Don't forget the insides of the spark-plug wire terminals in your search for corrosion and carbon tracks.

Check each plug wire for resistance with an ohmmeter, and replace it if it's over manufacturer's specifications.

Next, test the ignition coil. The simplest way is to unplug the wiring connector from the coil and make a coil tester from jumper wires and a set of breaker points with an integral condenser, which you can get for a few dollars from an auto parts store. Connect one jumper from the battery's positive terminal to the coil positive, and a second jumper from the coil negative to the terminal on the breaker-points assembly. Ground the plate of the breaker points, and flick open the breaker points with a screwdriver. You should see a spark jump a ½-in. gap in the spark tester. If there's no spark, the coil is defective.

If the distributor cap, rotor, and wires pass inspection and the ignition coil passes this test, go to the ignition primary circuit to continue diagnosis of a no-spark or intermittent spark problem.

Where the system has a simple electromagnetic pickup, there's gen-

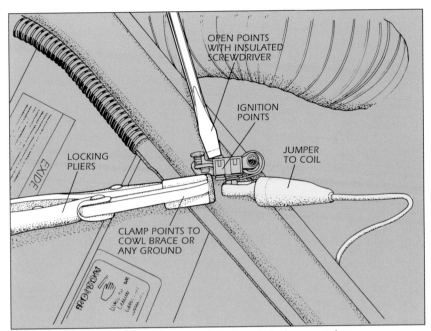

Use a spare set of old-style ignition points to switch the ground to the coil while performing tests. Just clamp the points someplace handy that's grounded.

erally a resistance test you can make across the pickup's wiring terminals. And if resistance is outside specs, the pickup is defective. This design usually has a trigger wheel with teeth.

However, more distributors today use a Hall-effect switch, which has a trigger wheel with shutter blades that pass through a U-shaped part (the Hall switch) and produce a sharp voltage change that signals the electronics.

The typical Hall switch has three wires; one to the ignition coil, one to provide a signal to the engine computer or ignition module, and a third to the ground (which also may be to the computer). Check the wiring diagram, unplug the wiring from the Hall switch, and hot-wire the switch to the battery (coil terminal to battery positive and ground to battery negative, a voltmeter positive lead to the signal terminal and the negative lead to ground). If a shutter blade from the trigger wheel is in the Hall-switch gap, the voltmeter should read close to battery voltage. Remove the trigger wheel, and it should drop to 1 volt or less.

A simpler check when there's no spark on Chrysler engines is to connect the ignition-coil wire to the spark tester and ground the tester. Unplug the wiring connector from the Hall switch and, with the ignition on, connect a jumper wire across terminals 2 and 3 of the harness. If there's now a solid spark, replace the Hall switch.

On Ford products with the Electronic Engine Control IV computer, there's a small ignition module (either on the distributor, or remotely mounted and connected to it). To test the pickup and ignition module, probe the tach terminal of the ignition coil with a grounded test light, crank the engine, and the light should flicker brightly. If it doesn't, make a second check with a voltmeter set on AC scale. Connect the

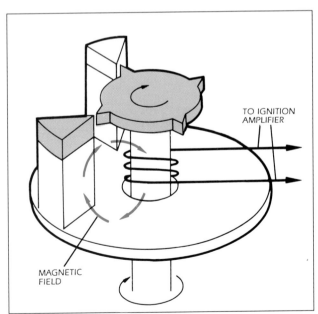

Electromagnetic distributor sensor uses a steel paddle wheel to generate the timing signal for the computer.

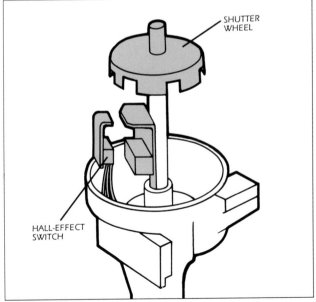

Solid-state Hall-effect sensor switches on and off the voltage signal from the engine computer with a metal shutter.

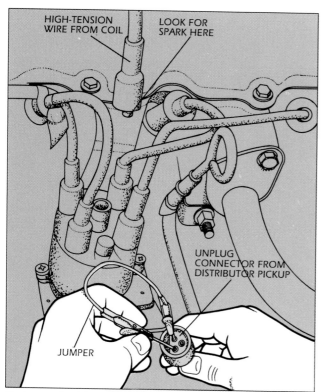

HIGH-TENSION
WIRE FROM COIL

LOOK FOR
SPARK HERE

UNPLUG
CONNECTOR FROM
DISTRIBUTOR PICKUP

JUMPER

Test some ignition systems by shorting
across the sensor terminals in the
harness and checking for spark at the coil wire.

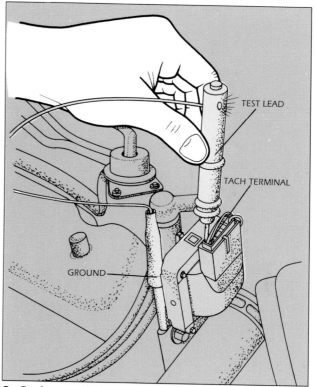

TEST LEAD

TACH TERMINAL

GROUND

On Fords, a test light on the tach
terminal should flash when cranking
over the engine, if the sensor is working.

voltmeter to the ignition module's pickup terminal and ground (refer to the circuit diagram). With the engine cranking, it should read between 3.0 and 8.5 volts, if the pickup is good. Normally, when the test light fails to flash, the cause is a bad ignition module, particularly the type mounted on the distributor, but it takes a special tester (more expensive than substituting a module) to be sure. If the Hall pickup looks physically good, try a new module.

Although there are electronic ignition testers that really check out the ignition module, they're professional quality ($) equipment. You generally can't return electronic parts once you walk out of the store. It's usually still more cost-effective to check the coil, harness wiring, and pickup, and if they're good, replace the ignition module if there's no spark or intermittent spark.

Occasionally, you can confirm that a module is the problem if the loss of spark is on a hot restart. Restart the engine when it's cool, then apply heat to the area of the module

with a hair dryer set on high, and if the engine starts misfiring shortly, that's a reasonably solid indication of a defective module.

Whenever you replace an ignition module, whether it's on a domestic or imported car, and the module rests on a flat surface, always apply a thick coat of silicone dielectric grease to the base. It improves heat transfer from the module, so it runs cooler.

DISTRIBUTORLESS IGNITION

Although there's no distributor cap to inspect, most distributorless ignition systems still have spark plug wires. The wires connect into double-end ignition coils, each lead feeding a separate spark plug—one firing near TDC exhaust and the other near TDC compression. Because the plug to the cylinder on the exhaust stroke should draw virtually no voltage, almost full voltage should go to the one on compression. However, if the plug on exhaust is badly worn, it may draw

enough voltage to cause the plug on compression to misfire. So the plug wire that is misfiring in your spark tester may not be in the problem area.

Always begin by unplugging the wires at the coil to inspect for corrosion, cracks, or carbon tracks inside the terminal.

To double-check what seems to be a misfiring plug wire, first ground the wire on the opposite end of the coil with a jumper wire, and if the plug now fires, remove the opposite wire's plug for inspection.

If a distributorless ignition module passes basic inspection (including current feeds and grounds) and there's misfire on the cylinders at just one coil, the likely problem is a bad coil. The bank of ignition coils normally can be replaced separately from the electronic module, so a coil is worth testing. Make a simple resistance check of the coil, often at the multiterminal of the module. Check the wiring diagram to identify the wire for that coil and the "common" wire that completes the circuit for all the coils on the mod-

233

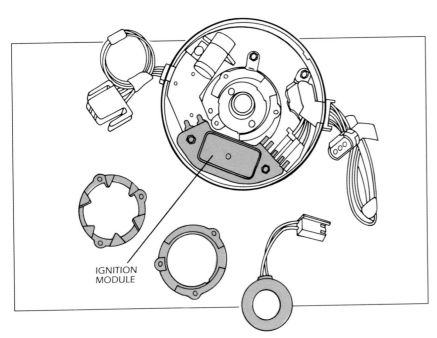

IGNITION MODULE

Use special heat-conductive grease under the replacement ignition module to ensure adequate cooling.

ule. Connect the ohmmeter across the terminals, and the reading should be less than 2 ohms.

Many distributorless ignition problems also are caused by defective crankshaft position sensors. The computer can identify some major failures in the sensor, but not all. To try to duplicate or eliminate an intermittent misfire, wiggle the wiring connector on the sensor, and if the problem is affected one way or the other, inspect the connector and wiring. If they're good, the sensor apparently is the problem.

How to Fix Your
HEATING/AIR-CONDITIONING SYSTEM

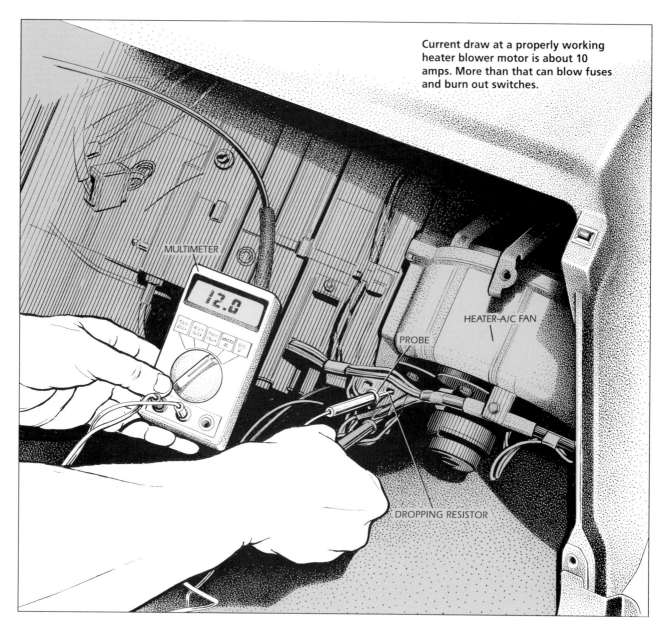

Current draw at a properly working heater blower motor is about 10 amps. More than that can blow fuses and burn out switches.

MULTIMETER

12.0

HEATER-A/C FAN

PROBE

DROPPING RESISTOR

It's a long drive home from Grandmother's house—a long drive indeed, in the dead of a frosty winter night with your car's heater producing only a trickle of tepid air. Soon your toes and fingers are numbing, interfering with proper operation of your car's controls.

Beyond comfort, your car's ventilation system is important to good driving and safety, almost as much as the brakes and steering. We tend not to think about the heater or a/c until they don't work—usually during the worst of weather conditions. Fortunately, regardless of your ve-

hicle's age, make, or model, care and repair of its heater/defroster/air-conditioning system is well within the scope of the competent Saturday mechanic.

Air enters the car through the fresh-air intake in the cowl, under the bottom edge of the windshield,

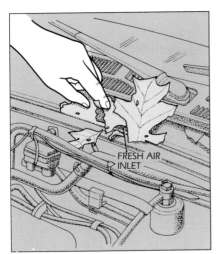

Clean out leaves, twigs, and other debris from the fresh-air intake.

through ductwork and dash-mounted outlets, and exits through vents in the C-pillars, at the base of the backlite, or both.

Therefore, the first step in guaranteeing proper ventilation is making certain that the air intake is clear. With the hood open, reach into the ventilation intake and remove leaves, twigs, and other debris. You may have to remove a grille cover or open the chamber by moving the vent control to FRESH. Clear the drain holes in the bottom of the plenum, and flush the chamber with water from a hose.

AIR DOORS

Small flapper-type blend-air doors located in the ductwork beneath the dash direct the airflow to the outlets you want. These doors typically are opened and closed via cables or vacuum diaphragms.

On cars with vacuum-operated systems, you should hear a slight hiss along with the sound of the doors opening and closing as you move the airflow selector switch. On cars with cable-operated doors, you should feel the resistance of the doors moving and hear a reassuring clunk as you move the selector. Besides directing the air between the various dash-mounted outlet vents, these doors also direct the flow of air around or through the heater core after the air passes the a/c evaporator. Cars with a RECIRC/FRESH switch utilize another door to allow air from the fresh-air intake into the system.

First, check that all the ductwork is connected. From underneath the dash, feel the backs of all the vents. Gaining access to the ducts may require removing the glove compartment and some trim panels. Either a solid, molded-plastic duct or a flexible, reinforced duct hose should be attached. Follow the duct back to the main heater outlet compartment, and be sure that end is also connected. Check that there are no tears in any of the ducts. Reconnect any loose ducts and patch any tears with duct tape.

If all the ductwork is intact but air is not getting to where it should, inspect the dashboard airflow selector switch. If there's no access to the rear of the switch from underneath the dash, you may have to remove the radio and some trim panels.

On vacuum-operated systems, make certain the selector lever bellcrank is properly attached to the vacuum switch and that all the vacuum hoses are connected to the vacuum switch or to a separate connector attached to the switch itself. Start the engine to determine which vacuum hose goes to the vacuum source.

If none of the hoses shows vacuum, check for a leak. Vacuum for the control panel is supplied by the engine, quite possibly by way of a vacuum reservoir mounted in the

engine compartment. Trace the source hose back to the engine compartment—the other hoses will run to the vacuum diaphragms mounted near the blend-air doors. Check that the hose is properly connected and that it has no cracks, kinks, or holes. If the hose is good, disconnect it at the source, and supply vacuum to it with a manual vacuum pump. If the hoses and the vacuum switch are good, the system will hold the vacuum, and the selector switch should move the doors. If so, inspect the vacuum reservoir for a leak and check that the vacuum port on the engine is clear. Check the hose connection between the vacuum port and the reservoir.

Replace any damaged hoses. Repair small holes or cracks with vinyl tape, or splice in a section of new hose.

If vacuum is getting to the switch or connector, but not to the individual diaphragms, apply vacuum to the individual diaphragms. Disconnect each hose in turn at the switch and connect it to a manual vacuum pump. Apply between 5 and 10 psi of vacuum. If the rod or link on the diaphragm does not move, check the diaphragm's hose for leaks. If the hose is bad, replace it. If the hose is good, attach the manual pump directly to the diaphragm and reapply the vacuum. If the diaphragm still does not move, or if the

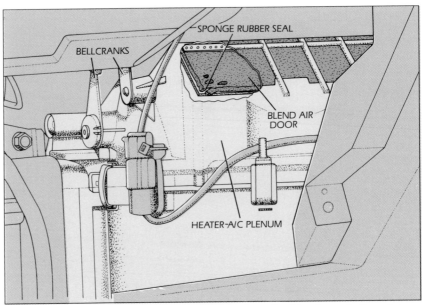

Check carefully under the dashboard for misadjusted cables, loose bellcranks, binding blend-air doors, or torn foam-rubber seals in the heater housing.

diaphragm cannot hold the vacuum reading, replace the diaphragm.

If the diaphragm link pulls on the door, but the door doesn't move, or barely moves, disconnect the diaphragm's link from the door and check that the door itself is free. A judicious application of penetrating oil may do the trick. Also inspect the door's seal. Glue down any tears or spots where it could be catching on the ductwork.

If each vacuum diaphragm works properly and none of the hoses is leaking, but the doors do not open or close as they should, replace the switch.

To check the operation of a cable-operated selector switch, first ascertain that the cable (or cables) is properly connected to the back of the selector lever. If not, reattach the cable and cinch it down, either by tightening its loop on the lever or by snugging down any retaining clips or clamps.

Next, check the other end of the cable. Again, if it is disconnected, reattach it. Next, be sure that the cable is properly clamped along its run from the selector to the door lever and that the cable is not binding en route.

If the cable and both levers are operating properly, check the adjustment of the cable. Disconnect the cable from the door-operating lever, and push the selector all the way to the end position. Slowly move the door-operating lever through all its detents, listening carefully to hear the doors open and close as you go. With the door-operating lever moved to its extreme position, reattach the cable. If the cable end does not match the door-operating lever position, loosen the cable's mounting clamp or cinch nut and then adjust the cable as necessary.

Reattach the cable, and move the selector lever back to the other extreme. Remove the cable from the door-operating lever, and ascertain that the door is also at the end of its travel. If the door lever can still move, adjust its linkage to meet the cable end. Perform this adjustment for each cable and its flapper door on systems with more than one cable. As with vacuum-operated doors, be sure that the doors are all free and are not binding on their hinges and that their seals are not torn or sticking.

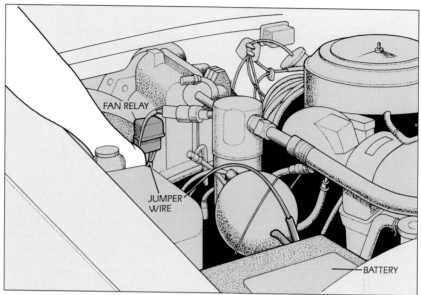

Run a 12-volt jumper wire directly to the blower motor or relay from the battery to check if the motor is in good running order.

BLOWER BASICS

If the blower does not work with the ignition and heating system turned on, check its fuse. If the fuse is blown, replace it. If the fuse is good, or if the new fuse blows, there is a problem in the fan's motor, switch, or the wiring between them.

To determine if the blower motor itself is the problem, connect a jumper wire directly to it from the battery. First, disconnect the blower motor from the wiring harness. If the wiring connector to the motor has two wires, one is hot and the other is ground. To test the motor, connect a jumper wire from a good ground to one terminal of the motor's connector and another directly from the battery's positive terminal to the other. Connect the wires only briefly—the motor should run, spinning the fan. If not, the motor is defective.

Before reconnecting the wiring to a good motor, inspect the wiring and its connectors, and clean corrosion from the connectors' terminals. If the motor, its fuse, and wiring are all good, but the fan still does not blow air, the problem is in the fan switch or its resistor. Since the resistor regulates current flow depending on switch setting, a fan that blows full tilt all the time, regardless of switch setting, probably indicates a bad resistor.

Depending on your car's system, current for the motor flows either from the fuse box to the control panel, then to the motor and then the fan switch and the resistor, or from the panel to the fan switch and the resistor and then to the blower. Check your wiring diagram to see exactly how your car's system is configured.

Check the fan switch to see that all the wires are connected and that the switch itself is not charred or obviously broken. Also check the resistor, typically mounted near the switch, to see that its coils are not burned out. If everything looks good, test the switch.

Depending on your car's system, you can test the switch without re-

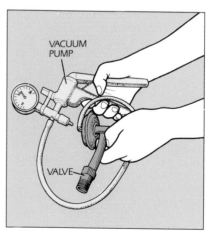

Verify a vacuum-operated heater control valve by applying 10 pounds of vacuum.

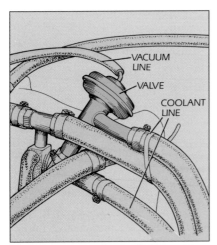

The heater control valve is located in the engine compartment, In the heater inlet hose.

moving it: Use a test light to determine which wire carries current to the switch, with the ignition and the heater on. Then, jump across from the hot wire to each of the other terminals on the switch. If the fan runs at each connection, the switch is defective. Replace it. If the fan doesn't run with the switch bypassed, the resistor is bad.

Some systems also incorporate a special high blower-speed fuse and/ or a relay in addition to the fuse in the fuse panel. If the blower runs only on low speed, check the fuse and relay.

HOT AND COLD

Last, the incoming air must be heated or cooled the way you want it. When the heater switch is at max, and the engine is fully warmed up, the air coming from the outlets should be well over 100°F, as much as 120°F or more. And cars with air-conditioning should be able to produce air that's cooled to a temperature that's at least 20°F cooler than the outside air. Place a thermometer in an outlet vent, run the heater at full heat and the a/c at full cold to check temperatures.

If the heated air is cool, first inspect the engine's cooling system. The heat for the heater is supplied by engine coolant circulating through the heater core, itself a small version of the engine's cooling radiator. Therefore, the engine must reach proper operating temperature. If the engine is running cool, check that the thermostat is not opening too early and the radiator's electric cooling fan is not switching on at too low a temperature or, on cars so equipped, that the clutch in a clutch-type fan has not locked up.

With engine coolant temperature correct for your car—typically about 200°F—but the heater still blowing cold, check the heater control valve, if your car has one. Most cars have a valve in the heater inlet hose, which runs from the heater core nipple at the firewall to the en-

gine. The valve may be mounted at the heater core.

To check that the valve is working, move the dash-mounted temperature selector to its coolest setting. With the engine running at operating temperature, feel the hose on both sides of the control valve, if accessible. The engine side should be hot, the heater side cool. Next, move the selector to maximum heat, and feel the hose. Both sides should now feel hot. If not, the valve or its switch is defective.

Heater control valves are actuated by either a cable or vacuum. Check the dash-mounted heater switch in the same manner you checked the airflow selector switch. To check a vacuum-controlled heater valve, with the engine running, apply vacuum from a manual vacuum pump directly to the valve. If the two sides of the heater hose are now equally hot, the valve is good. Make sure it is getting vacuum. If there is no temperature change, the valve is bad.

If the heater control valve is operating properly, but there's no heat, make sure that there is ample coolant flow through the heater core. With the engine cool and the temperature selector to full heat, briefly disconnect the heater outlet hose at the firewall. With the engine running, there should be a steady flow of coolant from the heater. If there is just a trickle, the heater is

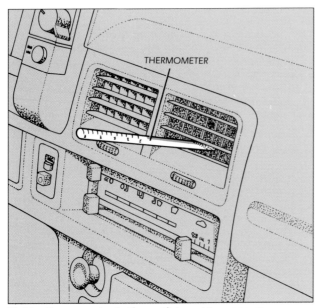

Hold a thermometer in the outlet vent to measure both heater and air-conditioning performance.

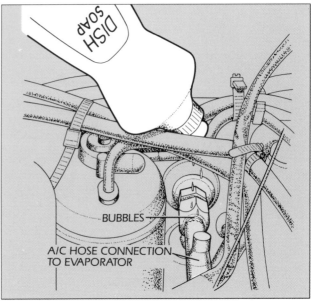

Soap dripped over a/c fittings will bubble if the system has a leak at that fitting.

blocked. You can attempt to back-flush the heater core, but keep water pressure less than 20 psi or you may damage the core. Otherwise, replace the heater core.

Cars without a heater control valve, such as those with automatic climate-control systems, regulate air temperature by directing cooled air from the air-conditioning evaporator past the heater core. If the air blows cold when it should be warm or warm when it should be cold, the doors directing the air past the heater core are not operating properly. Check them in the same manner that you checked the other air-flow doors. With full heat, all air should go through the chamber with the heater core. With full a/c, none should.

Tepid air or a defroster that does not remove humidity, regardless of temperature setting, indicates a problem with the air-conditioning system. Automotive air-conditioning systems have come under greater scrutiny since the relationship of the refrigerant R-12, known as Freon, with the depletion of the earth's ozone layer has become a major concern. Accordingly, repair of a/c systems should be left to a properly equipped pro. However, you can still make some checks of your car's a/c.

First, make sure that the compressor clutch engages when the air conditioner is switched on—either via its own switch as with many imports or via the setting of the heater switch—and that the engine is fully warmed and running. If you do not hear the click of the compressor switch or you can see that the clutch has not engaged, check the system's fuse, relays, and wiring. If the clutch engages, be sure that the drivebelt is not slipping.

If the compressor runs, but performance is weak, make sure there is good airflow through the condenser. The condenser is mounted against the engine's radiator. Use a soft brush, soap, and water to clear bugs and debris from the condenser fins.

Next, check all the tubing fittings for leaks. With the engine and the air conditioner running, cover the fittings with light oil or soapy water. A trickle or stream of bubbles indicates a leak. However, because overtightening the fitting can distort the sealing O-ring, leave the snugging of the fitting to a professional. You'll have to take the car to him anyway to have him recharge the system.

If your car's a/c system has a sight glass in the accumulator, check the glass while the engine is running with the air conditioner on. If you see bubbles in the refrigerant, the system's pressure is low and should be recharged. Again, recharging an automotive air-conditioning system should be done by the properly equipped pro who will capture all the old refrigerant and recycle it.

How to Diagnose
OXYGEN SENSORS

You're running late for work, again. Your car starts fine, runs perfectly for the first few frantic minutes. But just as you enter the highway, it starts to stumble, making you spill hot coffee on your pants. And when you press on the gas, the engine surges. Worst of all, the CHECK ENGINE light is on.

You know you don't need a tune-up. You're worried that the car's computer might be shot. It could be, but it's not likely. A likely culprit is the O_2 sensor, or it may be an engine problem that causes the sensor to act up.

THE SENSIBLE SENSOR

In a world of high-tech engines, it's nice to know that the O_2 sensor is extremely simple: It tells the engine computer how much oxygen is left in the exhaust.

By analyzing exhaust gas oxygen levels, the engine's computer can determine the best air/fuel ratio—something that became much more critical when cars got catalytic converters. For an internal combustion engine, complete burning occurs when there is about 14.7 parts air to 1 part fuel (by weight). The fancy

scientific name for this ideal 14.7:1 air/fuel ratio is *stoichiometry*.

If the O_2 sensor detects too little oxygen in the exhaust, it signals the computer that the engine's air/fuel mixture needs less fuel. Under these conditions, the engine is running rich. Too much oxygen indicates a lean mixture and the need for less fuel.

To perform its signal-sending feat, the O_2 sensor acts like a simple battery. The main portion of the sensor consists of a hollow ceramic finger. Outside air reaches the hollow inner portion of the sensor

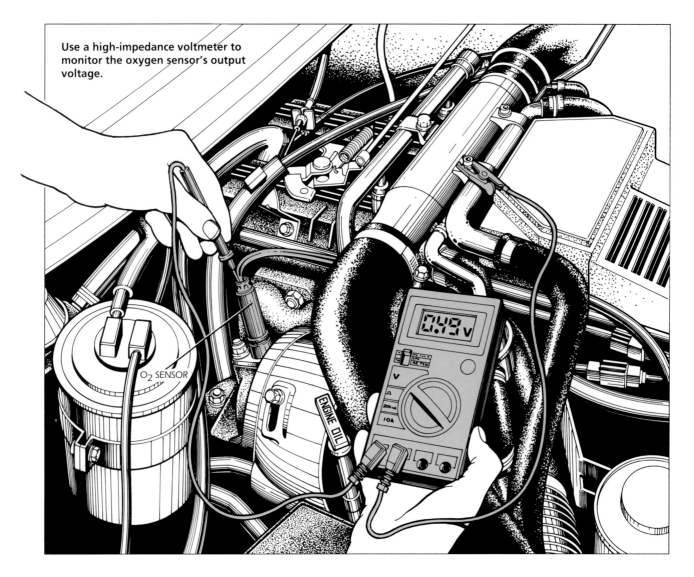

Use a high-impedance voltmeter to monitor the oxygen sensor's output voltage.

O₂ SENSOR

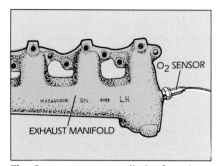

The O₂ sensor can usually be found at the rear of the exhaust manifold.

while the outer portion sits directly in the exhaust stream. Both sides of the finger are plated with a porous platinum alloy. When the engine is running rich, there is little oxygen in the exhaust. That allows oxygen ions from the fresh-air side of the ceramic to push their way to the exhaust side of the ceramic, which, in turn, creates an electrical signal of about 1 volt. To the computer, that's a clear message to make the mixture lean.

When the engine runs too lean, sensor voltage drops because oxygen is present in equal amounts on both sides of the sensor, and there is no transfer of ions—an equally clear message to the computer that the engine is rich.

An important thing to remember, however, is that an O₂ sensor doesn't do anything until it's really hot (about 600°F). So when the engine is cold, the computer ignores all inputs and governs the air/fuel ratio based on its own programming. During this warm-up phase, the engine is in open-loop mode.

Once the sensor is warm, the computer goes into closed loop, an endless cycle where the O₂ sensor switches back and forth between voltage (rich) to no voltage (lean), while the computer reads the switches and adjusts air and fuel accordingly.

A sensor can have as many as four wires coming out of it. If that's the case, two of the wires are simply grounds, the third wire is for sensor voltage, and the fourth wire supplies current to a built-in heater that warms the sensor so it can start sooner (about 400°F) when the engine is cold. It also warms the sensor when exhaust temperature isn't sufficient to do the job. Two- and three-wire sensors may, or may not,

have an auxiliary heater. Consult a manual to figure out which wire does what.

SENSOR TESTS

When there's a problem that relates to the O₂ sensor, the computer knows about it right away. And it lets you know by illuminating the CHECK ENGINE light and storing the appropriate trouble codes.

For example, on some GM cars, Code 13 indicates that the sensor is not switching back and forth, even when the engine is warm. Code 44 indicates the sensor is constantly telling the computer the engine is lean. Code 45 indicates the sensor is constantly telling the computer the engine is rich. Other cars have different trouble codes for the same problems.

A set trouble code is not an automatic indication that the O₂ sensor isn't working. In fact, the opposite may be true. The sensor might be working perfectly, and simply indicating that there are other problems. For example, a sensor that constantly indicates a lean mixture could mean that the engine is indeed really running lean all the time. The problem could be due to a vacuum leak, a bad EGR valve, or a malfunctioning carburetor or injector. The sensor will also indicate lean operation if a cylinder is misfiring—since a misfire dumps all the oxygen from the unburned charge directly into the exhaust.

If the O₂ sensor constantly indicates a rich mixture, the problem could be the sensor. Or a malfunctioning carburetor, dribbling injectors, or some other problem may be giving the engine too much fuel.

SENSOR CHECKS

If you suspect a sensor-related problem, verify whether the O₂ sensor is operating properly. Start by making a visual inspection. The electrical connection should be clean and tight. Many sensor problems have been cured by simply unplugging and replugging the sensor's connector—which does nothing more than clean the terminals sufficiently to reestablish an electrical connection.

Many sensors fail because the fresh-air intake on the outside of the sensor becomes plugged. Inspect the sensor for signs that the air intake is covered with engine oil, grease, dirt, or undercoating.

If the sensor appears to be okay visually, you can check to see whether it is operating properly by using a high-impedance digital voltmeter. Begin by connecting the voltmeter between ground and the sensor's connector. If you can't get to the sensor connector, you might have to rig a jumper wire between the sensor and the wire. In any event, *don't* pierce the wire to establish contact, because the wire will eventually corrode enough to ruin the connection.

On GM cars, the voltmeter should read 400 millivolts when the key is on and the engine is not running. This reference voltage is generated by the computer. If you don't see it, disconnect the wire from the sensor and see if the reference voltage appears at the wire. If you do, it indicates that the sensor is shorted out and should be replaced. If the voltage still doesn't appear, then there is a problem with the wiring or the computer.

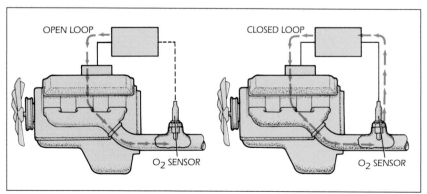

The computer relies on feedback from the O₂ sensor to maintain closed-loop operation.

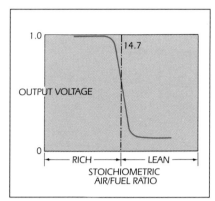

Sensor voltage swings sharply around the proper stoichiometric air/fuel ratio.

Once you've performed this test on General Motors cars, or you're working on another kind of car, start the engine and run it for a few minutes at about 3,000 rpm. This will assure that the engine has gone into closed-loop operation.

SWINGING THE SENSOR

If the sensor is working normally, voltage will swing between about zero and 1 volt. If you see this voltage swing, it means the sensor is working as it should and the computer is changing the air/fuel mixture between rich and lean.

If you don't see the swing, you can use a 1.5-volt flashlight battery to determine if the problem is engine related or if it's caused by the sensor itself. With the engine running, disconnect the sensor wire and connect the negative side of the flashlight battery to a good ground and the positive side of the battery to the sensor wire. This fools the computer into thinking the engine is running rich. So it leans things out and should make the engine speed drop or even stumble as it goes lean. At the same time, voltage at the sensor should stay low, as the sensor reads the lean mixture.

Conversely, if you disconnect the flashlight battery and then ground the sensor wire, the engine should go rich and the sensor voltage should rise dramatically as the sensor indicates the rich mixture. You can tell the sensor is bad if these tests cause changes in engine performance but the sensor readings indicated on the voltmeter show the sensor isn't responding.

Once you find a bad sensor, you can simply replace it. However, there's a good chance the sensor will go bad again—if you don't find and correct the problem that caused the sensor to malfunction in the first place.

SENSOR POISONING

A common cause of sensor failure is poisoning—the most likely candidates being lead, carbon, and silicon. When one of these elements coats the ceramic, it no longer gets oxygen and the sensor either fails completely or gives erroneous readings. Excessive oil consumption can also cause failure as the burned oil deposits plug the sensor.

Lead poisoning shouldn't be a problem, unless you've been using a funnel to gas up with leaded fuel.

Carbon fouling of the sensor is similar to carbon fouling of the spark plugs. It occurs when the mixture runs too rich, coating the ceramic with black, sooty carbon. Fortunately, the effect on the sensor is only temporary if you eliminate the cause of the problem, such as a stuck choke or other condition

that is causing the engine to receive too much fuel.

Silicon contamination causes the sensor to give false rich signals, which, in turn, cause the engine to run lean. Surges, high-idle, and poor running are the result. There are three primary causes of silicon contamination. One is gasoline that's contaminated with silicon. But a much more common cause has been the use of RTV gasket material when reassembling an engine. The gaseous residue given off by the fresh RTV gets into the oil and it is eventually sucked through the PCV and burned in the engine. Silicon contamination can also come from silicone lubricants that get into the engine intake when sprayed around throttle or choke linkages.

Unlike carbon contamination, silicon contamination is permanent and a new sensor must be installed. Use only RTV compounds that are labeled for use with engines that have O_2 sensors.

You can read an O_2 sensor for contamination in much the same way mechanics used to read a spark plug for proper air/fuel mixture. Silicon contamination appears on the

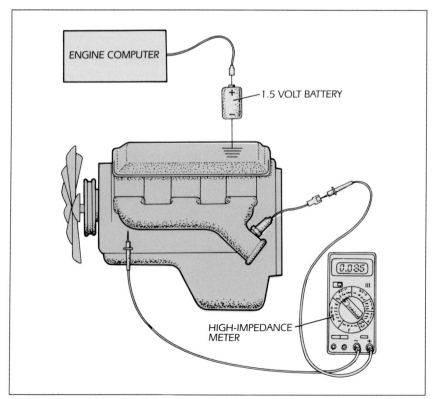

Fool the computer with a 1.5-volt battery to check for proper operation while using a voltmeter to monitor sensor output.

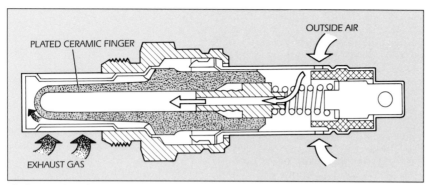

Platinum-plated ceramic electrode produces the signal voltage when heated to 600° F.

louvered part of the exhaust side of the sensor as a soapy film—ranging from a light haze on slightly contaminated sensors all the way to a heavy white coating. Lead contamination appears as a tan or shiny deposit. And carbon appears jet black, just as it does on a spark plug running in a rich mixture.

Sometimes sensors simply wear out or fracture—though a typical sensor will last at least 50,000 miles.

REPLACING A SENSOR

Replacing a sensor is almost like replacing a spark plug. All you do is disconnect the sensor wire and un-

screw the sensor. But because the sensor is mounted in the hot exhaust manifold, it is sometimes difficult to unscrew. If that's the case, heat the sensor and the manifold slightly by running the engine and then try to remove the sensor. You can also use penetrating oil to free the threads.

Before installing a new sensor, make sure the sensor threads are free of rust and corrosion by cleaning them with a wire brush or a spark plug thread chaser. New sensors usually come with high-temperature antiseize compound already in place. If you want to reinstall an old sensor, you'll have to install new compound. Dry-type, high-temp antiseize is available from AC-Delco.

After threading in the sensor by hand, be sure to torque it to the proper specification. When reconnecting the sensor wire, make sure the connector snaps fully in place.

How to Change
LIGHT BULBS

As you near your exit, you move the directional signal stalk up and steer to the right. You move to the right lane and onto the off-ramp, slicing between traffic that seems oblivious to your signaling. And as you instinctively glance down at the dashboard, you notice that the little arrow isn't blinking. It's glowing steadily. You're also aware of the flashing lights of the police car behind you. "What's the matter, pal?" asks the officer. "Doesn't this car have directional signals?"

Light bulbs, whether they're $20 halogen headlights or $1.59 directional signals, periodically burn out—no matter how well you care for your car. But this problem should never become more than a temporary irritation, because it's usually a simple matter to replace a burned-out lamp.

In fact, thanks to the sleek, aerodynamic noses of today's cars, replacing a headlight is easier than ever on many new cars. The designers' efforts to lower hoodlines with narrow headlights coincided with engineers' quests for reduced weight. The result was a change in the federal regulations concerning headlights that allowed the carmakers to develop stylish headlight housings, made of lightweight durable plastics, with separate, replaceable halogen bulbs. These composite headlights grace the noses of most new cars.

When a composite headlight stops shining, you need only change the bulb—not the complete unit. If you're not sure whether your new car has composite headlights, first check the headlight's shape. If it's not a rectangle or circle, the same size and shape as the standard sealed beam from a two-headlight setup, you've got a composite. You'll know for sure if you try to replace the headlight as though it

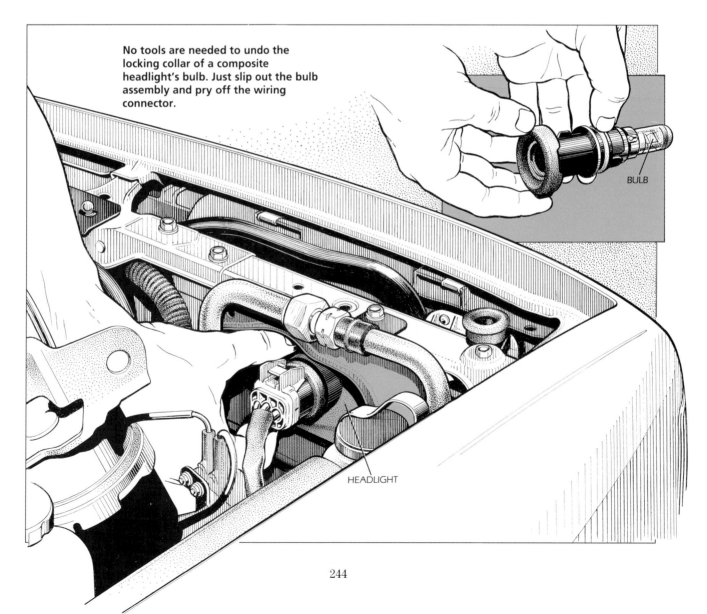

No tools are needed to undo the locking collar of a composite headlight's bulb. Just slip out the bulb assembly and pry off the wiring connector.

BULB

HEADLIGHT

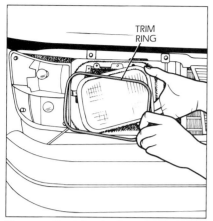

Unscrew the trim ring's mounting screws, and slip in a new sealed-beam headlamp.

base—this keeps moisture from getting inside the housing.

Unfortunately, these slimmer headlights are only part of the trimming done on new cars. Chances are you'll discover your new car has a crowded engine compartment that greatly limits your access to the rear of the headlight. It can be so cramped that you may not be able to contort your hand into a position to undo the bulb's locking collar or clip. So, even though the headlight bulb replacement itself requires no tools, you may need an assortment of wrenches to temporarily remove underhood components—the cruise control module or air-cleaner housing—mounted behind the headlight.

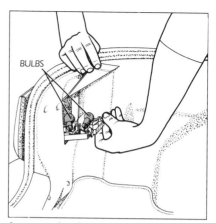

Some marker light assemblies are easily accessible from inside the trunk.

were a sealed beam and discover that you can't find any mounting screws or retaining ring holding the light.

Changing the bulb in a composite headlight doesn't require the removal of screws. In most cases, you don't even need any tools. Open the hood and reach into the engine compartment behind the headlight. You'll find either a plastic collar or a spring clip around the base of the bulb, protruding from the rear of the light's housing. Simply twist the collar counterclockwise or flip the spring clip to unlock it. Then pull the bulb out of the back of the light. Next disconnect the wiring connector from the bulb by lifting up on the connector's locking tab and gently rocking while pulling the connector off the bulb. If the bulb is the type that uses a locking collar, slip the collar off the bulb. Reverse the procedure to put in the new bulb.

Be careful, however, not to touch the glass of the bulb with bare fingers. Like all halogens, these bulbs burn brighter and hotter than standard headlights. The glass of the bulb is special to withstand the heat. But the oily deposit left on the glass by your skin creates a hot spot. That hot spot is all that's needed to cause the bulb to burn out again sooner than normal. Play it safe and, besides taking care to avoid touching the glass bulb, wear clean work gloves when handling the halogen bulb. The relatively large plastic base end of the bulb offers plenty of grab area. Also, take care not to pinch or cut the rubber O-ring on the new bulb's

SEALED BEAM STRATEGIES

If you own a pickup truck or a car that's a few years old, you still have traditional sealed beams to contend with. Replacing a burned-out sealed beam begins with buying the right replacement headlight. Your rig has either dual round or rectangular lights, or quad round or rectangular lights. If it's a quad setup, the low beams are the outer or upper headlights, and the high beams are the inner lights or lower ones. The sealed beams for a quad system are smaller than the ones for a two-light system. The headlights are not interchangeable from one system to another.

To remove your old headlight, first remove any trim ring or cover.

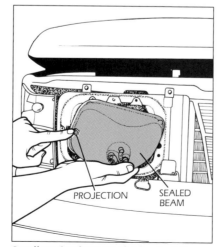

Small projections on the back of the bulb will mate with slots in the mounting bezel.

On some cars, you may even have to remove the grille or part of it, since the headlight trim is integral with the grille. The trim ring on some cars (GM models in particular) is held by a Torx fastener. You'll need a Torx driver to undo the screws. They're available at auto parts stores.

With the trim off, you have access to screws for the ring that holds the light. Round headlight retaining rings are held by three screws, and rectangular ones by four screws. Before you start loosening screws, however, make sure you know which are the mounting screws and which are the aiming screws. Rectangular sealed beams have an aiming screw either at the top or bottom and on one side or the other. Round ones typically have one screw at the twelve or six o'clock position and one at either three or nine o'clock. When replacing a sealed beam, there is no need to disturb the aiming screws.

And before you can loosen and remove the retaining screws, chances are you'll have to free them up since they've probably rusted in place. Treat the screws to a healthy dose of penetrating oil and allow the oil to sit for ten or fifteen minutes. Then attempt to loosen the screws. If they don't move, give them more penetrating oil and wait some more. If you maul the soft head of the screw and your screwdriver can't grip it, you'll have to drill out the screws, working in very cramped quarters. So be patient, and start off with a new, high-quality Phillips or Torx driver—one that hasn't been rounded off yet. While you've got

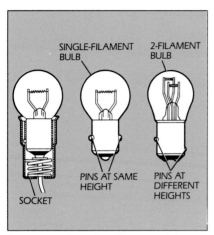

Be sure you're using the correct type of bulb when replacing tail/marker lights.

the penetrating oil out, give the aiming screws a squirt as well.

If you're having a really bad day, the screw-mounting tabs of the retaining ring will break off as you loosen the screws. Fortunately, replacement retaining rings are available at auto parts stores.

With all the screws out, you can lift off the retaining ring. As you do, the headlight will probably slide out of its housing. The light's wiring keeps it from falling. Grasp the headlight in one hand and the wiring connector in the other. Work back and forth while pulling to remove the connector.

Before installing the new light, check the condition of the connector and the wire. If there's corrosion inside the connector's terminals, clean the terminals with aerosol electrical contact cleaner, available at electronics supply stores. If the insulation of any of the wires is chafed or torn, wrap it with electrical tape, or splice in a replacement section of wire if the damage is bad enough.

To install the new sealed beam, push the connector fully onto the tabs on the back of the new light. Slip the headlight into its mounting housing, making certain that the light is right-side up. Small projections on the rear of the light go into notches in the receptacle to ensure proper mounting. Some sealed beams are marked to indicate which side is up. As a rule, the writing on the face of the light's lens should be right-side up. If you mount a sealed beam upside down, the light pattern

will not be thrown properly. Put a small dab of antiseize compound on the screw threads of the mounting screws so they'll come out easily next time, and then slip the retaining ring over the light and replace the screws. Tighten the screws halfway at first until all are caught. Be sure the light is seated properly in the housing before snugging up the screws.

Before replacing the trim ring, check the new light's aim. Though there's usually access to the aiming screws through the trim ring, it's an easier task with the ring still off. You should also check the aim of a newly replaced composite headlight bulb.

READY, AIM

Though sealed beams and composite headlights are designed not to have their aim altered when the bulb is replaced, it's good practice to verify proper headlight aim. If you've planned in advance knowing that someday you would have to check the headlight aim, you have already marked the wall of your garage with crosses where the bright spot of focused light hits when the car is twenty-five feet away. The marks should be made with the car on a level surface, no load in the trunk or seats, and the tires properly inflated. Then all you need to do is check that the focus of the new light corresponds with the old.

If you haven't marked your wall, pull up the car to the garage wall or any vertical smooth surface and put a dot on the wall directly opposite the middle of each headlight lens. Drive the car straight back twenty-five feet. Use masking tape or chalk to make crosses over each of the dots you made on the wall. Again, be sure that the car is on a flat, level surface, that the trunk isn't loaded, and that all the tires are properly inflated. Turn on the headlights. The bright spot of light should be just below the horizontal part of each cross and just to the right of vertical.

To adjust the aim of light, turn the adjusting screws in slight increments. The adjusting screws for composite lights may be accessible only with the hood open, either on the front or rear side of the headlight. After you've aimed the lights, reinstall the trim rings.

LIGHTING THE CORNERS

Replacing a directional signal, taillight, brake light, or marker light is equally simple. But there are a number of variations by the carmakers as to exactly how you have to go about it.

On some cars, you must remove the lens to gain access to the bulb. With others, the light's entire housing must be removed to gain access to the bulbs, and still others offer easy access via a removable trim panel inside the trunk or under a bumper.

The quickest way to tell how to get to a specific bulb is to check the light's lens and housing for screws. Screwheads in the lens itself indicate that you have to remove the lens. A lens housing with no retaining screws means that access is from inside the trunk or behind a fender or bumper. You may have to remove a trim panel—often there's an access flap, but sometimes you must remove some retaining screws for the trim panel—or if the bulbs' receptacles are exposed through the trim panel, there's nothing else to remove. Screwheads, possibly Torx-head ones, around the perimeter of the housing and the lack of any access from the inside of the car indicate that you must remove the entire light unit.

When removing a lens, take care to note which way it mounts. Also, be careful lifting it off the housing. In all likelihood, there's a gasket between the lens and housing. If you tear the gasket, moisture will enter the light and quickly corrode the socket. With the lens off, remove the bulb by gently pressing the bulb

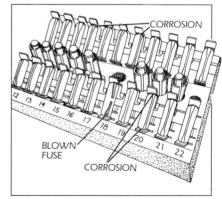

Check for blown or corroded fuses. You may need to probe with a test light.

Ground test light lead, and the light should light up when you touch a "hot" circuit.

into its socket while turning it counterclockwise to release it. Then pull out the bulb.

To remove a bulb from the back side of a housing, either through a trim panel or after removing the entire lamp housing from the car, twist the bulb's socket counterclockwise to release it, then pull out the socket. Remove the bulb by pressing it and twisting counterclockwise.

Before replacing the bulb, check that the socket isn't corroded. If it is, spray it with electrical contact cleaner and, if necessary, clean it with a small parts-cleaning brush. If the corrosion is serious, replace the socket with one from an auto parts store. Then note the grooves and retaining slots on the inside walls of the socket. If the bulb is a dual-filament one—a bulb that does double duty, typically as taillight and brake light—the retaining slots are at different heights inside the socket.

If the bulb has a single filament and performs only one task, the retaining slots are at equal heights. Be sure to install a dual-filament bulb correctly, with the lower locating pin aligned with the lower retaining slot. If the bulb doesn't lock into place with slight pressure as you push and twist clockwise, remove it and check that you're installing the correct type of bulb—single- or dual-filament—and that it's properly aligned.

When reinstalling the socket in the back of the housing, be sure that it locks properly in place and that any metal tabs on the socket make contact with the metal inside the housing. These contacts serve as the ground connection. Replace the housing or the trim panel.

When reinstalling a lens, be sure that the gasket is in place and not pinched. And don't overtighten the retaining screws or you might crack the lens.

PROBLEMS CONNECTING

If you've installed new bulbs or sealed beams and the light still doesn't work, first check that the replacement itself isn't defective. Either install the new light on the other side of the car, if the light on that side has been working, or briefly connect the new light directly to the battery using jumper wires. If the light works, your problem is in the circuit or connection.

If none of the lights in the circuit—both headlights, taillights, and so on—is working, check the fuse. Most cars have their fuse panel under the dash on the driver's side, often on the kick panel. If the fuse panel isn't under the dash, it may be under the hood on the firewall.

Most recent-model cars use color-coded, spade-type plastic fuses. You'll still find glass-tube fuses on older cars and possibly even ceramic ones on European imports.

You can check the fuse without struggling to get it out of a hard-to-reach fuse panel. Turn on the switch for the offending circuit. Ground the lead from the test light and probe both ends of the fuse. If the light goes on only at one end or the other of the fuse, the fuse has blown. Replace it with one of the correct amperage.

Fuses can blow due to circumstances that may not recur, and

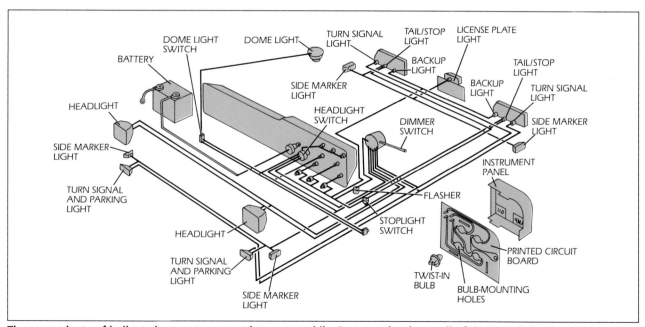

There are plenty of bulbs to burn out on a modern automobile. Fortunately, almost all of them can be replaced with simple hand tools like a screwdriver—or without any tools at all.

changing the fuse may be all that's necessary. If the new fuse blows, however, there's a short somewhere in the circuit, and until it's found and repaired, fuses will keep blowing. The most likely cause of a short in a lighting circuit is a chafed wire, typically somewhere near one of the lights. Check the wires where they go through the car's chassis and body for nicks or rubbed-off insulation. If the wire is otherwise good, but the insulation is missing, wrap it with electrical tape. If the wire itself is damaged, cut out the bad section and splice in a replacement. Be sure to match the gauge of the wire.

If the fuse is good but the lights still don't work, there's an open circuit, possibly caused by a defective switch. Check the switch by connecting a jumper wire directly from the light socket to the battery. If the light works, suspect the switch. Simple push/pull dashboard switches are easily replaced. However, the steering-column stalk-mounted switches popular in new cars require a fair bit of disassembly to replace.

If only one beam—high or low—of a headlight works, check the connector's terminals with a test light. Ground the test light.

With the light switch on and the dimmer switch set to low beam, probe all three of the connector's terminals. Repeat the test with the dimmer switch on high beam. The test light should not go on when you probe the ground terminal.

If the test light fails to light at all in either of the other terminals, either the connector is defective or there's a break in the wire to it. You can replace the three-pronged connector with individual female spade-type crimp connectors and splice in a longer section of wire to replace the wire to the connector in case there's a break.

AN OUNCE OF PREVENTION

You can reduce your chances of suffering the tension of a dimly lit night drive or unnecessary hassle of a ticket by giving your car a weekly inspection. You can do the inspection from the driver's seat while still in your garage. Turn on all the lights and check the reflections off the walls. Step on the brake pedal and watch that both brake lights, and the high-mounted stoplight on newer cars, go on. Check directional signal bulbs by turning on the four-way hazard flasher, which uses the same bulbs.

And be aware of changes while you're driving. A dashboard directional signal arrow that glows instead of flashes is a tip that one of the bulbs has blown. Dashboard lights that no longer light can indicate that the taillight fuse has blown. Spotting problems early can save you headaches later.

How to Repair the
WINDSHIELD WIPER SYSTEM

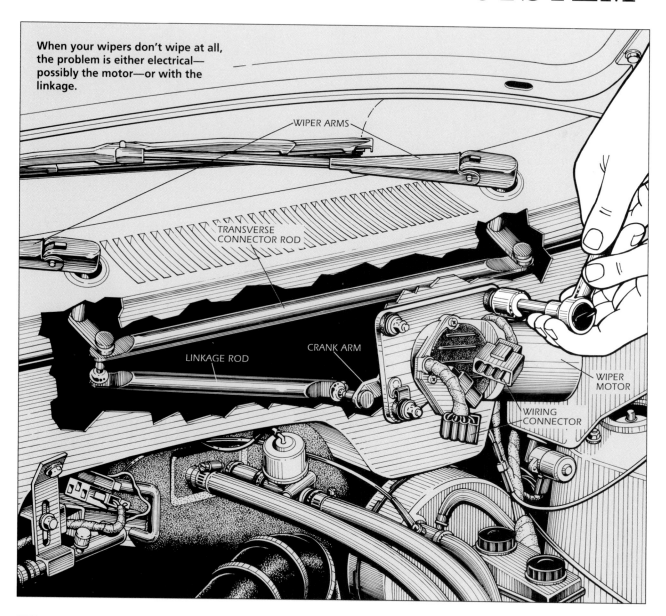

When your wipers don't wipe at all, the problem is either electrical—possibly the motor—or with the linkage.

WIPER ARMS

TRANSVERSE CONNECTOR ROD

LINKAGE ROD

CRANK ARM

WIPER MOTOR

WIRING CONNECTOR

The already ominous sky ahead is growing darker by the second and the traffic coming at you is all wet. Now you can clearly see that cars and trucks coming from where you're going all have their windshield wipers on—full tilt. Suddenly you know why, as you drive into a wall of water at 50 mph. "No problem," you say to yourself as you flick the lever to turn on your wipers. Wrong. You've got a big

problem—the wipers do not budge from their perch no matter what you do.

Or, while it may be less dramatic, it is no less dangerous when you turn on the wipers to clear the annoying muddy mist thrown up by traffic ahead of you after a rain, but all your wipers can do is chatter, bounce, and groan their way across the glass. And they do this despite the fact that you replaced the

rubber squeegees no more than a couple of weeks ago.

In both cases, you simply cannot see where you are driving. And, in both cases, you didn't even know you had a problem until you were face to face with it on the other side of your windshield.

Your car or truck's windshield wipers have been designed to perform one function, and it's a function that you may not utilize very often.

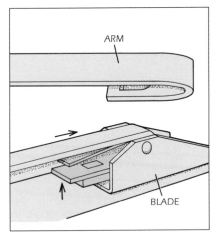

Remove blade from hook-type wiper arm by unlocking tab, slipping arm over pin.

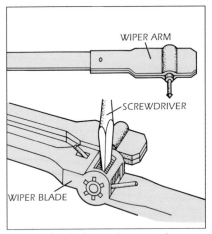

Remove blade from pin-type wiper arm by releasing catch, pulling blade away.

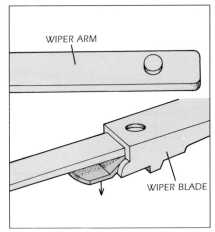

Remove blade from bayonet-type arm by lifting locking tab, pulling blade out.

Part of the trouble is, if you don't use your wipers, you won't know that there is a problem—until it rains.

And like the roof that stops leaking as soon as the rain stops, you may tend to put off repair and maintenance of the wipers when it's not raining.

However, once you discover a problem with the windshield wipers, and the system that operates them, pinpointing and repairing the trouble is simple and inexpensive.

The windshield wiper system actually has several components, many of which may be hidden behind your vehicle's cowl. The pieces that actually wipe the water from the glass are called the squeegees or rubber inserts. These are held by the wiper blade, which is the plastic or metal frame that is the same length as the squeegees. The blades are attached to the wiper arms, which sweep them back and forth across the glass. The wiper arms are spring-loaded to tension the blade and squeegee down on the glass even at highway speeds.

The wiper arms are attached to drive spindles. Typically, the spindles and the bases of the wiper arms are splined and have matching tapers for a press fit. In addition, the tips of many drive spindles are threaded to take a locknut and washer. Others may have a hidden retaining clip or spring. A cover may hide the locknut.

The spindles rotate as a trans-verse connecting rod moves back and forth across the base of the windshield. Small links between the spindles and the connecting rod force the spindles to rotate in one direction and then the other as the connecting rod moves back and forth.

The connecting rod is attached to a linkage rod, which is connected to a crank arm driven by an electric motor. As the shaft inside the electric wiper motor spins, it rotates the crank arm. As the crank arm spins, it pulls the linkage rod over center, converting the pulling motion into a pushing one, then back again.

A switch inside the motor allows the motor to continue running after you have shut off the wipers so the blades can continue through the remainder of their arc and park at the base of the windshield. In addition, a fuse or circuit breaker protects the electric motor from overload—such as when the wiper blades are frozen to the windshield or buried beneath heavy snow. And a relay allows for intermittent action.

A SMEAR JOB

Even if the wiper motor, its wiring, and its various linkage rods work perfectly for the life of your car, the rubber squeegees will have to be replaced periodically. Dirt, grit, and various airborne contaminants all work to destroy the squeegees. Even the ammonia in household window cleaner, along with various other environmental elements, will deteriorate natural rubber squeegees.

If the wipers streak, smear, or otherwise wipe unevenly, replace them. Naturally, if an inspection reveals tears, cracks, or chunks missing from the squeegee, it should be replaced.

While squeegees are available at auto parts stores and discount chains, you may have to replace the wiper blade as well as the squeegee if your car's original blade design does not take a replaceable insert. However, you may also choose to save money next time by replacing your original wiper blade/squeegee combination with an aftermarket blade designed to take replaceable rubber inserts. In addition, various carmakers and wiper manufacturers have different systems for securing the wiper blade to the wiper arm. All, however, allow the blade to be removed from the arm for replacement.

The most common attachment systems are the hook, locking pin, and bayonet. Naturally, there are variations on these themes.

Hook-type wiper arms have a 180° bend at the end, which attaches to the wiper blade. This hook wraps over a pin or tab at the center of the blade. Release the lock on the pin or tab, slip the hook off the pin, and thread the blade off the arm. Some of these blades must be flipped upside down in order to be removed.

Locking-pin wiper arms have a

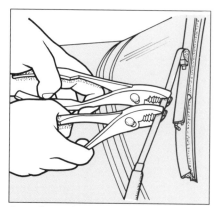

Cure chattering wipers by straightening a twisted wiper arm using two pairs of pliers. Arm must be parallel to the surface of the windshield.

small pin connecting the tip of the blade. The perpendicular pin keeps the wiper arm parallel to the center of the wiper blade. Disengage the lock that holds the pin and pull the blade away from the wiper arm. The lock and the pin may be located on either the blade or the wiper arm.

On a simple bayonet mount, the tip of the wiper arm slides into a sheath on the center of the wiper blade. Release a locking tab and pull off the blade.

If you are replacing the blade and the squeegee as a unit, reverse the process and you're done. If you are replacing the wiper blade with one from the aftermarket, select the appropriate adapter from the assortment packaged with the blade. First install the adapter on the blade, then install the blade on the arm.

If you are changing the rubber insert only, you must remove the squeegee from the wiper blade. There are essentially two ways that the rubber insert attaches to the wiper blade. In one system, you must squeeze or pry open locking tabs and slide the squeegee out of the blade. With the other, you must unlock one of the links of the wiper-blade frame from the rest of the blade—then slide the squeegee along with the locking link off the arm. Then remove the locking link.

If your car has wipers that park inaccessibly behind the lip of the hood, shut off the ignition while the wipers are in midstroke to stop them in the middle of the glass.

CHATTER

If the squeegees are new and in good shape—not hard or brittle—and are the correct ones for your car, they may still chatter or skip their way across the glass rather than wipe. This can be caused by a wiper arm that is bent or one that is improperly tensioned.

With the wipers parked in the middle of the windshield, look to see if the arm is parallel to the glass—and not twisted. If the arm looks twisted, use two pairs of pliers to reshape it. If this doesn't work, replace the arm.

If the arm is parallel, you may need to increase the arm's spring tension. Inexpensive spring helper clips are available at auto parts stores. If these don't do the trick, you have to replace the arm again.

While you can buy replacement wiper arms at an auto parts store or your new-car dealership, you may also be able to buy them at a scrap

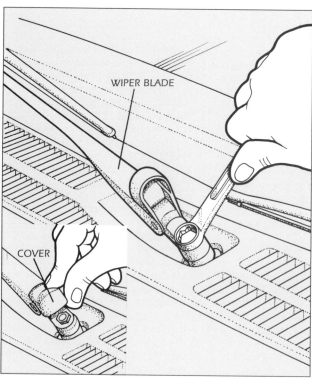

First, lift any dust cover over wiper drive spindle (left). Remove any nut and washer, then carefully pry arm off splines on spindle shaft.

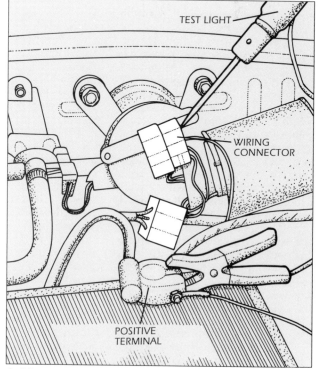

Quick-test wiper motor with jumper wire or test light from battery's positive terminal to wiper motor's wiring connector.

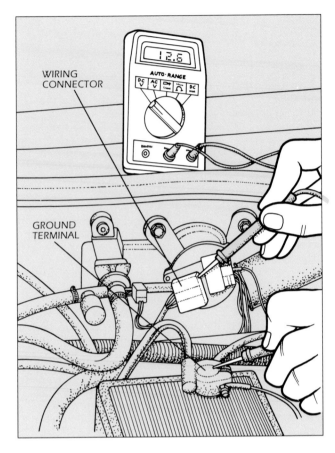

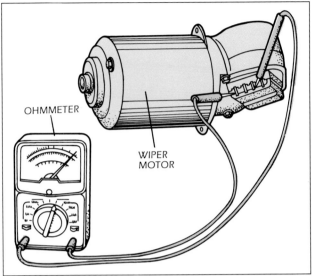

Bench-test a suspect wiper motor by checking its resistance with an ohmmeter. Check the readings at different terminals.

Test wiring, fuse, and switch by connecting voltmeter between battery's ground terminal and wiper motor's connector with the wiper switch on.

yard, particularly if you have a popular model car.

To replace the wiper arm, remove or raise any protective cover over the drive spindle. If there is a nut, remove the nut and then gently pry the arm off the spindle's splines.

If there is no nut, check the wiper arm for a small hole that may access a locking tab or retainer spring. If there is a hole, insert a scribe to release the lock. Pry up on the wiper arm.

Some wiper arms are simply pressed onto the drive spindles. If you cannot find evidence of a locking tab or other retainer, pry up on the base of the arm. Take care not to mar the finish or damage the plastic cowl or plastic trim cover, if your car has one.

Reverse the procedure to install the new arm. When installing a wiper arm, place the arm on the drive spindle so the blade will not foul against the windshield frame at either end of its stroke. If the blade does hit the frame, carefully remove the arm and reposition it by one or two splines on the spindle. Recheck.

TOTAL FAILURE

If your problem is a sluggish or erratic interval setting, check to see if your car uses a separate relay for the interval setting. The relay will be at the fuse or relay block, under the dash or in the engine compartment.

If the problem is more severe—namely that the wiper blades do not move at all when you switch on the wipers—there is either an electrical problem in the switch, wiring, fuse, or motor, or a mechanical problem with the crank arm, linkage, or connecting rods.

First check the fuse. If it is blown, replace it and see if it blows again. The fuse may have been done in by a temporary overload, as from trying to operate the wipers when the blades were frozen to the windshield. If the new fuse blows, there is either a short in the wiring or the electric motor, or an overload, as from a seized linkage or motor.

Isolate the motor from the linkage by disconnecting the motor from the crank arm. This may require removing a section of cowling

or other cover as well as the wiper arms.

If the motor now runs, the problem is with the linkage (assuming you've already replaced the fuse). If not, there's an electrical problem.

Try moving the linkage by hand by twisting the crank arm. If it's tight, disconnect the crank arm from the linkage rod and try again. Work your way from the motor to the individual drive spindles to pinpoint the problem.

In some cases, dirt, rust, or corrosion can be binding one of the ball joints or the sockets—possibly at the crank arm or either end of the linkage rod or connector rod. Disconnect the ball joint, wire-brush it clean, and reassemble it. Lubricate the joint with a dab of white grease.

If part of the linkage is bent or severely corroded, replace it.

However, if the disconnected linkage moves freely, check for an electrical problem at the switch, motor, or wiring circuit.

Unplug the motor's wiring connector and probe the wiring harness's connector with a grounded test lamp or voltmeter. With the ignition on, turn on the wiper switch. One of the connections to the motor should show current. Change the switch setting to a higher speed and a different terminal in the connector should show current. If there is no power to the connector with any switch setting and the fuse is good, there is either an open circuit or a bad switch.

Reconnect the motor's connector and bypass the wiper switch by connecting a jumper wire to the terminals on its back. If the motor now works, the switch is defective. If not, the problem is in the wiring or with the motor itself.

Test the motor by unplugging its wiring connector and attaching a jumper wire directly to the battery's positive terminal. Make sure that the wiper motor is grounded. If the motor runs—and at different speeds as you touch its different terminals—the problem is in the wiring circuit. Use a grounded test lamp to work your way back along the wiring until you find the broken connection.

If the motor does not run, it is defective.

Before replacing the motor, remove and test it. Your factory shop manual will have the amperage draw, resistance load, and other specific tests you can perform. The motor simply may have stuck, dirty, or defective brushes, or a tight bearing—all repairable on your workbench.

How to Repair
POWER WINDOWS

It may be no more than an annoying inconvenience for you to open your door to pay tolls or collect those Big Macs from the drive-through window because your car's power windows won't go down anymore.

Or, it may be a cold, wet, and noisy pain in the keister because one or more of the electrically operated windows will not go up all the way—if at all—letting all manner of weather into the car's interior.

Maybe you're faced with the worst-case scenario—you can't park your car unattended because one or more of the windows always stays wide open, no matter how you play with the buttons and switches that are supposed to operate them.

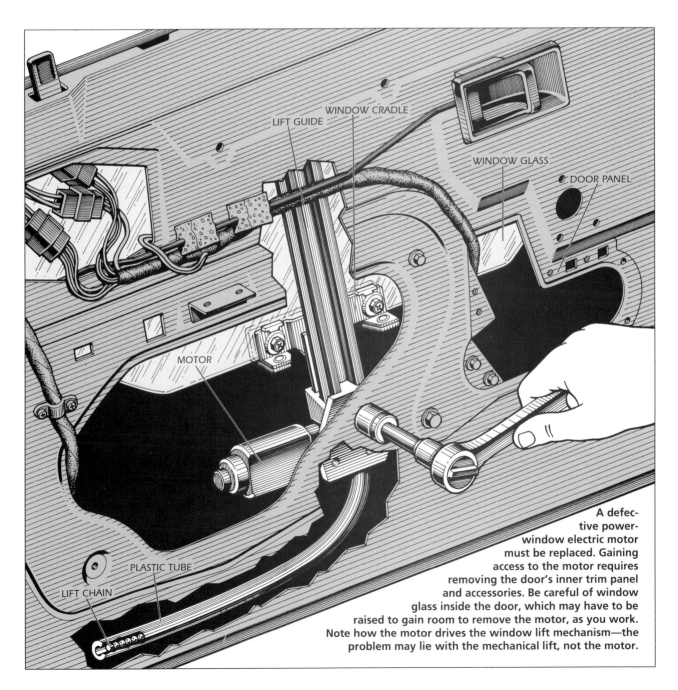

LIFT GUIDE

WINDOW CRADLE

WINDOW GLASS

DOOR PANEL

MOTOR

PLASTIC TUBE

LIFT CHAIN

A defective power-window electric motor must be replaced. Gaining access to the motor requires removing the door's inner trim panel and accessories. Be careful of window glass inside the door, which may have to be raised to gain room to remove the motor, as you work. Note how the motor drives the window lift mechanism—the problem may lie with the mechanical lift, not the motor.

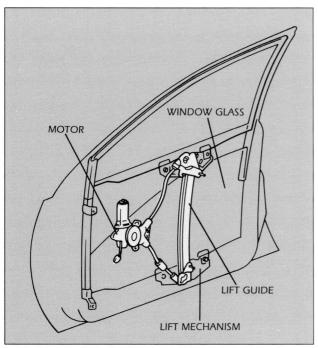

Typical system has electric motor, lift mechanism, and window cradle and guide.

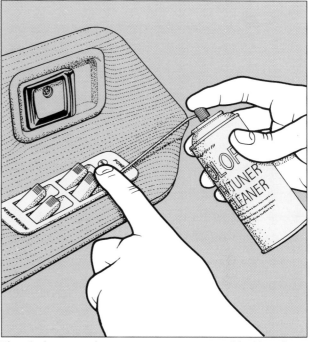

Electrical contact cleaner can remove current-blocking dirt and corrosion from contacts with the switch in place.

In any case, power windows are meant to be a convenience item on a car or truck. And chances are that you paid several hundred dollars for that convenience. You should enjoy it.

Fortunately, tracing and repairing problems with a power-window system are tasks well within the ability of the average Saturday mechanic. The time and effort spent on curing the problem makes living with it foolish.

POWER TO THE PEOPLE

Electric power windows work the same way as manual windows, except for the fact that with power windows an electric motor inside the door, rather than a handle on the door panel, turns the window crank to raise and lower the window glass.

Each door-mounted motor has its own switch, usually on the door near the window or on a center console. In addition, there are redundant switches for the passenger windows at the driver's position so the driver can operate any window when driving alone. The driver's switch panel also has a safety lockout switch, which can shut off power to the passenger windows to

keep small children from opening or closing them.

The system is protected by a fuse or a circuit breaker, and power for the system goes through an ignition-key-activated relay as well.

The individual electric motors either drive a gear, which meshes with a large sector gear to operate the glass-lift assembly, or run some variety of cable, chain, or tape through a drive gear to move the window glass.

BEGIN WITH THE BASICS

There are two elementary types of power-window problems—localized and universal. Localized problems affect only one or two windows or switches. Universal problems involve the whole system.

If none of the windows operates at all from any of the switches, assume there is a simple electrical problem. The trouble lies with the fuse or circuit breaker, relay, wiring, or possibly the driver's master switch.

Begin by checking the fuse or circuit breaker. If the fuse is blown, replace it. Reset a tripped circuit breaker. It may have been just one of those things. If the fuse blows again or the circuit breaker trips,

there is either a short circuit or an overload caused by a problem with one or more of the electric motors or the glass lift mechanism.

If one of the electric motors is beginning to fail, it may draw enough current to burn a fuse or trip a circuit breaker. And, if one of the window lift mechanisms is sticking in the door, it can create enough of an overload on its motor to blow the fuse as well. If this is the case, the fuse or breaker will fail only when the suspect window is being operated.

A simple way to check is to replace the fuse and operate each window in turn, isolating the window that is causing the trouble. If the fuse blows regardless of which window is being operated, the trouble probably lies elsewhere in the windows' electrical system.

If the fuse is good, double-check that it is getting current. Probe the fuse with either a grounded test light or an electric meter. Make sure that the ignition switch is turned on for this check.

If the fuse is not getting any current, locate and test the relay. Check your owner's manual for the location of the relay—it may be at the main fuse block or in a separate secondary fuse and relay bus. Re-

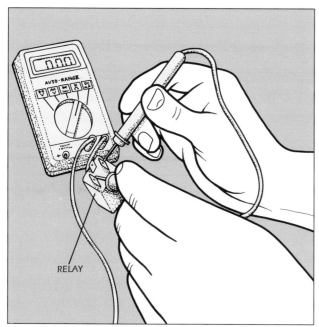

Check the operation of the relay by testing the continuity across its various terminals.

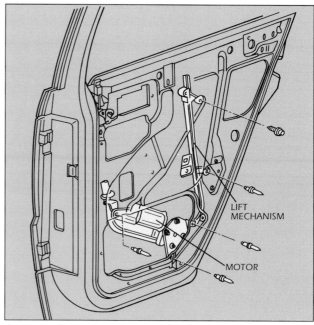

Space confines of smaller rear door may require a different lift arrangement.

move the relay by pulling it straight out. Use a volt/ohm/ammeter to check the relay by testing the continuity across its terminals according to the sequence in your shop manual.

If the relay is bad, replace it.

If it tests good, verify that it is getting power—again with the ignition system turned on. If not, check your owner's manual to see if there is a second relay—possibly from a factory-installed antitheft system—that may feed the power-window relay. Check that relay's operation.

Otherwise, trace the wiring from the relay to its power source from the ignition switch for an open circuit. If the relay is getting current with the ignition switch on, check the windows' master switch at the driver's control panel.

ONE SWITCH SERVES ALL

The passenger-window lockout switch at the driver's master switch passes current on to the individual window switches. If the driver's switch fails, none of the windows will operate from any position.

Before taking apart the door panel or center console to get to the driver's switch, consider cleaning the switch's contacts. And, depending on the specifics of your car's or

truck's system, you may be able to do that without removing anything. Spray some aerosol electrical contact cleaner (sold as radio- and television-tuner cleaner) through the gaps around the switch's rocker. Operate each of the rockers back and forth as you clean. Naturally, start with the separate button or rocker that locks out the individual window switches.

If cleaning does not help, check the operation of the driver's master switch. On some cars, you may have to remove a door inner trim panel or part of the center console for access. On other cars you may be able to simply depress a couple of locking tabs and lift out the switch assembly. Unplug the switch from its wiring connector.

Use an ohmmeter and follow the testing sequence in your shop manual, checking for continuity between the terminals on the switch.

If the switch assembly—or any of the individual switches—fails the test, replace it.

If the switch is good, check the wiring connector for current. Use a grounded test light or ammeter with the ignition turned on. If there is no current to the driver's switch, you must trace the wiring back to the fuse panel looking for a broken wire or another open circuit.

If there is current getting to the

driver's master switch, there must be an open circuit between the switch assembly and all of the window motors. Check the switches' wiring connectors for good contact. Use a pair of pliers—which have some tape on the jaws to pad them—to gently squeeze tight a loose connector. Clean any corrosion from the connector using the same electrical contact cleaner you used on the switch. If these steps don't cure the problem, you must check the continuity between the driver's master switch and each of the individual door switches, using an ohmmeter to find the open circuit.

MOTORIZED ACTUATION

If the problem is a local one—only one window does not operate—begin by checking that the motor is getting power. First check the window's switch—trying to clean it as you did the driver's master switch. Remove the switch and check it using an ohmmeter. If the switch is defective, replace it. If the switch is good, use a grounded test light or ammeter to verify that it is getting current with the ignition on.

If the switch is good and there is power to it, the next step is to check the motor.

To gain access to any of the window motors, or the glass lift mechanism, you have to remove that door's inner trim panel.

This means first removing the door-latch lever and possibly an armrest. You may also have to disconnect wiring for a courtesy light or stereo speaker from the back side of the door panel after you have removed all of its retaining screws and pins. Make sure that you have taken out all of the panel's retaining screws before trying to pry the panel off the door metal. Look carefully for screws hidden inside armrests and under trim pieces. Slide a thin, wide tool—either a door trim removal tool or a putty knife—between the trim panel and the door metal to find all of the retaining pins or clips. Gently pop out the pins or clips as you go.

With the door trim panel off, you may be faced with a plastic liner held by sealer. Gently peel back the liner, taking care to not tear it or fold it back on its sealer.

Locate the window's electric motor, and disconnect its wiring connector. With the ignition switch on, operate the window switch and check that power is getting to the motor's connector. If not, there is an open circuit between the door switch and the motor; replace the wiring.

If power is getting to the connector, make sure that the connector is clean and making good contact with the motor. If the motor still does not operate but the fuse has not blown, double-check that the motor's ground is good. If it is, the motor is defective—replace it.

If the motor operates sluggishly or if the fuse blows when you operate it, either the motor or the window glass itself is binding. To determine which, you must remove the motor from the door, disengaging it from the window lift mechanism.

If the motor simply drives a spur gear, which meshes with a large sector gear on the window lift mechanism, unbolt the motor from the door panel and take it out.

If the motor passes a cable, chain, or tape drive through it, you might have to remove the lift assembly along with the motor—which may mean supporting the window glass while you remove the drive mechanism. Or, depending on your car, you may be able to separate the

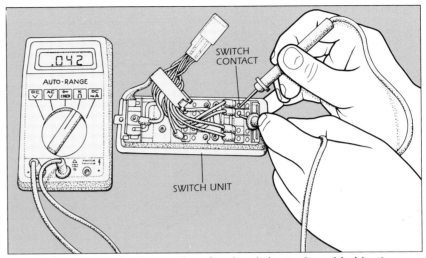

Use an ohmmeter to check operation of each switch, starting with driver's master switch.

motor from the drive drum or mechanism that moves the cable, chain, or tape.

In many cases, you may need the window in the fully up, closed position to get the necessary clearance inside the door to remove the motor. If the motor has failed with the window open and down, you will have to manually raise the window. If the motor has actually seized, you will first have to disengage the motor from the lift-mechanism drive to move the glass.

For a quick test of a disconnected

motor, simply attach it directly to the battery. The motor should spin. Reverse the polarity of the connections and the motor should spin in the other direction. For a more accurate test, attach an ammeter to the spinning motor to check its current draw. Compare that with specifications. Typically, a draw of more than about 15 amps, however, indicates internal drag in the motor. Replace it.

If the motor checks out properly—spinning freely in both directions and not consuming so much

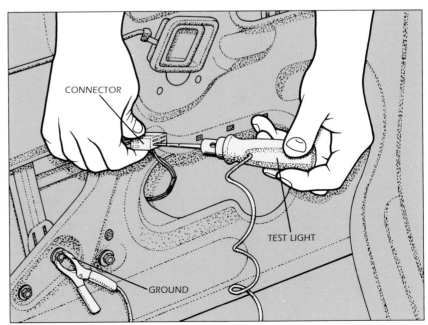

With the ignition switch on, use a test light or meter to check for current to each window switch at its wiring connector.

current in the process that it is going to blow the fuse—the problem lies in the mechanical components of the window, not the electrical components.

Before reinstalling the motor, check the operation of the window lift system. Various carmakers use different types of arrangements to raise and lower the window glass. They also employ various systems to guide the glass as it moves up and down.

If the lift mechanism is binding—due to a bent link, twisted or folded plastic tape, frayed cable, or mangled chain—it can put enough of a strain on the window's motor to cause an electrical overload. Like-

wise, if the glass itself is not properly aligned in its channels—front or back—it can create a serious problem. Also, verify that the glass is not getting hung up on some loose or torn weatherstripping.

Inspect the lift mechanism—as much of it as you can see through the access holes in the door's metal panel—looking for obvious physical damage. You may be able to make a quick and simple repair by straightening or reattaching a piece. You may also be able to replace the defective component of the lift mechanism. If the window lift mechanism is defective, you may be able to find a replacement for it at a scrap yard.

To check the alignment of the window glass itself, remove the inner panel of the door on the opposite side of the car. Compare the movement and alignment of the glass of the two windows, making adjustments to the balky window in small increments and rechecking its alignment.

Check that the lift mechanism is not corroded or dry—clean and lubricate the linkages as per your shop manual. Then reinstall the motor and reconnect its wiring. Replace the plastic door inner liner, reattach any courtesy light or stereo speakers, and reinstall the door trim panel.

CHASSIS 5

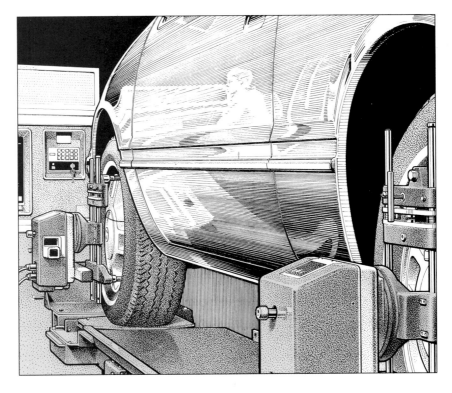

How to Maintain
DRUM BRAKES

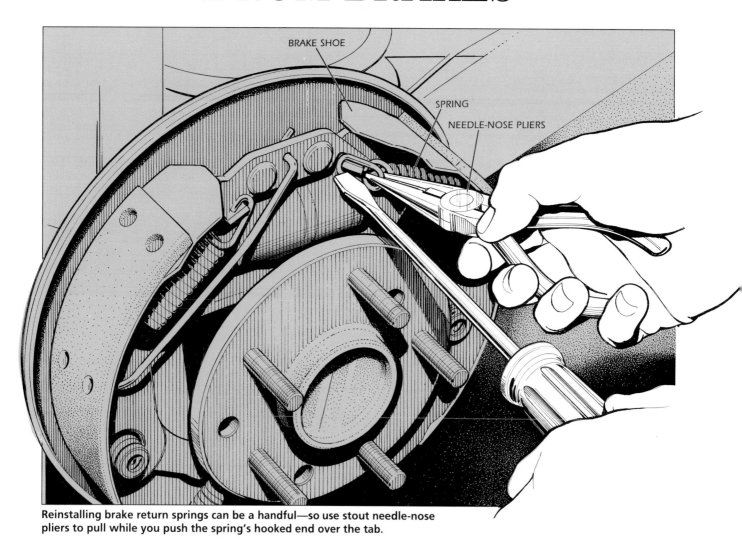

Reinstalling brake return springs can be a handful—so use stout needle-nose
pliers to pull while you push the spring's hooked end over the tab.

Pushing down on your brake pedal seems to mirror the sinking feeling in your stomach, as the pedal hovers dangerously close to the carpet when you try to slow down. And lately, it's been accompanied by a grinding noise. The front brakes look good—at least from what you can see by looking through the front wheels. It's time to check your rear brakes.

Most cars nowadays use front disc brakes. And with the front discs doing most of the work, there's good reason to use lighter, less expensive, low-rolling-friction

rear drum brakes. But even so, there's still some occasional maintenance to be done.

Only a few rear brakes have tiny lining inspection holes in the backing plates, so generally you've got to remove a drum to really see. It's absolutely worth doing.

Drum removal can be a minor pain on some cars, particularly if the drum is held by the wheel-bearing adjusting nut. Pick up a fresh cotter pin or tabbed nut, and a grease seal as well, and check a manual for the removal/installation/adjustment procedure. Don't forget,

you'll need some appropriate grease to repack the bearing if you remove the drum.

Most drums, however, are just on a hub, and with the wheel off, the drum slides off. There might be a metal clip or setscrew to keep the drum from falling off during wheel changes. If it doesn't pull right off, rotate the drum. If it's binding against the lining, that's usually because the device that moves the shoes to compensate for lining wear, called a star wheel adjuster, needs to be backed off to let the ridge inside the drum clear the

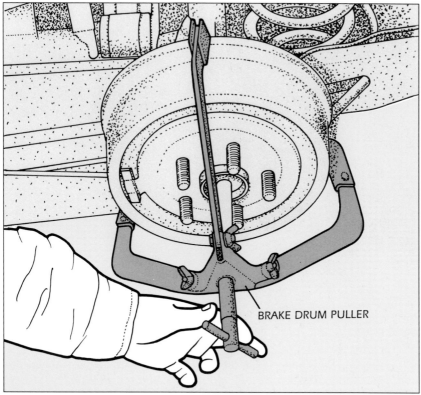

BRAKE DRUM PULLER

You can rent a brake drum puller at rental agencies or auto parts stores. Don't try to hammer the drum off—it may bend or crack.

shoes. Retract the brake shoes by releasing the adjuster, accessible through a hole in the backing plate.

If the drum is stuck to the hub, apply penetrating solvent to the rim of the joint, and if there are stud holes in the drum, apply it to them. Next, try a drum puller. Hammering on the hub or even using a torch on the drum (if it's beefy cast iron) are techniques, but you shouldn't need them. On some late-model Nissans, look for two threaded holes in the drum. Insert a couple of bolts, turn them down evenly, and they will thread through and push the drum off the hub. Where the drum fits to an axle flange, always make alignment marks to refit the drum for proper rear wheel balance.

If the linings are less than ⅛ in. thick, replace the shoes. If they're thicker, they can stay.

Replacing the shoes, which should be done on both sides for balanced braking, is straightforward. Take off the drum on the other side, so you have a mirror image of how everything goes back together.

The star wheel adjuster may be automatically turned by a lever, or perhaps with a cable. There may be one coil spring, one U-shaped spring, or a pair of coil springs to retract the shoes when you release the brakes. Most shoes are held to the backing plate by a spring, pin, and retainer; others are held by a pin and spring clip assembly.

Brake specialty tools are helpful in the removal and installation of springs, but a little patience and a good assortment of standard hand tools can get you through the work.

Begin by removing the shoe return spring(s), which you can usually disengage with needle-nose pliers. Don't waste your money on the old drum brake pliers, which just won't work on late-model cars. If you can't get the springs off with the needle-nose, you can use pliers with specially shaped tips for late models or a tool, such as the one for GM cars, that pivots on the rivetheads of a duo-servo anchor.

Next, take out the self-adjuster spring(s) if they are accessible at this point, and they usually are.

Then, disengage the shoe holddown springs. With needle-nose pliers (or a specialty tool), turn the pinhead 90° so it aligns with the slot in the retainer, and then the coil spring underneath will push the retainer up and out.

The shoes are now free of the backing plate, so spread them apart (they are connected together at the bottom in a servo design). Pull them away slightly from the backing plate, and disconnect the parking-brake cable from the parking-brake lever arm, which is pinned to one of the shoes.

Disconnect the lever from the shoe, typically by prying out an E- or C-shaped clip from a pivot pin in the shoe. That pin, and any others in the shoes, may not be included with the replacement shoes, so, if necessary, drive them out with a punch and insert them in the same holes in the new shoes. If any lever is supposed to pivot around a pin, be sure the pin is loose in the new part. Wire-brushing or light filing may be necessary to free corroded pins. Lubricate with a stingy dab of antiseize or grease.

The new shoes should be as close to a duplicate of the old as you can get, or better. If the original shoes have semimetallic linings, get them as a replacement. If it's not semi-metallic, don't "upgrade," as brakes are a balanced design of linings, drum materials, and provisions for transfer of heat. Many cars have asbestos linings, and if you can't get a replacement in asbestos today (because of the health issue, asbestos linings are being phased out), you should find one in another nonmetallic material (there are many combinations using aramid and fiberglass, among others). Always pick a name brand—and only that brand's premium lining. There have always been a lot of cheap linings out there, and although they stop a car, they can't compare with the good stuff for fade resistance, lining life, wet performance, and relatively low noise levels. A relined shoe may be fine, but a name-brand new shoe is best—and generally not a lot more money.

Always replace the springs. Weak springs allow shoes to drag, which affects brake smoothness and lining life. You should think hard about replacing all of the automatic adjuster

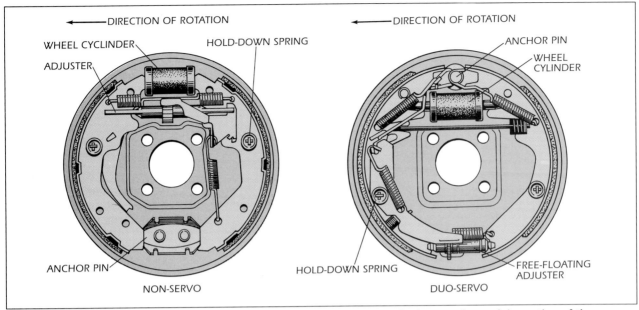

DIRECTION OF ROTATION

WHEEL CYCLINDER
ADJUSTER
HOLD-DOWN SPRING
ANCHOR PIN
NON-SERVO

DIRECTION OF ROTATION

ANCHOR PIN
WHEEL CYLINDER
HOLD-DOWN SPRING
FREE-FLOATING ADJUSTER
DUO-SERVO

Some cars use non-servo-type brakes, especially with power boosters. Servo brakes use the wedging action of the shoes to lower pedal effort. Service is essentially similar.

hardware and the holddown springs if they look heavily corroded. An auto parts store that sells shoes probably has a complete kit. If the star wheel adjuster has even one slightly damaged tooth, or if any strut or lever is bent or badly rusted, replace it.

Before you reassemble, clean the area. Remember that on all but a few of the newest cars, the brake dust is high in carcinogenic asbestos. Vacuum up or wet down the dust, and dispose of it properly. Lubricate the rotating shaft and threads of the self-adjuster with

wheel bearing or chassis grease, but if it's really frozen, replace it. Clean the backing plate with brake cleaner, a light solvent that leaves virtually no residue. Inspect the brake shoe platforms, those raised sections along which the shoe slides. Wire-brush if necessary to remove

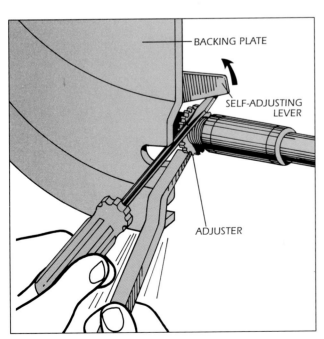

BACKING PLATE
SELF-ADJUSTING LEVER
ADJUSTER

To remove or adjust many self-adjusting brakes, you'll need to use a thin screwdriver to lift the self-adjuster away from the adjuster's star wheel in order to rotate the star wheel.

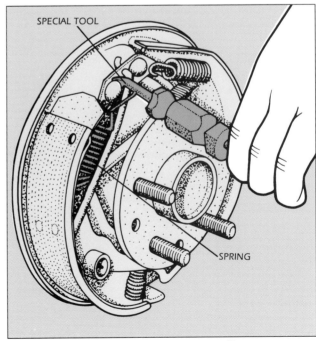

SPECIAL TOOL
SPRING

This special tool is a big help when reinstalling return springs on many GM cars.

rust, then apply a film of grease to them.

Pry back the wheel cylinder dust boots, and if there's any evidence of brake fluid inside them, replace the wheel cylinder. If you do have to replace a wheel cylinder, and the car's mileage is 50,000 or more, consider flushing the entire brake system with fresh fluid instead of just a simple bleeding. And as long as you have to loosen the bleeder valves anyway, unthread them and coat them with antiseize compound, so they'll still be free the next time.

Inspect the drum. If it's cracked, get a new one. If there are grooves deep enough to catch a fingernail, have the drum resurfaced at a machine shop. Even if the drum looks good, unevenly worn linings may indicate warpage. You may have

suspected this already if the brake pedal feels like it's doing the boogaloo under your foot. Have the drum measured for out-of-round (which should not exceed .002 in. on drums up to 7 in. in diameter, .004 in. on larger drums).

A tough part of reassembly is getting the hook eyes of springs into their holes or notches without using specialty tools or losing all the skin on your knuckles. If you're using needle-nose pliers, grasp the spring close to the coil, pull it until the hook end reaches the slot, and then push the hook in with a flat-blade screwdriver.

After you've reassembled, give the brakes a break-in. First, operate the automatic adjuster. On most cars, it works while the car is moving in reverse, so slowly back up the

car and firmly apply the brakes. On many cars, however, the rarely used parking brake operates the self-adjuster, so begin a new habit by applying it now.

If there's no self-adjusting function, you'll have to adjust the brakes manually. Turn the adjuster through the backing plate while rotating the wheel, until the wheel scrapes. Then spin the wheel rapidly, while a helper stabs the brakes sharply to seat the new brake shoes onto the arresting pins. Then readjust. You'll probably want to adjust within 100 miles or so as well, as the new shoes radius themselves to the larger diameter of the drum.

Then road-test the car, making several moderate stops from 30 to 40 mph, and the drums should be ready to make their contribution.

How to Cure
BRAKE SQUEAL

Y ou turn into the driveway of a very trendy restaurant. The attendant leaps from the curb, and the heads of a dozen chic patrons swivel toward you as you stop.

Unfortunately, they are swiveling not to admire your new Belchfire Road Eater, but to see where that awful squealing noise is coming from—and it's coming from your brakes. You are ashamed.

DEFINING THE PROBLEM

Actually, despite the ear-piercing squeal, your brakes work just fine. The noise seems to come and go at random. Is it normal? Or does it mean trouble? Or could it be a sign of trouble to come?

The quick answer is "possibly all of the above." But you want a more precise answer than that, so let's begin by explaining that the squeal is a high-pitch vibration. It isn't a

scrape, which is a dull metallic sound, and it isn't a howl, which is a low-pitch, deep noise. When the brakes on a new car squeal, the cause is almost always in the brake lining or friction material that the car's manufacturer has chosen to use. It is also possible that the squeal means the brakes need a better shim or silencing pad for the disc brake shoes that the carmaker had hoped was not necessary. If a lot of people complain, however, the fac-

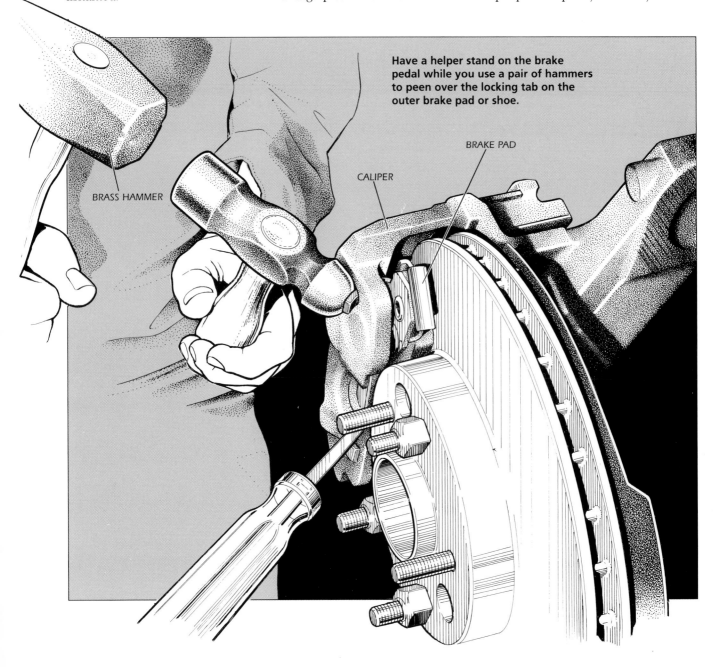

Have a helper stand on the brake pedal while you use a pair of hammers to peen over the locking tab on the outer brake pad or shoe.

BRASS HAMMER

CALIPER

BRAKE PAD

tory jumps on its brake supplier for a quieter replacement, and within six months or so, the dealer will get the replacement parts.

FINDING THE SOURCE

If you have a new car or truck and the squeal is endemic to its breed, fine. Sooner or later its maker will have a fix. If not, it's your problem.

Begin by accurately determining the source of the squeal. Use a mechanic's stethoscope to check the brake pedal and the master cylinder. If either has loose mounting bolts, it can emit a squeal when you apply the brakes. Tighten or replace loose bolts or nuts. Be sure that the pushrod between the brake pedal and the master cylinder is not dislocated—reposition it, if it is.

Once you're satisfied the noise is emanating from one of the wheels, determine which one. Applying the parking brake—gently—as you drive is a quick way to isolate the front and rear brakes. Otherwise, listen carefully through open windows as you apply the brake pedal.

After you trace the squeal to its source, you must next determine what is causing the squeal. Then you can decide whether or not it's a problem or merely an annoyance. As noted above, a squeal is caused by a high-frequency vibration and, ideally, the brake shoes should not vibrate at all. However, almost any brake lining will vibrate when there are major changes in the weather, such as dry to wet or cold to hot, because of the change in its friction characteristics. To further complicate the issue, every brand of brake lining has its own recipe, so every one is different. None is completely squeal-free under all conditions. A once-in-a-while squeal is normal if the overall braking is not affected. Discs are more prone than drums, although both suffer.

Still another factor: The widely used semimetallic linings conform less easily than the formerly used asbestos linings to irregularities in discs and drums, so otherwise minor deviations in these parts can result in occasional noise.

What if the brakes squeal frequently? For years, imported cars suffered this malady because over-

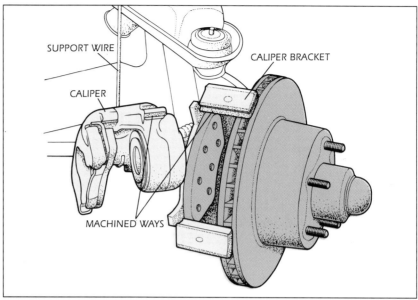

Wire-brush and lubricate the machined sliding ways on the caliper and bracket to allow the caliper to slide freely back and forth.

seas owners accepted squeal, and so the linings were formulated with less regard to noise. It was an easy tradeoff for other desired characteristics. Most Americans don't accept frequent squeal as normal, so linings for cars sold here are designed not to have the problem. If they do, it isn't normal.

Okay, but does it mean trouble? If the brake shoes are an economy replacement, a squeal on hard braking is probably telling you that the linings are fading, and you'd better not rely on them too much if you descend a mountain. Furthermore, that hard braking is causing some internal chemistry changes to the linings that not only will continue to reduce their performance, but will produce more squeal and less stopping power even in less severe use. Replace the economy shoes with premium-lined shoes. Premium doesn't mean shoes sold in speed shops for cars that may go on the racetrack. Even if these are squeal-free, they're designed for high-speed braking, and you may have to really mash the pedal to get them to work in normal driving.

A sudden onset of frequent squeal with a quality lining may be telling you that the design that keeps them quiet is not working. It could be a minor matter—the silencing pad, shim, or outboard shoe has come loose. However, you don't want to try any heavy-duty braking

until you find out, because the squeal could also be caused by a shoe out of position—something that affects the way the shoes are applied or how well they can stop the car.

Begin by looking at the shoes (also called pads by some car and brake manufacturers when used on disc brakes) with a wheel off. If the linings are worn, that could also easily be the cause, particularly if the linings are riveted to the shoes and are worn down to the rivet-heads. If the linings are more than $1/8$ in. thick, keep looking and checking.

CALIPERS

Check the caliper for tightness, because a loose caliper equals loose shoes. You may have to pry on the

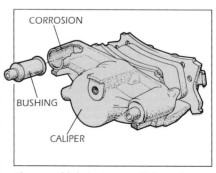

Clean and lubricate any sliding pins or bushings with antiseize compound.

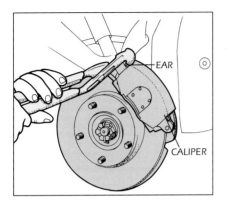

caliper to see if there's any free play, although calipers that slide through rubber bushings or plastic sleeves will have some give if you pry hard enough. Use a torque wrench on the caliper bolts and the bolts that hold the anchor plate to the suspension.

Eyeball the fit of the shoes in the caliper, looking for something

Some calipers use shoes with ears that can be crimped over with a large pair of pliers.

askew, such as linings that extend above or below the disc's contact surface into the unmachined rusty areas. Inspect the disc contact surface for circular "heat" spots, deep scores, or even phonograph-record-like grooves (which result from the machine shop's failure to properly finish the disc's resurfacing). A shoe squeals as it tries to follow these grooves.

Uneven movement of the caliper affects contact between the linings and the discs, producing squeal. Remove the caliper and hang it on the suspension. If the caliper slides in machined guides, check these guides for rust or corrosion—and if necessary, wire-brush them clean

and apply a thin coat of silicone dielectric grease. If the caliper slides along pins or bolts, similarly inspect them—and the rubber bushings or plastic guides through which they run. Replace damaged bushings or guides.

If bolts or pins on older cars are lightly corroded, they can be wire-brushed clean and lubricated. Most new-car bolts are coated against corrosion—so if there's corrosion, something's wrong and the best approach is to replace them. If the bushings are supposed to be a tight fit, make sure they aren't loose. If they're a push-in fit, sand away any corrosion, clean and lube the bores. Also lube the pins or bolts.

Even if the caliper moves smoothly, any extra movement of the shoes can produce squeal. Make certain that the brake shoes are properly installed. If the inboard

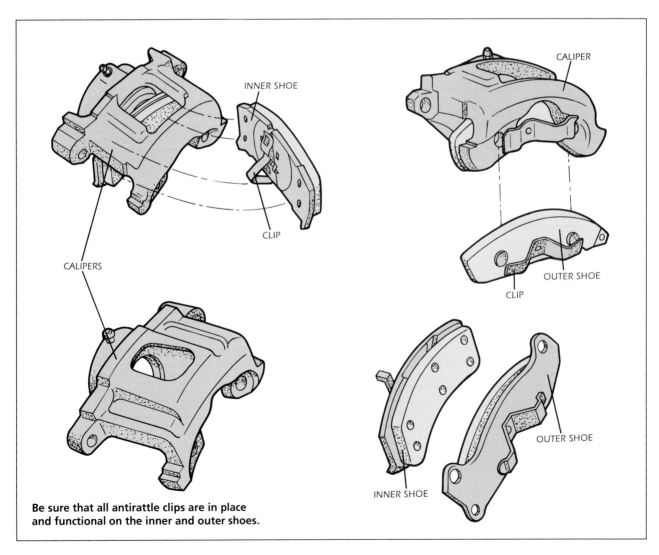

Be sure that all antirattle clips are in place and functional on the inner and outer shoes.

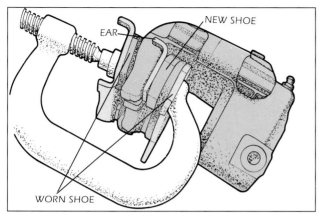

To press in new shoes, protect the friction material from the clamp with the old shoes.

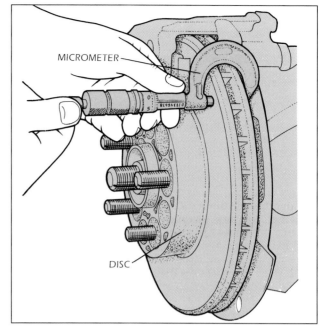

Check the brake disc for any thickness variations with an inexpensive micrometer.

shoe is supposed to have a clip holding it to the piston, make sure that the clip wasn't thrown away or bent during a previous brake job. Outboard shoes are almost always located positively in some way, and when that way isn't exactly to specs, squeal is the result.

In addition, there's often a steel shim or silencing pad attached to the back of the shoe. If the shim is out of position, put it back, perhaps using coats of moly grease or silicone paste on both sides (of the *shim*, not the brake friction material). The grease will hold it to the shoe and the caliper and add layers of silencing insulation. Or, install a silencing pad with self-stick adhesive on both sides. You can find these self-stick silencing pads at the auto parts store. You may need to trim them with sheet-metal shears.

If there's nothing on the shoe back, apply a thick coat of silicone paste, allow it to cure for about ten minutes, then install the shoe. This works much better—and longer—than the typical aerosol antisqueal spray.

Many GM cars have outboard shoes with locating ears that should be bent down over the ends of the caliper. Other GM cars may have tabs that go through slots in the caliper. Check these before you take off anything: Push on the back of the outboard brake shoe with your hand, and if there's any move-

ment at all, the shoe has to be retightened in position.

Wedge a chisel or screwdriver shank between the hub of the rotor and the bottom of the outboard shoe, then have a helper firmly apply and hold the brakes. Hold a ball-peen hammer against the top of the tab, then hammer on the back of the ball-peen with a brass hammer to bend the tab down to a 45° angle. Pull out the chisel, have the brakes released, and try to move the shoe again. If there's still movement, do it again.

On many Chrysler products, the outboard shoe has a thick ear that goes over the edge of the caliper to hold it. If that ear is even slightly loose, that's enough for the shoe to move and squeal. Want it right? Hammer down on the tab so the only way the shoe will go on is by forcing it with a C-clamp above. Use an old, worn-out set of shoes to prevent damaging the friction surface of the brake shoe with the clamp. That shoe should still get a silencing shim or coat of silicone paste.

LINING AND DISC PROBLEMS

Even if the linings are near full thickness, inspect the surface for a glossy look, called glaze, which can be caused by uneven contact with the disc or by abusive braking, par-

ticularly with economy linings. Glaze accelerates a problem of uneven contact, which may have been started by a disc that is unevenly thick or "wobbling" slightly, or a drum that is out-of-round. In this case, the squeal is an early warning of a developing brake performance problem. You can measure wobble, also called lateral runout. Attach a dial indicator to the suspension and rest its plunger against the lining contact surface. With the disc held securely by tightened lug nuts, rotate the disc while you watch the indicator needle. The maximum needle movement should be no more than .005 in.

Excessive runout could be caused by worn bearings or a disc worn unevenly. Check the disc thickness with an outside micrometer at a half-dozen points around the contact surface (maximum thickness variation should be no more than .0007 in.). An unevenly worn disc should be machined or replaced. You may be able to sand off glaze, but it often indicates a chemistry problem with the linings, so it's better to change the shoes.

Also, inspect the linings for oil or grease. You may be able to sand off a light touch of grease as well—but even if you can, don't reassemble until you find out where the oil or grease came from—probably a defective seal—and stop the seepage.

DRUM BRAKES

Although drum brakes are quieter than discs, they aren't immune to squeal. Check the outside of the drum first—there may be a sign that something is missing, such as a damper spring. Then pull the drum and look for an accumulation of brake dust. That alone can produce squeal, so just clean it out. But do so carefully.

Even though a large proportion of brake friction materials used today contain no asbestos, you should still take precautions. *Always* wear a disposable particle mask. Either wear a disposable smock or change your clothing immediately after finishing your brake work. Use a commercial, environmentally safe brake cleaner, not one of the older-style products based on chlorinated solvents. At the very least, soak the brake dust with water from a spritz bottle. Whatever you do, don't use compressed air to blow the dust all over. Sprinkle damp sawdust over the brake dust that does make it to the floor, and sweep it up before you track through it. Wash your hands.

Next, check for loose or broken shoe holddowns and other shoe hardware. Inspect the linings for uneven wear, which could be a sign of an out-of-round drum. Have the drum measured at a machine shop.

Still looking? Pry away the shoes and inspect the platforms along which they slide. If you see rust, remove the shoes, sand the platforms clean, and apply a film of silicone grease. Brakes are a balanced design system, and you should replace semimetallics with new semimetal-lics. Replace nonasbestos, nonmetallic linings with brand-name nonasbestos, nonmetallic linings that are recommended for use on your car.

LAST-DITCH EFFORTS

You've tried new shoes. You've got a shim or pad against the outboard shoe. The caliper or drum brake hardware is all new. But there's still squeal, so what do you do now besides give up? Make a last-ditch effort. Try some of our favorite demon tweaks:

- Make sure the noise isn't coming from the front or rear suspension by prying on all the parts in rubber bushings. If you can't find anything, try spraying the rubber bushings with silicone lube or glycerin anyway, just to eliminate the possibility. And eyeball all the front spring coils for shiny spots, just to make sure they aren't coming in contact.
- Chamfer the edge of the linings on discs or drums. Just grind off about ¼ in. at about a 45° angle. Remember, you're probably grinding asbestos—don't give yourself silicosis. If the squeal is originating from irregular edge contact, or if the problem is some shoe vibration you can't seem to trace, this just might work. One reason this often helps on disc brakes is that it also eliminates squeal resulting from slight relative movement between lining and caliper.

- Also try a coat of silicone paste over the backing of the inboard sides of the disc brake shoes.
- If the shoes you installed were relined, as is common with drums, try brand-new shoes. The relined shoes just might be off-shape enough to make uneven contact.
- Go back and recheck to see if the shoes you tightly installed have worked loose. There may be something worn in the hardware that could allow this.
- Some mechanics will tell you that all they have to do to eliminate squeal is change the shoes from bonded (glued-on) linings to riveted. It's true that riveted linings have a better history of low-squeal performance, although no one is sure why. However, there have also been cases where riveted shoes squeaked and the factory fix was replacement with bonded shoes.
- For reasons no one can explain, hacksawing a diagonal groove across the friction surface sometimes helps. This probably changes the resonant frequency of the system just enough.

Unless the car had a squeal problem when new, consider original equipment replacements from the car dealer (although be warned that the shoes will be expensive). However, if the linings once were squeal-free and now are not, there's a mechanical flaw you can find and correct.

How to Service
DISC BRAKES

Most of the routine service on disc brakes is a do-it-yourself job. You can certainly replace linings (pads)—plus the shims and antirattle springs or clips that may be attached to pads. You can probably rebuild calipers, too. If a caliper has to be replaced—another job you can do yourself—rebuilt units cost about $50 each.

It's when you get into disc brake *overhaul* that you'll need some professional help. For rotor work, for example, you'll need measuring instruments (a micrometer and dial gauge) and a $1000 rotor machining tool. Rather than make such an investment, most of us will admit the

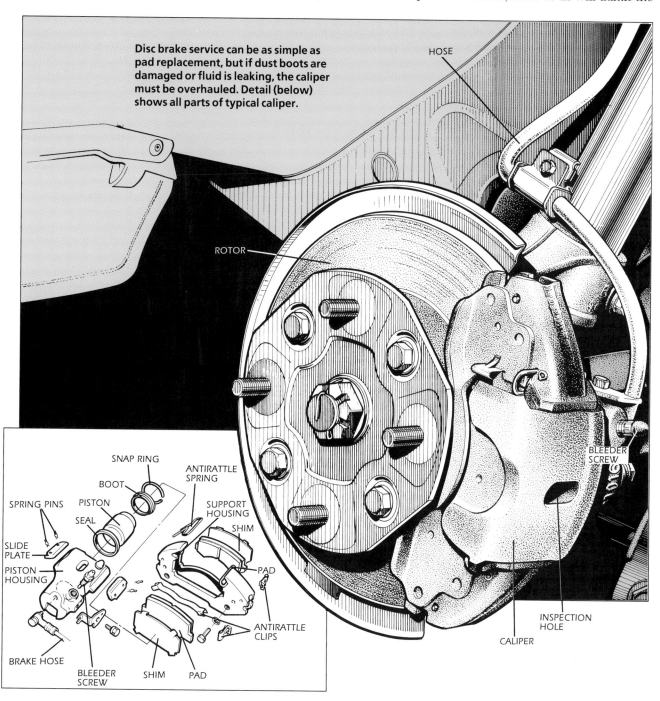

Disc brake service can be as simple as pad replacement, but if dust boots are damaged or fluid is leaking, the caliper must be overhauled. Detail (below) shows all parts of typical caliper.

HOSE

ROTOR

BLEEDER SCREW

INSPECTION HOLE

CALIPER

SNAP RING

BOOT

SPRING PINS

PISTON

SEAL

SLIDE PLATE

PISTON HOUSING

ANTIRATTLE SPRING

SUPPORT HOUSING

SHIM

PAD

ANTIRATTLE CLIPS

BRAKE HOSE

BLEEDER SCREW

SHIM

PAD

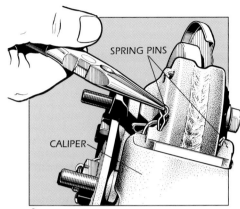

1 Two spring pins in each slide plate must be removed to release the caliper.

limitations of a home garage and pay to have the work done.

Before you start brake work it's suggested that you have the factory service manual or general auto repair manual for specific instructions, and specs for your car.

WHEN IS OVERHAUL NEEDED?

There are two ways to determine if disc brakes need repair before the linings are worn enough to cause extensive rotor damage. Brakes in Ford and GM cars and light trucks manufactured since the early seventies have pad-wear sensors. When a lining gets to within .03 inch of the rivetheads, this spring-steel sensor

comes in contact with the rotor and a high-frequency squeak is emitted. The warning sound continues until the brakes are applied and the sound changes pitch or ceases.

If the warning is ignored, wear progresses, but the raucous sound eventually ceases. By then, it's probably too late to save the rotor from extensive damage. A new rotor costs about $75 and, because pad wear often progresses equally on both front wheels, this means the damage costs you $150.

If your vehicle is a Chrysler model, it probably doesn't have wear sensors. Most imported cars don't have wear-sensor-equipped disc brakes either, although they have begun to appear on some of the newest models.

CHECKING WEAR VISUALLY

To find out if a vehicle without wear sensors requires pad replacement, remove the wheels and calipers and take out the pads to check the amount of friction material remaining. Nonmetallic pads should not be allowed to wear beyond the point where $1/16$ inch of friction material protrudes above the rivets. Semimetallic pads can wear to within $1/32$ inch of the rivets. If the pads are not riveted to the backing plates, the amount of friction material should equal the thickness of the backing plates.

If you have a late-model import vehicle, it may have a swivel-mount caliper. By removing a bolt, you can swivel the head of the caliper away from the main body. You can then measure the lining thickness without removing the pads. The swivel head also makes it easier to replace the pads, since you don't have to remove the caliper.

Inspect non-sensor-equipped pads at 30,000 miles. If they're okay, check them every 15,000 miles until they need replacing.

Most calipers equipped with non-sensor-type pads have inspection holes that let you view one or both linings, so you can judge the extent of wear without disassembling everything—if you know for certain that your pads are bonded to the backing plates and do not have rivets. *Caution:* To inspect and overhaul front disc brakes, have the vehicle resting on jack stands with the rear wheels blocked.

METAL OR PHENOLIC

Let's review some things you should know in order to remove pads for inspection and replacement. We'll only deal with single-piston disc brakes, which have been used on most cars since 1970.

The piston in the caliper, which is activated hydraulically and presses pads against the rotor when you step on the brake pedal, is made

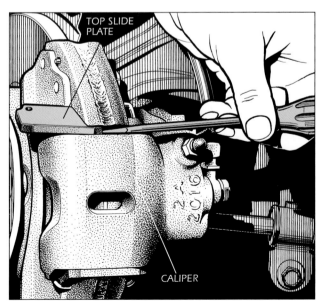

2 After the spring pins are removed, tap the top and bottom slide plates out sideways to disengage caliper.

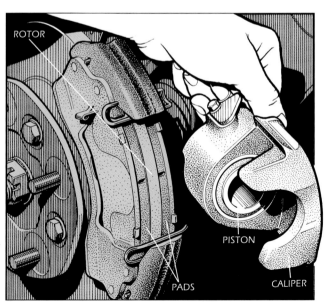

3 When caliper is removed, don't let it hang by the brake hose. Support it with a wire hooked to the chassis.

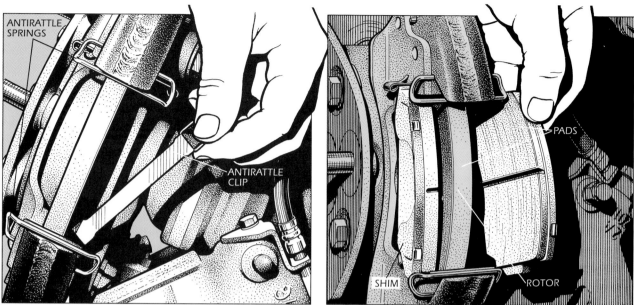

4 Clips that hold antirattle springs may require replacement. If so, they'll be supplied in the pad kit.

5 Before removing pads, sketch the exact position of all shims, hardware, retaining clips, and springs.

of nickel chrome-plated steel or plastic (a phenolic material similar in hardness and smoothness to Bakelite).

Introduced around 1975, phenolic pistons have been increasing in popularity. They weigh less, are less expensive, and provide better insulation than metal, thus protecting brake fluid from heat generated by metallic disc pads. And they don't corrode as metal pistons can. However, phenolic pistons have to be treated more gently than metal because they can crack and chip.

You can't easily distinguish piston composition with the disc brake unit assembled. So treat pistons as if they are phenolic unless you are certain that they aren't.

RETRACTING PISTONS

The caution to take is simple enough. When pushing the piston back into its bore, don't slip a screwdriver or pry bar under the pad so it's directly on a piston.

You have to push the piston into its bore to free the pads on GM vehicles. To do this, place a C-clamp so the flat on the end of the screw rests on the pad, and the stationary part of the clamp rests on the rear of the caliper. Tighten the clamp to push the piston back into its bore just enough for the pads to clear the rotor.

On Ford calipers, you'll need a

$3/4 \times 1 \times 2\frac{3}{4}$-in. block of wood to retract the piston once the caliper is off.

Note: Even if the piston is metal, it's not wise to push it back with a screwdriver. You might nick the plating.

Before pushing the piston into the bore, drain about half the fluid from the master cylinder. Discard it and have a *sealed* container of fresh brake fluid ready to add to the master cylinder when the job is done. Buy the brand of fluid recommended by the carmaker or another high-quality replacement that conforms to Department of Transportation (DOT) specification 3, 4, or 5.

ABOUT BRAKE FLUIDS

The significant difference between the three DOT grades is in boiling point—DOT 3 has the lowest boiling point, and DOT 5 the highest. DOT 3 will also thicken more readily in subzero weather.

The major benefit provided by DOT 4 and 5 fluids is in severe service conditions, such as hauling trailers. If you plan to keep your car for many years, you may benefit from using DOT 4 or 5 fluids, which offer greater corrosion protection.

Despite its inability to withstand extremes of temperature as well as the other two, DOT 3 fluid is recommended by most carmakers. However, most have no objection to

DOT 4 or DOT 5 fluid. Check your service manual for recommendations.

If you decide to upgrade from DOT 3 to DOT 4 or 5, empty the hydraulic system and flush with the new fluid before adding the final fill. Fluids may not mix chemically, especially the glycol-base DOT 3 and 4 fluids if they are mixed with the silicone-base DOT 5 fluid.

BOLTS OR PLATES

Most carmakers secure calipers to their supports in one of two ways: with bolts or with pin-held retaining plates.

If the calipers on your disc brakes use bolts, push the piston back into the bore and see if the bolts are fastened on the outboard end of the caliper with retaining clips. If so, pull them off. The outboard end of the caliper is the side resting on the outside surface of the rotor.

Determine how to remove the bolts. Those that have hex or Allen heads should be unscrewed with the appropriate wrench. Other bolts may be tapped out with a hammer and drift. These are the ones usually retained by clips.

If there are no bolts, the caliper is probably being retained at the top and bottom by slide plates. Look for spring pins holding these plates. There are probably four of them—

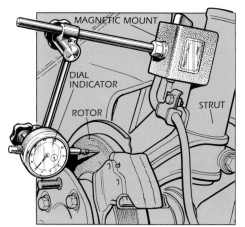

6 Rotor runout can be checked with a dial indicator while spinning the rotor by hand.

two holding the top slide plate and two holding the bottom plate. Pull the pin out and save them (see Fig. 1). Then, tap out the top and bottom slide plates (Fig. 2).

Many Ford and AMC calipers are retained on their machined guides by a support key and screw. After removing the screw, drive the key out of the anchor with a hammer and drift.

Again, check a service manual for specific instructions. If you're still not sure how to do the job, get professional help. Don't take chances when it comes to brake work.

When the bolts or slide plates have been removed, lift the caliper off the rotor (Fig. 3). You may have to push the caliper down and then pull it away from the rotor so it clears the antirattle springs. With some setups, you don't have to replace the antirattle springs. However, they may be held by clips that often have to be replaced (Fig. 4).

The best way to know which parts to replace and which to retain is by purchasing a brake pad kit for your particular vehicle. It will contain pads and all of the hardware that should be replaced when doing an overhaul. It also provides installation and lubrication instructions.

CALIPER CARE

If you're only replacing pads and hardware, you don't have to disconnect the brake hose from the caliper. However, if you do remove the caliper, don't let it hang by the brake hose, which can split under the weight. Fashion a hook from a wire coat hanger, slip one end into one of the caliper bolt holes, and hang the caliper on a part of the chassis.

Pads are held in calipers by support springs, retaining clips, or retaining pins. They may also have shims (Fig. 5). Before removing pieces of hardware, make a note or sketch of how they lie in relation to the pads. Then, take the old pads off and throw them away.

Check around the piston bore for signs of moisture, which indicate that fluid is leaking. Also, inspect the dust boot for cracks and cuts. If leaks are present or the boot is damaged, overhaul or replace the caliper.

OVERHAULING A CALIPER

Calipers have a small square-cut rubber O-ring that helps draw the piston back away from the pads when pressure on the brake pedal is released. If this O-ring loses elasticity, which it will in time, the piston won't draw back and the pads won't release. The result will be slight pad-to-rotor contact and premature pad wear, noise, fading, and/or uneven braking. For this reason it is wise, though not essential, to overhaul a caliper when replacing pads.

Now the question arises: Should you overhaul the calipers yourself, replace them with rebuilt units, or turn the job over to a pro? The least expensive approach is to overhaul them yourself. The next in line, cost-wise, is to install rebuilt calipers, which you can buy from an auto parts dealer. Obviously, a pro is going to be the most expensive.

OVERHAUL PROCEDURES

Here's a general idea of the overhauling procedure to help you decide whether you want to tackle the job. If you do it yourself, make sure you have specific instructions for your vehicle.

Note: If one caliper has to be overhauled or replaced, the caliper on the other side should also be overhauled or replaced. Also, when replacing pads, replace them on both sides of the car.

1. After removing the caliper from the rotor, keep the caliper on the car with the brake hose attached. Place a rag in the caliper to catch the piston and brake fluid. Make sure no one is near the car and carefully push on the brake pedal to ease the piston out of the bore. Don't get brake fluid on your car's fender—it will take off the paint.

This is a reasonably safe way to remove a piston and is recommended if calipers have phenolic pistons. If a caliper is already off the vehicle and has a metal piston, you can apply spurts of compressed air through the bleed screw to ease out the piston. Place a shop rag in the caliper to catch the piston and keep your fingers clear.

Much greater air pressure might be needed to get out a phenolic piston, but it could expel the piston with such force that it would be destroyed or else injure anyone in its way. To remove a phenolic piston from a caliper, it's best to attach the caliper to the brake hose and force the piston from the bore using hydraulic pressure.

In a few cars—Toyota Supra, for example—pistons have to be unscrewed using a special tool. They cannot be removed by applying hydraulic or air pressure.

2. Remove the caliper. When you disconnect the brake hose, cap it to prevent fluid loss.

3. Open the bleed screw to drain brake fluid. Remove the bleed screw and clean or replace it.

4. Remove the dust boot, following the manufacturer's instructions. Some dust boots are difficult to reinstall without special tools. In all cases, the dust boot must be replaced.

5. The rubber O-ring is more difficult to remove. Use a pointed wooden or plastic stick—a toothpick might work—to pry the seal out of the bore. Then, discard it.

Do not use a screwdriver or any other metal tool. You may scratch the bore or cause a burred edge on the O-ring groove and ruin the caliper.

6. Wash the caliper, bore, and piston with denatured alcohol

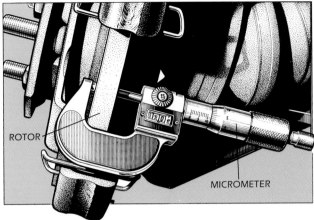

7 Check rotor parallelism by taking measurements on the circumference. Machine rotor if it doesn't meet specs.

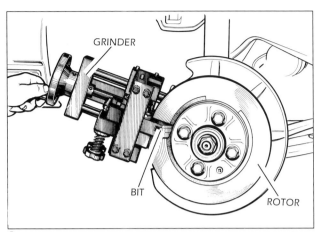

8 On-the-car rotor grinding is required on some models, notably Hondas, to get vibration-free brake operation.

or clean brake fluid. Don't use kerosene, gasoline, or any petroleum solvent. Residue left by these fluids can cause rubber brake parts to deteriorate.

Dry parts with a clean, lint-free cloth and an air hose aimed at the bore and other passages. If you don't have a compressor, let parts air-dry.

7. Examine the piston. If it is metal and is rusted, pitted, or scored, throw it away. If it's phenolic and chipped or cracked, get rid of it, too.
   Don't try to polish a metal piston. Any attempt to sand or buff away damage will destroy the plating.

8. Examine the bore. If it's scored or corroded, replace the caliper. But if it's only slightly stained, clean it by rotating a piece of crocus cloth, by hand, in the bore. Don't use a lot of pressure, and make sure you polish the bore all the way around. Don't slide the abrasive in and out, and don't use any abrasive except crocus cloth.
   Incidentally, black stains on the bore wall are not something to get alarmed over. They're caused by the O-ring seal and aren't harmful.

9. Reinstall the bleed screw and lubricate a new O-ring with clean brake fluid. Push the O-ring into place at one spot in the groove and then gently work it inch by inch into the groove with your fingers. Make sure you don't twist the O-ring.

10. After lubricating both parts, start the piston into the bore. You may have to fit the dust boot over the piston before pushing it in all the way. Check your service manual instructions. If you need a special tool for dust boot installation, it's probably available at the parts store where you bought the pads.

11. After the new pads and caliper are in place, bleed the brake system.

ROTOR SERVICE

Don't be misled by the fact that the rotors may look perfect. True, they might not be scored, but thickness variation (parallelism) and runout may be such that failure to catch something now will mean a problem like vibration or chatter later. You can't detect excessive parallelism or runout by eye. Measuring instruments are needed.

To find the extent of runout a pro will mount a dial indicator and slowly rotate the rotor, taking readings at several points (Fig. 6). He should also check parallelism by placing a micrometer at four or more points around the circumference of the rotor, each the same distance in from the edge of the rotor (Fig. 7). The findings should be checked against the manufacturer's allowable specification for the car. If the rotor fails to meet the spec, it will be machined.

When it comes to machining rotors, make sure your brake shop is aware of the latest technology. Rotors can be machined off the car on a brake lathe or on the car by using a special grinder. Some manufacturers—Honda, for one—require on-the-car grinding, since near-perfect parallelism is obtained with this equipment. Honda finds this necessary to eliminate a vibration that faulty parallelism causes.

When using an on-the-car grinder on a front-wheel-drive car, the transmission is placed in third gear or D after the grinder is attached and the rotating rotor turns against the grinder's machining bits. If the car has rear-wheel drive, a drive mechanism is used to turn the rotors.

Obviously, if you have a car equipped with rotors that *must* be ground on a car, let a pro handle the entire brake job. After machining a rotor, a pro should remeasure it to make sure grinding hasn't removed metal beyond the minimum dimension stamped on the rotor by the manufacturer. If the rotor is too thin, you must replace it.

How to Rebuild
BRAKE CALIPERS

You're clipping along at the speed limit. Several hundred feet down the road, a truck lazily pulls out from an adjoining highway. You stomp on the binders and your foot goes to the floor. Frantically, you pump the brake pedal. Pressure builds with maddening slowness, the brakes begin to apply, and, gradually, you come to a halt.

As you wipe the sweat from your brow, you vow to do something about those mushy brakes. No more procrastinating.

Mushy brakes are the result of air in the hydraulic system—air that's not supposed to be there. When you apply the brakes, the air compresses where hydraulic fluid would not—and the brake caliper's piston doesn't move.

Where does the air come from? Well, usually it's air that has replaced leaking brake fluid. And the most common cause of a brake fluid leak on disc brake systems is a leaking caliper.

Hone the interior walls of the caliper bore lightly with fine stones (or polish uniformly with crocus cloth) to remove any stains or discoloration.

CHECKING FOR BRAKE FLUID LEAKS

Your brake system could be leaking fluid without your knowing it.

To check, just run the engine at idle with the transmission in NEUTRAL. Then push on the brake pedal, holding constant pressure. If the pedal gradually drops, the hydraulic system is leaking. A few minutes on the creeper can confirm a leaking caliper. If the back of a tire is streaked with brake fluid, or if there's a strong brake fluid smell near a wheel, you can bet that you've got a leaker on your hands. If a caliper isn't the source of the hydraulic leak, trace all lines back toward the master cylinder until you find the offender.

If your calipers don't leak fluid and your car has more than 30,000 miles on the clock since your last caliper rebuild, you may just be riding on a bit of good luck. Because brake pad replacement will frequently cause a neglected caliper to leak, we recommend that you rebuild or replace your calipers whenever you renew your brake pads. Or,

at the very least, rebuild or replace calipers at every other brake job.

Replacing the calipers with after-market-rebuilt or new units can be costly. And, since the rebuild procedure is somewhat easy, it's a job that you probably will want to do yourself. In the following sections, we'll show you how. You'll need a few basic tools and a rebuilding kit for each caliper that you intend to service. You can purchase the rebuild kit at your auto parts store. You should have a supply of compressed air as well, but you can get along without it, if necessary.

Most cars with four-wheel disc brakes combine a parking-brake mechanism with the rear calipers. These vary widely in basic design and can be difficult to rebuild. For specific instructions on the rebuild-

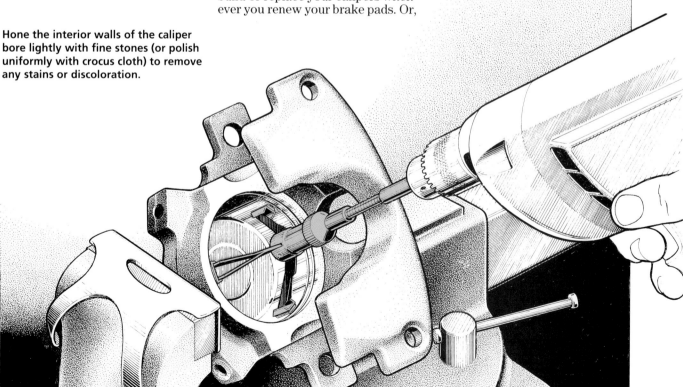

ing of rear calipers with integral parking-brake mechanisms, consult your factory service manual.

CALIPER REMOVAL

Before you even think about removing the caliper, you'll have to siphon about two-thirds of the brake fluid from the master cylinder, so that it won't overflow when you retract the pistons. A turkey baster comes in handy here. Discard the old fluid, and keep it away from the paint, as it's an excellent paint remover. It's also toxic if ingested.

Raise the car securely on jackstands, following the manufacturer's vehicle-support recommendations. Then mark the relationship of the wheel to the axle with a grease crayon or chalk. Remove the wheel and tire, and on front-drive cars reinstall a pair of lug nuts so the discs don't flop around.

Next, you'll need a C-clamp (7 in. or larger) or a pair of 12-in. adjustable water pump pliers to retract the pistons. What you have to do here is squeeze the piston back into the caliper until there's enough clearance between the pads and the rotor to remove the caliper (Fig. 1). On some applications, the C-clamp will work better. On others, the pliers will be more useful.

If you're using the C-clamp, position it so that the jackscrew rests against the inboard pad and the top of the clamp rests against the back of the caliper. Turn the jackscrew

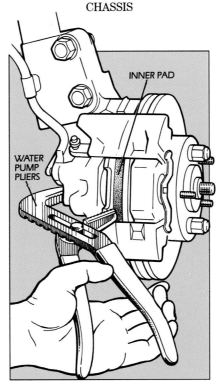

1 Before you can dislodge the caliper, you'll have to retract the piston in one direction or the other for clearance.

to retract the piston. If you opt for the pliers, just position them over the inboard brake shoe tab and the back of the caliper housing, and squeeze.

Next, disconnect the brake hose. On many calipers, you'll find that a bolt secures the inlet fitting to the caliper. By unscrewing this bolt, you can disconnect the hose and in-

let fitting from the caliper. Once the hose is off the caliper, plug the end of it with a plastic cap, or something similar.

At this point, you should carefully examine the brake hose. If it shows any signs of cracking, rubbing, or other deterioration, it must be replaced.

There used to be a whole grab bag of schemes for attaching the common single-piston floating brake caliper to the car. Fortunately, most makers have adapted a single strategy: pins that extend through bushings on the caliper and thread into the caliper mount (Fig. 2). But older cars may employ other means of attachment, so we'll cover several of the most common here.

THREADED-PIN CALIPERS

Threaded-pin calipers are found on almost all late-model cars and most GM cars with disc brakes, including the older models. On most early GM cars and many other late-model cars of other makes, a 3/8-in. hex key (Allen wrench) tightens or loosens the pins. You also might find a conventional capscrew head on some pins. The latest GM calipers are secured with internal Torx drive pins. You'll need a Torx drive key to remove them. Some tool companies package the specific driver you need and sell it as a brake tool. You should be able to find it at an auto parts store.

After removing the threaded pins, lift the caliper from the rotor.

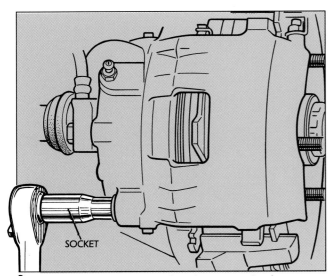

2 Most calipers are mounted to the suspension by means of threaded pins that are easily removed.

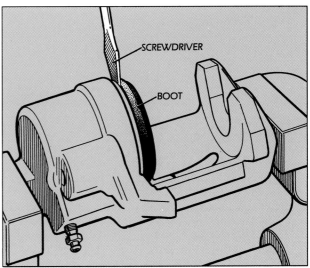

3 Carefully pry the old dust boot from the caliper housing without nicking the edge of the caliper bore.

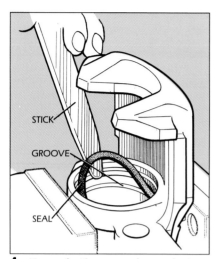

4 Use a plastic or wooden probe to lift the seal from its groove in the caliper bore.

If necessary, you can use a screwdriver to pry it away from the rotor.

MACHINED-WAY CALIPERS

Early Ford calipers slide on a machined surface and are retained by a key. A locking screw holds the key in place. To disengage the caliper, remove the locking screw and use a hammer and drift to drive the retaining key out of the caliper mount.

Some early Chrysler calipers slide on machined guides, or ways, and are retained by clips. These can be removed by disengaging the clips.

Up until a few years ago, most import calipers moved on machined guides, and were retained by pins and clips, or pins and pin bolts. These are removed by disengaging the clip or pin bolt from the pins.

On some early imports, you'll find machined metal pieces that fit between the guides and the machined surfaces of the caliper. Take note of their position as you remove the caliper. If you get confused, refer to your factory service manual. You may find that the caliper pins have corroded to the point where you have to cut through the pins to remove the calipers. In such cases, the calipers must be replaced.

CALIPER DISASSEMBLY

Once the calipers are off the car, remove the outer and inner pads and any support retaining springs.

On most threaded-pin calipers, you'll find sleeves on the inboard ears of the calipers and O-rings inside the caliper ears. Remove them.

On the pins of retainer-pin calipers, you'll find dust seals and rubber seals. Remove these as well.

On all calipers, any soft bushings or O-rings should be replaced with new parts at rebuild time.

Examine the retainer pins or threaded pins as well. If they show wear, corrosion, or galling, they should be replaced. Don't attempt to polish away corrosion, as it will only come back.

To remove the piston, position the caliper on the floor and place rags in position between the piston (which is covered by the dust boot) and the rear pad support of the caliper. Then *gradually* apply air pressure to the caliper inlet to force the piston out of the caliper bore. *Don't* try to catch the piston in your hand!

If you don't have an air compressor, you may have to ask your neighborhood mechanic or parts store counterman to give you a hand here. But, you also might use a portable air tank and air-gun attachment, as only a short blast of compressed air is needed.

A third alternative: Leave the brake line connected to the caliper, and suspend the caliper from the steering knuckle with a piece of wire coat hanger. After removing the pads, stuff some rags behind the piston and gently push on the brake pedal until the piston pops out of its bore. This is the recommended procedure when removing the phenolic (plastic) pistons, which might be damaged if they're expelled aggressively with air pressure.

Some phenolic pistons have been known to stick in their bores and have defied all attempts to remove them. If this proves to be the case, you'll have to replace the caliper assembly.

Use a screwdriver to pry the dust boot off the caliper bore. But be very careful not to damage the caliper bore surface (Fig. 3).

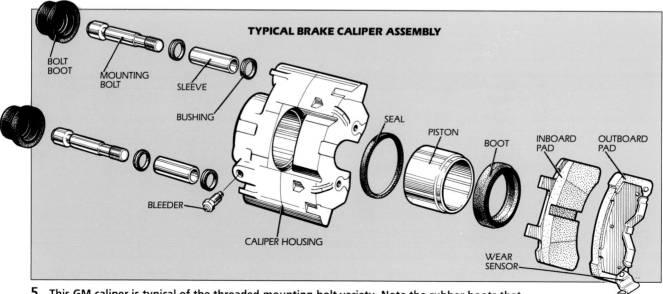

5 This GM caliper is typical of the threaded-mounting-bolt variety. Note the rubber boots that protect the bolts from corrosion.

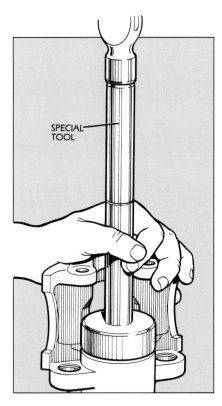

Use a plastic toothpick or pointed wooden probe to remove the seal from the groove in the caliper bore (Fig. 4).

CLEANUP AND INSPECTION

Wash all the metal caliper parts in brake cleaner or alcohol. Blow them off with air, if possible. But make sure the air supply is free of water or oil. You want to steadfastly avoid

6 Install steel-ringed dust boots with a driver that pushes on the edge of the seal.

contaminating any brake parts with moisture, as the brake fluid will quickly absorb moisture, leading to serious problems later on.

Carefully examine the caliper bore, the groove in the caliper bore, and all the passages in the bore for any lingering moisture.

Check the caliper bore for nicks, pitting, or scoring. If you find any metal distress, the caliper should be replaced. Pay particular attention to the seal groove. This is the business end of things. If the seal doesn't hold pressure, the caliper won't work.

If the caliper bore is stained or discolored, you can clean it up with a light honing or with a bit of crocus cloth. Take care not to overdo it with a hone, and make sure the stones don't clog by lubing liberally with a light machine oil.

Carefully check the piston for scoring, pitting, nicks, corrosion, and worn or damaged plating. If the piston is the least bit flawed, it *must* be replaced.

Phenolic pistons should only be reused if they are in perfect condition and were easily removed from the bore of calipers that weren't leaking. In every other case, replace them. Some mechanics automatically replace the phenolic pistons with steel pistons. But this practice

is questionable, as the steel piston transfers more heat to the brake fluid than a phenolic piston does. If a phenolic piston has given you good service to date, replace it with another phenolic one. Don't try to file or sandpaper phenolic pistons.

CALIPER REASSEMBLY

To reassemble a caliper, lubricate the cylinder bore and the piston seal with clean brake fluid (Fig. 5). The fluid must come from a new, freshly opened can.

Lube the outside surface of the piston with clean brake fluid and slip the dust boot over the end of the piston. Then, smoothly push down the piston to the bottom of the bore.

Don't force the piston. Use hand pressure only. If it won't move past the seal, the seal was inserted incorrectly or you have the wrong piston.

If the dust boot has a steel rim, tap it in place with a driver that aligns with the outer edge of the rim (Fig. 6). An old brake piston will work on some applications.

If the dust boot is solid rubber, use the flat side of a screwdriver or other blunt tool to press the boot into its groove. If you damage the boot, you'll have to get another one and try again. Make sure the boot seats fully in its groove.

Where applicable, apply a small amount of antiseize compound to

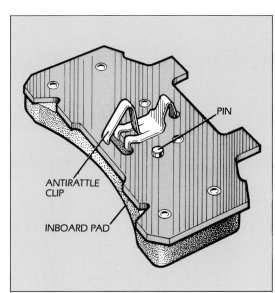

7 Avoid squealing brakes by installing all antirattle clips on the inboard pads.

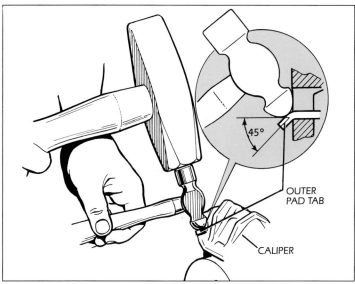

8 Have a helper depress the brake pedal while you clinch the pad tabs against the caliper body.

the caliper pin bores between the bushings. Then install new bushings and O-rings in the caliper ears or pin bores.

BOLTING EVERYTHING BACK TOGETHER

Of course, we're assuming here that you've completed the rest of the brake job, checking all other hydraulic components for leakage and examining and servicing the brake rotors as required.

If so, reinstall the new pads in the calipers with any antirattle springs or clips (Fig. 7). Check for possible left and right side designation on antirattle clips. Apply a narrow strip of noise-suppression compound to the center of the inboard pad, and a large round patch of the compound to each end of the outboard pad. Then install the pads in the caliper.

To reinstall a threaded-pin caliper, position the caliper on the rotor so that the holes in the caliper ears line up with the holes in the anchor. Insert the caliper pins, making sure they pass under the retaining ears on the inner plate. Then tighten the threaded pins to 25 to 35 lb.-ft.

Reattach the brake hose and torque the retaining bolt to 30 lb.-ft. *Note:* On brake pads equipped with tabs that fit over the caliper, you'll have to clinch the tabs after bleeding the brakes. On calipers with machined guides, use silicone grease sparingly to lube the guides. Locate the caliper in position and reinstall the pins or clips.

OUT WITH THE BAD AIR

Refill the master cylinder reservoirs with clean, fresh brake fluid. Make sure they remain at least half-full throughout the bleeding operation. Top off as necessary. If you find that the master cylinder is empty, you'll have to bleed it before proceeding. Check your service manual.

To bleed the calipers, find a box wrench that fits the bleeder valve and hang it from the valve. Connect a transparent tube to the bleeder valve of the right-rear caliper (or wheel cylinder if your car has drum brakes in the rear). Submerge the other end of the tube in a glass jar of brake fluid.

Have a helper push the brake slowly to the floor and hold it. Then loosen the bleeder valve and allow air and brake fluid to escape from the caliper's cylinder. Tighten the bleeder valve and slowly release the brake pedal. Wait at least fifteen seconds, then repeat the process. Continue to repeat the entire sequence, including the fifteen-second wait, until you stop getting bubbles. Don't let the fluid level get too low.

After bleeding the right rear, continue with the left front, left rear, and right front. When you've finished, there should be no hint of sponginess in the brake pedal, and the brake warning light should, of course, be off. If not, repeat the process.

If you have compressed air, a power bleeder will make this a faster, one-man job. Some auto parts stores and rental outfits have power bleeders for rent.

CLINCHING THE TABS

On many cars with threaded-pin calipers, including most GM models, you'll have to clinch the tabs of the brake pad backing plates onto the caliper after bleeding the system.

To do this, apply heavy pressure to the brake pedal (about 175 pounds) three times in a row. Then have a helper hold down the brake pedal with about 150 pounds of force. While he's holding the pedal, use two hammers to bend the tabs of the outboard shoe around the caliper body (Fig. 8). Never hit a steel hammer with a steel hammer—use a brass, lead, or plastic mallet.

How to Troubleshoot
ANTILOCK BRAKES

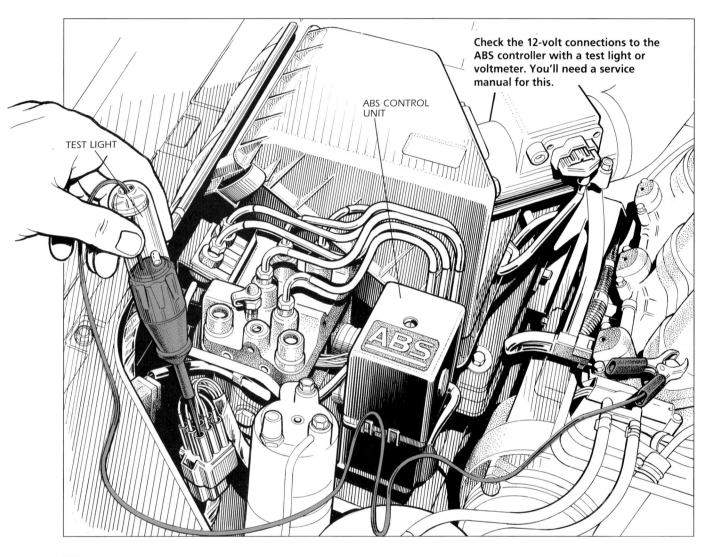

TEST LIGHT

ABS CONTROL
UNIT

Check the 12-volt connections to the
ABS controller with a test light or
voltmeter. You'll need a service
manual for this.

Y ou're winding your way home
from the rained-out Little League
game through a frog-choking thun-
dershower, depending on your new
car's antilock braking system to
keep you and the entire infield safely on the road. Suddenly, the ABS
WARNING light on the dashboard
winks at you. After a moment's panic, you realize that the normal service brakes should still be fine,
capable of stopping your car normally. But since you've come to rely
on the extra margin of safety of
ABS—you'll be extra careful until
you've found the source of the ABS
problem.

Despite the proliferation of air-
bags, rear-seat three-point seatbelts,
and improved passenger accident
protection, the most important
safety devices your car comes with
are still those things that help it
avoid an accident in the first place:
its acceleration, steering, and braking. And the most important safety
innovation of the last decade is
the development of antilock brakes
(ABS).

WHY YOU NEED ABS

Anti*lock* braking systems do exactly
that—they prevent the controlled

wheels from locking, even if you
push down on the brake pedal with
all of your might and with both feet.

You might ask: How can this be
good? Won't this make my car take
longer to stop? Shouldn't the brakes
lock in a panic stop?

Not necessarily. Under almost
every circumstance, a wheel should
continue to roll to maintain the
maximum deceleration. A tire that's
being scrubbed along the pavement
at speed without rotating actually
has a few percent less deceleration
than a tire that rotates at about 95
percent of the road speed. In practice, this doesn't amount to much

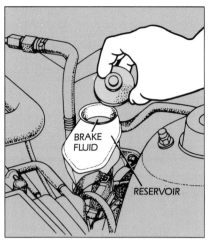

Check the brake master cylinder reservoir for fluid level at regular intervals.

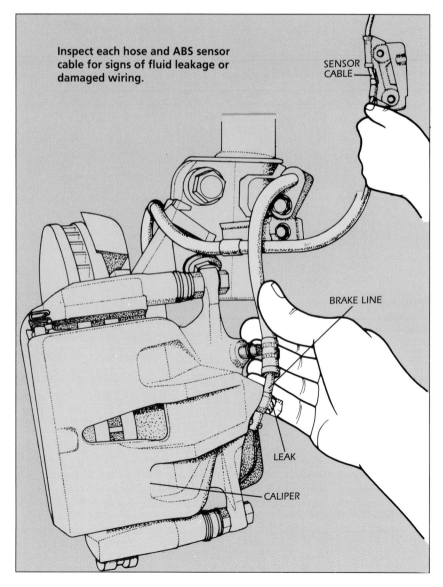

Inspect each hose and ABS sensor cable for signs of fluid leakage or damaged wiring.

difference, and braking distances on dry or wet pavement are within one to three feet, with or without antilock brakes.

But there's a much more important consideration than the raw stopping power, and it's a side effect of the ABS-braked tire's continued rotation. The tire will maintain its ability to steer the car.

A locked tire will have no directional stability. Lock the tire with the brakes, and you can turn the steering wheel any which way with no effect on the car's direction of travel—it will continue to head straight toward whatever it was heading for when you slammed on the binders.

But an ABS-retarded-but-still-rotating tire, even one that is hauling you down from high speed, will still permit you to make steering input and find some way to steer around an obstacle, or keep from driving off the outside of the curve you've entered at too high a speed.

APPLIED INTELLIGENCE

There are several different antilock brake systems currently on the road, from such diverse manufacturers as Bosch, Teves, Kelsey-Hayes, Bendix, Delco Moraine, and Nippon. Some of the systems are quite similar to one another, and others have major technical differences.

Some antilock brake systems, such as those on many pickup trucks, operate only on the rear brakes, while other systems—the ones appearing with greater frequency on passenger cars—work on all four wheels. But regardless of the differences in the brake systems, they all work in essentially the same way.

Antilock systems use a combination of electronic and hydraulic technology to modulate the brakes individually, keeping them from locking. The systems rely on wheel-speed sensors, a microprocessor or electronic control unit, and a sophisticated valve body called the hydraulic control unit. The wheel-speed sensors are located at each wheel, or in the differential carrier, where a sensor head reads the wheel's (or axle's) speed by way of a toothed ring. The electronic control unit constantly compares the relative speeds of all four wheels.

When the brakes are applied, the control unit determines if any one of the wheels is decelerating at a far greater rate than the others, indicating that that brake is beginning to lock. The microprocessor unit then directs the valves in the hydraulic control unit. These valves control fluid flow to that brake to release, hold, or reapply hydraulic pressure to the brake until that wheel is decelerating at the same rate as the others.

Most passenger-car antilock brake systems are of the three-channel variety, which, while monitoring the speed of each of the four wheels, controls brake-line pressure to the two rear brakes as though they were one, regardless of which wheel may have been lock-

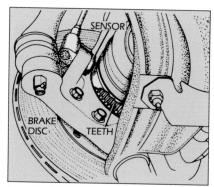

Inspect the sensors for missing or broken teeth on the speed ring in the hub.

ing. Some high-performance cars have four-channel systems that modulate the brakes on the rear wheels individually.

Because of the complexity of the electronics and hydraulics, all the antilock systems conduct a thorough self-check each time you start the engine. As the system is checking itself, the dashboard warning lights remain lit. If there are no detected problems, the lights go out. Some systems have two dashboard warning lights, one typically labeled ABS and the other labeled BRAKE. Some systems have only one warning light. However, the warning lights can be triggered by anything from a faulty parking brake or brake light switch to a failure of one of the wheel sensors or a failure of the electronic or hydraulic control units.

All ABS systems are designed so your car will still have normal, non-ABS-modulated braking *even if the ABS system itself fails.*

BACK TO BASICS

Begin diagnosing any antilock brake system problem the same way you would diagnose a problem on a car without ABS.

Check the master cylinder reservoir for a sudden fluid-level drop. As with all disc-brake systems, the fluid level in the master cylinder slowly goes down as the linings on the brake pads wear out. A precipitous drop in the fluid level indicates a leak.

Many antilock systems use hydraulic pressure to reduce brake-pedal effort instead of the vacuum assist on most disc-brake systems.

An electrically driven hydraulic pump pressurizes the brake system. In addition, there may be a separate accumulator that stores the pressurized brake fluid. Since the brake fluid in these systems is kept under high pressure, usually over about 35 psi, the chances for a leak are greater, and you must depressurize the brake lines and cylinder before working on the system.

If there is no large vacuum diaphragm attached to your car's master cylinder, look for an electric hydraulic pump and an accumulator. The accumulator typically resembles a cylinder or bulb, and is mounted near the master cylinder and the pump. The accumulator has a diaphragm separating it into an upper and lower chamber. The upper chamber is filled with an inert gas, such as nitrogen, and the lower chamber contains the brake fluid. The pump runs as necessary to fill the lower chamber, compressing the gas in the upper chamber. When you step on the brakes, the pressurized gas helps the brake fluid flow out toward the brakes.

Remember, before loosening any connections in a hydraulically boosted system, you must relieve pressure in the system. To reduce system pressure, first turn off the ignition or disconnect power to the hydraulic pump. Then step on the brake pedal as many times as needed—perhaps two dozen or so. Your leg will tell you—pedal effort dramatically increases. The increase in pedal effort indicates that the pressure is relieved.

Begin the search for leaks at the master cylinder, working your way to the hydraulic control unit and then to the wheels. Inspect the steel brake-line connections at each juncture. If you find signs of leakage—such as stains—at any of the fittings, undo the fitting nut and inspect the nut, the flare at the end of the brake line, and the mating surface inside the master cylinder or hydraulic control unit. Any cracks or splits mean the defective part must be replaced.

Make certain that the mating surfaces of the brake-line flare and master cylinder are perfectly clean. Then reattach the brake line, threading the nut into place by hand. Do *not* force it. Once you're sure the nut is being properly threaded, snug it up using the proper size flare-nut

wrench. Flare-nut wrenches resemble box wrenches with a small section of the box missing. Slip the wrench over the brake line and then slide it onto the flare nut. Flare-nut wrenches are sold in both metric and SAE sizes. Use the right one.

Inspect the brake-line connections at all the wheels next. Look for signs of leakage where the brake line attaches to the brake caliper as well as where the flexible brake hose connects to the steel brake line. Carefully inspect the brake hoses for signs of chafing, tearing, or bulging. Replace any suspect or clearly damaged brake hoses. If you find stains or brake fluid at any of the connections, undo, inspect, and clean the connection before reattaching it. If your car uses hydraulic pressure to reduce brake-pedal effort, also inspect the fluid-pressure accumulator for a leak. A leaking accumulator must be replaced.

LET IT BLEED

As with any brake system, if an antilock brake system has been leaking, you must bleed the trapped air from it after you've repaired the leak. But, in addition to bleeding an antilock brake system after a repair, you should regularly, at least every two years, totally flush, refill, and bleed the system.

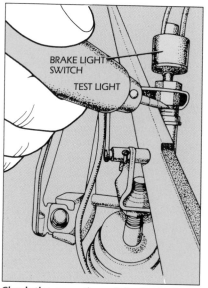

Check the operation of the brake light and parking brake switches with a test light.

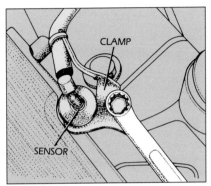

Tighten a loose wheel sensor to be sure it's the proper distance from the ring.

While it's a good idea to flush the brake fluid from any brake system every two years to remove moisture and contaminants, it's critical to do so with an antilock system. The dirt and moisture that can invade the hydraulic portion of an antilock brake system can seriously damage the expensive and complex hydraulic control unit.

Any time a brake system is flushed and refilled, the air must be bled from it. However, because of the complexity of the hydraulic circuits and valving in the hydraulic control units, the individual antilock systems have specific bleeding sequences. Some systems require a pressure brake bleeder. Others can be bled using the system's own hydraulic pump and accumulator to supply the pressure.

Some systems have bleeder screws at the hydraulic control unit which are part of the bleeding sequence. Bleeding the hydraulic control unit often entails disconnecting the electrical connector at the control unit.

Before attempting to bleed the brakes of your antilock system, check your car's factory service manual for the exact procedure.

When the ABS is activated, the pulsing of the valves in the hydraulic control unit may or may not be felt through the brake pedal, depending on the system. However, if the brake rotors or drums are warped or out-of-round, you will also feel a pulsing in the brake pedal. You'll feel the ABS-induced pulsing only when the system is activated by your overpowering the available traction and hitting the pedal hard enough to skid

at least one wheel. You'll feel warped rotors full-time whenever you're on the brakes.

To ascertain that the rotors are in good condition, check their thickness in at least four locations around the circumference using a micrometer. Check the factory service manual for allowed tolerances. Also check the runout of the disc, using a dial indicator. An out-of-round, warped, or otherwise defective rotor should be machined back to specifications or replaced.

Also inspect all the calipers for signs of rust, corrosion, bent slide pins, and other damage. Verify that the pad lining is wearing evenly on both pads on each disc—uneven wear indicates a sticking caliper.

SWITCH!

If there is no hydraulic problem, but the dashboard warning lights indicate something is wrong, check the mundane wiring before even inspecting the ABS components.

Make sure that the brake lights come on when you step on the brake pedal. If not, check the brake light switch. If they do turn on, check the switch for the parking brake warning light next.

Use a 12V test light and, with the ignition on, probe both sides of the suspect switch. The test light should show current on one side of the switch. With the brake pedal fully depressed or the parking brake lever fully engaged, there should be current to the other side of the switch as well. If not, check the adjustment of the switch—possibly its contact plunger or tab needs to be adjusted. Check the wiring connections and circuit for the suspect switch, looking for an open connection or broken or chafed wire.

If the switches prove to be working properly, the problem is likely to be in the antilock system.

DON'T OVERLOOK THE OBVIOUS

Despite the sealed electronic and computerized nature of the antilock system, you can still make simple mechanical checks to the system's components to find the problem.

First ascertain that the system's various relays and circuit breakers are in place and working. Check that the relays are tight and there is no

corrosion on any of the terminals. You can use a volt/ohmmeter to check the operation of the individual relays, following the diagnostic procedure and specifications listed in the factory shop manual. If you are satisfied that the relays, fuses, and circuit breakers are working properly, inspect the sensors at the brakes.

Check the sensor at each wheel. The sensors are not serviceable if they are defective. However, inspect the wiring to each sensor for cuts and chafes. The signal-carrying wire is typically covered in a thick protective sheath. Carefully inspect the sheathing for tears, slices, or other signs of damage.

Next, check to be sure that the sensor itself is securely in place. Road debris and stones could have dislodged or broken the sensor. Also be sure that the sensor's mounting bolt is snug. Be sure that the sensor head is squarely in position to read the wheel-speed ring on the hub.

Then, inspect the sensor ring itself. On some systems the ring is under a protective cover, on others it's exposed. In some systems it's inside the brake drum housing, on others it is visible and accessible behind the rotor. In some two-wheel ABS applications, the sensor and speed rings are inside the differential case. Carefully check the ring for broken or missing teeth. Be certain that

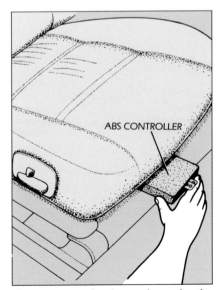

The ABS control unit may be under the seat, in the trunk, under the dash or hood.

there are no pebbles or other pieces of debris wedged into the teeth of the ring or between the ring and the sensor head. Last, be sure that the ring is tight in place on the hub and that it spins with the hub.

Next, check the wiring at the electronic control unit and at the hydraulic control unit.

The electronic control unit is a sealed box, mounted typically under a passenger seat, in the trunk, or on a shock tower under the hood.

Be sure that the control unit's wiring connector is solidly connected. Try tugging on the connector and its wiring loom. Also be sure that the control unit itself does not move while you tug at its wiring. Tighten the unit's mounting bolts if they're loose.

The hydraulic control unit is located in the engine compartment, either at the brake master cylinder or remotely. Check the wiring connector for looseness and corrosion.

Also inspect all the wires in the control unit's loom. There should be no looseness in the connection, and the wires should be in perfect condition.

If everything checks out, but the warning lights are still on, you must defer to the antilock system's self-diagnostic capabilities. Since this often requires a dedicated tester and always requires a trouble-code chart, it's also time to defer to the dealership's mechanic.

How to Replace
MACPHERSON STRUTS

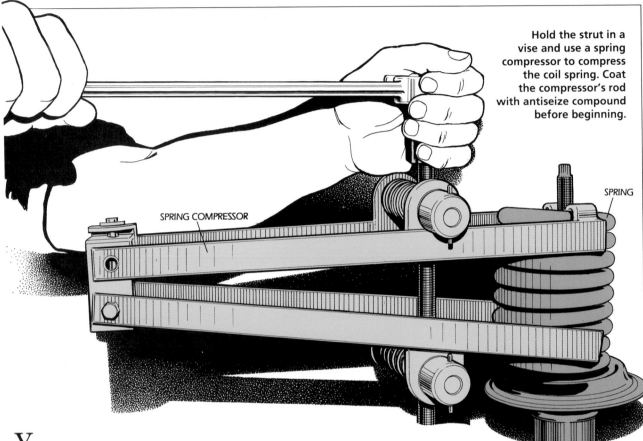

Hold the strut in a vise and use a spring compressor to compress the coil spring. Coat the compressor's rod with antiseize compound before beginning.

SPRING

SPRING COMPRESSOR

STRUT

You're clipping along on the interstate when some clown decides to move from his lane into yours. No problem—you cut the wheel left and then right and avoid serious bending of metal. But your car protests the maneuver by rocking and yawing and squealing the tires as you keep compensating with the steering wheel. You've taken quicker, more sudden evasive action in the past without such a fuss. It feels as though your car's suspension has gone to mush.

You've noticed that each time you come to a stop, regardless from what speed, your car nosedives for the blacktop. And then your rig bobs and rocks like a small boat on a rough sea.

These and other symptoms all point to worn shock absorbers. No big deal. Changing shocks is a simple couple-of-wrenches deal. You'll be back on the road before you and

your favorite dinner partner have to cancel those reservations. Except, what's this? Your car doesn't have simple shock absorbers at each wheel—it has MacPherson struts. Now what?

No problem. Be properly equipped and informed before you begin, and you'll still be rolling to dinner.

MacPherson struts are found attached to the front wheels of just about every front-drive car on the road and at the fronts of many rear-wheel-drive cars as well. And as more front-wheel-drive cars are being equipped with totally independent link-and-arm-type rear suspensions, the nearly ubiquitous struts are appearing there as well.

The MacPherson strut is a single unit that contains the shock absorber and coil spring. In addition, the strut acts as the upper arm in a typical suspension. The strut attaches to

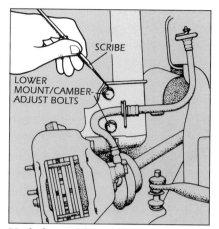

Mark the position of the lower mount bolt heads to keep alignment close to specs.

the chassis at its top, and to the wheel and lower control arm at its bottom. This simplicity and compactness make for an effective, inexpensive suspension. It also leaves room for other components, like a transverse engine and transmission sitting between the front wheels, or a wide rear seat between the rear wheels.

The strut's top mount consists of the coil spring mount and a swivel bearing which permits the entire strut to turn along with the front wheels as the driver commands via the steering wheel. The lower mount for the coil spring is integral with the strut housing, a metal tube that's heavy enough to support the load of one corner of the car. The bottom end of the strut can either

contain the wheel spindle, or bolt to the spindle and hub carrier, or be attached to the steering knuckle, possibly via a ball joint. Any antiroll bar attaches the left and right struts, either directly or via the lower control arm.

STRUTS SIMPLIFIED

Since the shock absorber is only one element of the strut assembly, replacing a worn strut-type shock absorber is more complex than replacing a simple shock absorber. But it's nothing to be afraid of either.

While a few older designs—such as the Dodge Colt and Plymouth Champ made by Mitsubishi—had repairable shock absorber units within the strut that had to be drained, disassembled, cleaned, and repaired, most cars have far simpler systems. In fact in many cars, replacing the shock absorber means merely replacing the strut unit. With others, the shock absorber is in the form of a cartridge contained in the strut housing's tube and simply slides out once the strut is removed and disassembled.

Begin strut repair or replacement as you would with a nonstrut shock absorber, by verifying that the shock absorbers are in fact worn. Push down on each corner of the car and let it rock. The car should come up, go down once, and come back to its original height. If it bounces more than twice at any corner, that shock absorber is worn.

Also lift the car on its suspension, extending the spring and letting it go. Again, more than two bounces indicates a problem. The car should settle to the same height—within ½ in.—after pushing down on the car and after lifting up on it.

Next, jack up and support the end of the car with the suspect shocks and remove the wheels and tires. Place safety stands under a frame member to support the car—*do not* work under a car that is sitting only on a jack.

With the wheels off, check the strut for damage—dents, cracks, or bends in the housing or spring seat. Look for signs of leaking shock oil on the shock absorber portion of the strut inside the coil spring. More than a trace of oil leaking from the shock is grounds for immediate replacement.

If you determine that any one of the struts is bad, you must replace its mate on the other side of the car. An exception here is if the strut is new or almost brand new and was damaged. Having one strut that's only a few miles younger than the other is not generally a problem. Otherwise, you must repair or replace both struts on the same axle.

TAKING IT OUT

To replace the shock absorber cartridge on most MacPherson struts, you must remove the entire strut unit from the car. There are exceptions, however, such as the Buick Regal and its brethren, which are

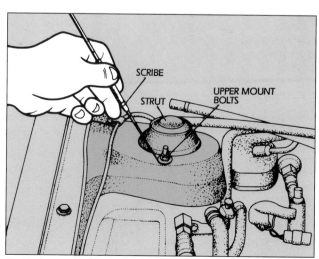

Similarly, mark the position of the upper mount bolts with a sharp tool before removing them.

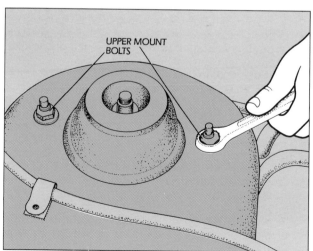

Remove the upper mount bolts or nuts. Don't loosen the large center nut yet—this nut holds the strut together.

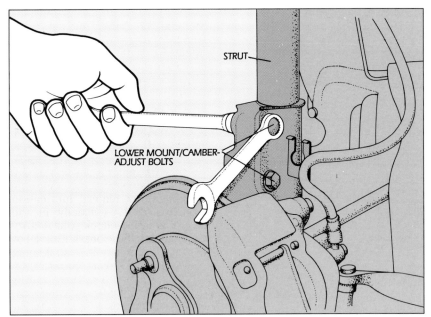

Remove lower mounting hardware. On some cars you'll be taking the ball joint apart instead.

designed for cartridge removal without strut removal. If you must remove the strut to repair or replace the shock absorber, first determine how the unit is mounted to the wheel.

In cases where the strut is attached to the front-wheel spindle and steering knuckle, you must remove the brake caliper and rotor, and disconnect the steering knuckle from the steering tie rod. In most cases you can remove the brake caliper without disconnecting the brake line. Use a piece of heavy wire (wire hanger or welding rod) to tie the caliper to part of the car so the weight of the caliper is not hanging on the brake hose. Disconnect any clips that may hold the brake hose to the strut as well.

If the strut is bolted to the steering knuckle or spindle carrier, check the bolts before loosening them. On many cars the lower bolt also serves as the camber adjustment. Before undoing the bolt, scribe matching marks on the head of the bolt and strut mount. Now you can undo the bolts.

In cases where the steering knuckle is integral with the bottom of the strut, you have to remove the steering tie rod end from the knuckle. This usually involves removing a cotter pin and nut. You may need a ball-joint fork to separate the tie rod from the

steering knuckle. A sharp blow to the fork with a heavy hammer should do the trick. Take care not to damage the rubber boot on the tie rod end.

With some cars you must also undo the antiroll-bar mount if it is attached to the strut's lower mount or the wheel spindle, so the strut can fall away from the lower control arm.

After you've disconnected the bottom of the strut, go to the top. Front struts are accessible from under the hood, at the tops of the strut towers. The upper mounts for rear struts may be hidden under a parcel shelf or trunk panel or behind the rear seat back.

To remove the strut, undo the two or three nuts that hold the top mount in place. Do not disturb the center nut—it holds the top mount in place on the strut and holds the coil spring compressed. But before loosening the top-mount nuts, ascertain if any of the upper mounting holes are slotted. Slotted holes indicate that moving the top of the strut along the slots adjusts wheel alignment. If the upper mounting position is part of the alignment procedure, use your scribe to mark the positions of the mounting studs against their spots on the strut tower. Now undo the nuts.

If your car has an electrically controlled suspension that alters the shock absorber valving in the

struts, the electric motor and controller are mounted at the top of the strut. You must undo the wiring and remove the motor and controller before disconnecting the strut's top mount. Consult your service manual first.

With both upper and lower mounts disconnected, you should be able to pull down the strut out of the strut tower—if the strut's own weight along with the weight of the lower suspension doesn't cause it to fall. Then lift the strut out of the steering knuckle or wheel spindle carrier.

A STRUT IN THE VISE

Place the strut in a bench vise, using two pieces of wood in the jaws to protect the strut. To gain access to the shock absorber, you have to remove the coil spring. You must use a coil spring compressor, one designed for use on MacPherson struts. These can be rented or purchased at any auto parts store, as well as many tool rental agencies.

Warning! Do *not* attempt to backyard-engineer any substitutes for a proper coil spring compressor. There's enough energy trapped in a compressed coil spring to punt your head into the neighbor's backyard—regardless of whether it's attached to your neck.

Position the compressor over the spring, coat the compressor's threaded rod with antiseize compound, and tighten down the rod to compress the spring. Use a long-

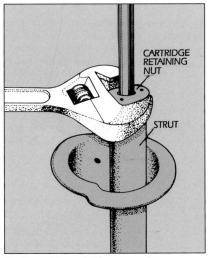

Replaceable cartridges require removing a large-diameter nut at the top of the strut.

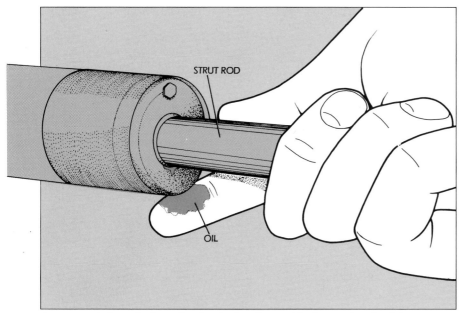

An accumulation of oil on the shock absorber rod indicates the shock is worn.

tact, with no cracks or deformation. Replace both springs if even one is defective. When reinstalling the coil spring, be sure to place it so the spring end is in the small recess or against the spring stop tab on the mount.

Also inspect the upper bearing plate and jounce rubber before reinstalling them. A new shock probably comes with a new jounce rubber and dust shield—use them. Check that the bearing moves smoothly. The bearings in the top strut mounts on some cars require lubrication upon reassembly—usually in the form of grease—check your factory shop manual. If the bearing sticks or feels rough, replace it. Also inspect the spring seat surface and the mounting studs. If there are cracks or a deformation of the spring seat, replace the mount. Likewise, if any of the mounting studs shows stripped threads.

With the strut reassembled, do not remove the spring compressor until you have tightened the upper mount nut to the correct torque specifications. Check your factory shop manual for the spec—it can run to well over 100 ft.-lb.

After the strut has been reassembled, reinstall it in the car, starting at the top. Do not overtighten the nuts on the top mounting studs. Take care to reposition the upper mount as per your scribe marks. Some cars require that new nuts be used.

With the top bearing in place, reassemble the bottom. Again, take care to align any marks you made on the strut's lower mount. And again, some carmakers recommend new

handled ratchet and socket on the spring compressor so you don't have to struggle with the spring. Work slowly and carefully. If the compressor starts to slip or walk on the spring coils, or if the spring begins distorting instead of compressing evenly, back off and reposition the compressor and start again. All the while you're working, stay out of the line of the spring.

Compress the spring until it is free of the upper mount. Once the spring pressure has been removed from the mount, you can undo the top nut. You may need a deeply offset box wrench to reach the nut, depending on your car. You will also need to hold the shock absorber's piston rod from turning along with the mounting nut. This may require an Allen wrench or a small hex wrench. If you have an air wrench handy, you can probably just spin the nut loose without even holding the rod. Remove the topmount nut, the upper spring mount, and the coil spring/compressor assembly. Set the spring/compressor assembly someplace out of the way where it won't be disturbed.

If there is a rubber jounce stopper and dust cover boot, slide them off the shock absorber's piston rod. Inspect the shock. Check the rod for deep nicks, scratches, and cuts. Check to see if the rod is bent. Hold the strut upright and pull the piston rod all the way up, out of the strut

housing. If oil spills out along with the rod, the shock is bad—some very slight seepage is normal, however. While still holding the strut upright, push the rod into the housing and pull it out again. If the rod sticks, pull the rod all the way out and turn the strut upside down and push the rod all the way in. Turn the strut right-side up and pull the rod out again. Turn it over and repeat the process. If the rod still hesitates or sticks, the unit is bad.

If the strut itself is bad—dented, bent, or the lower spring seat is cracked or deformed—or if the shock absorber is not a replaceable cartridge variety, you must replace the strut unit. Simply install the coil spring and upper mount on the new strut, and install it in place of the old.

However, if the strut itself is good and the shock absorber is a cartridge, you need only replace the shock absorber. Undo the large nut at the top of the shock absorber tube. This may require a special spanner or simply a large wrench. Unthread the nut and slip it up over the shock's piston rod. Then simply pull the old shock cartridge out of the strut housing. Slip the new shock into the housing in its place. Replace the nut and snug it down. Reinstall the spring and upper mount and reinstall the strut.

Before reinstalling the coil spring, be sure that the coils are in-

Inspect the strut's upper mounting plate and bearing before reinstalling it.

mounting nuts and bolts. Tighten them to specs. In some cases, you may have to slightly exceed the torque setting to align your scribe marks. Lubricate the threads and washers with oil or antiseize compound before tightening.

Reassemble the brake and wheel hub assembly and reconnect the steering knuckle to the tie rod. Reinstall the wheel and tire and put the car back on the ground. Despite your care in reassembly, you should have the wheel alignment checked soon.

EASY OUT, EASY IN

As carmakers become more comfortable with the nuances of building ease of service into front-drive cars, they have developed ways to replace the shock absorbers in MacPherson struts without the need for removing the strut unit. Besides being easier all around, replacing the shock absorber without removing the strut obviates the need for checking the alignment.

If your car has top-replaceable shocks, there is no need to jack up the car. In fact, the job must be done with the full weight of the car on the suspension, since the car's weight will keep the coil spring compressed between its lower seat on the strut and its upper seat. If the suspension were unloaded—as by having the car sitting on safety stands—the spring would extend, pushing down on the strut and the control arm, displacing itself out of its seats when you removed the upper mounting nut.

Working from under the hood, remove the cover at the top of the strut and undo the mounting nut at the top of the piston rod. With this nut off, you can remove any jounce stopper and then undo the shock cartridge's locking nut. However, to undo these you need special socket wrenches, available from either your dealer or auto parts store. Without the special tools, the job is impossible. Once the cartridge nut is off, you can slip the shock absorber cartridge out through the strut tower and slide in its replacement. Replace any jounce stopper, retorque the piston rod nut, and reinstall the cover. Close the hood, and you're ready to roll.

How to Replace
BALL JOINTS

A lot of Saturday mechanics are afraid to attempt steering linkage and chassis component repairs, thinking that these are jobs better left to a professional mechanic. Actually, they're among the easier jobs that the driveway technician might attempt.

On the following pages, we'll tell you how to diagnose and replace faulty ball joints, tie rod ends, idler arms, and sway bar components. Since steering angles can change significantly when new components are installed, a professional front end alignment will be a necessary procedure after ball joint or tie rod end replacement.

DIAGNOSING FRONT END PROBLEMS

You should suspect front end problems if your front tires wear abnormally, if your mechanic says he can't align your front wheels because steering linkage parts or ball joints are too loose, if you hear

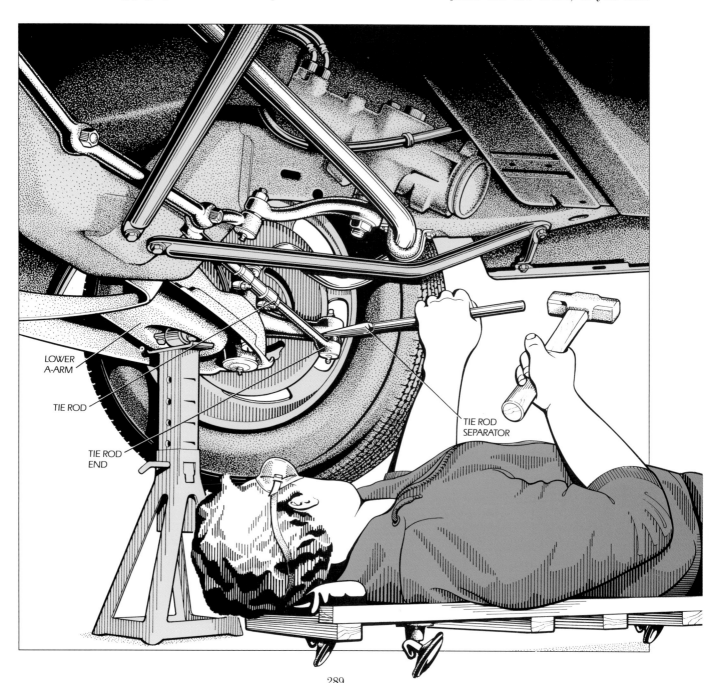

LOWER A-ARM

TIE ROD

TIE ROD END

TIE ROD SEPARATOR

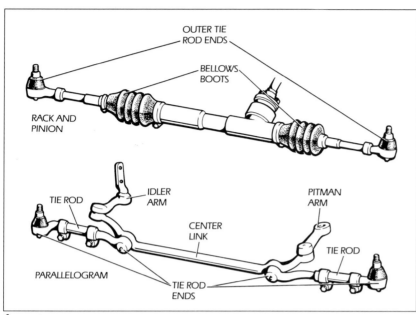

1 Rack-and-pinion steering systems, common on newer cars, have fewer parts to wear, but older-design parallelogram linkage can be rebuilt easily by a careful mechanic.

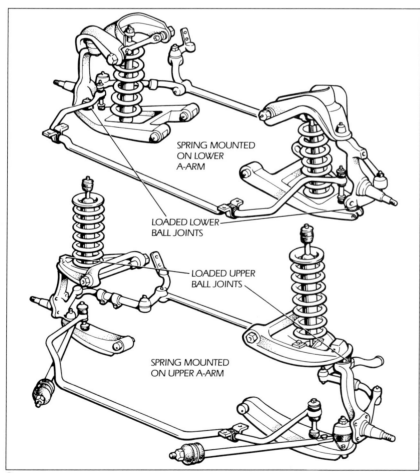

2 When springs are on the lower A-arm, weight is carried by lower ball joint. Upper A-arm mounted springs put load on upper ball joints.

clunks when you turn the wheels or corner, if there seems to be excessive free play in the steering mechanism, or if you experience wheel shimmy and/or vibration.

To confirm a suspected chassis part problem, you're going to have to spend some time under the greasy side. Before raising the car with your hydraulic floor jack or scissors jack, chock the rear wheels and apply the parking brake. Raise the car and locate jack stands in the recommended positions on the frame or frame/body structure. Lower the car until it is resting on the stands, leaving the floor jack in place for additional security.

Examine your steering linkage and front suspension. Most rear-wheel-drive cars use parallelogram linkage—a center link, two tie rods, an idler arm, and a pitman arm (see Fig. 1). This steering linkage is usually used with a coil spring mounted on the lower or upper control arm. Some cars with upper and lower arms have torsion bars in place of coil springs. Most front-drive and some rear-drive cars are equipped with rack-and-pinion steering. The steering arms on the wheel spindles are joined directly to the steering rack by a pair of tie rods. The idler arm and pitman arm are not used. Most front-wheel-drive cars and a few rear-drivers have only lower control arms. A MacPherson strut replaces the spring, shock absorber, and upper arm.

CHECKING BALL JOINTS

While cars with MacPherson struts have only one ball joint at each wheel, those with parallelogram steering linkage usually have both upper and lower ball joints. But the two joints don't wear out at the same rate, since only one ball joint carries the full load. If the coil spring is mounted on the lower control arm, the lower ball joint is the load carrier (Fig. 2). If the spring is mounted on the upper arm, the upper joint is the load carrier. When checking joints for wear, check the load carrier first. If it's okay and has never been replaced, you'll probably find that the unloaded joint is okay as well.

Before you check for wear, inspect the rubber seal of each ball joint. If it's torn, the joint must be replaced.

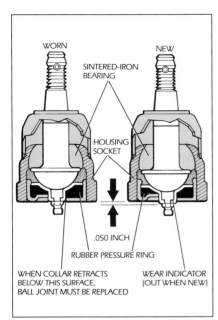

3 Wear-indicator ball joints show condition by position of grease fitting shoulder.

If your car has wear-indicator ball joints—as many produced after 1973 do—checking them is a simple matter. Before checking the joints, you must lower the car to the ground, or its wheels must be resting on ramps.

Most wear-indicator joints have a collar that protrudes from the lower surface of the joint and encircles the grease fitting (Fig. 3). As the joint wears, this collar sinks below the surface of the joint, indicating that replacement is necessary.

A second type of wear-indicator joint is used on some vehicles, including late-model Chryslers. On this type joint, you merely attempt to wiggle the grease fitting (Fig. 4). If you can move it with your hand, the joint is worn out.

If your car does not have wear-indicator ball joints, you'll have to measure free play with a dial indicator or check it by feel.

The ball joints of most front-wheel-drive cars that are equipped with MacPherson struts should be checked with the wheels off the ground and the car supported on jack stands. Grab each wheel at the top and bottom and shake it in and out while watching for movement of the steering knuckle relative to the ball joint. Any noticeable movement is grounds for replacement.

To induce movement in a loaded

joint, relieve the load. If your car has loaded lower joints (spring on lower arm), lift the car and relocate the jack stands under the lower control arms, as close to the ball joints as possible.

If your car has loaded upper joints, wedge a block of wood between each upper control arm and the frame, with the wheels resting on ramps or with jack stands under the lower control arms. Then lift the car, locate the jack stands under the frame, and lower the car to rest on them.

Ball joints are excessively worn if they permit too much sideways movement (radial play) or up and down movement (axial play). To measure axial movement, mount a dial indicator so that its stem rests against the bottom surface of the spindle assembly (knuckle). The stem should be parallel to an imaginary line that runs through the center of both ball joints. Insert a pry bar between the bottom of the tire and the floor and lift the wheel. Watch the indicator to see how much movement the joint permits. The figure should be less than the tolerance listed in your service manual.

To check radial movement, mount the indicator so that its stem is in contact with the edge of the wheel and perpendicular to the wheel. When checking an upper joint, locate the indicator at the top of the wheel. For a lower joint, locate it at the bottom of the wheel. Push the wheel in and out and watch the indicator. (Make sure that any motion is not the result of in-

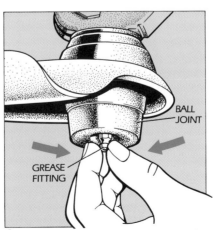

4 Other wear-indicator joints reveal their condition when you wiggle the grease fitting.

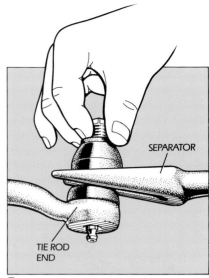

5 To prevent boot tearing, insert separator carefully between rod end and dust boot.

correct wheel bearing adjustment.) Radial movement maximum is 0.25 in., at the edge of the wheel.

CHECKING ROD ENDS, IDLER ARMS

For most cars, there are no specific procedures for checking tie rod ends and idler arms, but a little common sense is all that's needed. For the driveway technican, the most practical way to check the four tie rod ends of a car with parallelogram steering or the two outer rod ends of a rack-and-pinion system is to simply grab the tie rods and shake them vigorously. The tie rod ends should not be sloppy or loose. Rod ends must be preloaded, but even a brand new one allows some horizontal movement. A good joint should show little or no vertical movement. Missing or torn dust boots are also grounds for replacement.

To check an idler arm, push the end of the arm that is attached to the center link up and down. It should show little or no vertical movement.

Examine the bellows boots that cover the inner tie rod ends of rack-and-pinion cars for cracks, splits, or other physical damage. If they're not in good condition, replace them. On cars with power rack-and-pinion, fluid in the boot can be a sign of leaking seals. Manual racks with lubricant in the boot are normal.

To check the inner tie rod end, squeeze the bellows boot and feel around for the rod end. With one

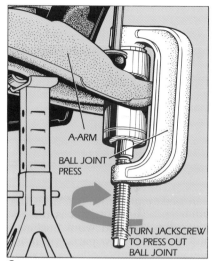

6 A screw-type ball joint press is required for servicing many GM and Chrysler cars.

hand on the rod end, push and pull on the tire. If the rod end seems to be loose, it should be replaced.

CHECKING SWAY BAR COMPONENTS

A loose sway bar will make a clunking noise every time you turn or hit a bump. Check the bushings and links that join it to the control arm and the bushings that secure it to the frame. If any are worn, broken, deteriorated, or missing, they must be replaced.

BALL JOINT REPLACEMENT

You'll need a ball joint separator—a wide-slot pickle fork—to replace ball joints on any car. For cars that have press-in type joints, you'll need a ball-joint press as well. This tool can usually be rented from the parts store when you purchase the new ball joints. Some Chrysler and Ford models have joints that are secured by rivets, so you'll need a good chisel to service these cars. The ball joints used on front-wheel-drive Fords and many Japanese imports cannot be removed. If joints are worn, replace lower control arms.

If you're not sure how the ball joints in your car are attached to the control arm, consult your service manual before attempting the job.

To replace load-carrying lower ball joints on most cars, loosen the lug nuts on both front wheels, and

lift the vehicle with your floor jack. Place a set of jack stands under the frame and remove the wheels. Lift the car, remove the stands from under the frame and relocate them under the lower control arms, as close to the ball joints as possible. Lower the car until it is resting on the stands.

Disengage the tie rod ends from the steering arm using a tie rod end separator or narrow pickle fork (Fig. 5). Insert the pickle fork between the rod end and its rubber boot so that you won't tear the boot when you knock the rod end off the steering arm. If you tear the boot, replace the rod end. A more expensive jackscrew-type separator is used for releasing rod ends that will be reused. This tool won't tear the boot.

Make sure that the lower control arm is firmly supported by the jack stand, then remove the cotter pin from the ball-joint retaining nut and unscrew the nut. Reinstall the nut approximately three turns, then insert your ball-joint separator between the steering knuckle and ball joint and hammer it in until the joint is disengaged from the knuckle. Unscrew the nut. If you can't unscrew it by hand, the jack stand is not supporting the control arm. Once the joint is completely disengaged from the knuckle, lift the knuckle and upper control arm assembly clear of the ball joint and support them.

If you're working on a car with pressed-in joints, install the ball-joint press on the joint and control arm, following the directions included with the press (Fig. 6). Then, tighten the jackscrew on the press until the ball joint drops out of the control arm. Inspect the tapered hole in the steering knuckle and remove any dirt. If the hole is out of round, the steering knuckle assembly must be replaced.

Once you're sure the knuckle is okay, reverse the press, and, using the appropriate adapters, install the new joint. Torque the nut to spec and install the cotter pin. Don't back off the nut to insert the pin; tighten it a bit more.

On cars with riveted joints, simply chisel the rivetheads off after disengaging the ball joint from the steering knuckle. Be careful not to damage the control arm with your chisel. Inspect the steering knuckle as described above. Then install a

new joint, using the bolts that came with it.

A third type of joint, much less common than the other two, has a threaded body and screws into the control arm. It can be removed with a large socket and breaker bar. The new joint must be torqued to spec.

The replacement of load-carrying upper joints is similar. A block of wood is wedged between the upper control arm and frame to relieve the load on the joint so it can be removed. If you're unable to support your upper control arm in this manner, check the service manual for specific instructions.

The replacement procedure for non-load-carrying upper joints is approximately the same as that for lower joints. Because the rivets used to hold many upper joints are on top of the control arm, you may not be able to reach them with a hammer and chisel. If this is the case, drill them out from below, using a 1/8-in. drill bit. Drill right in the center of each rivet to a depth of about 1/4-in., then drive the rivets out with a punch or drift.

To replace joints on most front-wheel-drive cars with removable joints, unscrew the clamp bolt that secures the ball-joint stud in the steering knuckle and disengage the joint from the knuckle (Fig. 7). You might have to tap it out with a mallet. Then, chisel off the rivets that secure the joint to the control arm or, on cars with pressed-in joints, remove and replace them with a ball-joint press.

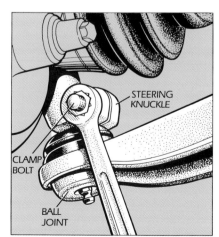

7 On many front-drive cars, ball joints are retained in the knuckle by a clamp bolt.

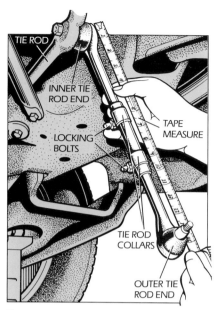

8 Measure existing tie rod length in order to get an approximate alignment setting.

REPLACING TIE ROD ENDS

A separator is needed for tie rod end service. Make sure you get a pickle fork with a narrow slot between the tangs.

To replace any of the four tie rod ends on a car with parallelogram steering linkage or an outer end on a car with rack-and-pinion steering, remove the nut that secures the rod end to the steering arm or center link. In most cases, you'll have to pull a cotter pin from the nut before you can loosen it. In some cases, you may find that the rod end is secured with a locking nut. Locking nuts cannot be reused.

Separate the rod end from the center link or steering arm by driving the pickle fork in between the rod end and its mount. On cars with parallelogram steering, measure from the center of the tie rod's other end to the center of the rod end you plan to replace and record this figure (Fig. 8). Then loosen the locking bolt on the tie rod collar and unscrew the faulty rod end.

On cars with rack-and-pinion steering, measure from the center of the outer rod end to the boot-retaining groove on the inner rod end, then unscrew the rod end.

Install the new tie rod end and screw it in until the rod length is equal to the measurement you recorded earlier. This will give you an approximate toe setting that will allow you to drive the car to an alignment shop.

Several types of inner tie rod ends are used on cars with rack-and-pinion steering. Procedures vary significantly, so consult your service manual.

REPLACING AN IDLER ARM

To replace a worn idler arm, remove the cotter pin and nut or the locking nut that secures it to the center link. Then, use your tie rod end separator to disengage it from the center link. Unbolt the bracket that joins the idler arm to the frame. On some cars, you'll have to access the nuts through holes in the frame. Install the new arm, tightening the retaining bolts to 35 lb.-ft. or the spec provided in your manual. Check the taper on the center link for damage before reattaching it to the arm.

REPLACING SWAY BAR BUSHINGS

To remove a typical sway bar link, hold the bolt head on one end of the link and remove the nut from the other end. Once the nut is off, remove the link and worn bushings and install the new parts. On most applications, the bushings are installed above and below the sway bar and the control arm. A washer backs up each bushing.

Repeat the procedure on the other side, then remove each frame-mount bracket and replace the rubber bushings that surround the sway bar. If you don't find any bushings when you remove the brackets, the old ones probably deteriorated and fell out. If this is the case, you've located the source of an annoying clunk.

Don't forget that an alignment check is essential following the replacement of tie rod ends or ball joints. Also, chassis parts are only part of the handling and steering equation. Equally important are the vehicle's ride height, springs and shocks, tires, and steering box.

How to Stop
STEERING SHIMMY

A ripple in the pavement ahead is a visual warning. You white-knuckle the steering wheel, and get ready. As soon as your tires meet it, a jarring, back-and-forth shimmy is transmitted through the steering linkage right to your sweaty palms. It's enough to make your hair gray and your tires bald.

A bottle of hair dye and a new set of tires are not the recommended fix. Instead, try a few hours on the creeper and, in most cases, a relatively modest investment in new parts.

NARROWING IT DOWN

The diagnosis of steering wheel shimmy is sometimes the toughest part of the job. Potential causes of the problem on both front- and rear-drive cars include tires or wheels that are out-of-balance or out-of-round, excessive wheel runout, a blister on a tire, loose wheel bearings, worn steering linkage parts, and worn ball joints.

When shimmy is induced by a pavement bump it usually indicates that steering linkage parts are at fault. Shimmy that is noticeable only at certain speeds may be the result of tire/wheel imbalance.

Shimmy induced by braking can sometimes be caused by loose wheel bearings. Shimmy that occurs constantly may well be the result of a runout or out-of-round problem.

But none of these are hard and fast rules. If, for example, the shimmy is most noticeable when one wheel hits a bump, jump ahead to the trouble-shooting procedure called "Steering Linkage Slop."

If you don't know where to start, begin at the beginning.

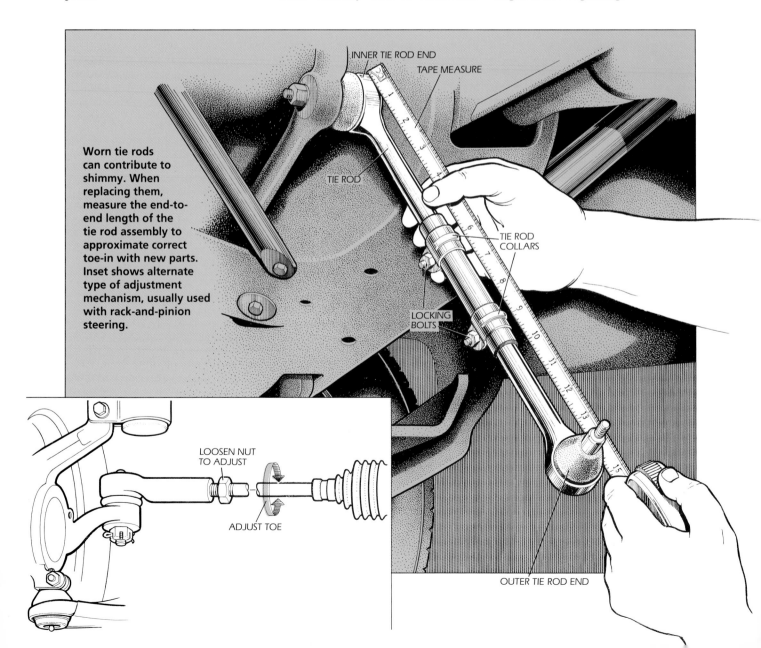

Worn tie rods can contribute to shimmy. When replacing them, measure the end-to-end length of the tie rod assembly to approximate correct toe-in with new parts. Inset shows alternate type of adjustment mechanism, usually used with rack-and-pinion steering.

INNER TIE ROD END
TAPE MEASURE
TIE ROD
TIE ROD COLLARS
LOCKING BOLTS
LOOSEN NUT TO ADJUST
ADJUST TOE
OUTER TIE ROD END

TIRES FIRST

A common cause of shimmy that is accompanied by vibration or a thumping noise is a tire bump or blister. So, before we start looking for more serious problems, lift the front end of the car and support it with sturdy jack stands in the jacking positions recommended in your owner's manual. With the wheels clear of the ground, carefully examine the tread and sidewalls of each front tire. A bump on the tread will usually cause uneven wear.

WHEEL BEARINGS

Because some of our other checks are dependent on proper front wheel bearing adjustment, and because a loose bearing can contribute to a shimmy problem, it's important to make sure the bearings are okay before moving on (Fig. 1).

To clean, adjust, and repack the front wheel bearings of a rear-drive car, remove the grease caps by gripping them with sliding-jaw pliers and rocking them back and forth slightly. Then remove the cotter pin, castellated nut lock, and outer bearing.

If your car is fitted with drum brakes, attempt to remove the drums. If they won't budge, use a brake adjusting tool to back off the adjustment. You'll have to lift the self-adjusting lever away from the star wheel with a small screwdriver.

To remove disc brake rotors, simply disengage the caliper assembly and suspend it from the steering knuckle arm with a piece of wire.

With the drum or rotor off its spindle, use a ¾-in. drift to drive the inner wheel bearing and seal out of the hub. Take care not to catch the edge of the bearing race with the drift. A few taps should disengage the bearing and seal. Clean the bearings in solvent and check them carefully for signs of pitting or other surface damage. Clean the races inside the hub and examine them as well. Some minor discoloration of race and bearing is okay, but any damage is grounds for replacement.

To repack a wheel bearing, scoop up a handful of wheel bearing grease, cup your hand, and push the side of the bearing cage into your palm. Force the grease past the rollers and continue until grease oozes

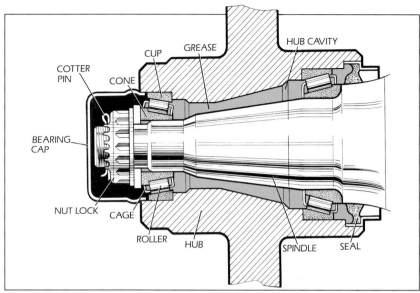

1 Adjust spindle nut, hidden under nut lock, to allow virtually no end play in bearing.

out of the top of the cage. Then rotate the bearing and do it again.

Reinstall the bearings with a new grease seal. Assemble all the parts carefully and tighten the hub nut to about 10 lb.-ft. while rotating the wheel. Then back the nut off and retighten it with your fingers. Position the nut lock slot so that it aligns with the hole in the spindle and install the cotter pin. End play should be almost imperceptible, about 0.001 to 0.003 in.

The front wheel bearings of front-drive cars are not serviceable or adjustable. If wheel looseness and/or noise indicates that a bearing has failed, the bearing assembly must be replaced. Special tools are required for this job, so you may want to delegate it to your mechanic. If you do decide to do it yourself, you'll need the factory service manual for your car.

TIRES AND WHEELS

Now that we're certain that the wheel bearings are in good condition and properly adjusted, let's check those tires and wheels for radial and lateral runout. Radial runout is the difference between the high and low points on the circumference—the tread area—of the tire. Lateral runout is the wobble of the wheel and/or tire.

Before making any measurements, drive the car a couple of miles to eliminate any temporary

flat spots on the tires. Raise the front end of the car and support it on jack stands, following all normal safety precautions and using the prescribed jacking points.

To check for radial runout, you'll need a runout gauge, which is nothing more than a dial indicator with a wheel on the bottom of its stem. Mount the indicator in such a way that its stem is perpendicular to the tire and its wheel is in contact with the center of the tread but in an area without grooves (Fig. 2).

Slowly rotate the wheel and tire. Radial runout of more than 0.060 in. will usually cause shimmy or shake. Sometimes, 0.045 is enough.

Now check for lateral runout. Place the runout gauge with the stem perpendicular to the tire's sidewall near the shoulder. It must be in contact with a smooth area all the way around. Rotate the wheel. Lateral runout of more than 0.080 in. could cause a steering shimmy.

If either of these measurements is out of spec, remove the wheel in question and clean the mounting face of both the wheel and hub. Rotate the wheel a half turn so that it will mount in a different position. Remount it, torquing all the wheel nuts down to spec in two steps. Torque in a cross pattern as indicated in Fig. 3. Lube the threads and chamfer with motor oil or antiseize compound. Look for the correct torque spec in your owner's manual. Repeat the runout checks. If the

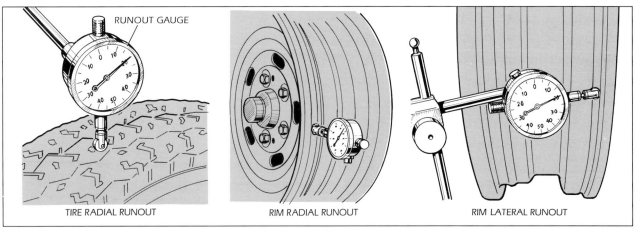

TIRE RADIAL RUNOUT   RIM RADIAL RUNOUT   RIM LATERAL RUNOUT

2 With runout gauge, measure radial runout with tire warm from short drive. Also measure lateral runout (see text). Then demount tire from rim and measure rim radial and lateral runout at tire-mounting flanges at inboard and outboard sides of the rim. Don't try to measure runout at the edge of the rim, as it has no effect on total rim/tire runout. Don't try to measure from center of rim without demounting tire. If rim shows excess runout, sometimes tire can be rotated relative to rim 180°, otherwise rim or tire must be replaced.

problem hasn't been solved by re-mounting the wheel, mark the point of maximum runout on the tire, wheel, and stud (Fig. 4).

Then have the tire removed from the wheel, remount the wheel in the same position relative to the hub as before, and measure lateral and radial runout on the wheel itself in the positions indicated in Fig. 2. If possible, check radial runout on the outboard side. If wheel design makes this impossible, check on the inboard side.

For steel wheels, radial runout should be no more than 0.040 in. while lateral runout should be no more than 0.045 in. For aluminum wheels, both lateral and radial runout should be less than 0.030 in.

- If either runout measurement is excessive with the tire mounted, but wheel runout is okay, replace tire.

- If lateral or radial runout was excessive on both the wheel and the tire, install a known good wheel and check runout on the wheel again. If it's still excessive, the brake disc or wheel hub is at fault and will have to be replaced.
- If runout is okay with a good wheel, installed, remount the tire on the good wheel and re-check. If runout is now within limits, your old wheel is defective and must be replaced.
- If the wheel is within spec but shows some radial runout and radial runout was excessive on the tire, you might be able to effect a cure by remounting the tire in a different position on the wheel.
- If wheel radial runout is greatest near the original chalk mark—the one you made when you checked tire

runout—remount the tire 180° from its original position and recheck runout. If it's still excessive you'll have to replace the tire, or have it trued on a tire-truing machine. Unless the tire is almost brand new, this will probably remove so much rubber that you will be better off just replacing the tire.

Once you're satisfied that your wheels and tires are true and free of bumps or blisters, have them dynamically balanced. A bubble balancer is not an acceptable substitute.

STEERING LINKAGE SLOP

If you haven't located the cause of your problem yet—or if the symptoms lead you to believe that the condition is steering linkage related—it's time to crawl under the greasy side and check linkage parts.

Your car is equipped with either rack-and-pinion or parallelogram steering (Fig. 5). It's easy to tell which. A parallelogram linkage consists of two outer tie rods that are joined to a center link on one end and to the wheel's steering knuckles on the other end. The center link is supported by an idler arm and pitman arm. The pitman arm is joined to a frame-mounted steering box.

A rack-and-pinion system consists of nothing more than the steering box itself. This long, tubular

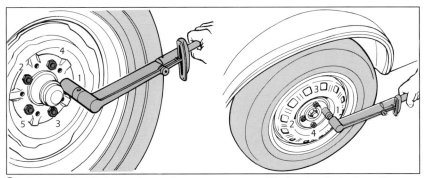

3 Torque wheels in an alternating pattern to avoid wheel or hub distortion. Check your owner's manual for the correct torque spec.

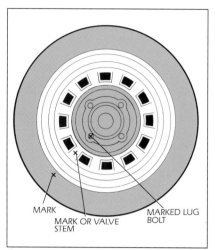

4 Before removing tire to check wheel runout, mark it relative to both wheel and hub.

component is fitted with bellows and tie rods at each end. The tie rods are joined directly to the steering knuckles.

After steering linkage repairs, you should have your wheels aligned at a shop equipped with a four-wheel alignment machine. Some repairs may change the alignment angles. What's more, the shimmy problem could be partially due to misalignment, particularly because misalignment can cause the linkage parts to wear prematurely.

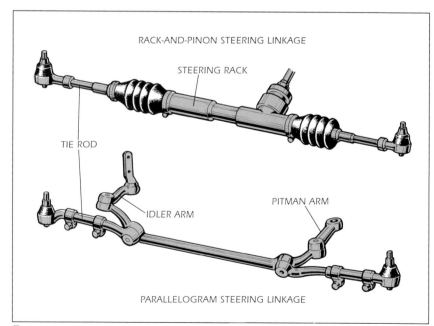

5 Parallelogram front-steering system has more moving parts, more places to wear out.

IDLER ARM SERVICE

To check the idler arm of a car with parallelogram steering, grab the end of the idler arm that is joined to the center link and push up and down as hard as you can. It should move only about ⅛ in. or less (Fig. 6). An idler arm that clunks ½ in. or so is a classic cause of violent intermittent shimmy.

To replace a defective idler arm, remove the nut that secures it to the center link. You'll need a tie rod end separator—commonly called a pickle fork—to disengage the idler from the center link. You can purchase one at any auto parts store for a modest amount. Disengage the idler by driving the pickle fork between it and the center link.

Next, unbolt the bracket that joins the idler arm to the frame. Install the new idler, tightening the bolts to the spec indicated in your factory service manual, probably around 35 lb.-ft.

Examine the hole in the center link. It should be tapered and uniformly shaped. If it's out-of-round or gouged, the center link should be replaced. Once you're certain that the center-link hole is okay, insert the rod end in the center link and reinstall the retaining nut and cotter pin. If your idler arm was attached with a locking nut, purchase a new one. *Never* reuse jam-type locking nuts.

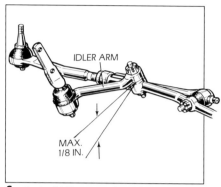

6 End of idler arm should show only slight up-and-down movement. GM specifies ⅛ in.

TIE ROD END SERVICE

To check the tie rod ends of a parallelogram linkage, grab the tie rods and shake them vigorously. The rod ends should not be preloaded, sloppy, or loose. Even a new rod end allows some horizontal movement but little or no vertical movement. Examine the rod end dust boots carefully. A tear is grounds for replacement.

With rack-and-pinion steering, check the bellows boots for cracks, splits, or other damage. If they're not in good condition, replace them. Check the outer rod ends for looseness by shaking them back and forth as described above. To check the inner rod ends, squeeze the boot and locate the rod end. Then, with one hand on the rod end, push and pull on the tire. If the rod end feels loose, it should be replaced.

To replace any of the four tie rod ends on a parallelogram linkage or the outer rod end on a rack-and-pinion system, remove the nut and cotter pin or locking nut from the rod end stud. To disengage the rod end from the center link and/or steering knuckle, drive your pickle fork between the rod end and its mounting point.

Before removing the rod end from the link, check the overall length of the link. On parallelogram systems, measure from the center of one rod end to the center of the other rod end (see illustration on page 294). On rack-and-pinion linkages, measure from the center of the outer end to the boot retaining groove on the inner rod end.

Once you've recorded the measurement, loosen the rod end clamps

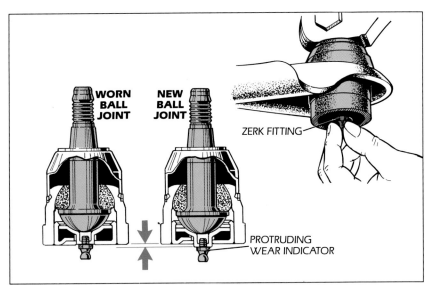

7 Wear-indicator ball joints provide visual evidence of wear. Check Chrysler-type by attempting to wiggle the Zerk fitting. If it moves, the joint is worn.

used on most parallelogram systems or the locking nut used on most rack-and-pinion linkages and unscrew the rod end. Install the new rod end, tightening it until the rod length is equal to the measurement you recorded.

CHECKING BALL JOINTS

The steering knuckles of almost all cars are attached to the control arm or control arms with ball joints. Most cars with strut-type suspension have only one ball joint. Most cars with dual control arm suspension have two ball joints.

Checking ball joints used to be a difficult task, but because most cars are now equipped with wear-indicator ball joints, it's now quite easy. To check wear-indicator ball joints, the car must be on the ground or resting on ramps. (If you find that your car is not equipped with wear-indicator joints, refer to your service manual for specific instructions on checking ball-joint condition.)

Two types of wear-indicator joints are commonly used (Fig. 7).

Both types utilize the grease fitting as a measurement device. On the most common wear-indicator joints, a collar protrudes from the lower surface of the joint and encircles the grease fitting. As the joint wears out, this collar gradually sinks below the surface of the joint. If you can see a collar around the grease fitting of the ball joint, but it's no longer protruding, the ball joint should be replaced.

A second type of wear-indicator joint is used on some vehicles, including late-model Chryslers. With this type, you can check the joint by attempting to wiggle the grease nipple, or Zerk fitting. If you can move it with your fingers, the joint is worn out.

Ball-joint replacement is relatively easy on cars that have riveted, bolted, or screw-in ball joints. On cars that have press-in ball joints, including most GM makes, it can be very difficult. Because the procedure varies, you'll need a service manual. You'll also need a ball-joint separator (a wide-slot pickle fork), and jack stands.

Read all the instructions in your factory service manual before you decide to attempt the job. You may find that expensive special tools are required. Some of these, like the ball-joint press required for press-in joints, may be available through tool-rental outlets or your auto parts store.

For less experienced Saturday mechanics, ball-joint replacement is probably best left to a professional.

How to Plug
POWER STEERING LEAKS

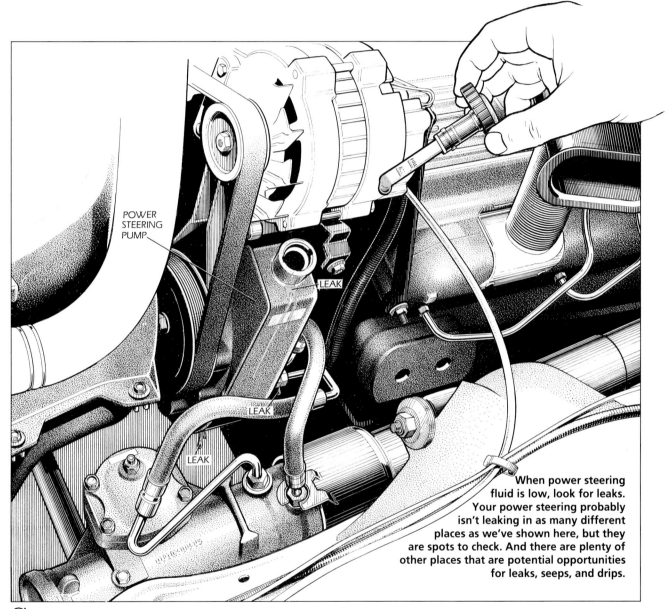

POWER
STEERING
PUMP

LEAK

LEAK

LEAK

When power steering
fluid is low, look for leaks.
Your power steering probably
isn't leaking in as many different
places as we've shown here, but they
are spots to check. And there are plenty of
other places that are potential opportunities
for leaks, seeps, and drips.

S moke billows out from under the hood of your car. The air fills with an obnoxious sulfur odor. Suddenly, the steering goes heavy. You feel as though you're at the tiller of a ten-ton truck.

You stop your car, leap out, and throw the hood up. Everything is covered with oil—the exhaust manifolds are smoking.

The cause of this mess? Quite possibly a big leak on the high-pressure side of your power steering system.

But power steering leaks may not always be quite so obvious. A leaking seal or low-pressure hose, for example, may only leave puddles of hydraulic fluid in your driveway. In either case, the fluid loss can cause a sudden loss of steering assist.

POWER STEERING BASICS

Although some power steering systems have grown more complex in efforts to improve "feel," basic operation is simple. When the engine is running, hydraulic fluid is pressurized by a belt-driven pump mounted on the engine and delivered to the steering box by a high-pressure hose. Within the steering box, a piston is connected to the steering linkage. When the steering wheel is turned, a valve routes high-pressure oil to the piston. This helps the driver move the steering gear and turn the wheels. Low-pressure oil is directed back to the steering pump reservoir through a return hose (Fig. 1).

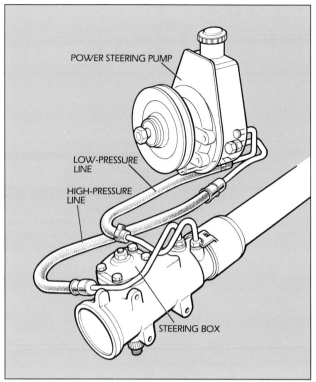

1 Typical system consists of steering box, pump, and high- and low-pressure hoses.

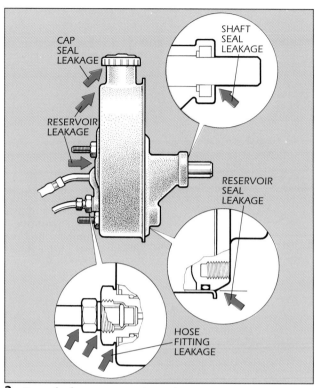

2 Pump leaks can occur at cap, hose connections, reservoir seal, and body or shaft seal.

On most cars, the pump reservoir is mounted directly on the pump. On some cars, primarily imports, the reservoir is remote-mounted and connected to the pump by means of a second return hose.

LOCATING A LEAK

Some power steering leaks will be obvious and easy to spot. Others may be quite elusive. To track down a leak, fill the reservoir with fluid. (Make sure you don't overfill it. If the reservoir is already overfilled, you may have located the source of your leak!)

Clean any areas that are covered with fluid. Then, with the engine idling, have a helper turn the steering wheel left to right and back several times.

Trace the system: pump to high-pressure hose to steering box, steering box to low-pressure hose to pump. On cars so equipped, carefully check the remote reservoir and its hose connections. In addition to all hoses and connections, check the front shaft seal area on the pump (behind the pulley), the junction between the pump and its attached reservoir (where applicable), and all seal areas on the steering box.

HOSES AND REMOTE RESERVOIRS

Both low- and high-pressure hoses are subject to failure, but it's easy to distinguish between the two. A leaking high-pressure hose will squirt fluid all over. A leaking low-pressure hose will only drip fluid.

The most common cause of a power steering fluid leak is a burst high-pressure hose. The hose separates from the metal collar and fitting. It may seem as though you can reattach the failed hose to its failed fitting, but believe us—you can't. It'll blow out again. Replacement is the only fix.

Before replacing the hose, disconnect the negative terminal of the battery and turn the front wheels to the straightahead position. Use a tubing wrench to unbolt the hose-end fittings from the power steering pump and the steering box. Catch spilled fluid as you disconnect the fittings.

Some power steering hoses are sealed by means of an O-ring in the pump or steering box fitting. If you find an O-ring, replace it with a new one. Use only the specified replacement O-ring, which is usually provided with the new hose. If you need only the O-ring, you should be able to purchase the right piece at the dealer's parts counter.

Reinstall the new hose in exactly the same position as the old one. If you use an aftermarket hose, it may be slightly longer than the old one. That's okay, but make sure the hose won't be subjected to chafing or other abuses. Don't twist the hose, and be sure it isn't in contact with other components.

Tighten the hose-end fittings with a tubing wrench. Don't overtighten the fittings: You could damage the tube nut wall or—where applicable—the O-ring seal, either of which will cause a leak. Use only firm wrist pressure. If you have a torque wrench and "crow-foot" open-end or tubing wrench attachment, torque the lines to the manufacturer's spec.

Like the high-pressure hoses, some low-pressure hoses are made with permanently attached fittings.

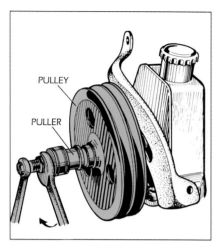

3 To remove pulley, hold pilot bolt while turning the shaft nut counterclockwise.

But most hoses are attached to steel tubing with crimped or worm-drive clamps. When you replace a low-pressure hose that is not equipped with permanent fittings, use worm-drive clamps to secure it in place. Don't attempt to reuse the crimped clamps from the original equipment.

A remote reservoir—one that's not attached to the pump—is obviously a prime candidate if your leak is a slow, steady drip. Replacement is simply a matter of removing the hoses and installing a new reservoir. Attach the hoses with worm-drive clamps.

After replacing hoses or a remote reservoir, bleed the system as described at the end of this article. The bleeding procedure should follow any power steering system repair in which fluid is released.

AT THE PUMP

The most common leak points on power steering pumps are the front shaft seal and the fluid reservoir or reservoir seal. But there are other possibilities to consider (Fig. 2). One is the cap gasket. Make sure it is in place before you start taking things apart, or you could turn a simple two-minute repair into a messy two-hour job. Other possibilities include loose rear cover bolts, if applicable, and a damaged or cracked pump body.

To remove the pump, disconnect the hoses at the pump. Hold a can under the fittings as you disconnect them to catch fluid. Once the hoses

have been disconnected, keep the free ends in a raised position to prevent oil spills. Then cap or tape the ends of the hoses to keep dirt out. Cap or tape the pump fittings as well.

With hoses disconnected, remove the pump belt. To do this you'll have to either loosen the pump-mounting bolts and rotate the pump toward the engine, or, on cars so equipped, loosen the pump jackscrew adjustment. Once the belt is off, remove the pump retaining bolts and lift the pump out of the engine compartment.

To remove a power steering pump pulley, you'll need a special hub puller designed specifically for power steering pumps (Fig. 3). A universal model that works on almost all cars is available from your better auto parts stores. The same tool is used to press the pulley back onto the shaft once repairs have been completed.

Before removing the pulley, drain as much fluid as possible from the pump through the reservoir neck. Then install the removal tool on the pulley hub. Make sure the tool's pilot bolt bottoms in the pump shaft by turning the nut all the way to the top of the pilot bolt. With most tools, you remove the pulley by holding the pilot bolt and turning the nut counterclockwise. The same tool is used to press the pulley back onto the shaft once repairs have been completed. To install the pulley, hold the pilot bolt and turn the nut clockwise.

The reservoir is usually attached to the pump by means of mounting studs and a rubber O-ring. In most cases, you'll have to remove the mounting brackets from the pump to get at the reservoir. Before attempting to remove the reservoir, clean the exterior of the pump and reservoir with solvent. Then clamp the pump in a bench vise with soft jaws. On most pumps you'll have to remove the outlet fitting. On Ford pumps you'll have to remove the flow control valve as well.

Use new O-ring seals in all locations when reinstalling a new reservoir. Use a pick to remove O-rings from valves or fittings (Fig. 4).

To reinstall the reservoir, locate a new O-ring seal on the housing. Apply petroleum jelly to the O-ring and the inside edge of the reservoir. Place the reservoir over the pump

and align any fitting holes with the respective holes in the pump. Push it into place.

To replace a leaking shaft seal on most pumps other than GM units, you'll have to completely disassemble and reassemble the pump. Unless you're very skilled at this type of work, we'd recommend buying the rebuilt unit. An aftermarket pump will probably cost quite a bit less than a new pump from the dealer.

You can, however, usually replace the pump shaft seal on a GM power steering pump without disassembling the pump itself.

First, you should protect the pump driveshaft with steel shim stock wrapped around the shaft and inserted between the shaft and the seal. Then use a chisel to cut the seal. Remove the shim stock. Then remove the old seal with pliers.

Coat the new seal with power steering fluid, and carefully drive the new seal into the pump housing using a seal driver or a deep well socket that will slip over the driveshaft but whose outer circumference rests on the metal seal carrier (Fig. 5).

AT THE BOX

The most common leak point on a recirculating-ball power steering box is the pitman shaft seal. If the seal is bad, fluid will drip or squirt from the shaft area. The underside of the car may be completely covered with power steering fluid.

Before you can extract the pitman shaft seal, you have to remove the pitman arm. Once again, a spe-

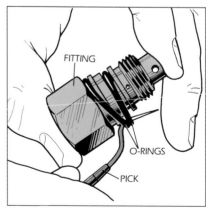

4 Remove old O-rings from a flow control valve or fitting with a sharp pick.

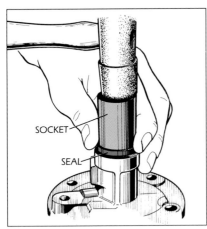

5 Install new seals with a mallet and a socket just slightly smaller than the seal.

cial tool is required. It's a simple hub-puller that fits snugly around the shaft end of the pitman arm. You can rent or buy one at most auto parts stores.

To remove the pitman arm, unscrew its retaining nut. It may be locked in place with a cotter pin or lockwasher. Then slip the pitman arm puller over the shaft end of the arm and use a socket wrench or box wrench to tighten the hub-puller's jackscrew against the end of the pitman shaft (Fig. 6).

Once the pitman arm has been removed, clean the exposed end of the pitman shaft and the steering box housing with solvent.

Within the shaft housing you'll find a snap ring holding the seal in place. Remove this ring with your snap ring pliers.

Place newspaper and a drain pan on the floor under the pitman shaft area. Top off the power steering fluid if it's low, then start the engine and turn the wheels fully to the left. This should force the seals and washer out. (Most are fitted with two seals.)

Once the seals have been removed, inspect the housing and shaft. If the shaft is worn, rough, or pitted, you'll probably have to replace the steering box. Choose an appropriate rebuilt.

Find something you can use to drive the new seals in place. A deep well socket that contacts the outer edge of the seal will work on many applications. If you can't find anything that will do the job, you may have to purchase a seal installer. In

any case, make sure you drive the seal in straight and true. As with any seal of this type, you'll ruin it if you cock it going in.

Reinstall the pitman arm, lockwasher, and nut. Torque the pitman nut to spec.

AT THE RACK

Some rack-and-pinion steering box leaks are merely the result of a leaking hydraulic cylinder line. These lines, sealed with O-rings, join the cylinder at one end of the rack to the valve at the other end (Fig. 7). If the leak is coming from one of these lines, you should be able to spot it while your helper turns the steering wheel back and forth. That is, you should be able to spot it if you can *see* the rack. On some cars, it's buried behind the engine.

If access is okay, try tightening the line slightly. Don't muscle it down. You could strip the threads and ruin your steering box. Manufacturers provide torque specs for these fittings. Your best bet is to tighten the fittings with that previously mentioned torque wrench and "crow-foot" open-end or tubing wrench.

If tightening the fittings doesn't stop the leak, replacement is necessary. Replacing the seals and, if

necessary, the lines is a simple job, executed with a tubing wrench. Use the torque wrench if possible.

Some rack-and-pinion leaks are due to failure of other, internal seals. Most rack-and-pinion steering box leaks are, unfortunately, a symptom of a failed rack. In most cases, steering effort gets hard before the leakage begins. This hard steering effort is most noticeable when the car is cold.

The fix? Replace the rack with an aftermarket rebuilt unit. These aftermarket rebuilds are a relatively good buy, as compared to a new factory unit. Rebuilding the old rack yourself is a possibility, but it's an extremely difficult job and not recommended. You're liable to expend much effort and agony, spend a lot on parts and special tools, and end up with a rack that leaks or—worse yet—doesn't steer very well.

On many cars, however, removing and replacing the rack is relatively easy. By checking the procedure in your service manual, you should be able to determine if it's a job that you feel comfortable with. But you must have a factory service manual and a good set of jack stands or ramps. Observe all normal precautions for jacking and supporting a car. Plan on having the toe-in reset at an alignment shop when you're finished.

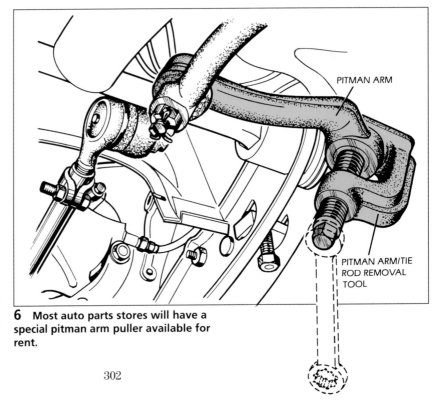

6 Most auto parts stores will have a special pitman arm puller available for rent.

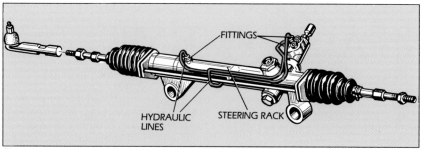

FITTINGS

HYDRAULIC LINES

STEERING RACK

7 Common leakage points include O-ring seals at either end of hydraulic cylinder lines.

BLEEDING THE SYSTEM

Following any steering repair in which hoses have been disconnected or parts removed, air will have to be bled from the system.

First, turn the wheels all the way to the left and add the manufacturer's recommended power steering fluid (see your owner's manual). Fill only to the COLD level as indicated on your steering reservoir dipstick.

Start the engine. With the engine at a fast idle speed, recheck the fluid level. If it's not up to the COLD level, add more fluid.

Turn the wheels from side to side several times without going all the way to full lock. Keep adding fluid gradually if necessary to maintain the level. Repeat this procedure until the fluid in the reservoir is normal in appearance. (Fluid with air in it will be lighter in color than normal fluid.)

Return the wheels to the center position, and run the engine for two or three minutes. Then road-test the car. Steering function should be normal and free of noise.

Recheck the fluid level and top off to the HOT level if necessary.

How to Check for Correct
WHEEL ALIGNMENT

While the basics of wheel alignment are within the scope of most Saturday mechanics, for lack of a $25,000 alignment rack and a place to set it up, most of us have to assign the job to a professional mechanic. But that doesn't have to mean turning one's back and hoping for the best. Alignment should be a joint venture between owner and technician.

Take care of the preliminaries. Be sure alignment is needed and make certain the job is done properly.

Many shops are using methods that are obsolete. If a technician speaks only in terms of *front*-wheel alignment, for instance, be wary. Front-wheel alignment is just about a dead issue, so unless it's a slip of the tongue, someone talking about front-wheel alignment is behind the times. Most cars today require alignment of all four wheels.

WHY ALIGNMENT?

Alignment—adjusting the suspension so the wheels roll straight and true—is a must if you want even tire wear, precise steering, and the most optimum fuel economy possible.

The second greatest cause of abnormal and/or rapid tire wear is misaligned wheels. (First, as it always has been, is underinflation.) Whatever the reason, abnormal tire wear can be spotted before it gets too bad by inspecting tires frequently (Fig. 1).

The most common symptom of misalignment is a drift or pull to one side. Other telltales are looseness in the steering wheel, a steering wheel

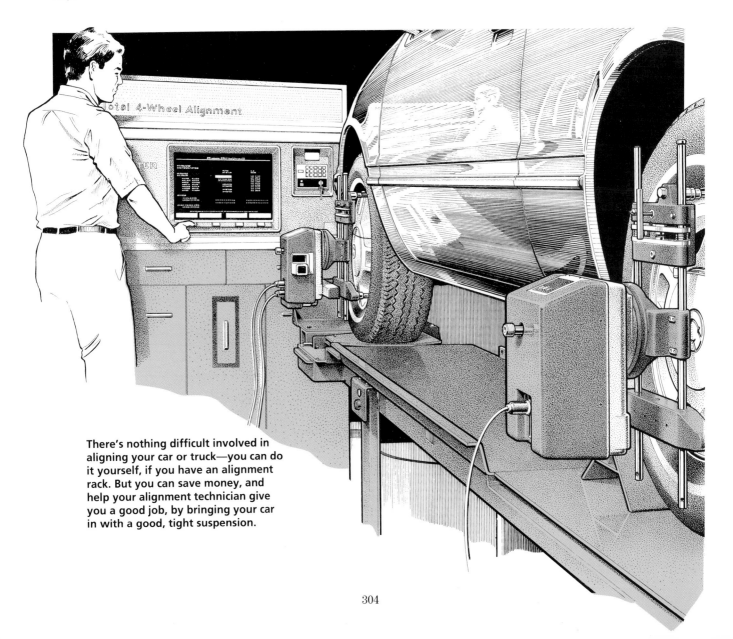

There's nothing difficult involved in aligning your car or truck—you can do it yourself, if you have an alignment rack. But you can save money, and help your alignment technician give you a good job, by bringing your car in with a good, tight suspension.

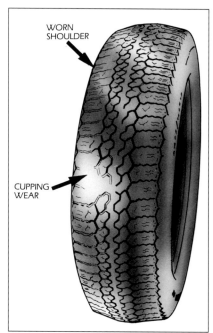

1 Cupping and rapid shoulder wear are probably from improperly adjusted toe-in.

that is off-center when front wheels are straight, a sensation that the car is wandering over the road, and high-effort steering. It's not unusual to feel misalignment at the steering wheel before tire wear becomes apparent, so that's the time to take care of it.

Vibration could also be symptomatic of misalignment, but misalignment is a secondary condition that crops up if vibration continues. Vibration is usually caused by unbalanced or out-of-round wheel/tire assemblies. Other reasons are excessive tire runout, drive shaft imbalance, and brake rotor/drum unevenness.

An unbalanced wheel/tire assembly—that is, an unequal weight distribution about the circumference of the assembly—and wheel misalignment are not the same thing, but they are interrelated. The constant bouncing of unbalanced wheel/tire assemblies will result in wear to suspension components, which in turn leads to misaligned wheels.

ROLL A FOUR

It's easy enough to determine if your car is a candidate for four-wheel alignment. If it's a front-wheel drive with independent or beam-axle sus-

pension at the rear, or if it's a rear-wheel-drive car equipped with independent rear suspension, you should have either a total four-wheel alignment or thrust-line alignment done (Fig. 2).

A thrust-line alignment measures the toe-angle of the rear wheels. The rear-wheel toe-angle measurement is used as a reference to adjust the alignment of the front wheels. The intent is to bring the front wheels into line with the rear wheels to assure more precise steering and the longest possible tire wear. If the toe-angle of the rear wheels doesn't meet the established specification, the rear suspension is damaged.

On cars with rear wheels whose camber-angle as well as toe-angle can be set, each wheel—front and rear—is adjusted individually to a precise position. This is called total four-wheel alignment. As long as suspension and steering components are not damaged, it automatically brings the thrust line of the rear wheels into line with the front wheels.

Owner's manuals aren't always clear whether total four-wheel alignment can be done for the particular car or if you must settle for thrust-line alignment, which is less

precise. If you don't know, ask your alignment shop or a dealer.

Some models in the four-wheel alignment category are Chrysler Corp. front-wheel-drive cars, Fo-MoCo front-wheel-drive cars except Fiesta, most full-size GM front-wheel-drive cars since '79 (also Corvette and Fiero), BMWs since '84, all Hondas except wagons, front-wheel-drive and '86–'87 rear-wheel-drive Mazdas, some Mitsubishi front- and rear-wheel-drive cars, Nissan Maxima and 300ZX, all Porsches, some Subarus, all Toyota front-wheel-drive cars as well as some rear-drive models, and rear-drive VWs.

Thrust-line alignment costs about $10 more than aligning the front wheels only, which owners of older rear-drive cars with solid rear-axle suspension systems still have done. Even they, however, can benefit from an occasional thrust-line alignment, because in time the rear wheels of cars with solid rear axles can go out of alignment.

Total four-wheel alignment costs about $10 more than thrust-line alignment, but this is only for putting the car on a four-wheel alignment machine and measuring angles. If alignment has to be reset, the charge

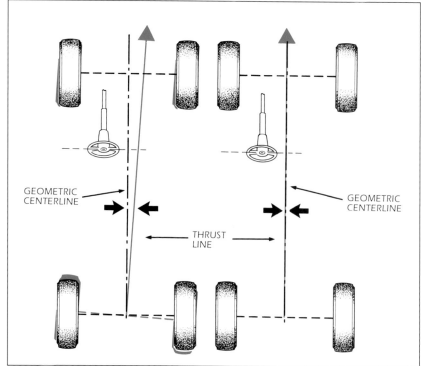

2 A complete four-wheel alignment is necessary to correct thrust that's off centerline.

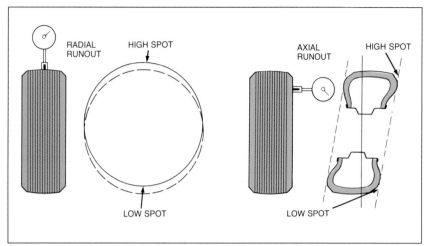

3 Radial or lateral runout is more likely to cause tire-shake than improper alignment.

is about $10 more per wheel—plus parts. It's not unusual, then, for a four-wheel alignment to cost almost $100.

WHAT YOU CAN DO YOURSELF

By doing some of the preliminary work on your own, you can assure yourself that the feel you're getting is really being caused by misalignment and not a condition that can be solved with a little air, for example.

An imbalance in tire inflation, which can cause drifting or pulling to one side, is easily detected. Just inflate both tires on the same end of the car to the same pressure.

A variance of a couple of pounds, even within the recommended spec range, can affect handling.

What about tire sizes and tread patterns? Are they the same, especially on the same end of the car? You can't expect good handling if tires are mismatched. Even replacing a partly worn tire with a new one—say for instance the spare—can make your car pull because of the difference in the diameter between the new and old tire. And don't get your car aligned when the tires are mismatched, because you'll be out of alignment again as soon as you replace them. The alignment rack assumes that all four tires are identical, and properly inflated.

Two kinds of sensations you'll feel coming through the steering wheel with modern cars are lateral drift and torque-steer pull. Lateral drift occurs when driving at a constant speed and indicates wheel misalignment. Torque-steer pull affects some front-wheel-drive cars only during quick acceleration.

Torque steer can be aggravated by misalignment. The car actually steers to the left or right unless you fight the steering wheel to keep it going straight.

To pin down lateral drift and torque-steer pull, drive the car on a straight and level surface. To test for lateral drift, maintain a constant speed, take your hands off the steering wheel briefly, and note the direction and severity of the drift. To test for torque steer, accelerate quickly to a speed of 40 to 50 mph from a speed of 10 to 15 mph and note the direction and severity of the pull.

Now, switch the front tires from side to side and do the test again. If the drift or pull is the same, you've probably got a vehicle-related problem—often misalignment, but maybe a steering or brake system malfunction. If the drift or pull has changed direction or its severity is reduced, it is being caused by the tires. In fact, just switching tires from side to side may get rid of the drift or reduce the pull to an acceptable level.

If not, return the tires to their original positions and then switch the right front and right rear. Does this get rid of or reduce the severity of the drift or pull? If the answer is no, put tires back where they were, switch the left front with the left rear, and test again. If the condition doesn't clear up, you can have the tires checked for runout. A tire with runout wants to roll in an arc, which can cause a car to drift or pull (Fig. 3).

Incidentally, car manufacturers specify in maintenance instructions how often tire rotation should be done to avoid the feel tire wear can present and also to get maximum mileage from tires. Where the tire rotation interval is not spelled out, rotate at 6,000 to 8,000 miles (assuming you're starting with a new set) and then every 18,000 to 24,000 miles. If your owner's manual doesn't state how to rotate tires, cross-rotation is recommended for all-season tires, front-to-rear for directional-tread tires.

ALIGNMENT? NOT YET

Whether you do it yourself or have a professional do it, all components in the front and rear of your car should be inspected before alignment. If a worn or bent part stays put, doing the alignment is a waste of money. The condition you hope to clear up will continue to ruin tires. All of the following must be in good shape to achieve accurate alignment:

- Coil and/or leaf springs or torsion bars.
- Tie-rod ends and sleeves, idler and pitman arms, rack-mounting bushings, sway bar, steering linkages, and steering gear.
- Wheel bearings, wheel spindles, and ball joints.
- Upper and lower front- and rear-control arm bushings, strut rod or brake reaction-rod bushings, and stabilizer link and frame bushings.
- Struts and shock absorbers, strut mountings and bearings, and shock mounting bolts and bushings.

It's possible to inspect all of the above in your driveway, but you'll need to safely set the car on jackstands. This unloads the suspension, allowing you to properly check for loose bushings and the like. It takes

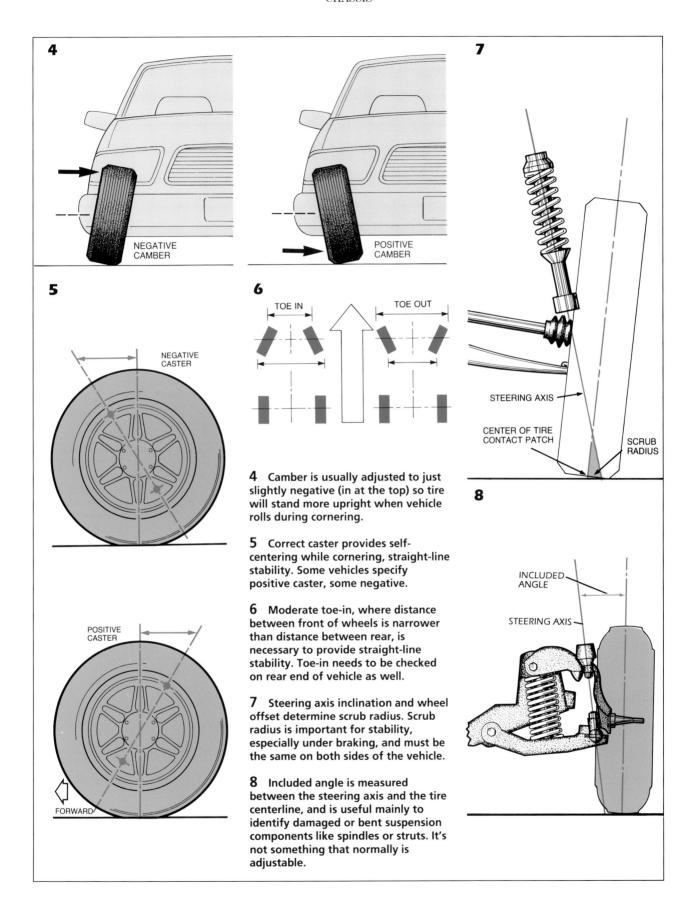

4 Camber is usually adjusted to just slightly negative (in at the top) so tire will stand more upright when vehicle rolls during cornering.

5 Correct caster provides self-centering while cornering, straight-line stability. Some vehicles specify positive caster, some negative.

6 Moderate toe-in, where distance between front of wheels is narrower than distance between rear, is necessary to provide straight-line stability. Toe-in needs to be checked on rear end of vehicle as well.

7 Steering axis inclination and wheel offset determine scrub radius. Scrub radius is important for stability, especially under braking, and must be the same on both sides of the vehicle.

8 Included angle is measured between the steering axis and the tire centerline, and is useful mainly to identify damaged or bent suspension components like spindles or struts. It's not something that normally is adjustable.

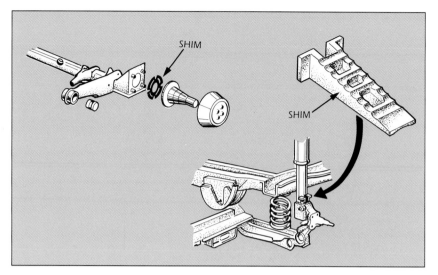

9 Rear-wheel alignment on some vehicles is adjusted by shimming the rear stub axle (far left and left). Sometimes both toe-in and camber are adjustable (far left), sometimes only camber (bottom). On some cars, adjustments can only be made by replacing components.

forty-five minutes to an hour to really inspect everything properly.

Before driving the car onto the alignment rack, discuss with the technician the way it should be loaded. For example, if you're a salesperson who keeps heavy carrying cases in the trunk, you'll want them in the trunk as alignment is being done. Removing them, having wheels aligned, and then returning them to the trunk will throw alignment off when you hit the road. If you're a 250-pounder, maybe you too should be in the car as alignment is being done. Most alignment shops keep sandbags around for just this purpose. Don't forget about that snowplow that's mounted to the front of your pickup all winter—it will certainly affect the way your alignment should be done.

FIGURING THE ANGLES

The angles that should be measured and, if necessary, reset are illustrated in Figures 4 through 8. Adjustments should be made to the car manufacturer's *preferred* settings, not simply to "within specifications."

If this will be your first-ever four-wheel alignment, and the car has adjustable rear wheels, you may be interested in knowing that the camber-angles of the rear wheels of some cars are set with shims or wedges (Fig. 9). Toe-angle settings are altered by using shims, turning tie-rod adjusters, or adjusting a cam.

Once alignment is done, the two most commonly unanswered questions are: "When next?" and "Can a pothole knock alignment out of whack?" According to Hunter Engineering Co., the major manufacturer of total four-wheel alignment racks, a car's alignment should be checked every 10,000 miles or once a year. And, yes, a pothole can knock alignment out of kilter, but usually only if the jolt damages a suspension or steering component.

Generally, day-in day-out wear and tear is the primary cause of misalignment—not a bout with a pothole. But after such an encounter, be especially critical of the way your car feels. If there's doubt about it, have the alignment checked.

INTERIOR AND EXTERIOR 6

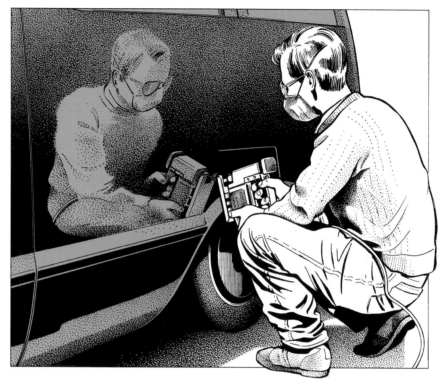

How to
WAX YOUR CAR

Use a clean, damp sponge to apply wax. Use long, linear strokes, rather than a circular motion, to minimize round swirl marks.

Y̲ou've finished cleaning up your car. You've dug all the crud from the suspension and hosed off the underbody. You've cleaned all the globs of road tar from behind the wheel openings. You've removed all the dead bugs and dried, caked-on bird droppings. And you've even dried the car with lint-free rags. Now you're ready to finish the job and put down a layer of wax. But something's wrong here—instead of that rich metallic paint shining through, the car is looking duller and duller as you work. What's wrong?

Or maybe after you've just washed your car, it still looks dirty. That screaming-red finish barely murmurs—it's hazy and chalky. And no matter how much wax you use, it *still* looks as dull as it did when you started. What's going on here?

What's going on is that you're learning there's more to waxing your car than just buying the most expensive finish-care product you can find. Besides having to select from pastes, liquids, aerosols, and even mousses, you've got to know which of the ever-expanding list of products is safe and appropriate. Do you need a wax, polish, or cleaner? And what are the differences among them?

You may have inadvertently discovered that using the wrong type of product can result in a less-than-showroom shine. And you may have also just discovered that using a product that's totally wrong can actually do more harm than good—perhaps to the point of actually damaging the paint surface.

Before you even start washing your car to prepare it for waxing, you need to understand what makes your car dirty and dull-looking. And you should understand what you need to make it shine—regardless of the type of finish the car has.

WEATHER AND PAINT

When your car rolls off the assembly line, the paint is glistening. But as

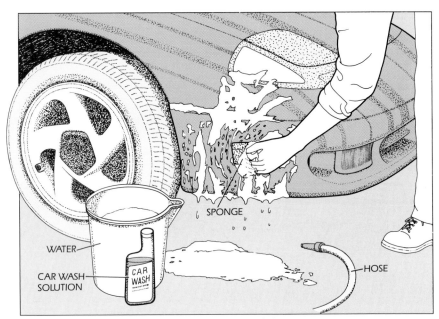

Start with a car wash preparation and plenty of clean water.

soon as the car leaves the factory, the glisten begins to fade. Once outside, your car's finish is attacked by the sun's rays, acid rain, industrial fallout, salt and dust in the wind, and plain old dirt.

The most harmful element on this list is the sun's ultraviolet rays. The UV causes the top layer of the finish to oxidize. With lacquer and enamel finishes, oxidation takes the form of "dead" paint, recognizable as a chalky, white film. The UV also oxidizes the top layer of clearcoat/basecoat paints, which are becoming very common on new cars.

The days when cars were all covered with lacquer paint are long gone. The popular clearcoat/base-coat paints have a layer of pigmented paint, usually an acrylic—often with tiny metallic particles in the mix—which gives the car its color. Over this is a layer of clear paint, which gives the car's finish a deep and lustrous look.

But since the clearcoat is out there against nature, it suffers the ravages. With time and exposure, the clearcoat stops looking so clear as a result of being etched by dirt and dust particles, and yellowing from exposure to the sun's UV rays.

Since a high-gloss, shiny look is one that reflects the most light, just like a mirror, the first steps in shining your car are smoothing and repairing the surface. Therefore, regard-less of the type of finish on your car—clearcoat/basecoat, enamel, or lacquer—you have to remove the oxidation from the finish to get it to shine. You also have to repair the damage done by dust, grit, and airborne corrosives. How you remove the oxidation and repair the damage, however, depends on what type of finish your car has.

Oxidation is removed from single-coat paints by rubbing the oxidized layer, using a very fine abrasive. The abrasive can be part of the formulation of the waxing product or a separate product. However, if you try rubbing off the oxidation from a clearcoat/basecoat with a product that's not meant specifically for clearcoats, you'll end up rubbing completely through the clear layer, exposing the less-than-shiny basecoat.

Accordingly, before you set out to buy the best finish-care product you can, you need to know what type of paint you're dealing with. If you don't know, check with your car dealer. You'll find the factory paint code listed somewhere on your car—possibly on a door jamb decal or on a plate under the hood. The code tells both the specific color of the paint and also the type of finish.

WAXY DEFINITIONS

Once you've determined what type of finish your car has and which type of abrasive or nonabrasive product to use, you're still faced with the dilemma of selecting from a host of liquids, pastes, and mousses that are marketed as

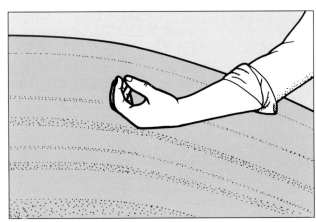

Check for oxidation by dragging the back of your hand across the suspect finish. The roof and hood are most prone to such damage.

Seriously oxidized finishes can be rescued with careful use of abrasives. The abrasives can be in the waxing product or separate.

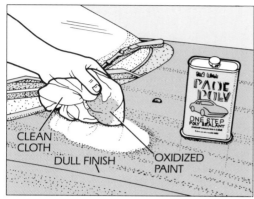

If color shows on the rag, you're removing at least some of the paint.

Black rubber and plastic parts can be shined with a cleaner/polish product that's intended for vinyl.

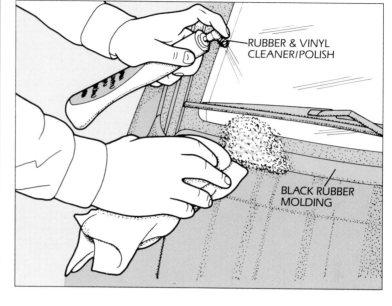

RUBBER & VINYL CLEANER/POLISH

BLACK RUBBER MOLDING

waxes, polishes, and cleaners. As you read the labels of the products, you'll even find some products that call themselves waxless waxes.

For the sake of clarity, think of waxes as products that do nothing but add shine and luster to the car's finish by leaving a layer of glossy material—possibly a genuine wax or a synthetic—over the finish. Polishes are products that contain very fine abrasives to smooth and brighten the surface. Cleaners remove surface damage either through abrasive action—possibly with coarser abrasives than those found in polishes—or chemically. The convenient one-step products combine waxes and cleaners or polishes to do the cleaning and shining all at once.

When you're looking through the bewildering array of waxes and one-step products, check the list of active ingredients. Some of the wax products actually do contain some wax, the most preferable being carnauba, derived from carnauba palm trees. Just about all quality products have silicone in them. However, all silicones are not equal. Most of the products have silicone fluids or oils that make the product easy to apply.

But better products also contain silicone resins or amino-active silicones. These give the polish a longer working life and add to the durability of the finish. And the more durable the protection you leave on the car's paint, the better for the paint under-

neath. You must understand that the layer of wax protecting the paint amounts to only a few *billionths* of an inch. The tougher the layer is and the longer it lasts, the better.

And while you're checking the labels, look for a product that has some sort of ultraviolet-ray blocker. Since most of the damage to your car's finish is from the sun, one of the most important developments in finish-care products is the UV blocker. Basically, these are the same kinds of sunscreen compounds found in modern suntan lotions. The UV blockers allow the light of the sun to pass through to your car's paint, so you can see the shine, but they filter out at least some of the UV, reducing oxidation. You'll find UV blockers in more and more waxes.

If you wash and wax your car regularly—at least three or four times a year—and you don't live or drive where there's an inordinate amount of airborne corrosives, one of the quality one-step products will do the job for you. If your car is subjected regularly to intense sunlight, acid rain, blowing sand and dust, or salt air, you may have to resort to performing individual cleaning, polishing, and shining steps to get your car to glisten the way you want it to.

STEP ONE: THE WASH

Okay, now that you know what type of finish your car has and what type of wax you need for it, you're ready

to shine your car. And to ensure that it glistens more brightly than ever before, start by washing it. If you wax a car that's anything less than perfectly clean, you'll scratch the finish as you shine.

Begin by parking your car in a shady spot, but not under a tree where it will be prone to sap and bird droppings. Try to start early in the day, when the car won't be hot from the sun and to ensure that you'll be able to finish the job long before dark—important so the wax can cure before dew starts to settle.

Hose the car down thoroughly, starting on the roof. Use plenty of water at high pressure. The idea is to float the dirt and grit off with the water rather than rub it into the finish with your wash rag. Periodically hose the car as you work, just to keep it wet and dust-free.

Next, start sudsing the car, using warm water and a special car wash cleaner—*not* household detergent. The car wash preparations have water-softening ingredients to prevent mineral deposits, and the mild cleansing agents won't strip too much of the wax that's already on the car. Start sudsing and washing the lower sections of the body first, rinsing each section as you go, to avoid streaks.

Work in small areas, washing and rinsing, working your way back up to the roof. Wring your sponge and change the water in your wash bucket frequently to avoid rubbing dirt into the finish as you wash.

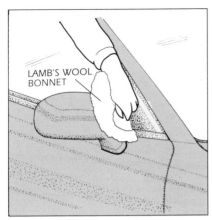

Use a fresh lamb's-wool bonnet or glove to complete buffing areas that are not accessible to the electric buffer.

Don't rub stubborn stains—you could rub through the finish, particularly a clearcoat. Any stains that won't come off with water and cleaner need to be removed chemically, using a special bug and tar remover. After you've cleaned a stain with bug and tar remover, wash the area with soap and water.

Once the car is washed, dry it thoroughly. You can use a chamois cloth—a tanned hide of sheep, lamb, or deer, or synthetic imitations—to dry the car. Or you can use an old terry-cloth towel. The older the towel the better, since old towels are softer than new ones and they leave less lint. Dry the car starting at the roof, and work your way down. Wring the drying cloth frequently to prevent droplets from spotting the finish.

PREWAX PREP

Before you wax the car, inspect it for any minor nicks or scratches in the paint. These should be tended to before you continue. Any rust spots should be sanded down to bare metal. Apply a primer to inhibit further rust. After the primer is dry, use touchup paint to hide the damage. Nicks in clearcoat cars require the additional step of having a layer of clear paint over the pigmented touchup.

Before you start polishing, determine how badly the finish is oxidized. If your car has enamel or lacquer paint and you can see that it looks hazy or chalky, you know you have to remove the oxidized

layer. If you can't see the oxidation, or if your car has a clearcoat, run the back of your hand over the roof and hood, the surfaces most prone to UV damage. If the clean surface feels rough and drags against your skin, you should attend to the oxidation before you wax.

Oxidation on a single-coat paint can be removed with a polish or abrasive cleaner. The severity of the oxidation determines how coarse an abrasive you need. If the oxidation is barely perceptible, a one-step wax and polish will do the job. If it's more severe, take the time to perform the extra step of polishing before you wax. Apply the polish and remove it by hand, working on small sections at a time. Your applicator cloth or sponge will turn the color of the car as you work since you are removing a fine layer of pigmented paint.

Do *not* use a product labeled as a rubbing compound. Rubbing compounds are fairly coarse abrasives and are used to remove deep scratches and to prepare for repainting. Rubbing compounds remove a heavy layer of your car's finish, not just the oxidized layer. And don't use a power buffer with a polish or cleaner because this too could remove more than the oxidation.

Cars with clearcoats can be cleansed of their oxidized layer with special nonabrasive chemical cleaners. These are labeled as safe for clearcoat finishes.

GLOSSING UP

Finally, with the oxidation and dirt removed, you can shine your car. Start on the roof and work your way down, taking small sections at a time. Don't wax an area larger than one-fourth of the roof before allowing it to dry to a haze and wiping it off. Frequently turn and rinse the applicator as you go. Again, don't be alarmed if the applicator comes up the color of your car when you're using a one-step polish/wax—these are designed to remove the layer of dead paint as they shine.

If you want your car to shine like a show car, try these tips from Johnny Zaino, maker of "Z" polish, Bronx, New York. Put the wax on and remove it in a linear rather than circular motion. By wiping in circles, you'll leave swirl marks, perceptible after the wax has cured. Always use a clean, damp applicator, since damp applicators have less friction than dry ones. This means they're easier to use and leave more wax on the surface. It's a good idea to buy a bag of small household sponges to use as applicators. They're small, easy to use, and you can keep changing sponges as you work. Remember to keep them damp with clean, lukewarm water.

If you're using a totally nonabrasive wax and don't mind subtle swirl marks, you can add to the luster by buffing the wax with a power buffer, orbital polisher, or even a polishing

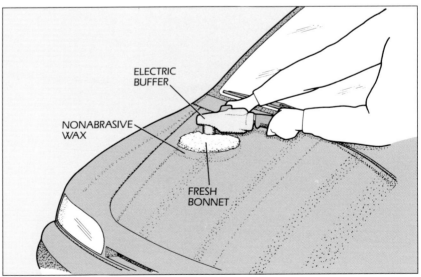

Try applying wax with an electric buffer. But stick to completing a small area before moving on to another section.

attachment on your power drill. It's essential that the bonnets be perfectly clean, so have at least three or four of them ready, and change them as you work. Again, a little dampness adds to the shine as you work by reducing friction between the bonnet and wax. Use the bonnet as a glove to buff areas inaccessible to the power buffer.

There are several products on the market now that actually have pigment to match your car's paint blended in with the wax. These have two advantages. The annoying little ridges of white waxy buildup in the gaps around the hood and doors can take a long time to chase and rub off. The colored products don't eliminate them—but they are certainly a lot less obtrusive. You will still probably have to go back and clean up after yourself, but not nearly as carefully.

But there's another fringe benefit. If there's a scratch or two in the paint, down through the clear, and even a little into the primer, pigment-matched waxes will actually mask the scratch. Depending on the exactness of the match on color, even major scratches are much less obtrusive. Just remember that bare metal or rust must be covered with primer.

In all cases, take care to keep wax off flat black and plastic surfaces. Wipe off any spillover immediately. These surfaces should be polished separately with products specifically formulated for them. Otherwise, you'll wind up with a white or pinkish haze instead of a shine.

MAKE IT LAST

No matter which type of product you've used, and no matter what type of finish it's on, sooner or later you will have to rewax the car. There are a few waxes advertised as lasting for about a year.

To know for sure if there's still wax on the car, sprinkle water on it: When water won't bead up on the car's surface, there's no wax left.

To help keep the finish from dulling, make the car wash a once-a-month maintenance habit. And make waxing a three-to-four-times-a-year project. You can also take some preventive steps to keep the finish shining like new.

First and foremost, garage your car to keep it from the sun's rays and airborne corrosives. If you can't garage it, make sure you park it under a carport or keep a car cover on it.

The other big destroyers of shine are grit and dirt, so hose off your car frequently to float away dirt.

And resist the temptation to wipe down a car that's been in the rain. Unless the car was deluged, there are all types of matter and grit in the water standing on the car. Wiping down the car with a towel will scratch the finish as you wipe off all that dirty water.

How to Find and Fix
WATER AND AIR LEAKS

Water that gets into your car makes a mess and can lead to long-term damage. Leaks start when your car's drainage system gets clogged, if seam-sealer between body panels crumbles, or if weatherstripping around doors and windows wears out or tears. Weatherstripping damage can also create cold-air leaks.

Considering the dozens of potential openings, how do you find the one that leaks? With a lot of patience, a little luck, and a few down-home tools, such as a garden hose and towels.

NATURAL DRAINAGE

A car's drainage system consists of holes and dart-shaped openings in the lower part of the windshield, in the cowl, at the base of doors, and under rocker/quarter panels. When it's functioning properly, the system disposes of the water that sneaks behind the vehicle's skin.

But if the drain holes and darts get plugged, water can run into the interior, accumulate in small enclosed areas, and cause rust.

Drain holes and darts frequently get blocked when the car is being repaired. Suppose that in the course of replacing a cracked windshield the glazier accidentally seals the drain holes at the base of the windshield. Rain won't be able to run off. Instead, it will flow down the bulkhead, seep through openings, and find its way into the car under the dash.

Another example: Suppose you get a leak after a body shop straightens the front of the car following an accident. The mechanic may have failed to reinstall the shields over

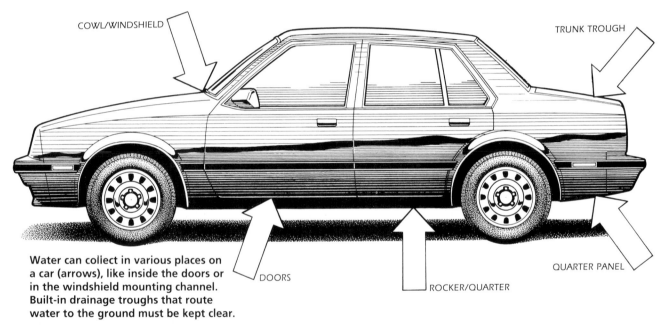

COWL/WINDSHIELD

TRUNK TROUGH

QUARTER PANEL

DOORS

ROCKER/QUARTER

Water can collect in various places on a car (arrows), like inside the doors or in the windshield mounting channel. Built-in drainage troughs that route water to the ground must be kept clear.

Flooding a suspected area is first step in hunting for a water leak.

You or a volunteer may have to get into the trunk to pinpoint leaks.

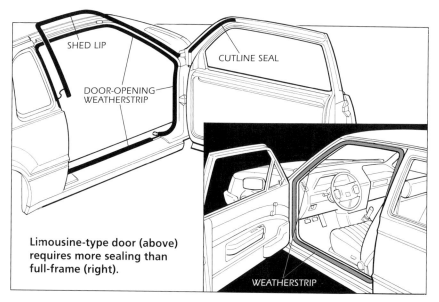

SHED LIP

CUTLINE SEAL

DOOR-OPENING
WEATHERSTRIP

WEATHERSTRIP

**Limousine-type door (above)
requires more sealing than
full-frame (right).**

the large drain holes on the left and right sides of the cowl, giving falling autumn leaves a resting place. Instead of then being able to run off through cowl holes, water may seep into the car.

Did a leak develop soon after you had the car rustproofed? Maybe drain holes and darts in the door and quarter/rocker panels have been blocked. To be sure they're open, poke them with an awl.

But, remember, if the rustproofing is applied thickly, and is still as gooey as it's supposed to be, it will probably melt and block the holes again on the next sunny day.

Also, over the years, drain holes and darts in doors and quarter/rocker panels can get clogged with sediment or leaf fragments that wash down with the water. It takes a few minutes to reopen them with a probe and thus ensure that rust won't develop because of water trapped between the panels.

WHITHER
WEATHERSTRIPPING?

Rear-wheel-drive cars are much more susceptible to damage to weatherstripping and seam-seals than front-wheel-drive cars. The stress on FWD vehicles by the pulling action of the transaxle is absorbed by structural members in the engine compartment—not by doors, windows, and sheet-metal joints as with a rear-wheel-drive powertrain.

Depending on the style of door—full-frame, limousine, or frame-

less—there are a number of things to keep in mind when tracing a leak that may be the result of damaged weatherstripping.

A full-frame door has a frame around the glass that seals the door to the body. A limousine door is the same as a full-frame door except that the top of the frame is extended and beveled to allow the door to become an integral part of the roof. (Limousine-type doors are found on other cars besides limousines.) Frameless doors, which are characteristic of hardtop, T-roof, and convertible models, lack frames around the windows.

With one exception, full-frame and limousine doors are weatherstripped the same way. That ex-

ception is the extended top frame member of limousine doors, which requires shed-lip and cut-line seals.

The shed-lip seal is a pliable flap along the front and top of the door frame opening that blocks water and air. The cut-line seal is located along the edge of the door to fill this cavity.

To determine if there's a water and/or air leak through weatherstripping of full-frame and limousine doors, first examine the material for tears, which can usually be repaired with silicone rubber sealant.

Next, gently pull on the weatherstripping to see if it has separated from the metal at some point. If it has, use rubber cement or liquid butyl sealer to resecure it.

To determine if weatherstripping is worn, put a crisp dollar bill on it, close the door, and pull. If there's no resistance, weatherstripping is worn in that spot, but don't be too fast to replace it. Worn weatherstripping can often be salvaged by cleaning the metal under the weatherstripping and placing a piece of double-sided polyethylene foam tape between the metal and the weatherstripping.

Note: Repair materials can be obtained from auto parts and hardware stores or car dealers.

SOUND ADVICE

There are several other points to remember about full-frame and limousine doors:

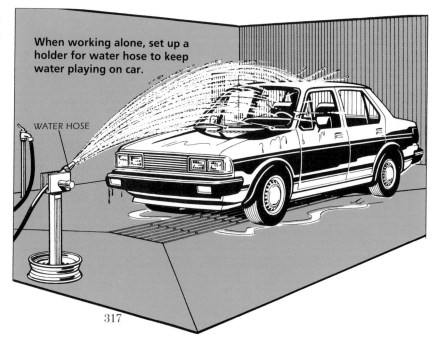

When working alone, set up a holder for water hose to keep water playing on car.

WATER HOSE

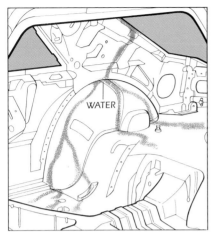

The entry point for rainwater can be a long way from where it puddles in the car.

- Spraying weatherstripping with silicone lubricant every six months will keep the material supple and prolong its life, often for as long as you own the car.
- Door alignment affects the performance of weatherstrip-

ping. If a door loses alignment, something that usually happens only after an accident, you'll get air and/or water leaks. A misaligned door, which can often be resquared by shimming and resecuring hinges, is apparent if the space between the door and B-pillar on one side of the car is wider than the corresponding space on the other side of the car.

- Wind noise can result if there is an irregularity in the surface of the door opening, such as a lump of solder or plastic body putty. Use a chisel or sandpaper to smooth the area.
- Three potential leaks around windows of full-frame and limousine doors are the flocked-run seal in the channel that surrounds the inside opening of the door, and through inner and outer beltline seals.

You can see at a glance whether inner and outer beltline seals are doing their jobs. They should hug the glass.

The flocked-run seal is another matter. Suppose there's a water leak around a window during a gale-driven rain or when the car is going through a car wash. Air can also leak into the car if this seal is worn.

You can't examine the flocked-run seal visually to see if it's worn. Instead, cut a length of foam tape to size, roll down the window, and insert it into the window channel under the seal. If the leak disappears, you've eliminated a troublesome spot.

Frameless doors of hardtop, T-roof, and convertible models rely on secure weatherstripping on the body flange and body trim to stop leaks. Door alignment is even more important on these models.

WATER TEST

Once you're confident the drainage system is clear and the doors and windows are doing their job, where else can water be entering the car? To find out, do a water test. Divide

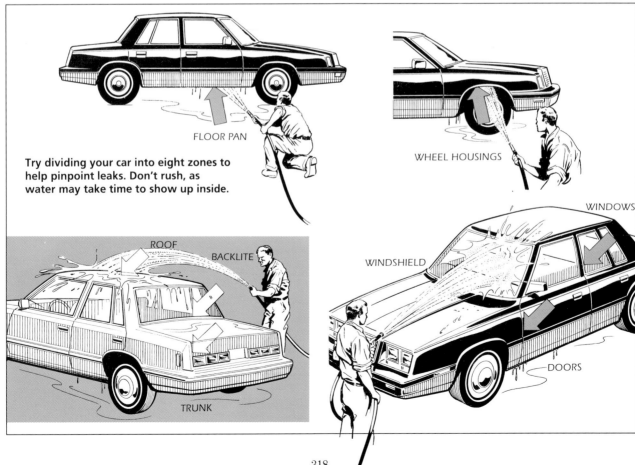

Try dividing your car into eight zones to help pinpoint leaks. Don't rush, as water may take time to show up inside.

FLOOR PAN

WHEEL HOUSINGS

ROOF

BACKLITE

TRUNK

WINDWSHIELD

WINDOWS

DOORS

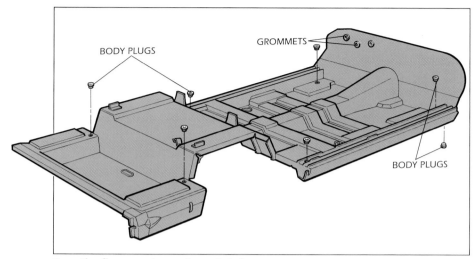

Even the floor pan has entry points for water. Check for missing grommets and plugs.

the car into eight zones and investigate one zone at a time. Be patient. It may take a long time for water to begin dripping during the test, so don't give an area just a quick spritz. Keep water flowing onto each spot for at least twenty minutes.

Keep in mind that water can be deceiving. Its point of entry doesn't always correlate directly with the wet spots. For example, a soggy carpet on the front floor could be caused by damage in the sunroof channel. Instead of rain falling on your head, as you might expect, it will take the path of least resistance which could be from the sunroof channel, down the windshield pillar, and onto the floor.

ZONING THE CAR

What you can anticipate finding in each zone is as follows:

Floor pan—If water leaks through the floor pan, making carpets soggy, the cause is loose or missing fasteners, such as brake-line clips, torsion bar bolts, seatbelt bolts, loose or missing floor pan grommets, and seal-seam gaps in floor pan panel joints. Tighten fasteners and seal them with auto body caulking, buy grommets for empty holes (seal them, too) and apply caulk to body seams and spot-weld joints. Just pull-

ing up the carpet can reveal plenty, since floor pans are just as prone to rusting away as exposed panels like fenders.

Wheel housings—Water leaking into the car through wheel wells will show up on the floor near A-, C-, and/or D-pillars, or in the trunk, depending on which housing has the leak. Tighten fasteners, such as rear seatbelt bolts and shock-mounting bolts, and reseal panel seams.

Doors—Although you've already checked weather-stripping and door alignment, there are other possible leaky spots. If water is showing up on the floor near doors and pillars, there may be a gap in a pillar seam, or perhaps loose hinge bolts or loose grommets around the A-pillar wires that pass from the engine compartment to power window motors.

Windshield—You can pinpoint leaks around the windshield by having an assistant with a mirror and flashlight sitting in the front seat. As you concentrate water on the zone, he can see if it drips down the bulkhead.

If there is a leak, make sure left and right cowl drain holes are clear and a shield covers each. Look for missing or loose grommets in the bulkhead. Tighten fasteners holding parts to the bulkhead, such as relays and the air conditioning/heater plenum.

That leaves the windshield itself. As mentioned before, drain holes at the base of the windshield could be clogged if you've had the windshield replaced. Otherwise, small gaps could have developed in the sealer around the windshield. If so, there's a chance you can reseal these from *inside* the car using a urethane sealer. Typically, it comes in a cartridge for use with a caulking gun.

Apply the material around the entire perimeter, but remember: *on the inside.* It won't work if you put it around the outside molding and could cause a problem, requiring removal of the molding to reseal the windshield.

Don't get windshield sealer into the clips. It'll make removing the trim almost impossible to do without damage, and if you haven't found the leak (or need to replace the windshield at some point later on), you might wind up replacing the trim.

If an inside-the-car resealing effort isn't successful, remove the molding using a windshield molding trim tool. Don't make do with something like a screwdriver—chances are you'll crack the glass. Slide the tool under the molding until it hits a clip. Then twist the tool gently until the molding pops off the clip.

After all moldings have been taken off, count the number of clips and buy new ones from an auto

319

Wind flutter in trim can be located by temporarily taping down suspect pieces.

A mirror and a flashlight will come in handy for restricted areas like the dash.

glass shop. Don't reuse old clips. They're not tight enough the second time around.

Put new clips in the same positions as the old ones, lay down a wide bead of windshield sealer (don't leave any gaps), place the molding over the clips, and press down until they're in place.

Backlite—Leaks from gaps in backlite sealer will necessitate removing moldings and resealing from the outside. But before going through this trouble, make sure the deck lid seal (that's the weatherstripping on the top lid inside the trunk) is firmly in place and gutters are secured to the body of the car.

Yes, gutters. Water can leak through a separation between a gutter and C-post, for example, and wind up inside the rear of the car.

Trunk—If you find water in the trunk, first check weatherstripping. Then tighten and apply sealer to all rear-end fasteners, such as taillight screws, license plate housing screws, and bumper or shield fasteners. Check gutter-to-body integrity and seal taillight and backup light assembly moldings with auto body caulk.

Windows and roof—Water-test windows in case you missed something before. Then, test the roof. Water found in the car after the roof has been given a going-over can be entering through gaps between a gutter and the body or a gap in pillar weld joints. If the car is equipped with a sunroof, suspect that. If sunroof channels were not equipped with drain tubes and sealed tightly at installation, remove and reseal properly.

WIND TIPS

Here are two tips that may save time in locating the source of a wind noise:

- As you test-drive the car with the windows tightly closed and the heater/air conditioner/vent system off, have an assistant press a towel against each window. If a wind noise disappears or changes pitch, you've got the area pinpointed.
- If the source of the wind noise seems to be outside the car, retract the radio antenna and drive the car. If the noise hasn't disappeared, tape small sections of molding with pressure-sensitive waterproof tape. Drive the car. Has the noise stopped? If so, remove the molding, fill its hollow back with auto body caulk, and reattach the strip securely to the body. When moldings have been tested, turn your attention to headlamp and taillight pieces and the grille. Patience pays.

How to Restore
FADED PAINT

Machine compounding is the most efficient method of restoring faded and oxidized paint. It looks easy, but don't try it yourself unless you're ready to repaint—because it's altogether too easy to overdo.

LAMB'S WOOL WHEEL

RUBBING COMPOUND

It's been a long cold winter, and you've been curled up, warm and dry, at the hearth. Your car, meanwhile, has been outside taking it on the chin. And it looks it. A little neglect (Hey! It's too cold to wash the car!) and a lot of acid rain and road salt have dulled your machine's once-brilliant shine. Your mission, on the first warm day of spring, is to resurrect that paint job.

Ultraviolet rays and corrosive salt fade and discolor the surface of automotive paints. Usually, however, the damage is only superficial. By removing the top layer of paint with a product that is compatible with the type of finish on your car, you can restore the original luster and color of the finish.

Resurrecting even a severely dull and faded paint job is certainly within the realm of things possible, but there are limits. First, the more faded and oxidized the surface, the harder you'll have to work to refurbish it. Second, if the layer of paint is too thin, you may rub all of the finish off before you find good paint. Of course, with a complete repaint being the only viable alternative, you have little to lose.

DIRT REMOVAL

This procedure, largely unknown to owners of cars with severely damaged paint, is known as "washing the car." For some of us, it's a drastic measure but a necessary one. It's also a practice you'll want to continue after the paint has been restored as it helps remove airborne

chemicals and muck before they damage the surface.

Do a thorough job, using a non-detergent soap that won't remove more oil from the paint. When washing a car that has already been waxed, this type of soap will not remove all of the wax—heavy detergents will. Soaps that are specially formulated for washing cars are available at most auto parts stores. One of our favorite nondetergent soaps is the widely available Murphy's Oil Soap. Liquid soap made for washing dishes by hand is okay, but it may remove some oil. Don't use liquid or powdered laundry detergent.

Before washing the car's body, blast the wheel wells and underbody with a strong stream of water to remove road salt and other cor-

1 Nondetergent soap removes dirt and restores the paint's shine.

3 Sometimes hot air helps loosen stickers or woodgrain vinyl trim.

rosive substances. If you're working at a carwash with a high-pressure wand, you can begin by spraying soap underneath, then rinse it off. After cleaning the underside, check for corrosion. And, if you find potential rust spots under the car, clean them up and apply an aerosol rustproofer.

Wash upper body surfaces in the shade. Have a hose on hand with a shutoff nozzle. Mix the soap in a bucket of lukewarm water. Use a big sponge and apply soapy water liberally (Fig. 1). Wash the roof first. Once the roof has been thoroughly cleaned, rinse it (Fig. 2) before pro-

ceeding with the hood and deck lid and, finally, the body sides and the front grille area and rear panel. Rinse every time you finish a section, so the soap doesn't have a chance to dry. Each time you rinse, rewet the surfaces that you rinsed previously. If you're rinsing or soaping up with the high-pressure wand at a commercial carwash, keep it well away from the painted surface.

Here's how to use a chamois to dry the car thoroughly. Soak the chamois in water for a few minutes and then wring it out completely. As you wipe up water from the surface, wring the chamois out from time to

time. As you work, you can tell when the chamois is saturated as it will begin to leave droplets on the surface. Once your paint has been restored, drying your car with a chamois is just about all you have to do to restore the luster.

Once the car is dry, check carefully for remaining spots of tar or other foul muck and remove same with a rag and a bottle of bug-and-tar solvent. This chemical cleaner is available at most auto parts stores. If the rear panel and bumpers are defaced with old peeling stickers, now would be a good time to remove them, as you'll probably be able to blend in the paint underneath them (which is less faded than the rest of the car) when you compound or polish. A hair dryer can sometimes help loosen the sticker's adhesive (Fig. 3).

ASSESSING THE DAMAGE

With all road dirt removed, you can evaluate the condition of your car's finish. How you deal with various problems depends, in part, on what type of paint was used to finish the car. If it's metallic without a clearcoat on top, avoid using any type of abrasive cleaners. Metallic paint surfaces are not uniform from top to bottom—so if you rub off the top layer, you'll be left with a mess. A nonabrasive polish, used before waxing, can remove dirt and oxidation without removing paint. But

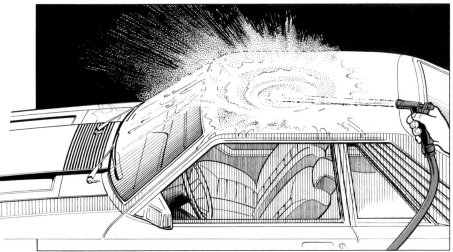

2 Wash and rinse the car from the roof down to avoid carrying loosened dirt into clean areas.

don't confuse nonabrasive polish with polishing compound. Any product referred to as a compound or cleaner wax contains abrasives that can ruin metallic finishes.

An example of a good nonabrasive polish that is suitable for metallic finishes is Show Car Polish for Clear-Coat (518-327-3043). Most other manufacturers of automotive wax sell similar products that are marked as suitable for metallic finishes.

Depending on the thickness of the top coat, clearcoat/basecoat finishes can sometimes be damaged when abrasive cleaners are used. If you remove all of the thin clearcoat over the base, a respray will be necessary. While these finishes aren't as susceptible to damage as the conventional metallic types, they still call for caution. Don't use an abrasive polish if you can restore the sheen with a non-abrasive. If you must use an abrasive to restore your clearcoat, try a cleaner wax rather than straight polishing or rubbing compound.

If your car has a finish other than metallic or clearcoat/basecoat, you can usually restore its original luster with polishing compound or rubbing compound. These products actually grind off the top layer of paint, leaving like-new paint below. In some cases where aggressive paint removal is necessary to restore a nice finish, you could end up removing too much paint—even if you're careful. But if your paint is in really bad shape, repainting might be the only alternative anyway.

If your paint is just slightly dull but has a relatively smooth surface, hand polishing will probably be sufficient to restore the luster. There are a number of polishing compound products available on the shelf of your neighborhood auto parts store that are intended for hand application. These usually differ from machine-applied products in that they are much more liquid and not as difficult to remove. They are not likely to remove too much paint as their abrasive power is limited by the application method.

Not all manufacturers use the same nomenclature for their products. For example, polish and polishing compound are usually not the same thing. Some products described as polish contain no abrasives and can be used on clearcoat paints—others may be nothing more than polishing compound in a more liquid form. Some have names that confuse the distinction. So don't rely on the name alone. Make sure you read the label before purchasing polish or polishing compound. If the label doesn't tell whether abrasives are included, rub some onto a painted surface (not necessarily your car) and look for color to be transferred to your cloth.

If the paint is severely faded and its surface resembles primer or is heavily scratched, compounding will be necessary. The product used for this operation is called rubbing compound. For the inexperienced, compounding is probably best done by hand, but it's a big job. Some of the rubbing compound sold in retail auto parts departments is intended

for hand application only and should not be applied by machine, as severe rub-through can result. Rubbing compound for hand application is available in both paste and liquid form. Liquid types are easier to use, but you won't get as much compound for your money.

Machine compounding is easier and faster than hand compounding—but chances of damaging the finish are increased considerably. It's not a job recommended for the uninitiated unless the only alternative is repainting.

If you do decide on machine compounding, use rubbing compound specifically formulated for machine application. You can buy it at an auto parts store that specializes in body shop supplies. It will be available in different abrasive grades, and if you're trying machine compounding for the first time, use a light grade, which will cut more slowly.

The counterman can also help you select the right type of polishing pad. A lamb's-wool pad is most often used for compounding. You'll probably need two to finish the job. You can rent a power polishing machine at most tool rental stores.

HAND POLISHING

Whether you're using an abrasive hand-applied polishing compound on faded conventional paint or a nonabrasive polish on clearcoat or metallic paint, work in the shade or wait for a cloudy day. Apply the polish to a small area—about two feet square. If an applicator pad didn't

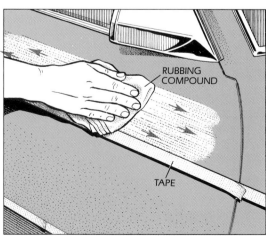

4 Before you compound, use masking tape to protect raised edges.

5 Hold the leading edge of the pad slightly above the surface of the area being compounded.

come with the polish, use a piece of soft terry cloth. The instructions on the product package may tell you to dampen the applicator.

If you're using abrasive polishing compound, you should start to see some of the removed pigment on your applicator. Work with a very light touch when polishing edges. It's easy to rub right through the paint on a raised edge. Use a clean, soft, terry-cloth rag to buff the surface.

HAND COMPOUNDING

As noted above, hand compounding is hard work. A lot of elbow grease is required to do the job right. Do a two-feet-square area at a time. If the damage is severe and includes relatively deep scratches and substantial discoloration, begin by lightly wet-sanding the area with 600- or 800-grit wet-or-dry sandpaper folded into quarters. Keep the paper fully saturated with water and don't get carried away. This is not recommended for clearcoat/basecoat or metallics, unless you're at the last-resort stages of trying to rescue a loser. Before you begin, apply a thin strip of masking tape to raised edges and creases.

Apply the compound with a soft terry-cloth rag that has been folded into a pad. Or, if the product came with an applicator pad, use that. Using medium pressure, apply the compound with straight back-and-forth strokes (Fig. 4). Following the directions, remove the compound with a dry rag.

If the surface isn't glossy once the compound is off, you haven't removed enough paint, and should repeat the compounding part of the procedure.

Once you've finished all other body parts, remove the masking tape from the edges and creases and compound these areas. Avoid applying compound with any significant degree of enthusiasm on raised edges to avoid rub-through. If you do rub all the way through the paint, refinishing is the only satisfactory fix.

MACHINE COMPOUNDING

As we've already said, rub-through is a considerable risk when compounding a car using a professional polishing machine. However, machine compounding is much faster and considerably more effective than hand compounding. So if your paint is a total disaster and you're not willing to spend what *could* be all weekend trying to compound it by hand, you might want to do the job the way the pros do it. Remember, however, that machine compounding removes quite a bit of paint and if the paint is thin, you may have to repaint the car.

Make sure you wear old clothes, as the compound will fly all over when you turn on the machine. You'll also need safety goggles and a dust-type respirator. These are not optional. Compound can seriously damage your eyes and lungs. Don't take chances.

Before you begin, take some precautions to prevent rub-through. Since raised surfaces rub through first, apply a thin strip of masking tape to creases, raised edges, or sharp corners on painted surfaces of the body. This will help reduce the likelihood of excessive paint removal.

When you're ready to start, read the instructions on the rubbing compound package and mix the paste with water if the instructions so indicate. With most types of rubbing compound, you should periodically add water to the mix as you work to compensate for evaporation and for the tendency of the compound to become less liquid toward the bottom of the container. Apply compound to a two by two-foot area of the car with a medium-sized paintbrush or just toss a handful in the center of the area you're working on. Use just enough to achieve uniform distribution.

Without turning the polishing machine on, spread the compound evenly over the area with the polishing machine's pad. Don't apply compound directly to the polishing pad.

Drape the cord to the polisher over your shoulder, away from the spinning wheel, as it will take only a heartbeat to wrap the cord around the shaft if it touches the pad's edge. The polisher will rip itself out of your hands, and do a remarkably destructive whirligig death dance on your hood.

Turn the polisher on and smoothly stroke the area to be compounded left to right and then right to left. When moving the machine from left to right, lift the right half of the pad a little bit. When you stroke from right to left, lift the left half of the pad a bit. In other words, the leading edge should be slightly above the surface of the area being compounded (Fig. 5). Each full stroke should overlap the stroke directly above or below by about half its width. Don't apply pressure as you stroke. Instead, just rest the machine against the surface. Let the

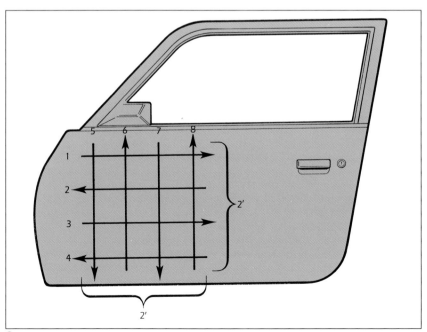

6 To compound a two × two-foot area, stroke horizontally. Repeat vertically.

weight of the machine do the work.

Once you've fully covered the area with horizontal strokes (it should take about four strokes), repeat the procedure using vertical strokes, but don't apply more compound. Figure 6 illustrates how eight strokes cover a two by two-feet section of door. If the compound is all used up before you've finished, you didn't use enough. If there's a lot of compound left on the surface, you used too much. In other words, by the time you've finished compounding vertically and horizontally, the compound should have disappeared and you should see a glossy surface. Or at least a glossier surface. If the damage is severe, and you're using the recommended fine-grade compound, it might take more passes. Patience is called for, as you can't go back after you grind down to the primer.

As you work, you'll have to clean the pad from time to time to prevent buildup of compound. To do so, lay the machine on the ground, pad facing up, and turn it on. Grip the machine firmly and scrape compound buildup from the pad by passing a dull screwdriver over the pad as the machine runs. Move the screwdriver from the outer edge of the pad toward its center.

After you've compounded all exposed areas of the paint surface, remove the masking tape from the raised edges and corners and compound these spots by hand. You'll also have to hand-compound areas under the edge of bumpers or spots that can't be reached with the machine.

PROTECTING THE FINISH

Once the car has been compounded or polished, rinse it thoroughly with warm water and dry it with a chamois. To make your car shine as brightly as it would if a professional detailer had restored the finish, apply pure carnauba wax. Be sure to allow sufficient time for the car to dry. The carnauba will provide a layer of protection. It is essential that the wax does not contain any abrasive or it will remove more paint. Rub a bit between your fingers before you use it. As with the compound, apply wax to one small area at a time. Polish with a soft cloth.

How to Repair
MINOR BODY DAMAGE

Your family wagon isn't quite the glamorous machine that it once was. The effects of use, road salt, pollution, parking lot mishaps, and a variety of other hazards have taken their toll.

Where it was once bright and shiny, it is now dull and fading. The paint is chipped behind the front and rear fenderwells, and a couple of long scratches cross the door panels. A professional bodyshop repair job would be a very expensive proposition. Can you do it yourself?

Unlike mechanical work, success in bodywork can be measured in degrees. With a mechanical job, either you can do it or you can't. When it comes to bodywork, however, even a feeble effort may make the car look better than it does right now, and if you can't afford a pro job, you have little to lose.

In the following sections, we'll outline some simple exterior repairs. Refer to page 321 for directions on restoring faded paint.

REPAIRING CHIPS AND NICKS

Perhaps the toughest part of repairing chips and nicks is deciding how

Dull paint can sometimes be refurbished with a compounding treatment, either by hand or by machine.

1 Use a sanding block and 80-grit paper for the first sanding of a nicked area. Follow that with the 240-grit, and then wet-sand with 400-grit.

you want to do it. Small nicks can be repaired "temporarily" in just a few minutes (more on that later). But if you want to restore the area to like-new condition, complex techniques are recommended for the various types of finishes used by carmakers today.

If you don't have a spray gun and compressor and don't want to rent one, you'll have to have a body shop finish up the job once you have repaired the nick. However, you can still save a lot of money by doing the body repair yourself.

Don't try to refinish part of a panel with touch-up spray cans. You won't get a good match. On a small panel that is not particularly visible, such as the lower half of a rear quarter that is split by a trim line, you may decide to have a go at refinishing with touch-up spray. The results may not please you, however.

To produce a professional-looking nick repair you'll need a sanding block, 80-, 240-, and 400-grit sandpaper, zinc chromate primer, finishing primer, wax-removing solvent, a tack cloth, glazing putty, and a rubber contour squeegee. You should be able to purchase all of these products at any well-stocked auto parts store. If you can't find them there, you can try a parts store that specializes in body shop supplies.

You'll also find a knowledgeable bodywork-oriented counterman at these establishments who will be willing to help you with problems.

Before you begin the repair of a nick, clean the entire panel with a wax-removing solvent. Wipe it dry.

Using 80-grit sandpaper on a hand sanding block, sand the area until the edges of the nick or chip have been smoothed out and the surface is totally free of rust (Fig. 1). Hold the sanding block flat against the panel and apply moderate pressure. Work with a back-and-forth motion over an area that is sufficiently large to allow complete feathering of surrounding paint.

Continue working until you can't feel the edges of the nick. Insert a piece of 240-grit paper and sand until the surface is free of deep sanding scratches, then wet-sand lightly with 400-grit paper until the surface is satin smooth. Wash with water, dry with a cloth rag, and then wipe the entire panel with a tack cloth.

Next, mask any trim near the repair area or the edges of any adjoining panels that are close enough to be threatened by overspray (Fig. 2). Then coat the bare metal and the sanded paint with zinc chromate primer. Hold the spray can parallel to the surface and at a distance of about 10 in. Move the can back and forth, keeping it the same distance from the surface at all times.

Once the primer has dried, put a lump of glazing putty on the edge of the contour squeegee and apply it to the prime-coated repair area (Fig. 3). Apply with moderate pressure, move quickly and in one direction only. Don't attempt a second pass with the squeegee. If you don't like the results of your first attempt, remove all the glazing putty and try it again with a fresh lump of putty.

FINISHING PUTTY REPAIRS

Let the putty dry overnight, or as specified on the product label, then sand with 240-grit paper in a sanding block until the repair area is completely level with the surrounding area. Feel for any high spots and sand some more if necessary. Inspect the puttied area carefully for pits, low spots, or rough areas, and apply glazing putty again if necessary, resanding as above.

Finally, insert a piece of 400-grit paper in the sanding block and wet-sand the area until it is satin smooth. Flush the area with lots of water as you sand to avoid leaving scratches.

Wash the panel with water, dry it, and wipe it with the tack cloth. Then apply a final finish primer that is compatible with the color coat that will be applied.

TEMPORARY TOUCH-UP

If your car is nicked and chipped but you don't want to get involved in a repair that will necessitate the

2 After the nick has been sanded smooth, mask adjoining areas. Then coat nick with a rust-inhibiting primer.

3 After applying a rust-inhibiting primer, coat the area with glazing putty, using a flexible squeegee. Apply the putty with a single stroke.

refinishing of a panel, you can do a temporary touch-up.

Buy a can of touch-up paint that is an exact match for the color of your car (vehicle type and year as well as the name of the color are listed on the can of paint). The best type is the brush-applied touch-up paint, but this is sometimes hard to find. You'll probably have to settle for a spray can.

Remove all rust from the nick area, but don't attempt to feather the edges. A pocket knife used as a scraper works well for this.

Once all the rust has been removed, spray some of the paint into the cover of the spray can and let it sit for about five minutes until it thickens a bit. (If you have bottled brush-type paint, use it as it comes.) Use a matchstick to apply the paint. Dip the end of the match that is not coated with sulphur in the paint and dab it onto the chipped area. Try to apply a heavy coat on the first attempt to completely fill the nick. Make sure that you have covered all of the bare metal.

In conspicuous places, this type of repair won't produce very satisfactory results, but it is far better than simply spraying touch-up paint over an unrepaired chip. In less conspicuous places, it will serve quite well to protect the metal until a more extensive repair can be completed.

REPAIRING SCRATCHES

Deep scratches can be repaired following the same procedures recommended for repair of chips and nicks. And, of course, surface scratches that have no depth to speak of can usually be removed with rubbing compound. Scratches that fall in between—not deep enough to have reached bare metal but too deep to be removed with rubbing compound—can be repaired with glazing putty.

You'll need glazing putty, finishing primer, a tack cloth, a squeegee, masking paper and tape, 240- and 400-grit sandpaper, rags, and wax-remover solvent.

Clean the scratched area with the solvent, then lightly sand the scratch with the 240-grit paper. Fold the paper into quarters or smaller, and sand only enough to slightly roughen the area directly around the scratch. Sand evenly along the length of the scratch. Don't concentrate on one area.

Wash the area with a wet rag, dry it, and then wipe it with the tack cloth. Apply a dab of the putty to the edge of your squeegee and smoothly wipe it across the scratch, making one pass next to the other, all along the length of the scratch. As before, don't attempt a second pass. If you're not satisfied with your first attempt, remove the putty and try again.

Allow the putty to dry overnight or as specified, then sand the area with 240-grit paper on a sanding block. Sand evenly to avoid creating low spots. Wash the area with water, dry it, and wipe with the tack cloth.

Don't be alarmed if there are low spots or if parts of the scratch are not completely filled with putty. Simply reapply another coat of the putty as before. Repeat the application of putty as many

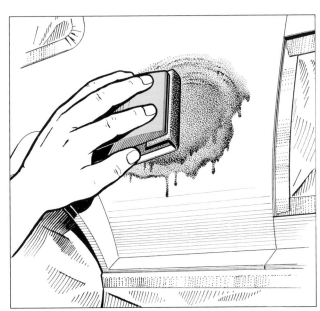

4 When the glazing putty has dried, wet-sand with 400-grit paper. Splash water on the area as you sand to flush away sludge and keep the paper fresh.

5 Once the surface has been sanded to a shiny smoothness, apply a finishing primer that will be compatible with the final color coat.

times as necessary to effect a smooth repair.

Once you're satisfied that the repair is perfect, sand with 400-grit paper in a sanding block, wetting the paper and the repair area with water (Fig. 4). Keep splashing water on as you sand to flush away sanding residue. Use long strokes and sand until the area is perfectly smooth. Then, rinse, dry, and wipe with the tack cloth.

To complete the repair, coat the area with the right type of finishing primer, depending on what type of paint will be used to color coat (Fig. 5).

As we pointed out earlier, spot repair of automotive finishes can be complicated. To find out what type of color coat or primer must be used, you'll have to visit a body shop supply store. Before you do, make sure you know the color code for your vehicle. You can find this code on the body identification plate.

Each of the various carmakers has its own name for this plate. On GM cars, other than Corvette, the body number plate is under the hood on the front or upper surface of the firewall shroud. On Corvettes, it's on the dashboard brace below the glove box or on the left door hinge pillar.

On Fords the vehicle certification label is on the lock face panel of the driver's door.

On Chrysler products, the body code plate is under the hood on or near the left front fenderwell, or on the radiator support.

On some cars, it's quite obvious which of the many numbers on the body plate is the paint code. On other cars, you'll need the assistance of a factory service manual or the counterman in the body supply store. If you have to, make a sketch of the whole tag and let him pick out the correct paint code.

PRIMER AND COLOR COAT

Once the code has been determined, the man in the body supply store can check it against the color chart for your year and model car. The chart will tell him exactly what type of finishing primer and color coat should be used. For most types of automotive finish, the final color is applied in a number of coats. The first coat is sprayed so it covers an area only as large as the spot repair. Each subsequent coat covers a slightly larger area.

For some types of paint as many as six coats are necessary. Spray gun pressure usually is altered for the final coats. This technique blends the new paint into the old.

Don't attempt to do this yourself without specific instructions for your type of finish. You might be able to get instructional literature from the auto body supply store. Various books are also available.

Remember that patience is the key to successful body and paint work.

If you apply paint haphazardly, your car won't look any better than it did before the damage was repaired. If you concentrate sanding efforts in one area in an attempt to remove an imperfection quickly, you will create a low spot. And if you sand before filler, glaze, or primer has had a chance to dry properly, you'll create a real mess.

How to Repair
PLASTIC BODY PANELS

SCUFF BACK
OF PANEL

GLUE TABS
TO BACK OF
PANEL

Rigid plastic panels are easily repaired by cutting a section from another panel, and then scuff-sanding and gluing tabs to the back of the repair area. After this adhesive sets, glue in the replacement section.

You're backing out of the garage one morning after a late night at the bowling alley. Your mind is on that last 7–10 split, while your right foot eases on the throttle. But after a few feet, all motion to the rear ceases. Hmmm. What gives?

Uh-oh. Number-two son's MX bike has managed to move itself across the garage and directly into your flight path. ("Honest, Dad—I left it in the bike rack!") And the steel handlebars have punched a

hole right through the side of your car's fender.

Hole? Not a dent, but a nasty ragged hole in the metal. Wait, it's not metal—it's *plastic!* There are lots of little fibers hanging out of the hole, and there's no evidence of the panel being bent—just the hole.

You already know how to repair a hole in a metal fender—screwing, riveting, or better yet, welding a patch over the hole, carefully dollying and hammering the metal back

to its original contour. Add a little filler, and number-two son won't have to remain grounded until he starts college. But plastic? How do you weld that?

If this seems like a scenario from *Back to the Future*, look again. There are plenty of at least partially plastic cars out there. The aerodynamic noses on cars like the Chevy Beretta, Toyota Celica, and GEO Storm are made of flexible plastic. In fact, it's getting harder and harder to find a

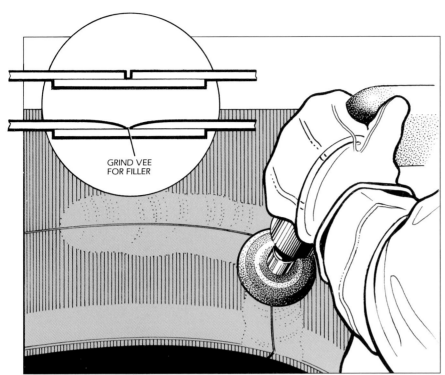

GRIND VEE
FOR FILLER

1 Use 36-grit sandpaper disc to vee out the exterior panel for application of filler material.

modern car that doesn't have flexible plastic panels, at least for the front and rear fascias or bumpers.

You'll find rigid plastic makes up the tailgate on later-model Jeep Wagoneers and on both the hood and tailgate of the Ford Aerostar.

There are also several totally plastic-bodied cars out there. General Motors' GM200 minivan (Chevy Lumina APV, Pontiac Trans Sport, and Olds Silhouette) has an entire body made of rigid plastic panels. The panels are glued to a steel cage welded up from sheet-metal stampings, and the whole structure provides strength that is equal to that of a similar all-steel design. Remember the Fiero? It used both rigid and flexible panels, although they weren't structural parts of the car, but merely bolted on. In theory, you could drive a Fiero around without its skin, something that's not true of the newer plastic-bodied minivans.

The repair techniques are the same whether the panel is structural or not—although you might consider how good a job you're doing in light of whether the panel represents merely a cosmetic face or is an integral part of the car's structure.

So how do you fix plastic body parts? Throw away your hammer and dolly. You can't beat this stuff back into shape. But thanks to several new products, repairing both rigid and flexible plastic parts is fairly easy. And figuring out where the plastic body parts are on your car is no more difficult than grabbing a magnet from your refrigerator. If it doesn't stick to the car, you've found plastic.

RIGID PLASTIC REPAIRS

Rigid plastic body panels are hardly a new idea. The 1953 Corvette was made of fiberglass, and Corvette bodybuilding didn't change much until 1984, when Chevrolet switched the Corvette to a new plastic material that's called sheet molding compound (SMC). Now, SMC is the plastic of choice when carmakers build rigid plastic body panels.

Like fiberglass, SMC is impregnated with glass fibers for structural strength. However, fiberglass is laid or sprayed into a mold and cured by a catalyst additive. Fiberglass repair is a completely different topic. We're not going to discuss fiberglass repair here at all, as the techniques and materials are completely different.

Sheet molding compound, on the other hand, is made up of two preformed, partially cured plastic sheets. Glass fibers and resins are sandwiched in between, and the whole affair is pressed into shape in male and female molds before the SMC is heat cured. The result is a plastic body panel that's quicker to make, smooth on both sides, and dimensionally accurate. More important, the side that shows has a better surface finish than fiberglass.

In an accident, an SMC panel retains its shape—until it's hit hard enough to gouge, rip, tear, or crack. Then the undamaged portion of the panel will spring back into shape by itself.

Devcon makes an epoxy filler designed for consumer use. It's good for repairing minor gouges and scratches in both SMC plastic and fiberglass. It's available at auto parts stores. To use it, grind out the damaged area with a coarse sanding disc, then scrub the area with Plexus cleaner or lacquer thinner. Next, mix equal parts of A and B until it reaches a uniform gray color.

Fill the damaged area so it's slightly higher than the surrounding body. The filler hardens in about a half-hour. Once it's hard, sand the area with 180-grit paper to level the repair and achieve a smooth contour. If there are any pinholes, mix more filler and apply a skim coat. When it's dry, resand the filler and feather-edge the paint with 240-grit paper, followed by 320-grit paper, until the repair is perfectly smooth.

You can't use lacquer- or enamel-based primers/surfacers to prime SMC repairs—or any plastic repairs, for that matter—because the solvents will cause the repair to bleed through. Then, after it's painted, the area will have what body men call a bull's-eye.

To get around this problem, Devcon's Plexus primer is specifically formulated for plastic parts. It comes in a five-ounce aerosol can. To cover the area sufficiently, apply several thin coats, allowing the primer to dry for five to ten minutes between coats. Finish-paint the area to match, using the paint manufacturer's recommendations for painting plastic parts.

For more serious damage, you'll want to use 3M's Rigid Parts Repair system. This is the stuff that body

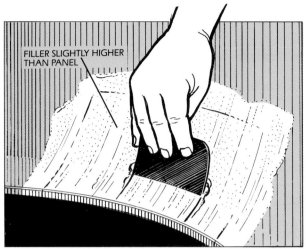

2 Spread the filler material slightly higher than the surrounding plastic panel. Allow the filler to cure completely before sanding.

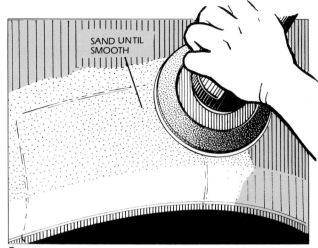

3 Block-sand filler for proper contours, and feather-edge back into the original panel. Then use plastic primer and finish-paint the area to match.

shops use and it should be available at auto parts and paint stores where professional body and paint supplies are sold. In spite of the For Professional Use Only tag on the box, the counter staff should be happy to sell you some, and also will be able to answer any questions you might have.

Be sure to follow the manufacturer's recommendations about wearing particle masks and respirators, and maintaining proper ventilation of your shop area.

The 3M system, in addition to having a filler that's similar to Devcon's, also has an adhesive. It can be used for gluing broken SMC panels back together again using a scrap of SMC as a backup patch. You can also use the adhesive to section new pieces in place, after damaged pieces are cut away (see illustration on page 330).

Where do you get the new piece? You can always buy a replacement panel from the dealer. A cheaper alternative is to go to the local salvage lot with a cordless saber saw. A little searching and some luck should turn up an identical, undamaged panel, or at least a panel that doesn't have damage in the area you need to make your repairs.

To section a new piece in place, remove any inner panels and move any wiring out of the way. Cut away the damaged portion with a saber saw, then cut the new piece so it fits into the hole. Use the old panel to fashion bonding strips. They should be at least 3 in. wide, follow the original body contour as closely as possible, and run the entire length of the repair. (It's okay to use multiple pieces.)

Clean the inside of the car's panel, the bonding strips, and the new piece with 3M General Purpose Adhesive Cleaner. Next, scuff-sand all bonding surfaces with 80-grit sandpaper, then clean scuffed areas with lacquer thinner (top inset to illustration on page 330).

Mix equal parts of A and B of the 3M adhesive, then glue the bonding strips to the hole in the body. The strips should form flanges to hold the repair piece. Allow the adhesive to cure for thirty minutes, then remove the clamps. Apply adhesive to the scuffed portion of the repair piece and glue it onto the body. Use clamps to locate the panel properly.

After the adhesive has hardened, remove the clamps, then grind out V-notches at the repair seams using a 36-grit disc (Fig. 1). The V should taper back from the seam about 1½ in. to provide enough surface area for the filler to adhere adequately.

The 3M filler is applied in the same manner as Devcon's filler (Figs. 2 and 3). After the filler is applied, sanded, and feathered, use plastic primer, then paint to match.

FLEXIBLE PLASTIC REPAIR

For years, repairing flexible plastic fascias, spoilers, and skirts has been incredibly easy, but horribly expensive. That's because the only choice has been to throw away the old piece and bolt on a new one.

That's changed recently with the introduction of flexible plastic repair materials. Both Devcon and 3M have systems that make invisible repairs to splits, gouges, and tears without compromising the part's flexibility.

Like Devcon's Plexus rigid plastic repair system, the Plexus flexible system consists of an epoxy filler. The main difference is that this filler remains pliable after it has cured. The same is true of the 3M filler.

With both systems, you simply grind out and fill minor gouges (Figs. 4 and 5). For splits and tears,

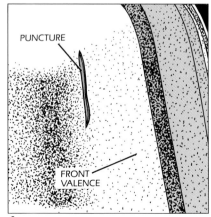

4 This scrape may need to be reinforced from the back if the flexible plastic panel has torn all the way through.

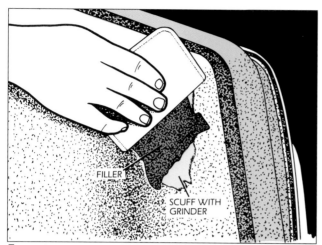

5 If the damage is superficial, simply clean, scuff-sand, and fill with the appropriate flexible panel filler material.

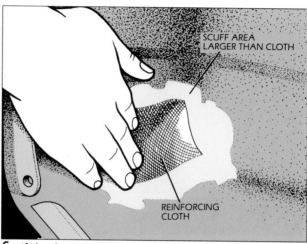

6 If the damage penetrates, then cut a piece of fiberglass cloth to use as a reinforcement. Scuff-sand the area.

remove the part and add a fiberglass reinforcing patch to the back. But before we start, there's something you need to know about flexible plastic.

Most flexible plastic parts are based on polyurethane. But some are based on polyolefin. It's important to know which one you're working with because the filler won't adhere to polyolefin unless an adhesion promoter is used.

How can you tell one poly from another? Grind it with a high-speed (at least 3,600 rpm) 36-grit disc. Polyurethane will grind cleanly, with no melting or smearing. Polyolefin, on the other hand, melts and smears as it's ground.

Devcon doesn't make an adhesion promoter, but 3M does. Keep this in mind when you find plastic that melts when you grind. To repair a cut or split with the Devcon system, start by removing the part, or at least getting easy access to both sides of the damaged area. It's hard on your back and knees, so you may find it ultimately much easier to remove the part.

Clean both sides with soap and water, then clean the damaged area on both sides with Plexus cleaner.

Grind the back side with a 36-grit disc, then cut a fiberglass patch to fit over the area (Fig. 6). Mix equal parts of A and B of the flexible filler, and coat the scuffed area, then apply the fiberglass patch (Fig. 7). Spread more filler over the patch and smooth out any wrinkles or bubbles.

After the backside patch has cured for about thirty minutes, use a 36-grit disc to grind a V in the front of the part. Mix more filler, then spread it over the damaged area so it is slightly higher than the undamaged surface (refer back to Fig. 4).

After thirty minutes' curing time, sand the area with 180-grit sandpaper to establish the proper contour. Then use an oscillating sander or a rubber block with 240-grit sandpaper to feather the edges and remove scratches. If there are any pinholes, apply a skim coat of filler and resand after it has cured. Before prim-

ing the area with Plexus primer, wet-sand with a rubber block and 320-grit or 400-grit sandpaper.

The procedures for using the 3M system are essentially the same. However, you'll have to use a spray gun to apply 3M's primer, called flexible parts coating. And if you're working on polyolefin, you'll have to spray adhesion promoter over the area being repaired every time you sand or grind the part. After priming, paint the area to match, using the paint manufacturer's instructions for painting plastic.

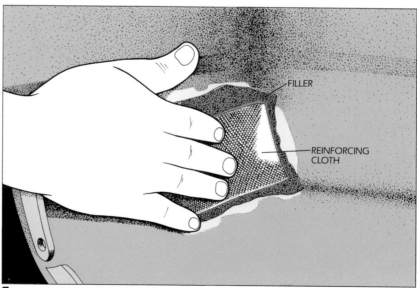

7 Lay on the flexible filler, press the fiberglass patch into it, and then cover immediately with a little more filler. Allow the area to cure for thirty minutes.

How to Replace
WINDSHIELDS

The double-bottomed gravel truck lumbering along in front of you runs over a pothole in the road, shedding several bushels of fifty-caliber pieces of limestone. And, sure enough, several of them ricochet off the surface of your windshield.

There goes your deductible.

Insurance is fine, but what's worse is that it doesn't cover everything. Moldings are notorious for allowing moisture to gather and erode the rubber seals that hold the windshield against its mounting. Even the twisting motion of today's car bodies can be enough, over time, to break the seal and cause leaks.

How do you know when your windshield seal is shot? Your windshield is actually a sandwich of two molded glass panels around a thick sheet of Mylar—a small amount of damage to regular window glass is amplified by this type of composite glass. A BB-hole or stone chip quickly expands when moisture or air between the two panels forces them apart.

Indicators of a broken seal at the windshield's edge include increased wind noise and the appearance of grit or soil between your car's headliner and the inside windshield joint. But the most obvious sign is a leaky windshield. To prevent the inside of your car from becoming a miniature rain forest, it is necessary to remove, reseal, and, if necessary, replace the front glass panel.

FINDING A REPLACEMENT

For vehicles made in 1980 and on, it is recommended that you use Original Equipment Manufacturer's re-

Safely remove salvageable or broken windshields by carefully sawing them loose from the seal with a piece of steel wire.

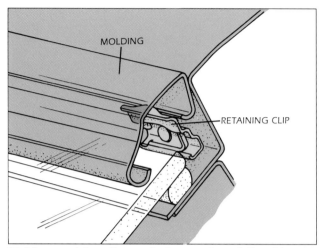

Molding retaining clips can be loosened carefully with a special tool or flat blade. You may need to replace the clips afterward.

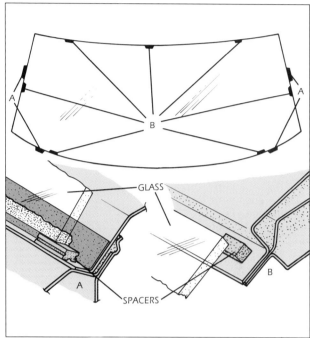

Small plastic shims can be used to center and support the windshield in the opening. Some may need to be removed to install the molding.

placement glass. Auto companies (and licensed OEM glass manufacturers) spend millions in research and development to keep themselves on the cutting edge. The 25 to 40 percent you save on aftermarket products may cost you in mismatched tints, blemishes in the windshield, and other surface imperfections.

Yet, the best source of a replacement windshield may not be an aftermarket catalog or a dealership. Saturday mechanics will be pleased by the variety and low cost of original glass available at their local junkyards. (Sorry—local auto-parts recycling centers in today's ecology-conscious climate.) And since removing a junker's windshield is a lot like removing your car's, we will handle both together.

If your old windshield is broken already, we suggest practicing your removal techniques on this first, before trying them on the keeper you'll be paying for, successfully removed or not.

REMOVING THE WINDSHIELD

You should first prepare your car for the removal and installation. Tape off painted areas that will come in contact with tools. A tarp or large cloth will protect your interior from glass shards and messy urethane

sealants. Unscrew and remove the antenna if it's in the way.

On most cars, a chrome or plastic decorative molding covers the outer seal. Moldings on GM cars are attached by studded retaining clips, and must be removed with a special tool that removes the tension as you lift off the molding. Insert the point of the tool behind the clip and rock it gently back and forth until you can free the clip. Repeat this section by section as you pull away the molding.

On some cars, upper or lower reveal moldings are held in place by screws, which must be loosened before the trim can be removed. Your car's service manual will tell you which tools and removal techniques to use.

Now you are ready for the trickiest part of windshield repair, a stage that separates tinkerers from artists. You should notice a layer of rubber insulation covering the bond between the windshield and the front pillars. The bad seal must be removed by cutting the glass from its seating.

A small amount of the solvent methyl-ethyl-ketone (MEK) will soften the glue holding together your car's urethane sealant. MEK evaporates so quickly that it should *not* damage painted surfaces on the body pillar. Try it on an unimportant area first. Factory paint should be

fine—but we have no idea what's been sprayed onto your car. You can lay down a line of solvent with a clean oilcan. Do *not* use gasoline because it evaporates more slowly and can inhibit the bonding of the urethane sealant later.

You will now need about two feet of piano wire, two handles, and the help of a steady-handed friend. Using a sharp windshield knife (available at auto parts and hardware stores), cut a pathway for the wire through one of the windshield corners near the base of the glass. Tie one end of the wire around a wooden handle. Then use needle-nose pliers to insert the free end of the wire through the caulking, and attach this to the other handle.

Working lumberjack style, saw around the perimeter of the glass until you have completely cut through. Apply even pressure and keep the tension on the wire as you cut. Kinks or breaks in the wire can force you to start over.

Before cutting the glass free, apply a piece of masking tape over each corner, and attach the tape to the car body pillar. Slit the tape, which will become your alignment point for installation.

Now the person inside applies even pressure without trying to force the glass. With the outside person supporting the glass, light outward pressure will separate the windshield from the body pillar. Remove the glass.

If you are simply resealing your original windshield or installing a used one, you want to leave a healthy bead of adhesive on the car. Urethane bonds well to itself, and old caulking works in favor of a strong seal.

You will also want to check the type of sealing material your manufacturer uses. Some older windshields are sealed with polysulfide, which can be determined by burning a small amount in a well-ventilated area. Polysulfide burns clear with a strong sulfurous odor, while urethane emits a dirty black flame with little odor.

If there's no damage to the seal, the old sealant can serve as a basis for the new seal. Note here that you must take care to leave a uniform bead for bonding when cutting the windshield. Tape off the edge of the replacement glass to within ¼ in. of the seal to protect the surface.

Windshield adhesive kits are available from your auto parts store. Prime the perimeter of the glass outside your taped boundary, and allow five minutes for the primer to dry. Then, lay a smooth bead of adhesive over the primer—no more than three-sixteenths. Your adhesive kit contains a nozzle to help direct the adhesive flow.

If your windshield sealant must be replaced entirely, or if you are installing a new windshield, the procedure has a few extra steps. Check the lower windshield glass supports and clean away any excess caulking. Replace any molding clips that are bent more than 1/32 in. away from the body metal. Small plastic shims will let you space the glass evenly from side-to-side and top-to-bottom, as well as ensuring the correct thickness of sealer as curing progresses.

Test the glass in position before sealing it—gap space should be no more than ¼ in. between the glass and body. Prime the glass, and caulk a ⅜-in.-high bead of sealant in a smooth, continuous line.

Now you can reposition the glass with a helper. Each of you supports the windshield on the sides with one hand in front, the other behind the glass. Gently lower the glass in the horizontal position, center it on the lower shims, then ease sides and top into place.

Make sure the glass is properly aligned with your tape markings. Then press the glass firmly to set the adhesive caulking.

You can immediately water-test the car. Direct a cold-water spray away from the adhesive joints, and notice if any leaks exist. You can then paddle in adhesive at the leak point with a sharp, flat tool.

OTHER WINDOWS

You've been thinking about that broken rear window, haven't you?

Thinking that you ought to be able to use the same procedures to replace *that* glass as well.

Almost. The back window is often attached to the car by a similar adhesive. But the windscreen is laminated safety glass, capable of shedding rocks without shattering. It's also much more resistant to the vagaries of being handled.

If you've got a rear window that's only cracked, we're surprised. It's made of tempered single-layer glass, and almost any surface trauma will leave you with a bushel-basket's worth of dime-size shards. So guess what will happen when you try to remove it and stress it just a little too much? It's worth a try. Just remember to wear safety glasses and gloves.

REMOVING SCRATCHES

A close inspection of your windshield may reveal lots of small scratches from rocks, worn wiper blades, and that last trip to the sandy shore.

If scratches are too shallow to catch your fingernail, they can often be buffed out. You'll need a low-speed polisher or drill, a felt polishing wheel, and a jar of fine-grain cerium-oxide windshield polishing powder. This is similar to a jeweler's rouge.

Dilute the polishing compound 2:1 with water to form a slurry. Soak the felt wheel in water for one hour

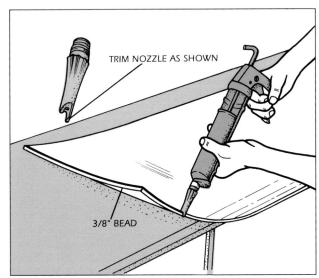

Use the appropriate windshield sealer and a caulking gun to re-cement the glass to the body. Use the right primer for the sealer.

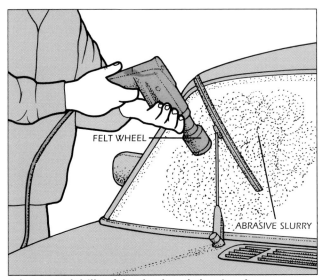

A low-speed drill, a felt wheel, and abrasive slurry can safely polish out scratches. Try Brookstone, Eastwood, or an auto parts store for the kit.

and then mount it on the buffer. Be sure to thoroughly wash the windshield first. Dirt and grit can actually scratch the glass as you buff it.

Spread the slurry over a one-foot-square area of your windshield and liberally apply the elbow grease as you begin buffing. Use circular movements, and don't let the oxide dry out as you move across the windshield. You may buff several times before you're happy with the results. The polishing compound washes away with soap and water.

Remember that deep scratches or stone chips cannot be buffed out. (Chips are air pockets where the glass separates from the inner Mylar layer.) Trying to rub these out will create surface imperfections that may impair visibility.

How To
TUNE UP YOUR INTERIOR

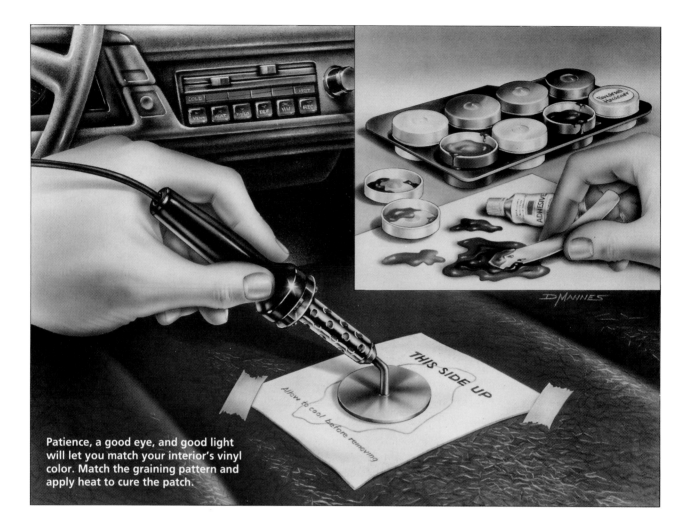

Patience, a good eye, and good light will let you match your interior's vinyl color. Match the graining pattern and apply heat to cure the patch.

Each time you take to the road, your butt is in the driver's seat, your hands are holding the steering wheel and operating all the controls, and your eyes are looking through the windshield, at the mirrors, and at the dashboard. So, if for no other reason than your own comfort and pleasure, you should take the time and effort to keep your car's interior as clean, fresh, and functional as possible. After all, you spend hundreds—maybe thousands—of hours inside that passenger compartment each year.

Of course, it's an added bonus that a like-new interior most favorably impresses your passengers and helps maintain your car's worth.

The first step to tuning up the interior of your car is cleaning it. In fact, if there is nothing damaged in the passenger compartment, a thorough cleaning may be all that is needed to restore it to its original showroom condition. This is especially true if your car or truck has been subjected to the ravages of a particularly sloppy winter—one complete with lots of tramped-in snow, salt, and sand.

Begin by vacuuming the seats, floors, and cargo area. Use a pointed nozzle attachment, if your vacuum cleaner has one, to clean in the crevices between the seat back and cushion, under the seats, and between the seats and center console. Vacu-

um the insides of door and seat-back pockets, as well as any other storage bins.

Move the front seats all the way forward and vacuum the floor behind them, then run them all the way back and vacuum the floor in front. If your car has removable mats or carpet, remove them to vacuum them and the floor beneath. After you've vacuumed, club the seats—a Little Leaguer's baseball bat is the perfect-size club—and carpet to shake loose ground-in dirt. Then vacuum it all again.

If your car has vinyl upholstery, you can clean it with some household cleaner mixed in warm water or with a spray cleaner. Leather up-

338

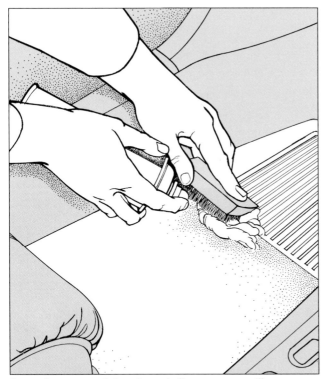

Foam cleaner, scrub brush, and elbow grease will remove stubborn stains from floor mats and carpeting.

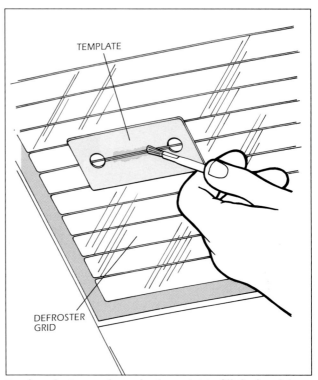

TEMPLATE

DEFROSTER GRID

Brush on just enough conductive paint to fill the break in the defroster grid. Clean thoroughly with solvent first.

holstery should be cleaned with a special leather-care product. Cloth upholstery may be cleaned with household upholstery cleaner.

If there are stains on the upholstery, remove them using the appropriate method and cleaning product. Dried food and other water-based stains may be carefully scraped up using the edge of a spoon and then cleaned. Chewing gum can be stiffened by chilling with an ice cube and then scraped off. Butter, oil, and other grease-based stains should be scraped and treated with a solvent-type stain remover, according to the directions of the solvent's maker. Try to work from the edge of the stain toward the center to avoid leaving a ring.

Reclean the upholstery after removing any stains. Treat clean cloth upholstery with a fabric protector.

Remove the floor mats, scrub them, hose them clean, and let them dry before putting them back on the floor. Carpeting and nonremovable mats should be cleaned, using either warm water and a household cleaner or a special carpet cleaner.

Stubborn dirt and grime stains on the floor may need an old-fashioned scrubbing. White salt stains can be neutralized with some vinegar and warm water.

Vinegar and warm water can also be used to clean smoke-scum-covered windows. Otherwise, use a quality window cleaner and clean, lint-free cloth or paper toweling to clean windows. Be sure to lower the windows an inch or two and clean their edges. When cleaning the inside of the rear window, take care not to damage the defroster grid lines.

Also use glass cleaner to clean the rearview mirror, visor vanity mirror, and the instrument lenses or cover.

Last, clean and polish the dashboard, windowsills, armrests, center console, and door and interior trim panels. Use a mild cleaning solution or one of the special cleaners.

Take care to clean window winders, door handles, dashboard switches, shift lever, steering wheel, steering column cover, radio and heater controls, direction-signal lever, and the louvers for the dashboard vents. You can add luster to the cleaned surface by following the cleaning with a coat of special protectant. Do not treat the accelerator, brake, or clutch pedals, steering wheel, or shift lever with a product that leaves them slippery.

As you clean the interior, note any damage that needs to be repaired. Tears or holes in the seat upholstery, cracks in the dashboard, armrests, or vinyl door panels, and missing or broken switches or controls ruin the effect of your concours-clean interior.

Small tears, cracks, or holes in vinyl—seats, dash, or trim panels—can be neatly patched using a special repair kit. Mix the supplied ingredients and add appropriate coloring pigments to match the color of your interior. Then select the graining paper from the kit that matches the surface finish of the damaged area. Smear the repair mixture over the damaged area, lay the graining paper over the mixture, and use the kit's heating iron to cure the repair.

Severely weatherbeaten, torn, or cracked dashboards can be improved by covering them with a preformed, molded dash cover.

Loose interior door trim panels can be reattached by replacing the broken pushclips with new ones available at auto parts stores, particularly those stores that specialize in

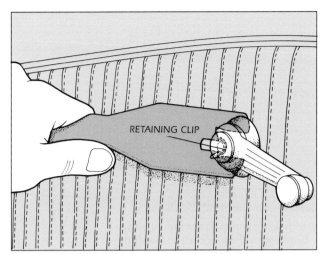

Window cranks on some GM and other vehicles are held by a retaining clip. Push out the clip using this slim tool.

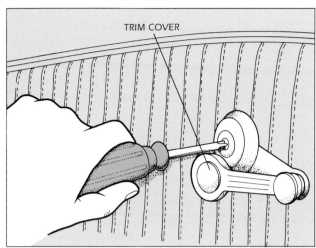

A window-crank screw may be hidden behind a vinyl or plastic cover. Pop off the cover to gain access to the screw.

body repair. If a small section of a trim panel is neatly torn, you can reattach it to its backing using trim adhesive.

Spray trim adhesive can also be used to reattach sagging headliner fabric by spraying the adhesive through a small slit that you cut in the headliner fabric.

Replace badly worn or damaged controls—armrests, window-winder cranks, radio controls—with new pieces. Duplicates are available at your dealership's parts department, while near-duplicate replacements are available at auto parts stores.

While some switch covers and buttons may pull off and snap on, most have a small setscrew or retaining clip. Look carefully before you pry.

Window-winder cranks have either a center-mounted retaining screw—possibly hidden under a pry-up cover—or a hidden retaining clip. To replace a window-winder crank, remove either the screw —which may be Phillips, Torx, or Allen—or the retaining clip. To remove a hidden retaining clip, slide a special tool between the winder crank and door panel and push out the clip. To install the replacement, install the clip on the back of the crank and snap it into place on its shaft.

Also tighten and repair loose or damaged interior components such as sun visors, rearview mirror, heater/defroster ducts, and rear-window defroster.

You may be able to tighten a loose rearview mirror on its mount by tightening a setscrew. You can reattach a loose mount to the windshield using special mirror-mount adhesive. Thoroughly clean the glass with some isopropyl alcohol before attempting to reattach the mirror.

If the rear-window defroster has not been clearing the glass at all, check its fuse. If the fuse is good, check the wiring connections to the defroster grid. Clean any corrosion from the connections and recrimp loose connectors. Be sure that the ground connection is solid and corrosion-free. On hatchbacks and station wagons, be sure that the hatch itself is grounded securely to the rest of the vehicle.

If only one or a few of the lines of the rear-window defroster grid are not clearing, carefully check those nonworking lines for breaks. If you cannot see or feel the physical break or see where the grid may have come away from the glass, use a voltmeter to find the problem spot. Switch on the defroster and hold one of the voltmeter leads to the power buss at one end of the grid. Slowly move the other lead along the grid line. The voltage reading will drop very slowly as you move the lead. However, when the voltage drops precipitously, you have found the break in the grid line.

If the grid line has merely detached itself from the glass but has not broken, carefully clean the glass around the grid line—without tearing the defroster grid—with isopropyl alcohol on a lint-free cloth. Then reattach the grid line to the glass by brushing either a thin film of clear nail polish or special defroster repair paint over it.

If the grid is broken, you can repair the break using an inexpensive repair kit available at auto parts stores. The repair kit contains a special conductive paint, a thin brush, and an adhesive template. Place the template over the broken spot in the grid line, aligning the slot in the template with the grid. Brush a small amount of liquid over the damaged area. Allow it to dry.

After a thorough cleaning, the interior of your car or truck should smell as fresh as it is pristine. However, after a long winter of closed-window driving, the carpeting and upholstery may hold some stale odors—as from wet pets, cigars, and spilled food. Wet feet and other moisture may also create a mild mildew odor.

Rather than resorting to heavy perfumes to mask these odors—all the cleaning products have their own scents—try to locate any sources of mildewing carpet and dry—using an electric hairdryer if necessary—and disinfect them. Then trap the odor by placing small open containers of baking soda under the seat cushions and inside the trunk. Replace the containers once a month until the condition is alleviated.

GLOSSARY

accelerator pump: a small pump in the carburetor that is activated to spray extra fuel through specific nozzle(s) when the accelerator pedal is suddenly and quickly pressed to the floor on sharp acceleration.

air aspirator valve: a device that uses a diaphragm to draw air into the exhaust system to reduce emissions. If a large volume of air is needed, an air pump is used instead.

air cleaner: a housing that holds a filter element that removes dirt from the air flowing into the throttle body, before it is mixed with fuel to form the air-fuel mixture that is burned in the cylinders.

air cleaner intake: the neck, called a snorkel, into which air flows en route to the throttle body.

airflow sensor: see MASS AIRFLOW SENSOR

air-fuel mixture: the mixture of air and fuel necessary to produce power when ignited by a spark plug and burned in a cylinder. The normal mixture is 14.7 parts of air for each part of gasoline.

air pump: a belt-driven or electrical pump that delivers compressed air to the exhaust system to reduce emissions. Also called *secondary air injection* and *Thermactor.*

alternator: see GENERATOR

ammeter: a test meter that reads amps in a circuit.

amps (or amperes): the measurement of the energy content of the electricity in a circuit. Also see VOLTS and OHMS.

antifreeze and summer coolant: a fluid of ethylene glycol and special additives that when mixed with water lowers its freezing point in winter and raises its boiling point in summer.

antilock brakes: a braking system with electronic and electromechanical components that prevents the wheels from locking up and causing the car to skid when traction at the wheels is uneven.

antiseize compound: a paste that is applied to metal parts to keep them from sticking to other metal parts, particularly threaded surfaces such as spark plug threads and wheel studs and bolts.

automatic choke: a carburetor choke that operates automatically, according to engine temperature.

axle, axle housing: a power transfer component with a ball-shaped center section and often two tubes at a 180° angle to each other. In the center section is a gearbox called a differential, with joints for a shaft that goes through each tube. In an automobile, each shaft goes (through a tube if used) to a wheel to power the car. Or more simply, there is just a suspension assembly that supports the front or rear wheels.

backfire: an abnormal form of combustion of the air-fuel mixture. The flame may shoot back from the cylinder into the intake manifold and possibly the throttle body. Or it may be delayed until the fuel reaches the exhaust system, in which case it causes a popping sound.

ball joint: a pivot joint, typically used in an automobile's suspension system.

battery: a component that stores electrical energy in the form of chemical energy.

battery terminals: A battery has two terminals, one labeled positive, the other negative, to which thick wires called *cables* are attached. These cables distribute electrical energy to various systems in the car.

bearing: a smoothly finished round metal sleeve, or a sleeve with smoothly finished metal balls or rollers, to reduce the friction between two parts. In an engine and other components a simple sleeve may be split in two half-circle sections for ease of installation. Also see BUSHING.

bearing cap: a bolt-down cap used to hold a crankshaft and bearing in position.

bellhousing: the area behind the engine, covered by the front of the transmission, that holds the manual clutch assembly or the torque converter of an automatic transmission.

block: see ENGINE BLOCK.

bore: the diameter of a cylinder, such as the engine's cylinders or the brake cylinders.

brake bleeder: a valve that can be opened as part of a procedure ("bleeding") to expel air from the hydraulic braking system, so the action of the brake pedal is free of sponginess.

brake caliper: a C-clamp-like hydraulic device with a piston or pistons to press the brake shoes against a disc to stop the wheel when the driver steps on the brake pedal.

brake drag: failure of the brakes to release completely when the driver's foot is removed from the pedal.

brake fluid: a special fluid used in the hydraulic braking system. For automobiles, only a fluid labeled DOT 3, DOT 4, or DOTS should be used.

brake lining wear sensor: a device on a brake shoe that signals the driver when the lining of friction material is worn.

brake master cylinder: the source of the hydraulic pressure transmitted to the brake system at each wheel. The pressure is developed in this component by the driver stepping on the brake pedal.

brake shoes: steel plates, either curved or straight depending on the system, to which friction material called brake lining is bonded or riveted. Also see DRUM BRAKE and DISC BRAKE.

breaker points: see POINTS AND CONDENSER.

bushing: a cylindrical sleeve of metal, plastic, or rubber placed between two parts to isolate them from each other. The bushing may absorb shock or help locate the parts.

cam: a lobe on a camshaft.

camber: a mounting angle of the wheel relative to the road.

camshaft: a rotating shaft with eccentric lobes that push open the valves for each cylinder. The lobes operate against cylindrical parts called *lifters*.

camshaft sensor: a sensor that signals to the engine control module the rotational position of the camshaft. This enables the computer to more precisely time the fuel injection and ignition systems for faster starting of the engine.

camshaft timing belt (or chain): the rubber belt or metal chain that transfers power from the crankshaft to the camshaft to operate it. The chain or belt must be installed so it maintains the relationship between the camshaft and crankshaft, so the valves for each cylinder open and close at the right time for proper engine operation, a factor called *camshaft timing*.

carbon canister: a canister filled with activated charcoal. When the engine is off, it absorbs vapors from the fuel system that would otherwise cause air pollution. These vapors are drawn into the engine and burned when the engine is running.

carbon tracks: fine lines from burned carbon (such as from oil film) that may be found in a distributor cap. Carbon tracks may cause engine misfire.

carburetor: a device that atomizes fuel in air, and meters the air-fuel mixture that results, into the intake manifold. It also includes a throttle body.

carburetor air horn: the top part of the carburetor, in which the choke is located.

carburetor base: the lower part of the carburetor, in which the throttle plate is located.

carburetor choke: see CHOKE.

carburetor cleaner: a petroleum solvent for cleaning the carburetor.

carburetor float: a device much like the float in a household toilet tank that regulates the amount of fuel in the carburetor fuel bowl.

carburetor fuel bowl: a small fuel storage area in the carburetor, at the carburetor fuel inlet. Also called the *float bowl*, because it contains the carburetor float.

carburetor fuel bowl vent: a vent on the bowl. It typically is connected to a carbon canister, which absorbs vapors when the engine is off, and it also may be vented to the atmosphere when the engine is running.

carburetor fuel inlet: the threaded fitting on the side of the carburetor, to which tubing from the fuel pump is connected. Fuel enters the carburetor at this point.

carburetor needle and seat valve: a valve at the carburetor fuel inlet that is controlled by the up-and-down movement of the carburetor float. When open it allows fuel to enter the carburetor fuel bowl. When closed, it stops the flow of fuel.

caster: an angular relationship between a wheel and its suspension.

catalytic converter: a component in the exhaust system in which harmful emissions are converted to water and carbon dioxide.

chassis: the frame or floor pan, suspension, brakes, and steering of a car.

Check Engine light (also called *Malfunction Indicator Lamp*): a dashboard light that goes on when the engine control module indicates a failure. It may also be capable of indicating diagnostic trouble codes.

choke: a thermostatically controlled plate/flap that pivots to restrict the flow of air through the carburetor when the engine is cold, to improve driveability by temporarily providing a rich fuel mixture. In a radio, a noise suppression device.

circuit: a complete path for the flow of electricity, such as from a battery, through wiring, to a lamp, motor, etc., and then back to the battery.

Clear Flood Mode: a situation in which a carburetor or fuel injection system increases the amount of air or reduces the amount of fuel when necessary to correct a problem called *flooding*.

clutch: a device used to join moving parts together and disengage them when desired. In a car, a manual clutch, operated by a driver pedal, disengages the engine from the transmission. It consists of a disc coated with friction material, and held in place by a spring-loaded metal plate.

coil: a winding of wire. See IGNITION COIL for example.

Cold Cranking Amps: a measure of the electrical energy a battery can deliver to start ("crank") the engine when it is cold.

combustion chamber: the area in the cylinder above the piston, where ignition of the air-fuel mixture occurs.

compression (*compression stroke*): the squeezing of the air-fuel mixture by the upward movement of the piston into a small space, with the valves closed. It is one of the strokes of the engine. The greater the compression pressure (within limits), the greater is the power produced by the engine when the compressed mixture is burned on its power stroke.

compression ratio: the volume of the combustion chamber with the piston on its compression stroke versus the volume of the cylinder with the piston at the bottom of its stroke.

connecting rod: a rod that connects the piston to the crankshaft.

contact: in an electric switch, the terminals that are bridged or brought together to close the switch.

coolant: a mixture of water and antifreeze that absorbs excess heat from the engine and dissipates it into the atmosphere.

cooling system: a system for circulating coolant through the engine, a radiator, and the heater using a water pump to keep the engine from running too hot, and to provide heat for the passenger compartment.

crank, cranking: the act of starting the engine, in which the starting motor turns a gear on the crankshaft to turn the flywheel fast enough for fuel and ignition systems to quickly go to work and enable the engine to continue running on its own.

crankshaft: a rotating shaft that moves the pistons up and down in the cylinders. When it is rotated by the downward force of burning air-fuel mixture on the pistons, it provides the power that is eventually transferred through the transmission to the wheels to propel the car.

crankshaft balancer (also called *harmonic balancer*): a circular device at the front end of the crankshaft, designed to dampen some of the impulses from the combustion events in the cylinders.

crankshaft journals: smoothly finished circular surfaces on the crankshaft, some of which are used with bearings to mate the crankshaft to the engine block. These are called *main bearing journals*. Others, also with bearings, mate to the connecting rods and are called *rod journals*.

cylinder head: the top part of the engine that contains the cylinder ports, the intake and exhaust valves, on most engines the combustion chamber, and on many engines, the camshaft.

cylinder head gasket: a gasket between the cylinder head and the engine block.

cylinder ports: passages in the cylinder head, two for each cylinder—one to bring the air-fuel mixture into the cylinder, the other to carry out burned exhaust gases.

diagnostic trouble code (also *trouble code*): a number stored by the engine control module when it detects a failure in a particular electrical circuit or mechanical system it is capable of monitoring. This number is a useful guide to diagnosis.

dielectric grease (also called *silicone dielectric grease*): a lubricant that repels moisture and has the property of adhering very well to surfaces.

differential: a set of gears that accepts power from the transmission and transfers it to the wheels to drive the car.

disc brake: a hydraulic braking system in which flat steel plates coated with a lining of friction material (called *brake shoes* or *pads*) are pressed by a brake caliper, against the sides of a metal disc to which the wheel is attached. The friction material rubs against the sides of the disc to stop the wheel when the brakes are applied.

distributor: in an ignition system, an electromechanical device that contains a sensor to signal an electronic ignition unit to activate the ignition system, and a rotor to distribute high-voltage electricity to the appropriate spark plug wire, through a cap into which the spark plug wires are fitted.

distributor advance (weights): a pair of spring-loaded centrifugal weights that cause a change in ignition timing at higher engine speeds by pivoting a plate within the distributor; on older cars only.

distributor cap: a plastic cover over the distributor. It holds the wires from the spark plugs and the ignition coil.

distributor drive gear: a gear on the distributor that meshes with a gear on the camshaft to cause a shaft in the distributor to turn. The gear is held to the shaft by a pin.

distributorless ignition: a form of electronic ignition in which the distributor is replaced by an electronic module and a special sensor in the engine.

drivebelt: a rubber belt that transfers power from a pulley on the engine to a pulley on an accessory to operate the accessory. Also see V-BELT.

driveshaft: a shaft from a transmission, either to a wheel or to an axle housing, to transfer power. When used to transfer power to a rear axle housing, it also is called a *propeller shaft*.

drum brake: a hydraulic braking system in which half-moon-shaped brake shoes are pushed by pistons in a wheel cylinder against the inside cylindrical surface of a part called the *drum*, to which the wheel is attached. The brake shoes are coated with a lining of friction material that rubs against the drum surface to stop the wheel when the brakes are applied.

ECM: see ENGINE CONTROL MODULE

EGR: see EXHAUST GAS RECIRCULATION

electromagnetic pickup: see PICKUP

electronic ignition: the modern type of ignition system, in which electronic components replace some of the electromechanical switches previously used. On new cars it refers to DISTRIBUTORLESS IGNITION.

electronic ignition module: see IGNITION CONTROL MODULE

emissions (exhaust): those compounds in the exhaust gases that are harmful to air quality. Typically measured are carbon monoxide and unburned hydrocarbons (gasoline particles). Soon to be measured, in addition, are oxides of nitrogen, which is a component of ground-level "smog."

engine block: the lower part of the engine, in which the cylinders, pistons, and crankshaft are located.

engine control module (ECM): the electronic computer that takes readings from various electronic sensors on the engine and possibly the transmission, and performs such functions as controlling idle speed, turning on the air-conditioning, regulating fuel mixture and ignition timing, and triggering various emission control devices, such as exhaust gas recirculation and positive crankcase ventilation.

engine idle speed: the rotational speed at which the engine runs when the driver's foot is off the gas pedal. The speed, regulated by the engine control module on late-model cars, is higher when the engine is cold.

engine oil gallery: a series of passages, usually drilled, through which oil circulates to key sections of the engine and to the crankshaft.

engine overheating: occurs when the coolant in the cooling system is so hot the metals in the engine are at a temperature that may cause damage to them. In addition, the engine runs very poorly and usually stalls.

evaporative emissions canister: see CARBON CANISTER

exhaust gas recirculation (EGR): a system, featuring the EGR valve, that controls exhaust gas flow. It meters a small amount of burned gases from the exhaust system back into the cylinders to combine with the air-fuel mixture, diluting it. This reduces the fuel mixture combustion temperatures, to reduce formation of oxides of nitrogen.

exhaust manifold: a component with chambers that carry burned exhaust gases from the cylinders into pipes that allow them to flow to the catalytic converter and through that to the muffler and tailpipe.

exhaust stroke: When the piston is moving up in the cylinder, the exhaust valve is open and burned gases are being pushed out into the exhaust system.

exhaust system: the series of parts that carries burned gases from the cylinder head of the engine out into the atmosphere. It includes one or two exhaust manifolds, on recent-model cars one or two catalytic converters, interconnecting pipes, a muffler, and a final pipe called the *tailpipe*.

exhaust valve: a valve that when open allows the flow of burned gases from the air-fuel mixture to flow into the exhaust system.

firing order: the sequence in which spark is delivered to the cylinders, which are numbered according to position in the engine. The sequence is determined by what is necessary to provide a smooth flow of power to the crankshaft. A firing order for a six-cylinder engine might be 1-5-3-6-2-4.

flooding: a condition in which there is excess fuel flowing from the carburetor or fuel injectors. It may cause the engine to stall or run very poorly.

flushing tee: a device with three hose necks laid out in the shape of the letter *T* that is spliced into a heater hose, secured with hose clamps. The neck on the stem is covered with a threaded cap, which is removed and a household water hose attached (with a special adapter) to run water through the cooling system to flush out dirt, rust, etc.

flywheel: a heavy wheel at the rear of the crankshaft that smooths out its transfer of power to the transmission. It has a gear around the circumference, which meshes with a gear on the starter so the turning of the starter cranks the engine.

four-stroke engine: the typical auto engine, with intake, compression, power, and exhaust strokes to form one complete cycle in two complete revolutions of the engine.

fuel-air mixture: see AIR-FUEL MIXTURE

fuel filter: a filter to remove dirt and some water from the fuel. If the filter is installed in the line between the fuel pump and the carburetor or fuel injection system, it is called an *in-line filter*.

fuel injection: a system that uses fuel injectors to deliver fuel to the cylinders. Also see MULTIPORT FUEL INJECTION and THROTTLE-BODY FUEL INJECTION.

fuel injector: a device that sprays fuel into a cylinder port or a throttle body. Although most injectors are electromechanical devices, some are purely mechanical.

fuel pressure: the pressure, measured in pounds per square inch or kilopascals, of the fuel in the line from the fuel pump to the carburetor or fuel injection system. It is measured with a special gauge.

fuel pump: a pump that draws fuel from the tank and delivers it under pressure to the carburetor or fuel injection system. It may be mechanical, operated by the engine, or electrical.

fuel rail: in a multiport fuel injection system, a line of tubing at the engine to which the fuel injectors are attached and from which they receive the fuel they inject into the cylinder ports.

gasket: a flat material designed to compensate for irregularities and therefore prevent leaks between mating surfaces.

gearbox: a housing with gears, such as a transmission.

generator: a device powered by a drivebelt that converts the mechanical energy of the engine into electrical energy for electrical devices and to recharge the car battery.

grease fitting: a small nipple containing a spring-loaded valve, threaded into a part that needs periodic lubrication with grease. The nipple is shaped to accept the tip of a grease gun.

grease gun: a service tool that injects grease, usually into a grease fitting, but also into hinge joints.

grounding (such as grounding a tester): attaching a wire (such as from a tester) to a ground, a metal part of the engine or car body, or the negative terminal of the car battery.

grounds: the negative terminals of modern automotive circuits. Typically, the engine and metal car body serve this purpose.

Hall (effect) **switch:** an electronic switch often used as a sensor, such as a type of pickup.

harness: see WIRING HARNESS

head gasket: see CYLINDER HEAD GASKET

hydraulic braking system: This is the braking system on every modern car. When the driver steps on the pedal, he/she pushes on a piston inside a brake master cylinder filled with fluid. This motion is transferred through the fluid in lines to each wheel, where a disc or drum brake stops the wheel. Use of fluid under pressure to perform work is called *hydraulics.*

hydrometer: a tester for measuring the freeze protection of the engine coolant, also the specific gravity of battery electrolyte.

idle speed: see ENGINE IDLE SPEED

ignition coil: a voltage transformer for the ignition system. It converts the 12-volt current from the battery into the high voltage necessary to fire across the spark plugs. The voltage needed typically ranges from under 10,000 to as much as 50,000 volts.

ignition control module: an electronic module that controls the ignition system, perhaps in conjunction with the engine control module.

ignition pickup: see PICKUP

ignition primary: the low-voltage part of the ignition circuit, such as part of the ignition coil wiring, the pickup, electronic ignition module, and engine control module.

ignition secondary: the high-voltage part of the ignition circuit, such as part of the ignition coil wiring, spark plugs, spark plug wires, distributor cap and rotor, and part of the wiring of the ignition coil.

ignition system: a group of components in a circuit that transforms the 12-volt battery electricity to 30,000–40,000 volts, and delivers that electricity to each cylinder at the correct instant to ignite the air-fuel mixture.

ignition timing: see TIMING

inlet sock: a coarse fuel filter in the fuel tank, designed to remove only very large dirt particles; it can last the life of the car.

intake manifold: a component with passages that lead from the throttle body to the combustion chamber intake port for each cylinder. It carries the air-fuel mixture on engines with carburetors or throttle-body fuel injection, or just the air on engines with a fuel injector at each cylinder (multiport fuel injection).

intake stroke: when the piston is going down in the cylinder, and the intake valve is open, so the downward movement creates a vacuum that draws in air-fuel mixture.

intake valve: a valve that when open allows the flow of air-fuel mixture through the cylinder port into the cylinder.

jumped time: a situation in which ignition or camshaft timing is incorrect because of a mechanical malfunction.

jumper: a wire with a clip at each end. It is used to make a temporary electrical connection.

knock: a knocking sound. It may be produced by worn engine parts, by an ignition system with excessive spark advance, or by low-octane gasoline.

knock sensor: a device that senses knock and reports this to the engine control module, which adjusts ignition timing to eliminate it.

lean fuel mixture: an air-fuel mixture that contains an excessive amount of air, and thus affects combustion of the mixture in the cylinders.

malfunction indicator lamp: see CHECK ENGINE LIGHT

manifold heat control valve: a thermostatic valve that controls the flow of exhaust gases so they heat the air-fuel mixture when the engine is cold for better driveability.

mass airflow sensor: a sensor that measures the amount of air flowing to the throttle body in a fuel injection system, and reports this information to the engine control module.

micrometer: a precision measuring instrument.

microprocessor: a small computer.

misfire: erratic operation of an engine caused by failure of one or more cylinders to contribute power. The problem could be in a mechanical system, in the air-fuel delivery, or in the ignition system.

miss: see MISFIRE

muffler: a part of the exhaust system that contains baffles or special materials to muffle the sound of exhaust gases moving out of the engine.

multiport fuel injection (also called *multipoint fuel injection*): a fuel delivery system in which there is one injector for each cylinder, and that injector is located at the cylinder port.

negative terminal, negative circuit: as opposed to the positive terminal and positive circuit, it is the one that completes the circuit, typically to an electrical *ground*.

ohm: the measurement of resistance in an electrical circuit. See RESISTANCE; also AMPS and VOLTS.

ohmmeter: a meter that reads resistance, measured in ohms, in an electrical circuit or wire.

open circuit: a wiring circuit that is interrupted, such as by an open switch, a bad wiring connection, or an internal break in the wiring.

overhead-camshaft: a type of engine in which the camshaft is mounted in the cylinder head. This design eliminates the use of pushrods.

oxides of nitrogen: an exhaust emission formed by nitrogen in the air at very high fuel mixture combustion temperatures in the combustion chamber.

oxygen sensor: an electronic device threaded into the exhaust system to measure oxygen content in the exhaust gases. High content usually indicates a lean fuel mixture was burned in the combustion chamber; low content usually indicates a rich fuel mixture.

PCV: see POSITIVE CRANKCASE VENTILATION

pickup: the sensor in the ignition system's distributor. Also a term that may be applied to any sensor or sending unit.

pintle: the tip of some types of valves.

piston: a cylindrical cap-shaped part that moves from one end to the other in a cylinder, such as in an engine to compress the air-fuel mixture. When the piston moves down under pressure from the burning, expanding mixture, it turns the crankshaft. A piston may also be used to transfer hydraulic force, as in the hydraulic braking system.

piston slap: a slapping noise in the engine caused by piston wear.

Plastigage: a plastic material that compresses to the thickness of the clearance between a crankshaft journal and a bearing when the bearing retaining cap is installed, so the clearance can be checked against specifications.

points and condenser: a simple electromechanical system in which a distributor-controlled switch (the points) and an electrical charge storage device (the condenser) were the control parts for an automobile ignition system. They were replaced by electronic components beginning in the 1960s, although some cars had points and condenser in the early 1980s.

positive crankcase ventilation (PCV): an emissions control system for unburned gasoline droplets that slip past the piston rings and go into the engine crankcase. A PCV valve controls the flow of the unburned fuel back into the cylinders for burning, so that the flow increases with engine speed. If the valve is stuck open, it can upset the engine idle speed.

positive terminal, positive circuit: the source of current flow in an automobile. Also see NEGATIVE TERMINAL, NEGATIVE CIRCUIT.

power brake: a device that provides an assist to the driver when the brake pedal is depressed. Although most power brake units are vacuum-operated, some use hydraulic pressure.

power stroke: occurs when the piston is pushed down by the expansion of the burning air-fuel mixture in the cylinder.

powertrain control module: an engine control module that also controls the automatic transmission.

preignition: ignition of the air-fuel mixture in the cylinders that occurs prior to the arrival of the spark. It may be caused by a hot spot in the combustion chamber.

pushrod: a part of the engine valve system in a "pushrod valve" arrangement. In this system (see CAMSHAFT) the camshaft is in the middle of the engine and the pushrod rests in the lifter. The opposite end of the pushrod pushes against a device in the cylinder head called a *rocker*, which pivots to push open a valve.

radiator: a heat exchanger that dissipates into the atmosphere the heat absorbed by the coolant as it circulates through the engine.

ram tubes: tubes of a specific length and shape in the intake manifold that promote performance at certain engine speeds by "ramming" air into the cylinders.

recharge: as to recharge a battery, which means to restore the electrical energy dissipated in starting the engine and other uses.

relay: an electrical switching device that allows a small amount of current in one circuit to control a much larger flow of current in another circuit.

resistance: a measurement, in a unit called *ohms*, of the resistance of electricity to flow in a circuit. It equals the voltage in that circuit divided by the amperes.

resistor: a device that restricts the flow of current in a circuit.

rich fuel mixture: an air-fuel mixture that contains more fuel than is necessary for efficient combustion in the cylinders, and so reduces gas mileage. A rich mixture, however, is necessary for easier cold starting.

rocker: a pivot installed in the cylinder head. When one end is pushed, the rocker pivots to push open a valve.

rotor: another name for the disc in a braking system. See DISC BRAKE. Also the term for a rotating part inside the ignition distributor, which serves to distribute high-voltage electricity to the spark plug wires.

rpm: revolutions per minute, the measurement of engine speed.

run-on: the tendency of an engine to run for a brief period after the ignition key is turned off. Also called *dieseling* and *after-run*. It may be caused by an engine malfunction or low-octane gasoline.

safety stand (also called *jack stand*): a device that can be securely locked at a choice of heights, so it can be placed under specific parts of the car underbody to support the weight of the car that has been raised with a jack and keep the car safely in place.

Schrader valve: a valve with a spring-loaded pin, in which the pin is depressed to open the valve. A Schrader valve is used at each tire, on most air-conditioning systems, and on some fuel injection systems.

sending unit: a device that senses something. On the car it may sense oil pressure in the engine, coolant temperature, air temperature, transmission oil temperature, and fuel level.

sensor: a sending unit. Also an electronic device that senses something and reports its reading to an electronic control unit, such as an engine control module. See OXYGEN SENSOR, THROTTLE POSITION SENSOR, MASS AIRFLOW SENSOR.

shock absorber: a device that forces fluid through narrow openings to dissipate the energy absorbed by the car's springs when the wheels ride over bumps in the road.

shoes: see BRAKE SHOES.

short circuit (or shorted circuit): a wiring circuit that ends short of its completed path because of a wiring fault.

solenoid: an electromagnetic switch with an arm or a shaft that can perform a mechanical function when electricity is applied. Most fuel injectors contain a solenoid.

spark: in an engine, the high-voltage electricity that jumps an air gap in a spark plug. A check of the delivery of this spark from the end of the spark plug wire is called a *check for spark* and is a basic automotive test when an engine fails to start.

spark advance: a change in ignition timing, so it occurs earlier than it did, for better performance and to prevent knock.

spark knock: see KNOCK

spark plug: a part with two electrodes, with a ceramic between them as an insulator, and the electrode tips separated by an air gap, threaded into each cylinder. When high-voltage electricity is applied, it jumps through the air gap between the electrode tips and ignites the air-fuel mixture.

spark plug boot: the nipple end of the plug wire jacket. It covers the terminal that goes on the end of the plug itself.

spark plug cable: another common name for spark plug wire.

spark plug electrode: one of two electrical contacts at the tip of a conventional spark plug. The *spark* is the high-voltage arc that bridges the air gap between them.

spark plug heat range: a spark plug design factor. It refers to the spark plug's ability to dissipate heat.

spark plug wire (also called *ignition wire*): a wire with thick rubber insulation that carries the high-voltage spark from the ignition coil to the spark plug.

spark retard: a change in ignition timing so it occurs later than it previously did, either because of a malfunction or intentionally to stop engine knock caused by the ignition system.

spec, specification: a number that is a standard of performance or service adjustment.

starter, starting motor: the motor that is activated by battery current to start the engine.

starter relay: a relay used in the starting system.

starter solenoid: a solenoid used in the starting system, typically built onto the starting motor.

suspension: a system of bars, springs, and shock absorbers to which the wheels are attached, and which supports the car body and the underbody frame on which it may sit.

tachometer: an instrument for measuring rpm.

tailpipe: a pipe that follows the muffler and is the end of the exhaust system.

temperature-sensitive bimetal coil: a part made of dissimilar metals that cause the coil to flex with changes in temperature. The flexing bimetal can operate a temperature-sensitive device, such as a carburetor choke.

test light: a device used to test electrical circuits. It contains a bulb or electronic equivalent, such as a light-emitting diode (LED), that goes on when a circuit is complete and carrying electricity.

thermodynamics: the science that deals with heat and heat transfer.

thermostat: a temperature-sensitive valve that regulates the flow of coolant between radiator and engine.

thermostatic air cleaner: an air cleaner housing with a flap valve that is controlled by a thermostatic device. In one position, it ducts hot air from the area of the exhaust system into the engine for smooth operation when the engine is cold. In the other position, it ducts cool, more dense air from the front of the car into the engine when it is warm for more power.

thermostatic switch: a switch that opens or closes at a certain temperature.

throttle body: the part of the fuel system that holds a flat, generally round plate (the throttle valve) that regulates the flow of air into the cylinders in response to how much the driver steps down on the accelerator. The throttle body may be part of a fuel injection or carburetor fuel system. Regulating the air flow controls the speed of the engine and therefore the amount of power it produces.

throttle-body fuel injection: a simplified fuel injection system with one or two fuel injectors positioned above the throttle valve.

throttle position sensor: a sensor that determines how far the gas pedal has been depressed, and signals that information to the engine control module.

thrust angle: a locational relationship between the front and rear sets of wheels.

time: the state of timing. See JUMPED TIME.

timing: the regulation of the ignition system such that it produces a spark at the spark plug at the correct instant for combustion; the regulation of the camshaft such that it opens and closes the valves to admit air-fuel mixture and allow exhaust gases to exit the cylinder.

timing gun: see TIMING LIGHT

timing light: a special type of light that when aimed at a mark on a rotating part lights only when a spark plug is triggered, so the mark seems to stand still. The instantaneous alignment of this mark with a fixed mark on the engine permits a check of ignition timing, and adjustment if necessary. See TIMING MARKS.

timing marks: a fixed mark on the engine and a second mark on a part that turns with the crankshaft (such as a belt pulley in front or the engine flywheel in the rear). When these marks align (as checked with a timing light) is an indication of the adjustment of the ignition system.

toe: a measurement of whether the wheels at front or rear point toward each other (called *toe-in*) or away (called *toe-out*).

Top Dead Center (TDC): when the piston is at the very top of its upward movement.

torque converter: a fluid-filled device with fanlike members that couples an engine to an automatic transmission.

torque wrench: a wrench with a dial that reads in a measurement of twisting force, such as pound-feet or ounce-inches.

torsion bar: a spring in the shape of a bar. It has been used in the suspensions of many cars.

Torx: a type of screwhead that requires a specific size Torx wrench to loosen or tighten.

transmission: a component with gears and shafts that takes the power of the engine and transmits it, through external shafts, to the wheels to move the car. The gears have different ratios to move the car at different speeds.

trigger wheel: in the ignition system, a wheel with flat, square "teeth," operated by a shaft in the distributor. It often is used to trigger a Hall-effect pickup to produce a signal to the engine control module.

trouble code: see DIAGNOSTIC TROUBLE CODE.

TVRS wire: a type of resistance wire used for spark plug wires. It minimizes ignition system interference with the radio and other electronic components on the car.

vacuum: pressure that is lower than atmospheric, produced by the engine or a pumping device, measured in inches or millimeters (mm) of mercury. The engine produces about 17–22 inches (approximately 430–560 mm) at engine idle speed. Engine vacuum normally is measured at a hose neck on the intake manifold.

vacuum gauge: a gauge that reads vacuum, such as that produced by an engine.

vacuum hose: a hose that connects a source of vacuum, such as on the engine's intake manifold, to a device that uses it, such as a power brake unit.

vacuum leak: a loss of vacuum from a leaking hose or defective gasket.

valve clearance: an air gap that exists between the tip of a valve and the part that opens it when the valve is fully closed. In some engines this gap is adjustable and must be set to specifications.

valve lifter: a valve train component. In OHV engines, the lifter is positioned between the cam lobe and the pushrod. In some overhead camshaft engines, the lifter is positioned between the cam lobe and the valve stem.

valve seat: a surface against which a valve seats when closed.

valve spring: a spring that keeps an engine valve closed until pushed open by a rocker or by the valve lifter.

valve train: the system of parts that operates (and includes) the intake and exhaust valves.

V-belt: a drivebelt with the cross-sectional shape of the letter *V* that rides in a similar-shaped pulley. Also see DRIVEBELT.

volts (or voltage): a measurement of electrical pressure. The automobile today uses an electrical system that operates on approximately 12 volts. Most engine control modules and their associated parts contain both 5-volt and 12-volt circuits. A car's ignition system can develop 30,000–40,000 volts. Also see AMPS and OHMS.

voltmeter: a test meter that measures volts.

V-type engine: an engine with two banks of cylinders set at an angle, such as a V4, V6, V8, V10, and V12. The number following the *V* is the total number of cylinders, such as two banks of two cylinders in a V4.

water jacket: passages in an engine through which coolant is circulated.

wheel alignment: adjustment of the suspension and steering of a car so it rides straight down the road and responds predictably in turns. The measurements adjusted or checked include toe, caster, camber, and thrust angle.

wheel bearing: a ball or roller bearing assembly that supports whatever part to which the wheel is mounted, so the wheel can spin freely as the car rolls down the road. See BEARING.

wheel chock: a triangular piece of metal or wood that can be wedged between a tire and the ground to keep the car from rolling.

wheel spindle: a flange that holds the wheel bearing assembly. It may be the end of a driveshaft.

wiring diagram: a diagram that shows how the wires in the car, or an individual circuit, are connected to components and to one another.

wiring harness: a group of wires bundled together and covered by a protective jacket.

wiring harness connector: a single connector with many terminals for electrical wiring connections.

Index

Page numbers in *italics* refer to illustrations